Kay Poir.

October 6

I hope that you will enjoy reading my book.

Nancy E. Neal

A United Empire Loyalist Family

The Life and Times of Thomas Hooper, of Bedeque, Prince Edward Island, Canada, And His Descendants 1734 - 2004,

Nancy E. Neal

Published by
Nancy E. Neal
in association with

2006

 All correspondence, queries, comments, and book orders are to be addressed solely to her: Nancy E. Neal, 10 Peterborough Drive, Northport, N.Y. 11768 U.S.A. Telephone: 631-757-7191; e-mail: NancyENeal@aol.com. Her Prince Edward Island summer address (June to October) is: Nancy E. Neal, Albany R.R. 2, P.E.I., Canada C0B 1A0; Telephone: 902-887-3785; e-mail: NancyENeal@aol.com

---

Library and Archives Canada Cataloguing in Publication

Neal, Nancy E.
A United Empire Loyalist family : the life and times of Thomas Hooper of Bedeque, Prince Edward Island, Canada, and his descendants 1734-2004 / Nancy E. Neal.

At head of title: The genealogy of Thomas Hooper and his descendants, 1734-2004.
Includes bibliographical references and index.
ISBN 0-9691824-8-1

1. Hooper, Thomas—Family. 2. Hooper family. 3. United Empire loyalists—Genealogy. 4. Prince Edward Island—Genealogy. 5. Canada—Genealogy. I. Title.

CS90.H5952 2006 929'.2'0971 C2006-900082-4

The dust jacket design displays the pre-1801 Union Jack flag of Great Britain

Printed and bound in Canada by Taylor Printing Group Inc., 225A Alison Blvd., Fredericton, N.B. Canada E3C 2S5

This book was published by the author in association with Crescent Isle Publishers, 157 Victoria Road, Summerside, PE Canada C1N 2G6. Telephone: (902) 436-8518; Fax: (902) 436-7717; and e-mail: c.morrison@pei.sympatico.ca

Contents

Acknowledgements

Saying "Thank You" is always difficult, and in this instance may be even a bit risky for fear I might exclude someone. Nevertheless, I feel it is imperative that I attempt to acknowledge the primary contributions made by several people over a period of years. If I have omitted anyone, I do so unknowingly and with contrition.

I would like, especially, to acknowledge the support, assistance and encouragement of Muriel Hooper, Kensington; Michael Schurman, Summerside/Charlottetown; Malcolm and Edith Bradshaw, Searletown; Fred MacQuarrie, Searletown; and Arnold McGrath, North Carleton.

Without the meticulous and comprehensive research on the history of the Bedeque area of P.E.I., conducted by the following talented writers and researchers, this book on the Hooper family would have been much more difficult: Marjorie McCallum Gay, Ross Graves, Doris Haslam, Henry H. Hooper, L.U. Fowler, Orlo Jones, George A. Leard, Jean MacFadyen, and Ada MacLeod.

Any errors or omissions in the genealogical information within this book are strictly unintentional, and the author accepts full responsibility for any such occurrences.

About the Author

Nancy E. Neal, a retired teacher, and her husband, Alden (also a retired teacher), have been summer residents at Chelton, P.E.I. for the past seventeen years. They reside at Northport, New York, from October to June.

Nancy obtained her bachelor's degree from Boston University and her master's degree from Emory University, at Atlanta, Georgia. Her interest in genealogy, especially her husband's lineage, goes back thirty years, when she and Alden and their children would travel to Saugus, Massachusetts to visit his parents. Nancy and "Grammy Neal" would sometimes stay up, after everyone else had gone to bed, and talk. Ada had left Prince Edward Island when she was about seventeen years of age (c.1913), and had gone to Haverhill, MA to work. Nancy would ask her husband's Island-born mother about her early life on Prince Edward Island, her family there, and such topics as her pregnancies and deliveries. Perhaps because Nancy was a nurse, as well as a teacher, or perhaps just because she was an interested person, her mother-in-law gave her a lot of information, and sowed the seed that would eventually grow into this book.

This genealogy is a "labour of love," as are most genealogies. Countless hours of research, reading, and sharing information with others, has consumed much of Nancy's (and Alden's) life since this project began back in the 1970s. It is Nancy's hope that others will enjoy and benefit from her work.

List of Maps and Illustrations

Background of the Hooper Surname

The Hoopers are thought to have been residents of the county of Devonshire, England since prior to the Norman Con quest in 1066, which took place under Duke William at the Battle of Hastings. The name is apparently derived from either the term for a maker of iron hoops, or else a marshland enclosure containing structures constructed above ground on elevated posts or stilts.

The name first appears in Pennsylvania as Hoopes, a name change possibly due to religious persecution under the reign of King Charles II and Queen Mary of England, since the Pennsylvania Hooper immigrants were Quakers. Mary, better known as the "Bloody Queen," arranged the execution of over three hundred people.

One of Queen Mary's victims was Oxford-educated and converted Protestant, Bishop John Hooper, who was born in Somersetshire, England about 1495. In order to escape religious persecution under King Henry VIII, John Hooper had lived in Zurich, Switzerland. He later became Bishop of Gloucester after returning to London upon the death of King Henry in 1547. When Henry's daughter, Mary, assumed the throne as Queen Mary I in 1553 she had Hooper condemned as a heretic. Refusing to recant, Bishop John Hooper was burned at the stake. About this time, it is believed the Hooper family in England chose several variations of the spelling of the surname in order to escape Queen Mary's vengeance.(See Chapter 1, "James Hooper," for further background information on the Hooper surname, and the life and death of Bishop John Hooper.)

Alden Neal, the author's husband, standing beside the gravestone of Thomas Hooper, his great-great-great-grandfather, a United Empire Loyalist, who is buried at Lower Bedeque, Prince Edward Island. Hooper settled at Bedeque in 1784. Thomas Hooper's son, Elisha (died March 18, 1860, aged 78) and his wife, Margaret Crosby (died May 31, 1843, aged 62 years) are also buried there. The stone was erected by Jane P. Hooper. Two years before this photograph was taken, the cemetery stones and monuments were cleaned beautifully. What a difference it made in reading the old stones!

This book is dedicated to United Empire Loyalists everywhere,
especially loyalist Thomas Hooper, of New Jersey.
Thomas Hooper, like his loyalist counterparts,
made the emotional and difficult decision
to leave his homeland in the British Thirteen
Colonies after the American Revolution.
Determined to remain loyal to the British Government,
he and his family oftentimes travelled through danger
and the unknown, in pioneer times, to eventually
reach Prince Edward Island to begin a new life.

Introduction

My name is Nancy Elizabeth Ellis Neal; I am also known as Mrs. Alden Hooper Neal. I started life as Nancy Elizabeth Ellis and, as you can surmise, took the beautiful name of Neal when I married Alden in 1955. I have been interested in genealogy for years and am in the process of investigating families, both Alden's and mine, involving dozens of surnames.

Well over thirty years ago, when Alden and I and the children went to Saugus to visit Grammy and Grampy Neal, Grammy and I would sometimes stay up after everyone else had gone to bed and talk. My wish is that I had written down what she had told me, for as with any conversations, time has a way of losing many specifics. Fortunately, many of the things we talked about were unimportant to the genealogical study which I have undertaken of the Hooper family, the ancestry of Grammy's father.

Only one of the many relatives, to whom we have spoken, knew about the fascinating facts that I found surrounding the history of the Hooper family: man's inhumanity to man, loyalty to country, sicknesses, fires, death, a degree of affluence and then poverty, separation of family, and on and on. All of this was promoted, primarily, by one man, starting about the year 1775, as a result of the war between Great Britain and the Thirteen Colonies. Unfortunately, I am one of the few people in Alden's immediate family who is interested in what I find to be a fascinating history. Therefore, I am preserving it for my children, and for anyone else who might have interest. It is one of those things which I MUST do! Besides making numerous visits to the public archives of Prince Edward Island, churches, relatives, cemeteries, and painstakingly searching the archives in Trenton, New

Jersey, Alden and I talked over thirty years ago to many "old-timers" in Prince Edward Island who knew the parents of Grammy Neal. It is from these old-timers that we got meat on the bones of the skeletons of the ancestors one generation beyond Grammy (two generations beyond Alden). We found out something of the physical appearance, the personality, and the morés of the times. The old-timers were a most interesting and valuable asset in my search. I am certain that these old-timers did not know anything of the origin of the Hooper family beyond Prince Edward Island, as I am sure Grammy herself did not.

In addition to conversations with the "old-timers," in September 2002 Malcolm and Edith Bradshaw (he is a brother-in-law to Gladys Lowther Bradshaw Henderson, a second cousin of Alden's) gave me about eighty-five pages of copies of newspaper articles which his family had saved, and which she selected (from what I am certain is their vast collection) and carefully duplicated so that each page was full of interesting articles from the 1800s and 1900s. This information greatly enlarged and enhanced the genealogical section, and provided interesting stories that helped in the preservation of the way of life in P.E.I. in the 18th and 19th centuries. Conversation with Malcolm, who is himself becoming an "old-timer" in the area, was interesting.

Primarily because I do not consider myself a professional writer, I decided not to paraphrase much of the published research I have used in this book. Instead, I have elected to use excerpts or passages directly from the works cited in the bibliography. I consequently feel secure in the knowledge that I have my story narratives correct since they came "direct from the horse's mouth." Also, by excerpting sections of previously published historical writing I believe I am providing the reading public with an opportunity to see for themselves the writing skill and research of many excellent Island historians, especially since many of their works have long been out of print. I have provided footnotes, also, to indicate those passages I have taken directly from the published sources.

Nancy E. Neal, Northport, N.Y.,
and Chelton, P.E.I.

The line of descent of my husband, Alden Neal, eight generations from the progenitor of this Hooper genealogy:

1. **Stephen,** in the Staten Island census, 1696
2. **Clement** (1700-1778) and **Mary Stillwell Journé** (1701/1702-1778), Staten Island early 1700s; New Jersey latter part of 1700s
3. **Thomas** (1734-1816) and **Mrs. Hooper** (d. 1782), New Jersey, Thomas went to Nova Scotia, Canada, to explore possibilities for moving his family, and went to live in Prince Edward Island in 1784 as a United Empire Loyalist.
4. **Major** (1764-1838) and **Catherine Urquhart**, second wife of Major, (1783-1866), lived in Lower Bedeque, Prince Edward Island
5. **John Keir** (1809) and **Jane Walker** (1821) in North Carleton, P.E.I.
6. **Major Charles** (1853) (baptismal name Elijah Charles) and **Mary Ann Mac/McDonald** (1865) in North Carleton, P.E.I.
7. **Ada Ann** (baptismal name Annie Eva), born in 1896 in North Carleton, P.E.I. and married **Charles Stone O'Neil** of Boston, MA, U.S.A.
8. **Alden Hooper Neal,** born January 30, 1931 in Lynn, MA, married **Nancy Elizabeth Ellis,** born January 21, 1932

The descendants of Alden Hooper Neal and Nancy Elizabeth Ellis:

1. **Sally Rebecca Neal** (born March 8, 1958)
2. **Charles Ellis Neal** (born April 20, 1961) and **Nathalie Daubin**

The descendants of Charles and Nathalie Neal:

2.1 **Juliette Daubin Neal** (born October 2, 1995)
2.2 **Rosalie Louise Neal** (born September 8, 1997)

A Map of Northern New Jersey in 1775 showing the areas where the Hooper family originated prior to their arrival on P.E.I. in 1784

CHAPTER 1

Generations One, Two, and Three

It was in the early 1990's in searching records at the Prince Edward Island Museum and Heritage Foundation in Charlottetown, P.E.I., that this writer first came upon the information that the Hoopers were United Empire Loyalists in the late 18th century. Broken down to some basic details, here is their story: Living on Staten Island, New York, in 1706 was the Hooper family. [Actually the parents, Stephen and his wife, had been there in 1696. I have not been able to find out if they were the first of their families in this country or from where they came.] At that time (1706), Stephen and Maria Hooper had two sons, Stephen and Clement.[1] I will call **Stephen** (the father) **GENERATION ONE** as I do not know his ancestors. It would appear, however, that they came from England, staying in Holland for several years. In 2002 when I was researching the origin of the Hoopers in this country at the New York Public Library's Genealogical Room, I found by implication that Maria was a Huguenot, but her surname was not given. The Huguenot influence was very strong in Staten Island and Manhattan in the late 1600s and the early 1700s. **Clement** and his brother Stephen, about whom I know nothing other than he was the son of Stephen, are **GENERATION TWO**. There may have been other children born after Stephen and Clement, but I have no evidence yet to back that possibility.

7	milking cows	12 shillings	0 pence
1	yearling	03 shillings	0 pence
3	two-year olds	01 shilling	0 pence
1	black heifer	04 shillings	0 pence
1	mug	obliterated	torn paper
1	steer	obliterated	obliterated
	half of wheat	3 shillings	10 pence
1	corn harrow	1 shilling	10 pence
1	farlow harrow	0 shillings	10 pence
1	plow	0 shillings	15 pence
3	hogs	0 shillings	10 pence
	press and cider mill	3 shillings	15 pence
1	tub	1 shilling	0 pence
1	wooden wheel	0 shillings	10 pence
1	saddle	0 shillings	5 pence
	keg and chain	0 shillings	5 pence
	Table Hand jars Dung Shovel	0 shillings	10 pence
1	farmer Cupboard	0 shillings	3 pence
1	chiss	1 shilling	5 pence
1	tea table	0 shilling	5 pence
1	feather bed	1 shilling	0 pence
1	pane and iron	5 shillings	0 pence
	illegible	illegible	10 pence
1	lantern	0 shillings	02 pence
	mortar and pestle	0 shillings	07 pence
1	quart pot		02 pence
9	chairs	0 shillings	15 pence
2	trammels	0 shillings	10 pence
2	kettles	illegible	illegible
1	pot	illegible	illegible
	lovel tongs and lavle		illegible
1	gridiron	0 shillings	02 pence
	knife box and 12 forks and 7 knives	0 shillings	10 pence
9	sheep	3 shillings	10 pence
1	sop tub	0 shillings	4 pence
1	pail and juggin	0 shillings	1 pence
1	butter tub and juggin	0 shillings	5 pence
1	churn	0 shillings	2 pence
4	milk pans, 1 earthern pot	0 shillings	9 pence
2	milk tools	illegible	illegible
1	pail	illegible	illegible
1	large iron kettle	illegible	illegible
2	wooden chairs	0 shillings	10 pence
2	pewter plates, 1 basin, 1 platter	0 shillings	8 pence
1	looking glass	0 shillings	10 pence
4	pewter plates	0 shillings	06 penct
1	bed, two bolsters converted into bed and bedhead	2 shillings	10 pence
2	coverlets blanket and chest	1 shilling	5 pence
1	bed bolster, 2 pillows and a cot	4 shillings	0 pence
1	pillow and a bee quilt	0 shillings	10 pence
1	spinning wheel	0 shillings	7 pence
1	brass kettle	0 shillings	5 pence
2	hatchets	0 shillings	5 pence
1	whiling pot	0 shillings	5 pence
	drawing knife and illegible	illegible	illegible
2	hoggs head	illegible	illegible
	cronk and grain stone	illegible	illegible
	candle sticks	illegible	illegible
	old wagon	illegible	illegible

Clement Hooper's inventory in 1774, before the American Revolution began

Clement Hooper (1700-1778) married Mary Stillwell Journé (1701/1702-fl1774), the daughter of Thomas Stillwell, Jr. [fourth generation in the colonies] and Mary Poillon (another source reads "Martha" Poillon),[2] and moved near present-day Trenton, New Jersey [I have amassed a wealth of information on the Stillwells and hope to do a Stillwell document]. I have in my possession a copy of a deed for the sale of property from William Robertson to Clement Hooper. The heading reads: "County of (?) Middlesex Loan Office to Clement Hooper, recorded March 3, 1748." The beginning is decidedly different from modern-day versions: "This indenture made the fourteenth day of June in the twenty-second year of the Reign of Our Sovereign Lord George the Second by the Grace of God of Great Britain, France, and Ireland — King, Defender of the Faith or ano Dom One thousand Seven hundred and forty eight."

Mary, many of whose ancestors were Huguenots from Holland, had been married previously to a Mr. Journé and with him had two daughters, Mary and Elizabeth.[3] Clement's step-children are not mentioned in his will. Clement and Mary had seven children in **GENERATION THREE**. The names of their children, all born in New Jersey, with spouses and dates which I know, follow:

Stephen Hooper of Middlesex County, N.J., married Catrine Clayton, of Monmouth County, on March 31, 1767.[4] "Stephen Hooper [in the three generations, he is the third Stephen!] of Windsor, Middlesex County, and John Embly, Monmouth County, gave 500 pounds to His Excellency William Franklin, Esquire, Governor of New Jersey, for a marriage license sealed and delivered in the presence of Mary Leonard, March 31, 1767.

Nicholas Hooper, no information available

Ann Hooper, born on November 4, 1728; married Isaac Coberley, of Burlington, N.J., on December 7, 1749 (another source reads "Isaac Cubberly on December 16, 1749"); died in 1815.

Martha Hooper, married Levi Updike [Senior], the son of William, son of Lawrence, son of Johannes, son of Louris. Levi was born about 1730 and died in 1807. A fifth generation Updyke from Holland,[5] he was a prosperous farmer in West Windsor Township, Middlesex (now Mercer) County, N.J. and "considerably increased his paternal inheritance for he gave to his sons their full share of his estate before his death, and by his will he bequeathed to his daughter and granddaughter legacies which were large for those days."[6] They had two sons: William and Clement; a daughter Ann Slaback; a granddaughter, Mary South, consort [wife] of Ezekiel South, and a grandson, Levi Updike.[7]

* **Thomas Hooper,**[8] born 1734, married (name unknown).

I am in possession of a document "Colonial Laws, 1774," a small part of which I would like to quote:

> An ACT to enable the Owners and Possessors of the low Lands, Meadows and Swamps on both Sides of Assunpink Brook, from the Line commonly called George Keith's to the Lands of John Ely, to remove the Obstructions to the free Course of the Waters of the same Brook. . . . And be it further enacted by the Authority aforesaid, That it shall and may be lawful for the said Owners and Possessors of the said Meadows, low Lands and Swamps, or as many as shall choose to attend, to meet at the Dwelling-House of **Thomas Hooper**, in the Township of Windsor, on the fourth Tuesday in May aforesaid [1774], and yearly and every Year for-ever thereafter, or at such other Place as the Managers for the Time being shall appoint....[9]

Thomas did not attend yearly forever thereafter. This story, laid out to the best of my knowledge and ability after years of research, will give the reader some insights into the life and decisions of Thomas Hooper, Alden's great-great-great-grandfather who died in 1816 at age 82 in Lower Bedeque, Prince Edward Island, Canada. The story will also point out some of the hardships to his wife, children, and other descendants, difficulties that came as a result of his decisions, arrived at with honesty and careful thought. Because of the turmoil of the times, and his own strong feelings of loyalty to the British Crown, even though he himself was not a radical, but a quiet

farmer who would live and let live, his personally-held belief changed his life and that of his family forever. His grave is in the (Methodist) cemetery at Lower Bedeque with a rather tall stone near the street in the middle of the cemetery.

Recently (1997) work has been done in the cemetery, and moss has been removed from the stones. Thomas Hooper's house and property were just beyond this site. On Callbeck Road, opposite the old Callbeck store in Central Bedeque, about two miles from the cemetery, is a small park with a monument bearing a memorial plaque recognizing a few United Empire Loyalists. Sited on the monument are Richard Robins of English ancestry, coming to Bedeque in the Island of St. John, as it was known in those days, from outside Amboy, New Jersey where he owned a farm and a comfortable home;[10] William Schurman (c. 1743 - 1819) of New Rochelle, New York, a Huguenot town, of Dutch ancestry whose family had been for several generations in "the Colonies";[11] and William Wright from Westchester County, New York, near where Westchester County borders Connecticut, about 25 miles northeast of the present New York City.[12] Thomas's wife, whose name we do not know, died in 1782 in New Jersey (See further particulars of her tragic death elsewhere in this history).

Rachel Hooper, baptized on Staten Island, on April 6, 1735.[13]

James Hooper, married Agnes (surname unknown). St. Michael's Church, Trenton, N.J. lists baptisms for June 27, 1773 of Stephen, age 30 months, and Clement, age 7 months, sons to James and Mary Hooper. On the same date John Hooper, age 15, was baptized as an adult. We do NOT know the year of the birth of James who married Agnes. I would assume that he was older than Thomas. Perhaps John was the son of a first wife and Mary was the second wife? Or perhaps James was the son of the first James, and Stephen and Clement were the grandsons of James and Agnes. We *do* know, from the will of Clement, that James, the brother of Stephen, Nicholas, Ann, Martha, Thomas, and Rachel, had a son, Clement.

The State of New Jersey furnished to the continental army, Joseph and Phillip, from Middlesex County, and four others from different parts, two being from an adjourning county. One of these was a brother James, I think. Who the father was is not clear, but the strongest evidence I have been able to obtain is in favor of Clement."[14]

As a bit of background on the surname, Hooper is an English name derived from "Hoopmaker." The expression is that Hooper's hoops fit on Cooper's barrels. It is probable that the surname Hooper was first used in England about the year 1275. There is no record to show that it is older than this date. In 1275 William le Hopore possessed lands in Dorset, England. In 1325 the name Hooper is found in the county of Somerset. The name of Hooper was the Norman French term for a cloth merchant."[15] John Hooper (written also hup´er and höp´er) was an English Protestant bishop. All authorities agree that he was born in Somersetshire, in England, about the year 1495. This Bishop Hooper is the most distinguished member of the English family of Hoopers.[16] While a student at Oxford, he was converted to the Protestant faith. In 1539, to escape the Bloody Statutes of Henry VIII, he retired from England and passed several years in Zurich." In his *Book of Martyrs*, John Fox writes that John Hooper was married in Zurich to a Burgonian.[17] At the death of King Henry VIII, he settled in London, where he became Bishop of Gloucester, and in 1552 received the bishopric of Worcester *in commendam.* Soon after the accession of Mary, he was condemned as a heretic, and, refusing to recant his Protestant belief, was burned at the stake in 1553."[18] Fox states that the fire had to be started three times as the wood was very green![19] I do not know yet the relationship of Bishop John Hooper to Clement Hooper. There are over 200 years between their births (1495 - 1700).

On July 13, 1635, the ship *James* sailed from London, England, for New England with William Hooper, age 18, the father of the Hoopers in America. He went to Reading, MA.[20] There was a William Hooper living on Staten Island in the 1630s. I do not know his relationship to Stephen, if any.

In the will of Clement Hooper, proved August 14, 1778, he left one-third of his estate to his dearly beloved wife, Mary. To his son, Stephen, and to his heirs, executors, and administrator, he left 200 pounds current lawful money of New Jersey to be paid to him or his heirs at the end of six months after his wife's decease; to his son Nicholas, £100; to his daughter Ann, £100; to his daughter Martha, £100; to his grandson Clement Hooper, James's son, £16; to his grandson, Clement Updike, Martha's son, £16 when they reached 21 years of age; to his sons Thomas and James his plantation where he lived and his meadow in Maidenhead; and to his sons Thomas and Stephen, who were executors, (illegible). We have a copy of this will which is on file at the present state capitol in Trenton, N.J. as well as a copy of his inventory, which was transcribed for this document, taken soon after his death. Interestingly Rachel is not mentioned in the will.

Of particular note is a portion of his will from which I would like to quote. This is apparently not a "form will," as I have seen others of this era which are not the same. I am sure that portions came directly from the Anglican Book of Prayer, 1728, and I think that his will shows something about him as a person and an Anglican:

In the name of God, AMEN. The fifth day of May in the year of our Lord one thousand seven hundred and seventy three, I, Clement Hooper of Windsor Township and County of Middlesex, being sick in body, but of good and perfect memory, thanks be to Almighty God, and calling to remembrance the uncertain estate of this transitory life and that all flesh must yield unto Death when it shall please God the call to make, constitute, ordain and declare this my last will and testament in manner and form following, revoking and annulling by these presents all and every testament and testaments, will, and wills heretofore made and declared either by word or by writing; and this is to be taken only by my last will and testament and none other; and first being penitent and sorry from the bottom of my heart for my sins past, most humbly desiring forgiveness for the same, I give and commit my Soul unto Almighty God, My Savior and Redeemer in Whom by the merits of Jesus Christ I trust and believe assuredly to be saved and to have full remission and forgiveness of all my sins and that my soul with my body at the General Day of Resurrection shall rise again with Joy, and through the merits of Christ's death and passion possess and inherit the Kingdom of Heaven prepared for his elect and chosen and my body to be buried in such place where it shall please my executors heretofore named to appoint and ______ (ask?) for the settling of my temporal affairs and estate and such goods and chattles and debts as it pleased God for above my desserts to bestow upon me....

In 1996 Alden and I went to St. Michael's Anglican Church in Trenton, near the State Capitol building, to look for the graves of Clement and Mary. The church in the diocese of New Jersey was founded in 1703. We had telephoned the church clergy in advance. We were unable to find a stone or stones for Clement and Mary in the churchyard cemetery and we gathered from the information given to us by the clergy that the old burial ground was toward the sides and the back of the church. Since the early days the cemetery has been enlarged. When the need for expansion of the church building took place, the edifice was erected over gravesites. It would appear that the reason that Clement and Mary's graves aren't visible might be that the church extension is on top of them!

St. Michael's is an historic Parish, founded in 1703. During the Revolutionary War services were suspended; members were divided by Tory and Patriotic sympathies. Hessian troops were quartered in the church, destroying pews for firewood. The Battle of Trenton, December 26, 1777, raged around the church walls. The graveyard contains many 18th and 19th century personages.[21]

Several Hoopers (Robert Lettis Hooper, Sr., Robert Lettis Hooper II, and Robert Lettis Hooper III and Jacob Roeters Hooper, brother of Robert Lettis III) were all Vestry members at St. Michael's. A Sarah Hooper of Kingsbury, N. J. married William Pidgeon in 1758. Mr. Pidgeon was admitted to the N. J. bar [as a lawyer] at the August term, 1750. He was a Vestryman for several years and a Warden in 1761. He was a Justice of the Peace for the counties of Burlington and Monmouth. He was a person of substance, having an advertisement for the sale of his house on February 15, 1776: *Trenton: To be sold - A handsome, well-furnished brick house, a convenient kitchen with quarters for servants, stable, garden and small piece of meadow ground, situate in King Street, in Trenton. The purchaser may have*

possession the first of March. (Signed) William Pidgeon. [William Pidgeon was a well-known citizen of Trenton during the War period. The brick house referred to was situated on the east side of what is now Warren Street, midway between what is now East Hanover and State Street]."[22] I do not know how these people were related to Clement, but I am certain that there was a rather close familial relationship.

The land that Clement Hooper owned was at Maidenhead [now called Lawrenceville], Hunterdon County, and at Windsor, Middlesex County, N.J. According to old records, Thomas Hooper, who lived near Windsor in Middlesex County, owned 100 acres of land and two smaller pieces of ten acres each which he bought from his father. The deed was dated October 8, 1769. The purchase of fourteen acres quite near the other property was dated January 25, 1775. With the death of his father in 1778, he received the home plantation as well as the "Meadow in Maidenhead," in Hunterdon County, which he shared with his brother, James. The home plantation consisted of a tavern, noted as the place where all public business was transacted, as well as farming land.

I have a copy of the inventory of Clement Hooper taken in 1778 after his death. The inventory was found in the New Jersey Archives in the State House.

The author of this genealogy has in her possession the copy of a letter from Harry Hooper, written in May 1985, questioning if Mary Stillwell Hooper had died before Clement, and had he perhaps married another Mary. He asks, "If Mary was living at the time her grandmother wrote her will, why was she passed over in favor of just her Journé children?

Notes

1 Census of Staten Island in the Year 1706 lists (men) Stephen Hoper; (Women) Elizabeth Hoper, (boyes) Stephen Hoper and Claman Hopper. Index clarification reads HOOPER (HOPER, HOPPER) and CLEMENT HOOPER.
2 Register of Early Settlers of King's County by Teunis G. Bryant, 1973
3 John E. Stillwill, M.D., *Stillwell Genealogy* (N.Y.: 1930), p. 279 (according to the will of Martha [Biljouw Stillwell] deBonrepos, grandmother of Mary Hooper, written 3 March, 1734).
4 N.J. Archives, First Series, Vol XX11, Marriage Records, 1665-1800
5 Charles Wilson Opdike, *The OPDyck Genealogy* (Albany, N.Y.: Weed, Parsons & Co, 1889)
6 Ibid., p. 243
7 New Jersey Colonial Documents: Calendar of Wills 1806 - 1809, 1806, July 24, Levi Updike, p. 342
8 The asterisk represents those persons in direct-line ancestry to Alden Hooper Neal; the round bullets symbolize the siblings, nieces and nephews of the direct-line ancestors.
9 *Colonial Laws, 1774*, pp. 265-267
10 *An Island Refuge. Loyalists and Disbanded Troops on the Island of Saint John.* Orlo Jones and Doris Haslam (Abeqweit Branch of the United Empire Loyalist Assoc. of Canada, 1983), p. 237
11 Ibid., p. 256
12 Ibid., p. 317
13 The Dutch Church Record, Staten Island, 1728 - 1735, p. 83
14 H. H. Hooper, "Bedeque and Its People," *The Prince Edward Island Magazine*, August and September, 1900
15 Mrs. William Sumner Crosby, *William Hooper, 1635 - 1883, A Biographical Sketch of Eight Generations of Hoopers (*Brookline, MA: 1906), p. 4
16 Ibid., p. 5
17 John Fox, *Book of Martyrs*, p. 323
18 Ibid., p. 5
19 Ibid., p. 212
20 Mrs. William Crosby, op. cit.
21 Synopsis of St. Michael's Church, Church Bulletin, April 14, 1996
22 *History of St. Michael's Church*. Biographical Sketches. Series A, p. 105

Addendum to Chapter One

In September 2003, a "genealogist neighbor" of ours, Bill Good, in Chelton, Prince Edward Island, found three more generations of Hoopers on the internet. The name of the wife of Stephen, in the first generation, is incorrect according to the internet information. The new and apparently correct information follows: Stephen Hooper (b. 1666) married Maria Mellet (b. 1667) whose father was John Peterson Mellet and whose mother was Maria Bellemaine [Research on ancesters of Orval McFadyen by Sarah McFadyen]. **Stephen and Maria Hooper** had six children, four girls and two boys all born on Staten Island, New York (surname Hooper):

Elizabeth, born 1688; **Marie**, born 1689; **Anna**, born 1690; **Martha**, born 1692; **Stephen**, born 1695; and **Clement**, born 1700

The father of Stephen, husband of Maria, was **George Hooper Jr.**, born on April 14, 1625 at St. James, London, England (Our British friend stated that St. James is a well-to-do, posh end of London). George's wife was Elizabeth (surname unknown). George and Elizabeth were married c.1646. How many children they had I do not know.

The father of George Hooper Jr. was **George Hooper Sr.**, born on August 11, 1583 in Mauldon, Bedfordshire, England, a southern county close to London. The names and numbers of children in this family I do not know other than the George mentioned above.

The father of George Hooper Sr., born in 1583, was **Thomas Hooper**, who was born in 1539. The mother of this George Hooper was Margaret Poole, birthdate unknown. The area of residence for Thomas Hooper is not stated.

CHAPTER 2

The Changing Times of the Island of St. John in the Mid-Eighteenth Century, and Thomas Hooper's Seven Children - The Fourth Generation

The early historical background of Prince Edward Island, 1752-1771, prior to the arrival of Thomas Hooper from New Jersey

John O'London once wrote: "There is something called history, but the long, long voice of tradition whispers down every corridor that has not been closed, or it reaches us, we know not how, through the wall or the rent in the wall, and through 'man's ancient heart.' We are members, not only of one and another, but of all who have passed before us."

The well-known, early Twentieth Century Island historian, Ada MacLeod, of Summerside [her historical research dates from the 1920s], penned a beautiful, descriptive narrative of Prince Edward Island's history during the 1700s. Her writing style remains primarily unchanged in a book edited and published by Marjorie McCallum Gay in 1980, called *Roads to Summerside. The Story of Early Summerside and the Surrounding Area.* I quote verbatim from their work, in the hope that it will introduce the reader to their wonderful research and writing talents:

A UNITED EMPIRE LOYALIST FAMILY

In the hot noon of an August day in 1752...there alighted from a canoe that had just landed at the head of the coast-water now known as Raynor's Creek, a fine French gentleman with his attendants. He set out briskly along the shady beaten path that from time immemorial had been the main Indian trail across the Island at this point (where the highway now runs past Read's Corner to Bedeque), and as he walked he glanced ever about him with the eye of the trained observer. Scholar he was and diplomat, Thomas Pichon by name, formerly of Marseilles, but at this time secretary to the French Governor of Louisburg, and commissioned by him to report on the Island of St. John, chiefly as to its harbors and navigable rivers. But for all his learning and graces he was false at heart, a traitor to La Belle France, selling her secrets to the English for money and fine raiment, so that in the end he was compelled to spend his days in hiding in the city of London.

Nevertheless, while there he published under an assumed name a record of his travels in Cape Breton and St. John's Island, and from an extract out of this book, translated some years ago for the Prince Edward Island Magazine by Miss Amy Pope (Madame Berlingquet) we glean the following account of Bedeque Bay as to its surroundings: "From Malpec we set out in a canoe and after crossing a bay three leagues we landed near a small rivulet entirely fed by the filtration of the waters which lodge themselves in this low marshy neighborhood. From the head of this rivulet we directed our course by a way that runs a league to the southward. The earth was covered with beech and especially with a prodigious quantity of French beans, and a kind of pine-tree. At length we arrived at Bedec. The harbour of Bedec is inhabited by eight families which by our computation makes four and forty souls. It is situate in the south side of the Island within sixteen leagues of Port de la Joie, and eighteen of the Green Bay of Acadia. The soil is very proper from culture and the borders adorned with beautiful meadows. After doubling the Isle of Bedec the harbour divides itself into two branches. In both you may cast anchor for four or five fathoms at low water, but for greater safety you had better move to the southward side which is thoroughly protected from the wind."

Further details as to the contour of the harbor and its currents complete his observations at this point. He notes the gum-chewing habit of the sqaws by which "their teeth are rendered exceeding white," but wrongly attributes the source of the gum to "an incense distilled from the white cedar." He is much "incommoded with marignoins or gnats whose stings are more pungent here than in any other part of the country. They bite with such venom and fury that persons not accustomed to their insolence are apt to lose all patients,"[sic] but adds philosophically, "there is no place without some sort of inconvenience." [Author's Note: Might these gnats be mosquitoes for which Bedeque is infamous today?]

In the autumn of the same year, 1752, the French governor, realizing the growing importance of St. John's Island, sent another officer, Sieur La Pichon sailing along the north coast to Malpec where he was "amazed at the excellence of the timber, consisting of all kinds of hardwoods such as maple, black birch, and oak, fit

for use in the construction of schooners," then portaged across to the south side. "Not far from the harbor of Bedec," he wrote, "is a great grove in which are cedars of four feet in diameter and two toises and a half in circumference." [That is the equivalent of fifteen feet]

LaRoque's record shows there were 2014 settlers on the Island at this time, none of them apparently having been born here, but described as "natives of Acadia." They were "poor but contented." Only one person had more than one horse, cows were scarce, but oxen and pigs fairly common.

To these settlers, particularly those about Malpaque, had come "three years of anguish" when their crops in successive years had been destroyed by field mice, locusts, and scald. A certain man by the name of St. Germain from Perigord in France was accused by the Indians of bringing about these calamities by witchcraft, and was killed and buried "on the isle that lies to the larboard as you enter Port la Joye."

The journals of these two surveyors are without doubt the first words ever penned about this section of the Island.[34]

The *Journal Pioneer* published, in the July 28, 2000 edition, the following short article: "The Council of Nova Scotia decided to deport Acadians 245 years ago today, in 1755, under the pretext that they had refused the oath of allegiance to Britain. Over the next few years most of the Acadians, who were the descendants of French settlers, were rounded up and deported. Others managed to flee to Quebec or hide. It is estimated about one-half of them died during the expulsion."

Returning to, *Roads to Summerside. The Story of Early Summerside and the Surrounding Area,* I quote:

And so LaRoque and Pichon sailed away, and the Acadian children stood in wondering groups on the shore to see them depart; but these had grown to men and women and faced bitter tragedy before the next ship recorded by history sailed into Bedeque Bay - and it bore the flag of another and a victorious race. It was the two hundred ton ship *Canceaux* from Plymouth, well armed, with a crew of forty sailors, carrying Surveyor-General Samuel Holland and his assistants on this, the first stage of their survey of the North American possessions of His Majesty George III.

In the cabin of the vessel stood a tall and beautiful mahogany clock which was used "by Holland in all his surveys as the chronometer on which his observations were based...."

On account of Holland's place as a foundation-builder in our Province, he is worthy of more than a passing notice. Not only did he bestow on the Island its first English place-name, but, as Sir Andrew MacPhail has said, "His survey still governs every transaction in the sale and purchase of land. Even the houses are set to Captain Holland's compass, that is, to the magnetic north of his time, which, it may be added, lay some seven degrees to the eastward of the present direction."

He was born in England in 1717, and having been left an orphan at an early age was brought up by some maiden aunts who planned for him a clerical career. But his adventurous spirit rebelled at the prospect, and he finally obtained their consent to finish his education in Holland at one of the famous military colleges where he became an expert engineer.[34]

Crossing the Atlantic as Captain of Artillery with the Royal American Regiment, he was sent to join Wolfe, taking part as his aide-de-camp in the siege of Louisburg, and leading successfully the attack on the west gate. Shortly after, the famous Captain Cook visited this port in command of the "Mercury," and received instructions from Holland on the working of several new mathematical instruments brought from England by the latter.

In 1759 Holland sailed for Quebec with the historic fleet which was destined to play such an important part in the conquest of Canada. He was on board the "Pembroke" under Captain Simcoe (father of Governor Simcoe), but this gallant officer died while sailing up the Gulf; and it was Holland who afterwards told the Governor of his father's dying command to his men - worthy of the old British sea-dog - "Just wrap me in an old sail-cloth and drop my body over the side. Save your lead for the enemy, and your pitch to mend the rents in the ship."

Holland was engaged in the taking of Quebec. On the very day of the battle, Wolfe had presented him with a pair of pistols bearing the following inscription on the barrels: "The gift of Major-General James Wolfe to Captain Samuel Holland." These weapons were afterwards used in a duel that took place near Montreal between his son, Lieut. Samuel Holland, and Capt. Shoedde, both of the 49th Regiment, in which young Holland was killed and Shoedde badly wounded....

In October 1764 Holland and his survey party landed on the Island [on the *Canceaux*] and he spent the winter in a hastily built shanty at "Observation Cove." With him was his beautiful and accomplished young wife, Marie Josette Rolet - and here amid these rude surroundings was born their eldest son (afterwards Colonel John Holland), the first child of resident British parents to be born on Prince Edward Island....

Within a year he had finished the survey of the Island and dispatched the plans to the "Lords of Trade and Plantations" in England, and so warm was their letter of commendation that he declared he "could now climb the rocks and wade the waters without thinking of danger or weariness."

While Holland was conducting surveys in New Hampshire, the American Revolution broke out and he was offered a high command in the "Continental Army." On refusing this offer, he was thrown into prison, but escaped, and on reaching Quebec, entered service again on behalf of the Motherland.

At the close of the war...he held the office of Surveyor-General for fifty years, and at the time of his death in 1801 was a member of the Executive and Legislative Assembly of Quebec. His son, Colonel John (called by him "St. John Jack" because he was born on the Island), followed in his footsteps and in 1787 was appointed with two others to establish the line between Nova Scotia and New Brunswick, and also between Quebec and New Brunswick.

The early Micmac and Acadian place-names of the Island were altogether of a descriptive nature such as Baslooakade (Cape Traverse) "landing place," and Tulakadik (Tracadie) "the camping place"; or Point Prime "the first point of the compass," and Point Naufrage which carried the memory of an ancient shipwreck.

Holland on the other hand was wont to commemorate the names of distinguished friends in his English place-names, and thus the list of capes and coast waters on his beautifully executed map of St. John's Island forms a veritable "who's who" of the prominent people of that time.

It was his custom to designate a large bay by the leading title of a certain nobleman, and then distribute his lesser titles among the tributary streams and creeks. Thus, the harbour of Summerside was called by him Halifax Bay after his superior officer, the Earl of Halifax, President of the "Lords of Trade and Plantations" and Secretary of State at that time, who was also termed "the father of the coloneis." His name was George Montagu Dunk and his second title was Viscount Sunbury, which explains the origin of Dunk River and Sunbury Cove. Wilmot River is named from Lt. Col. Montagu Wilmot, Governor of Nova Scotia at the time of the survey. Although the official title of Halifax Bay still appears on modem maps, the old Indian name of Bedeque Bay has always persisted (Bedec meaning "sultry place").

One fancies that some incident must lurk in the name Salutation Cove (Seacow Head), and it may well be that some of the same Acadians who in their childhood had called farewell from the Bedeque shore to the departing French explorers now stood in a group on the same cliff, and sadly yet courteously waved a greeting to this vanguard of another race. Graham Head (McCallum's Point) is from Lt. Col. Gordon Graham, Major of the 42nd in America, who in 1767 received a grant of one-half of Lot 47....

From the time when the *Canceaux* sailed into Bedeque Bay a full score of years had gone by ere the next ship recorded by history made its appearance, and it was the bearer of part of that "epic migration" of the Loyalists of whom 35,000, driven from their homes, took refuge in the Maritime Provinces.

on Wilmot Creek, the rest back land on Lot 19. They preferred taking leases from the proprietors in a place which the French Acadians had formerly inhabited with quite large clearings, small houses and orchards, in what is now Lower Bedeque. John and his sister, Isabella, lived in one of these houses.

It was not until May 1792 that the one hundred acres they were living on was conveyed to John and Mary Robins from the proprietors of Lot 26, Anthony and Robert Gordon, of the Islands of Dominica and Saint Vincent. Later that year Mr. Gordon arrived on the schooner *Betsey* from Halifax to inspect his property and meet his tenants.

In January 1794, John appeared before the Legislative Council asking that the grant given to his father, Richard Robins, be distributed to his descendants residing on the Island. His petition was granted on May 6, 1803. In 1793, when England was at war with France, the Island of Saint John Corps of Volunteers was formed with John Robins among the Prince County Regiment's officers. When he was baptized by Rev. DesBrisay, on October 17, 1796, he was described as "late" lieutenant. He died less than a year later, leaving six small children for his wife Mary (Hooper) to bring up on their one hundred acres in Lower Bedeque.[5]

Thomas Hooper, called Tommy (4, Thomas 3, Clement 2, Stephen 1) was born in 1772 in New Jersey; he married, in 1807, Elizabeth Cole (called Betsy), who was born c.1788, the daughter of Benjamin Cole and Isabella Robins (the young lady mentioned above). Note the disparity of years between husband and wife). She died on June 10, 1866 at age 78, in Lower Bedeque.[6] Thomas and Eizabeth lived in Lower Bedeque, P.E.I. Thomas died on February 16, 1837.[7] Thomas was the lad of 13 or thereabouts who came with his father and brother, Major, to seek a new life in Canada.

Rachel Hooper (4, Thomas 3, Clement 2, Stephen 1), birthdate unknown; she did not marry, but made her home with Elisha (who had inherited his father's home and property) in later years. Apparently she lived with her father until his death in 1816. [The longer I study this family and think about Rachel the more I wonder if she was a

real person. There seems to be NO information about her. Her birth and death dates are unknown, and there seems to be no mention of her anywhere except in the notes of Muriel Hooper Blanchard. All that is listed there is her name and the fact that she lived with her father until his death, and that she then stayed on in the house which Elisha inherited. There is no stone for her in the Lower Bedeque Cemetery in P.E.I .]

Elisha Hooper (4, Thomas 3, Clement 2, Stephen 1) born in Windsor, Middlesex County in 1782; married, on June 30, 1809, Margaret Crosby, who was born in 1781, the daughter of William Crosby of Meadowbank, P.E.I.; she died on March 31, 1843. The reader will remember that Elisha was the baby born to Mrs. Hooper just before the Patriots caused her death. Elisha came with his sisters to P.E.I. when he was about 4 years old; he was baptized on October 8, 1812 by the Rev. T. Debrissay. [The Rev. Theophilus Desbrisay was the rector of the parish of St. Paul's in Charlottetown from 1773-1823][8] [Because the dates of birth of only five of the seven children are known, it is possible that Mary was the fifth child and the births went something like this: Major 1764; Sarah 1767; Ann 1770; Thomas 1772; Mary 1774 or 1775; Rachel 1778; and Elisha 1782. It would appear, however, as Mary had six children in 1797 when her husband died, that she was born before 1775. The reader will ascertain later that Isabella Robins Cole came to the Island of St. John in May of 1784. Isabella said that four years later her marriage and her brother John's to Mary Hooper took place close together in time. If Mary was married in the spring of 1788 she would have been 13 or 14. Her children were said to be between the ages of 8 and 2 when her husband died in 1797. They would therefore have been born between 1789 and 1795]

H. H. Hooper has a commission issued by William Townsend appointing Elisha Hooper a Lieutenant in the South Battalion of Prince County militia commanded by the Hon. Harry Compton. It is signed by Thomas Desbrisay, Secretary, and J. F. Holland, Military Adj. General, and dated the 23rd day of January, 1813. Also, one dated

April 19, 1858, signed by Charles Desbrisay, issued by the Governor, appointing Elisha High Sheriff of Prince County. Owing to poor health he declined to accept the office, and two years later he died, aged seventy-eight.

Thomas told his children that his grandmother was a French Huguenot.[9] The mother of Mary Stillwell Journé Hooper (who was Clement's wife and Thomas's mother) was Mary (Maria) Poillon, the daughter of a French Huguenot, Martha Biljouw (Billew), who was born in Leyden, Holland, after her father and mother, Pierre and François (DuBois) Biljouw fled to Leyden for refuge.[10] Also, the census of Staten Island in 1706 listed Clement Hooper's mother as a French Huguenot, born in Tifilis, France.[11] Thomas's two grandmothers, then, would have been French Huguenots!

Notes

1 Obituary, The *Royal Gazette*, Tues., Feb. 27, 1838; and Orlo Jones and Doris Haslam, eds., *An Island Refuge. Loyalists and Disbanded Troops on the Island of Saint John* (Abegweit Branch of the United Empire Loyalist Association of Canada, 1983), p. 138

2 Ibid., p. 138

3 Ibid., p. 139

4 Ibid., p. 238

5 Ibid., pp. 238-239

6 Doris Haslam, *The Wrights of Bedeque, Prince Edward Island* (Summerside, P.E.I.: Doris Muncey Haslam, 1978), p. 831

7 Information compiled by Dave Hunter, Charlottetown, PEI

8 *A Concise History of St. Paul's Churches*. (Charlottetown, PEI: St. Paul's, 1978)

9 Orlo Jones and Doris Haslam, op. cit., p. 137

10 John E. Stillwell, M.D., *The History of Captain Nicholas Stillwell* (N.Y. City: 1930)

11 Records of Muriel Hooper Blanchard

CHAPTER 3

The Struggle in the Colonies Between 1775 and 1784, and Some Implications

The Thirteen colonies were under the rule of the British. In 1733 when Benjamin Franklin wrote "Poor Richard's Almanac" about 70 percent of the population of the Colonies was of English descent. The Revolutionary War in America started on April 19, 1775 when a group of colonists fought British soldiers at Lexington, MA. Hours later in nearby Concord, colonists fired "the shot that was heard around the world" when these "minutemen," so called because they were farmers ready to engage in fighting at a moment's notice, battled the British near a bridge. The war lasted for eight years.

Bad feelings had been festering for more than ten years. After the French and Indian War ended in 1763, the British gained control over nearly all of France's empire in North America. At this time, the majority of the colonists was undoubtedly loyal to Britain, their "mother country." Twelve years later, however, Americans rebelled against the British rule.

There was fear of French encroachment so the colonies had stuck with Britain, but when the French were routed, this question was asked: "Do we need to be governed by a pipsqueak island?" The French War left Britain with a huge debt. The British paid taxes 25 times higher than the Colonists. The British had tried to restore their authority over the American colonies and to tax them more heavily shortly after the war with France. The Americans, who had enjoyed quite a bit of self-government, wanted even greater freedom. The Whigs/Patriots resisted British taxes in 1760. They refused to pay the Stamp Tax of 1765 and the Townshend duties on imports in 1767.

Citizens of Boston organized a "tea party" in December 1773 to dump incoming tea into Boston Harbor rather than pay a tax on it. Colonists dressed as Indians raided three British ships and threw their cargoes of tea overboard. Twenty-three thousand pounds of tea were thrown into the harbor, and several British vessels were burned. The tax on tea was three pence a pound. If a person drank a gallon of tea a day, he would pay $1.00 at the end of the year! Obviously there was a fear of being controlled by the British.

Britain sent troops to support its authority. As the British tried to tighten their grip on the colonies in many directions, the Americans resisted. For example, Britain attempted to manage Indian affairs from London and to slow down the westward expansion of the colonies. A tax on sugar and molasses was ordered. Americans were required to provide quarters, fuel, candles, cider or beer, and transportation for British troops. The Stamp Act required colonists to buy tax stamps and put them on newspapers, playing cards, diplomas, and various legal documents. The colonists refused to allow the stamps to be sold, saying "Taxation without representation is tyranny!" [a feisty bunch, they!] These words were strictly a slogan in a war of ideas. The radicals of the Patriots knew that they didn't want representation as they would be outvoted. Lord Frederick Nelson was the prime minister of Britain at the time when America challenged the British parliamentary constitution. The British government decided that something drastic needed to be done to assert its authority. It passed the Intolerable Acts in 1774. These new laws closed Boston Harbor to commerce until the city showed repentance for its "tea party."

The First Continental Congress met in Philadelphia in September 1774, and demanded that the British abandon their efforts to make Massachusetts bow to British authority. It asked Britain to admit that parliament had no right to tax the colonists for revenue. General

Thomas Gage, military governor of the colony of Massachusetts, reported to the British cabinet that Massachusetts had revolted and asked for orders. The cabinet ordered Gage to arrest the colonial leaders in Massachusetts, break up the "mobs," organize a Tory militia, and use the troops in Boston. Gage sent troops from Boston to Concord to destroy the Patriots' main supply depot. This is when Paul Revere and two other horsemen went on the ride that Longfellow wrote about ... "On the 19th of April in '75, hardly a man is now alive who remembers that famous day and year!" For his decision, Gage was relieved of his command by King George III of England, and Major General William Howe was put in charge of the redcoat forces in the American colonies.

Boston appeared to be the hot bed of rebellion and other areas reluctantly joined.[1] Sam Adams and John Hancock [small mind, deep pockets][2] were radicals against the British. Sam Adams was the agitator, the "mouth." He spent full-time doing it. The Sons of Liberty was a Political Action Group. The Patriots were a mob and cunning. John Adams, Samuel's cousin, was the Boston Massacre trial lawyer, one of the finest in the country.

This war was really a civil war between the Patriots and the Loyalists, especially in the American south where the feelings were very fierce. Benjamin Franklin's family was torn apart; his illegitimate son, William, in his 20's, was very close to Benjamin. Franklin supported King George III for a long time, then the disenchantment grew, and the love affair ended! In 1767 William, a strong Loyalist, was the royal governor of New Jersey. By then Benjamin Franklin was more of a Patriot. In 1774, he split with England in time to avoid arrest for Lexington. [He was at sea then on his way home] What followed was a terrible disassociation with his son.

According to *World Book Encyclopedia*, 1987 Edition, about one-fourth of the colonists supported the redcoats. These Loyalists or Tories [a derogatory term] stirred the bitter hatred of the Patriots. As time went on, the Patriots became bolder. Hot tar was used to cover

the bodies of the Loyalists, then chicken feathers were put on and the men were paraded up and down the main street of the town. One can imagine the burned skin, the pain, and the disgrace of this treatment!

On the 19th of April, in '75, when Paul Revere took his midnight ride, weapons and ammunition had been stored. One-third of the militia were minutemen, ready to fight at a moment's notice. There were 11,000 militiamen and minutemen from Massachusetts colony; and 4,000 came to Lexington/Concord! Only one in 300 musket balls met its mark; they were notoriously inaccurate. The British general yelled, "Lay down your arms, you damn rebels, or you will all be shot!" Eight colonists were dead, and one was wounded. One British soldier had a flesh wound.

Four cities in the colonies had over 10,000 population: Boston, New York, Philadelphia, and Charleston. The major powers in the world would become involved in this war. General George Washington became the commander-in-chief of the rebel forces in the eight-year war.

The Patriots thought that one big battle would win the war. They built a fort on the Charlestown peninsula where the battle of Reed's Hill was fought on June 16, 1775. Reed's Hill was closer to the water than Bunker Hill. A young Patriot was decapitated by a bullet. Some Patriots left, but 1,200 stayed. Thick white smoke covered the battlefield. The Colonists' supplies were limited; their powder was gone. On the third try of the British soldiers, one-half of the 3,300 landing force were dead or wounded. "Success is too dearly bought," said General Howe. The war continued, however, for six more years.

The Second Continental Congress adopted the Declaration of Independence on July 4, 1776. Ties between the colonies and the mother country had now been cut. Britain launched a great offensive to crush the rebellion. In 1778 the colonies acquired an active ally when France recognized the independence of the United States and entered the war. Spain declared war on Britain in 1779, as did Holland in 1780. Faced with so many enemies, Britain found it difficult

to assemble an army powerful enough to destroy the Patriot forces. Britain hired mercenaries, soldiers paid to fight its battles, primarily Hessians from Germany. At sea American privateers captured British ships. The surrender of Cornwallis at Yorktown on October 19, 1781 marked the war's last major action. Then the British gave up all hope of conquering the Patriots.

The British military forces included regulars (redcoats), Loyalists (Tories), mercenaries (hired soldiers of other countries), and Indian tribes (particularly the Six Nations and the Cherokee). At peak strength the British army had about 50,000 soldiers. The British navy reached its peak strength of 468 ships in 1783. In contrast, the fighting forces of the Patriots consisted of militiamen and volunteers in the Continental Army, which reached its peak strength of 20,000 men, more than enough to defend themselves. The Continental Navy at its height had about 50 ships, aided by about 2,000 privateers. The colonists had large advantages in that they did not have to transport supplies across the ocean. They also knew the terrain and could easily retreat to places where the British had difficulty reaching them. In addition, the colonists were almost wagering that Britain's enemies in Europe would enter the fight against Britain.[3] Both patriots and redcoats relied primarily on the musket and the bayonet. Some Colonists used rifles.

In 1995 Alden's dear cousin, Gladys Henderson, took us to lunch at the Loyalist Inn, Prince William Dining Room, in Summerside. The Loyalist story was told on the front cover of the menu, with more illumination:

> The American Revolution began at Lexington and Concord, Massachusetts in the spring of 1775 and, after six years of bloody civil strife, ended with the surrender of the British forces at Yorktown, Virginia in 1781. The former British Thirteen Colonies then officially became the United States of America.
>
> Fought between the rebel Patriots, who wanted independence from British rule, and British forces trying to subdue their rebellion, the Revolutionary War pitted friends against friends, even dividing families in its course. Caught in the middle were thousands of "Loyalists" who chose to support the British cause over that of their rebel neighbors.

A UNITED EMPIRE LOYALIST FAMILY

The Loyalists or Tories supported the government of King George III for a variety of reasons. Not all were recent British immigrants to the Thirteen Colonies. Several minority groups, particularly those of German or Dutch descent, also chose to carry the Loyalist banner. The recent British immigrants supported Britain, understandably, out of a deep sense of loyalty, whereas the minority groups became Loyalists out of fear for the eventual loss of their language, religion, and customs because of the democratic principle of Representation by Population advocated by the rebels.

Throughout the revolution Loyalist sympathizers were shunned and mistreated by rebel supporters who frequently forced their Loyalist captives to endure the disgrace of being publicly "tarred and feathered." [The skin was smeared with tar and then covered with feathers. You can imagine the discomfort in trying to remove the feathers. If the tar was hot, the skin would be burned and terribly painful. It's possible death may have occurred from using this procedure] The British government made every effort to protect these Loyalist supporters, and King George's son, Prince William, openly championed their cause and publicly worked to ease their suffering. However, with the eventual victory of the rebel forces led by George Washington, the Loyalists were forced to abandon all their material belongings and flee for their lives. The Loyalists came by the tens of thousands to Nova Scotia, New Brunswick, and Prince Edward Island. One of the main Loyalist settlements in P.E.I. was established at Bedeque during the 1780s, and before long these Loyalist settlers fanned out over the surrounding area where they were instrumental in settling much of this part of Prince County. Such names as Darby, Green, **Hooper**, Linkletter, Robins, Schurman, Small, and Wright became prominent in the later development of the region.

One local Loyalist family, the Schurmans, fled from New Rochelle, N.Y. where William Schurman is said to have escaped from a rebel jail where he was incarcerated for several months for his Loyalist convictions. William, his wife Elizabeth Hyatt, their 10 children and 2 faithful slaves set out for the Isle of St. John. While en route to safety, family history relates that the Schurmans sought refuge in a cave from their pursuers. While hiding during the night, it is said that spiders spun webs across the cave opening thus deceiving the rebel soldiers into believing the cave was empty. It is said that ever after, Mrs. Schurman would not allow any of her family to kill a spider.[4] They eventually reached Bedeque in 1784. Another Loyalist settler, Daniel Green, gave his name to Green's Shore which later became known as Summerside.

The Loyalist tradition remains vibrant and strong in the Summerside area yet, and numerous families still proudly claim Loyalist ancestry.

After the close of the war in 1782, the Government of the United States extended no amnesty to those who had been loyal to Britain,

but treated them with marked vindictiveness - very different from the spirit which the North evinced towards the South after the great civil war in the nineteenth century. The unfortunate Loyalists were proscribed, despoiled, and forced into exile. As New York had been in British hands throughout the war, it naturally became a place of refuge for all who were under the ban of the Government. Massachusetts and New York were the most severe of all the states....All legal rights were denied a Loyalist. He might be assaulted, blackmailed, or slandered, without having any recourse in law. Washington, himself, approved of the harsh treatment which was meted out. Many unfortunates were imprisoned on the slightest provocation. The story of the Simsbury mine in Connecticut is far more terrible than the Black Hole of Calcutta, for many people were placed there under the most revolting conditions, which caused a frightful mortality. When it was realized that only punishment and misery would be the lot of the persecuted Loyalists if they dared to remain in their own country, the British Government offered them an asylum in Canada, and under the organizing genius of Sir Guy Carleton and others, arrangements were made for the removal of some seventy thousand people.[5]

St. Michael's Church and congregation, in Trenton, New Jersey [where Clement and Mary Hooper are presumably buried, and where several family members were baptized], suffered greatly during the Revolutionary War: "[It] was closed by action of the vestry from July 1776 to October 1783, a period of seven years....The Rector, wardens, and vestry of St. Michael's Church in Trenton, deeply affected with the situation of Public Affairs, by which, among other unhappy Circumstances, the Public Home of Worship of a Church of the most Catholic & Benevolent Principles has become incompatible with the safety of the Person of the Rector & Members of the Church, and the Exercise of it may thereby be attended with Inconveniences which for the Peace of the Church & society they wish to avoid. And as no alteration therein can take place, but by a Particular Authority competent only for that purpose, in order to avoid the Inconveniences

aforesed, the Rector, Church wardens & vestry agree to a Temporary Suspension of Public Worship 'till God in his Providence shall so order that it can be performed agreeably to the Principles & Constitution of the Church.'"

The "alteration" referred to concerned the obligation to include the "Prayer for the King" as set forth in the liturgy.[6]

Most of the writers of our American history books, especially the earlier ones, in dealing with the War of the Revolution, show a disposition to magnify unduly the characters of those who espoused the cause of the Patriots, and to belittle and disparage those who adhered to the mother country. Certainly the Loyalists in our histories are too seldom accorded fair treatment, rather are their motives aspersed, and their characters as men of honor and lovers of justice and liberty bitterly assailed. Nothing could be more unfair or more subversive of the actual facts in many cases. For example, the men in the vestry of St. Michael's Church who, in 1776, threw in their fortunes with the royal cause, were undoubtedly at least equal in conscience and character to their associates who supported the cause of the Patriots. It was a time that tried men's souls, and those equally intelligent and conscientious saw their duty differently.

Of those who favored the British cause, many in New Jersey and elsewhere were men of position and substance, like Daniel Coxe IV, who had been appointed by order of the King to a seat in the Council of the Province of New Jersey, May 1, 1771, and who assumed the same at Burlington on November 21 of the same year.

The minutes of the Council show that, after his appointment in 1771, Coxe was regular and faithful in his attendance until the close of that body's existence in 1773. He was a zealous Tory, and in a letter dated July 4, 1775, viewed with prophetic foresight the cruel plight to which such as he would be reduced.

Nelson, a biographer and genealogist, wrote: "What then have men of property not to fear and apprehend, and particularly those who happen and are known to differ in sentiment from the generality? They become a mark for popular fury, and those who are esteemed friends to Government devoted for destruction. They are not even allowed to preserve a neutrality, and passiveness becomes a crime."[7]

At the time that Alden and I went to school, the sentiment was totally "rah, rah Patriots!" It was not until I was a middle-aged adult that I began to think more objectively about the situation and the conflict. I believe that I very well might have been a Loyalist, knowing my personality as I do. On Long Island and, of course, in many other places in New York, as well as in Connecticut, Rhode Island, Massachusetts, and New Jersey, there were many enclaves of Loyalists.

Notes

1 Video, "American Revolution, Vol. 1, The Conflict Ignites," Graystone Comunications, Inc., 1990
2 Ibid.
3 *Word Book Encyclopedia,* Vol. "R", (WB Publisher, 1987), pp. 252-260
4 Orlo Jones and Doris Haslam, eds. *An Island Refuge* (n.p.: Abegweit Branch of the United Empire Loyalists Association of Canada, 1983), p. 374
5 Graves, Ross, *William Schurman, Loyalist of Bedeque, Prince Edward Isladnd, and His Descendants*, (Summerside, P.E.I.: Harold B. Schurman, 1973), pp. 20-21
6 *History of St. Michael's Church*, Chapter X, "St. Michael's and the War," p. 75 (Trenton, N.J.)
7 Nelson, *Biographical and Genealogical Notes*, p. 84

CHAPTER 4

The Difficult Decisions of Thomas Hooper, United Empire Loyalist

To give some background on Thomas Hooper, the son of Clement and Mary, I will quote from an article which appeared in the *Charlottetown Guardian* shortly after the turn of the twentieth century:

A TROUBLED LOYALIST. Through the courtesy of Messrs. J. M. Dent and Sons, Publishers, of Toronto, the writer is permitted to make use of the selection bearing the above title from the book *In Pioneer Days,* written by Dr. D. L. Dickie, and published by Messrs. J. M. Dent:

Thomas Hooper lived in New Jersey. He had a hundred acre farm, a large house and barn, a wife, and a happy, growing family. When the war came [the Revolutionary War], Hooper, feeling that he could not fight against his flag, refused to join the American Army; he remained quietly on his farm taking neither side. His American neighbors and relatives were angry at his loyalty to Britain. They helped themselves to his cattle, pigs, and fowl whenever they needed them; they stripped his place of oxen.

The war dragged through nine weary years; by 1782 it was plain that peace was near and that Britain would give the struggling colonies their freedom. Hooper was a shrewd man. He wished to live in a British country, and he felt sure that the Americans who had treated him badly during the war would not be kinder when they had all power in their own hands. He decided that it would be best for him to go to Nova Scotia or Prince Edward Island.

Early in the spring [of 1782] he set out to find a new home. He went to the Maritime Provinces and travelled about examining the country for he wanted a good farm. The Governor of Halifax had already promised farms to all Loyalists

who wished to leave the United States. Hooper was everywhere kindly received and in July [1782] returned to his home full of hope.

Matters had not been going well in his absence. His American neighbors had grown bolder than ever. They pretended to think he was hiding a spy, went often to his place, plundered his house and thrust their bayonets through the furniture, curtains, and hay-filled bed-ticks. He also found his wife and two children sick of a fever.

According to Orlo Jones and Doris Haslam, in their book, *An Island Refuge*, we read:

He had planned to move his family to the Island that fall, but he had to change his plans. He left alone for the long treck back to Shelburne [Nova Scotia]. He worked in the Port saving his money for his new home. He returned to New Jersey, but again disaster had struck. It is said that the soldiers had returned, and not finding Thomas, they took their revenge."[1]

The historian, Dr. D.L. Dickie, in his book, *In Pioneer Days*, elaborated on the events:

At last one morning, they came in and took the bed from under Mrs. Hooper who was still an invalid [from recently giving birth to a baby boy]. They carried her out and, laying her down on the floor of an outhouse, they made off with the bed. Mrs. Hooper took cold and died." [I believe that this version is a polite one. You will soon read that she was subjected to "cruel indignities." I believe that they raped her and that she hemorrhaged and died leaving seven children, one an infant. After that Thomas Hooper hated the Americans].

He was watched, but he managed to escape with his two sons, lads of nineteen and ten. He left behind him four girls and his baby boy. To do so must have been a trial for the poor father, but he had, as yet, no home to which to take them.

Hooper and his sons got safely to Shelburne [Nova Scotia] which was then building. Thomas worked and saved for two years. By this time, he thought he had enough money to take a farm, and he begged Governor Patterson of Prince Edward Island to get him a grant of land. The Governor arranged that Hooper, Robins, and Schurman should be granted a lease of land at Bedeque in Township No. 1 containing 1250 acres which was the western division of the half of Lot No. 26. The following rates applied: first year 2 pence for each acre granted, second year 4 pence, third year 6 pence, and the fourth year 8 pence and so on. Hooper and Schurman had six months to apply for the grants. It was also stated that if they applied within a year to purchase the land, they would be able to do so for two Spanish dollars for each acre.

Research by Haslam and Jones stated: "Thomas selected his land on Bedeque Bay which was formerly farmed by an Acadian settler who had cleared several acres. He built a log cabin and put in provisions for winter, and then headed back to New Jersey to bring out the girls."[2]

According to Willard Moase, educator and local historian, there was not enough good farmland in Nova Scotia, and many loyalists left Shelburne to earn a living elsewhere. The Island of Saint John needed settlers, and land agents went to Shelburne to offer land claims; they also advertised for settlers in the *Royal American Gazette* and weekly *Intelligencer*, the first newspapers printed in 1787 by James Robertson, a Loyalist who had come to Charlottetown by way of Shelburne.[3] The Loyalists, then, did not stay long in Shelburne. It was a town created for Loyalist settlement, begun in 1783 with the arrival of three thousand refugees, growing to a population of about sixteen thousand, then disintegrating within a decade.[4]

Dr. D. L. Dickie's account continued:

> Hooper and his sons crossed to the Island in 1784. Thomas was a careful man, but in the end he found just the farm he wanted. The land was rich; the sea abounded with fish, the river with wild fowl. Hooper hoped that at last he might build a little home and gather his family about him again.
>
> In New Jersey Ann, the oldest daughter [my records show that she was the second after Sarah who had chosen to marry a Patriot and stay in New Jersey] who had had charge of the farm and the children, now prepared to move. [She would have been about 14 at the time!] She held an auction sale. Three months' credit was allowed to all those who bought more than ten shillings' worth. The goods were sold for a third of their value, but they were sold and the family began to pack up and make ready. Records show that Ann was born in 1770 making her 12 years old when her mother died and about 16 when she moved the family to P.E.I.

Thomas must have been reminded many times of a similar situation with his mother's family in France, perhaps two generations earlier. Like his Huguenot ancestors, he knew the choice that he had to make, and he made it, under continuously difficult circumstances, for the safety of his family and for his own mental health.

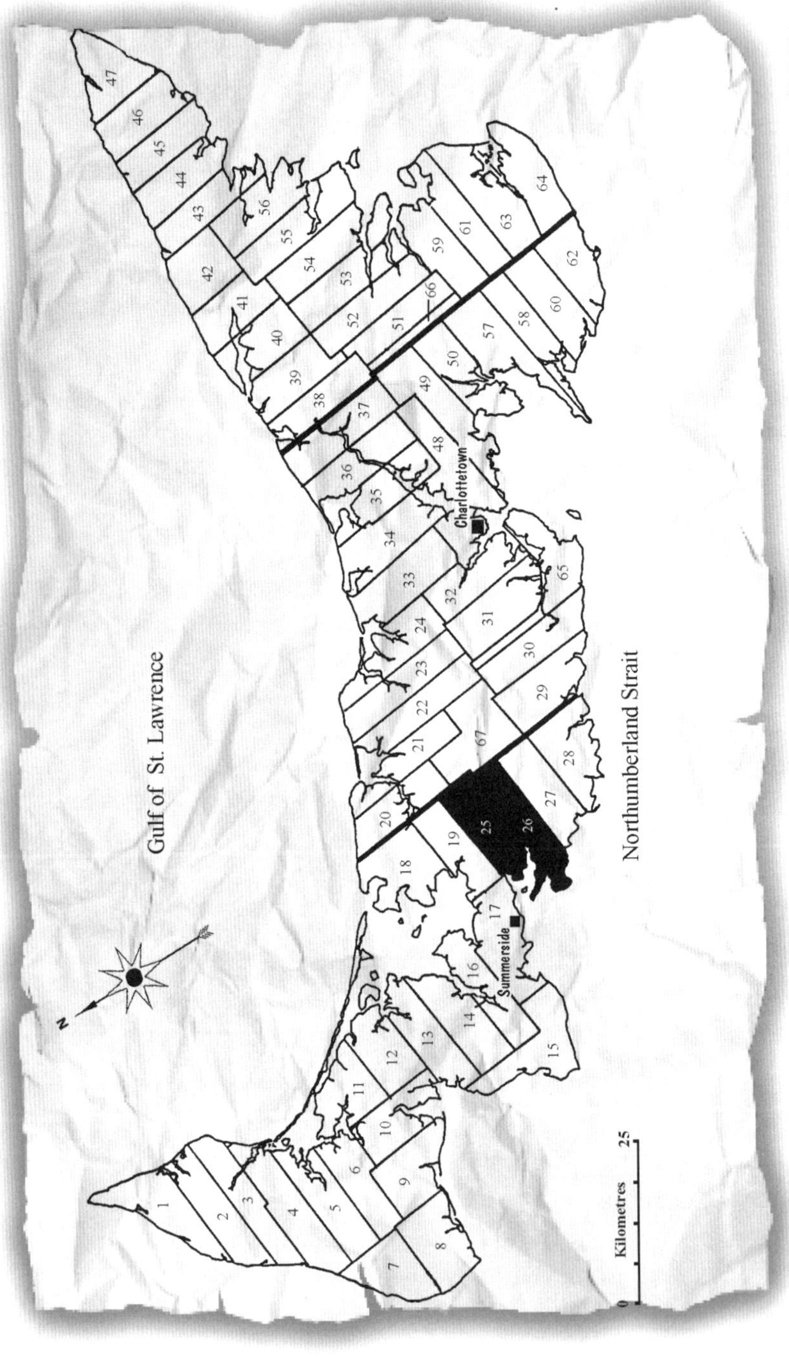

Graphics by Crescent Isle Publishers

Lots 25 and 26, Prince Edward Island, where several Hooper families eventually settled

About 1784 or 1785 William Schurman and fellow-Loyalist Thomas Hooper sailed to Shelburne in William Schurman's ship to transport refugees to the Island. Schurman may have purchased the small ship after he sold his home and furnishings in New Rochelle, N.Y. Among these refugees who became neighbors on the Island of St. John were the Wrights, the Strangs, and the Sillikers [the latter living on the property where the present Lower Bedeque Cemetery stands].[5]

In May 1784 William Schurman and Thomas Hooper appeared before the Executive Council of the Island of St. John and asked that land in the Bedeque area be reserved for them and for other settlers whom they would bring to the Island. The Council agreed to hold it until August first. Then William sailed to Shelburne and brought a group of refugees back with him. They arrived on the Island of St. John on July 26, five days before the deadline. On July 29 lots were allocated to the Schurman company, generally 500 acres to a married man and 300 acres to a single man.

Most of the refugees whom William Schurman brought to the Island in his ship did not settle permanently on the lands reserved for them. Exceptions were William Wright, William Schurman, Thomas Hooper, Jesse Strang, and Jacob Silliker. Ross Graves, in *William Schurman, Loyalist ...*, wrote that there were fourteen single men, thirteen married men, and twenty-nine children.[6] At that time Bedeque took in the whole area around the shores of Bedeque Bay. It was gradually being settled with log houses and barns widely scattered from each other.

The following letter, taken from MacLeod and Gay's *Roads to Summerside*, to one of his brothers in New Jersey, tells of the result of Thomas's search:[7]

Bedeque Harbour
Island St. John, Sept. 19, 1785

Dear Brother,

I take this opportunity to let you know that we have arrived safe to this place after a passage of four weeks. We came by the way of St. John where we remained three days for a passage to Cumberland and from thence we got teams to cross the land to the Bay of Verte, and there stayed six days waiting for a passage to the Island, which we performed the next day, and found everything agreeable to our expectations.

I have drawn 500 acres of land in two divisions, 250 on the above harbour where I can take every kind of shell-fish within ¼ of a mile from my door, and oysters in particular, a great abundance. The land appears to be good, and has about eight or ten acres cleared, formerly a French settlement. We have begun to build. Major and myself are at Charlottetown in order to get the articles allowed us by the Government. The Governor pays us great attention, and serves us in every respect.

Major and Tommy are well and very hearty. They like the place well, and think themselves happy if their sisters and brother were with them, which would be a great blessing to me. . . . I purpose to apply for Major's land which he is entitled to, three hundred acres, before I leave the town.

About 1900, H. H. Hooper wrote: "This letter he no doubt started at home and finished in Charlottetown. He returned to Nova Scotia in the fall and left Major and Tommy alone all winter. They amused themselves by fishing and hunting; occasionally they would take a hand sled and go to the French Village in Lot 17 and procure potatoes and other necessary provisions."[8]

H.H. Hooper provided greater detail about Thomas Hooper's first house:

When Thomas Hooper and his two sons Major and Thomas settled on the farm, they built a log house on the site of the present shop. It was used as a dwelling until the summer of 1790 when the present house was built. They had a genuine "house warm" when it was complete and the family moved into it. It was also the scene of many of the celebrated "fulling bees." The old log house was burnt late in the fall

of 1833.... Near the site have been found broken dishes, pieces of iron, and some thirty years ago, a peculiarly shaped axe, and later a French subsidiary coin of 1747. The French had cleared the land beyond the site of the present house and had quite a large orchard a few rods in a northeasterly direction.[9]

One can imagine Thomas seeing in his mind's eye the smoldering of a rough house, the woods cleared stump by stump for house and garden space, the panic of the frantic departure of the French family who lived on his acreage. He may also have thought of the French Roman Catholics who had driven his French Protestant grandparents and great-grandparents into exile in France. Now it was he who was the refugee, driven from his own country by descendants of the people who had accepted his grandparents and great-grandparents, settled on property of Roman Catholic French dispossessed by Protestant English!

According to H.H. Hooper, writing in, *In Pioneer Days*, "Major built his house, the homestead lately occupied by Artemas, in 1804. He, like his father, was also appointed a Justice of the Peace by Governor Patterson. Thomas Junior built a few years later in 1806 opposite his father."

In the summer of 1999 Ed Pearson told the author that Major's home was across the road from the 1976 home and farm of Dick VanHerk. That would make Major's property start just after the big right angle turn in the road going to Lower Bedeque. Ed also explained that Thomas, Jr. lived on the farm now owned by Ray Barrett (the second farm beyond the cemetery), and the third son, Elisha, settled on the home farm [the property of Thomas] owned in 1976 by Conrad Plomp, which is the next farm beyond the cemetery on the same side of the road. That description would make the three properties between the river and the present road belong to the Hooper family, all of them on the river side of the road, with only one interruption, that being where the cemetery is. That property was originally owned or rented by Jacob Silliker [or his son]. As one would turn the sharp corner on the road to Lower Bedeque, Major's prop-

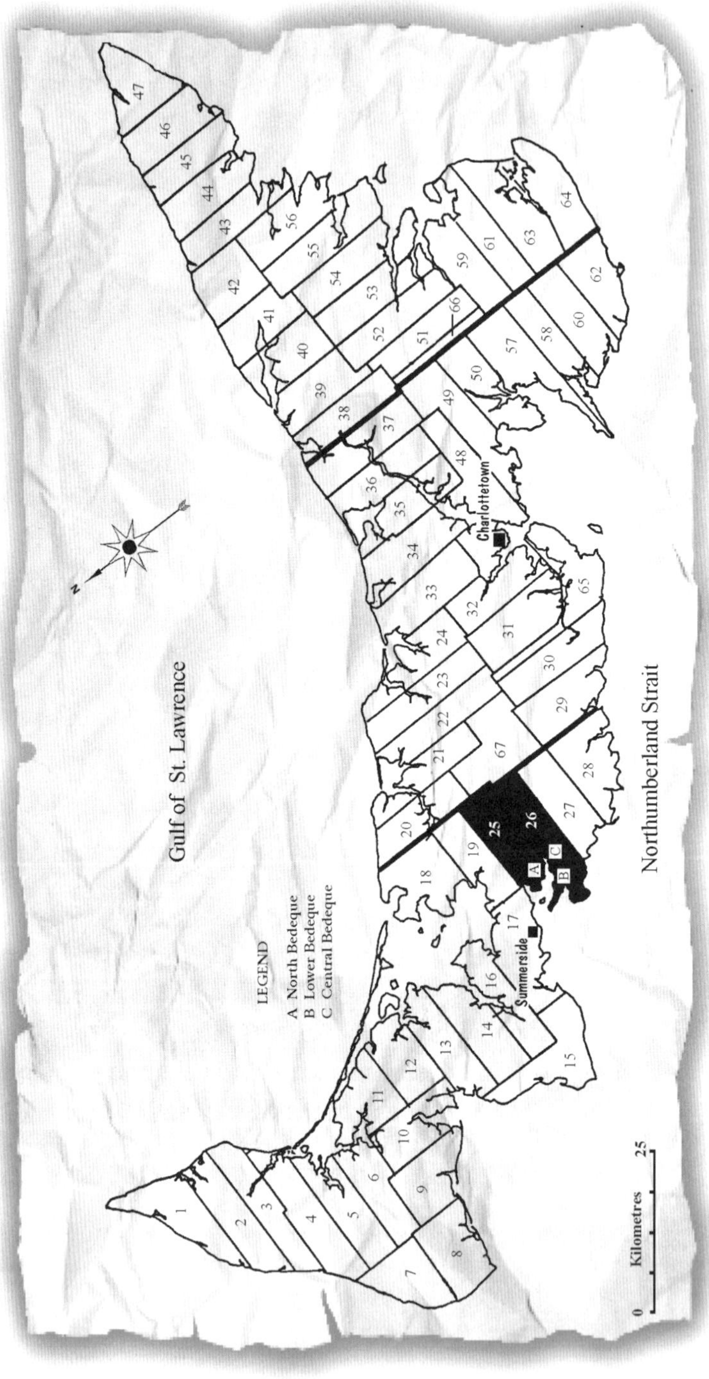

LEGEND
A North Bedeque
B Lower Bedeque
C Central Bedeque

Graphics by Crescent Isle Publishers

The "Three Bedeques," situated in Lots 25 and 26, P.E.I.

erty would come first on the right, then Silliker's which became the cemetery, then Thomas Hooper's which went to Elisha which went to Lemuel, then Thomas Junior's. Mary Hooper Robins also lived further down the same road.

According to H.H. Hooper:

Thomas Hooper died in 1820, aged eighty-two. [My information states that Thomas was born in 1734 and died in 1816 at the age of 82] Major married (i) Miss Patterson and had two children, and (ii) Miss Catherine Urquhart, and had eleven children, making a total of thirteen children for Major ....Thomas, Jr. married Elizabeth Cole [and had seven children]. Elisha married Margaret Crosby and had [seven] children. Mary married John Robins, Ann married John Montgomery; both had large families. Rachel never married. [As I have stated previously, I believe that Rachel did not exist in this family, but was the SISTER of Thomas Hooper, the Loyalist. Nowhere have I seen evidence of a child named Rachel. Only in the writings of Muriel Hooper does Rachel appear as Thomas's daughter] It is strange how antipathy can take such a deep hold on a person that a father can ostracize and forget a child. Sarah who was left behind in New Jersey and married a whig [Patriot] was forgotten and no correspondence passed between the family and her for many years. They did not even know where she lived. We find as late as 1841 Elisha corresponding in order to find her, and was informed that she had died on June 4, 1828, leaving four sons and four daughters. Her descendants live in the same place in New Jersey. The others [the girls and Elisha] reached Bedeque in Prince Edward Island in December 1786 [another source later in the document says November 1786]. The baby was now quite a big boy [about 4 ½ years old]; his father would not have known him. The rough little cabin in the bush was a poor place after their fine home in New Jersey, but they were all together once more, and in the joy of reunion they cared about little else.[10]

In the spring of 1786, Governor Patterson sent him [Thomas] the following document, dated May 2, 1786:

To Thomas Hooper, Esq. Greeting -
By virtue of the power and authority to me intrusted by His Majesty's commission and Royal instructions reposing special trust and confidence in your loyality, fidelity, and good conduct, I do by these presents appoint you, the said Thomas Hooper, one of his Majesty's Justices of the Peace.
Signed by His Honors command
Isaac Swan, Dep. Provincial Secretary.[11]

Orlo Jones and Doris Haslam effectively described the situation with respect to the institution of marriage in pioneer times on the Island:

Strictly interpreted, the original law of the Colony had confined the marriage ceremony to clergy of the Established Church, though all governors from the first, recognizing the inability of Parson Desbrisay, for many years sole Anglican clergyman on the Island, to take care of the situation, issued a license to any interested couple directing a specified justice of the peace to perform the ceremony according to the rites of the Church of England.... Later, when the Methodist ministers followed the Bedeque circuit, the custom of magistrate marriages had been so well established that it continued as a social custom for nearly the first hundred years of Bedeque history. **Thomas Hooper, Sr., Major Hooper,** and Alexander Anderson were among the favourite joiners [those who performed the wedding ceremony] of the early years. However, any parties desiring the blessing of the church were married by the Methodist ministers with no compunctions as to the legality of same. The earliest legal marriage by a Methodist minister in Bedeque was performed on September 20, 1832, when Gabriel Strang, settled on a farm later to be known as the Major Lowther property in the newly opened Searletown district, was married at Centreville to Ann Wright after publishing the banns.[12]

From an earlier time, the following letter will be of interest:

Charl'Town Aug. 3rd, 1801
Sir- Application having been made to me for a license to marry Isaac Schurman and Mary Baker of Bedeque, and the messenger being in a hurry to return, and the Governor being engaged with Captain Fenwick just arrived from Halifax on public business, it is impossible to procure a license in time through the necessary forms. I therefore take the liberty to inform you that I think you may venture to perform the ceremony and I will procure license when more convenient.
I am, Sir, Your most humble and obedient servant, Robert Gray.[13]

H.H. Hooper also stated: "**Thomas** [**Hooper, Sr.**] held the position of High Sheriff also. In a letter from Governor Patterson dated November 22, 1786, he congratulated Thomas on his safe arrival on the Island with his family."

In the archives at Trenton, N.J. I found the following information on the claim on confiscation of his property:

Thomas Hooper, a son of Clement Hooper (who died in 1777) [1774 is the correct date] and owner of a plantation in Windsor township, in Middlesex County, New Jersey, of which there is a description with a copy of the inquisition against him. He also kept a tavern, noted as the place where all public business was transacted. There is an estimate of his losses and a deposition in his favor by Gilbert Giberson (q.v.) and Richard Robins (q.v.), dated December 12, 1783, from Shelburne, Nova Scotia, where he was himself a refugee at that time (A.O. 13:18; A.O. 12:16, ff. 55 - 60; A.O. 12:62, f.67). In 1786 he was living in Prince Edward Island. He was allowed 497 pounds from his claim of 825 pounds (A. 12:109).

In 1787 **Thomas Hooper** was satisfied that the British government had allowed him 317 pounds 18 shillings as compensation for the loss of his farm, but so far as we know it was never paid. According to Dickie, who was cited previously, "As regards the compensation, it is more than likely that it was paid and reached the Island, but did not reach Hooper. The history of the early days recounts many episodes in which public officials did not appear in any good light."

At the archives in Trenton, N.J., I found another document in flourishing handwriting (parts of which are hard to read) which was photocopied for me. I quote:

Account of the Estate of Thomas Hooper, late, of the County of Middlesex and State of N.J., confiscated for joining the Army of the King of Great Britain and sold by the Commissioners and agent of forfeited Estates for said County returned to this office.

Date of Sales	Purpose	Pounds	Shilling	Pence
Nov. 10th, 1777	To amount of Personal Estate	64	12	4
April 4th, 1779	Ditto of Real Estate	564	0	0
May 5th, 1784	Ditto. . . . . Ditto	900	0	0

__________ from the Publick Books in my office, given under my hand this twentieth day of September, one thousand seven Hundred and Eighty-six- 1786.
[signed] Aaron Dunham
N.J.

Another article with information on Thomas Hooper appeared in "Bedeque and Its People," in *The Prince Edward Island Magazine*, for August and September 1900. As we have read already, Thomas's wife died before the family left New Jersey. A descendant, H. Henry Hooper, gives another interesting account of the "indignities of a cruel nature" she had endured:

> The soldiers were making things rather uncomfortable for the Loyalists. Several called at his [Thomas Hooper's] place and made a search through the house and barn where they jabbed their bayonets into beds, hay mows, or any likely hiding place. One of his brothers was very bitter against him for being a Loyalist. [Both James and either Stephen or Nicholas were in the Tory Army of George Washington.] It was about this time that his [Thomas's] wife had given birth to another son and was still confined to bed. Exasperated at not finding the husband, or for pure revenge, they actually took the bed from under her and subjected her to indignities of a cruel nature. She was, however, removed to an outhouse and concealed, but the intense excitement and removal incident thereto caused her death, and from that time until his dying day, Thomas entertained nothing but the bitterest hatred and contempt for everything belonging to the States.

The relationship of H.H. (Henry) Hooper to the loyalist Hoopers from New Jersey is unclear. There is a Henry Hooper, whose wife's name was Johanna, and who had a son Fred *Jesse* Hooper, born on April 4, 1873 in Trowbridge, England, and died on October 6, 1948 in Liberty, Maine. It may be that this is the Henry Hooper who wrote the article, "Bedeque and Its People," in *The Prince Edward Island Magazine* in 1900, although I am not sure. Catherine Frances Pearson, called Kate, of Chelton, born December 4, 1862, married (the second time) the above-stated Fred *Jesse* Hooper and had one son, Fred Witcher Hooper, born July 5, 1906 in Amesbury, MA; Fred Witcher Hooper married Mary Ella Adams. Kate Pearson was the daughter of Edward Pearson, granddaughter of Lydia Wright, great-granddaughter of Stephen Wright, and great-great-granddaughter of William Wright, Loyalist.

Dr. D.L. Dickie, previously cited, wrote:

The 1798 census shows that **Thomas Hooper**, now distinguished from the rest of the residents of Lot 26 by the title Esquire, was still on his farm at Bedeque. With him were his two younger sons [Tommy and Elisha] and a woman - probably his daughter Ann. Not far away lived **Major Hooper** with his wife and two daughters, the latter being under 10 years. [This would be the youth aged 19 who left New Jersey in 1782 and who would be 35 when the census was taken] The name **Hooper** still survives on the Island, both as a surname and a baptismal name, and always with honorable mention.[14]

Attempting to personally tie historian Dickie into the Lot 26 scene, and perhaps thus giving his research greater credence, H[enry]. H. Hooper wrote: "I do not know the present location of Dr. D.J. Dickie, author of *In Pioneer Days*, but was told in 1915 that a family of that name lived in Lot 26.

Probate Records show Thomas's will, dated August 17, 1812, was proved July 11, 1816. He was 82 years old when he died. Thomas Hooper, Esq. was the first Justice of the Peace appointed in Bedeque.[15] [My records show that he was born in 1734. Had he written his will in early to middle 1812, he would have been 78 at that time. Had he died in 1816, when his will was proved [in July, 1816], he would have been 82 years old.

With all the traumas and hardships of his life, not to mention the hard work or the tentativeness of his existence at times, Thomas must have had a strong constitution, a steady resolve, and a good cardiovascular system! I hope Thomas can hear my somewhat belated eulogy: "Thomas, this writer, who is the wife of your greatgreatgreatgrandson, and is chronicling your family, has tremendous admiration for your resolve and persistence in finding harbor for your Loyalist spirit and in building a new life for yourself and your family in a land new to you."

The Island of St. John became known as Prince Edward Island in 1799.[16]

Notes

1 Doris Haslam and Orlo Jones, eds., *An Island Refuge, Loyalists and Disbanded Troops on the Island of Saint John* (n.p.: Abegweit Branch of the United Empire Loyalist Association of Canada, 1983), p. 136.
2 Ibid., pp. 136-137
3 Ibid., p. 373
4 Graves, Ross, *William Schurman, Loyalist of Bedeque, Prince Edward Island and His Descendants*, (Summerside, P.E.I.: Harold B. Schurman, 1973), p. 23
5 *An Island Refuge*, op. cit., p. 257
6 Ross Graves, *op.cit.,* p. 25
7 Ada MacLeod, *Roads to Summerside, the Sotry of Early Summerside and the Surrounding Area,* edited by Marjorie McCallum Gay, 1980, pp. 12-13
8 H. H. Hooper, "Bedeque and Its People," *The Prince Edward Island Magazine*, August and September, 1900
9 Ibid.
10 Ibid., Chapter 4
11 Orlo Jones and Doris Haslam, op. cit., p. 137
12 Ibid., p. 39
13 H. H. Hooper, op. cit.
14 Dr. D.L.Dickie, *In Pioneer Days* (Messrs. J. M. Dent)
15 George A. Leard, *Historic Bedeque* (Bedeque, P.E.I.: Bedeque United Church, 1948), p. 21
16 George A. Leard, op. cit., pp. 7-12

CHAPTER 5

Early Settlers in the Bedeque Area of Prince Edward Island

The history about the land on which **Thomas Hooper** and some other Loyalists settled is interesting. Long before the white man came to Bedeque, the Micmac Indians knew the river, its green marshes and fine timbered shore as Eptek, "the hot place." When the French came in 1750 they must have found it warm, too, for they changed the original name only slightly, at first calling it Bedec which soon evolved into the typical French form of Bedeque. Still later in 1764 when the English came to map the Island, Captain Holland, Chief Surveyor, though he named one hundred and fifty prominent Island features for numerous acquaintances from his clockmaker to his king, must, too, have found the place warm because he retained the name Bedeque as an alternate title for the waters adjoining the Hot Place, naming it Halifax or Bedeque Bay.

George A. Leard, a meticulous and talented Island historian, provides an exciting account of the early history of Bedeque. To attempt to paraphrase his wonderful writing style would be to do him an undeserved injustice:

> The Abegweit Micmacs knew Bedeque best as a place passed through on their way to New Brunswick. Their chief village on the north of the Island, Makpaak (Large Bay), from which the French evolved the name Malpeque, was the frequent starting point of canoe trips to New Brunswick. Paddling through "Large Bay, they

would ascend what is now Raynor's Creek, portage across the country to Wilmot Creek and float down the Bay of the "Hot Place" to the straits where, hugging the coast as far as Cape Traverse, they would finally make the dash to Tormentine [N.B.].

The first white settlers to disturb the red man's solitude came to Bedeque in 1750. They were "plowmen" from Acadia with their wives and children, pawns of the game of empire, who, induced by the offer of three years' subsistence and compensation for their losses, were persuaded to forsake their pleasant homes in Nova Scotia which came under British sovereignty in 1748 and to preserve their French citizenship in the Island of St. John which was still a domain of the king of France. Though thrifty and hard-working, they invariably settled near the marsh-lands of our various Island bays and rivers, obviously for the marsh hay which could be gathered with comparative ease.

In 1752 four families were settled along the shore of North Bedeque with four on the south side making a total of forty-two persons in all. The last French census taken in 1753 showed a population of one hundred and one. What it was in 1758 may only be surmised, probably no more than one hundred and fifty. This was the year of the capture of Louisburg and the surrender of the Island of Saint John to the British with the evacuation in October of practically all its Acadian inhabitants. War in any aspect is cruel, but never more so than in its dealings with the innocent toilers of the soil. Bedeque's first settlers enjoyed at the most only an eight-year stay. Induced to its shores by their own super-patriots who did not wish them to take the oath of allegiance to the British in Nova Scotia, they were this time given no choice of becoming British subjects, but bundled into transports, some of which foundered en route, and were unceremoniously returned to the shores of their unwelcoming mother country.

Throughout the Island the homes, stores, and churches of the Acadians were burned to the ground in accordance with the orders issued to the troops, but in several places the careless soldier failed to raze the buildings, and, in Bedeque for one, they remained desolate reminders to the Indians passing up and down the bay of friends who had come and gone. Some of the thirty-year-old French houses were still more or less habitable when the first English- speaking settlers came to Bedeque in 1784. From old plans of townships number 25 and 26 in the Registry office at Charlottetown, it may be surmised that there were probably fifteen or sixteen French buildings still standing in Bedeque in 1782 with the largest number on the south side, and clearings of two hundred acres or more overgrown again with young trees. In 1752 shortly after Bedeque had been settled by the Acadians, the largest clearing had been on the north side where one family with six men over eighteen years of age (a very unusual family- five being unmarried) had cleared sufficient land to sow sixteen bushels of wheat; while neighboring houses with only one to chop and hoe had but a garden each. To these deserted houses and overgrown gardens came the United Empire Loyalists. The **Hoopers**, Robins,

Schurmans, and Wrights as typical Loyalist families had much in common with the Bedeque Acadians, the LeJeunes, Robichauds, and Terriauds into whose labors they had entered. Both alike as refugees knew the bitter taste of defeat, the cruel severance of well-loved ties which bind a farmer to the soil, and the heart-breaking toil of starting anew in the wilderness.[1]

From H.H. Hooper's, "Bedeque and Its People," written in 1900, we get an interesting description of the site of Thomas Hooper's new home on P.E.I.:

Prior to the arrival of Thomas Hooper, the former owner had lived in a house that stood on a hill a few rods from the shore, being near to a spring, which at that time was quite a distance from the shore, and a pleasant walk through the woods was necessary before reaching it, but the elements have washed away the bank so that today it is on the shore. Here, too, many a crank used his "mineral rod" and spade, delving for the celebrated Captain Kidds's hidden treasure, and like most cases, ended in failure.

Here on this hill overlooking the beautiful bay where the salt sea breezes blow surrounded by the dense and scarcely unbroken forest, once stood the humble home of the hardy Acadian. No doubt it was the scene of many festivities, many happy and unrecorded events save that stored in the vivid memory of childhood. Here the merry children played on the shore

And built their castles of dissolving sand
To watch them overflowed, or swallowed up
And flying the white breakers, daily left
The little foot prints daily washed away.

Undoubtedly it was also the scene of many a hard winter's struggle. It must have cost them, as it did the Loyalists, many a pang at parting and leaving behind the fruit of years of toil.

At the time of the arrival of Thomas Hooper all that remained was the blackened site. The evidence is still there [1948] though not so distinct as it was a hundred and fifteen years ago. It seems as if ashes of the past are the only visible token as no hand was stretched forth at that time to save the events, its interest to history, from oblivion. The civic pride and patriotic sacrifices of the people of that time may well be recalled for encouragement and imitation of both present and future. While the deportation of the eighteen thousand simple agricultural Acadians, the burning of their homes and crops before their eyes, and the separation of families may well be looked upon as one of the most grievous wrongs ever perpetrated in the new world, it may not have given the few settlers reason to abandon their homes, but like all such acts, tended to cement the race still firmer together.

In viewing the spot where once stood the happy home, we become interested in the past and the carefully stored tales of childhood. The half-fanciful legends of long ago are recalled, and we stand in meditation and picture the past. Awaking from our daydream, we realize how true are the beautiful lines of Kingsley:

So fleet the works of men, back to the earth again
Ancient and holy things fade as a dream.[2]

H.H. Hooper went on to elaborate on the names of the early Loyalists in the Bedeque area:

Who were the first Loyalists to settle in Bedeque? We do not know. Ensign John Robins of the King's Rangers came to "Charlotte Town," March 17, 1782 as junior officer of the garrison. A letter signed by him and several of his fellow officers which appeared in a New York newspaper of April 1782 advising prospective emigrants that our Island "soil was good, the water excellent, the harbours spacious, the government mild, the cattle plenty..." was doubtless instrumental in attracting a number of Loyalists here. Ensign Robins, his father Richard Robins, **Thomas Hooper**, and William Schurman, late of Shelburne, were at Charlottetown early in May of 1784 presenting a memorial to the Governor-in-Council and asking for "singular choice" in different lots of land to be granted to refugees. They had been doubtless looking over Bedeque because the governor in his reply offered **Hooper** and Schurman ("and any others they may choose for partners") leases of large areas of Lot 26 with the option of buying in twelve months' time at the rate of two dollars an acre. These men were evidently a delegation acting on behalf of other Loyalists temporarily settled at Shelburne. The first large body of settlers came to Bedeque by ship from Shelburne in July of 1784 [No doubt these refugees were transported in William Schurman's ship accompanied by **Thomas Hooper** as mentioned earlier].

There were ten families of Loyalists or "Loyal Refugees": William Wright, John McDonald, Jacob Silliker, Nathaniel Wetherell, John Murray, David Stags, Sarah Palmer, and William Stairman (Schurman?), **Thomas Hooper**, and Richard Robins. In addition there were the following unmarried Loyalists: Robert Hancock, Lawrence Berry, John Murray, Andrew Eastman, James Wharf (Waugh?), Jesse Strang, and Nathaniel Wright. Also in the same ship were the following disbanded soldiers: George Malby (Mabey?) and wife, Richard Moorfield and wife; and single men: John Shilfox, Dudley Wells, Robert Hancock, Thomas Gould, John Chambers, William Sauchaback (Sencabaugh?), Richard Price, Joseph Wood, and Richard Garrett. Not all of these settled at Bedeque and indeed not all stayed on

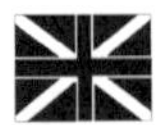

the Island. It is conservatively estimated that by the fall of 1786 over half of the Loyalists who came to the Island in the period 1783-1785 had left on learning how the landlords were interpreting the apparently generous terms on which the government had offered the land.

When the Loyalists came to Bedeque in 1784, they entered on a relatively short period of hardship, but for a people who had been settled in the American colonies for at least two generations and had arrived at considerable affluence, it was like turning back a page in their history to re-enact their father's and grandfather's pioneering in New York, New Jersey, and other American colonies. Small families in two-roomed log cabins lived luxuriously the first winter while large families in one-roomed homes found the conditions crowded. Some foods were plentiful: bar clams, quahaugs, grandfather lobsters weighing ten pounds each, the choicest oysters of the continent, trout, salmon, and eels could be had in and around the Dunk or other nearby harbours without anyone's leave or license. Those without flour took their wheat to Tryon where John Gouldrup ran one of the early grist mills of Prince County. Stone fireplaces for heating and cooking had chimneys made of "cat-and-clay" on frames of wood. Hoes and axes and a few other tools were supplied through a government rehabilitation grant, together with food supplies sufficient for a year, but as nearly all the Bedeque Loyalists had wasted upwards of a year at Shelburne, their grants were exhausted shortly after their arrival.

Jesse Strang, one of the Loyalist refugees, was born in Westchester County, New York, probably around 1764. Sarah Wright, daughter of William Wright, Loyalist, was also born in Westchester County, New York, These two people were issued a marriage license on October 24, 1787.

According to Doris Haslam, in her book, *The Wrights of Bedeque*, "Jesse was almost certainly the son of Daniel Strang, a Revolutionary counteragent for Loyalist Col. Robert Rogers. Daniel was captured near the rebel camp at Peekskill, New York, and hanged by revolutionary forces on Oak Hill, Peekskill, on January 27, 1777. Mary, one of his children, became the wife of Jacob Silliker."[3] He had come to Bedeque via Shelburne in 1784.

Stephen Wright, the son of William, the Loyalist, and brother of the above-mentioned Sarah (Wright) Strang, was born about 1768 in Westchester County, New York. Doris Haslam described his experiences prior to coming to the Island:

Stephen was a lad in his teens living on the home farm in Westchester County during the American Revolution. No doubt he and his mother were left in charge because his father was imprisoned for his Patriot sympathies by the Rebels and his brother Nathaniel was away much of the time fighting in the militia. His father returned to find his family deprived of much of their property by the Rebels, with only one bed left in what had been a comfortable farm home, and his wife and children all sick with yellow fever. Stephen came by sea with his family to Shelburne and thence to the Island of St. John in 1784."[4]

Doris Haslam also wrote of Stephen's brother-in-law (his sister Sarah's husband):

Jessey Strange (as he was listed on the "Muster Roll of Disbanded and Discharged Soldiers and Loyalists") was granted 300 acres on the first day of April, 1789, 40 acres "situate lying near the head of the Dunk or Bedeque Bay along the front on the water side and extending East 48 chains," and the remaining 260 acres lying inland. The 40 acre lot lay next to the farm of William Wright who had come with his family on the same vessel from Shelburne so it was not surprising that in the autumn of 1787 Jesse married Sarah, second daughter in the Wright home. Five of their nine sons married back into the Wrights.

Jesse was one of the original elders of the Bedeque Presbyterian Church in the Princetown congregation, having been ordained in 1801 or 1802. He donated the site for the Presbyterian Church in Bedeque. The first church stood in the middle of the present cemetery. He was one of the right-hand men of Rev. John Keir [the long-time minister of the North Bedeque Presbyterian Church]

Sarah and Jesse had nine sons and three daughters who were all married and making their own way in the nearby pioneer settlements when Jesse died suddenly just a few days after making out his will.

Late autumn to early spring were not slack times for the early settlers. Most of the winter the pioneers spent working in their lumberwoods.

H.H. Hooper's article in 1900, cited elsewhere, recorded Willliam Schurman's operation of Bedeque's first store:

In Bedeque's first store, William Schurman, from November on, was prepared to help the settlers with moderate amounts of credit. He supplied the community with broadcloth, bohea tea, salt, strap iron, leather, lumber, scythes, West India brown sugar, West India rum, calico, handkerchiefs, and ribbons. Tea and salt may

have been considered most essential, but rum and ribbons were most popular. Rum and ribbons, the stimulant and vanity of the Bedequers of 1785, were given a place in the community no different from that accorded them in other places of pioneer settlement where a change of ribbon made an old homespun dress seem new, and rum was the popular beverage for all occasions.

In 1798 when the first English census was taken, only the southern part of the Township was settled. It is quite possible that all those people mentioned below lived in Bedeque:[6]

Head of Family	Number in Family
William Schurman	2
Samuel Chatterton	7
Peter Schurman	4
John Baker	10
Major Hooper	4
William Silliker	4
William Barret	4
Thomas Hooper	4
Peter Maybe	10
John Strickland	6
Nathanial Wetherall	4
Widow Robins	7
[Mary Hooper Robins]	
Benjamin Cole	8
Richard Price	5
Moses Hines	5
Alexander Anderson	4
Archibald MacCallum	6
Angus MacDonald	5
Ronald MacDonald	6
Samual Rix	4
William Wright	8
Jesse Strang	5
John Murray	8
David Murray	0

George A. Leard's, *Historic Bedeque,* contains an interesting account of early settlement in Bedeque, beginnning with the granting of Township 26 in 1767, and concluding with the arrival of the Loyalists in the early-mid 1780s:

Bedeque as an address covered a large area in the early days: any farm bordering the bay was in Bedeque whether in Lot 17, 19, 25, or 26, but most of the early farms fringed the Dunk [River] to take advantage of the French clearings and the marshes. From reference to early maps and deeds, farm settlement in both Lot 25 and Lot 26 was of a moving pattern for the first few years, and not till 1798, which saw the first English census for the Island and the completion of Bedeque's first fifteen years of British settlement, does the pattern seem stabilized.[7] ...At North Bedeque in 1798 there were five beautiful shore farms corresponding roughly to the present day [1948] holdings of the McMurdos, Staverts, Clarks, and Bakers. The patriarchs of the settlement, John Murray and William Wright, both over sixty years of age, were surrounded by their children's homes. William Wright, on what is now [1948] the Heath Clark place, lived with his son Stephen and family; his eldest daughter Hannah was married nearby to William Murray; while Jesse Strang married to Sarah Wright and Samuel Rix who had Lydia Wright to wife, were neighbors. John Murray's eldest son David, married to Nancy Penman, rounded out the little settlement with a home of his own. The settlers on Lot 25 had been granted their lands by Governor Patterson who by an order-in-council in 1782 divided this township calling the southern half the "refugee share."

The northern part was designated as that of James Campbell who, with A. Kennedy, had been granted the lot in 1767. Neither of the landlords ever made any settlements or improvements as they were by ownership bound; in fact, they never registered their titles. James Campbell eventually sold the northern half of the lot to Captain Allan MacDonald of Rhetland, and the 1798 census shows two Macdonalds on the northern half of this lot, Angus and Ronald, who were married to sisters of Captain Allan Macdonald and in possession of one thousand acres each. Disputes regarding titles in this lot were to hinder settlement for many years.

The largest settlement of Loyalists was on the south shore of the Dunk [River] in Lot 26 which was owned by Lieut. John Stewart of England and Major Peter Gordon of St. Vincent in the West Indies. William Schurman, one of the most wealthy and enterprising of the Loyalists, was settled on 350 acres in the Central Bedeque of today. His farm would comprise the present [1948] Leonard Schurman, Edwin Lord, Charles Green, and Weldon Crossman properties. L.U. Fowler, writing in *The Prince Edward Island Magazine* of June 1900 (*Bedeque and Its People*, p. 121), tells very interestingly of Schurman coming to the Island in 1783 and spending the first winter at Tryon where he whipsawed lumber for the Charlottetown market and hauled it over the ice to the capital on hand-sleds.

It's a story which has found its way into different newspaper and magazine articles on Bedeque, and would be hard to dispute; yet in the list of Loyalists who landed from Shelburne at Bedeque on the 26th of July 1784, the name William Stairman stands out as a possible misspelling of William Schurman, added to which the list of children by ages - two over ten and three under ten - agrees exactly with

the Schurman record. Again William Schurman's Island of Saint John account book, still preserved in a North Bedeque home, is dated from 1784, not 1783 as one would suppose if he had been doing business previously. The date of his arrival may be a trifle uncertain, but there is nothing doubtful about the fact that William Schurman was Bedeque's first store-keeper and first representative in the Legislative Assembly.

To the south of Schurman lived John Baker who according to some was a former fellow-citizen of Schurman's in New Rochelle, New York, but believed by others to have been a native of Philadelphia. He was not only a farmer, but also Bedeque's first blacksmith, occupying a solid block of three hundred acres which extended from Schurman's south line to what later was known as the "old mill hill road."

Please allow a bit of digression as I quote from another undocumented source, which outlines in greater detail the story of John Baker, Loyalist neighbour of the Hoopers, Schurmans and others:

John Baker (c.1748-1821) of Goshen, Pennsylvania, was a Quaker who was loyal to England during the American Rebellion. John's ancestor, for whom he was named, came out from England to Pennsylvania in 1684. There he bought five hundred acres of land and was appointed a constable for Gilead. He was also influential in changing the name of the township from Gilead to Egmont in memory of the Royal Manor of Egmont in his native county, Shropshire.

Loyalist John Baker was issued a license to marry Hannah Lewis on December 23, 1773 by the Secretary of State at New York. Most Quaker marriages were performed in the traditional Meeting House; one might conclude that John's wife was not a Quaker. Four children were born to the couple before they decided to leave their strife-torn native land and migrate northward to Nova Scotia. They received a grant of land in Remsheg, now known as Wallace, prior to settling on the Island of Saint John.

The precise date of the Baker's arrival on the Island is not known. It was possibly during the late 1780s that the family settled at Bedeque on land adjacent to that of another Loyalist, William Schurman. The proprietors of this land were the Gordon brothers, Robert and Anthony, who lived in the West Indies. The three hundred acre solid block extended from Schurman's south line to what was known later as the "old mill road." A lease for it was signed in 1792. The terms demanded for it were two pence sterling per acre in the first year, four pence the second year, six pence the third year, and eight pence in the fourth and subsequent years.

John Baker was a farmer and Bedeque's first blacksmith. It is recounted that in the early days the French Acadian settlers of Tignish occasionally would journey more than fifty miles to have work done at John Baker's forge. A cinder heap, added to by his successors and still evident years later in one of the fields near the creek, marked the site of this forge. That property in Central Bedeque is owned at present by Robert Linkletter." [This biography was written perhaps fifty years ago, but Robert or his son is still the owner of the property which is situated beyond the Baptist Church in Central Bedeque on the same side of the road as well as across the road beyond the cemetery]

The Bedeque Bakers corresponded with their Quaker relatives in Pennsylvania after the Rebellion, and Loyalist John paid them an impromptu visit when he went to Philadelphia to have a leg amputated. After several years John, junior, brought his father home to Central Bedeque where he died on December 17, 1821. At that time all of his children were married and established on farms nearly. Joseph inherited the homestead. John Baker and Hannah, his wife, whose death is unrecorded, had a family of eight children, six sons and two daughters," only the first will be profiled here.

John Baker Jr. (1776 – 1852) was born in 1776 and died on October 22, 1852 at North Bedeque. On July 20, 1798, he married Alice Lord, daughter of John and Elizabeth Cottrell Lord of Tryon. She was born in 1777 and died on March 4, 1809. John and Alice bought land from the MacDonald family in North Bedeque where he was a blacksmith as well as a farmer. They had six children, two of whom lived only a few months.

John's second marriage was to Ann Cole, a daughter of Benjamin and Isabella Robins Cole of Lower Bedeque. She was born on May 9, 1794 and died on December 2, 1866. John and Ann had twelve children.

Still extant is the copy of a letter which John wrote on October 11, 1827 to a cousin in Pennsylvania. In it he expresses thanks for letters received from this Uncle Andrew, tells about his father's death and gives various bits of family news. In closing he writes: "I have been building me a large house [that] cost me about Five hundred pounds. Please give my love to all my relations and tell them I expect to see them yet." He never did. His property was worked 30-50 years ago by a great-great-grandson, J. Donald Baker.[8]

Nathaniel Wright, later known as the father of Methodism in Prince County, had a three hundred acre Loyalist grant in Lot 26, one hundred and fifty of which was at Centreville, comprising the present [1948] Noonan property east of the church and extending south to include the valuable mill site. In 1798, however, these lands were

vacant: Nathaniel Wright had settled in Tryon. The farms west of Wright's, towards Lower Bedeque, were long, leggy ones which bathed their feet in the Dunk and butted their well-treed heads against the middle division line of Lot twenty-six.

I continue to quote from the above-mentioned, unrecorded source :

A 1784 plan with possibly a few later additions showed the following settlers from Centreville west to Hurd's Point: Richard Hancock, George Mawby, **Thomas Hooper**, **Major Hooper**, Sam Jameson, Robert Elmer, R. Hoge, W. Wetherell, R. and T. Robins. By 1798 the names had changed considerably. The Hancock, Jameson, Elmer, and Hogg families had moved on and William Barret, John Strickland, and Moses Hives (Ives) had moved in. Joseph Seliker, whose father Jacob had died shortly after coming to Bedeque, owned the farm on which the Lower Bedeque cemetery is located.

The Robins property further down the Lower Bedeque road was in 1798 occupied by Bedeque's one recorded widow, **Mary Hooper Robins**, relict of John Robins, one time ensign of the King's Rangers and later Lieutenant in H.M. Island of Saint John's Corps of Volunteers. Having six children under sixteen made her position anything but an enviable one. [Actually she had six children between the ages of 2 and 9.] On the other half of the Robins' Loyalist grant lived Benjamin Cole and wife, Isabella Robins Cole, who had come into part of the property of her father Richard Robins, the first of the Bedeque Loyalists to die on the Island.

Doris M. Haslam in her 1978 book, *The Wrights of Bedeque*, included this interesting narrative on the Coles-Robins families, as recalled by Isabella (Robins) Cole, daughter of Loyalist, Richard Robins:

Isabella Robins (1768-1855), later Mrs. Benjamin Cole of Bedeque, P.E.I. and ancestor of many Wright descendants, was the daughter of Richard Robins of Amboy, New Jersey. Richard illustrated in various ways his allegiance to the British Crown during the Revolutionary War and was punished by the rebels through imprisonment, confiscation, etc. His daughter related her memories to her offspring and a record thereof was printed in Summerside's *The Pioneer* in 1896 and in *A Sketch Book* by John McKinnon:

A UNITED EMPIRE LOYALIST FAMILY

I was born in the state of New Jersey, then a British province, in the year 1768, but our people had been in America a century previous to that date. My father, who was in very comfortable circumstances, cultivated a farm near the town of Amboy [now known as Perth Amboy] and had a number of slaves, slavery being practised at that time there as well as farther south. My earliest recollection was of hearing the violent political discussions about the "Stamp Act," and a lot of things of which I had but very vague ideas. My father taking sides with the British, I, of course, considered the "rebels" to be a pack of thieves and robbers without one redeeming feature. I was eight years old when actual war broke out and the war lasted seven years. To give any idea of the misery and horror resulting from a hostile army occupying and quartering on the country is something hard to do. Often, and well, do I remember of ten or a dozen at a time, of rough fellows, coming in and ordering dinner "quick," and after getting it they would carry off anything they took a fancy to- sometimes a fat sheep, bag of flour or other provisions. I recollect once five or six fellows coming to the field where my brother Ben (a big resolute fellow) was plowing with a team of valuable horses, in which he took great pride. They ordered him to unhitch and give the horses to them. "No," says Ben, "If you take them, you take them over my dead body!" And after some parleying and blasphemy they went off. Of course, they knew if such conduct was represented to Gen. Washington they would receive punishment, but the Loyalists were too independent to recognize the American party so much as to lodge complaints. [Another source speaks of Isabella's childhood years being filled with misery and horror resulting from abuse by the rebels....Her father joined the British army, and his daughter Elizabeth who died in Bedeque in 1851, told of the persecution that the family endured. Crowds of rebels used to come to the house and compel the family to prepare meals for them. Then after the meal was eaten, they would carry off whatever they could lay their hands on! You can fancy how our nice place would go to ruin in seven years of such as this.

"My mother died and brother Ben went to Kentucky, then a wilderness. My father, hearing and getting assurance from the British authorities that Loyalists would get free grants of land in Nova Scotia or "Island St. John," as P.E.I. was then called, made ready in the summer of 1783 and started to find a place. There was no regular mail to any place on the Island but Charlottetown, and we got no word from him till late in the fall when my brother received a letter describing the place father had selected and directing him to come and bring his sister Isabella with him as early in the spring as possible. John was 22 years of age. He had been a lieutenant in the New Jersey militia and did service under the British, so he was entitled to draw land as well as father. To come from there to this colony at that time meant more than going to Australia does now. However, we went about making preparations. At this time I was only 16 years old. John found a vessel leaving New York in which we embarked in April, 1784, and we had a fair passage. The vessel had to call at Passamaquoddy to discharge some cargo where we were detained for two

weeks, which seemed to me like so many years. After leaving there the weather was delightful and, coming into the harbor of Bedeque - which was to be my residence for the remainder of a long life - on a lovely day in June, all nature looking at its best, was most charming. The peculiar red banks along the Island coast in contrast with the sombre gray of Nova Scotia had been a subject of remark as we sailed along the Straits of Northumberland, but on nearing the land, after passing the low thickly-wooded place where the town of Summerside now stands, and the lovely green opposite that place, we sighted a clearance. My brother thought, I suppose, to cheer my spirits, which had been pretty low during the voyage, by pointing to the place and saying, "Father has selected a handsome place anyhow," and by a good deal of light banter succeeded in getting me to acknowledge (what I really thought) the place to be very beautiful. As soon as our vessel was sighted two young men came off from the shore to meet us. When I thought it possible that my father was in the boat my heart seemed to come to my throat, but I soon saw that he was not there. I fancied those men's countenances wore a sad expression to welcome new arrivals. My brother inquired if they knew a man named Richard Robins. "Yes, but alas! He is dead," they replied. If I had been struck in the head with an axe the effect at the time could have been no more severe. Everything appeared to turn around and I fell, but rallied soon. John tried to comfort me as best he could by assuring me we would return home. I then learned that my father the previous winter in company with several others had started to Charlottetown around the shore - there was no other road then. [The date of the storm is often given as February 1784, but this cannot be reconciled with a petition to the Governor signed by Richard Robins in May of 1784. The correct date is doubtless February of the next year, 1785.] There had been a snowstorm terminating with a silver thaw which formed a crust having water under the ice which made it hard work to travel upon. My father, being a heavy man and not used to that kind of thing, gave out about the place now called Carleton. They concluded to return and he travelled with them to Sea Cow Head, when he declared he could go no further. The men who were with him stuck to him for a good while and helped him along, but at last he prevailed on them to go on and leave him. On arriving home the only horse in the place was taken to bring my father, but they found him dead. He was buried in the field near where I was destined to live, and sometimes in my loneliness the first four years of my residence here I would take my work and sit on the grave. The land which was set apart for the Loyalists - at least the parts drawn by my father and brother - were at that time in a wilderness state; fifty acres for each bounded on the river and twenty-five acres "back land" seven miles distant, without a road. They preferred taking leases from the proprietors in a place which the French Acadians had formerly inhabited and had quite large clearings, small houses, orchards,& c. John and I went into one of these houses. When I would be alone the first few winters the bears would come and put their paws on the banking and look in the window, and for many years it was difficult to raise sheep, bears and wild cats were so

numerous. John and I were both married near the same time about four years after our arrival. To tell the ups and downs of my life in raising a large family would be uninteresting and commonplace. My brother died before this century (19th) commenced and before he was 40 years of age, leaving a family of little children while I have lived to tell this story to my great-grandchildren.

Isabella Robins Cole died at Bedeque on 27 August 1855. Her obituary in The *Islander* noted: "She emigrated from the State of New Jersey at the close of the Revolutionary War. The deceased had 11 children, 85 grandchildren, 144 great-grandchildren, and 2 great-great-grandchildren."[9]

In George A. Leard's *Historic Bedeque*, for the period 1785-1798, in Lot 26, we get a brief overview of the nature of the land, problems associated with the proprietary system, early Hooper settlers, and the last Loyalist settler to take up residence there:

All these farms had a fringe of more or less cleared land: heritage from the French settlement which extended from Hurd's Point to Wright's mill stream, with clearings roughly corresponding to the land north of the present [1948] Lower Bedeque road in that section.

Thomas Hooper, Esq., the first Justice of the Peace for Bedeque and only Lot 26 resident over sixty years of age in 1798, writing from Bedeque Harbour September 19, 1785, spoke of the land as being good. (He had 300 acres west of Silliker's and his son **Major** had 150 acres nearby with eight or ten cleared acres of the French settlement) and noted happily the abundance of oysters a quarter of a mile from his door [The reader will remember that Joseph Silliker, whose father Jacob had died shortly after coming to Bedeque, owned the farm on which the Lower Bedeque Cemetery is located].

The Lot twenty-six Loyalists found shortly after they had settled that despite some of the governor's conveyances they still had a landlord, Peter Gordon, who had drawn the northern half of the lot as his share. He was not content to let the refugees pick the choicest portions of his property for free settlement. An inland tract of eight hundred and seventy-five acres in present-day Fernwood was designated a "Refugee share," but settlers on the river front, the only highway of the day, could not appreciate a backwoods farm and preferred to become tenants. Tenants they were, paying rent for many, many years. The location was near the shore for the practical reason that travel was largely by water, there being no roads, only trails.

The last of the Loyalists to reach Bedeque was Alexander Anderson, who, settling first at Rustico in 1789 where he married Margaret MacCallum of Brackley Point, came to Bedeque in 1797. He secured six or seven hundred acres, the greater part of the previously mentioned "Refugee tract" earmarked for Loyalist settlement, with a home site on the marshes near the southern shore of Salutation Cove. [As noted later, Mr. Anderson was one of the original members of the Session of the North Bedeque Presbyterian Church.] On a nearby clearing lived a Loyalist ex-soldier whose red-coat and bayonet are present-day treasures in a Fernwood home. His Bible, inscribed on the fly-leaf "Donald MacFarlane His Book", is preserved by descendants in Denver, Colorado. The Archibald MacCallum family who came about the same time, also by way of Rustico, settled at Indian Point.[11]

Notes

1 George A. Leard, *Historic Bedeque. The Loyalists at Work and Worship in Prince Edward Island* (Bedeque, P.E.I.: Bedeque United Church, 1948, amended 1973), pp. 8-9

2 H. H. Hooper, "Bedeque and Its People," *The Prince Edward Island Magazine*, August and September, 1900

3 Doris Haslam, *The Wrights of Bedeque, Prince Edward Island. A Loyalist Family* (Summerside, P.E.I.: Doris Muncey Haslam, 1978), p. 16

4 Ibid., p. 12

5 Ibid., p. 16

6 "Bedeque and its People," *The Prince Edward Island Magazine*, July 1900

7 George A. Leard, op. cit., pp. 10-11

8 Unknown source, pp. 28-29

9 Haslam, Doris, op. cit., pp. 832-833

10 Doris Haslam and Orlo Jones, *An Island Refuge. Loyalists and Disbanded Troops on the Island of Saint John* (n.p.: Abegweit Branch of the United Empire Loyalist Association of Canada, 1983), p. 239

11 George A. Leard, op. cit., pp. 7-12

CHAPTER 6

Life in the Bedeque Area of Prince Edward Island in the First Half of the Nineteenth Century

About the time of Waterloo [1815] early settlers in the Bedeque-Summerside area appear to have escaped the dreadful forest fires that devastated other parts of the Island. They also did not suffer as severely during the famine years. The famine years were known as the "mouse years" because all the growing crops were destroyed by the innumerable hordes of field mice. Deep ditches were dug around the potato patches in hope of saving the tubers, but that did not help much! Souris, at the eastern end of the Island, got its name from the mice. The eastern end of the Island was dealt a more severe influx of the vermin. An older man, however, in the Bedeque area, told of "seeing the bodies of the drowned rodents lying like great rolls of seaweed along the shore near his home at Wilmot Valley"[1]

The very nature of the hardships experienced by the early Loyalist settlers in the Bedeque area helped to foster a profound respect for God and the institution of organized religion. In basically a physically comfortless society an emotional and spiritual attachment to their religion allowed the pioneers to cope with the elements of nature and to find comfort in the midst of privation and despair. Noted Island historian, George A. Leard, described the early history of religion in Bedeque, in his book, *Historic Bedeque*, written in 1948:

The Island of Saint John, which became Prince Edward Island in 1799, had but little organized religion in the 18th century. The parish of St. Paul's [Anglican] in Charlottetown had for some time the only clergy of any denomination on the Island, whose natives were described by a pious visitor as being for the most part "profane and unsaved." In Bedeque the state of religion among the early settlers was probably but little different from anywhere else. One authentic note comes from the account book of William Schurman, Bedeque's first merchant, who on April 1, 1786, sold William Wright one cow for four pounds ($16.00) and one "Bibel" for one pound three shillings ($4.60), which in present day [1948] cattle values would be around $25.00 for a Bible. The price suggests not only a high value placed on the Word of God by storekeeper and purchaser alike, but also a big Book for public worship.

William Wright was a Quaker, but, having married a Presbyterian and having fought in the Revolutionary War, he would no longer be considered a member of the Society of Friends. Bedeque's early settlers, excluding a sprinkling of Quakers and Anglicans and two Roman Catholic MacDonald families, were Presbyterian so it was to be expected that the first sermon preached in the community would be Presbyterian. Dr. James MacGregor of Pictou, N. S., the most famous Presbyterian Divine in the Maritime colonies, came to the Island in the summer of 1794 on a missionary visit and supplied "several new places" including Bedeque and Tryon River with services.

The older community of Princetown in 1794 erected a log building, which, serving as church and school, was the first Presbyterian establishment on the Island. Bedeque Church (Methodist) may easily have been the second though no date of its erection has been preserved. Most accounts of the present North Bedeque United Church, successor to Bedeque Presbyterian Church, fail to mention the earliest church of all, built on land owned by William Wright's son-in-law, Jesse Strang, of which the present cemetery [in North Bedeque] marks the site, and which as a guess was built in the closing years of the eighteenth century or the opening ones of the next.[2]

The first Presbyterian minister to settle on the Island was Rev. John Urquhart of the Church of Scotland who, coming in 1800, made Princetown his headquarters, according to L.U. Fowler in his artcile, *Bedeque and Its People*. He emphasized the seriousness with which individuals took their religion in those early days:

The Church of Scotland was the Kirk, the official Presbyterian Church as opposed to the free church. Mr. Urquhart organized a congregation which, including Bedeque on the south, extended from Cavendish on the east, to Lot 13 on the west. This congregation was governed by an elected body of elders who, though drawn from various parts of the congregation, exercised their office in the different churches of the congregation without regard to the district they represented. Of the eleven original members of this very first Prince Edward Island Session four were Bedeque Loyalists whose names should be remembered: Alexander Anderson, **Major Hooper,** David Murray, and Jesse Strang.

[There is a humorous little story, compliments of L. U. Fowler, about Jacob Schurman and his wife who lived at the northern end of Lot 25.] The settlement is now known as Norborough [Norboro] and here the family . . . was born. [Jacob] was a good man in his way, but did not see eye to eye in religious matters with his wife who was a strict Presbyterian and a member of Rev. Dr. Keir's church. Mrs. Schurman asked her husband for a shilling as the Sabbath was sacrament day. He told her that he would not give the shilling unless he found it. He was at the time making public roads, stumping the trees out, etc. One evening upon his return home from work, he gave his wife the shilling, telling her that he had found it in a hollow hemlock tree that he had taken out of the new road. Although there were those then living who did not believe this story, it has passed into the family history as a well attested fact and is firmly believed.[3]

As an aside, L[ouis] U[rquhart] Fowler wrote a series of articles called, "Bedeque and Its People," for *The Prince Edward Island Magazine*, around 1900. He married Anna Isabella (called Belle) Rogers, daughter of David and Mary Wright Rogers, born in 1860. One wonders Mr. Fowler's relationship to Mr. Urquhart, the Presbyterian minister and perhaps the person for whom his middle name was given. Mr. Urquhart's daughter, Catherine, was Major Hooper's second wife.

In his book, *Historic Bedeque*, George A. Leard provided some background to Rev. Mr. Urquhart and his family:

Mr. Urquhart's stay on the Island was short. He removed in 1802 to Chatham, New Brunswick. His work was not under the official supervision of the Church, but his organization of the congregation was recognized as being truly Presbyterian when on November 9, 1807, the Session met at Princetown and was constituted by Rev'd Peter Gordon, the first officially settled Prebyterian pastor on Prince Edward Island....

In Bedeque the Rev. John Urquhart is remembered best by his descendants. His daughter Catherine, who married **Major Hooper** in the early years of the new century, succeeded a governor's daughter in the Hooper home. (Major had married Ann Patterson in 1794) and had the honor of bringing up six [my sources say that there were only two] of Governor Patterson's grandchildren in addition to a large number of her own, all of whom turned out to her credit. With her manse background it is perhaps little wonder that her husband was one of the original elders in Bedeque [Presbyterian] church.[4]

George A. Leard was truly a masterful local historian, and was wonderful at documenting the lives of ordinary people, or people who otherwise would be forgotten to history if it were not for his personal interest in preserving their stories and lives for posterity. He wrote:

Early settlers who left no descendants were quickly forgotton in the collective memory of the community. The first resident doctor at Bedeque was a striking example of this. James Graham, a forty-two-year-old bachelor of Edinburgh, who began a thirty-five year practice at Bedeque in 1814 which ended only with his death, was entirely forgotten a hundred years later, though at least one man, James Graham Wright of Crapaud (second son of William Wright and his wife Isabella Cole of South Shore), had the honour of carrying his name through life. Dr. Graham lived at **Major Hooper's** with a practice even larger than the Methodist missionary's circuit.

The doctor saw many weary eyes close for the last time. The Loyalist pioneers were going Home. **Thomas Hooper Sr.**, who had been appointed Bedeque's first Justice of the Peace thirty years previously, died in 1816 at the age of eighty-two[5] [1734-1816].

The obelisk at the Lower Bedeque Cemetery has inscriptions on all four sides. Side one: "Sacred to the memory of Thomas Hooper, United Empire Loyalist. Settled in Bedeque 1785. Also his son Elisha, died Mar. 8, 1860, aet. [aged] 78 and his wife Margaret Crosby, died May 31, 1843, aet. 62. Erected by Jayne P. Hooper." Side two: "William, son of Elisha Hooper Drowned Aug. 12, 1874, AET 59." [This was "Black William" who burned a barn and pulled the plug in the boat when he was out on the Dunk River, filling the boat with water and thereby drowning. He was mentally handicapped and alcoholic according to Muriel Hooper Blanchard.] Third side: "Jane

Payne Hooper died Feb. 10, 1912 AET 88." [She had lived some years in Victoria with a relative, probably Major Hooper Wright.] Fourth side: "Mathilda Ann, wife of H. N. Hope and daughter of Elisha Hooper, died October 15, 1854, aet. 44." She died following the birth of her thirteenth child.

In his book, *Historic Bedeque*, Leard wrote of the passing of the two Williams - William Wright and William Schurman - two of the most prominent of all the Bedeque loyalists:

> ... At North Bedeque William Wright, who had heard the Word of God read from the Treasured Book with which he had furnished his home, finished out his days in February of 1819. Further along the shore at Wilmot Grove, William Schurman, who had sold the Book in Bedeque's first store, paid his debt to nature the same year when the leaves began to fall, leaving legacies totaling nearly one thousand pounds to his daughters, farm lands in excess of twenty-seven hundred acres to his sons and grandsons and three thousand acres of woodland earmarked for sale on behalf of his estate.
>
> William Schurman in his last will and testament directed his body to be buried near the church (Presbyterian) at Bedeque and from this it might be surmised that the first church stood in the middle of the present cemetery [which it did]. His Negro servant, Susannah Schurman, was to be provided for in the family as long as she lived, or if she wished to leave was to receive fifty pounds. Sook, as she was commonly known, has become a legend in Bedeque. Her beautiful voice, typical of one of her race's gifts to humanity, led the singer of the Psalms in the old Church at North Bedeque for well nigh a quarter of a century.[6]

At the time of his death Mr. Schurman was quite wealthy, and to his energy and enterprise many of the descendants owe the valuable homesteads they now occupy. His will was dated July 21, 1819 with a codicil added on August 2nd; it was proved on September 29th, 1819.

The tombstone that marks his resting place in the Presbyterian cemetery at North Bedeque bears the following inscription:

> In this place are interred the remains of
> William Schurman
> Undeviating in honesty and sincerity,
> Faithful as a Magistrate,
> Affectionate as a husband and father,
> Kind as a friend through life.
> He exchanged it for eternity on the 15th day of Sept., 1819 Aged 76 years.

Mr. Schurman's obituary appeared in the *Prince Edward Island Gazette* for Wednesday, September 23, 1819. He died in that part of Bedeque called Wilmot Valley:

DIED. On the 14th inst, at his House in Bedeque, WILLIAM SHUREMAN, Esq., an old and respectable Magistrate for Prince County. He was one of the oldest Loyalist Inhabitants of that settlement. His public duty as a Member of the Assembly and as a Magistrate were ever of a piece with his other conduct, marked with strong discernment and vigorous activity of mind, which were always evinced by his purity of intention and sound judgment. As a husband and parent he was no less conspicuous. His numerous family, whom he lived to see flourishing around him, with his numerous and attached neighbours must ever retain a truly affectionate and grateful remembrance of the virtues of a good father and a staunch, undeviating friend.

On the 15th at the same place, Mrs. Moyse [died]. Mrs. M. was upon her way mounted on horse-back, to Mr. Schureman's House, to visit the afflicted family, having dismounted to tighten the Girth of her Saddle, expired upon the spot.[7] [The account of this last death appears later in this genealogy]

From L.U. Fowler's, *Bedeque and Its People*, I will give a brief account of what became of the two Black slaves, Bill and Sook, who Mr. Schurman brought from the States with him. Their real names were Billinger and Susanna:

Some people have told me that those two were man and wife; this, however, is not correct. Bill was quite willing, in fact anxious, at one time to have Sook for a wife. And he, with that diplomacy so characteristic of him, secured the consent of all the friends. After a time he was asked when the wedding would take place. Bill gravely replied that "it would never take place." "Why?" he was asked. "Is not Mr. Schurman willing?" "Yes, everyone is willing but Sook." This saying has passed into a byword used by the generation when certain, particularly love, affairs do not come out as hoped for, someone may smilingly ask you if you have secured the consent of Sook!

Bill remained with the Schurmans until the year 1800 [another source says 1792]. Some believe that Sook made a wise decision for in 1794 a record was found of "William Bellinger, a black man" tried for theft in Charlottetown, found guilty, and sentenced to be whipped. Some time later he went to the United States, staying there for a time, then returning to Charlottetown. Two years before Mr. Schurman's death, Bill was again tried for theft, found guilty, and sentenced to be

brought in front of the Charlottetown gaol and receive thirty-nine lashes, then to be taken opposite the town stocks and receive thirty-nine more; then to be taken to the public market for thirty-nine more. The court record shows that the item stolen was an axe. Bill would be seventy years old at the time that he received his 117 lashes!

Sook, after the death of Mr. Schurman, went to River John, N.S. and lived with John Schurman's youngest son. She made a visit to the Island, an old lady. Residents told of the nice, silvert-haired old lady who had a kind word and a pleasant smile for everyone, praised all her friends, especially Mr. Schurman who had remembered her so generously in his will . . . . She died at River Phillip, N.S.[8]

Within a relatively short period of time, Richard Robins, **Thomas Hooper, Sr.,** William Wright, and William Schurman, four of the early Loyalists to leave New Jersey and New York for Prince Edward Island, had all passed to their eternal reward.

Hard work was a prerequisite to survival, and only after decades of toil and planning was it followed by material success. With lives caught up in this struggle to clear land, raise a family, and reap nature's bounty, it was to be expected that the early generations of settlers placed great importance on social activities as a means of relaxation, sharing and communication with neighbours. In *Roads to Summerside* we read from Ada MacLeod and Marjorie McCallum Gay's work:

The first builders of the Province, who with heroic labour transformed a wilderness into productive fields and comfortable homesteads, suffered their full share of privation, but were not without their seasons of relaxation and good cheer.

Indeed it seems as if they entered into both work and play with a zest that is foreign to these modern and more artificial times; and they had a unique method of combining work and pleasure in the community system of "frolics." Was there a frame to be raised or wood to be hauled, or a piece of ground to be stumped or plowed? The accepted method of getting it done was by gathering neighbours to a "frolic."

... An editorial in an old copy of the "Islander" laments the advent of the "fulling mills" which supplanted this old-time custom and lessened the number of social gatherings: "The time of general morality would be much raised if we could go back to the days of thickening frolics when all well-behaved people met on an equality.

It was in gatherings such as this that the first dwellers in Green's Shore [Summerside] found their social pleasure. In the winter time, there was much interchange of visits between them and the people of Bedeque. Pleasant indeed it was to gather around the huge fireplace with its blazing backlog and frontlogs on the andiron; and Penn Green used to recall their trials of skill in frying pancakes. The frying pan had a handle a yard in length, and the cake had to be turned by throwing it high over the crane and catching it in its descent with the proper side up.

This was the "Ballad Age" when people used to congregate in certain homes to hear solos - not three verses as today - but consisting of forty or fifty stanzas, usually the tale of some tragedy. The singer was always a man....

Then there were the ever-popular stories, and it was only natural that in a seaport such as this, where there lived so many who "went down to the sea in ships," that a large number of them should be traditional yarns of the deep.

Such, for instance, as the tale of the spectral "Lightship of Tryon" that used to hoist her shadowy sails and set forth over her old cruising ground up and down the Straits. She had been a French cruiser and once sailed in these waters, but one dark and stormy night she went ashore on Tryon Bar. All through the darkness her minute guns flashed and boomed, but no help came, and before morning an unusually high tide lifted her over the bar, and with her masts cut away and her crew at quarters, she went down in deep water. No wreckage ever washed up; no bodies ever drifted ashore. In that shifting sand, the sunken ship was soon filled with silt, and there she remains until this day with every man at his post as when the boatswain's whistle summoned them that night.

But, ever after on the wild nights unfit for mortal navigation, watchers on the shore could see first a speck of lurid light about two miles off at sea, then a bluish glare in which would become gradually visible the outline of a ship with broad hull, high prow, and heavy spars - all clearly defined to the eye, with men on deck and outlying on the yards.

Never was the spectral ship seen in so many places as at the time of the terrible "Yankee gale." While fishing vessels were pounding to fragments on the rocks, and battered bodies were being cast up on all our shores, she was seen by many eyes, scudding under full canvas in the very height of the tempest over the scene of the disaster, searching, as it was said, for the souls of the lost....

There are still living many elderly people who can repeat with much enjoyment the rhymes in which it was customary in the days of their youth to record the happenings of a community, and these men protest that young people nowadays do not even begin to have this fun they used to have. There was always someone in every settlement who possessed the art - more or less - of "putting things together," and these verses became at once the common property of all who gathered around the mud-diggers, the forum of that time. Woe betide the man who tried sharp

practice of a weaker neighbor. His case might be upheld by the law, yet if it ran counter to the community sense of justice, his nights would be made miserable by hearing a metrical version of his most intimate family history sung lustily by passing gangs to the tune of "Molly Darling" or "Long, Long Ago."

Hospitality abounded in those days, and folk did not wait for an invitation to dinner or afternoon tea. It was the custom for a party of several women to start out in the morning with their black luster aprons and their knitting, and drop in at some house to spend the day. This was sometimes rather embarrassing as, for instance, where the impromptu hostess happened to be a young bride, called upon for the first time to run the gauntlet of all these experienced cooks, and small wonder if, in her nervous haste, she would empty the peppermint bottle into the pudding instead of lemon flavor.

The old-time family servant who, unlike the transitory hired man of today, lived for years in the same situation, claimed many family privileges, and often furnished impromptu entertainment. Thus, for example was the quick-witted Mattie Shea. Rev. Cecil Wiggins (for nearly fifty years Rector of Sackville) tells of Mattie, an Irishman who was man-for-all-work for his father, "Parson" Wiggins at St. Eleanor's. He had been sent one day to hoe the family potato patch, but, visiting first the all too convenient grog shop across the road, was found some hours later lying between two rows, fast asleep. On being summarily wakened, he rose to his feet with what dignity he could muster, and, raising his hand for silence, said, "Wheest, master! It's the divil's own crop of petaties you will be after havin' this year! I was just listenin' here, wid me ear to the ground, and I heard wan big fellow say to the next one: 'Quit your crowdin'. Can't ye lie over an' make room?'"

On another occasion, Parson Wiggins was passing through the Rectory kitchen while Mattie was having his dinner. It was in the late spring when the family stock of potatoes had got low and only the small ones were left. "Begobs," said Mattie, "it's the quare pirates ye do be givin' us now, master. A man has to be lookin' for one, an' paling one, an' atin'one, all at the same time."

The "church tea" has ever been an institution of this Province. The cakes which used to appear there in bygone days, were wonders of architecture with their decorations of multi-colored fringed tissue-paper and their "ornaments," imported from England, of sugar hearts, roses, strawberries and other devices; and the cake itself usually proved worthy of its fine exterior although one case is on record where a Summerside lady bought at a church tea a handsome-looking structure of three stories only to discover that its center was composed of unadultered cornmeal.

... Singing schools were well-attended though not always with the object of learning to sing. Nathaniel Huestis was the first teacher of singing in Summerside.

The favorite ladies' magazines of that day were "Godey's Lady's Book" and "Demorest's Monthly," while the melodrama now provided by the movies was found in the fascinating pages of the "New York Ledger," usually kept hidden from the eyes of critical husbands under the rocking chair cushion.[9]

Across the river the Methodist meeting-house [apparently in Lower Bedeque], so near by ice in winter and so far away by road in summer, was soon a strong rival to the long-established Kirk. The Methodists had an urgency in their message and a popular appeal in their hymns of worship which the more staid service of the Scottish church lacked."[10]

The founding of Bedeque United Church was recorded in Jean MacFadyen's *For The Sake Of The Record*: "Its origin can be traced to Nathaniel Wright who was converted during mission services conducted in Tryon by an itinerant Methodist missionary from Nova Scotia. He was responsible for the coming of Rev. William Black to the province in 1794. Mr. Black's visit resulted in the organization of a Wesleyan Society of twenty members. The services were held in Mr. Wright's barn."[11]

George A. Leard provides an interesting account of the conversion of Nathaniel "Nattie" Wright:

> [In 1788 Nathaniel] married Nancy Lord of Tryon River and settled on a farm in the older community near her father where some land was cleared and the comfortable farm home had a large room left without partitions for frolics and dances. Nattie, William Wright's oldest son, had taken his Loyalist grant in Lot 26 and probably had even made some improvements on his property as his lease demanded. It seems that he left that property in North Bedeque to live in Tryon. In 1792 the Rev. William Grandin, an itinerant Methodist minister, came from Nova Scotia, and for several weeks spoke powerful, disturbing words to the assembled Tryon folk about sin and repentance, justification, and adoption until many were uneasy, and a few at least ready to adopt a new way of life. This first revival on the Island left a marked impression on the minds and souls of the young couple.... Their conversion marked the beginning of the Methodist churches in Tryon and Bedeque.
>
> After Grandin's departure other preachers came to the frolic room at Wright's with doctrines that troubled the newly-won Methodists, doctrines of predestination and election which seemed to say that lives of virtue and good works were not necessary for the Christian life. Being but slightly grounded in his new faith, Nathaniel with one of his relatives went to Nova Scotia in 1794 and brought back the saintly William Black, bishop of Methodism in the Atlantic colonies, who strengthened the wavering Wesleyan forces with convincing sermons and talks,

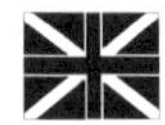

formed eight or ten into a society (really a church in the sense of it being a body of believers) who thereafter met regularly in class and baptized Nathaniel Wright and his three oldest sons, John (later to be known as "Squire John" of Searletown), William (later of Chelton), and Nathaniel of Bedeque.[12]

In 1807 Nattie returned to Bedeque and, settling on his one hundred and fifty acres at Centreville, through which ran the south creek of the Dunk River, soon built a grist mill and vied with William Taylor as the most popular Bedeque miller. It is uncertain why he left Tryon to return to Bedeque. He may have been in danger of losing his Loyalist grant if he was not settled there. Also two of Nancy's sisters had gone to Bedeque to live: Fanny in 1791 as wife of Nattie's brother Stephen, and Alice in 1798 as the bride of John Baker, Jr. In the Presbyterian stronghold of Bedeque, two lone women needed reinforcement of the Lords who were strong Methodists!

The Methodist Church grew and prospered in Bedeque in the nineteenth century. George A. Leard wrote about the major benefit of Methodism over Presbyterianism:

[The] Rev. James Bulpit, the Methodist preacher on the Island in 1807, belonged to an itinerant ministry, one which believed that a new broom sweeps clean and that both pastor and circuit benefited by frequent changes as opposed to the permanent ministry of the Presbyterian system which held that a pastorate without time limit allowed the church and minister to grow together in close relationship.

It would appear that the Bedeque circuit followed that belief for the next 150 years as most of the ministers stayed not more than three years until the 1950's.

In August 1815, the Rev. John Hick arrived in Charlottetown, and Tryon and Bedeque were made preaching appointments of the Charlottetown circuit. Sometimes on foot and sometimes on horseback, the preacher made the rounds of his large circuit. Writing in the spring of 1816 in a report to the Missionary secretary in England, Mr. Hick said: "At Bedeque our congregations are remarkably large, but our society is the smallest of any in the Island, the generality of them being Presbyterians.... But I am not without hopes of seeing

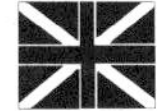

good days here also. Speaking more generally of the Island, he found the bulk of the people very poor, yet he had no doubt that a young man on the circuit would be amply provided for. The Bedeque society or church of which Mr. Hick was writing had a membership of only six at this time of whom we can be sure Nathaniel Wright and his wife formed a third."[13]

In George A. Leard's *Historic Bedeque* the author gave a complete and interesting account of early Methodism in Bedeque:

Bedeque's best-known and best-loved pioneer preacher, the Rev. John B. Strong, came to Bedeque on Saturday, 24th August, 1816, guided through the dense woods from Tryon by Jane Callbeck, eighteen-year-old daughter of Phillips Morris Callbeck, who was later Mrs. Joseph Silliker of Bedeque. The bridle-path, which only politeness could call a road, had no farm homes on it, but was arched all the way with trees which lent welcome shade for a summer day. On Sunday Mr. Strong preached his first sermon in Nathaniel Wright's barn at Centreville (there being apparently no "frolic room" in the Wright house at Bedeque similar to the Tryon one) from the text, "This is life eternal, that they might know Thee, the only true God and Jesus Christ Whom Thou hast sent." Mr. Strong, recently from Montreal where he had been fifth pastor of St. James Methodist Church, had exchanged circuits with Mr. Hick of Charlottetown. The twenty-six-year-old minister, who eventually rounded out his days in Prince Edward Island and who with his family was to be very intimately connected with the Bedeque circuit, made his headquarters at Charlottetown, visiting Tryon River and Bedeque once every six weeks.

During his December visit of 1816, Mr. Strong, who had a year-old chapel in Murray Harbour and a six-months-old one in Charlottetown, held meetings in both Tryon and Bedeque to plan the erection of the first Methodist meeting house in Prince County. It was determined in both centers to get out the frames that winter, with friends giving either work or material. In Tryon, according to schedule, the men went to work in March and by the first of June had quite a creditable building which, though lacking pews, windows, pulpit, and plaster, was considered a fitting place for the first sermon of their pastor following District Meeting in 1817. Their pastor then was no longer the Rev. John B. Strong of Charlottetown for they were no longer a part of the Charlottetown circuit. Tryon and Bedeque had become a separate circuit with the Rev. John Fishpool as missionary in charge. Writing in August of 1817, a few weeks after his arrival, Mr. Fishpool said: "Tryon and Bedeque is the present extent of any circuit and notwithstanding the paucity and

poverty of this people, they are doing great things and then went on to tell how he had preached his first sermon in the unfinished church at Tryon, later going on a begging expedition to Sackville and Wallace where he secured a stove and glass and money to spare to make Tryon meeting house truly a Maritime affair.

The proposed chapel at Bedeque did not make such speedy progress. Nathaniel Wright and his little band were growing; his own family of eleven children, two daughters-in-law, and four grandchildren made a sizable gathering in themselves, but the Methodists were not nearly so numerous in Bedeque as Tryon. Not enough of them turned out in the winter of 1817 to cut sufficient Bedeque pine to erect the chapel that year. In the meantime the end of the conference year saw another change of missionaries. Mr. Fishpool and Mr. Strong exchanged circuits in June of 1818 so that Mr. Strong who had proposed the chapel in December of 1816 was back in time to see it built. Still thirty years in the future another Bedeque church was to be built under his guidance.

The 1818 chapel was built with skill and dispatch by men of the shipyards to whom the smell of pine chips and the feel of the adze were the breath of life. Shipbuilding in Bedeque Bay, not unknown from 1791 when William Baker built a forty-four ton square-sterned schooner..., did not flourish until the beginning of the new century when William Schurman built the schooner "Lovely" to replace the "Mary" which for many years was Bedeque's chief link of communication with both Charlottetown and the mainland. In 1803 Schurman built the brigantine "William," a ship of one hundred and sixty-seven tons, which was not exceeded in size in the Bedeque shipyards for many years. The same year Alexander Campbell of Wilmot built a seventy-six ton schooner, the "Eliza," which was followed by a succession of sister schooners, "Jane," "Sally," and "Feronia," but not till 1814 did he try a square-rigger when he built the "Sophia," a brig slightly larger than Schurman's "William."

Many of the Bedeque farmers built small schooners or shallops which, like the motor trucks of their descendants, were used for both business and pleasure. The Wrights, Prices, Murrays, MacFarlanes, MacCallums, Greens, and others all owned boats of varying sizes in which they tempted Providence at various times. For the merchants, of course, ships were the essential carriers of commerce which made or lost fortunes depending on weather and markets. Names of early merchants of Bedeque, otherwise long forgotten, as culled from shipping registers include Samuel Welsford, Thomas Townshend, and Charles Stowe, all of them probably living in Lot 25.

The commercial history of Centreville and Lower Bedeque may be dated from the arrival of the Popes in 1818. The Popes of Plymouth [England] were merchants and shipbuilders, but above all they were Methodists, and their arrival in Bedeque was perhaps one of the turning points in the history of the Methodist Church. Thomas Pope the elder, of Plymouth, had six sons, three of them were

famous preachers in the Wesleyan church and three merchants and shipbuilders who worked very successfully in a family partnership. One of the sons, John Pope, with his brother, William, came to Bedeque in 1818 with a shipload of artisans and labourers to build ships and cut pine deal for the British market, both of which found a ready sale on the other side of the Atlantic. The Pope residence, later to become the Summerside Kirk, was built near the corner of the Lower Bedeque road and for many years served as a mariner's landmark for those sailing up the channel. Probably the same men who built the Pope home (one of them chalked the name 'George Price 1818' on a beam) helped at the new church which was built under the direction of John Pope. It was built to the east of the then small cemetery which had been started at Lower Bedeque and its site is now covered with the graves of its first attendants.

Most Bedequers [in 1948] can remember the old church reduced at last to warehouse status behind Bowness' store where it burned to the ground in the fire of 1938. A plain low-posted building 30 X 40 (a shade bigger than Tryon's 39 X 27 chapel) with gothic windows and, in its day, galleries and porch, it made no pretensions to being a cathedral, but for the Loyalists entering their first Methodist chapel in Bedeque, even for the minister but two years removed from a Montreal pastorate, and for the Plymouth Popes who knew the larger meeting-houses of the old country, it was doubtless a considerable achievement in church building. The chapel, when completed with gallery and some crowding of fat folks, was officially reckoned as having three hundred and six sittings with forty of them free; but where they tucked them all in is just difficult to say.[14]

...travelers who wrote of their Island experiences in this period were Englishmen and Irishmen of an itinerant ministry whose missionary society sponsored and paid the missionary travelers in their wide field of labour and charged them to "keep a journal and send frequent and copious extracts without high colouring of facts" to the parent Society. From these reports we have the earliest mention of Bedeque Methodist church. Mr. Fishpool writing of his year's stay at Tryon and Bedeque (1817-1818) described it as the most fruitful of his labours with "many dark minds enlightened and hard hearts softened." Mr. Strong's letter to the missionary Committee written from Bedeque in 1818 told of hardships of Island travel: bogged in a swamp - lost at times for hours on lonely wood trails - and twice broken through the ice in winter with three fathoms of icy water beneath - circuit work which demanded indeed a **Strong** minister.

The third pastor of the Prince County circuit was George Miller who came in 1819 and stayed two years....Tryon and Bedeque appeared in the list of foreign mission fields together with other circuits in Nova Scotia, Africa, New Brunswick, and India. For many years succeeding pastors in the circuit signed their names as Wesleyan Missionaries and for nearly forty years Bedeque continued to be listed as a foreign mission circuit in North America....

Rev'd Thomas Payne came to Bedeque in 1821. He was a little more methodical than his predecessors, starting a baptismal and marriage register which, apart from St. Paul's Anglican records at Charlottetown, is the oldest Protestant one on the Island. Mr. Payne and his wife Jane stayed at Nathaniel Wright's home which, like many since, had a spare room downstairs (generally off the parlor) known as the minister's room. Mr. Fishpool, the first minister on the circuit, had stayed at Tryon, but all succeeding pastors lived at Bedeque; Mr. Strong and Mr. Miller moving about from home to home. Beginning, however in 1820 (a date which may have marked the erection of a new home - later to be known as the Noonan Cottage), the minister and his family were the permanent, free guests of the Wrights at Centreville.

[The] Rev. George Jackson, who succeeded Mr. Payne in 1823, had eighty-two baptisms during his two year pastorate... Mr. Jackson, though small in stature, had energy enough for two. He was in Bedeque but a short time when he decided the Methodists should have a preacher's house. Nathaniel Wright, the father of Methodism in Prince County, was failing and it did not seem fair for the minister to continue to impose on the Wright's hospitality. Accordingly in the spring of 1824 a small log house arose near the present cemetery, and though for many years unfinished and unfurnished, it was from the start the Wesleyan Parsonage or Mission house and here the missionary lived.

During Mr. Jackson's pastorate a deed to the church property was drawm up and reigistered. Joseph Silliker and wife Jane... sold for five shillings [or $1.00] a half acre of freehold land directly east of land then appropriated for a burying ground. The trustees in this typical Wesleyan Methodist deed were charged to hold the property in trust for the people called Methodists. Only Methodist preachers were to have use of the chapel and the preachers were to be conference appointees and preach only from Wesley's Notes on the New Testament.

All monies collected and received, so the deed went on, were to be used in discharging debts and taxes on the premises and towards the support of the preachers... The trustees named in the original deed were Nathaniel Wright Sr., Stephen Wright Sr., Nathaniel Wright Jr., Stephen Wright Jr., Joseph Wood, **Elisha Hooper**, and Jesse Strang Sr. Only two of this number, Joseph Wood of Tryon who represented the circuit's interest in the property and Elisha Hooper of Bedeque, were not members of the Wright family.

... Nathaniel Wright Senior's name was, of course, first on the list. He was the father of the church in Prince County, the earliest member, the most liberal supporter, and the first class-leader. His sons, Nathaniel Jr. who was also a class leader, having been appointed in 1820, and Stephen Jr., were the youngest members of the board, the latter being but twenty-three. Stephen Wright Sr., brother of Nathaniel Wright Sr., had doubtless been led into the Methodist fold through the efforts of his wife, Frances Lord, and his brother Nathaniel.

Jesse Strang, whose name appeared last on the deed, was one of the original elders of the Bedeque Presbyterian Church in the Princetown Congregation, having been ordained in 1801 or 1802. He and Joseph Silliker at Silliker's Brook, Lower Bedeque, shared a mother (they were half-brothers) and also shared the honour of donating the sites for the respective Methodist and Presbyerian churches in Bedeque. Jesse Strang's father is presumed to have been Daniel Strang (a British recruiting agent shot as a spy with the approval of General Washington) whose widow married Jacob Silliker shortly before they came to the Island.

Just how a Presbyterian elder on whose land the church stood could stray so far in the Wesleyan way as to become a Methodist trustee seems almost unexplainable until it is known that Jesse Strang was a brother-in-law of Nathaniel Wright. A faithful elder for upwards of seventeen years, Jesse Strang was one of the right-hand men of Rev. John Keir, who had been inducted into the large Princetown Parish in 1810 and sat in many meetings of session when straying members of the Presbyterian flock were cited to appear and account for conduct unbecoming in followers of Christ. Many offences, including "failure to support the gospel in this congregation," quarreling, stealing, Sabbath breaking, and the more carnal sins were charged to church members who, if guilty, were expected to show true contrition and after being publicly rebuked before either the session or congregation, were "absolved from the scandel of their sin." The guilty, unpenitent member was "suspended from the sealing ordinances of the church" for a time and later, if continuing in sin, was "excommunicated."

Elders as well as members were under strict discipline of session and in 1817 and 1818 when Jesse Strang commenced attending the Methodist meeting house more often than his own, he doubtless expected the reproof of his fellow elders. The Session which met following the June Communion of 1818, which together with the fall communion of 1817 had been marked with Jesse Strang's absence, spoke of one of their elders walking disorderly (i.e. attending Methodist services in preference to Presbyterian ones) and appointed David Murray and Alexander Anderson to interview him and report at the next meeting.

A year later, June 9, 1819, the assembled session heard from their committee that elder Jesse Strang's reason for leaving the church and going with the Methodists was "because he could receive more benefit from their preaching." The report was calmly received by the Moderator of the session, the eloquent preacher and learned graduate of Glasgow University, Rev. John Keir, who next Sabbath told the congregation that because of his conduct Jesse Strang was no longer considered a member of the church or session.

The new Methodist member served faithfully in the Wesleyan church for the remainder of his days, little dreaming that less than ninety years after his death the church, to which in his life he had divided his allegiance, should be members of one great United Church, neither Presbyterian nor Methodist, but both, the off-

spring of the most significant ecclesiastical marriage in Canadian history. Many of Jesse Strang's family followed in the father's footsteps, and for many years after his death in 1836, his son Gabriel Strang of Searletown occupied the Strang seat on the trustee board.[15]

... Strictly interpreted, the original law of the Colony had confined the marriage ceremony to clergy of the Established Church, though all governors from the first, recognizing the inability of parson Desbrisay, for many years sole Anglican clergyman on the Island, to take care of the situation, issued a license to any interested couple directing a specified justice of the peace to perform the ceremony according to the rites of the Church of England. Two of these licenses (now Museum pieces), Nathaniel Wright's, issued in 1788, and Stephen Wright's 1790, were preserved in Bedeque up till very recently [1948]. Later when the Methodist ministers followed the Bedeque circuit, the custom of magistrate marriages had been so well established that it continued as a social custom for nearly the first hundred years of Bedeque history. **Thomas Hooper Sr., Major Hooper,** and Alexander Anderson were among the favourite joiners [magistrates] of the early years. However, any parties desiring the blessing of the church were married by the Methodist ministers with no compunctions as to the legality of same. Rev. Thomas Payne who commenced the circuit records, started well in 1822 by marrying two couples on New Year's day.[16]

By about 1830 there was also an Anglican clergyman in St. Eleanor's. George A. Leard continued his account with reference to a noticeable competition between the Baptists and the Methodists also, as well as between the Methodists and the Presbyterians already alluded to:

... Bedeque Methodist homes may have lacked for money in the early days, yet for the most part they considered themselves to be of respectable birth and would have been shocked (as are their descendants) to know that probably ninety-five per cent of the Methodist children born in Bedeque up till 1832 were illegitimate, when in that year the Colonial Government rather belatedly passed a law (William IV Cap. 14. 1832), to confirm marriages made by non-conformist clergy, or by justices of the peace by virtue of licenses from the Lieutenant Governor, and to make the issue of such marriages legitimate to all intents and purposes.

... The earliest legal marriage by a Methodist minister in Bedeque was performed by Rev. Wm. Webb on the 20th day of September, 1832, when Gabriel Strang, settled on a farm later to be known as the Major Lowther property [the father of Gladys Henderson and the son of Adella Hooper Lowther], in the newly opened Searletown district, was married at Centreville to Ann Wright after publishing of banns.[17]

... The early pastors of all the Bedeque churches appeared to be men of considerable stamina. They traveled over the incredibly poor roads preaching incredibly long sermons four or five times a week in addition to performing the many chores incidental to pioneer existence. Rev. George Jackson, the Methodist minister of this period, wielded a ready pen which was not confined to obituaries and sermons. Just previous to coming to Bedeque he had written a lengthy pamphlet entitled "An Humble Attempt to Substantiate the Legitimacy of Infant Baptism and of Sprinkling as a Scriptural Mode" which was directed rather apologetically as the title suggests against the teaching of the Baptist brethren. It, of course, was not allowed to go unchallenged and was answered by William Elder, first pastor of the Baptist Church at Bridgetown, Nova Scotia. In rebuttal, Mr. Jackson, in his spare moments at Bedeque, wrote a two hundred page book entitled, "A Further Attempt to Substantiate the Legitimacy of Infant Baptism" and the battle of Baptist was on. Rev. Charles Tupper (father of Sir Charles Tupper) who was later to be the first ordained Baptist minister residing on the Bedeque charge and Alexander Crawford of Tryon, rushed into print in defense of the "gospel mode" of baptism and so the wordy war continues. None ever knew who won, though Mr Jackson's Methodist supporters claimed a victory for their side inasmuch as Rev. Wm. Elder of the Bridgetown Baptist Church was won over by Mr. Jackson's book. He offered his services to the Methodist ministry which had to be declined on a technicality, and eventually ended up as first Anglican rector at Sydney Mines. The loss of Rev. Wm. Elder, the Baptists countered, was not unexpected; he was trying all the ministries, having started as a Congregational preacher.[18]

During the decade of the 1820s, while Methodism was becoming entrenched in the Bedeque settlement, George A. Leard lamented the death of several noteworthy Bedeque pioneers:

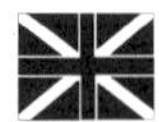

Death kept visiting the homes of the Bedeque pioneers. John Baker's anvil rang no more to his hammer blows after 1821 for Bedeque's first blacksmith was gone to his rest. His cinder heap added to by his successors and still evident years later in one of Offie Inman's fields, marked the site of his forge. At Lower Bedeque, Benjamin Cole [who had married Isabella Robins and shared a lot with John Robins and Mary Hooper a ways beyond the cemetery in Lower Bedeque], whose family name would be perpetuated in a wharf for many years, died in 1825.

At Central Bedeque in February of 1824, the aged and enfeebled wife of William Taylor, the miller, fell in the fire and was burned to death, a type of accident which was to be repeated at various times in the community's history as long as there were open fires and the aged, crippled, or infant folk were left unattended. That William Taylor found the milling business not without profit was seen by his new home (later to be known as the Howard Schurman residence) erected around 1830. His second marriage in 1829 at the age of seventy-five to seventy-year-old widow Chappell, received due recognition from the press of that day.

Nathaniel Wright, whose earthly pilgrimage commenced on the borders of New England twenty miles from New York, and whose youthful years knew war and revolution and yellow fever, finished his journey in Bedeque on April 25, 1825, at the early age of sixty. Thrift and hard work had made for comfort and plenty in the Wright home whose furnishings according to an inventory in 1825 would not be amiss in many homes of 1950. The barn population of draft oxen, horses, swine, stirks, and neat cattle showed a prosperous farmer. Down on the mill stream, the grist mill had company of another, the earliest carding mill in Bedeque, but the miller was dead, the community mourned a great loss. In less than twenty years's residence, Nathaniel Wright had made his mark on Bedeque which is still evident [1948]. Beginning with a flaming faith and two or three members, his barn serving for church services, his home as the minister's dwelling, he saw before his death a well-established church in Bedeque and a parsonage nearing completion.

It was an achievement worthy of "well done, good and faithful servant" which indeed was given him in an extensive memoir written by his pastor, George Jackson, which appeared in the Wesleyan Methodist Magazine of 1825. No other Islander before or since has had the honour of a full length obituary in this oldest of religious periodicals in the world. A presentation copy of this 1825 volume, still treasured in the Searletown home of a descendant, has the following inscription: "From George Jackson, Wesleyan Missionary, to Mrs. Nathaniel Wright Senior, as a token of Christian regard for her and her dear departed husband whose memoir is contained in this volume.
Halifax, N.S.
June 2, 1826."[19]

Mrs. Nathaniel Wright [Ann] is buried in the Lower Bedeque Cemetery, as becomes a Methodist, after her death on March 20, 1838 at age 70.

George A. Leard, in *Historic Bedeque*, also commented on the problems experienced by the Bedeque Methodist Sunday School program in the 1820s:

The Bedeque Sunday School ... suffers an interruption of six months in the year due to the road and weather [from the Missionary report of 1826]. In this department of our labours, we suffer most for the want of local help, and these institutions languish for want of books. Had not the missionary purchased them at his own expense, there could have been no school at Bedeque ... For the church year June 1, 1825-May 30, 1826, the absence of baptismal entries in the Bedeque records and the dearth of reports for this period make it uncertain as to whether there was a missionary stationed at Bedeque at this time. Rev. John Marshall who followed Mr. Jackson reported thirty-one members at Bedeque for 1827 with "three backsliders reclaimed...." The Sunday School at Bedeque in 1827 still suffered from the lack of teachers which had so discouraged Johnstone in 1821. The twenty-eight pupils enrolled had the missionary and his wife as teachers. Bedeque circuit, twenty-three miles in extent, had six preaching places which the pastor visited eleven times a fortnight.[20]

According to L.U. Fowler's article, "Bedeque and Its People," by 1900 there were great changes in the appearance of Bedeque since the days of Nathaniel Wright and the old generation of Loyalist pioneers in the 1780s:

At a quick glance, the Bedeque of Nathaniel Wright's time differed from that of one hundred and twenty-five years later, not so much by the smaller homes and barns as by the large stretches of virgin forest through which wound roads which did not merit the name. In the fall of 1824 tenders were called for the opening of a new road to Bedeque, "commencing near the 17th mile of the old Tryon Road and running ten miles to the South West branch of Bedeque River." The following work was required: "All trees and stump roots in way of surveyor's line to be taken out and thrown a distance of ten feet on each side of the line. The ground to be leveled four feet wide upon the line to make a bridle road."

Such was the pioneer road. Little wonder that Nathaniel Wright did not live to see a carriage in Prince County. The first four-wheel carriage was brought to Bedeque in 1826 from Providence, Rhode Island, and its proud owner, unknown to history, took it to church the first Sunday where the young Bedequers gazed in awe and wonder, while the wag of the day remarked it was poorly constructed, for if driven fast he knew the hind wheels would overtake and run down the fore wheels!

The new road proposed for Bedeque in 1824 naturally preceded an election by a month or two, and Nathaniel Wright's last vote was polled in his own barn on December 27, 1824 when four members for Prince County (still one polling district) were elected. The poll had opened at Princetown on December 20th with six candidates, and had adjourned to Bedeque (the only other polling center) on the 27th, closing that evening with Alexander Campbell of Bedeque House, Wilmot, leading the poll, and Wright's brother-in-law, John Lord of Tryon, James B. Palmer, lawyer of Charlottetown, and Samuel Green of St. Eleanor's, among the also-rans. The Register (Charlottetown's only paper) called the election "a warm contest" featuring bloody noses, smashed hats, and hoisting and pulling down of 88 banners and flags.

Wright's barn was for many years the polling center of Bedeque, and long after its walls had forgotten the echoes of the prayers and hymns of the first Methodist services, they retained faint memories of strident political speeches and the hoarse three cheers for the Governonr and four cheers for King William which closed the elections.

Alexander Campbell, Esq. was an important man in his time: farmer, Justice of the Peace, merchant, ship builder. He was also for some time Island Treasurer. He had a large house, and visitors to the settlement always put up at Campbell's.

It would fill a book to write all the stories that are told of the time when Campbell was a merchant. What is now Summerside was at that time simply Green's Shore without harborage or accommodation of any kind, while there was good anchorage at the foot of Campbell's farm. Here for many years vessels landed, cargoes of general merchandise including iron, dry goods, and rum, and were loaded with lumber for the markets of Nova Scotia and Great Britain by Mr. Campbell or Mr. Schurman. In the absence of telegraphic or other modern communication and with a very ineffective and irregular mail service, it quite frequently happened that vessels arrived for lumber without any notice to the shippers of their coming. On such occasions so abundant was the lumber that a sufficient number of men could be collected to cut down, hew into timber, and load a vessel in one day. On one occasion a large cargo of salt in bulk was imported. Mr. Campbell had no building large enough to store it. After some delay it was hauled up and piled in a field. Brush was placed all over and around it. The brush was then burned, the heat from the fire melting the salt, thus forming a crust and serving as a protection from the weather.

The land bought from Mr. McDonald by Mr. Schurman, for which he gave eight hundred pounds, was covered with the best of pine and hardwood trees. A large number of men were constantly employed cutting, hewing, hauling, or rolling the timber into the river.[21]

Though politics secured the ardent loyalty of many Bedequers, it was generally second to the loyalty given their churches. The third church to be established in Bedeque was the Baptist. Rev. Charles Tupper, a missionary of that persuasion, preached throughout the Island in the summer of 1825 with considerable success. The following year at Bedeque, under the leadership of Rev. Theodore Seth Harding, the first Regular Baptist Church in Prince Edward Island was organized on Calvinistic principles under the rules and articles of the Baptist Association of Nova Scotia. This Baptist congregation, which included members in both Tryon and Bedeque was the first **Regular** Baptist Church, but had been preceded some years by a **Scotch** Baptist Church which ... was found to be in a disorganized state when the communities of Tryon and Bedeque were first visited by Mr. Tupper in 1825, and the next year by Rev. Joseph Crandall, and Rev. T. S. Harding, all of whom helped in the founding of the Regular Church by each baptizing a number of the original members.

Like the Presbyterian and the Methodist, the site of the first Baptist Church is covered with the graves of its early membership. The first Church, built it is believed in 1826, stood in the middle of the present [Baptist] cemetery. In Bedeque's early history, Isaac Bradshaw was to the Baptist Church what Nathaniel Wright was to the Methodist. Coming to Bedeque from Sackville, N.B., in 1805, with his wife, Sybil Emerson, he settled on a farm at Central Bedeque. His pleasant home, built on the hill overlooking the creek which for many years carried his surname, was the first headquarters of the Regular Baptist Church on the Island, with Mr Bradshaw serving very effectively as local preacher in Bedeque and Tryon.... The church when organized in 1826 had a membership of twenty-eight with Isaac Bradshaw the first deacon. The earlier ministers resided in Tryon.[22]

In North Bedeque the Presbyterians stood to pray and sat for the lining and singing of the metrical psalms as led by the presentor. Across the Dunk [River] the Methodists in Centreville stood to sing the lively tunes and hymns in Wesley's Book. When led in prayer, by preacher and prayer-leader, they knelt as though in private devotion with their backs toward the pulpit, the seat of the pew often supporting devout hearts in tired bodies which sometimes slept if the prayers were too long.

Other customs which a hundred years would bring to a uniformity though not necessarily an improvement in either case, included the dispension and reception of the sacraments. Summer Communion at North Bedeque was always the biggest event of the year in the Presbyterian calendar which strenuously excluded all holy days or religious anniversaries. Preceded by preparatory services for two days, the faithful gathered on Sunday, outdoors if it were fine, around an actual table spread

for the Lord. The table was "fenced" by the minister in a sermon setting forth the significance of the sacrament and the danger of receiving it unworthily. Afterwards the faithful drew near, each with a metal token of admission received the previous day at a preparatory service from one of the session who now proceeded to assist the minister in servicing succeeding tables. A service of thanksgiving on the next day completed the solemn service of remembrance.

Methodist preparation for the Quarterly Communion was a matter of right living, right thinking, and right believing. If a member of the Society had walked aright with love towards his fellow-men, attending regularly upon preaching-services and class-meetings, he received a quarterly ticket with his name on it signed by the pastor admitting him to Communion. The symbols of our Saviour's death, served by the minister, were received kneeling at the altar rail, one of the few survivals of Anglican church order in Methodist procedure.

The Baptists, too, at this period stood for prayer and it was not till the latter third of the century that the congregation needed to be reminded that standing or kneeling was the suitable posture for prayer ...The trustees for this "certain body of Christians at Bedeque called Calvinistic Baptists" consisted of five members: Philip Baker, Solomon D. Schurman, Joseph Bradshaw, **Artemas Hooper** [Major's son who married a Baker], and Albert Casswell....[23]

Methodism was making considerable progress, and in 1816 Rev. John Hick took steps toward the erection of a chapel.... The church was completed in 1818 on a part of that plot of ground which forms the cemetery [in Lower Bedeque], the land being donated by Joseph Silliker. [The reader will recall that he owned the farm on which the Lower Bedeque Cemetery is located. On either side of this farm was the property of Major Hooper and Thomas Hooper.] The location was near the shore for the practical reason that travel was largely by water, there being no roads, only trails. The building was 30 feet by 40 feet with Gothic windows, gallery and porch. The first Trustee Board of this Wesleyan property consisted of Nathaniel Wright, Sr., Nathaniel Wright, Jr., Stephen Wright, Sr., Stephen Wright, Jr., **Elisha Hooper**, Joseph Wood, and Jesse Strang, Sr.[24]

Ann Lord Wright's attachment to Methodism showed in her wish that her children should marry only Methodists. "Her son Stephen, the mill owner at Centreville, married [for the second time, his first wife, Martha Hooper, having died] six months later into one of the most prominent Anglican families of the colony when Millicent, second daughter of the late James B. Palmer, became his bride with the St. Paul's (Charlottetown Anglican Church) rector officiating. The first two children of the marriage were taken to Charlottetown to receive baptism at the hand of the rector, and it looked as though the wishes of the Mother of Bedeque Methodism were being flouted. However, Stephen Wright always remained the loyal son of his mother's church and with his wife Millicent and their children occupied one of the prominent pews in the old church which in time they all grew to love and serve."[25]

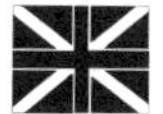

Obviously, there was s strong Methodist heritage in the Bedeque area, and the pioneers placed a great importance on religion. George A. Leard wrote about the visit of Walter Johnstone from Dumfries, Scotland in the early 1820s. Despite the strong religious presence, Mr. Johnstone's impressions of the settlement were not all positive:

> Bedeque had its first adverse press notice in 1822. Walter Johnstone, one time shoe-maker of Dumfriesshire, Scotland, who came to the Island in 1820 selling straw bonnets and religious tracts and organizing Sunday Schools, published an account of his visit to the Island in which he spoke of Bedeque as "truly an excellent, well-cleared settlement. The settlers, however, are both ignorant and indolent farmers and much of the land is running wild and barren under their management." He had very little success in starting a Sabbath School. Mr. Johnstone did note, however, that "the Methodists of the Island seldom lacked a sermon at all their preaching places, because they had so many excellent local preachers. It must be acknowledged that wherever Methodists abound, vice and immorality are made in a great measure to hide their head, and every man and woman is taught to pray.
>
> ... Mr. Johnstone, who was not a total abstainer himself, condemned the Island custom of drinking rum: deploring very much the fact that even those with only a short way to return from Sabbath worship must need "refresh" themselves at a tavern. The common charge at the Island Inns was six pence (10 cents) for bed and one shilling (20 cents) for supper. Not only the drinking habits of the settlers but their whole bill of fare was frowned on by this Scottish traveller.... He noted the women as being "uncommonly fruitful," dressed mostly in homespun druffles, stuffs and druggetts dyed blue, and wrote, "a wife that is a good spinner, knitter, and sewer is a great acquisition here." The girls, he thought, had nice figures, but the rosy cheeks of North Britain lassies were never evident for which he blamed the tanning of the summer sun and the bleaching of the great fires in winter. "The men," he said in slightly critical tones, "were for the most part tall and well-made in their persons, but too fond of riding and roving about, frolicking and drinking rum, eating fish and fishing" to ever make really good farmers.[26]

Merchant William Schurman, Loyalist, had a store at Bedeque. Ross Graves, in *William Schurman, Loyalist ...*, gave a detailed account of the variety of goods available to his pioneer neighbours:

The two hundred customers generally lived within a dozen miles of William's house. In the earliest years they would come by water to William's wharf or by land on horseback through the woods to where the lane to his house branched off the trail, later replaced by a road. We can get an idea of what they went to purchase by the accounts charged up against them when they had no cash and nothing to barter. First there were food supplies: molasses, sugar (either maple or brown), tea, coffee, (mentioned only once in 1784), salt, rum, codfish, wheat, barley, potatoes, and spices: nutmeg, cinnamon sticks, pepper, ginger, and allspice. Sold for use in the pioneer household were cutlery, cups and saucers, tin cups, pint mugs, noggins, firkins, kegs, pails, buckets, barrels, tubs, churns, cards (for the wool), spools (for the spinning wheel), iron pots (for the crane), lanterns, oil, ink (powdered), paper, and an occasional Bible. Yardgoods he stocked at various times were broadcloth, linen, serge, flannel, calico, cotton, corduroy, camlet, muslin, baize, cambric, and gauze, and other supplies for the pioneer housewife included pins, needles, thread (sold not on a spool but by the skein), binding, lining, buttons, and indigo. William also carried the occasional item of ready-made clothing (twice), in addition to shoes, shoe leather, soles, moccasins, and snowshoes. Several items are mentioned only occasionally, for they were rarely bought. The housewife made her own soap, candles, butter, cheese, stockings, and mittens, and the farm produced its own lamb and mutton, veal and beef, pork, wool, lard, turnips, and flour; yet all these were sold by William to those in short supply during his thirty-five years of storekeeping in Bedeque. For the pioneer farmer William carried scythes, cradles (for the scythe), sickles, hayrakes, ploughs, harrows, axes, awl blades, files, sheepshears, chains, steel and iron bars, hoops, flax-seed, sieves (for sifting grain) sieve hoops, and pocketknives. Occasionally he sold livestock and fowl off his farm: oxen, cows, pigs, sheep, turkeys, geese. If the pioneer wanted to build, he could buy lumber, shingles, spikes, nails, tacks, hinges, and (though rarely) glass from the Schurman store; if (like many) he used the water as a means of travel, William would gladly sell him canvas, sailcloth, cordage, and pitch. Did he need powder and shot? Sulphur? A new chair or a new chest? The Schurman store had them and more. And there were a few items of luxury: tobacco for both men and women; pipes, the white clay kind which generally sold for a penny each and were bought by the dozen; combs, much needed in that era of long hair for all the family; large handkerchiefs, both plain and silk, worn by men as scarves to give a bit of colour to homespun clothes; ribbons by the score; and for the extravagant, a bottle of lavender (once in 1806) and a set of "fidel strings," (once in 1795). The foregoing includes several items mentioned once, as well as ones which appear many times, and the variety in William's stock would probably never be half as large as the list suggests. Three that he did carry all the time, three that together outsold all the rest, were tea, tobacco, and rum.[27]

The Scottish traveller, Walter Johnstone, visiting the Island in 1821, also commented on agricultural conditions. George A. Leard wrote: "P.E.I. cart wheels in 1821 were seldom shod and ploughing was done most with oxen. The horses, small and light, seemed very hardy and were used mostly for riding. The black-horned cattle on the Island were fed only wheat straw all winter supplemented with what they got by foraging in the woods. Most of them appeared stunted."[28] [A critical fellow, he!]

The Rev. Robert Sim Patterson, M.A., came to the Island in 1825 and was inducted as pastor of the Bedeque congregation in 1826. He had the longest unbroken pastorate in the history of the Canadian Presbyterian Church. His ministry ended with his death in his fifty-eighth year of ministry. He is credited with organizing the first temperance society on the Island, in Bedeque, in 1827. It was probably very much needed, according to George A. Leard:

> The tremendous consumption of raw and ardent spirits by English-speaking people in both the old country and North America during the latter part of the eighteenth century and the early years of the nineteenth century has probably never been exceeded by any other people in any other period. It was a time when gin dispensers in England advertised that you could get "drunk for a penny- dead drunk for two pence, straw provided free." Rum sellers in Bedeque thought nothing of selling five gallons at a time at $1.00 to $1.50 a gallon.
>
> Almost everyone drank at least some type of intoxicating beverage in early Bedeque from the home-made wines which the women of the household took liberally and allegedly for their health, to the port and peach brandy on the genteel sideboards. The homes were generously supplied with intoxicants without the taverns' whiskeys and rum which consumed on the premises by the gil were carried home by the gallon. Little wonder that the earliest pledge of the Bedeque Temperance Society called for less than total abstinence, excepting certain occasions such as Christmas and election day when the flesh might be weak. However, it was long before practical experience showed that only the total abstainer was truly temperate, and eventually the pledges were amended accordingly. Discipline in both the Methodist and the Prebyterian churches forbad drunkenness. At North Bedeque the drunkard was reasoned with by some of the elders and sometimes cited to appear before the session. If truly sorry for his sin, he was publicly rebuked, sometimes before the entire congregation, and thus absolved from the scandal he had

caused; but if inpenitent, he was suspended from the sealing ordinances of the church. With the Methodists, a class leader occupied somewhat the same role as elder and less formally than the Presbyterians would decide in consultation with the pastor whether the guilty one's name should remain on the church roll.[29]

L.U. Fowler reiterated Leard's comments and provided more information on the rum-sellers in the Bedeque area:

The men drank plenty of what they called good rum, and it was told for a fact that years after, when the land was being cleared for the plow, a goodly number of empty bottles were found among the trees and stumps.... The account book of Mr. William Schurman of the Island of St. John ... for June 15, 1785 read 1 gallon rum 10 shillings... and for July 1, ½ pint of rum, 10 pence... Most of the customers bought rum. It was evidently considered a necessary article in those days.[30]

Bedeque had its share of drinking and sometimes it would seem almost more than its quota of taverns. **Thomas Hooper's** (son of Major, (1804-1879) licensed Inn at Centreville provided bed, board, and alcoholic refreshment for all travelers in the period from early in the eighteen-thirties until the eighteen-and-fifties. Trueman's Corner was a tavern site very early in Searletown history with Matthew Atkinson the Inn-keeper in 1848 when his farm was for sale. The very earliest licenses to sell liquor in Bedeque of which there are records were those issued in 1794 to Peter Maybey, Bedeque Tavern and Mary Brancomb, Bedeque Tavern.[31]

Thomas Hooper's licensed Inn provided free alcoholic beverage at election time with a bucket in front of the Inn and a sign to "Help yourself!" Ada MacLeod, Summerside historian, wrote: "It is customary, nowadays, to hold up hands of horror at the tales of the drinking at these old-time elections. But we must remember that, although reeling voters might make a lot of noise and engage in many personal combats, not one of them ever carried home in the pocket of his homespun trousers a one pound note as the price of his manhood's right. Free drinking was merely the accompaniment of an exciting political contest where all was square and above board. The noxious weed of bribery was a plant of entirely later growth.[32]

In the latter part of the first half of the nineteenth century, the excessive use of alcohol was a problem. Although none of the newspaper articles I obtained from Malcolm and Edith Bradshaw are dated, several are about the abuses of alcohol and will be quoted here:

SAVED BY HIS CHILDREN Rev. Theordore L. Cuyler tells the story of a physician who escaped ruin by the mimicking of his children. He began his professional life with the brightest prospects, and being thoroughly educated and skillful, soon won a large and fashionable practice. His danger was in the baneful custom of social wine drinking in fashionable gatherings and at aristocratic dinners. The young physician was witty and agreeable, a welcome guest everywhere. The rich petted him. At their tables he found the social glass. He drank. His appetite was aroused. It grew strong. Soon he could not control it. He neglected his business, sank lower, losing patrons and friends till he became a staggering drunkard. His wife and children wanted the necessaries of life. Close before him and them waited the pauper's inevitable fate.

One Sunday, when, half-sobered after a night of excess, he was likely to remain awhile at home, his wife went to church and left him with his two boys. While the children played about the room, he lay upon a lounge and sank into a torpid sleep. Presently their noise awoke and angered him, but on opening his eyes he saw what struck him dumb. His little six-year-old son was staggering across the floor and tumbling down in exact imitation of an intoxicated man. The other boy, older than he, laughed with delight at the performance. "That's just like papa: let's both play drunk!" he cried and then joined his brother in the sport. How the agony of conscience awoke in that father's breast! Had he lived to become such an infamous pattern to those innocent little ones? When next the wretched man left his house, it was not to go to the dram-shop nor to visit a patient. He had no patient. He went forth to suffer his own accusing, and think of his own sadly-needed cure. In misery he wandered through the fields. The sight he had seen exposed him to himself, smiting him with ceaseless rebukes. But it *saved* him, for it broke his heart and drove him to the divine Healer for help and grace. Alone with God he registered a vow that he would drink no more. He was still young, and recovery and returning prosperity rewarded the keeping of his solemn pledge.

LICENSED — TO DO WHAT?

Licensed - - - to make the strong man weak;
Licensed - - - to make the wise man low.
Licensed - - - a wife's fond heart to break and make her children's tears to flow.
Licensed - - - to do thy neighbor harm;
Licensed - - - to kindle hate and strife.

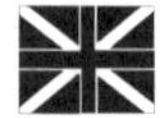

Licensed - - - to nerve the robber's arm;
Licensed - - - to whet the murderer's knife.
Licensed - - - thy neighbor's purse to drain and rob him of his very last;
Licensed - - - to heat his feverish brain till madness crown thy work at last.
Licensed - - - like spider for a fly, to spread thy nets for men, thy prey.
To mock his struggles - - - suck him dry, then cast the worthless hulk away.
Licensed - - - where peace and quiet dwell to bring disease and want and woe;
Licensed - - - to make this world a hell and fit man for a hell below."

WHERE IS MY WIFE?
I missed my wife. Where could she be? And strangers in her room.
I heard them say, "Poor thing, she's dead; she led a wretched life.
'Twas grief and want that broke her heart. Who'd be a drunkard's wife?"
I saw my children weeping 'round. I scarce could draw my breath.
They called and kissed her once warm lips forever cold in death,
Crying, "Father, dear, pray, wake her up! The neighbors say she's dead!
O, make her smile and speak once more and we'll never cry for bread!"
"She is not dead!" I frantically cried, and rushed to where she lay
And madly kissed her once warm lips forever cold as clay.
"Mary, speak one word to me! I'll never cause you pain.
I'll never grieve your loving heart or ever drink again!
O, Mary speak! It's Derlin's call" – "Why, so I do," she cried.
And then I woke - my Mary dear was kneeling by my side.
I pressed her to my throbbing heart while joyful tears did stream,
And ever since I've Heaven blessed for sending me that dream!"

THE BAR ROOM
A Bar to heaven, a Door to Hell - whoever named it, named it well!
A Bar to Manliness and Wealth. A door to want and broken health.
A Bar to honor, pride and fame. A Door to sorrow, sin, and shame.
A Bar to hope, a Bar to prayer. A Door to darkness and despair.
A Bar to honored, useful life, A Door to brawling, senseless strife.
A Bar to all that's true and brave, A Door to every drunkard's grave.
A Bar to joy that home imparts, A Door to tears and broken hearts.
A Bar to heaven, a Door to Hell - Whoever named it, named it well.

TICKETS TO SELL
There's a road all completed in perfect condition
Running straight with no turns from the earth to perdition.
There are trains starting out every hour in the day.
There is room for all souls that are going that way,

And the depots are scattered, broadcast over the land.
There are men everywhere who wait your command
With tickets to sell! Tickets to sell!
Tickets to ticket you right through to HELL.
There are first-class tickets, a glass of old wine!
And Bacchys smile up from the "nectar divine."
Drink it, young man! Drink it, it's a No.1 pass!
It will carry you through to perdition first-class.
You will enter the palace car - ah! But the end
Unto you and the street sot will be the same, friend.
Tickets! First, second, and third class to sell,"
Tickets to ticket you straight through to HELL.
Third and second - ale, whiskey, rum, brandy, and beer,
Cheap as dirt - come and buy! They are all for sale here.
Are you troubled with baggage? No matter, you know;
It will lessen and lighten the farther you go.
Is the road safe? Yes, friend, buy a ticket and you
Cannot fail of the station you're ticket to.
Tickets to sell!! Tickets to sell!!
They'll see you safe through to perdition and HELL.
Swift, swift from the highlands of peace, truth and light,
Down, down through the marshes of mildew and blight,
Through the tunnel of sorrow, of terror, and pain,
Through the lowlands of shame and o'er poverty plain;
Through crimes, grief and sin, to the valley of death
Doth the engine speed down with its hot scorching breath.
All aboard! Wait, show me your ticket! 'Tis well!
It will carry you through to destruction and HELL!

Many people in the second half of the nineteenth century were opposed to the sale and use of beverage alcohol, but the vote against its use was not strong enough to pass, as will be seen in Chapter Eight.

In the early days of Bedeque's settlement communication with the Old Country, especially, was slow and unreliable at best. Even communication with distant neighbours or relatives and friends elsewhere in the colony of Prince Edward Island was backward. Eventually, a system of mail delivery was more or less perfected by the early 1800s. In George A. Leard's, *Historic Bedeque,* we get a brief summary of the community's early postal history:

Bedeque's first post master was William Baker. For many years the only post office on the Island was at Charlottetown where Bedequers called two or three times a year for their mail or received it through the kindness of their neighbors. In 1827 a Western mail carrier was appointed to deliver the mail - once a week in summer and once a fortnight in the winter at four Prince County centres. The people were informed through the *Register* that all mail for Cascumpec, Tignish, and Malpeque would be left with Mr. Fowle, the schoolmaster at George Bearisto's, Princetown. Residents of St. Eleanors, Miscouche, and West Point were to get their mail at John Townshend's Inn, Traveller's Rest, while South Side Bedequers (Chelton) had to go to William Baker's, and Crapaud residents received their mail at James Bulpit's Union Inn. Tryon Inland post of two pence on letters and ha'pence on newspapers, seldom if ever paid in advance, kept the weekly Prince County mail to what a man on horseback could carry. The first Western mail carrier, Richard Bagnall, host at the Hazel Grove Inn, the famous half-way house on the Princetown Road, was to become well-known to the travelling public of Prince County when beginning around 1830 he ran the first stage coach for passengers and mail between Charlottetown and Princetown. The first postmaster at Bedeque, Capt. William Baker, no relation to the Loyalist blacksmith family of the same name, died Sept. 30, 1828, only a year after his appointment at the age of 82.[33]

George A. Leard also provided an interesting account of early education in Bedeque:

Though a school had been established in Bedeque previous to 1800, its history is difficult to trace. Schurman's store at Central Bedeque, and later at Wilmot Grove, generally sold "1 Bible and 1 schooling" together which may indicate the course of studies. Teachers, however, were often a problem: the majority of them being driven to the poorly-paid task by an inability to perform heavy manual labor, and for this reason, too, given to the consolation of drink. An advertsement in the *Royal Gazette* of Tuesday, August 4, 1835, would point to this: "WANTED for Bedeque district school a teacher of second or third (highest) class. None need offer who cannot produce testimonials of sobriety and good moral conduct. Apply to Joseph Pope, Esq., Bedeque."

The first Bedeque school was possibly somewhere on the Leonard Schurman property to which came scholars from as far as Lower Bedeque, Freetown, Centreville, and North Bedeque. The teacher secured at this time taught in the oldest of Bedeque schools. He was William Nelis, one-time master at Princetown, whose daughter Emily Rev. William Wilson baptized in 1837. At this time Mr. Wilson commenced signing his official title as "Wesleyan Minister": a significant trend in Bedeque's history when the Methodist pastors started dropping the title of Missionary. The Bedeque school at this period, so the first report of John McNeil,

district visitor of schools, informs us, was among the best on the Island, the pupils having "an extensive knowledge of the signification of words." Mr. Nelis left Bedeque in 1839 to take the No. 1 teaching position on the Island - mastership of the Normal School at Charlottetown, yet such was the pay of school teachers of that period (and the next hundred years was to see no very marked improvement) that in 1850 when age had overtaken him, the Legislature found it necessary to grant him eight pounds to carry him to his friends in the United States.

Schoolmasters in Bedeque in the eighteen hundred and thirties ... all taught the twelve month year for their board and twelve dollars a month. The teacher's contract at this time generally called for half the salary to be paid in potatoes at one shilling a bushel with the remainer in oats, wheat and barley at market prices, and pork, beef and mutton at three pence a pound, all to be delivered at some convenient wharf.

School kept from nine to twelve in the mornings and one to four in the afternoons with generally a two hour dinner period in the summer when the afternoon session was from two to five. Heat was provided by each scholar bringing a cord of wood. The master's room in the community was not a trailer, yet moved from time to time, and from house to house, and if the contract was carried out, was "comfortable with firewood furnished."

[The year] 1840 was Bedeque's big year for erection of schools. Upper Bedeque (probably present North Bedeque) had twenty-four pupils in a new school building which was "neat and comfortable." At Bedeque, a school, which opened early in this year and was situated near the marsh, south of the road and east of the bridge at Centreville, had twenty-three pupils with J. B. Newcome as master. Lower Bedeque's school where the enrollment was thirty, was three months younger again with Allan MacPhee as the first teacher. "Bedeque Road Lot 27" folk (undoubtedly Searletowners of a later day) dated their school history from 1840 with a neat house, newly erected, and a teacher whose name Charles R. Stuart echoed royalty.[34]

Next to education, and many would undoubtedly agree before education, was the value of the church in the community. Leard in his *Historic Bedeque* (p. 38) recorded the names of the Bedeque subscribers of the Methodist circuit about 1832 : "... Joseph Pope, member of the House of Assembly; John R. Gardiner [husband of Mary Hooper, the first child of Major and Ann (Paterson) Hooper], merchant and tavern owner; Rev. John Snowball, missionary; and Stephen Wright, Centreville, carding-mill owner, as contributing a pound or more each. Fifteen Wrights appear on the list including two Nathaniels, two Stephens, two Williams, and three Anns. Oth-

ers include Joseph Black, Henry Boulter, Avery Baker, John Bowey, Eliza College, William Condell, Richard Cole, Elizabeth Clark, William Clark, James Clark, John Campbell, William Downing, William Glasby, Nathaniel Huestis, **Elisha Hooper, Margaret Hooper, Catheine Hooper**, John Hall, Newton Lea, Thomas Moyse, John Mallet, William Maxfield, Timothy Maxfield, Donald McFarlane, Malcolm McFarlane, Alexander Murray, Eliza Pope, George Price, James Price, Mary Price, Richard Price, Jesse Strang, Stephen Strang and John Soby."

As the congregation [at the Bedeque Methodist Church] increased, it was essential that a larger church be built. This was done in 1848 on the site occupied by the present edifice, the land being given by Thomas Wright [Haslam states that "the new chapel was built on land owned by Thomas Hoooper."[35] Hooper had died in 1816. This location was about a hundred yards from the Wright barn where the first Methodist services were held. The old church [which was located in the present cemetery and built in 1818] was moved to the village and used as a school. George A. Leard described the new Bedeque Methodist Church's appearance:

> The new chapel at Bedeque, built in New England style, faced the road. The fourteen foot square porch which centered the south of the church had a double door entrance on the east side. Stairs opposite the door led to the gallery. The steeple, topped with a weather vane and looking out over many miles of countryside from its seventy-four foot height, made a much observed landmark for many years. Inside, single and double pews on the main floor, with single seats in the gallery which extend on both sides and the south end of the church, gave a seating capacity of five hundred people. Tallow candles on brackets curved like the letter S with little pitty-pan holders on their forward tips, lit the evening meetings in the winter time. These lights were economically spaced, one on each post supporting the gallery. The lamps, which came later burned a heavier oil than kerosene. Three wood stoves, rectangular in shape, about three by two feet, familiarly known as Scott Stoves, were strategically situated, one at the front just outside the communion rail, and one each, in the back corners of the church. Iron brackets attached to the gallery supported long black arms of stove pipe which stretched warmly from the far corners to meet in a drum on the pipe which ran straight up to the flue from the front stove.

The high pulpit on six foot posts was attached to the wall with a winding stair leading up to it. A door guarded the entrance to the desk where the Word of God, always the focal point of the Methodist meeting house, lay in waiting to be shared with all who would hear. The Communion set was kept in a little built-in closet under the pulpit stairs. A large church clock hung in front of the gallery at the back of the church directly opposite the pulpit. It was the gift of the Speaker of the House, Hon. Joseph Pope, who the previous year, while on a visit to Liverpool, acquired the first clock for the Methodist Church and a third wife for himself.

The day after the opening of the church a "grand bazaar" was held in the old chapel at Lower Bedeque under the auspices of certain women of the congregation, undoubtedly the forerunner of the Ladies Aid. Contributions, according to an advertisement in the *Gazette* were to be left with the missionary's wife, Mrs. Strong, Mrs. Stephen Wright, and the **Misses Hooper.** A great variety of fancy and useful articles were sold and the proceeds, lumped with Sunday's opening day collections amounted to forty pounds which, said Mr. Strong, thinking doubtless of potato disease and other distressful conditions, "must be considered very liberal in the unprecedented pressure of the times." The church costing over eight hundred pounds, was financed by the bazaar, two previous "tea-meetings" and the sale of sixty-six pews which brought nearly seven hundred and fifty pounds.[36]

Jean MacFadyen's history, *For the Sake of the Record*, provides concise historical summaries of many Island churches, such as the Bedeque Methodist Church (now United Church) built in 1848:

The new meeting house was large, 50 feet by 38 feet with a high pulpit and a winding stair leading up to it; galleries extended along two sides and across one end which was used by the choir. Rev. John B. Strong, pastor of the circuit, reported that on July 15 a "new and elegant chapel" in Bedeque had been dedicated "to the worship of the Triune God." For this dedication people came from almost every direction, even some in boats from Cape Tormentine to Cape Traverse to throng the church at every service.[37]

Island historian, George A. Leard, had an almost encyclopedic knowledge of the customs and traditions of Methodism in the Bedeque circuit of the nineteenth century:

Though none of the churches planned for the circuit was completed in his pastorate, Mr. Wilson [whose pastorate was from 1834-1837] was pleased to represent the Bedeque circuit at the opening services in Charlottetown of the new Methodist chapel which replaced the first one. His text for that Sunday afternoon

of July 9th, 1835, was "Holiness becometh Thy house, O Lord, forever." The circuit of which he was superintendent had a larger membership than Charlottetown at this time. The phenomenal growth in the Prince County societies from sixty-eight in 1828 to three hundred and five in 1832 could not be expected to keep up; indeed revival growth was always followed by revival recession; and the membership for several years continued to decline as the fickly and the factious found the Wesleyan way too hard to travel. A membership of two hundred and seventy in 1833 was reduced by 1835 to two hundred and six stalwarts which compared to Charlottetown's one hundred and eighty-seven for the latter year.

The donation in 1835 to the Methodist mission of eight acres of land at Searletown, where later the Searletown church and parsonage were to be established, received prominent mention in the missionary report of that year.... In 1835 Sunday School work had yet to become popular in Bedeque.... Mr. Wilson was happy, however, in the forming of a small society six miles west of Bedeque in what is probably present-day Fernwood.[38]

... Most typical of Methodist meetings around New Year's was the Watch Night Service on New Year's Eve when at midnight, the Methodists, following a custom inaugurated by John Wesley who greatly deprecated the greeting of the new year with revelry and drunkness, met for prayer and praise and rededication of their lives for the coming year. Hymns suitable to the occasion were sung, such as the one beginning:

Join, all ye ransom'd sons of grace,
The holy joy prolong,
And shout to the Redeemer's praise
A solemn midnight song.
Blessings and thanks and love and might
Be to our Jesus given,
Who turns our darkness into light,
Who turns our hell to heaven.

The hymn book used in Centreville Chapel and all Methodist churches in the Maritimes was still Wesley's "Collection of Hymns for the use of the People called Methodists" in very much the same form as in 1779 when John Wesley had published it. In its popular edition Wesley's Hymn Book with John Wesley's picture as frontispiece was quite small and thick (2" wide, 3 ½ inches long and 1 ½ inches thick) having only a little over one hymn to the page - seven hundred and sixty-nine hymns on six hundred and eighty-eight pages. This book which served as both a liturgy and confession of faith in the young church commenced with a hymn which has ever since been first in every Methodist hymn book, the stirring, soul-rousing words of Charles Wesley's:

O for a thousand tongues to sing
My great Redeemer's praise.

The glories of my God and King,
The triumphs of His grace.

The Methodists of early Bedeque knew their hymn books almost as well as their Bibles; their everyday speech, letters, death-bed testimonies and epitaphs showed it. Rev. John Prince, who returned to Bedeque as an old man for a farewell visit, as remembered by Thomas Moyse, stood in the high pulpit of the second chapel, and, to a depleted circle of familiar faces, quoted lines of comfort and assurance whose context made them richer still:

Part of His host have crossed the flood
And part are crossing now.

from the lovely hymn, "Come, Let Us Join Our Friends Above."

At conference and district Meeting, a hymn from the old Collection, which was often sung, commenced:

And are we yet alive
And see each other's face?
Glory and praise to Jesus give
For His redeeming grace!

Boasting no literary merit, but filled with that joy and liveliness which characterized so many of Charles Wesley's hymns, it had its special place; and in England, where customs cling longer, it continues to be the opening hymn for General Conference. The hymns of Wesley's book were mainly Wesley hymns, written by Rev. Charles Wesley and his brother John with a small sprinkling of the inspired verse of Watts, Addison, Cowper, Ken, and others....

An old Methodist funeral custom observed for many years in some parts of the Island was the singing of a hymn at the open grave before the reading of the committal service. Hymns such as "O God, Our Help in Ages Past" or "Again We Lift Our Voice and Shout Our Solemn Joys" were deeply moving to hear; and for those who could forget their sorrow in the joyous belief of a loved one safely Home, they were songs of triumph with a deep undernote of comfort helping to heal the broken pattern of life.[39]

Death's harvest, the surest of all, continued to fill the granaries of eternity and the graveyards of Bedeque. The father of the Middleton Wrights was gone in his seventy-fifth year. His neighbor to the north, Ronald Macdonald, died the previous month, aged 78. **Thomas Hooper, Jr.** died February 14, 1837, aged 65. His older brother, **Major**, aged 74, went a year later leaving vacancies in the Kirk session and His Majesty's Commission of the Peace.

Death was no fearsome thing for the aged pioneer facing it with dignified expectancy or even faint welcome; only when it struck at youth in the seeming callousness of accident or epidemic did terror and horror fill the minds of those who were left. Nothing in Bedeque of the nineteenth century seemed so utterly wanton in its destruction as "black diphtheria" which took its dread toll most among the children. Many examples might be given, but none more typical than in 1843 in the home of Nathaniel Huestis of South West Bedeque where five children, Elizabeth, Jesse, Martha, Stephen, and William died from diphtheria in three weeks. Gifted with the best voice among Bedeque Methodists, Nathaniel Huestis made his living as a farmer, kept singing-school as a hobby and was choir master for the sheer joy of it. But how could he sing the joyful hymns of Methodism in those dark days of March while just outside the church door five red clay mounds made contrast with the last snow of winter? Yet he had faith to go on, sharing with his wife, Betsy, eldest daughter of Nathaniel Wright of Centreville, the conviction that though God's hand might not always be apparent in the epidemics of mankind, it was His will for them that they should not leave His gifts unused, and trusting some day to know more fully, he returned to his place in the gallery of the Lower Bedeque Church and gave the beat for the singing of the hymns from Wesley's Book, probably such a song as Number 224:

I'll praise my Maker while I've breath;
And when my voice is lost in death
Praise shall employ my nobler powers:
My days of praise shall ne'er be past
While life and thought and being last
Or immortality endures.[40]

Revivals were important from the social viewpoint. Meeting every night for several weeks, under the stimulating influence of the mission services, people came to know each other better and in the sharing of the great experiences of conversion, justification, and regeneration and eventually membership in the body of Christ, they could not help but have their whole viewpoint of life enlarged and broadened. Revivals, so the old people said, brought marriages in their train. Perhaps the greater opportunities for meeting frequently helped to speed acquaintanceship. Certainly the emotional experience of revivals, where self-consciousness was often forgotten, developed self-assurance in the meek and shy.[41]

Bedeque had two great revivals, the first in the 1820s and the second about 1844. In the spring of 1828 a woman preacher by the name of Martha Jago arrived in Bedeque from Jacobstowe, Cornwall, England. She had come to a Bedeque home to serve as a serv-

ant girl. According to George A. Leard, "She was a member of the Bible Christian church, a branch of the Methodists, so-called from the fact that early in his ministry John Wesley with others had 're-solved to be Bible Christians and preach plain old Bible Christian-ity.'"

George A. Leard's *Historic Bedeque* gave a good account of this servant girl's influence on Bedeque Methodists in the third decade of the nineteenth century:

> The church, much in advance of the times, encouraged the women to preach, and Martha Jago was one of their preachers. No record is preserved of sermons delivered in Bedeque, but she was doubtless heard from the Methodist pulpit. The Charlottetown *Register* of February 24, 1829 tells how this twenty-five year old maid in napt cloak and bonnet came to Charlottetown and preached to crowded congregations in the market house and the Wesleyan Chapel. At a time when men wrote wrathful letters to the newspapers protesting the sacrilege of allowing a woman to ursurp male prerogatives, she could stand demurely in a Charlottetown pulpit and without any embarrassment give out a hymn beginning
>
> Shall I for fear of feeble man
> The Spirit's course in me restrain?
> Or undismay'd in deed or word
> Be a true witness to my Lord?
>
> Martha Jago retired from preaching in 1830 to devote her talents to homemaking in King's County. In Bedeque those who liked female preaching could attend services held by one of their own settlers lately arrived from England. Both John Adams and his wife, who lived in South West Bedeque, had been Bible Christian preachers before coming to the Island. They welcomed the arrival of Francis Metherell, the first ordained Bible Christian minister to come to Canada, who commenced a life-long mission on Prince Edward Island in 1832. Mr. Metherell preached at South West occasionally and encouraged Mr. and Mrs. Adams to conduct preaching services in their own little community. The results were gratifying. A revival of considerable scope took place at which many were converted. However, with a Methodist Church so near, both geographically and doctrinally, the Adams and their converts were advised to unite with the Methodists rather than form a new society.[42]

Bedeque's growth and development in the first half of the nineteenth century was impressive, and it was undoubtedly one of the most progressive rural communities on the Island at that time. George A. Leard's *Historic Bedeque*, describing the growth of the militia and agriculture, bore witness to Bedeque's progress:

As the older settlements of Bedeque and Tryon became crowded under the pressure of large families, the population slowly spread into the inland districts. South West (later called Middleton) had tossed off its woody cloak to the axes of the Wrights, Kinleys, Craigs, and others, displaying fields as fertile as the shore farms of Bedeque Bay. Searletown, too, was opening up quickly with the children of Nathaniel Wright at Centreville forming an important part of its population as compared to South West where the Wrights were of the Stephen and Frances Wright family.[43]

... Another newspaper advertisement of this period told of Jesse Wright wanting a miller who understood milling oats and wheat. Liberal wages were promised in return "for soberness and industry." The appointment of sub-collectors of Customs and Excise at various points on the Island was provided for in a bill passed in 1837, and it is thought that the Customs House, which was on Hurd's Wharf up till 1856 or later, was built around this time.[44]

... In Bedeque of long ago, two duties devolved on every able-bodied man from sixteen to sixty: to work on the roads and train in the militia. The three days road work required each year was seldom begrudged, but orders to turn out for militia parades, whether for training or the Queen's Birthday, were often complied with very reluctantly. Militia training on the Island dates back to the formation of Philips Callbeck's Company for the protection of the colony in 1780, but it is doubtful if Bedeque had much share in it till 1793, when, the mother country at war with France, H. M. Island of St. John Corps of Volunteers was formed with David Murray of North Bedeque and John Robins (Mary Hooper's husband) of Lower Bedeque among the Prince County Regiment officers. Later, during the period 1809 – 1814, when for a time the war with the Americans stimulated militia training, Capt. David Murray and Ensign Peter Schurman were active in military affairs. In 1825 Squire John Wright (whose first wife was Elizabeth Robins) and Isaac Schurman received commissions in the 2nd battalion of Militia....

The most ambitious organization of Militia came in 1833 when twelve Regiments of militia were established on the Island with the Second Prince County Regiment, made up of men from townships 26, 27, and 28, having headquarters at Tryon, where the landlord Frederick B. Holland was major commanding. Though the majority of officers at this time were from Lot 28, Bedeque was fairly well

represented by Captain Joseph Pope, Captain John Wright, John Black, Lieutenant John Lee and Ensign James Cole and Alexander Anderson. The surgeon of this Regiment was Dr. White with Bedeque's Dr. Graham listed as surgeon of the 3rd Prince County Regiment which had headquarters at St. Eleanor's.

The Bedequers of Lot 25 mustered with the 1st Prince County Regiment which, commanded by Major Thomas MacNutt, had headquarters at Princetowon and surprisingly enough had no commissioned officers from North Bedeque. Headquarters for the 2nd Prince County Regiment moved to Bedeque in 1837 when on the death of Major Holland, Captain Pope received his majority and succeeded to the command.... On Friday, 14th August, 1840, the 2nd Prince County Regiment was called to Captain James Clark's place at Bedeque for inspection parade which in the interval between haying and harvest marked the climax of the year's training, after which the drudgery of drills was over for another year.

Another drudgery, threshing by hand, was on the way out at this time. In July, 1841, thirteen years after the first threshing machine came to the Island, James Narraway, farm machinery agent, came to Bedeque, and erecting a threshing machine at Nathaniel Wright's, informed the people of the Island through the press that he was ready to take orders for same. From Bible times, threshing had been done on the barn floor; the doors open for the wind to blow out the chaff while the threshers rhythmically beat a tattoo on the floor with their flails.

One of the Loyalists, Stephen Wright the elder, of North Bedeque, a mighty thresher in his day, did not live to see the successor to the flail. Speaking rather boastfully of his health in his barn on January 19, 1841, and saying that he intended to thresh all the grain there himself, Stephen Wright suddently dropped to the floor dead. The father of the Middleton Wrights was gone in his seventy-fifth year. His neighbor to the north, Ronald Macdonald, died the previous month, aged 78. Death's harvest, the surest of all, continued to fill the granaries of eternity and the graveyards of Bedeque. **Thomas Hooper** died Feb. 14, 1837, aged 65. His older brother, **Major,** aged 74 [1764-1838 – incorrectly written aged 82] went a year later leaving vacancies in the Kirk session and His Majesty's Commission of the Peace.

Leard went on to remark on the interesting custom of the early Bedeque Loyalists in passing on Christian names to their offspring. A prime example was the descendants of Major Thomas Hooper: "... who carry or have carried the name Major: Major Lowther, Major Townshend, Major Linkletter, Major MacIntosh, Major Huestis, Major Wright, Major Strong, and many others in the last hundred and fifty years have revealed their Hooper descent in their first names.[45]

To the list could also be added Major Hooper Clark, Major Gardiner Hooper, Major Craig, Major Wright Huestis and many others, including Alden's grandfather, **Major Hooper**. The name also spread outside the family and in the neighborhood as in Major Schurman and Major Linkletter.

Although progressive in many ways, the community of Bedeque by 1850 was still deficient in a number of amenities necessary to guarantee continued growth and prosperity; two of these were money and medicine. "Money was an ever present problem in this Island colony in the early days when everything from leather notes of exchange to silver dollars with holes punched in them were used to stabilize the currency," wrote George A. Leard in his book *Historic Bedeque*:

> Rev. William Smith who came in 1833 for his second short pastorate at Bedeque, claimed he could not pay for his book order in 1834 because of the inability to exchange P.E.I. currency in Nova Scotia except at a discount of ten per cent. Not willing to lose this, he left the bill unpaid and was forthwith charged ten percent as an overdue account so it was little wonder that he loudly declared himself a victim of circumstances.
>
> For many years afterwards the lack of money continued to be a very grave handicap as shown by an 1846 minute in the District (or Conference) Book: "In some cases where money is a thing unknown or unseen, produce has to be taken to the great inconvenience of the preachers, some of whom now have wheat, deal and maple sugar on hand for which they have given credit on their circuit accounts and in this proportion they are unable to meet their just debts.[46]

According to Doris Haslam in *The Wrights of Bedeque*, there also was very little medicine in the first half of the nineteen century, aside from alcohol, which was sometimes used medicinally. However, perhaps in the 1820s, some Balm of Gilead saplings were planted by John Wright near the log cabin built by him in Middleton. Salve made from the buds of Balm of Gilead was one of the old-time remedies used in the John Wright family for generations. Another pioneer remedy was pine salve. A notch was cut on the side of one of the pine trees on the property. The sun would draw out the balsam which was scraped off into a container, boiled to a certain thickness

and held in readiness. When an accident occurred the salve was spread on a rag and bound around the wound which would start to heal immediately. Pine balsam was used to check blood poisoning and was especially effective for punctures and cuts.[47]

The Bedeque people were proud of their farms, adorning their homes with fanciful names, not unlike their British counterparts in the Old Country. By the 1830s this custom was used widely, with the following properties (with the owners) falling into that category:

"Thorndale Cottage," Chelton	Benjamin Cole Wright
"Castalia Grove," Centreville	Jesse Wright (and **Sally Hooper**)
"Elmvale," Centreville	Stephen Wright (and **Martha Hooper)**
"Fairhaven Farms" Lower Bedeque	**Alexander Hooper,** Horace Wright, Horace Melville Wright
"Avondale Cottage" Central Bedeque	Mrs. Joseph Schurman's home
"Sunset View Farm,"	Earle Pearson (Ed Pearson's father)
"Riverview" (adjoined "Elmvale")	Charles Stephen Wright, son of Stephen Wright by his second wife, Millicent
"Noonan Cottage," Centreville	Nathaniel Wright and Nancy Lord
"Mill Grove Farm," Southwest Bedeque	John Wright (Crabbed John) and Jane Schurman Wright
"Birch Grove," Searletown	John Wright and **Elizabeth Robins**
"Newark Cottage," Centreville	Nathaniel Wright, Frederick Strong and Martha Wright (Millicent's daughter)
"Maplethorpe," Centreville	**Major Wright**

"The Willows," Searletown	Christopher and **Adella Lowther, Major** and Addie **Lowther, Gladys** and Neil **Bradshaw**
"Brownstone Hermitage"	Lemuel Vickerson and **Harriet Ethel-Linda,** daughter of Jesse and Sally Hooper Wright
"Centreville House"	formerly **Thomas Hooper's Tavern**, home of Lorenzo and Mary Wright, brother of Jesse Wright
"Gordon Grove"	John Gardiner and **Mary Hooper** (2nd wife)
"Fair View"	Christiana and Nathaniel Wrght, Bedeque
"Holland Grove"	A.E.C. Holland
"Riverside Residence"	John Alexander MacLeod Wright and Margaret Leard
"Potato Grove"	John Gardiner and Eunice, his wife

It would seem that the late 1840s were difficult times for Islanders as there was a potato blight for which no one knew the cause or the cure. Many thought that it would disappear, but it did not go quickly. George A. Leard wrote: "[The year] 1848 was known as the "year of distress" on Prince Edward Island because there was almost total failure of the potato crop and partial failure of other harvests. Little flour was ground in the Island mills in 1848, and most of the bread baked in Bedeque ovens that year was made of flour hauled from the Bedeque wharf and paid for in cold, scarce cash."[48]

The half-century, from 1800-1850, witnessed much change on the Island. No where was this more evident than in the settlement of Bedeque. The early pioneers, many of whom were Loyalists who arrived in the 1780s, had gone on to their heavenly reward, leaving their children and grandchildren with established farms, businesses, and social institutions intact. During this interval the foundation was laid for a promising future.

Notes

1 Ada MacLeod, *Roads to Sumerside, The Story of Early Summerside and the Surrounding Area.* Edited by Marjorie McCallum Gay, 1980 (Schurman Publishing, 1980), p. 47

2 George A. Leard, *Historic Bedeque. The Loyalists at Work and Worship in Prince Edward Island.* (Bedeque, P.E.I.: Bedeque United Church, 1948, amended 1973), pp. 12-13

3 L. U. Fowler, *"Bedeque and Its People,"* Chapter 5, compliments of Muriel Hooper Blanchard

4 George A. Leard, George, op. cit., pp. 16-17

5 Ibid., pp. 20-21

6 Ibid., pp. 7- 21

7 Ross Graves, *William Schurman, Loyalist of Bedeque, Prince Edward Island, and His Descendants* (Summerside, P.E.I.: Harold B. Schurman, 1973), pp. 34-35

8 L.U. Fowler, op. cit.

9 Ada MacLeod, op. cit., pp. 117-120

10 George A. Leard, op. cit., p. 21

11 Jean MacFadyen, *For the Sake of the Record* (Summerside, P.E.I.: Williams and Crue, Ltd, n.d.), p. 21

12 George A. Leard, op. cit., pp. 13 and 15

13 Ibid., p. 17

14 Ibid., pp. 18-20

15 Ibid., pp. 24-27

16 Ibid., p. 39

17 Ibid., pp. 29-30

18 Ibid., pp, 27-28

19 Ibid., pp. 31-32

20 *The Prince Edward Island Magazine*, July 1900; and L.U. Fowler, op. cit.
21 Ibid., pp. 28-29
22 Ibid., p. 62
23 Ibid., p. 26
24 Ibid., p. 44
25 George A. Leard, op. cit., pp. 22-24
26 Ibid., pp. 22-23
27 Ross Graves, op. cit., pp. 31-32
28 George A. Leard, op. cit., p. 24
29 Ibid., p. 34
30 L.U. Fowler, op. cit.
31 Ibid.
32 Ross Graves, op. cit., p. 32
33 George A. Leard, op. cit., p. 32
34 Ibid., pp. 42-43
35 Doris Haslam, op. cit., p. 39
36 Geoerge A. Leard, op. cit., pp. 52-53
37 Jean MacFadyen, op. cit., p. 22
38 George A. Leard, op. cit., p. 41
39 Ibid., pp. 89-90
40 Ibid., p. 47
41 Ibid., pp. 36-37
42 Ibid., pp. 36-37
43 Ibid., p. 40
44 Ibid., p. 43
45 Ibid., pp. 27, 46-47
46 Ibid, p. 39
47 Doris Haslam, op. cit., pp. 352-353
48. George A. Leard, op. cit., p. 51

CHAPTER 7

Generations Five and Six: Some Background on the Grandchildren and Great-Grandchildren of Thomas Hooper and His Wife

The asterisks (*) show sons and daughters from whom Alden Hooper Neal is directly descended. The numeral in front of the ancestor's name stands for the birth order of the child in that particular family.

*1.0 **Major Hooper** (4, Thomas 3, Clement 2, Stephen 1) and Ann Patterson (daughter of Walter Patterson, the first Governor of Prince Edward Island when it was made a separate colony in 1769, and his mistress, Margaret Hyde) were married on November 16, 1794. Major was 30 and Ann was 20. "Young Major evidently made good use of his time while in the capital [Charlottetown, where he went with his father in 1785 to see the Governor] for not only did he secure his acres from the governor, but the heart of the governor's daughter in the bargain; and not very long after, we find Ann Patterson coming through the forest aisles on her bridal tour, mounted on the same horse behind her husband, to her cosy new log home in Bedeque."[1] Major and Ann had two children (fifth generation, surname Hooper):

1.1 Eliza Hooper (5, Major 4, Thomas 3, Clement 2, Stephen 1), was born about 1795 in Bedeque; she died on October 10, 1825 at Miramachi, New Brunswick. Her obituary appeared in *The P.E.I. Register* in October 1825, the year of the great Miramichi Fire in New Brunswick.

George A. Leard wrote: "[The year] 1825 was remembered longest in Bedeque as the year of the Miramichi fire." In his wonderful book, *Historic Bedeque*, he gave an account of the terrible natural disaster which befell the pioneer settlers along the banks of this northern New Brunswick river:

...Everything for many years dated from that terrible catastrophe which not only filled the Bedeque atmosphere with cinders and smoke, but brought the sorrow of bereavement to several Bedeque homes. The Miramichi, no distant unknown place, was Bedeque's best market for potatoes and oats supplied to the big lumbering centre by the schooner trade each spring and fall. [Northeastern New Brunswick was a lumbering center that was made prosperous because of the timber trade.] John Wright of Middleton, eldest son of Stephen Wright and Frances Lord, was at the Miramichi with oats and early potatoes in the first week of October, 1825, when the unseasonably hot, dry weather made ideal conditions for the great fury of fire which, accompanied by a high wind, swept down on Newcastle on the evening of the 7th. Of two hundred and sixty stores and houses only twelve remained. One hundred and sixty people were burned to death.

Several Bedequers in Newcastle were rescued by John Wright and his crew. [John and his brother William owned between them a small vessel, the *Lovely,* a 14-ton square stern schooner with one deck and two masts. It was used by the brothers for trade between Bedeque and Miramichi, a lumber region in northeastern New Brunswick. As the reader can tell, John played a large part in the rescue of many people in the catastrophic fire.] George Price, who with his wife and children, were found next morning in the river, where they had spent the night almost totally immersed to avoid the searing gasses and heat, were given passage back to their native Bedeque. They had lost everything and Mrs. Price died soon afterwards from the effects of the fire. **Eliza Hooper**, eldest daughter of Major Hooper of Centreville, who was visiting in Newcastle, guest of her grandfather, Rev. John Urquhart, the first Presbyterian minister of PEI [he was her step-grandfather], was so unfortunate as to be ill with scarlet fever during the fire, from whose flames she escaped only to die from the effects of being moved."[2]

A very interesting story was preserved by a relative regarding John Wright's "observations" following the fire. The reader should not confuse this John Wright, called, "Crabbed John," who married Jane Schurman and was the son of Stephen and Frances Lord Wright, with John Wright, the husband of Elizabeth Robins. Actually there were several John Wrights and sometimes to distinguish him from others he used "T" as a middle initial. George A. Leard retold the interesting story from the great Miramichi fire:

John Wright's own account, heard many years later from the lips of an imaginative grandson, described how he saw the ball of fire strike down judgment upon the wicked town, and how he was kept busy for hours ferrying people to the other side of the river. When the ashes were partly cooled, he was able to search for a shoemaker friend whom he had not seen during the rescue. Going to the lot where the shoemaker's cottage had stood, he saw only smouldering ruins and a chimney, like many others, pointing a finger heavenwards. As he approached through the smoky haze, his old friend the shoemaker became visible sitting on the hearth stone in the blackened ruins, indicating by signs that his Bedeque friend should tip up the hearthstone, after which he faded away in the smoke.

John Wright unearthed a pot of gold coins and soon found evidence that the shoemaker had been burned to death. Was he entitled to the money? Deep down in his Methodist conscience, he knew that regardless of the vision, the money was not his, but belonged to the shoemaker's only heir, a daughter whose whereabouts was unknown, having married against her father's wishes and moved away many years previously. Counting himself a ghost-appointed executor, Wright advertised for the missing heir to the estate, but the lst daughter was never heard from. The coins, kept in a treasured bowl on a Bedeque sideboard for many years, eventually were divided to the daughters of Mill Grove Farm [John Wright's property] as part of their doweries.[3]

Doris Haslam recorded in greater detail what happened to the coins, and their whereabouts today (1978), in her book, *The Wrights of Bedeque*:

At least three of these gold guineas are still in possession of Island descendants. One, owned by a North Bedeque granddaughter of John's daughter Sarah Ann, is dated 1785; a second, given to John's daughter Jane, is prized in the Springfield home of her great-granddaughter and is dated 1775; a third, dated 1795, is owned by John's great-grandson on the home place in Middleton - who remembers yet

that inquisitive little boys were not allowed to play with the bowl of shiny coins kept on Grandfather Jesse's dresser. By then the number of coins in the bowl had been greatly reduced. They were used mainly for charitable purposes, a good many going to help build the little MacDonaldite church in Searletown on a lot deeded to the MacDonaldites by John's son-in-law Alf."[4]

John and Jane had settled in Middleton - then called South West Bedeque, or, more commonly, Sou'West - where he started a sawmill on the brook that flowed through his property. It was a new settlement at the time, with prime standing timber, hardly touched. They lived on the farm, on a portion of which, in the 1970s, the family of Eldon Wright and Joan Craig lived [Joan still lives on Mill Grove in 2004]. John and Jane called their farm "Mill Grove Farm." They lived first in a log house (the depression from which showed the site that was visible until about the 1960s). Later they built a frame house. Down the hill and south of the road was John's sawmill of the up-and-down variety. For a time John, and later his son, Jesse, operated a shingle mill in connection with the saw mill. Lumber was sawed in the mill until 1955. John was a Justice of the Peace for many years. One of his last acts in this capacity was to perform the marriage ceremony for his niece Lizzie, Job's daughter.

1.2 Martha Hooper, the second child of Major and Ann, was born in 1797 in Lower Bedeque. On December 31, 1824 she married Stephen Wright, born in 1801, the son of Nathaniel Wright and Ann NANCY Lord. The marriage license was issued December 31, 1824 to Phillips M. Callbeck, Justice of the Peace. The *P.E.I. Register* for February 5, 1825, carried the following: "Married at Bedeque, Mr. Stephen Wright and Miss Martha Hooper, 2nd daughter of Major Hooper, Esq." [5] [The designation of Esquire is an esteemed one and came after Major was appointed Justice of the Peace and acted as a magistrate in Bedeque. To be allowed to use the prized abbreviation Esq. was indeed an honor.]

Stephen was a farmer at Bedeque and operated a carding mill and saw and shingle mills. Doris Haslam provided a complete account of his life in her book, *The Wrights of Bedeque*:

He and Martha settled on his father's carding mill property. After his father's death in 1825 Stephen shared with his mother the profits of the mill and assumed full ownership of the mill and machinery when she passed away in 1839.

Nathaniel's will reads: "I give and bequeath to my dear son Stephen all the land possessed by me on the East of the Mill stream above the mill, which land is now considered a part of the farm on which I now live, provided nevertheless that he purchase or rent for my dear son Thomas an equal quantity of woodland on the Tryon Road ... or an equal quantity of woodland in the nearest possible situation to the farm on which I now live; and provided, also, that my dear son Stephen shall allow a space of three hundred feet to the south of the corn mill, for the convenience of both mills and a "road to the property hereby bequeathed to my dear son Jesse." Stephen also inherited his father's eight-day clock.

In the 1841 census Stephen was listed as a merchant, and held 430 acres in fee simple. *Lake's* map, 1863, shows he was operating the carding mill, also a saw and a shingle mill. He was appointed Justice of the Peace in an age when local disputes were usually settled by such officials, and for some years he served as High Sheriff for Prince County. He bought and sold a good deal of land. At one time he owned well over a thousand acres in Lot 8 - purchased in tracts of varying size at sheriffs' sales - and he acquired various mill sites in Lot 19 as well. According to an elderly gentleman, Edward Strong of Summerside, who was interviewed years ago, "The Bedeque Wrights (that is, the Centreville branch) always thought themselves a cut above others." They were sometimes called "those proud Bedeque Wrights," and Aunt Mollie Schurman claimed they referred to their own double-first cousins as "the queer Middleton Wrights." Why queer? Perhaps because the Middleton Wrights had married into the Schurmans and their children tended to be Baptists or MacDonaldites, rather than Methodists. When the daughter of one of the Bedeque Wrights (Nathaniel, Jr.'s daughter Jane) wanted to marry a MacFadyen, a Macdonaldite, her father is reported to have said he would rather follow her to her grave than see her marry a man of such a sect....

Stephen's death notice appeared in the *Pioneer* for May 2, 1883: "Stephen Wright, Esq., died at his home, Elm Vale, Bedeque, after a lingering illness. Until age began to steal over him, he was the leading man of the neighbourhood and in his church. His funeral took place yesterday afternoon and was one of the largest ever seen in that neighbourhood. The casket in which his remains were interred was got up by Doull Bros. of this place. It was made of black walnut trimmed with silver, altogether the handsomest ever got up in Summerside."[6]

Stephen's death date was actually April 27, 1883. [One account says in Miramichi, N. B.] Another news clipping reads, "At Middleton, Lot 27, of inflammation of the lungs, in 83rd year, Stephen Wright, an

from *The Wrights of Bedeque*, p. 32

"Elm Vale," home of Stephen W. and Martha (Hooper) Wright, Centreville Bedeque, P.E.I.

old and respected inhabitant of this locality." The writer believes that this notice is about Sally's husband as the dates 1801 - 1883 [in 83rd year] coincide; he was old and respected, and both Middleton and Bedeque were in Lot 27.

Martha had died of tuberculosis in 1838 in Miramichi, N.B., although they resided in Bedeque. Martha's gravestone says that she died on June 10, 1838, aged 43, but *The P.E.I. Royal Gazette* for Tuesday, July 3, 1838, printed: "At Bedeque, on Monday the 25th ult., aged 41, Martha, wife of Mr. Stephen Wright, Jr. of Bedeque, and daughter of the late Major Hooper, Esq. Her end was peace." Martha and Stephen had one daughter and three sons (sixth generation, surname Wright):

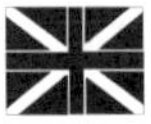

1.21 Major Wright I (6, Martha 5, Major 4, Thomas 3, Clement 2, Stephen 1) born on November 18, 1825; died on February 10, 1829 in Centreville Bedeque.

1.22 Charles Nathaniel Wright (6, Martha 5, Major 4, Thomas 3, Clement 2, Stephen 1) born c.1828 in Centreville Bedeque; died in 1850 in California, aged 22 [in another account he was born c.1829, died at age 20 years].

Early in 1849 he caught the California gold fever and by the payment of £100 became a member of the California Association, a group of forty Islanders bound for California via Cape Horn on the brig *Fanny*. In the list of shareholders, he is called a miller. [The other Bedequers appearing on the list are James Alfred Gardiner, passenger, and James College Pope, shipbuilder, who was to become a Father of Confederation and Premier of P.E.I.] They set sail November 12, 1849 and arrived at San Francisco on July 3, 1850. Four letters written home by Charles have been preserved and give us, as they did his family, a vivid picture of the young man's journey to a far country. It is hard to give excerpts when passage after passage calls out for quotation, but here are four:

At daylight we saw a sail ahead steering the same course as ourselves. We soon found that we were gaining upon her; before night we came up and spoke to her. She was a barque called the *Stephen* from St. Andrews, New Brunswick, and like ourselves, bound for California. Judge of our feelings, from home four thousand miles, and meeting with friends from our own Country and set upon the same expedition. As soon as this intelligence was received, three deafening cheers burst from the decks of the *Fanny*, which was responded to by the Barque with equal enthusiasm. We shortened our sail to keep beside her while various questions were asked and answered on both sides. We had thought our passage uncommonly long up to this time, and no doubt is was; but when we heard she had nearly as long a one and crossed the Equator a long way to the Eastward of where we did, it gave us fresh courage, and tended in some measure to do away with the prejudices against our Captain. It was coming on night when we parted company with her, and the next morning she was out of sight.... I promised in the preceeding part to tell you how I came off in regard of *sea sickness*. If I had not it to perfection then it's no matter. I had a longer seige at it than anyone on board. It was not until Christmas that I can date my recovery. Since then I've been quite healthy and have joined the "watch," and am just the same as they who signed "Articles." I am very much obliged for the

kind letters that I found at the bottom of my cake bag. They expressed a wish that I might be over my sickness before I should read them; but, I assure you, I was bad enough when I found them, but they raised my spirits wonderfully.... To make a long story short, after a tedious passage of seven months and a half we are safely landed on California's Golden Shores; among the dust in reality, but it is not all *Gold Dust* that is here; which we find out facing up the street in the afternoon. The wind blows hard every day from ten to twelve o'clock until night, and in one direction all the dry season, and the dust or sand which abounds in this City flies in clouds.... The mines are all a lottery - a good many do well, but a great many more do nothing. Although I have not done much yet, my anticipations are just as great as when I left home. I'm bound to make the pile, or I'll stick to it like *"Wax to a Cobbler."* As you have heard, I was taken sick shortly after our arrival; and did not regain my usual health until a week ago, but now I'm thankful to say I have excellent health and appetitie enough "to eat a man off horseback." I was not sick enough to lay up, and bought a team of horses, and went trucking about Town, a business that hitherto has paid well; but I was rather unfortunate. One of the *horses turned out to be a mare,* and she had a foal on me not long after I got them. The other one, a splendid horse, was claimed shortly after by a Spaniard, from whom he had been stolen, and taken from me....

I would be much obliged if you would write the next mail after you receive this and give me all the news, those who have got married, and those who intend to. I hear Horatio (Wright) is spliced, and I believe got a good wife. Well, I'm glad of it for he's deserving of one, and I hope he'll have a jolly lot of young Horatios. I hope Theodore (Wright) and wife are well, and in a *thriving* way. How I should like to have a gallop round my *favorite* route and a look at you all again, but everything will come round in its season. If I can get time, I shall write a few lines home; but in case I should not, you can tell them I am well, and bound for the "Diggins" by tomorrow's boat.

The last letter is dated September 11, 1850. Soon after writing it, Charles came down with yellow fever and died before the close of the year, at the age of twenty-two.[7] A poem entitled, "The Dying Californian," was sent to the newspaper. Several young men died of Yellow Fever on one ship, the *Fanny,* so one is not certain about whom it was written:

Come, brothers, gather round my bed for I am dying now.
The last bright gleam of hope has fled and clammy is my brow.
While reason still retains her throne, Oh, list to what I say,
And bear this message to my home: my home far, far away.

Go tell my father not to blame his wayward, erring child,
But kindly speak of his dear name on whom in youth he smiled.
To breathe that well-remembered prayer I learned beside her knee.
And when I'm dead, take off this ring And bear it to the shore;
Tell Mary 'tis an offering from him who wakes no more;
And tell her in the courts above I'll think of that dear hour
When first she pledged to me her love in that bright sunny bower.
But this dear tress her own hand gave with it I cannot part.
And when you lay me in my grave place it upon my heart
For, oh! I feel I could not sleep if it were wanting there,
And still in death I fain would keep a gift from one so fair.
Brothers, you soon must close my eyes and make my last cold bed,
For ere the morning sun doth rise I shall be counted dead.
Loved ones, farewell! My happy home I ne'er shall see you more, For I must slumber all alone on San Francisco's shore.

1.23 Major Wright II (6, Martha 5, Major 4, Thomas 3, Clement 2, Stephen 1) was born on April 17, 1830 in Centreville Bedeque. On October 12, 1870, he married Adah [or Ada – her name has been spelled both ways] Mary Shrieve, the second daughter of the Rev. Charles Jerson Shrieve and Harriet Hartshorne, who was born on September 9, 1846 in Guysboro, Nova Scotia. Major and Adah were married in St. Stephen's Anglican Church, Chester, N.S. The reader will note that Major is the second child of the same name of Martha and Stephen Wright, the first child dying at age 3. [Major Wright and John Keir Hooper were first cousins making Ada Hooper Neal, Alden's mother, a first cousin once removed to Major Wright]

Major and Adah lived in Centreville where he was a merchant. They had four children (seventh generation). He died on October 7, 1907; Adah died on February 26, 1906 in Centreville Bedeque after a lingering illness. Adah's obituary appeared in the newspaper as follows: "The death of Mrs. Major Wright occurred at her home, Centreville Bedeque, on Monday 26th inst., after a lingering illess. Deceased was a daughter of the late Rev. C. J. Shrieve and was fifty-nine years of age. She is survived by her husband, one son, Richmond, and two daughters, Misses Millicent and May, all at home. The funeral will be held on Thursday afternoon at 2:30 o'clock." Doris Haslam's genealogy, *The Wrights of Bedeque*, stated:

Major had been named for his grandfather, one of the many descendants to bear the given name of Loyalist Major Hooper. The story has been told that on Major Wright's first trip to the U.S.A. he signed the hotel register where he was staying "Major Wright" without any intention that it should be regarded as a military rank, but before he realized what was happening, the clerks were paying him every deference with their "Major, would you like this?" "Major, can I get you that?" and he did not know how to stop it, but had to suffer it in great embarrassment. His fine appearance and erect carriage but added fuel to the impression that the written word "Major" had created. Never again in the States did he sign "Major Wright," but always "M. Wright."

Mary Beatrice, called May, died on April 18, 1906, less than 2 months after her mother's death. Major Wright, who was 16 ½ years older than his wife, died just over a year and seven months after her. His obituary appeared in the *Guardian*, a Charlottetown newspaper:

Many *Guardian* readers will learn with regret of the death of Major Wright, Centreville, which occurred yesterday evening about five o'clock after an illness of only a few days. The deceased was 77 years of age and had conducted business in Centerville for forty years retiring a few years ago. His wife, nee Miss Ada Shreeves, Chester, N.S., predeceased him a little over a year ago [actually it was just over one year and seven months], and a few weeks afterward his daughter May passed away. One daughter, Miss Millicent, and one son, Richmond, survive. The latter at present is on his way home from Vancouver, B. C. The *Guardian* extends sympathy to his family.

Doris Haslam recalled in *The Wrights of Bedeque*:

The Bedeque Wrights were very proud of their connections. Stephen's first wife, Martha Hooper, was the granddaughter of Walter Patterson, the Island's first governor; his second wife, Millicent, was the daughter of a prominent Charlottetown lawyer, James Bardin Palmer, and sister to two other lawyers. When his twins were displayed to a visitor Stephen boasted, "There's Palmer blood in these." The wife of Major (son of Stephen and Martha), Ada Mary Shrieve, the daughter of an Anglican rector in Nova Scotia, was extremely proud of her English and Anglican background. Her youngest daughter, May, once remarked to the maid-of-all work, "We are high bo'n English ladies."

Doris Haslam also gave an interesting account of Major Wright, in her two volume genealogy, *The Wrights of Bedeque*:

An 1862 list shows him [Major Wright] an ensign in the Volunteer Artillery Company in which his Uncle John was a captain. As early as 1863 he was postmaster and in business with his cousin, Charles C. Gardiner (under the name "Wright and Gardiner, General Dealers") in the village of Centreville [Charles Coulson Gardiner was the son of Mary Hooper Gardiner, the daughter of Major Hooper]. Through time, he [Major Wright] became sole proprietor and continued his merchantile business until the turn of the century when he was succeeded by his son, Richmond. The store was situated next to his large and imposing residence, "Maplethorpe." The store was the home of Mrs. Robert Burns [in the mid -1970s] and the house was owned by Mrs. Hubert Arsenault.

In 1866 His Excellency the Lieutenant Governor, in Council, was pleased to make Major a Justice of the Peace for Prince County, another position of importance he held for many years.... He was a prominent man of affairs in his church and his community and a successful business man, leaving an estate valued at over a hundred thousand dollars to be divided between his daughter Millicent and his son Richard Harold, who by then was living in Vancouver, B. C.[8]

On October 18, 1892 an item appeared in the local daily newspaper: "Major Wright, wife and daughter of Bedeque have returned from the World's Fair."

Doris Haslam wrote, "Adah's brother, Rev. Cannon Richmond Shreve, D. D., was rector at Sherbrooke, Quebec, for many years and also Canon of Quebec Cathedral. Her sister and husband, Dr. J. H. Jamieson, lived in Centreville in the house occupied in 1976 by Herbert Stright. His dispensary, a small building between their house and Major's store, was known as Jamieson's Apothecary Shop. Dr. Jamieson died in Centreville and was buried in the Lower Bedeque Cemetery."[9]

On October 1, 2002, I had the pleasure of meeting the new owner of Maplethorpe. Next door in the building that was Dr. Jamieson's apothecary and beyond that Major's store has been for several years the home and beauty shop of Brenda Beaton which is the shop where I go nearly weekly to have my hair done. In the summer of 2002 I noticed a sign in front of the house next door that read, "Maplethorpe Bed and Breakfast." The house was being renovated after years of apparent neglect. Brenda and her husband had built a new home behind their old one and she had established a hair dressing salon

there. October 1st was the day that Alden and I were leaving P.E.I. for home and I dearly wanted to find out about the new B & B that was named the same as the home of "Alden's cousin twice removed."

After knocking at the door I had the pleasure of meeting the new owner of Maplethorpe, an educator from Montana, U.S.A. and his wife, also an educator, both of whom had retired and bought the run-down property in December 2001. They have been improving it and restoring it ever since. His wife was away, but I look forward to meeting her next year. They have four bedrooms and baths, living room, dining room, and kitchen, all beautifully restored as a bed and breakfast at the front of the house. The family quarters are in the rear of the house. He and his wife had obviously done a great deal of research on the house.

Interestingly, only that day (October 1, 2002) the old house next to Maplethorpe, owned by Brenda and Brian Beaton, was demolished. Being nostalgic, I was somewhat sorrowful to know that this building where Alden's relatives, Major Wright and Charles Gardiner, moved about and worked was being demolished.

1.24 Ann *Eliza* Wright (6, Martha 5 [and Stephen Wright], Major 4, Thomas 3, Clement 2, Stephen 1), was born July 16, 1834 in Centerville Bedeque and died there on September 1, 1894. She married Martin Gay Black, the son of Joseph Black and Sarah Canfield, on March 13, 1856. Martin was born on September 8, 1819 in Nova Scotia and died on June 3, 1887 in Centreville Bedeque. As an aside, Martin's sister was Beria Stewart Black (1837 – 1910), the daughter of Joseph and Sarah Canfield Black, and married (i) Frederick John Edmund Wright. A newspaper article, thanks to Mr. and Mrs. Bradshaw, describes her bridal reception: "One of the prettiest bridal receptions this season was that of Mrs. Fred J. E. Wright at her home in Summerside on Friday of last week. Looking handsome in a becoming gown of sand satin and georgette, Mrs. Wright was assisted in receiving by Miss Wright while Miss Bird Wright ushered the callers. The dining room was exquisitely arranged with pink carnations and similax, the tea table being presided over by Mrs. Pritchard and

Miss Eva McNeill, assisted in waiting by Miss Jessie Sharp and Miss Ethel Strong of Summerside and Miss Sadie Smith and Miss Lois Hooper of Charlottetown. There were quite a number of callers to offer congratulations and extend a welcome to Mrs. Wright."

Dugald Wright, whose name will appear in Chapter Eight, was Beria's second husband. Again as an aside, Joseph's parents, Richard Black (1762-1834) and Sally Chapman (1767-1820), were both born in Yorkshire, England. Richard's father, William Black (1727 - 1820) was born in Paisley, Scotland. He and his first wife, Elizabeth Stocks, who died in 1776, came from Yorkshire to Nova Scotia in 1775 by chartered vessel. Joseph married Sarah, the daughter of Stephen Canfield of Wallace, N.S. They lived near River Philip, N.S. until they crossed the Strait to settle in Searletown.[10] Martin was a farmer; they lived in Black's Hill, P.E.I. Martin was from a most prominent Maritime Methodist family of whom the best known were Bishop William and the Rev. John Black.[11] Doris Haslam wrote of Martin G. Black, Eliza's husband:

> Martin had come with his parents to Searletown in 1822 and grew to manhood there. When the first Roman Catholic Church in Kinkora was built in 1847, Martin was the carpenter who put up the frame. By 1863 he was the miller at Jesse Wright's grist mill, and he and Eliza were living on the southwest corner of Castalia Street near the mill. By 1880 he owned a one hundred and seventy acre property, stretching from the West Branch of the Dunk River to South Shore (now Chelton). His house was on the brow of the hill on the main road from Bedeque to Searletown. The hill was called, for many years, Black's Hill.
>
> Martin, being a true Black, was devoted to the church of his fathers. He was a member of the trustee board which encouraged the construction of a new Methodist church (the third to be built in Bedeque), but did not live to see its completion in 1888.[12]

Eliza and Martin Black had seven children (seventh generation, surname Black). They were both buried in the Lower Bedeque Cemetery.

After Martha's death in 1838, Stephen married a second time, on October 3, 1839, Millicent Palmer (1814-1872), daughter of James Bardin Palmer and Millicent Jones.[13] Stephen and Millicent had six daughters and four sons. Although they would not be Hooper relatives, I include their names and minimal data (surname Wright) as it would appear that Millicent would have had responsibility for continuing to raise Martha's children:

- **Louisa Palmer Wright**, born July 2, 1840, married Dr. Francis Dyer Beer, a graduate of Harvard Medical School. Dr. Frank (as he was called) practiced medicine from 1860 - 1864 in Centreville Bedeque where his brother John was a merchant.[14] They had five children, all born in Charlottetown, P.E.I. Louisa's obituary appeared in two local newspapers on February 9, 1919 and is included here, thanks to Mr. and Mrs. Bradshaw for sharing their newspaper articles:

The death occurred in Charlottetown on Sunday, at the age of 78 years, of Mrs. Beer, wife of the late Dr. F. D. Beer, of Charlottetown. The deceased was the eldest daughter of the late Mr. Stephen Wright of Bedeque, and with her late husband had resided in Charlottetown from her young womanhood until her death. There are left to mourn two daughters, Mrs. Alexander Anderson of Albany, N.Y. and Mrs. John Longworth of Brandon, Manitoba, and two sons, Mr. F. Robert Beer of Seattle and Col. George S. Beer, Bloemfontain, S. A. Two sisters and four brothers survive her, namely Mrs. F. W. Strong of Summerside; Miss Mary Wright, Charlottetown; Mr. Henry E. Wright, formerly of Summerside now of Minto, N. B.; Mr. Edward Wright, New Annan; Mr. Charles S. Wright, Victoria, P.E.I.; and Mr. Maurice Wright, Vancouver, B. C.

BEER On Sunday, Feb. 16th inst., Louisa Palmer Wright, aged 78 years, widow of the late Frank D. Beer, M. D. Funeral Tuesday by train to Sherwood, leaving G. D. Wright's parlors at 1:50 p.m.

- **Millicent Palmer Wright**, b. March 20, 1842; d. Sept. 20, 1856, Centreville, Bedeque, P.E.I.
- **Sarah Palmer Wright** (Patience in family Bible), born October 11, 1843; died September 20, 1862 in Centreville Bedeque.

- **Alice Mary Wright**, born Sept. 12, 1845 in Centreville Bedeque; married Rev. Joseph Pascoe, on July 28, 1875, and had two sons, Joseph Benson, and Stephen Wright who became a partner in the firm of Harrison Pascoe Co. which specialized in dehydrating cranberries. She died in Centreville on September 27, 1883.
- **Henry Ernest Wright**, born Jan. 29, 1847; married Margaret Theodosia Chappel Wright, his first cousin, the daughter of George Miller and Betsy (Butcher) Wright, born c.1849. He studied law with his Palmer uncles in Charlottetown, then practiced law in Summerside. Mrs. Wright's obituary, taken from a local newspaper, appeared on March 18, 1916:

A wide circle of our readers will join us in sincere regret at the death of Mrs. Henry E. Wright, which sad event took place at her residence in Summerside on Thursday morning after a short illness. The deceased lady was a daughter of the late Mr. George M. Wright of Bedeque and has for years been an honored member of the society at Summerside where she has taken a prominent part in all work connected with the Episcopal [Anglican] Church, and up to the time of her illness was an ardent worker for the Red Cross and every good cause in the community. There are left to mourn a sorrowing husband, Stipendiary Wright, the oldest practicing member of the Bar in this province, and two sons, Mr. Stephen Wright, now a mining engineer in Mexico, and Mr. Rowan Wright of the Bank of Nova Scotia at Paspebiac, N.S., who is now home for the funeral; also three sisters, Mrs. Charles Full of California, Mrs. (Rev. Dr.) Steele of St. John, N.B.; and Mrs. David Rogers of Summerside, and two brothers, Messrs Mark Wright of Vancouver, B. C. and G. D. Wright of Charlottetown, to all of whom our deepest sympathy is extended. The funeral takes place on Sunday afternoon to St. Mary's Church at 2 o'clock and thence to St. John's Cemetery at St. Eleanors.

The obituary of another daughter of George M. and Betsy Butcher Wright, Isabella Christina, called Belle, also appeared in a local newspaper:

The many friends, in all these provinces, of Rev. Dr. Steele, Supt. of Missions, have learned with deep regret of the sad bereavement which has come to him in the decease of Mrs. Steele, which occurred at St. John on the 20th inst., after a lengthened illness. She was the daughter of Mr. and Mrs. George Wright of Wright's Mills, Prince Co., P.E.I. In early life she became a devoted Christian and took a

deep interest in all the activities of the church. In 1892 she was united in marriage with Rev. George Steele and took charge of his four boys who four years previous to this had lost their mother. With great tact and true motherly devotion she devoted herself to the training of these boys who loyally returned her affection.

Still another obituary for Belle, obtained from Mr. and Mrs. Bradshaw, dated April 1921, reads:

Many friends will regret to learn of the death in St.[sic] John, N. B. this week of Mrs. (Rev.) George Steele. The deceased was a sister of Mr. G. D. Wright and Mrs. David Rogers [apparently wife #3] of Charlottetown, and was well-known, her husband having been pastor of the Upper Prince Street Methodist Church for some years. Another brother is Mr. Mark Wright, Vancouver, and another sister is Mrs. Charles Full of North Dakota. The late Mrs. Henry Wright of Summerside, was a sister.

• **Edward John Wright**, born May 11, 1850 at "Elmvale" in Centreville Bedeque; married Euphemia (called Phemie) Townsend (October 24, 1854 - May 21, 1941), daughter of James and Eliza (Walker) Townsend of New Annan, on May 26, 1878 [Phemie would be the great-great niece of Jane Walker Hooper]. Phemie and Edward had five children: four daughters and one son. Doris Haslam's research in, *The Wrights of Bedeque* (pp. 94-95), reads:

Ed had attended Mount Allison Academy and returned to Bedeque to assist in the family mill operation. When the Jamieson Mills on the banks of the Barbary Weed Creek, New Annan, came up for sale in 1878, his father (Stephen Wright) bought them and established Ed there as proprietor of flour, carding, cloth, and grist mills. The property included a farm and a very fine farm home in which Ed and Phemie brought up their family of four daughters and one son.

The parents of Mr. Malcolm Bradshaw had saved the newspaper record of the marriage of a daughter of Edward and Phemie:

The marriage [of their daughter Harriet] was celebrated at the home of the bride's parents, New Annan, Wednesday, January 24th [1912], of Miss Harriet Florence, daughter of Mr. and Mrs. E. J. Wright, to Mr. J. Harry Brown of Margate. The ceremony was performed by the Rev. E. Johnson, Kensington, in the presence of

about thirty guests. The bride, who was given away by her father, wore a dress of dainty white eolienne over silk, with veil of tulle fastened by a coronet of orange blossoms, and was unattended. Miss Ethel Strong, cousin of the bride, played the wedding march. After the ceremony, the bridal party and guests repaired to the dining room where supper was served. The bride was the recipient of many beautiful presents. After a very pleasant evening Mr. and Mrs. Brown left for their home in Margate followed by the good wishes of their friends.

Doris Haslam's book, *The Wrights of Bedeque*, contains more information on New Annan's Jamieson's Mills:

New Annan was named by Squire William Jamieson who was born in Annan, Dumfriesshire, Scotland. He built the mills which the Wrights bought in 1878.... A saw mill on the property had already been closed when Ed took over management. The carding mill continued to operate during the warm weather, turning out rolls and batts until home spinning and weaving went out of fashion. Dyeing cloth was another operation carried on at this mill, a great convenience to the home weavers. The grist mill was in business for many years. Here the farmers brought their grain to be stone ground into "Island" flour, whole wheat flour, cream of wheat, oatmeal, bran, and shorts. Grain for livestock was also crushed at the grist mill. The Wright mill pond in New Annan was a place of recreation, in summer for trout fishing and in winter for jolly skating parties.

Edward J. "Ed" Wright died in New Annan, P.E.I. on January 16, 1929.

- **Martha Isabelle Wright** (a twin, called Mattie) was born June 16, 1852 in Centerville Bedeque; she married Frederick William Strong (called Fred), the son of the Honorable William Gambee and Sarah Jane (Bousfield) Strong, on October 10, 1876 [Haslam writes that Fred was the son of the Rev. John Bass Strong and Elizabeth Gambel]. According to Father Nigel Bousfield, St. Johns Episcopal Church in Huntington, New York, on 3/15/04, Bousfield is a rare British name]. Fred was born on Oct. 19, 1845 in Newark-on-Trent, Nottinghamshire, England. They had four sons and two daughters. One son was named Major Everett Strong and was born in

Summerside, P.E.I., on February 20, 1889. A news item dated June 3, 1914, in the *Summerside Journal* reads: "Major Strong, for some time a member of the staff of the Bank of Nova Scotia in St. John, has been transferred to the staff of the Toronto office."

Once more, Mr. and Mrs. Bradshaw shared another newspaper account from their scrapbook collection, this time of Major Strong's wedding:

WEDDING BELLS - A wedding of interest to a great many friends was solemnized yesterday in St. Paul's Church, St. John, when the Rector Rev. J. H. A. Holmes united in marriage Major Everett Strong of Toronto and Miss Constance Porter Reed of West St. John. The bride was given away by her brother-in-law, H. W. Ketchum. After a wedding trip to Moncton and P.E.Island Mr. and Mrs. Strong will go to their future home in Toronto. Major Strong was formerly of the Royal Bank of Canada, Summerside, but at present is on the staff of the Bank of Nova Scotia, Toronto. Major Strong, a son of the late Mr. F. W. Strong, Suummerside, arrived in Summerside with his bride on Thursday.

Major was employed by the Bank of Nova Scotia in the head office. His wife, Constance Porter Reed, who he married on September 1, 1920, was born on September 1, 1890 in Saint John, N. B. and died on October 13, 1967 in St. Catherines, Ontario. They had one daughter, Joyce Porter, born December 21, 1929, who married Frederick Alexander Ure.

- **Mary Amelia Wright** (a twin of Martha) born June 26, 1852; did not marry; died April 2, 1938. After her parents died, she went to live with her invalid sister, Louisa, in Charlottetown and was her constant companions until Louisa's death in 1919. Then she became an honored and dearly-loved member of the family of her twin sister Martha. Fred (the husband of Martha) was born in Newark-on-Trent, Nottinghamshire, England, but moved with his family to P.E.I. in 1847, living in Central Bedeque in the Weatherbe house until their new house, "Newark Cottage," was built. Fred attended Bedeque

School, situated midway between the two "corners," then called Weatherbe's and Hooper's. Fred established a business at the corner of Water Street and Central Street in Summerside and lived then on the corner of Central and Winter Streets.

- **Charles Stephen Wright**, born July 15, 1854; married his cousin, Wilhelmina Wright, on October 21, 1890. Charlie farmed his property, "River View," which adjoined "Elm Vale." His house was situated on the road connecting the mills with New Road from Central Bedeque to Searletown. [The "new road" would connect the road that in 2004 goes between Brenda Beaton's house and Malcolm Bradshaw's house] Charlie died on April 14, 1933.
- **John *Morice* Wright,** born July 20, 1857; married Bessie Salter Jost, and had five children. Morice and Bessie lived at "Elm Vale," the homestead which Morice inherited from his father. He and his brother, Charlie, ran the carding, saw and shingle mills on the West Branch of the Dunk River in Centerville Bedeque. The carding mill ceased operating about 1890. They ran the other two mills for ten years before selling in 1893. Before Morice moved to Vancouver he was an agent for Miller Bros, a Charlottetown firm selling musical instruments. In Vancouver he was also a salesman. On February 14, 1907 he deeded to Patrick Connolly (for his son Wilfred) the 146 acre farm property, known for so many years as "Elm Vale." In the 1970's it was owned by Campbell and Burns, Ltd.[15] It was almost opposite the Callbeck Store in Central Bedeque in 1999. Morice died in 1927 in Vancouver, B. C. His obituary, dated March 26, 1927, follows:

Death in Vancouver of Mr. J. M. Wright

A wide circle of old friends here will regret to learn of the death of Mr. J. Morris Wright, son of the late Mr. and Mrs. Stephen Wright [Millicent] of Elmdale Farm, [it was actually Elm Vale] Bedeque, which took place in Vancouver, B. C., on Thursday last, following a serious operation at the age of 69 years. The deceased was one of the best known and most progressive farmers of Bedeque, a man of many sterling qualities and a leader in the Methodist Church, who left the Island in 1906 and has since resided in Vancouver where he was held in high esteem. There are left to mourn a sorrowing widow (nee Miss Bessie Jost of Charlottetown), two sons and two daughters, namely Roy of Vancouver, Vickers of Toronto, Mrs. Harry

Henderson of Vancouver, and Miss Dora at home; also two brothers, Mr. E. J. Wright of New Annan, and Mr. Charles S. Wright of Central Bedeque, and two sisters, Mrs. F. W. Strong and Miss Mary A. Wright [the twins] of Summerside. Mr. Arnold Henderson of Bedeque is a grandson of the deceased, and three other grandchildren reside in Vancouver where the funeral takes place this (Tuesday) afternoon upon the arrival of his son Vickers from Toronto.

The *Summerside Journal*, September 5, 1906, gives this account of the family reunion held at "Elm Vale" to bid farewell to Morice and his daughter, Allie: "The tables were spread under the grand old trees, some nearly one hundred years old. Thirty members of the family were present and a very pleasant day was spent roaming over the old homestead." Bessie and the rest of the family joined Morice and Allie in Vancouver at a later date."[16]

from *The Wrights of Bedeque*, p. 98

J. Morice Wright (1857-1927), son of Stephen W. (c.1801-1883) and Millicent (Palmer) Wright (1814-1872)

from *The Wrights of Bedeque*, p. 98

J. Morice Wright and his wife, Bessie Salter Jost (1858-1927), residents of "Elm Vale," Centreville Bedeque

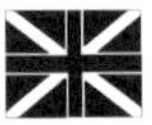

Mabel Louise Wright (born 1883/1884) was the firstborn of Morris and Bessie Wright. She married James Francis (Jimmy) Henderson and had a son, Arnold Henderson, who married Gladys Bradshaw in 1978. His marriage to Gladys made him not only a "cousin" to my husband, Alden Neal, but a good friend as well.[17]

Perhaps Stephen Wright did have something of which to be proud in the ancestry of both of his wives. Martha's father, Major, had come to P.E.I. in 1784 with his father, Thomas Hooper, a Loyalist from near Princeton, New Jersey. Major married, first, Ann Patterson, mother of Martha and daughter of Walter Patterson, Governor of the Island of St. John from 1769 until 1787. Stephen's second wife was Millicent Palmer whose grandparents, Joseph and Susannah (Bardin) Palmer of Capel Street, Dublin, had James Bardin Palmer, a lawyer who came to PEI in 1802. James had married in 1803 Millicent Jones, daughter of Benjamin Jones, L.L.D., of London, England.

The First Marriage of Major Hooper

Ann Patterson Hooper was born about 1774, the daughter of the former Governor of P.E.I., Walter Patterson, and his mistress, Margaret Hyde. The wife of Major, and the mother of two small children [Eliza and Martha], died on August 26, 1800. I believe that I read that Ann died in childbirth with her third child (who obviously did not survive).

I would like to chronicle some of the events in the life of Walter Patterson, Governor of Prince Edward Island and the grandfather of Ann and Major's two children. The last chapter in the book, *Bedeque and Its People,* apparently written by L.U. Fowler and H.H. Hooper, and given to me by Muriel Hooper Blanchard in 1998, is a brief biography on Walter Patterson. The heading of the chapter is puzzling to me as I do not know the background of Gov. Patterson's wife or his mistress. I will copy it as it is written; perhaps the reader will be more acquainted with the subject than I am. [This biography was written probably about 1900]

CARLYLE'S FIRST LOVE
Margaret Gordon
Lady Bannerman

Raymond Clare Archibald on July 23, 1767

Lot 19 granted to the brothers Walter Patterson Esq. and Captain John Patterson.

On Feb. 2, 1769 Captain Walter Patterson was appointed Captain General and Governor-in-Chief in His Majesty's Island of St. John.

Aug. 30, 1770 Governor Patterson arrived in Charlotte Town, the capital of the Island.

He was accompanied by his brother John who acted as his private secretary.

Both brothers had seen army service and it seems highly probable that the Walter Patterson, who as a volunteer was commissioned Ensign (1757) and Lieutenant (1760) in the 80th Regiment and served with his regiment in America, was he who was afterwards to become a Colonial Governor.

Walter Patterson was an Irishman and his father was known as "William Patterson of Fox Hall," County Donegal, although his ancestors lived and were buried in the not far-distant town of Rothmelton on the border of the Fanad Peninsula. Fox Hall was a leased estate of about 170 acres in the parish of Cornwall, some 30 miles from Bundrena.

Walter Patterson lived in an old house of the French Governors on the "Fort Lot" (now called Rocky Point). Fanning lived in the same house for some time. In this house between 1771 and 1775 Patterson's daughters Margaret and Ann [1774] were born. Their mother was Margaret (?) Hyde, daughter of Thomas Hyde who came from Clare Island to Prince Edward Island in 1770. He brought his family with him and settled at West River. Miss Hyde was not Patterson's wife. He married on March 9, 1770 Miss Hester Warren of Stratford, Essex, England. They had at least four children.

The "Fort Lot" which includes the site of the old French capital of the Island was developed by Patterson into a brightly productive farm. It is beautifully situated on undulating hills near the harbour's entrance and across the mouths of the North and West Rivers from Charlottetown, the present capital.

In 1775, Gov. Patterson was granted leave of absence and he left Charlottetown for England on August 2. He did not again return till June 28, 1780, in the ship *Two Friends*. The next few months were stormy ones in Patterson's administration, and in 1786 complaints had become so numerous [that] his recall was ordered, and Lt. Gov. Fanning, then at Halifax, was sent to take his place. Patterson's fight to retain office forms an interesting episode in the history of the Island.

For several months, this Island with scarce 4,000 inhabitants was ruled by two governors as Patterson, who had a large number of friends, refused to give up to his successor the great seal, public documents, and official papers. But on April 5, 1787 a preemptory order was sent by the Secretary of State to Patterson to deliver to Fanning all the public documents and instructions in his possession, the King having no longer need of his services.

After an absence of a few months in Quebec, Patterson returned to the Island and set up a systematic opposition to the administration of his successor, and this he continued until his return to England in 1788.

It is evident that " Patterson was a broken and ruined man, soured by misfortune and his long struggle to ordinance his own and the province's interests. He had invested his fortune in the Island and lost it. That he acted most indiscretely in his dealings with Fanning is evident. It was the conduct of a soured and disappointed man." In 1790 he was appealing to the Government for help, but there is no evidence that he received assistance. He never returned to P.E.I., and died in poverty at his lodgings in Castle St., Oxford Market, London, on Sept. 6, 1798.

Governor 1770-1786

A 24 volume work on historical and constitutional aspects of English history which was in Patterson's library in P.E.I. is still preserved by a gentleman in Charlottetown, and each sleeve bears the book plate.

This early history of Prince Edward Island is a preface to the introduction of the Thomas Hooper family who had arrived on Prince Edward Island in 1784. Major, the oldest child who left New Jersey for Prince Edward Island, was about 17. He and his father built a "house" out of the trees on their property.

*In 1801 after Ann's death, **Major Hooper** (4, Thomas 3, Clement 2, Stephen 1) married for the second time. His new wife, **Catherine Urquhart**, born 1783, was 19 years Major's junior and only 18 at the time). They were married by Dr. Wiggins. Catherine was the daughter of the Rev. John Urquhart and Mary MacIntyre; she died on May 17, 1866. She shares a gravestone with Major in the North Bedeque Cemetery (former Presbyterian). The stone reads: "In memory of Major Hooper, Esq., died Feb. 24, 1838 AET 74 Also his wife Catherine Urquhart, died May 17, 1866, AET 83." They

lived in Bedeque and had 11 children (fifth generation), surname Hooper. The birth order numbering will continue in Major's line, not his wife's. [Eliza was 1.1 and Martha was 1.2, the two children of Ann Patterson and Major Hooper]

Mary Hooper (5, Major 4, Thomas 3, Clement 2, Stephen 1) was born in 1802 in Lower Bedeque and died on January 25, 1890 at Summerside, P.E.I., at the home of her daughter Adelaide and her son-in-law, Mr. Charles McNeill. Mrs. Gardiner, relict of the late J. Rhodes Gardiner [was] in the 88th year of her age [taken from a Summerside newspaper, dated February 1890]. She married John Rhodes Gardiner (as his second wife) on March 9, 1831. John Rhodes was born on April 24, 1798 in Rhode Island, U.S.A., the son of John Gardiner and Eunice Haszard, and died on September 10, 1874 in Summerside, P.E.I. He had three brothers and three sisters, two of whom are included in this document: Ann Matilda, the wife of James Bagnall whose relatives moved from the Hazel Grove area of P.E.I. to Saugus, MA and Marion (should be spelled Maria), wife of Thomas Hooper, son of Major. Maria and Thomas ran a bed, board, and alcoholic refreshments arrangement in Centreville Bedeque c.1830-1850.

John Gardiner, Loyalist, who was a sixth generation Gardiner in New England, and his wife, who, it is believed, accompanied Eunice's parents, Thomas and Eunice Rhodes Haszard, to the Island of St. John, came from Rhode Island to P.E.I. in 1786 and was a descendant of Roger Williams. John was the father of Rhodes and six other children. [Rhodes was named for his great-grandmother whose family name was Rhodes.[18] The wife of James Douglas Bagnall, Ann Matilda Gardiner, was the daughter of John Gardiner, Loyalist, from Rhode Island. James lived and worked in Charlottetown where he was King's Printer and a Member of the House of Assembly. He died in Central Bedeque at the home of his son Samuel, one of his eight children][19]

When John Rhodes was about 20 years old he visited his relatives in Rhode Island where he met and married his first cousin, Mary

Gardiner. John and his bride returned to his native district, North River, shortly after their marriage. After living there for three years, the family moved to Bedeque. After Mary's death [I assume], John married Mary Hooper, daughter and first child of Major and Catherine Hooper. Mary and John lived in Lower Bedeque and Summerside. In Lower Bedeque John had owned property known as Gordon Grove as well as the Gardiner homestead.[20] On the Gordon Grove property John Rhodes farmed 350 acres from 1836 until 1866 when he moved to Summerside.[21] The property had been divided into three lots, two of which, including the Gardiner homestead, were sold to Joseph Cottle Morris.[22] Mr. Morris, born in 1831, died at the age of 65 on Jan. 24, 1896 and is buried in the Lower Bedeque Cemetery. His wife was Ann Wright (1840-1921).

John Gardiner was a tavern keeper and a Member of Parliament. [As mentioned above, Thomas, the son of Major, married the sister of John Rhodes Gardiner so we might say that brother and sister married sister and brother!] According to George A. Leard, "At Lower Bedeque John R. Gardiner was building up a general business and giving his support to the Methodist Church, but he too, would later move across the harbour and eventually become president of the Summerside Bank."[23] John and Mary are buried in the Lower Bedeque Cemetery. The names of their eight children (surname Gardiner, sixth generation), all born in Lower Bedeque follow:

1.31 George Henry Gardiner (6, Mary 5, Major 4, Thomas 3, Clement 2, Stephen 1), born January 1, 1832, married Sarah Reid on January 1, 1857. George and Sarah, who was from Crapaud, lived in Bedeque where he was a farmer. He was listed as a trader when they moved to Summerside. They had three sons and one daughter.

1.32 Adelaide Gardiner (6, Mary 5, Major 4, Thomas 3, Clement 2, Stephen 1), born September 27, 1833 in Bedeque; married Charles B. MacNeill, who was born about 1835, on November 24, 1859; and died on March 11, 1905 in Summerside. Adelaide and Charles lived in Summerside.

1.33 Charles Coulson Gardiner (6, Mary 5, Major 4, Thomas 3, Clement 2, Stephen 1), born September 10, 1835 in Bedeque. He married, first, Martha Jane Cox, who was born in 1840, on September 22, 1868. Charles was a merchant in Bedeque, Summerside, and Charlottetown. According to Rufus Bagnall, Charlie kept store with Major Wright in Centerville. This statement agrees with the information which was gleaned from other sources. Charlie's second wife was Lucy Narraway, the obituary of whom follows and is the only source for information about her. Her lengthy obituary was dated Charlottetown, January 1896:

Mrs. C. C. Gardiner

Lucy Narraway, beloved wife of C. C. Gardiner, Esq., was born in Pictou, N.S. and died of heart disease at Charlottetown Dec. 18th, 1895. The funeral services were held in Canso where at her request she was laid at rest beside her beloved mother. Mrs. Gardiner was the youngest daughter of H. R. Narraway, Esq. of Canso who has for many years faithfully served his church and was a member of the last General Conference. Her mother was a most godly and "elect lady" whose devoted life and happy health were an impressive gospel; and from her youth our departed sister was surrounded by the atmosphere of loyalty to Christ and His Church. Well-endowed mentally and receiving liberal culture, she became a most valuable member of society. At the opening of the Wesleyan Academy in Charlottetown, she was appointed one of the staff, discharging creditably the duties of her position until her marriage with Mr. Gardiner.

About twenty-three years ago, a very dear younger brother was lost at sea and from that time her mind was greatly impressed with the importance of preparation for death. This period of thoughtfulness was followed by her union with the First Methodist Church. She was constant in her attendance at the means of grace - always in her place when health permitted. Her piety was genuine, and her experience was like the flow of a deep, noiseless river whose sources were in living mountain springs. In godly sincerity she had her conversion - endearing herself to the congregation by her quiet graces and "good works" performed "in His name." Domestic in inclination, averse to display, sweet and simple in her manners, she devoted her gifts and graces to her home and Church. And so noiselessly were the countless threads of deeds and words that made up her character woven together, that we only realized the continuous service she rendered when death finished the work; but in the light streaming through the gates ajar we now see the beauty of the life and realize the power for good she exercised in the Church and city.

Greatly interested in the property of the Church, she was one of the promoters of the "Mite Society" and other agencies employed to free the First Church of debt. An intelligent supporter of Christian missions, she identified herself with the Woman's Missionary Society at its formation and as Corresponding Secretary and in other relations had much to do with the Auxillary's growth and success.

A few days before her death she requested Mr. Gardiner to make her a life-member of the Society and also forward the President the amount of her usual Easter offering. He at once hastened to fulfill her desire in this as in all other matters affecting her happiness and work. Recalling the regular meeting of the Auxiliary she said to a dear friend, "give the members my dying earthly love and undying heavenly love." This was her farewell message.

During her short, severe illness, patience had indeed its perfect work. There was unquestioning submission to the Divine will. At all times her sick room was a place of sweetness and light, of cheerfulness and glad resignation of rejoicing in the Holy Spirit with true Christian fortitude. And as the end drew near we were greatly comforted by her deepening consecration and full committal into the hands of God. Walking through the valley she feared no evil. Her one absorbing desire was to meet her dear friends in heaven, and from the margin of the river she sent messages, beautiful and tender, to those she loved so well - her aged father, sisters and brother. After this her life gradually ebbed away. As the grey dawn of the morning was stealing gently in, the great silence of the death-moment came, "she fell asleep in Jesus," and through the gates of the morning, entered the rest that remains for the people of God. Therefore her friends have no dirge to chant, and if any tokens of feeling were exhibited, it would be that of grateful triumphant – the symbol of the white-robed throng, the palm branch emblem of the secured victory. So thin the ranks on this side the flood. So swell the hosts above.

The pure life and triumphant death bear to the bereaved the comfort that is needed. Yet in behalf of all who sympathize with the sorrowing husband and friends, I write this word of consolation - for I would be as one who "comforteth the mourner." The teaching of Scripture and the "consolation of Christ" are that our departed friends have entered upon an enlarged and happier state, and that one day the weeping bereaved shall join the happy departed in that land where the labors, cares, and limitations of this earthly pilgrimage shall terminate in the undisturbed tranquility and the perfect blessedness "of the presence where there is joy, and the right hand where there are pleasures forever more. Wherefore comfort one another with these words.

Charles married a third time, to a lady called Minnie, who was a talented vocalist. [No more information available]

In the Wednesday, October 28, 1914 edition of the Summerside *Journal Pioneer* the following article was published: "C. C. Gardiner and wife who spent the summer in Charlottetown, crossed by the *Empress* a few days ago on return to their home in Los Angeles, California. They were accompanied as far as Point Duchene by Miss Eva McNeil of Summerside."

1.34 Mary Sophia Gardiner (6, Mary 5, Major 4, Thomas 3, Clement 2, Stephen 1), born July 18, 1837; died April 24, 1920. Mary was unmarried. Her obituary appeared in the Summerside paper on April 24, 1920:

Late Miss Gardiner

The death occurred on Saturday morning of Miss Mary Gardiner, for many years a resident of Summerside, at the age of 86 years. The deceased who had succumbed to an illness of some months had been residing with Miss Eva McNeill, Summer Street. [Eva was Mary's sister Adelaide's daughter.] She leaves one sister, Mrs. (Dr.) Price [Catherine] in the United States, and one brother, Charles, in Charlottetown. The funeral took place this afternoon (Tuesday) to the People's Cemetery. Rev. H. C. Rice officiated.

1.35 Eliza Jane Gardiner (6, Mary 5, Major 4, Thomas 3, Clement 2, Stephen 1), born August 30, 1839 in Bedeque. On October 14, 1864 Eliza Jane married James Mark Butcher, who was baptized on January 3, 1839. James is the son of the Charlottetown furniture and cabinet maker, Mark Butcher, the husband of Catherine Pope Hooper, Elisha's daughter. Eliza Jane and James moved to Denver, Colorado. [No further information is available]

1.36 Catherine Gardiner (6, Mary 5, Major 4, Thomas 3, Clement 2, Stephen 1), born February 20, 1842, married J. E. Price, M.D. of Summerside on November 20, 1868. Just after they moved to Hartford, CT., about November 1891, a newly married couple, David McMurdo and Bertha Walker McMurdo, moved into the home recently vacated by Dr. and Mrs. Price. They were still living in the United States when Catherine's sister, Mary, died in 1920.

1.37 Sarah Charlotte Gardiner (6, Mary 5, Major 4, Thomas 3, Clement 2, Stephen 1), born May 3, 1843; died December 9, 1847 at age 4 ½, buried in Lower Bedeque Cemetery.
1.38 Charlotte Elizabeth Gardiner (6, Mary 5, Major 4, Thomas 3, Clement 2, Stephen 1) [No information available, except that her grave is in the Lower Bedeque Cemetery]

2.0 Thomas Hooper (5, Major 4, Thomas 3, Clement 2, Stephen 1), born in 1804 in Lower Bedeque. Thomas was a tavern keeper by Hooper's Corner in Centreville. This home is now in excellent repair and condition and occupied and owned (1998) by Anthony and Claire Lockhart. On January 14, 1832 Thomas married Maria Waitsill Gardiner (the sister of John Rhodes Gardiner, husband of Mary Hooper), born on April 7, 1806 to John Gardiner and Eunice Haszard. She died on December 14, 1878. The *Summerside Journal* of December 26, 1878 lists the death at Lot 14 of Maria Gardiner Hooper, in her 73rd year, the wife of Thomas Hooper. Thomas died on December 19, 1879. In their later years they lived in Birch Hill, P.E.I. From the early 1830s until the 1850s Thomas Hooper's licensed Inn at Centreville provided bed, board, and alcoholic refreshment for all travellers. It seemed at that time that Bedeque had its share of drinking and sometimes it would seem almost more than its quota of taverns.[24] The children of Thomas and Maria, all born at Bedeque (surname Hooper, sixth generation) were:

2.1 Sarah Sophia Hooper (6, Thomas 5, Major 4, Thomas 3, Clement 2, Stephen 1), born March 12, 1834 in Bedeque; married Archibald MacIntosh on January 16, 1862 with John Hooper [he is not my husband, Alden's, great-grandfather as he died in 1854, but he *might* be the John C. Hooper whose grave is beside Major's in the North Bedeque Cemetery] as the witness and Henry Birchfield Swabey as the officiating minister,[25] died in 1899, in Charlottetown.

Archibald was born in 1818, the son of John MacIntosh and Barbara Campbell. "Archie" died on April 28, 1901 in Stanley Bridge, P.E.I. Archibald was a farmer and a hotel keeper. He and Sarah Sophia lived in Stanley Bridge.

2.2 Sarah Hooper (6, Thomas 5, Major 4, Thomas 3, Clement 2, Stephen 1), born November 8, 1835 [No further information available]

2.3 Catherine Hooper (6, Thomas 5, Major 4, Thomas 3, Clement 2, Stephen 1), born August 30, 1836 in Bedeque; married Archibald Campbell, born in Lot 16 in 1832, the son of Donald Campbell and Jane MacGregor; died in Lot 16 in 1884. He was a farmer in Lot 16. Catherine and Archibald had no children. Catherine died in Lot 16 in 1884.

2.4 Major Gardiner Hooper (6, Thomas 5, Major 4, Thomas 3, Clement 2, Stephen 1), born December 8, 1837 in Bedeque; married Pocahontas Millan, who was born on June 15, 1847, the daughter of J.B. Millan, on February 21, 1870 in Lancaster, Iowa. Major died on January 22, 1925 in Chariton, Iowa. Pocahontas died on March 9, 1911 in Chariton, Iowa. They had four sons (seventh generation, surname Hooper).

2.5 John Gardiner Hooper (6, Thomas 5, Major 4, Thomas 3, Clement 2, Stephen 1, born March 8, 1841. [No further information]

2.6 Ann Matilda Hooper (6, Thomas 5, Major 4, Thomas 3, Clement 2, Stephen 1), born May 2, 1844 in Bedeque; married Andrew Campbell on April 19, 1865; died on May 12, 1897 in Spokane, Washington, U.S.A. They had 10 children (seventh generation). Ann and Andrew's residence was in Spokane, Washington, U.S.A.

2.7 Charles Haszard Hooper (6, Thomas 5, Major 4, Thomas 3, Clement 2, Stephen 1), born August 29, 1845 in Bedeque; married Christina Ann Birch, on January 6, 1866; died on February 14, 1920 in Schuyler, Nebraska, U.S.A. Christina was born on March 25, 1841 in Port Hill, P.E.I., the daughter of Prussia Birch and Margaret Montgomery. Christina died on April 14, 1928 in Schuyler, Nebraska.

Charles was a farmer and a rancher. He and Christina had eight children (seventh generation). Not only did Christina leave Prince Edward Island and go west, but her brother, John, did as well, as indicated in his obituary from a P.E.I. newspaper:

Islander Dead

The death took place on October 10th [1926] at the residence of his son, Herbert W., Bentley, Alta., of John Birch at the age of 76 years and 6 months [John and two sons, Herbert and Ted (Theodore) operated a blacksmith shop at Ross's Corner in North Bedeque until they sold it in 1896 when the family left to seek their fortunes in Alberta. John lived with his son, Herb, in Bentley and Charlie went to Edmonton to be a tailor]. Deceased was born at Port Hill, P.E.Island. He left there about thirty-five years ago for Boston, U.S.A. where he had resided until three years and six months ago when he removed to Alberta. He leaves to mourn one daughter and four sons: Miss Margaret I. [named for her grandmother, probably Margaret Montgomery Birch, relationship to Ann Hooper Montgomery not known] ; Herbert W. of Bentley, Alta; Brandford L. of Los Angeles, CA; Theodore W. of Lamont, Alta; and Charles S. of Edmonton, Alta. Also one sister Mrs. Charles Hooper of Schuyler, Nebraska. The deceased was laid to rest in the Bentley Cemetery. The pall bearers were N. E. Carruthers, R. L. Ramsay, D. M Reeves, R. R. Hucheson, J. G. Blish, and Wm. Weise. The first three named were formerly natives of P. E. Island.

2.8 Colin MacLennon Hooper (6, Thomas 5, Major 4, Thomas 3, Clement 2, Stephen 1), born March 2, 1848 in Centreville Bedeque; married Mary Agnes Connally on January 6, 1866; died on April 7, 1926 in Lincoln, Nebraska, U.S.A. Mary Agnes was born on March 27, 1850 in Nova Scotia to John Connally and his wife, Anne [surname unknown], and died on October 25, 1935 in Nebraska. Colin and Mary Agnes had four children (seventh generation).

2.9 Major Hooper (6, Thomas 5, Major 4, Thomas 3, Clement 2, Stephen 1) I found this baptismal date and name of which I am not certain. I will list it here anyway. Baptismal date, Nov. 27, 1844 at Bedeque Church; father Thomas (Book 1, page 10), mother Maria. [Might he be the 6th child, or a twin with Ann Matilda, born on May 2, 1844. Or is he the fourth child who married Pocahontas and who may have been baptized when he was almost eigth years old? No further information]

5.0 Ann, called Nancy, Hooper (5, Major 4, Thomas 3, Clement 2, Stephen 1), born about 1806 in Lower Bedeque; married James A. Clark on February 20 (or March 11), 1830 [Nancy and Harriet, her sister, married brothers with the surname Clark]; James was born on June 19, 1805 at North Bedeque and baptized on November 27, 1805; he was the son of William Clark and Elizabeth Crosby. He was a farmer/surveyor in North Bedeque. After Nancy's death, James married, second, Amy Ann Linkletter; they had one daughter, Mary Ann, (born in 1847, died on January 7, 1861, age 14), who would not be a Hooper relative. After James's death, Amy married second John Townsend. Nancy and James's children (surname Clark, sixth generation) are as follows:

5.1 Sarah Clark (6, Nancy 5, Major 4, Thomas 3, Clement 2, Stephen 1), born in 1838 at North Bedeque; married Arthur Craig, who was born on August 23, 1833 in Bedeque, the first child of John Craig and his second wife, Elizabeth Lee Owen. Sarah and Arthur lived in Bedeque where he was probably a farmer. She died on January 12, 1861. There were no children. [I have no information on a death date for Arthur Craig, but Muriel Hooper has notes about a second marriage for Sarah to Wesley Arthur Madison, who died on August 5, 1873. After Sarah Clark Craig's death, apparently Wesley married (ii) another Sarah, Sarah Green, daughter of Charles Green of Tignish, formerly of St. Eleanors. She died on December 4, 1872 at Springfield, MA]

5.2 No information available

5.3 Ann Clark, called Nancy (6, Nancy 5, Major 4, Thomas 3, Clement 2, Stephen 1), born January 1, 1842 at North Bedeque and died on September 26, 1892 at Cape Traverse, P.E.I. She married Nelson Clark, who was born on March 23, 1842, the son of Isaac Clark and Mary Manson; they were married on January 28, 1865; she died on November 28, 1904 at Cape Traverse. He married (ii) Charlotte Jane Rowe, who died in 1907. He was a farmer. Nancy and Nelson had three boys and two girls (seventh generation).

5.4 a son; no information available

6.0 John Keir Hooper (5, Major 4, Thomas 3, Clement 2, Stephen 1) was named for the Princetown Presbyterian clergyman, the "eloquent preacher and learned graduate of Glasgow University," the Rev. John Keir, who was in Malpeque in April, 1852. [Jane, John's wife, was probably a Presbyterian before her marriage] Apparently there was no resemblance between the two men other than the name, from what I have read! John was born in 1809; on February 20, 1851 when he was 41, he married Jane Walker, aged 29 or 30, the second child and second daughter of John Walker (1795 - 1882) and Jane Davidson Weir (1789 - 1889) of New Annan. [John Walker was the son of David Walker, born January 25, 1762 in Annandale, Scotland and died in 1845 in New Annan, P.E.I. and Margaret Hetherington, born in Scotland]. The record states, "John Hooper, bachelor, and Jane Walker, spinster, married February 20, 1851 by license. Witnesses: Norman Ramsay and Helen Patterson. Married by Rev. Robert S. Patterson, minister; recorded June 5, 1851."[27] John Keir died on October 24, 1854 [according to Muriel Blanchard, "in his wagon in his barn, drunk"].

It is interesting to me that the second child, Jane, and the sixth child, John, both married Hoopers. Jane Walker and John Walker were born six years apart. [Those interested in the Walker genealogy may refer to the research done by Harold Cairns of Stanley Bridge, P.E.I.]

John Keir was a farmer who had a 100 acre farm in North Carleton. The house and property were sold several times in the intervening years. It was once known (after John Keir's and then his son Major's deaths) as the Hudson Lowther farm. In the summer of 1998 it was sold to Fulton Hamill of Searleton who lives up the road from the property. For many years prior to 1998 the VanVliets had owned the house and property. About 6 years ago, the big barn, which I'm sure at least Major, John's son, used and perhaps John did, too, collapsed from lack of maintenance. In 1998 the property would have been more valuable than the house which was in a state of disrepair, but it is good to know that Alden's relatives worked, played, and wandered through this house which is still standing. The house is now being

rebuilt and repaired (1999) by a new owner from Borden-Carleton. One summer day this writer asked the carpenter for the privilege of looking through the inside of the house as it was where my mother-in-law was raised. At the back of the house there was a kind of attached shed where the milk might have been kept cool. The large eat-in kitchen would have been big enough for the growing family. The living room was toward the front of the house. From it a staircase went to the three bedrooms upstairs all of which were being rebuilt. The newell posts going up the stairs were beautiful and presumably were going to be retained.

I believe that Mr. Hamill has kept some property for his use. John and Jane's three children (surname Hooper, sixth generation) were:

6.1 Adella Jane Hooper (6, John 5, Major 4, Thomas 3, Clement 2, Stephen 1), born 1852; married Christopher Lowther (1850 – October 3, 1923); died on Feb. 1, 1936, buried at Searletown Cemetery. Their tombstone reads, "Asleep in Jesus, blessed sleep from which none ever wake to weep." In September 1999, Gladys Henderson, Adella's granddaughter, told me that her grandmother was blind for a long time before she died, perhaps five years. In those days (she died in 1936 when Gladys was about 22), they called the cause of the blindness "a nerve disease." I wonder if it was macular degeneration, which Dorothy Adella MacKenzie, another granddaughter, has.

In the summer of 2002 Dorothy gave me a description of her grandparents. She said that her grandmother was a small woman with white hair. She loved to have her grandchildren comb her long hair while she sat in a rocking chair. Christopher, she said, was a big man with broad shoulders, side-burns and a moustache. He and Adella lived in "The Willows," a beautiful home in Searletown. In time their son Major and his wife Addie lived in the "big house" and built an addition in the back. Dot said that the dining room was beautiful, with a white linen cloth on the table and big linen napkins. Dot had one of those napkins until she moved from her home in Kensington to Andrews Lodge two years ago. Christopher had 100 acres by

Hooper's Mill (where the home is located) and 100 acres across the road. He hired help. He had arthritis in his fingers and back. He raised hens, chickens, cows, pigs, and horses. Dot said that he had "high thinking and simple living!"

Gladys, Dot's cousin, and another granddaughter, told me that at a later time the addition that was put on the back of the house was moved to Carleton and is now a house nearly opposite Bernice Harper's home (2001).

6.2 Major Charles Hooper (6, John 5, Major 4, Thomas 3, Clement 2, Stephen 1) [notice the repeat of names from generation to generation] was born in 1853 [baptismal name was Elijah Charles]. The 1881 census listed him, age 28, and Sarah [his sister] age 25, as living on the farm. His mother had been remarried for several years and moved to Albany, P.E.I. with her second husband, Charles Crossman. Major was recorded as a farmer, and a Methodist. He married Mary Ann MacDonald on November 25, 1886 of North Carleton [probably McDonald's Point], P.E.I. [Mr. Arnold McGrath, who lived across from the Seven Mile Bay Church, said that her family was from the Brook Road, the first road, unpaved, going west after the church. One turns left (south) on that road, goes down perhaps ½ mile to a junction in the road, and Mary Ann's family is supposed to have lived near the northwest corner of that junction [1991 interview]. Major died in 1914, at age 61. Their marriage certificate, which was copied for me, is in the Coles Building, 4th floor, Charlottetown, P.E.I. [PARO - Public Archives and Records Office for Prince Edward Island]. They were married by Finlay McNeill, Esq., Justice of the Peace, in Summerside. David Stewart was the bondsman. The witnesses were David Stewart, Mrs. David Stewart, William Gould, Mrs. William Gould, and Mrs. McKinnon. I have a copy of the marriage license of Major and Mary Ann, as follows:[28]

BY HIS HONOR THE HONORABLE ANDREW ARCHIBALD MACDONALD, Lieutenant Governor of the Province of Prince Edward Island. Major C. Hooper of North Carleton, Lot 27 (Bachelor) and Mary Ann McDonald of North Carleton Lot 27 (Spinster). **Whereas**, it hath been signified unto us that you have resolved to

proceed to the solemnization of true and lawful Matrimony, and are desirous to have the same solemnized without proclamation of Banns, and we being willing that these your good intentions shall take effect, and under and by virtue of an Act of the General Assembly of the said Island, made and passed in the second year of the reign of His late Majesty King William the Fourth, intitled "An Act to confirm and render valid certain Marriages heretofore solemnized within this Island, and also to declare by whom and in what manner Marriages shall be celebrated in future, and to provide for the public registry of the same," do hereby grant this our License and Faculty, as well to you the parties contracting as to *Finlay McNeill, Esquire* in the said Island, to solemnize the said Marriage openly, without publishing Banns; Provided there shall hereafter appear no lawful impediment, by reason of consanguinity, affinity, or any other cause whatever, and if in case hereafter appear any such impediment, then these presents shall be void and of no effect in law, inhibiting you the said *Finlay McNeill, Esquire* if any of the premises come to your knowledge, from proceeding to the celebration of the Marriage. *Given under my hand and Seal, at Charlottetown, this 25th day of November in the year of our Lord One Thousand Eight Hundred and Eighty-six. By Command, Arthur Newbery, Assistant Provincial Secretary. Dominion of Canada*, Province of PRINCE EDWARD ISLAND, *A. A. Macdonald, LIEUTENANT GOVERNOR William T. Hunt, Deputy Probationary, Prince County.* I hereby certify that the within named parties Major C. Hooper and Mary Ann McDonald were married by me this 25th November, 1886, at Summerside in the presence of David Stewart, Mrs. David Stewart, William Gould, Mrs. William Gould, and Mrs. Capt John McKinnon. Finlay McNeill, J. P. Date of License Nov. 25th, 1886 Date of Celebration Nov. 25, 1886. Filed May 3rd, 1887

W. R. Underhay, of 27 Hawthorne Avenue, Charlottetown, wrote to Alden on September 8, 1970 in response to Alden's inquiry into the name of Mary Ann's mother. He obviously [from his letter] had done some research. He says that John McDonald was the father of Mary Ann and Julia McKinnon was her mother. Mary Ann was born on November 27, 1864 and baptized on May 2, 1865. He continues: "It is not clear where Mary Ann McDonald was born, but H. M. Creek is given after the name of parents so I presume this was the location of the home." Just now [April 3, 2000] do I notice, interestingly, that a Mrs. McKinnon and Mrs. Capt. John McKinnon [no doubt the same person] were witnesses to the marriage.

The Federal Census of 1891 reveals that Major Hooper was Canadian Presbyterian [10 years earlier he was listed as Methodist], that his wife was of the Church of Scotland, and that they could both read and write. Herman Walker, a domestic, age 12, was living with them. He also could read and write. One wonders if Herman was a relative of Major's mother, Jane Walker Hooper Crossman. The two children were Jane, age 3, and Melvina, age 1.

Mary Ann, born c.1864, died of the effects of measles on Dec. 11, 1905. The *Summerside Journal* ran her obituary on page 8 in the December 20, 1905 issue as follows:

The death occurred on Monday, Dec. 11, 1905 of Mrs. Major Hooper, Searletown, who passed away very suddenly at the age of 42 years [actually, she was only 40 or 41 years old]. The deceased leaves a husband, three daughters, and two sons to mourn the loss of a kind wife and loving mother. She died as she lived: a true Christian. Death had no terror for her; she bid her family farewell and passed out as one having finished a race. With the sorrowing husband and children, the *Journal* joins in sympathy.

Mr. Fred MacQuarrie had told me nearly 30 years ago that his sister, Mary, had gone to take care of the Hoopers who had the measles (perhaps others in the family were also sick with the same disease). Anyway, he said that she had shaken rugs out the door, got the measles, and died of the after-effects. I think that the shaking of the rugs was an incidental thing; the point was that she was in contact with the person/people who had a communicable disease and caught it. In 1999 I was talking with Viola Taylor about her Aunt Mary. She *did* know that her death was caused by the complications of measles (perhaps pneumonia?) at age 21, but she *did not* know that she got measles from the Hoopers. The MacQuarries and the Hoopers were neighbors, with just one farm between the properties; the MacQuarries were closer to Searletown on the other side of the road.

Another article in the Wednesday, Dec. 13, 1905, edition of the same newspaper bears out the verbal account of Ada Hooper Neal, Alden's mother, of the terrible snowstorm surrounding the time of her mother's death. She described it as being "the dead of winter"

when her mother died. Ada, the fourth of five children, was only 9 years old:

The first real snow storm of the winter came on Sunday, December 10. During the day a northeast blizzard raged, turning to rain about dark, but in a few hours was followed by another storm which continued throughout the night. The great storm in the west completely blocked the roads Sunday night, and they are not much more opened up yet. It was the worst "Beginner" the oldest inhabitant remembers.

6.3 Sarah Katherine Hooper (6, John 5, Major 4, Thomas 3, Clement 2, Stephen 1), was probably born in 1855, a few months after her father, John Keir, died. Very little is known of Sarah's childhood other than that she grew up in the house of her father on the Searletown Road in North Carleton. Sarah married James Edwin Allen, bachelor, on April 8, 1886, with the Rev. William Scott, minister of the Presbyterian Church in North Bedeque, officiating. The witnesses were Major Craig [born 1841] and Major Hooper, obviously relatives of Sarah.[29] After Sarah's marriage to James Edwin Allen from New Brunswick, her brother, Major, who had the 100 acre farm of his father, gave them two acres adjacent to his acreage on the east on which to build a house. Ed Allen, a wheelwright, built the house for his wife where they raised their five children.

In the 1891 census James E. Allen was listed as age 25, born in New Brunswick, as was his father and mother, a Methodist, a farmer and carriage builder. The report said that he employed an average number of 18 hands during the year. Sarah was 33 years old, born on P.E.I., a Canadian Presbyterian, and they could both read and write. The children were Keir, age 5, Reuben, age 2; and James E. age 1. [I have no child James E. in the genealogical history for this family. The next child would be Bert or Lila. It is probably an error of the census enumerator.]

When the children were small (I believe Vera, the youngest, was about 4 years old) Sarah's husband left his family and returned to Nova Scotia. He did not support them. Sarah died on November 26, 1921. The inscription on her tombstone in the Searletown Cemetery

reads, "A tender mother and a faithful friend." Thelma Clark, her granddaughter, described her this way: "She had hair as black as a crow. She had arthritis so badly that she was in a chair all day. When she was moved from the chair to her bed, it was very, very painful. Lila [her daughter who had returned from Massachusetts to care for her] put a white apron on her every day. Thelma's father [Sarah's son Rube in Nova Scotia who had gone to work when he was about 12 years old] sent $50.00 a month to care for them."

I am in possession of some recollections, compliments of Muriel Hooper Blanchard, apparently quoted verbatim, on two already mentioned Hoopers, the wife of Thomas, the innkeeper of Centreville Bedeque, and John Keir. In September 1952, apparently Rufus Bagnall was reminiscing. Rufus Gordon Bagnall was a brother to Bessie Bagnall, who married Edward Hooper. Rufus was born on November 16, 1866 and married Jane MacFarlane.[30] Acccording to the stone at the Baptist Cemetery in Central Bedeque, Rufus was born on Nov. 16, 1855 and died on January 18, 1953, which would make him 98 at death! Rufus reminisced:

> I am 87 next month. [This quote must have been about 1942, but neither of the above birth dates coincides with the age that he gave] I knew old Auntie Hooper [Maria Waitsill Gardiner, the wife of Thomas who ran the tavern]. Yes, she sold rum one time ... lived here at Centreville. On election days they carried it out in a bucket, put a tin mug nearby and said, "Go to it!" I didn't know Thomas, but we always called her "Auntie Hooper." [According to Mr. Bagnall, "all the Gardiners were very high-tempered men who thought themselves something]. I've been reading lately of Richard Gardiner in Lot 16 who has lived 70 years with one woman... a world's record, they say! I think she [Maria Gardiner Hooper] would be buried in North Bedeque. I remember her visiting at our place... an aunt to father. Her son, Major Hooper [who married Pocahontas], lived out in Lot 16 or somewhere. That's where Auntie Hooper lived her last days [the dates do not coincide, but Rufus' memory may have been faulty]... she may be buried there. They were very poor.
>
> The family, one was Mrs. MacIntosh. I can't remember her name. [I'm sure he meant Sarah Sophia, Thomas and Maria's first child and the wife of Archibald MacIntosh] She kinda lost her head at times, go queer... There was Ann Matilda [6th child of Thomas and Maria]... two boys went out to the western states [Charles

Haszard and Colin MacLennon went to Nebraska]. In the MacIntosh family there were two girls. Alice was one. Aw, some of them Hoopers drank a lot. Artemas Hooper, he's buried down in the Baptist cemetery, used to say, "I would have been just as bad as any of them only I was so fond of the cents!"

One Hooper (his son lived on Hudson Lowther's place) came home dead drunk one night. They found him next morning in the carriage, not dead drunk, but dead. [He is referring to John Keir, Alden's great-grandfather!]

The above-mentioned John Hooper, one of the old men, was so given to drink that his family tried to keep it from him. One day he got a bottle when they were away and someone came into the house to find him sucking a nearly empty bottle and talking to himself, "Now, John, if your mother's millk was as good as that, you'd be sucking yet!"

I heard from a relative that John's death was caused by a hunting accident, but Muriel Hooper Blanchard, my great and accurate source of genealogical information, says that he died in the barn in his wagon, drunk, of a heart attack and was found in the morning! She says that he was a poor farmer according to family tradition. John is buried in the Presbyterian Cemetery in North Bedeque. His stone reads, "In loving memory of John K. Hooper, died Oct. 24, 1854 AET 45 years" Next to his grave is the grave of John C. Hooper. We have no idea who John C. is; the decoration on his stone is like a beautiful tree, but there is no date to help us to decipher his background.

Poor dear Jane Walker Hooper had a toddler, an infant, and a third in utero with no means of support and a hundred acre farm! According to the 1861 census, she had a 12-year-old farmhand living with her by the surname of Walker, perhaps a nephew or a much younger brother to help with the chores. In time she married Charles Crossman (1831-1896) from New Brunswick. The records at the Public Archives and Records Office in Charlottetown show that he had had a son John, born in New Brunswick, by a first marriage.

According to family tradition, Jane and Charles moved out of the North Carleton farm when Major was old enough to run it, which Gladys Henderson speculates might be when he was about age 16, c.1869. Jane and Charles Crossman moved to a farm in Albany. Now

this farm is on route 1 or 1A going east toward Tryon on the left-hand side of the road across the street from the house that has a large display of lawn ornaments in the yard (1999). Gladys thinks that originally the Crossman property probably had 100 acres. There are still large fields behind the house and beyond the house on the Tryon side. Gladys said that at the top of the hill there used to be a Baptist chapel which perhaps Jane and Charles attended.

I am pursuing information about Jane Walker Hooper Crossman and Charles Crossman's family, not because they are Hooper blood relatives, but because of the Walker connection which Harold Cairns is working on (2000). In the census of 1881 the Crossman family of Lot 28 (Albany) is listed as follows: Charles Crossman, age 50, born P.E.I.; Jane Crossman, age 60, born P.E.I.; John Crossman, age 25, born New Brunswick; Eliza Crossman, age 16, born P.E.I. Charles was a farmer and was listed as Baptist. The 1880 *Meacham Atlas* has Charles Crossman at Bedeque Road, Albany, a farmer, born P.E.I. in 1831 (as opposed to being born in New Brunswick). Charles and Jane had one daughter, Eliza Ann Crossman, who married Richard Large [buried in the cemetery at the People's Church (United) in Tryon, site 313].

Liza and Richard had 9 children [surname Large]. Gladys was not sure of the order of all of them: Wilmot, Cleve (Cleveland), Reuben, Urbille (or Orville?), Jane (the oldest girl), Josie, Florence (called Flossie), Aletha (called Letha), the youngest daughter, and Eldon, the youngest child. Here is what she told me about them: Flossie didn't marry; Jane was "different," and a great cook. She married a Kennedy from up west and was the child who was with Liza, her mother, when Liza died of cancer of the stomach. Gladys had taken us to meet Letha when we first came in 1970. Letha, who seemed like an old lady to me then, lived in Crapaud on the south side of route 1 (or 1A). Raspberry bushes were in the back of her property. Aletha had married Arthur Simmons; they had a daughter Glenda who married Wendell [surname not known]and lived in Charlottetown. Aletha probably had Alzheimer's disease and died in a manor before 1985.

Alder Large, Gladys' second cousin, is the son of Reuben, the only child of Reuben and Ada Moase. Reuben Large owned 125 acres along the Wilmot River just east of the Blueshank Road, extending across Taylor Road.[31] Alder married Janet Sinclair, a first cousin to Gladys [Janet died in Summerside in late May 2000 at Andrews Lodge where she was a room-mate of Dot MacKenzie]. Alder and Janet have one daughter Pauline who is married to Gregory Deighan (pronounced Deean), a Progressive Conservative member of the provincial legislature for P.E.I. Pauline's father, Alder, is a strong Liberal. Alder and Janet, who celebrated their 60th wedding anniversary in 1999, lived in Wilmot. The Sinclairs were all Liberals in the federal parliament in Ottawa.

Orville, of rural route Albany, married Edna Simmons and had two children, Wyman and Elma. He had 98 acres in Lot 28 bordering the Bedeque Road.[32] Wilmot of Albany married Hazel Simmons. He was a school trustee. School trustees were apparently the people who hired and fired teachers and custodians, and were responsible for the maintenance of the buildings; they also decided what children would be suspended. In other words, the position carried a measure of responsibility. Wilmot owned 100 acres in Albany, Lot 27 at the junction of Lot 28, Carleton.[33] Wilmot and Hazel had a child, Elworth.[34] Josie Large (1891 – 1958) married Harry Osborne Curtis (born Dec. 19, 1890) from Wilmot Valley. They had one daughter, Jean, who married a Miller; she died and he remarried. Jane Walker Hooper Crossman died around 1889; I have not been able to find the accurate date nor do I know where she is buried.

Charles Crossman was married a third time to Mary Lefurgey Curtis (Mrs. William Curtis) of Wilmot. The marriage license was issued March 15, 1892.[35] One wonders if she was related to Josie Large's husband, Harry Curtis. Charles Crossman died about 1896. His will, dated November 3, 1892, gave his wife, Mary, two cows and a buggy; daughter Eliza (now Mrs. Large) her mother's bed, "which I now use [and] bedding. My three daughters by previous

marriage [were they wife #1's children?]: Maria, Mary Lovenia, Adelaide, my son John (born in New Brunswick) the farm."[36] [It would appear that Liza and wife #3 did not do nearly as well as son John and three daughters by a previous marriage!]

There was also a Charles Crossman whose post office address was Carleton. He owned 70 acres inland from Traverse Cove; his post office address was Carleton. His wife's name was Ada Gould, and their children were Edwin and Willa.[37]

1.7 Major Hooper, Jr (5, Major 4, Thomas 3, Clement 2, Stephen 1) was born in 1811 in Lower Bedeque. On March 26, 1834 he married Sarah Green, the daughter of Samuel Green and Elizabeth Cox of St. Eleanor's. They resided in St. Eleanor's until the 1850s when they moved to Portsmouth, N.H. where Major died on March 14, 1861. In the April 5, 1861 edition of *The Islander* (page 5) his death notice was published as follows: "At Portsmouth, New Hampshire, on the 14th March, Major Hooper, Esquire, aged 50, formerly of Bedeque, Prince Edward Island."[38] Major and Sarah had the following four children (sixth generation, surname Hooper):

1.71 **Samuel G. Hooper** (6, Major Jr. 5, Major 4, Thomas 3, Clement 2, Stephen 1)
1.72 **Catherine Hooper** (6, Major Jr. 5, Major 4, Thomas 3, Clement 2, Stephen 1)
1.73 Infant daughter
1.74 **Isaac ? Hooper** (6, Major Jr. 5, Major 4, Thomas 3, Clement 2, Stephen 1)

In October 2002, Alden and I stopped at the old cemetery in Portsmouth, N.H., but the cemetery is so big that we could never find graves unescorted. We found the address of the caretaker whom we were told would know where all the graves were. Alas, he was not at home. He did not respond to a letter of inquiry written after we returned home.

1.8 Sarah Hooper, called Sally (5, Major 4, Thomas 3, Clement 2, Stephen 1) was born on August 11, 1812 in Lower Bedeque. On February 8, 1838, she married Jesse Wright, the son of Nathaniel Wright and Ann "Nancy" Lord. Sally died in Centreville Bedeque in 1879. Jesse (April 11, 1808 - July 17, 1894) was a grist miller/farmer. In 1880 his business was listed as "and Son." Jesse called his farm "Castalia Grove." It extended from the mill to the main road, called Main Street, in the village of Centreville Bedeque. Doris Haslam remarked in her book, *The Wrights of Bedeque*: "To look at the property now (1976) one would never dream that Castalia Grove was once beautifully situated amidst tall ornamental trees surrounded by luxuriant gardens, a hospitable home housing three generations. The house is now owned by Austin Gaudet."[39] Haslam continued: "On January 27, 1866, Jesse Wright (who owned the land from the Mill Road to the main road in Centreville) sold them [apparently referring to his brother Lorenzo et al] the corner lot directly opposite the present day Bowness store (1976), on which they built a store. At that time Lorenzo and Mary were living next to the store in "Centreville House," a former tavern run by Thomas Hooper.[40]

Sarah (Sally), the wife of Jesse, died on December 3, 1879 in Centreville Bedeque where they lived. Sally is the only early relative of whom I have a picture. Ada Neal, Alden's mother, looked like her great aunt Sally! Sally was a half-sister to Martha Hooper, first wife of Jesse's brother Stephen. Sally was a granddaughter not only of Thomas Hooper, Loyalist, but also of the Rev. John Urquhart, the first Presbyterian minister to settle on the Island. In the year 1800 the Rev. John Urquhart and his wife, Margaret Milligan, and their family arrived in Prince Edward Island from the U.S.A. He was originally from Scotland, a minister of the Kirk of Scotland. His wife was believed to have been a relative of John Quincy Adams, 6th president of the United States. The Reverend Urquhart was the minister in Princetown (Malpeque) and took under his charge not only the Presbyterians of that community, but also of New London, Bedeque, and the west side of Richmond Bay. In 1802 he moved to Miramichi, N.B. Sometime later when crossing the river in a canoe

which upset, he was either drowned or died afterwards from the effects of the accident.[41] He is cited, however, as living when his son-in-law's (Major's) daughter Eliza (by his first wife, Ann) died from the effects of a fire in Miramichi in 1825. Doris Haslam stated in *The Wrights of Bedeque*:

> Jesse and Sally lived on part of his father's original grant on the West Branch of the Dunk River where Nathaniel had erected a grist and saw mill. When he died Jesse became full owner of the grist mill. Nathaniel's will reads: "I give and bequeath to my dear son Jesse the corn mill and fifty acres of land I hold by a (?) from the agent of Hon. Robert Gordon above the said mill, provided nevertheless, that all my children shall have their grain ground toll free, in case they assist in repairing the mill dam at any time it requires repairing, and the mill when any extra ordinary accident may occur to damage the said mill, as they have heretofore done on such occasions. According to the 1841 census Jesse had increased his acreage to one hundred acres held in fee simple. He was primarily a farmer hiring a miller who understood milling oats and wheat. Liberal wages were promised for soberness and industry. In the early days the grist was taken to the mill on horseback. One of the Wrights, Nathaniel or Jesse, had a reputation of taking heavy toll for grinding."[42]

For many years Jesse was leader of a Methodist class which met every Sunday morning after service in the chapel. He was the last of his generation (grandchild of William Wright, Loyalist) to pass away. Sally and Jesse had two sons and five daughters (surname Wright, sixth generation) all born in Centreville Bedeque:

1.81 Martha Ann Wright (6, Sally 5, Major 4, Thomas 3, Clement 2, Stephen 1), born November 29, 1838; married Charles Wesley Strong [a Methodist!], son of the Rev. John Bass and Elizabeth (Gambee) Strong, in 1861; died on May 17, 1870 in Summerside, P.E.I. Charles was born on June 2, 1829 in Saint John, N. B. and died on May 19, 1919 in Summerside. Doris Haslam stated, in *The Wrights of Bedeque*, "Martha did not lack the blessing of the church on her marriage to Charles, for ministers of three denominations helped perform the ceremony." According to the *Islander* for May 10, 1861: "At Castalia Grove on Thursday 2nd May by Rev. John B. Strong,

assisted by Rev. Messers Prince, Patterson and Ross, Mr. Charles W. Strong, merchant, to Martha A., daughter of Jesse Wright, Esq., all of Bedeque."[43] Martha and Charles had five children (seventh generation). After Martha's death on May 17, 1870 in Summerside, Charles married (ii) Charlotte Maria Treadwell of Fredericton, N. B. in July 1876. They had no children. In *The Wrights of Bedeque*, we read:

In 1813 Charles' father, the Rev. John Bass Strong, a native of Bingham, a small town in Nottinghamshire, England, was sent to the city of Quebec by the British Wesleyan Missionary Conference. He was the first missionary sent out by the Wesleyans to that area. He was in Three Rivers, Quebec, for four years, and while there met and married Elizabeth Gambee, daughter of Luke Gambee. He was then sent to the Maritime Provinces where their children were born. When Charles, the sixth child, was eight years old, Rev. John returned to visit friends in England. On his return trip to Canada, a storm dismantled the ship and she had to put in to the Cove of Cork, Ireland. John returned to Nottingham and his friends persuaded him to take a circuit there. He sent for his family and they settled at Newark-on- Trent, Nottinghamshire. But they did not like England as well as they had expected and soon sailed from Liverpool to Charlottetown, a passage which took forty or fifty days. Being a child of the mission house, Charles moved with his parents to different circuits. When quite young, he clerked in Charlottetown, in Fredericton, N.B. where his elder sister, Sarah (Mrs. Hale) lived, and then in the Central Bedeque store his brother William G. had bought from Jonathan Weatherbe. While in Central Bedeque, he and his bride lived in the Weatherbe house which still stands on the same location [1976], opposite Campbell and Burns Cannery. In Hutchinson's Directory of 1864 Charles is listed as a trader living on Water Street near St. Stephens Street, Summerside. In 1869 he was a publisher. [Martha died in 1870.] He had become joint proprietor of the *Summerside Journal*, but sold out in 1873 and became collector of customs for the port of Summerside, a position he held until he was superannuated. He was superintendent of the Methodist Sunday School there for fifty years."[44]

His obituary follows from a Summerside newspaper:

Death of Mr. C. W. Strong

Mr. C. W. Strong, one of the oldest and most highly respected residents of Summerside, passed away at an early hour on Monday morning after an illness of several weeks at the good old age of 89 years and 10 months. His father was the late Rev. John Strong, Methodist Minister, born in Bingham, Nottinghamshire,

England, who came to Canada in 1813. Mr. C. W. Strong was born on July 2nd, 1829 and educated at Woodhouse Grove School, Yorkshire, Eng., and in the various public schools [which to our western way of thinking are private] of the town in which his father was stationed. He engaged in mercantile pursuits for several years in Charlottetown, P.E.I., Fredericton, N.B., Bedeque, P.E.I. and Summerside. In 1870 he became joint proprietor of the *Summerside Journal* which he assisted to conduct with much success. In 1873 he disposed of his interest in that paper and became Collector of Customs for Summerside until superannuated some years ago. In 1861 Mr. Strong married Miss Martha A. Wright of Bedeque by whom he had five children, two of whom are living: Allen Wilmot Strong, BSc, of Montreal and Miss Jessie W. Strong, residing at home. In May, 1870 Mrs. Strong died and in July, 1876, he married Miss Charlotte M. Treadwell of Fredericton, N.B. who survives. As a member of the Methodist Church Mr. Strong was for many years devoted to its varied interests and for 50 years he was Superintendent of the Sunday School. As a citizen he was interested in all that appertained to the welfare of the community. He was optimistic in temperament. Being well read and possessed of a rich vein of humor, he was a very interesting conversationalist. In his passing the community suffers a distinct loss. The funeral will leave the house for the Methodist Church on Wednesday afternoon at 1:45; interment in the Peoples' Cemetery [Summerside].

1.82 Archibald Montgomery Wright (6, Sally 5, Major 4, Thomas 3, Clement 2, Stephen 1), called Archibald M. and A. M., was born May 22, 1840; married Catherine Tufts, called Kate, the daughter of Henry Gershom and ____ (Ellis) Tufts. Archibald met Kate when she came over to visit her aunt, Mrs. Joseph Schurman. Their marriage was solemnized at the Schurman home, Avondale Cottage, Central Bedeque. Kate was born in 1845 in Halifax, N.S. and died January 28, 1930 in Westboro, MA. A.M. died in Westboro, MA on March 9, 1924. He was called A.M. to differentiate him from his cousin Archibald Thomas Wright, the son of Mary Wright and the grandson of Ann Hooper Montgomery, who was called A.T. It is Archibald M. who was in the mill business with his father Jesse, managing the grist mill and farm. He gradually branched out into larger interests as a trader and commission merchant. *Hutchinson's Directory of P.E.I. 1864* listed Archibald as a trader. *Frederick's Di-*

rectory, 1889, carried the following full page advertisement: "A.M.Wright, Commission Merchant General West India and Produce Merchant and dealer in Flour, Meal, etc. Agent for Corson's Anti-Corrosive Paints Water Street Summerside"

He had warehouses at Cole's Wharf, Lower Bedeque, where he bought and shipped by vessel the farmers' produce. Mr. Jesse Wright's (A.M.'s father's) diary records:

Sept. 15, 1883 Cleaning and bagging oats. here p.m. Left bags for oats.
May 4, 1885 Isaac Schurman [his Aunt Fanny's son] hauling up his potatoes to ship by scow.
May 5, Took his potatoes over to the Wharf [Cole's]
May 7, Isaac and I went after scow to take her home. Then ran to Summerside.

Jesse had his own scow and sail boat. In 1896 after his father died, A. M. deeded the mill to his son Frederick. A.M. and Kate had five children (seventh generation). [See Chapter 9] Doris Haslam wrote in *The Wrights of Bedeque*:

The failure of A. M.'s business c.1896 was a great blow not only to the farmers who had sold him their produce and to his creditors, but also to the Methodists for he was one of the head men in the church at Centreville and in the district at large. He left Prince Edward Island immediately and permanently for Massachusetts to be followed soon after by his wife and daughter. His cousin, Elisha H. Wright, and Kate's cousin, Isaac Newton Schurman, were appointed assignees and trustees of the estate. His land and residence at Castalia Grove were sold and resold. During the ownership of Bernard Connolly, the house was destroyed by fire. The farm land is now owned by Campbell and Burns (1976).[45]

1.83 Catherine Hooper Wright, called Kate, (6, Sally 5, Major 4, Thomas 3, Clement 2, Stephen 1)**,** born July 24, 1842; did not marry; died Dec. 3, 1901 in Central Bedeqeue

1.84 Harriet Ethelinda Wright (6, Sally 5, Major 4, Thomas 3, Clement 2, Stephen 1), born June 11, 1844 at Castalia Grove, Centerville Bedeque and died there on May 27, 1925. She married Lemuel Vickerson, son of Conrod and Jessie (Robertson) Vickerson, who was born on June 20, 1837 in Marshfield, P.E.I. and died on Decem-

ber 28, 1873 in Summerside, P.E.I. Conrad was the third child of Georg from Germany and the first child to be born on Prince Edward Island. Lemuel's grandfather, Johann Georg Vickerson was born on 2 January, 1756 in Willinghausen, Hassen Kassel, Germany, about sixty miles northeast of the present day Frankfurt.

King George III had an arrangement with the principality of Germany where Weckesser lived to provide Hessian troops to fight with England in the American Rebellion. He enlisted as a private and was later promoted to grenadier [a soldier who threw hand grenades]. Eventually his company landed on the Island of Saint John where they were forced to spend the winter. After the hostilities were over, Georg returned to Germany for a while before bringing his wife and two children around 1787 to settle on the Island of St. John where he applied for Loyalist benefits, and by 1790 had settled in Marshfield, Lot 34.[46]

Lemuel left the home farm, "Brownston" in Hermitage to take over his brother Henry's business in Summerside when the latter died in 1864. The business was a general store situated on Water Street near Queens Wharf. We know from reading his diary that is in possession of his great-grandson Frederick Vickerson, that Lemuel was active in religious life in Summerside and Bedeque as well as with the Masonic Mount Lebanon Lodge. He was the collector of excise and light duties for Summerside when he died at the early age of thirty-six. His obituary follows from a Summerside newspaper: "**Vickerson:** At his residence on Sunday evening, the 28th ult., after an illness of a few weeks, Lemuel Vickerson, Esq., aged 36 years, leaving a wife and three children to mourn the loss of an affectionate husband and loving parent."

Harriet returned with her three small children to Castalia Grove to live with her parents and sister Kate [Harriet had had four children (seventh generation), but one, a twin, died at age six months]. She was, like many of her Wright cousins, a devout Methodist. She was a teacher in the Sunday School, a charter member of the Women's Missionary Society, and a faithful worker throughout her long life.[47]

A Summerside newspaper published Harriet Vickerson's obituary:

In Memoriam Mrs. Harriett Vickerson

In the eighty-second year of her age, Mrs. Harriet Vickerson of Bedeque, P.E.I. , on May 27, 1925, passed to her home in heaven. She had lived the great portion of her long life in about the same locality.

Her husband having died when the family were young, she had added responsibilities and many times she praised God who heard her prayers and kindly led her through the decades of trial, sickness and perplexity.

For some years she was unable to attend the public means of grace, but to visit her home was an inspiration for the ministers and an incentive to many a troubled soul.

She was a woman of devotion, sincerity, strong faith, kind heart and of deep piety.

During her last illness, which was of months' duration, and on different occasions, she seemed at death's door; her great prayer was to be spared until her son Henry (who was her great concern during his lifetime and was very ill during the winter) was taken to be with Jesus.

This prayer was answered; she rallied. Henry went to his Heavenly home on March 17 and from that time she longed to go to be with her loved ones waiting for her in the Heavenly Home.

Mrs. Vickerson leaves to mourn the loss of a devoted mother and consecrated Christian, one son Herbert in Montreal and one daughter Mrs. Seymour in California.

Up to the last, Mrs. Vickerson had a deep interest in all the departments of the church which she supported liberally financially, being a faithful Christian Steward, and all organizations received their due share. Her prayers for the Revival services and her earnest desire to see God's Kingdom prosper reveal what can be done in a quiet way by the "shut-ins."

In the earlier days she was very prominently identified with the A.M.S. activities for tithing and to this movement the present standard of efficiency in missionary matters on this circuit is due largely.

Her spiritual life was deep, thorough, and conscientious.

Owing to the inability of her pastor to reach P.E. Island from the mainland on Monday in time for the funeral, the services were conducted by Rev. D. K. Ross of the Presbyterian Church assisted by Rev. N. A Whitman of the Baptist Church.

She has gone to higher regions
Safe from every grief and care.
We shall meet again in heaven
And never more be parted there."

With the help of research by C.W. Vickerson, and Dr. Frederick Vickerson, Doris Haslam wrote in *The Wrights of Bedeque*:

A fine example of an early Island craft, a coverlet, called a draft rug, woven by Harriet, has been donated to the P.E.I. Heritage Foundation by her grandson George Vickerson and his wife Anne.

Lemuel's ancestor [grandfather], Johann Georg Weckesser (anglicized George Vickerson), a native of Willingshausen in Hessen, an army officer in the American Revolutionary War while enroute with the British troops to Quebec was forced by fall storms to winter in Charlottetown. Here he met and married Ann Barbara Younker. After the war, they returned to the Island of St. John eventually settling in Marshfield where their son Conrod was born. Conrod married Jessie Robertson who was born in Perth, Scotland, daughter of James and Jean (Miller) Robertson. James and his son Alex immigrated to P.E.I. in 1818 and settled in Marshfield. His wife and family followed in 1819. Conrod and Jessie moved to the Brownston farm in Hermitage in 1842.[48]

1.85 Charlotte Mary Wright (6, Sally 5, Major 4, Thomas 3, Clement 2, Stephen 1), born November 18, 1847; married Rev. Edward Fade Goff, son of John and Elizabeth (Hayden) Goff, on July 4, 1876; Charlotte, called Lottie, died on January 10, 1924 in Riverside, California, U.S.A. Edward was born October 28, 1850 at "Woodville," Cardigan, P.E.I. and died on May 13, 1917 in Claremont, Riverside, California. Rev. Goff was the minister of various Congregational Churches in the U.S.A. While pastor of First Congregational Church in Riverside, CA, on the occasion of their 25th wedding anniversary, the congregation presented a sterling silver teapot filled with silver dollars. This teapot has been given to the Confederation Art Gallery, Charlottetown, by a nephew and namesake, Edward F. Goff, formerly of Woodville, Cardigan, P.E.I., now residing in B.C. (1976). The first P.E.I. Goff ancestor was Fade Goff who was born in Bryanstown, County Wexford, Ireland in 1780. In 1810 he settled in Erindale, P.E.I. where he built and operated mills.[49] A P.E.I. newspaper printed Mr. Goff's obituary:

Rev. E. F. Goff of Claremont, Cal., passed away last Sunday morning after an operation. The late Mr. Goff was 68 years of age and was the oldest son of the late Mr. John Goff of Woodville Mills, this province. He leaves to mourn his widow, formerly Miss Lottie Wright, daughter of the late Mr. Jesse Wright, Bedeque; also his aged mother residing in California, and five brothers and three sisters, namely Louis W. and Dr. H. Neville Goff in San Diego; W. P. in Montana; R. C. in Charlottetown, and George E. on the homestead Woodville Mills; Mrs. Charles Strangman, Montreal; Mrs. Arthur Jenks, Berkley, Cal.; and Mrs. (Dr.) J. A. McKinnon, Seattle, Wash.

1.86 Jane Eliza Wright (6, Sally 5, Major 4, Thomas 3, Clement 2, Stephen 1), born September 1851; died on March 11, 1864 at age 12 ½ of diphtheria.

1.87 Charles Elijah Wright (6, Sally 5, Major 4, Thomas 3, Clement 2, Stephen 1), born December 7, 1853, [here is a reversal of the baptismal name of John Keir's son] died on August 16, 1863 of "brain fever" [encephalitis?].

1.9 Jane Eliza Hooper (5, Major 4, Thomas 3, Clement 2, Stephen 1), b. 1815, d. 1890; married on February 8, 1838, William Craig (1813-1860), a farmer from Midddleton, the son of John Craig and Ann Robins of Lower Bedeque. [Jane married a first cousin.] William was the grandson of William Craig who arrived in Charlottetown on August 30, 1770 and was the teacher to the children of Governor Walter Patterson. William had been a school teacher in Scotland. He was a member of the first legislative assembly in 1773. He and his wife Kennedy (Copeland) Craig (c.1753-1828) had a son John who married in 1810, as his first wife, Ann Robins (c.1790-1827) (fifth generation), a daughter of John and Mary (Hooper) Robins. The obituary of Jane was in a Summerside newspaper on March 9, 1890 as follows: "CRAIG - At Middleton on the 9th inst. after a lingering illness, Jane Hooper, beloved wife of the late William Craig, in the 76th year of her age."

William and Jane had nine children (sixth generation, surname Craig) as follows:

1.91 Major Craig (6, Jane 5, Major 4, Thomas 3, Clement 2, Stephen 1), 1841-1905; married (i) Ann Wright, daughter of Ethelinda and Job Wright, born on December 20, 1840 in Middleton, P.E.I. Ann and Major married on February 26, 1868. They had one child (Etha) (seventh generation). Ann died on July 20, 1871. The obituary from a Summerside newspaper reads: "At her residence, Middleton, Lot 27, on Thursday the 20th, inst., after a lingering illness which she bore with resignation to the Divine Will, Ann the beloved wife of Mr. Major Craig, aged 30 years [died]."

Major married (ii) Elizabeth Campbell (1842-November 1, 1879) from Cape Breton, N.S. They had two children (seventh generation).

1.92 Elizabeth Craig (6, Jane 5, Major 4, Thomas 3, Clement 2, Stephen 1) b. 1841, d. 1860. [Were they twins?] The only other information that I have on Elizabeth Craig is from a newspaper, compliments of Mr. and Mrs. Bradshaw. Although the dates given are different from what are written above, I tend to think that the Elizabeth Craig of the poem is the daughter of Jane and Major Craig.

Lines written on the death of the late Elizabeth Craig of Middleton:

Weeks and months have flown away and days gone fleeting by
Since a fair one left her earthly home for a happy one on high.
Her mother cherished fondest hopes upon her circle fair;
Had she not trusted in her God who does the way prepare?
To relieve the sorrow-stricken heart bereft of dearest ties,
She would have fallen beneath the load of mortal agonies.
As Heaven is higher than the earth and far beyond our gaze
In illimitable unknown space His ways are not our ways.
He knows His own, He them does call. (No earthly hand can stay)
Their earthly pilgimage is done. They quit this mortal clay.
Her mother to her bedside came to hear those accents true:
I now must leave my earthly home; I cannot stay with you.
My Master's call I must obey. He dwells in heaven above.
O, dearest mother, I cannot stay; I feel His dying love.
She called the circle to her side, the family, compact, true.
She gave them kind, endearing words, to earth then bade adieu.
Before she closed her eyes in death, they rested on one near.
That look, so meaning in itself, called forth a silent tear.

This world is full of vanity," the unstable mind decoys;
I would you all could come with me, leave earth's remorseless joys.
Many were the hours of ... we did anxiously pursue.
They were the hours of happiness; they never pleasure knew.
O vain and transitory world! Who can in thee delight?
When thou dost —— the sweetest hope, the fairest prospects blight.
There is a home, a happy home, where reigns enjoyment true.
O seek that home, and with me come. I bid you all ADIEU!
Methinks I see that pleasant smile, that mild, complacent look
That ever graced her friendly home ere she the earth forsook.
Intrepid monster, cruel death, unseen by mortal eye.
Thy mission is to break the bands that bind sweet friendship's tie.
[Middleton, Feb. 11, 1867]

There is much emotion in this poem: sadness, acceptance, confusion, and anger.

1.93 John Craig (6, Jane 5, Major 4, Thomas 3, Clement 2, Stephen 1) born October 2, 1842 in Middleton; married January 6, 1869 Jane Schurman Wright (Thomas Wright [3], Nathaniel Wright [2], William Wright [1]) [and on her mother's side Jane Schurman [3], Isaac [2], William [1]] who was born October 18, 1843 [family Bible says October 19], and died in Middleton September 11, 1880. John died there on August 6, 1925. Apparently Jane was 37 years old when she died, and John was 83 at the time of his death; there is not a mention of a second marriage. John and Jane had a 150 acre farm in Middleton on the road which connected Middleton to Searletown. It was owned in 1976 by their great-grandson, Arthur [who died about 1998]. The house is the summer home (2000) of Arthur's sister Louise and her husband, Gregory Corbett.

John was a prayer leader, circuit steward, trustee and class leader on the Bedeque Methodist circuit. Nearly fifty years ago, when funds were being solicited for the erection of a church hall in Centreville Bedeque, John's son Bert made a contribution on the condition that the hall be named for his father. This offer was accepted and a plaque in the hall reads: "John Craig Memorial Hall. Dedicated to the glory of God and the Upbuilding of His Kingdom, this Hall stands as a

memorial to those who by their gifts, work, and encouragement made real a dream of many years. November 9th, 1954." Alden and I had seen this plaque many times in the church hall, but never knew that the donation was in the name of his relative. I guess that Ada and John would be first cousins once removed or something like that.

1.94 Albert Craig (6, Jane 5, Major 4, Thomas 3, Clement 2, Stephen 1) born 1844; married Emeline Crosby(1852-1919); died in 1912. Albert and Emeline had three children (surname Craig) in the seventh generation.

1.95 Charles Craig (6, Jane 5, Major 4, Thomas 3, Clement 2, Stephen 1) b. 1849; married Anne Montgomery (1860-1944); d. 1915. Charles and Ann had three children. [Ann was no doubt a relative of Ann Hooper who had sold their possessions in New Jersey to come to Lower Bedeque, P.E.I., in 1786. Perhaps she was a grandchild of Hugh, Archibald, or Donald Montgomery, Ann Hooper Montgomery's sons]

A newspaper article, dated October 1896, has been preserved and recorded Charles's involvement with the Middleton Lodge:

News from Middleton Lodge is gladly welcomed in the Good Templar column. An esteemed correspondent from that section writes as follows: A concert and ice cream social was held at Middleton on Tuesday evening the 27th October under the auspices of Middleton Lodge. The chairman, Bro Charles Craig, in a few well-chosen remarks opened the meeting after which quite a lengthy program was carried out by different members of the Lodge apparently to the entire satisfaction of all present. After the program had been exhausted, ice cream and cake were passed around and judging from the frequency with which several of the saucers were refilled, it was evident that the ice cream and cake were as much enjoyed as the literary part of the program. Although the Middleton Lodge cannot boast of a very large membership, yet the meetings are generally full of interest, and with the newly elected efficient staff of officers a successful quarter is looked forward to.

Charles Craig's obituary appeared in a local Island newspaper in 1915:

There passed away on the morning of the 31st of August Mr. Charles Craig of Middleton in the 66th year of his age. His funeral which was very largely attended took place on Thursday the 2nd September to the beautiful Cemetery of North Bedeque.

The solemn and impressive service was held at the home, the Pastor, the Rev. Alex MacKay, leading the service and giving a most practicable and appropriate address founded on the words "I have a desire to depart and to be with Christ which is far better." The Rev. Messrs. Ayers and Calder took part in the service. A male quartette sang excellently and with effect some choice musical selections. Miss Edna MacMurdo was organist. The elders, Members of the Session, acted as pall bearers. The immediate mourners, the widow and family, comprising Norman and Earle living on adjoining and splendid homesteads and Mrs. James Norton whose husband is in the employ of the I.C.R. [Intercolonial Railway], Moncton, have the sympathy of a wide circle of relatives and friends which was very evident from the large number who came together to pay their last respects to the dead. The deceased at an early age obeyed the injunction "Give Me thine heart" and when quite a young man was elected to the eldership in the Presbyterian Church, Bedeque. He took a lively interest in all matters pertaining to the welfare of the Church. Up to the time his health failed, although living seven miles or more from the church, he was seldom absent from the sanctuary. The same may be said of his attendance at the meetings of session and congregation. As a member of session he was a large factor in moulding the policy of the church. He was remarkably loyal to the honor taken upon entering the church and session. Whatever tended to the betterment of the community received heartily his loyal support. With him to know was to do. In politics he was a Liberal, but by no means a strong party man. He took strong ground on the question of temperance and the purity of the ballot. He would break with his party upon the slightest suspicion that they were shady on those two questions. There is but one member of quite a large family now living in the person of Mr. John Craig of Middleton. It is comforting to know that the bereaved are not called upon to sorrow as those who have no hope. "Blessed are the dead who die in the Lord."

1.96 Sarah Craig (6, Jane 5, Major 4, Thomas 3, Clement 2, Stephen 1) b. 1851; did not marry; d. 1886. Sarah's obituary appeared in an area newspaper and will be copied here, thanks to Mr. and Mrs. Bradshaw: "At Middleton, July 10th [1886], after an illness of 7 weeks, Sarah, beloved daughter of the late Wm. Craig, Esq., aged 35. She fell asleep in Jesus. "Blessed are the dead that die in the Lord."

A poem was written anonymously, given in memory of Sarah and sent from Dorchester, N. B. on July 27, 1886. One wonders if the author was one of her sisters or sister-in-law. The poem had been printed in a local newspaper and was given for this genealogy by Mr. and Mrs. Bradshaw:

Just at the morn of life, midst summer's balmy air,
From scenes devoid of strife to mansions bright and fair,
Dear Sarah passed from earth to yonder home above
To share immortal work where spirits live in love.

Her spirit clad in white soar'd far above the skies
To bathe in seas of light where joys celestial rise;
Resplendent in attire, adorn'd with robes divine,
She strikes her golden lyre within the glorious shrine.
She was, while here below, with many virtues blessed.
Her glory who can know, not entered into rest?
Made pure from earthly stain, from sin and sorrow free,
She shall with God remain throughout eternity.

While nature sheds a tear for her, now passed away,
We would her name revere and to her memory pay
That tribute of respect her virtues would demand;
Nor will we e'er neglect to plant with loving hands

Upon her grave the rose and gentle lily, too,
Which shall in spring disclose their beauty to our view.
These flowers shall adorn with emblematic grace
The grave of her we mourn, enshrined in memory's space.

But, far above the skies, in Heaven's eternal home
Her monument shall rise 'Neath the celestial dome;
Her grace with glory crowned by her Redeemer's love
Where joys for aye abound in yonder world above.

Although we bid adieu to Sarah, from us gone,
We shall again renew our friendships round the throne
Of our redeeming Lord, our Saviour and our King
Who will fulfill His Word and us to glory bring.

Then let us say "farewell" to sight and sorrows past.
Though life's rough billows swell, we shall be safe at last,
Safe in the arms of God beyond the swelling flood.
Then let us kiss the rod designed by God for good.

Dear Saviour, give us grace to bow to Thy command;
We shall behold Thy face in Canaan's happy land.

Thou wilt the work complete of grace and glory, too;
Our joy will be replete when we its fullness know.

1.97 Patterson Craig (6, Jane 5, Major 4, Thomas 3, Clement 2, Stephen 1) b. 1854; married Fannie Parlee; had one child Laura; d. 1895.
1.98 Artemas Craig (6, Jane 5, Major 4, Thomas 3, Clement 2, Stephen 1) (1856-1860)
1.99 William Craig (6, Jane 5, Major 4, Thomas 3, Clement 2, Stephen 1) (1860-1860)

1.100 Artemas Hooper (5, Major 4, Thomas 3, Clement 2, Stephen 1) (1818-1904) was a farmer who lived in Centreville, P.E.I. On March 22, 1843 he married Mary Ann Baker (June 20, 1821 - June 5, 1902), daughter of Lewis Baker and Adah Farrow. Artemas and Mary Ann lived in Centreville where he farmed. They were the parents of one son who died at six months, and of four daughters. Artemas and Mary Ann and two of their young children, as well as a married daughter, are buried in the Baptist Cemetery in Central Bedeque.

The tombstones at the Artemas Hooper site in the Baptist Cemetery at Central Bedeque give the following information: "Artemas Hooper 1818 - 1904; In memory of Mary Ann Baker, wife of Artemas Hooper, died June 5, 1902, AET 81; Their daughter Ada J. [probably named for her mother's mother, Adah Farrow Baker], wife of Dr. J. B. McDonald 1848 - 1906; also their children Archibald M. [perhaps named for his Aunt Sally's son, Archibald M.], died Mar. 2, 1846, age 6 months; Sarah W. P., died July 11, 1861, aged 5 yr and 6 mo. Of such is the Kingdom of Heaven."

The *Charlottetown Guardian* on October 20, 1904 published Artemas's death notice. It was found in the Public Archives and Records Office of P.E.I. in Charlottetown:

The death of **Artemas Hooper** which occurred at Lower Montague on Friday last removes one of the oldest and best-known residents of Bedeque where he spent most of his life. The deceased is a son of the late **Major Hooper** who was one of the earliest Justices of the Peace in Prince County and who, with his father [Tho-

mas Hooper], a British Loyalist, came to this province from New Jersey. The deceased was in his 86th year. He was a most exemplary man and a devoted member of the Baptist Church. The last few years of his life were spent with his daughter, Mrs. A. J. Robertson of Lower Montague, besides whom the rest of his family surviving him are Mrs. (Dr.) MacDonald, lately of Spokane, Wash., and Mrs. Newsome of Chicago, Illinois.

Mary Ann's parents were Lewis Baker (c.1777-1844) and Adah Farrow, daughter of Joseph and Judith Partridge Farrow (1787-1859). Adah was born at Broad Bay. They farmed at Central Bedeque and had eight children of whom Mary Ann was the sixth.[50]

A man in the community who must have been a friend of Artemas Hooper's was Mr. Solomon Schurman whose obituary was found by Mr. and Mrs. Bradshaw.

The death occurred on Sunday, March 2nd[1902], of Mr. Solomon Schurman, one of the oldest and most respected residents of Bedeque. He had been in failing health for some time, but no serious results had been anticipated, and it was hoped he would again recover his wanted strength, but it was otherwise willed and he passed away as above stated at the ripe old age of 84. Mr. Schurman was one of the first members of the Baptist Church of Bedeque, for years an honored deacon and all through his long life a consistent Christian gentleman, loved and respected by all who knew him. Besides a host of friends, one son, Mr. Albert Schurman, Bedeque, and three daughters, one of whom is Mrs. Rufus Wright, Middleton, are left to mourn. The funeral which took place on Tuesday was largely attended. Rev. E. P. Calder conducted the funeral service.

Solomon was born in 1818/1819 and died in 1902. His one remaining daughter, Mrs. Rufus Wright [Alice], died in 1916, and her obituary was given by Mr. and Mrs. Bradshaw to this writer:

In the death of Mrs. Alice M. Wright, wife of Mr. Rufus S. Wright of Middleton, that community loses one of its most valued residents. Deceased was the daughter of the late Mr. Solomon Schurman of Central Bedeque, and at the time of her death, Jan. 21st [1916], was slightly past seventy one years old. [*Alice* Maud was born Oct. 16, 1844] Mrs. Wright was noted for her kind and helpful disposition, and had a large number of friends. Her death was due to internal cancer, but her spirit of Christian resignation made a beautiful closing to such a well-spent life. Besides her husband, she leaves three sons, Harold, Clifford, and Ernest, all living in

Middleton, and Mrs. E. W. Schurman of Central Bedeque. She was one of the oldest and most valued members of the Bedeque Baptist Church. The funeral took place at her late residence on Jan. 23rd, interment in the Baptist Cemetery, Central Bedeque. The service was conducted by Rev. E. P. Calder, pastor of Bedeque Baptist Church.

To summarize, the children of Artemas Hooper and Mary Ann Baker (surname Hooper, sixth generation) were:

1.101 Archibald M. Hooper (6, Artemas 5, Major 4, Thomas 3, Clement 2, Stephen 1) b. 1845, d. March 2, 1846.[51]
1.102 Ada J. Hooper (6, Artemas 5, Major 4, Thomas 3, Clement 2, Stephen 1) (1848-1906); married Dr. J. B. McDonald; lived in Spokane, Washington, U.S.A. after leaving Summerside.
1.103 Harriet Hooper (6, Artema.s 5, Major 4, Thomas 3, Clement 2, Stephen 1) (1854 - 1922) married A. J. Robertson and lived in Lower Montague, P.E.I., and with whom Artemas lived for the last few years of his life. According to research done by Orlo Jones, on June 30, 1982 (found as an abstract in the Coles Building in Charlottetown), Harriet Robertson, the wife of Amos J. Robertson, whose parents were James and Margaret Robertson, had no children and lived in the U.S.A. One wonders if her years in the U.S.A.were after or before her father died. [The source was Athol Robertson of Montague]
1.104 a daughter (6, Artemas 5, Major 4, Thomas 3, Clement 2, Stephen 1) married Mr. Newsome and lived in Chicago, Illinois, U.S.A.
1.105 Sarah W. P. Hooper (6, Artemas 5, Major 4, Thomas 3, Clement 2, Stephen 1) born January 1856; died July 11, 1861. She died at 5 years, 6 months and is buried in the Baptist Cemetery in Central Bedeque.

11.0 Harriett Hooper (5, Major 4, Thomas 3, Clement 2, Stephen 1) b. 1822, d. March 9, 1901) married Richard Clark, born 1813, the son of William Clark and Elizabeth Crosby, on March 23, 1843, by the Rev. R. S. Patterson. He was a farmer; they resided in North Bedeque. [Harriett and her sister Nancy married brothers] Richard died on Sept. 18, 1868 in North Bedeque. Harriett, age 80, was buried in the North Bedeque Cemetery. The eight children of Harriett and Richard (sixth generation, surname Clark), are:

11.1 Elizabeth Clark (6, Harriett 5, Major 4, Thomas 3, Clement 2, Stephen 1) born c.1844 in North Bedeque; died December 21, 1865, at age 21

11.2 Major Hooper Clark (6, Harriett 5, Major 4, Thomas 3, Clement 2, Stephen 1) born December 5,1845; moved to New Zealand and apparently did not contact his relatives in P.E.I. as there was no further information. In 1980 there were still Hoopers in New Zealand according to a letter to the P.E.I. Archives from a person who wanted to know about her ancestors on P.E.I.! In 2003 this writer tried to make contact, but was unable to do so at that time.

Interesting information about New Zealand was recorded nearly one hundred and fifty years ago:

> Robert Clare, a son of James Douglas Haszard [who may have been related to Eunice Haszard Gardiner - see p. 26], was a principal organizer of an expedition to New Zealand in November, 1858. Reports of the favourable New Zealand climate could have been an inducement to emigrate; also, with decreasing opportunities at home, many Islanders were seeking greener pastures. Land was a major political issue, much of it being in tenures which restricted the access to farming for young Islanders. Thus, many of the more ambitious ones moved to accept the offer made by the recently appointed New Zealand agent in Prince Edward Island of "Land Orders to all persons of Good Character and Sober Steady Habits who will Emigrate at their own Cost from this Island to Auckland." "Waste land" was land bought from the Maori by the Crown for the purpose of settlement and each emigrant over 18 years was to select 40 acres of this land on paying 10 pounds Agents Fee. Children received 20 acres on application from a guardian.

A suitable ship was a first requirement and a brig of 174 tons was being built in Summerside by the shipyard of James C. Pope. She was the 67th ship registered in the Island in 1858 and was named *Prince Edward.*

The captain of the *Prince Edward* on its 14,000 mile voyage to New Zealand was Edward Nowlan. The ship's doctor was Dr. A. H. Boswall. They arrived in Auckland via the Cape of Good Hope, May 13, 1859 with ninety-eight passengers including children, thirteen of whom were Haszards.[52]

A son of Richard Bagnall was a member of the Legislative Assembly prior to emigrating with his family to New Zealand in 1862. They had eight sons and four daughters, two of whom were born in New Zealand where George died in 1889.[53]

On February 12, 2004 this writer received an e-mail from Judith Newell, the great-granddaughter of Major Hooper Clark. Judy lives in New Zealand and in the early 1980s brought her grandfather to P.E.I. She has researched her New Zealand family and promised to send information on her branch of the family for this genealogy. This is exciting, but unfortunately the correspondence by e-mail did not continue long.

The above-named ship was not the one that Major Hooper Clark took to New Zealand. Judy's great-grandfather went to Chicago when he was approximately 13 years old. How long he stayed there this author is not sure. Please see Chapter 9 for more information about Major Hooper Clark.

11.3 Charles Clark (6, Harriett 5, Major 4, Thomas 3, Clement 2, Stephen 1) dates of birth and death and place of burial are unknown. He may have been the fifth child! He lived in St. John.

11.4 Artemas Clark (6, Harriett 5, Major 4, Thomas 3, Clement 2, Stephen 1) b. c.1850; lived in Lot 25 and was a farmer.

11.5 Robert Clark (6, Harriett 5, Major 4, Thomas 3, Clement 2, Stephen 1) No information is available on his birth, marriage, or death. Lived in California. He may have been the third child!

11.6 Sarah J. Clark (6, Harriett 5, Major 4, Thomas 3, Clement 2, Stephen 1) born July 15, 1856; married (no date given) James Carruthers (born December 5, 1842; died March 4, 1917; buried in North Bedeque); she died on November 29, 1927, buried in North Bedeque.

11.7 John Clark (6, Harriett 5, Major 4, Thomas 3, Clement 2, Stephen 1) No information given except that John was the youngest son.

11.8 Jessie Clark (6, Harriett 5, Major 4, Thomas 3, Clement 2, Stephen 1) b. c.1859; married D. K. Currie; died on November 8, 1891 at age 32. Buried in North Bedeque.[54]

12.0 Charles Hooper (5, Major 4, Thomas 3, Clement 2, Stephen 1) born c.1827, died c.1849; I have no more information about him.

13.0 James Hooper (5, Major 4, Thomas 3, Clement 2, Stephen 1) born c.1827; went to Portsmouth, N. H. before 1838 (when he was only 11 years old?). James's brother Major Jr. moved from St. Eleanor's to Portsmouth, N. H. in the 1850s, perhaps following the lead of James. No more is known of James.

Sarah Hooper (4, Thomas 3, Clement 2, Stephen 1) b. June 4, 1767; d. June 4, 1828; married William D. Jewell and stayed in New Jersey, lived in Trenton. She was the eldest daughter in the family of Thomas Hooper, Loyalist. They had eight children (fifth generation).

Sarah (June 4, 1767-June 4, 1828) was the one child of Thomas and Mrs. Hooper who stayed in New Jersey, living all the rest of her life in Princeton, and did not go to P.E.I. with her father and her siblings. Only once did she and Rebecca write after the family left. That is the only communication that Thomas's family received from them *ever.* One of Sarah's siblings, Elisha, wrote to inquire about her several years after she had died unbeknownst to the sibling. As the reader can see, not much is known about Sarah's and William's children except their names and the fact that they were married or

unmarried. Feelings must have been very strained between father and daughter and perhaps between Sarah and her sisters, probably as a result of Sarah's marriage to a Patriot soldier in the State Troops of the Continental Army!

They had eight children (fifth generation, surname Jewell), as follows:

2.1 Ann Jewell (5, Sarah 4, Thomas 3, Clement 2, Stephen 1) married; died in 1831
2.2 Kenneth Jewell (5, Sarah 4, Thomas 3, Clement 2, Stephen 1) married and had two daughters; died in 1829; his widow remarried.
2.3 Elisha Jewell (5, Sarah 4, Thomas 3, Clement 2, Stephen 1) married and had 7 children, one named Thomas.
2.4 Margaret Jewell (5, Sarah 4, Thomas 3, Clement 2, Stephen 1) married.
2.5 Thomas Jewell (5, Sarah 4, Thomas 3, Clement 2, Stephen 1), married and had a daughter named Sarah.
2.6 Mary Jewell (5, Sarah 4, Thomas 3, Clement 2, Stephen 1), unmarried.
2.7 William Jewell (5, Sarah 4, Thomas 3, Clement 2, Stephen 1), married and had a son named William.
2.8 Rebecca Jewell (5, Sarah 4, Thomas 3, Clement 2, Stephen 1), was unmarried.[55]

The reader will notice that four of Sarah's eight children were given names of her siblings: Ann, Elisha, Thomas, and Mary.

Ann Hooper (4, Thomas 3, Clement 2, Stephen 1), second daughter of Thomas Hooper, Loyalist, married John Montgomery and lived on a farm in Lower Bedeque near her father, and founded the Bedeque Montgomery line. Ann was born in 1770 in New Jersey; she died on March 7, 1835 in Lower Bedeque, Prince Edward Island. John was born c.1763 and died in 1845, the son of Hugh and Mary McShannon Montgomery of Princetown, P.E.I. Another source says

that John Montgomery left Scotland as a boy with his parents, Hugh and Mary (McShannon) Montgomery on a ship bound for Quebec.[56] Enroute the water supply became low and the vessel put in at Richmond Bay for a fresh supply. Mrs. Montgomery was so delighted with the beauties of the bay and its numerous islands that she persuaded her husband to disembark and settle on what was then and for years after called Fox Point. Another version of the story given in *Cavendish, Its History, Its People*, by Harold H. Simpson, relates that she had been so seasick that she went ashore and refused to continue on to Quebec.

Ann is the only member of the family known to have been in touch with her sister Sarah in New Jersey. Ann was the daughter who was in charge of the selling of the household articles in New Jersey prior to their journey north. A letter from Sarah, with the seal, dated February 18, 1811, is brief. She evidently had not heard from the family for a long time. Sarah's daughter, Rebecca, also wrote sending her best regards to her grandfather and relatives.

The seven [probably not eight] children (fifth generation) of Ann Hooper and John Montgomery, were [surname Montgomery]:

3.1 Ann Montgomery (5, Ann 4, Thomas 3, Clement 2, Stephen 1) (c.1795-April 11, 1870); married John Townsend who was born c.1776, the son of James and Elizabeth Townsend; he died on September 5, 1866 at the age of ninety years.
3.11 a daughter (6, Ann 5, Ann 4, Thomas 3, Clement 2, Stephen 1) born 1795. No more information was available except that she lived and married and had a grandchild and a greatgrandchild. (See Chapter 9)
3.2 Major Montgomery (5, Ann 4, Thomas 3, Clement 2, Stephen 1) resided near Chaleur Bay, New Brunswick. I have no further information.
3.3 Hugh Montgomery (named for his grandfather Montgomery) (5, Ann 4, Thomas 3, Clement 2, Stephen 1) (c.1803-1873); married Elizabeth Murray (1809-1864), a twin, and the daughter of David Murray and Elizabeth Penman of North Bedeque, P.E.I. A license

was issued on July 29, 1833 for their marriage. They were probably married in the Presbyterian Church of North Bedeque where they are both buried. Elizabeth was a twin of Lucy Maud Montgomery's grandmother. Hugh and Elizabeth lived and farmed at Lower Bedeque. They had five sons and two daughters (sixth generation).[57] I do not know the details of these children. Five children are mentioned in Hugh's will.[58]

3.4 Mary Montgomery (5, Ann 4, Thomas 3, Clement 2, Stephen 1) born December 28, 1804 in Lower Bedeque; died February 3, 1877 in Centreville Bedeque; married Oct. 10, 1828 [another account reads Nov. 27, 1827] to James (called Jim) Wright (born June 14, 1803 in Tryon; died January 19, 1893 in Centreville Bedeque), son of Nathaniel Wright and Ann "Nancy" Lord. He was a farmer and they lived in Tryon, P.E.I. Mary was a cousin to the wives of James's brothers: John, Stephen, and Jesse, all granddaughters of Thomas Hooper, Loyalist.

James was a farmer. In 1832 he bought from John Stewart of Mount Stewart, one of the proprietors of Lot 26, 150 acres on the road from Bedeque to Tryon. In 1837, he bought from the Commissioners of Glebe Lands an adjoining 65 acres. The 1841 census shows him the owner of 230 acres in fee simple and the head of a household of seven: one Presbyterian (Mary) and six Methodists (James, their sons John M., Albert, Jesse, Norman, and infant daughter Ann). When the 1861 census was taken, the family had increased to eight. The 1880 *Meacham Atlas* shows James had given his son Jesse 100 acres and was living with his son Archibald T. on an adjoining 125 acres.

His two oldest sons, John M. and Albert, [actually his first and fourth sons] had gone to California at the time of the Gold Rush, c.1849. John M. contracted measles while in California but continued his work of carrying heavy timber over uneven ground. He took a very heavy weight and died soon after. Albert died a number of years later in Sacramento. Jim and Mary had ten children (surname Wright, sixth generation), all born in Bedeque:

3.41 John M. Wright (6, Mary 5, Ann 4, Thomas 3, Clement 2, Stephen 1) born July 23, 1829; did not marry; died Nov. 17, 1858 in California.

3.42 Albert L. Wright (6, Mary 5, Ann 4, Thomas 3, Clement 2, Stephen1) born Nov. 8, 1830; died June 26, 1833 in Bedeque.

3.43 Jesse Nathaniel Wright (6, Mary 5, Ann 4, Thomas 3, Clement 2, Stephen 1) born Oct. 6, 1832; married Lavinia Davies Wright [daughter of William and Isabella (Cole) Wright] on July 22, 1876 as his third wife. Lavinia was born on September 27, 1838 Chelton, P.E.I. and died on March 5, 1924 in Centreville Bedeque.[59] Jesse N. and Lavinia were first cousins. This was her first marriage; she would have two more. According to Doris Haslam, "She was named for the minister's wife, Mrs. Davies, a common practice with the Wrights. He was named for his Uncle Jesse and his grandfather Wright [Nathaniel], another common and confusing practice, not confined entirely to the early Wright families."[60] He died in May 1892 in Bedeque. In Haslam's, *The Wrights of Bedeque*, we read:

> Lavinia was the youngest daughter and remained in the home with her parents until they passed away within six months of one another. Later she went to Maine where she worked as a housekeeper in the home of a judge. When she came to the Island on her vacation visiting friends and relatives, Jesse was available to drive her here and there [with horse and wagon, not car!] but her diary does not mention a wedding date. When she returned to the Island at a later date, however, she had brought with her shutters for their new home. This home was the farm next to Jesse's father, James, in Centreville Bedeque. The shutters are still [1976] a pleasing addition to the house which is now the residence of Mrs. Irving Toombs and the farm is owned by Mrs. Toombs's son Garth.[61]

[Garth Toombs is the man from whom we bought our property in 1987!] The couple had a son in generation seven. About ten years later Jesse died and was buried beside his little son. Lavinia was left alone. She married another Jesse Wright (John Jesse), a second cousin of hers, on March 31, 1896. Doris Haslam wrote: "On

April 19, 1898 Lavinia and John *Jesse* Wright sold her 100 acre farm to John Galbraith. In 1905 he sold it to Archibald T. Wright, Jesse Nathaniel's brother, for Archibald's son Charlie. Once again the farm was in the Wright name."[62]

An interesting observation, and one which could easily confuse a person not familiar with the Wrights, is the one involving Jesse Nathaniel and Lavinia: So we see that Jesse Wright of Middleton married, first, his second cousin, Sarah Clark. He married, second, his first wife's first cousin, Agnes Clark. He married, third, his second cousin, Lavinia DaviesWright, who had married first her first cousin, another Jesse Wright, a second cousin to the Jesse Wright who was her second husband. Lavinia thus became Mrs. Lavinia Davies Wright Wright Wright. After the death of her second husband, the first Jesse Wright, she married , third, John Howatt who had married first, Mary Rogers whose brother David had married Lavinia's sister as the first of his three wives, all of whom were Wrights.[63] [In case the reader is hopelessly confused by all these marriages, this simplified explanation may help: Lavinia married Jesse Wright of Middleton as his third wife; he was her second husband!] Jesse's obituary appeared in two newspapers:

Wright - At his home in Bedeque on Thursday last, the 12th inst [May 1892], of la grippe, Jesse N. Wright in the 60th year of his age, leaving a widow and a large circle of friends to mourn their loss. Deceased was a brother to Mr. Elisha Wright of the firm of Wright Bros. of this town.

We are sorry to record the death of Jesse N. Wright of Bedeque who departed this life on Thursday last. He was seized with la grippe and succumbed after only a short illness at the age of 60. The funeral took place last Saturday and his remains were followed to their last resting place in the Centreville burying ground by a very large concourse of people. The deceased was an upright and consistent member of the Methodist Church and was universally esteemed by his neighbors for miles around. We tender to the surviving friends our condolence in their sorrow.

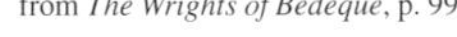

from *The Wrights of Bedeque*, p. 99

Jesse N. Wright (1832-1892)

from *The Wrights of Bedeque*, p. 99

Lavinia (Davis) Wright (1838-1924), third wife of Jesse N. Wright

[As an aside, and because Jesse N. Wright, who had as his third wife, Lavinia, has been included elsewhere in this book, the following information will be given]: Lavinia also was married three times, first in 1876 to Jesse N. Wright, son of James and Mary (Montgomery) Wright; they had one son Norman who died when he was three years old. She married second the above Jesse Wright who died in 1900. The third marriage was to John Howatt, a widower with married children.

3.44 Albert Lewis Wright (6, Mary 5, Ann 4, Thomas 3, Clement 2, Stephen 1) born Apr. 2, 1834; did not marry; died Oct. 9, 1865 in Sacramento, California

3.45 Norman R. Wright (6, Mary 5, Ann 4, Thomas 3, Clement 2, Stephen 1) born Jan. 15, 1836; married Margaret Matilda Wadman, called Tillie, daughter of Henry and Catherine (Webster) Wadman. Tillie was born Feb. 28, 1863 in Crapaud and died July 17, 1948 in Summerside where she lived after Norman's death for many years

with a housekeeper-companion. Norman had died Sept. 24, 1913 in Summerside. Norman was a merchant in partnership with his brother Elisha. They operated a business under the name Wright Bros. Commission and General Shipping Merchants, on Water Street, Summerside, with a branch in Victoria, P.E.I. Norman opened the business in Victoria and lived there until he moved back to Summerside. He and Tillie had no family, but he was a popular uncle, having more than half a dozen namesakes.

His obituary appeared in a Summerside newspaper on September 24, 1913:

A wide circle of our readers, especially the older generation, will learn with sorrow of the death of Mr. Norman R. Wright which sad event took place at Summerside on Wednesday at the age of 77 years after a lingering illness. The deceased was in former years one of the leading business men of the province. He was born in Bedeque and as a young man started with his brother, Mr. Elisha Wright, the widely known firm of Messrs. Wright Bro. at Summerside. Later he removed to Crapaud to manage the firm's business there and married Miss Wadman of that place. He retired from business thirteen years ago and took up his residence in Summerisde. There are left to mourn a widow, the brother above mentioned and two sisters. Mr. R. R. Newsom of Charlottetown is a nephew of the deceased. The funeral takes place this (Friday) afternoon at 3 o'clock to the Methodist Church, and thence to the Peoples' Cemetery [Summerside].

An obituary for Norman's mother-in-law, Catherine Webster, was preserved. She died in 1904, aged about 82 years. The reader will notice that many of the same names are given:

The Late Mrs. Henry Wadman

The funeral of the late Mrs. Henry Wadman, Crapaud, took place on Saturday the 9th inst at 12 o'clock from the residence of her daughter, Mrs. D. T. Louther, North Carleton. The service at the house was conducted by Rev. E. Rice, pastor of the Summerside Methodist Church, after which the funeral procession left for Victoria where services were held in the Methodist Church, conducted by Rev. G. M. Young, the choir rendering beautiful music. Many tears were shed as the dear old lady was a general favorite and will be sadly missed by all her relatives and friends. The interment was made in the old Crapaud Cemetery beside her estimable husband who predeceased her several years ago. She leaves to mourn four daughters:

Mrs. N. R. Wright, Summerside; Mrs. Peter Newson, Charlottetown; Mrs. I. Louther, Kensington; and Mrs. D. I. Louther, North Carleton; also two sons: Mr. O. B. Wadman, Crapaud; and Rev. Dr. Wadman, Honolulu, Hawaii. The following six grandchildren of the deceased were the pall bearers: W. R. Newson, Charlottetown; Louis Louther, Kensington; E. Gardiner, Chelton; B. Hogg, Kensington; and Leigh and Harry Louther, North Carleton.

Chelton had been called South Shore Bedeque or South Shore, and it wasn't until 1892 that it was named Chelton.

3.46 Thomas A. Wright (6, Mary 5, Ann 4, Thomas 3, Clement 2, Stephen 1) born Apr. 14, 1838; died Feb. 12, 1839 in Bedeque.

3.47 Ann Wright (6, Mary 5, Ann 4, Thomas 3, Clement 2, Stephen 1) born Jan. 29, 1840 in Centreville Bedeque, P.E.I.; married Joseph Cottle Morris of Millvale, now called North Granville, P.E.I., on June 1, 1866. They later moved to Lower Bedeque. Ann died in 1921. Joseph died on January 24, 1896 at the age of 65 years, having been born on November 3, 1830 to John and Maria (Young) Morris of North Granville. Ann and Joseph are buried in the Lower Bedeque Cemetery.

"When Ann married Joseph he was a widower with two small children, living in what his account book calls Mill Vale (present day North Granville)," wrote Doris Haslam, in *The Wrights of Bedeque*:

His first wife was Ann Rendle Tuplin, a daughter of William Braginton and Christiana (Rendle) Tuplin who had emigrated from Devon with their family of eight children on the "British Lady." They landed on June 3, 1837 on the Montgomery Farm on the North Shore of P.E.I. after seven weeks at sea. Joseph's father, John Morris, was a native of Bristol, England, and may have been acquainted there with Joseph Cottle, the poet for whom he named his son....[64]

At times Joseph and his brother Cyrus accompanied their father's brigs to England where the vessels were usually sold.... Joseph was a boat builder who built and rigged six brigs during the period from 1862 to 1866, two of them in 1864, two in 1865, and two in 1866... Joseph also had a store where he sold oatmeal and flour ground in his own mill and molasses hauled in puncheons from Summerside or Charlottetown by local farmers. These, with tea and tobacco and dry goods were the staples exchanged for planks, beams, and hardwood timber needed to build a brig. Other customers paid Joseph by working in his mills, on his farm, on his wharves, and in his shipyard. The account books name Joseph's blacksmith, caulker, sparmaker, blockmaker, planmaker, rigger and shipwright as well as the neighboring farmers with whom he had his business transactions. In 1866 Barbara Campbell earned 1.3 shillings a month for service in the Morris home. At the end of four months she had a credit balance of two pounds, twelve shillings, but when she outfitted herself with the clothing from the store her bill came to three pounds, four shillings, nine and one-half pence.

Crescent Isle Publishers/Ken F. Parry

A Brig A Brigantine

Vessels were named according to their rigging. Brigs had two masts, with square sails on both. Brigantines also had two masts, with square sails on the foremast and fore an' aft sails on the main mast. These were the types of vessels built by Joseph C. Morris, husband of Ann Wright.

Eventually Joseph sold the mills and moved to Lower Bedeque where he purchased two of the three lots that had been made of the John Rhodes Gardiner property known as Gordon Grove. He lived on the portions that had the Gardiner homestead and later sold the other lot to Curtis Lord and the one on which Joseph dwelt. Joseph built at least one brigantine on the bank of his farm at Lower Bedeque. He lost money on it, however, because the brig settled in the shallow water and he had to have a large trench dug to get it out into the deep water. It was taken to Cole's wharf at Lower Bedeque for rigging, sailed to England, and sold.[65]

3.48 Sarah Montgomery Wright (6, Mary 5, Ann 4, Thomas 3, Clement 2, Stephen 1) born June 23, 1842 in Centreville Bedeque; married William *Cyrus* Morris, son of John and Marie (Young) Morris, on November 1, 1870, in Halifax, Nova Scotia where the Rev. P.

Presswood performed the ceremony. Sarah died in North Granville, P.E.I., on July 20, 1923. Cyrus was born on October 29, 1841 in North Granville and died there on November 10, 1922. Ann and Sarah married brothers.

Doris Haslam's research for *The Wrights of Bedeque* revealed: "The Morris family were shipbuilders located on the left bank of the Trout River just above its confluence with the Stanley River on a lot of 150 acres in Lot 26 leased to John Morris in 1829 by William Pleace." According to Mrs. Haslam:

> It is marked on Lake's 1863 map with John Morris's house to the right of the yard. By 1880, when Meacham's Atlas was printed, Cyrus had built his large house on the hill above the shipyard. It is still standing [in the mid-1970s] foursquare, commanding one of the most delightful views in Prince Edward Island. By then the Morrises had given up the shipyard and Cyrus was farming a two hundred and ten acre farm in North Granville. (Granville really should be Grenville; it is spelled Grenville on early maps and lay in Grenville parish, one of fourteen parishes into which the Island was divided by Capt. Samuel Holland when he surveyed the Island in 1764-1765. Cyrus' youngest son, Ray, inherited his father's property and it is still (mid - 1970s) owned by Ray's descendants.[66]

Sarah and Cyrus had seven children (seventh generation, surname Morris). Please see Chapter 9.

3.49 Thomas Archibald (or Archibald Thomas) Wright called A. T. (6, Mary 5, Ann 4, Thomas 3, Clement 2, Stephen 1) born June 27, 1844 in Centreville Bedeque, P.E.I.; married Harriet Susannah Beer, oldest daughter of John and Jennie (MacCallum) Beer, on March 28, 1871. A. T. died on December 2, 1913 in Centreville Bedeque. Harriet was born Setpember 10, 1847 in Charlottetown, P.E.I. and died November 30, 1936 in Middleton, P.E.I. She had been sent to the private boarding school in Charlottetown of the Misses Ann and Matilda Muncey. At that period very few rural daughters were given the advantage of attending a private school or a convent.[67]

He was called A.T. to distinguish himself from his cousin A.M. or Archibald M,, the merchant trader. Doris Haslam wrote:

... A.T. inherited the family homestead and lived there with his parents, his wife, seven sons (three of whom were triplets), and two daughters. The arrival of the triplets in 1884 created a sensation and many were the interested and curious callers who dropped into the Wright home on the main road from Bedeque to Tryon."[68]

... A. T. was one of the adventurous Wrights who was lured to the Klondike. Harriet was not very enthusiastic about this venture, and when he returned empty-handed, her welcoming remark was only, "Well, Archibald!" After their first son died, the homestead was sold. Harriet and A. T. moved to the village to live in the house which in the mid-seventies was the home of their grandson, Walter Craig [painted raspberry in 2000, midway between the corner store and the Methodist Church]. A. T., like the rest of his Wright cousins, did his duty by his church [Methodist] and served in the various church offices to which he was appointed. Harriet taught for many years the infant class in the Methodist Sunday School. When she was quite young, her father came from Charlottetown to take over the business of Colin MacLellan in Centreville Bedeque. The family lived in a house next to the store which was situated on the right hand corner of the road from Central Bedeque to Tryon. [It must have been the first house after the corner on the road going toward the Methodist Church]

Alden and Nancy Neal Coll.

The Wright triplets, children of A.T. Wright and his wife, Harriet S. Beer.
Left to Right: Frank, Morris, and Jesse

3.410 Elisha Hooper Wright (6, Mary 5, Ann 4, Thomas 3, Clement 2, Stephen 1) born Feb. 20, 1846; married (i) Margaret Elizabeth Clark, called Maggie, daughter of William Ewan Clark, M.L.A. and Sarah Jewel (Hooper) Clark. She was born c.1848 in Darnley, P.E.I., and died February 6, 1917, aged 68, in Summerside. They had seven children (generation seven). In *The Wrights of Bedeque*, we read:

> Elisha was named for his granduncle, Elisha Hooper, the grandfather of his future wife, Maggie Clark. When he was sixteen, he started his business as a clerk in the Bedeque store of his cousin, Major Wright. Seven years later, he went into partnership with his brother, Norman, to conduct a general mercantile business under the name of Wright Bros. in Summerside. This little town, formerly known as Green's Shore on Bedeque Bay, owed its growth to the shipbuilding trade. In the 1880s Norman left Summerside to establish a branch business, Wright Bros. in Victoria, one of the larger shipping centers of Prince Edward Island at that period. In 1898 the Summerside business was changed to Wright Bros. Commission and General Shipping Merchants. Elisha was owner of the "Jubilee," a schooner of 76 tons, built in Georgetown in 1887. When his cousin, A. M. Wright's General Produce and Shipping business failed, Elisha and Isaac N. Schurman were appointed assignees and trustees of the estate, an appointment which entailed considerable work for the trustees. In McAlpine's P.E.I. Directory for 1909, he is listed manager of Hall Mfg. Co. as well as of Wright Bros. on Water St. with a home on Euston Street. Elisha moved to Victoria in 1911 to take charge of the business there. He and Maggie lived on Russel St., Victoria, in the large house he had bought from Capt. Archibald Lord, owned in the mid-seventies by Mrs. Don Sherren who operated "Dawndona," a home for the elderly. Following Elisha's death Claudine and the senior clerk, Miner MacNevin, took over the business in partnership until Miner became the sole owner."[69]

Elisha married (ii) Mrs. Claudina (Smith) Taylor, daughter of Hon. Matthew and Sarah Elizabeth (Lea) Smith, on July 1, 1922 (he was aged 76 years). She died in March 1970 in Charlottetown, P.E.I. A newspaper clipping was available for the latter marriage:

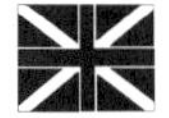

A very interesting event occurred on Saturday last when the quiet and pretty wedding took place at 7 a.m. in the Methodist Parsonage at Tryon, Rev. Mr. Fitzpatrick officiating, of Mr. Elisha H. Wright of Victoria to Mrs. Claudine Taylor. Both bride and groom were unattended and left after the wedding breakfast for a honeymoon trip to various points of interest in the United States. Mr. and Mrs. Wright enjoyed the esteem of a very exceptionally wide circle of friends with whom we join in wishing them long life and every happiness.

3.5 Archibald Montgomery (5, Ann 4, Thomas 3, Clement 2, Stephen 1) married Mary Knight [or McKnight] who was born in Halifax, Nova Scotia. Archibald was a farmer and they resided in Lower Bedeque. They had three sons and two daughters (surname Montgomery, sixth generation), only one of whose names I know:

3.51 Norman Ramsey Montgomery (6, Archibald 5, Ann 4, Thomas 3, Clement 2, Stephen1) No other information available.

3.6 Donald/Daniel Montgomery (5, Ann 4, Thomas 3, Clement 2, Stephen 1) married Sarah Cole, daughter of Benjamin and Isabella Robins Cole of Lower Bedeque. They settled on a farm in Traveller's Rest and had a family of two sons and three or four daughters; only one daughter's name has apparently been preserved. Donald was born in Lower Bedeque and died in Travellers Rest.

An interesting sideline on the names Donald/Daniel came to my attention. Daniel is considered English and therefore more proper than the Scottish Donald.[70]

The daughter of Daniel and Sarah (surname Montgomery, sixth generation) whose name I know is:

3.61 Margaret Montgomery (6, Daniel 5, Ann 4, Thomas 3, Clement 2, Stephen 1) born 1841; married Archibald Ellison, who was born in 1826 and died on June 8, 1891, buried in the Malpeque People's Cemetery, P.E.I. Margaret died on October 16, 1908 and was also buried in the Malpeque People's Cemetery. They had five children (surname Ellison, seventh generation).

3.7 Sarah Montgomery (5, Ann 4, Thomas 3, Clement 2, Stephen 1) born 1810; died August 4, 1872; I know nothing more about her. It would appear that she was named for her mother's sister who did not leave New Jersey with her father and siblings.
3.8 (?) Daniel Montgomery, probably is the Donald already mentioned above because both names were frequently used for the same person. Ross Graves, author of *William Schurman, Loyalist ...*, states that John Montgomery's *brother,* Donald, was the great-grandfather of Lucy Maud Montgomery (Mrs. Ewen MacDonald), author of *Anne of Green Gables* and other Island-based novels).[71]

Mary Hooper (4, Thomas 3, Clement 2, Stephen 1) the fourth child of Thomas, married Loyalist, John Robins, in Bedeque in 1788. In Jones and Haslam's, *An Island Refuge ...*, we read:

> John was born in Amboy, New Jersey and died in Lower Bedeque. He was an ensign in His Majesty's King's Rangers, and was stationed in Charlotte Town with the First Battalion as a junior officer of the garrison on March 17, 1782. A letter signed by John and several of his fellow officers, which appeared in a New York newspaper of April, 1782, advised prospective emigrants that on the Island "soil was good, the water excellent, the harbours spacious, the government mild, the cattle plentiful." The battalion was disbanded in 1783 and John Robins returned to the Colonies to invite more Loyalists to settle on the Island, and also to escort his sister Isabella to their new home in Lower Bedeque.
>
> According to the Muster Roll, John Robins drew a land grant of 500 acres at Bedeque Bay, Lot 26, on June 4, 1784. There was another grant on Lot 19 which was drawn on August 4. He had received twelve months provisions at Halifax. The land which was set apart for the Loyalists, at least the parts drawn by John and his father, was at that time a wilderness and each parcel consisted of fifty acres, bounded on Wilmot Creek, the rest back land on Lot 19. They preferred taking leases from the proprietors in a place which the French Acadians had formerly inhabited with quite large clearnings, small houses and orchards, in what is now Lower Bedeque. John and his sister Isabella lived in one of these houses.[72]

The six children of Mary Hooper and John Robins, who died very shortly after the sixth child was born in 1798, are as follows (surname Robins, fifth generation):

4.1 Elizabeth Robins (5, Mary 4, Thomas 3, Clement 2, Stephen 1), born in 1789 in Lower Bedeque, married John Wright [sometimes called John M. Wright and Squire John Wright] the son of Nathaniel and Nancy Lord Wright, born c.1789 in Tryon; died December 2, 1875 in Searletown, P.E.I. and was buried in the Searletown Cemetery. Elizabeth died in 1827 at the young age of 38 years, perhaps a year after her seventh child was born.

On November 16, 1831, John married (ii) Mary Stewart, the daughter of Dugald and Elizabeth (Craig) Stewart, who, with John, had two children (surname Wright) - a daughter, Elizabeth Ann, and a son, Dugald Stewart [See information later in this chapter]. John's obituary from the local newspaper will be duplicated here, thanks to Mr. and Mrs. Bradshaw:

Died at Searletown on Dec. 2nd, 1875, the Hon. John Wright in the 87th year of his age. He was the eldest of a family of eleven children. His parents were worthy and pious persons whose first desire for their children was that they might grow up in the fear and love of God. The Rev. George Jackson, the author of his father's (Mr. Nath. Wright's) biography, speaking of his anxiety for his children, says: "The piercing prayer, the piercing look, the earnest exhortation, whenever they came to his bedside, all bespoke the anxiety of his heart for their present and eternal salvation." Shortly after their conversion, the manner in which they prized the preaching of the Word was evinced by Mr. N. Wright and one of his relatives going with a vessel to Nova Scotia for the Rev. W. Black who, after his coming, baptized Mr. W. and three of his children, formed eight or ten into a society, administered the sacrament of the Lord's supper, and then returned to his station in Halifax.

Brought up thus breathing the atmosphere of an earnest piety, Mr. Jno. Wright early in life gave his heart to God and joined the class, but after a few years for some reason withdrew from the society and did not again unite with the Church until seventeen years ago under the ministry of the Rev. Mr. Barrett, since which all who have had the pleasure of his acquaintance can witness his exemplary and uniform Christian deportment. His piety was of the calm and quiet sort. It rather shunned than courted the notice of the world, exhibiting its genuineness and vitality in undoubted fruits; for his many virtues bore all of them, pre-eminently the Christian stamp. Nor did he ever manifest the fervour or impassioned zeal which is sometimes considered the only sure indication of deep religious feeling. But being naturally modest and retiring all this was foreign from his nature, and ... it would have been impossible for such a man to assume. He was punctual in his attendance at the means of grace and even after his hearing was so far impaired that he could

not receive benefit from the preached word, he still felt it his duty to attend the worship of God. He had an amiable disposition and it was the natural impulse of his spirit to render everybody around him happy. This feature of his character was strikingly manifested during his last illness, for though suffering intensely he ever sought the comfort and enquired after the welfare of others. His house was a welcome receptacle for the stranger, his heart was open to his friends, and his bounty was cheerfully administered to relieve the wants of the needy and to aid in the spread of religious truth and therefore, he was universally beloved and respected.

In his public capacity he was elected ... Lieutenant Colonel of the Militia, Justice of the Peace, Coroner, and also a Representative to the Legislative Council.

His last illness was very distressing, but God enabled him to bear the application with patience and submission. The last time I visited him he appeared very happy trusting in Jesus. It seemed as though the Lord was perfecting his servant through suffering, for as he drew nearer to his end the actings of his soul were more and more victorious so that his exit from this world was calm, peaceful, and glorious.

Elizabeth, who died in 1827, was a cousin of John's five Wright sisters-in-law, granddaughters of Richard Robins and of Thomas Hooper, both Loyalists [Appropriate spouses were apparently not easy to find!]. When John and Elizabeth were first married, they lived in the Central Bedeque area, it is believed, before settling in the newly-opened Searletown district. John was one of the first settlers to take land there. On June 13, 1829, Horatio and Isabella Mann, through the offices of Joseph Pope of Bedeque, merchant and attorney, conveyed to John Wright, Bedeque farmer, for 50 pounds one hundred acres of land in Township 27 on the west side of the Tryon Road. The 50 pounds was sealed and delivered in the presence of Joseph Black, David Schurman, and William Wright, John's brother. This land formed the nucleus of his "Birch Grove" property which grew considerably during the years.[73] Elizabeth and John had five sons and two daughters (surname Wright) all born in Bedeque. She died when her oldest child was 13 or 14 and the youngest was about 1 year old.

4.11 John Robins Wright (6, Elizabeth 5, Mary 4, Thomas 3, Clement 2, Stephen 1) born c.1813 [and named for Elizabeth's father]; married his cousin Sophia Ann Craig, the daughter of John and Ann (Robins) Craig. Sophia was born on August 30, 1819 in Lower Bedeque and died on July 3, 1898 in Searletown. John died on February 23, 1890 in his 76th year in Searletown.[74] His obituary states:

> [He was] the father of our respected townsman, Mr. Jas. C. Wright, [and] breathed his last about noon on Sunday, the 23rd inst. at Searletown where he has resided for many years. Mr. Wright was a consistent member of the Methodist Church [holding offices on the church trustee and quarterly boards] and was always on the side of every good cause. He was a general favorite in the neighborhood and was highly esteemed by all those who had the pleasure of his acquaintance. In politics he was a decided Liberal, and was at all times an outspoken advocate of reform principles. He leaves behind him a widow and six children to whom we extend our heartfelt sympathies in their sadness.

Another obituary tells us that he died of "Bronchitis superinduced by La Grippe ..., leaving a wife and six children and a large circle of relatives and friends to mourn the loss of a kind and affectionate husband, father, and neighbor."

4.12 Harriet Wright (6, Elizabeth 5, Mary 4, Thomas 3, Clement 2, Stephen 1) born May 28, 1815 in Bedeque; married Job Wright, son of Stephen Wright and grandson of the Loyalist William Wright, on February 2, 1846. Harriet was Job's second wife, the first being Ethelinda Wright, daughter of Nathaniel and Ann (Lord) Wright. Ethelinda was born in July 1817 in Centreville and died on November 19, 1843, less than a month after the birth of their third child, Jesse Alexander McLeod Wright. Jesse A., the new baby when Ethelinda died, was brought up by Ethelinda's sister Ann (called "big Nancy"), and her husband Nathaniel Wright, a brother to Job, and grew up on the Wright homestead in North Bedeque. "Jesse was an unusually bright child and became a great pride and joy to his foster parents, but Nathaniel did not live long enough to see the boy reach

manhood. He died in 1855, the year Jesse was twelve. Nancy was a widow for almost forty years, managing the farm until Jesse was old enough to take charge. Jesse was the fourth generation on that farm and the last Wright to till its acres.[75] He was not a Hooper relative.

Job's and Ethelinda's middle child was Ann (sixth generation), born December 20, 1840 in Middleton. She married, on February 26, 1868 Major Craig, son of William and Jane (Hooper) Craig. [Major Craig was a Hooper descendant and this branch of the family will be included in Chapter Nine]

The first child of Job and Ethelinda was Nelson Nathaniel Wright, born on January 10, 1839 in Middleton and died there on September 8, 1908. As he was less than four years old when his mother died, he and his sister Ann must have been raised by their stepmother and so he will be mentioned here. He married, first, Mary Watt [Provincial record is Mary Wate] on January 12, 1869. They had two daughters. He married second Sarah (Wiggins) Taylor Hopper, called Sally. She was born in the St. Eleanor's area, the daughter of James Gilbert and Eleanor (Green) Wiggins. They had one son. Sally died in western Canada. Doris Haslam provides background information on Nelson Wright in her genealogy, *The Wrights of Bedeque* (p. 134):

> When Nelson's father gave the homestead to Nelson's half sister, Lizzie, and her husband, Nelson received a smaller place nearby on which he and Mary settled. After some years, she left him, taking the two little girls with her. Nelson was a grass widower until he married about 1880 Mrs. Sally Hopper who had already been twice widowed. She had married Nov. 19, 1861, Isaac C. B. Taylor of St. Eleanor's. Isaac died with T.B. and left her with daughters and his insurance. Then she married a Mr. Hopper who left her with two sons, but took the insurance money. She brought the two boys with her to Middleton. One son, James Arthur Hopper, died Mar. 11, 1904 at the age of 26 and was buried in Searleton. The other Hopper son married a Miss Horseman from Ontario and left the Island.
>
> Nelson appears to have spent considerable time in North Bedeque, working with his brother, Jesse. Jesse's diary refers to Nelson being there in the spring to dig mud and help build a barn, in the summer to work at the haying in upland and marsh, and in the fall helping with harvesting the potatoes with their potato digger and hauling seaweed for banking.

After Nelson and their son Gordon died, Sally kept house for Mr. Tommy Robins in Central Bedeque until he required nursing care. [As a young man he was in an accident in Summerside, which is highlighted from newspaper articles in this document] . The house in Middleton was sold to Herb Mulligan, the Kinkora cheesemaker, and Sally went to live in western Canada with her Taylor daughter, Maggie, Mrs. Jim Oliver.

The children of Nelson N. Wright by his first wife, Mary Watt (or Wate), were both born in Middleton, P.E.I.(surname Wright): Ethelinda Ann, born November 17, 1870; and a daughter child. By his second wife, Sarah "Sally" Wiggins Taylor Hopper, he had a son, Gordon Major Nelson, born March 1, 1888; died July 1910 with heart trouble. It is interesting to note that the name *Major* continues to be used even outside the family.

Before leaving Job and his first wife Ethelinda (who are not Hooper descendants) the writer would like to sidetrack a bit and record a somewhat lengthy newspaper account of the 50th wedding anniversary of Jesse Wright and his wife Margaret. It will be obvious to the reader that his life transitioned between the old and the new Prince Edward Island civilization as few lives have been recorded to have done:

Presentation

To Mr. and Mrs. Jesse Wright, Bedeque, P.E. Island:

Dear Mr. and Mrs. Wright: On this the evening of your golden wedding anniversary, we, your friends and neighbors, have come to rejoice with you because today you have reached the 50th milestone along the journey of married life. We join with you in graditude and praise to Almighty God for His goodness and mercy in sparing your lives to see this golden day.

From this golden milestone on life's pathway you can look backward tonight over the half-century of life and work to the 19th day of October in the year 1876 when an adventurous youth and a blushing maiden joined hands at the marriage altar and started down life's way together as husband and wife.

Tonight as we review your life's story and try to estimate what you have meant to us, there are certain things that stand out prominently in our minds and we wish you now to understand why we are here and why we are interested in your welfare.

You have been model citizens of whom any community might be proud. Your farm has been a model of neatness and your labors have been crowned with success. By your intelligent methods, wise planning and diligent study, you have kept abreast of the times and have been able to help others to operate successfully in this part of the Island.

Your home has always been a model home. A home in which all the modern conveniences that skill and effort could produce were to be found. As we look around your beautiful residence tonight we see a model of neatness and convenience, a well-arranged and well-equipped home with everything that genius and industry can produce, ministering to your comfort and happiness in these latter years of your married life.

Your table has always been large and well-stocked with tempting delicacies, and no hotel in the land could produce a more appetizing and inviting bill of fare. Many of us here tonight will have to confess that we had the same failing when at your table as the boy at the dinner table who was always "first in and last out."[76]

Your garden has always be a model for the country-side, and poor indeed must that mortal be who never had the pleasure of sitting down to a meal of Jesse Wright's corn or partaking of the queen of ... strawberry, and dull indeed must be the esthetic taste of the man who has never feasted his eyes on the hedge of crimson dahlias and the rose bushes in full bloom and the sweet-scented peas. All these have made your garden a charmed spot! [Jesse's brother Nelson spent considerable time working on his brother's garden in North Bedeque. Jesse's diary refers to Nelson being there in the spring to dig mud and help build a barn, in the summer to work at the haying in upland and marsh, and in the fall to help with the harvesting of potatoes with their potato digger and haul seaweed for banking.]

We would not have mentioned these things if you had selfishly kept them all for yourselves. You have not been narrow in your use of the blessings God gave you, and have taken great delight in sharing these blessings with others.

The dahlias from your garden have adorned the pulpit of the church at your door [Presbyterian] and have been the admiration of many friends and visitors during the summer, and many people from far and near have enjoyed fellowship around your hospitable table.

We are here tonight to testify that during all the years of the past half century you have lived the friendly life. People come here as they would come to their own parents, and they confide in you. Many people not related by any family ties at all call you by the endearing term of "Uncle Jesse" and "Aunt Margaret."

Another thing that we admire about you both is your youthful spirit. We are delighted to see that the weight of years has not crushed your youthful and optimistic spirit. You have grown with the years and have kept pace with the progress of the best in life today. You began life with your horse and wagon and when the auto came, you purchased a "Chev" and have kept it humming, spick and span as it is today. No matter what mishap may come your way, you still persevere and keep sweet.

Our friend John Stewart may, out of the greatness of his heart, cause your tank to overflow and produce a conflagration that destroys your comfortable cushions and hood, but soon all is as good as new. Heath Clark's man may put up his pole to stop the horses, but he cannot stop you. Your windshield may be broken, but you yourselves are intact, and with the same unconquerable spirit, you secure the necessary repairs and appear out at church on Sunday as if nothing had happened.

That same spirit of yours was in your heart the day you hoisted your radio antennae wires to the breeze and began to catch the thousand voices of other lands and climes, and many people are greatly indebted to you for splendid radio programmes which they have enjoyed as they sat in your cozy music hall. This spirit of youth you both possess, and what an asset it is in any community! It challenges us to keep abreast of the times, to refuse to live in the past, and to press on to better things.... As an evidence of your youthful, hopeful attitude, we might cite your attitude toward the United Church of Canada. We appreciate very highly your spirit of unity and co-operation. You saw in the church at your door, a church with the same high ideals and progressive outlook as your own and you helped us in many ways.

We ought not to forget the debt we owe to you, Mr. Wright, for your helpful vocal instruction. For many years you have inspired our people with a love for good music. Music with harmony in it, accurate as to time, and true to tune. You have inspired many to try and reach out to better things in the musical line; for all have admired your thoroughness and accuracy, and your help in the training of our choirs will not be forgotten.

We may add also that apart from all these duties which you have rendered so winningly for the good of all, you have taken a deep interest in the public school. You have acted in the capacity of secretary of Trustees for many years and have done the work with satisfaction to all. In this section where there is no Women's Institute to assist the Trustees in keeping the school up to the standard, you have a school that is abreast of the times in every way, and part of the credit must at least be accorded to you.

We regret that Mrs. Whidden, the daughter of the home here, is not able to be with us tonight and to join with us in this celebration, but we are sure that she would like to be here and soon will be here to bring her good cheer and best wishes to those who tonight commemorate the 50th anniversary of their married life. [Bertha was an adopted daughter.]

In conclusion, permit us to remind you of the goodness and mercy of God, the Heavenly Father, in permitting you both to see this day of your golden wedding and to see, too, your many friends gathered together with warm feelings toward you and as an evidence of our affection and gratification that you have been permitted to celebrate your golden wedding, you will please accept these gifts: a gold – headed cane, wrist watch, cut flowers, and gold pieces; these are tokens of our friendship and good will and may you long be spared to use them and as you do, may they remind you of the golden friendships of your many friends who rejoice with you in this golden anniversary of your wedding day.

Signed on behalf of your many friends.
Clement Carruthers

Jessie Clark
Mrs. Clark MacQuarrie

Another newspaper article much more briefly covered the anniversary, as follows:

On the evening of October 19, 1926, the many friends of Mr. and Mrs. Jesse Wright of North Bedeque to the number of 125 gathered at his beautiful and com-

The Wrights of Bedeque, p. 135

Jesse A. M. Wright (1843-1927)

The Wrights of Bedeque, p. 135

Margaret (Leard) Wright (1850-1934), wife of Jesse A. M. Wright

fortable "Riverside Residence" to commemorate the fiftieth anniversary of their marriage. They were married in Charlottetown on October 19, 1876 by Rev. J. M. McLeod who was then pastor of Zion Church [Methodist]. The address was read by Miss Jessie Clark and the gifts were handed to Mr. and Mrs. Wright by Alex and Muriel Lefurgey and Miss Bradshaw. The bouquets were magnificent and so was the gold-headed walking stick and gold wrist watch and the purse of well-filled gold coins. The speeches were all good. Dr. Sinclair's was short and to the point. Good speeches were also made by D. D. McDonald, Wm. Callbeck, T. J. Humphrey, Arthur Wright, and W. J. Reid and others. Refreshments were served and an excellent programme of music enjoyed. The Summerside quartette and Huestis Bros and the young lady musicians all did well and the evening was very enjoyable.

Less than five months later, Jesse Wright died. A local newspaper gave this information:

Wright - At North Bedeque, March 3, 1927, Jesse A. Wright, aged 84 years. We record with extreme sorrow the death of Mr. Jesse A. Wright which took place at his residence at North Bedeque on Thursday at the ripe age of over four score years. The deceased, who was a native and life-long resident of the district, was one of nature's gentlemen. He was an up-to-date farmer and a model citizen of whom any community might be proud. Both his farm and his hospitable home were furnished with the most modern implements and conveniences and his garden was a model to the surrounding country-side. He was possessed of a cheerful nature and never grew old in spirit. He drove his car to the close of last season and kept right abreast of the times even after his health began to fail during the present winter. He was fond of music and was for years a leader of the choir. As secretary of the School Trustees, he helped to keep up the standard of education and throughout his long life was prominent in every progressive movement for the benefit of the community. On October 19th last Mr. and Mrs. Wright (nee Margaret Leard) celebrated their golden wedding amidst many tokens of friendship and goodwill from a host of friends and neighbors. There are left to mourn a sorrowing widow and one adopted daughter, Mrs. Atwood Whidden of California, to whom our sincere sympathy is extended. The funeral takes place today (Saturday) when services will be held in the North Bedeque Church at 1 p.m. and in the church at Centreville at 3 p.m.

Gladys Henderson told this writer that Jesse and Margaret had lived near the North Bedeque Presbyterian Church. As one approaches the church the road goes on either side of the church. If one takes the right turn, the home of Jesse and Margaret was on the left side of the

road up two or three lots. It must have been a very neat and magnificently landscaped piece of property! This author was hopeful of seeing the home, but on driving there all one saw were acres and acres and acres of potato fields! The home and beautiful grounds were long gone!

Job and his second wife, Harriet, had two daughters (seventh generation). Harriet and Job were frequent visitors at the old Wright homestead in North Bedeque according to the diary of their son, Jesse. Job died there at the place of his birth at the age of 84 on his way back from a visit to Harriet's brother, Theodore, in Lot 7. His death notice read: "WRIGHT. At the residence of his son [by the first marriage], Mr. Jesse A. Wright, North Bedeque, on Monday the 10th inst., Mr. Job Wright of Middleton, aged 85 years."

This is thc son who lived in the homestead with Nancy Wright who died in Middleton on October 27, 1893. [From Mr. and Mrs. Bradshaw's newspaper collection comes the obituary of "little" Nancy Wright, the daughter-in-law of "big" Nancy Wright, the wife of Nathaniel of the second generation in Prince Edward Island]:

We are sorry to learn by telephone that Mrs. Nathaniel Wright died at the residence of her adopted son, Mr. Jesse A. Wright of North Bedeque, last Tuesday night at the advanced age of 84 years. The deceased was a resident of the house in which she died for 57 years, and was universally respected by a large circle of friends and acquaintances. She had been ailing for some months and her death was not unexpected. Her remains will be laid to rest in the cemetery at Centreville on Thursday, the funeral leaving at 2 p.m. We tender our sympathies to all the sorrowing friends.

An obituary published in a local newspaper in December 1888, for Job Wright, reads:

It is our sad duty this week to record the death, at the ripe old age of 85 years, of Mr. Job Wright of Middleton, which sorrowful event took place after a brief illness at the residence of his son, Mr. Jesse A. Wright, North Bedeque, early last Monday.

The deceased whose home was in Middleton, lately went on a visit to Mr. Theodore Wright of Lot 7 and was on his way home again when he called to see his son, where he took ill. A strange coincidence was that the place where he died was also the place of his birth. His remains were buried in the Methodist Cemetery at Centreville last Wednesday [Dec. 12]. We mingle our tears with the sorrowing relatives on the loss of their venerable parent.

Another obituary from a different local newspaper provided the following information on Job's death:

While we feel deeply the loss of those members of our church who are young in years, we also feel very deeply the loss of our old members. They are so connected with the former times, with the days when we were a feeble folk, with the beginning of Methodism in our Province.

Bro. Job Wright, one of our oldest members, has, in the providence of God, been called to his heavenly reward in the 85th year of his age. A man of retiring habits, he lived rather than talked his religion. All his business transactions were in accordance with the golden rule. He did unto others as he wished others to do unto him. He was a man of wonderful faith and prayer. Away by himself in the field or barn, it was his constant habit to plead with God in prayer.

His sickness was most severe. Wearisome days and nights were appointed unto him. He bore up through it all with Christian fortitude until he obtained his rest, Sabbath Dec. 9. [He actually died on Monday, Dec. 10.] "Blessed are the dead who died in the Lord, yea, saith the Spirit; they rest from their labors and their works do follow them."[77]

Job was one of four brothers who settled in South West Bedeque, later called Middleton. His first home, like theirs, was a log cabin. His farm adjoined his brother Stephen's as one long lane led to their buildings located on opposite sides of the lane. The old log house was still in use as a storehouse when the farm was sold in 1945. The second house was built with low beamed ceilings in the kitchen and the dining room. Job was more "clannish" in choosing a wife than were his Middleton brothers. Both of his wives were his Wright cousins. Ethelinda was a daughter of his Uncle, Nathaniel, and Harriet was a daughter of his cousin, Squire John, who lived in Searletown, and his first wife, Elizabeth Robins.

Harriet died on October 27, 1893 in Middleton, on a Friday evening, at age 75. Her obituary reads:

HARRIET WRIGHT, relict of the late Job Wright, of Middleton, in her 77th year. [A bit of discrepancy exits] Our sister was another of the converts of the Rev. Mr. Snowball about 63 years ago. During all those years she remained a faithful member of the Methodist Church. Her house was always open to the minister and she was ever trying to make the servant of God happy in his work. Her experience was [one of] constant rest, calm, and peace in Jesus. She was ever ready to render help to the cause of God. During her last illness the writer had the privilege of visiting her and talking about the things of God. She loved dearly to talk about Jesus and His love and never once expressed any fear of death. She was longing to go home where she would be at rest with the Saviour whom she loved. She was of a retiring disposition and thus was never amongst the public workers, but hers was a service of love and charity to all. She literally fell asleep and her sun set in calmness and peace.

Another obituary follows: "The friends will be sorry to learn that Mrs. Job Wright breathed her last at Middleton about 7o'clock last Friday evening. The deceased was the mother of Mr. Jesse A. Wright [actually the step-mother] and Mrs. Wallace Bradshaw. The funeral will take place from her late residence today (Monday) at 2 o'clock p.m. 'Sleep, mother, quietly sleep. The rolling years go by; Thy memory, mother, we will keep Until we meet on high.'"

"That Wright home in North Bedeque was a most hospitable one," wrote Doris Haslam: "... a veritable halfway house, entertaining relatives and friends from near and far. Rarely a day passed when there were not several guests joining the family for a meal as well as occupying the guest rooms in the large house which was built prior to 1837.... [Nancy's] family tradition of hospitality was a strong one. Nancy's childhood home had been headquarters for the early ministers, and the doors of her Wright home in North Bedeque were ever open to welcome the resident and visiting clergy and their families."[78]

The home in Central Bedeque is now owned by Sidney Green and his wife and is in magnificent condition. A tour was given through the Bedeqeue United Church in 2001 of six local homes of which the Green's was one. It is beautifully decorated and maintained.

We will continue with the children of Elizabeth and John (surname Wright, sixth generation):

4.13 Albert Wright (6, Elizabeth 5, Mary 4, Thomas 3, Clement 2, Stephen 1) born 1818; died 1828
4.14 Solomon Dibble Wright (6, Elizabeth 5, Mary 4, Thomas 3, Clement 2, Stephen 1) born c.1820; did not marry; died in Summerside, Wednesday evening, April 29, 1896, as reported in a local newspaper.

According to Doris Haslam, "Solomon farmed in Searletown until about 1889 when he sold his farm to Johnson Leard. He moved to a cottage on Willow Ave. in Summerside, where he and his housekeeper, Elizabeth Dobson, lived. He had been a Methodist Class leader for many years in Searletown. The bulk of his estate was bequeathed to foreign and general missions of the Methodist Church with substantial sums being left to the Methodist churches in Summerside and Searletown, and to the fund for widows of "deposed" ministers. Solomon was named for the husband of his grand-aunt who was married and remained behind when the Wrights sailed to Shelburne, N.S."[79] Two obituaries, that describe the man that Solomon was, follow:

Solomon Wright was born in Searletown, Bedeque, P.E.I. in the year 1820; converted to God when a young man during the ministry of Rev. Alexander McLeod and entered upon the consistent and conscientious Christian life which came to its earthly termination at Summerside on Wednesday evening, April 29th, when his immortal spirit was introduced into the Saviour's presence.

No sooner did Mr. Wright experience a change of heart than he at once devoted his life to the Master's service and in due time identified himself with the Methodist Church. Living in a home which did not until that time enjoy the inestimable boon of family worship, with the consent of parents, he erected the altar whence the incense of household devotion ascended daily to the throne of God.

A Christian life so well begun could scarcely eventuate in other than a continuous career of loving attachment and honorable service, and from that day, whether found in the prayer meeting, in the class meeting, in the Sabbath School, or in the public services, he was steadfast and immovable, his affections centered in loving devotion upon Christ and his faith firm, fixed in the great eternal principles which

underlie all true Christian character. Such steadfastness naturally involved responsibilities both in regard to the spiritual and temporal interests of the Church, and whether as leader in devotional service, or administering with others financial concerns as a trustee of the Church property in his native community, and more recently as a member of the Trust Board of our new church [which was dedicated in 1888] in this town [Bedeque], he was ever faithful in the discharge of his duty and generous in the support of all the interests of the Church. In addition to several bequests to our local objects, Mr. Wright generously made the Church his beneficiary to the amount of one thousand dollars willed to the General Missionary Society, and two hundred dollars to our Supernumerary Fund. [The local newspaper read, "We are informed that by the will of the late Solomon Wright he bequeathed $1,000 to the women's foreign missions of the Methodist Church and $1,000 to the general missions of the same body. His will also contains something substantial to the building fund of the Summerside Methodist Church, to the Searletown Methodist Church and to the fund for the widows of deceased ministers." Beginning as a young man, he remained a useful, consistent and respected member of the church up to the ripe age of seventy-six years when the Master called him home and "he was not for God took him."

The second obituary provided extra details:

Many of our readers will be pained to hear of the death of Mr. Solomon Wright. He died at his home on Wednesday evening full of years, good acts, and kindly words. Having decided to retire from farming seven years ago, he sold his beautiful homestead in Searletown to Mr. Johnson Laird and removed to this town [Summerside]. He purchased a comfortable cottage from Mrs. Dr. Jamieson on Willow Avenue whose hospitable doors were ever open to his friends. Mr. Wright was one of our best citizens - his influence and vote were ever on the side of right. His clear judgment and rare good sense made one of the most desirable companions. His delicate health prevented his regular attendance at meetings of his church which was his chief delight. His familiar voice was listened to with delight in prayer meeting and when he lifted it up to God in prayer, in which he was especially gifted, the congregation felt that he had power with his Saviour. Few men in their 77th year were so well posted in the current events of the world, and his admiration of the Queen and loyalty to the British nation knew no bounds. His sympathy for the oppressed, not only in Armenia, but everywhere, and his heart's desire to see the gospel sent to "every land," his last will and testament bears substantial proof. Mr. Wright was a son of the late Hon. John R. Wright, a brother of Mr. Theo. Wright, Burton; Mr. Thomas Wright, Fulton, N.Y.; and Mr. D. S. Wright, Searletown, and the late Mr. John R. Wright and Mr. Job Wright, Middleton, the latter two with himself having all died in their 77th year.

Unveil thy bosom, faithful tomb; Take this new treasure to thy trust,
And give these sacred relics room to slumber in the silent dust.

4.15 Richard *Theodore* Wright (6, Elizabeth 5, Mary 4, Thomas 3, Clement 2, Stephen 1) born December 16, 1821 in Searletown; married his first cousin, Sarah Montgomery Wright, the daughter of Nathaniel and Christiana (Cole) Wright of Searletown [Nathaniel was in the third generation of Wrights in P.E.I., the grandson of William, the Loyalist], at the Mission House in Searletown on July 11, 1849. Sarah was born on April 23, 1828 in Cetnreville Bedeque and died March 8, 1896 in Burton, P.E.I. He died on February 21, 1914. In just over 2 months, he would have been 93 years old. In *The Wrights of Bedeque* (p. 57) we read:

... About 1858 they moved to a rather new settlement in Lot 7, Prince County, where Theodore built mills, on Bear Pond, above Seal Point. For many years he ran the grist and carding mills there and carried on considerable farming as well. The school district established in 1865 was called Mount Pleasant, but was renamed Burton in 1886 by Theodore because the use of the name Mount Pleasant would have caused misdirection of mail. The name Burton possibly comes from Haliburton Road since the next district was at its north end. Theodore was the postmaster, Justice of the Peace, and leader in the new community. He also operated a lobster factory there. There was no harbour in that part of Northumberland Strait so shipping stages, called "blocks" had to be built in the water. At low tide the shipments were hauled by horse and sloven, unloaded, and stacked on the block. When the tide was high, rowboats and dories transported the goods to the waiting schooners. According to *Meacham's Atlas*, 1880, Theodore also had mills at Campbellton, Lot 4, on the county line between Lots 7 and 4. Here he had another farm of one hundred acres, a saw mill, and a shingle mill. When the house at Burton was destroyed by fire, he moved to the Campbellton property and carried on both farming and milling operations.

Theodore took a deep interest in the Methodist cause in that area and served as class leader, Sunday School Superintendent and member of the Trustee and Quarterly Boards of the Cape Wolfe circuit. Sarah and all but two of their children are buried beside him in the Cape Wolfe United Church cemetery.

Theodore and Sarah Wright had six children (surname Wright, seventh generation). His obituary appeared in a local newspaper:

In Memoriam
R. Theodore Wright

When on the evening of Saturday, the 21st of February last R. Theodore Wright departed this life, the village of Campbellton, Prince Co., P.E.I. lost one of its oldest and most highly respected residents, and the Cape Wolfe Circuit, its oldest and one of its most loyal members. In December, 1821, he was born at Searletown, P.E.I., a son of the late John Wright. He was married to Sarah, daughter of the late Nathaniel Wright, of Searletown. There were born to them a family of five children, the two first of whom died in childhood. About eighteen years ago [March 8, 1896] the devoted wife and mother passed to her eternal reward. The surviving members of the family are two daughters, Mrs. Henry Wroth and Mrs. James Huestis of Boston, Mass., and one son, Ingham S., at home in Campbellton.

Nearly sixty years ago, Mr. Wright moved from Searletown to a beautiful spot on the Western shore of the Island in Lot 7 which at that time was a comparatively new settlement, but is now a thickly inhabited community known by the name of Burton. There he built mills, and for many years ran a grist mill, carding mill and saw mill and also carried on considerable farming. Mr. Wright was an energetic and industrious man, and by his good management, business ability, and the blessing of God, he became one of the most prosperous and well-to-do men in that section of the country. A few years ago, his home at Burton was destroyed by fire with most of its contents. After the fire he moved to the village of Campbellton where he spent the remainder of his days being lovingly and tenderly cared for in his declining years by his son Ingham and his estimable wife.

In early life, while at Searletown, Theodore Wright accepted Christ as his personal Saviour and united with the Methodist Church of which he continued a consistent and faithful member. Being a man of strong convictions, of sound judgment, of earnest purpose, and of upright Christian character, he became, under God, a very useful and honored citizen in the community and a "tower of strength" in the church. After his removal to Lot 7, he took a deep interest in the erection of a new Methodist Church there, to the support of which he continued to give willing service and generous financial help. Acting in his official capacity, he served the church at different times as class leader, S. S. Superintendent, and a member of Trustee and Quarterly Official Boards. The pastors who have labored on the Cape Wolfe Circuit and those who years ago were stationed on the Alberton charge will doubtless cherish pleasant and grateful memories of their happy and helpful associations with Br. Theodore Wright, and the warm welcome and exceeding kindness of his hospitable home.

For some time past on account of age and infirmity, our departed brother was unable to be present at the services of the sanctuary, but he drew near to God in the quiet of his own home and found daily nourishment in the inspired pages of his precious Bible; and thus by waiting upon the Lord, he renewed his spiritual strength.

At the throne of grace he didn't forget the interests of his church for while lying on his death-bed, he was praying for the success of revival services being conducted in the Cape Wolfe church at that time.

In common with others, Brother Theodore Wright had his spiritual conflicts, but he "fought the good fight," he "finished the course," he "kept the faith." He met the last enemy calmly and bravely, leaving behind him for the help and comfort of his sorrowing dear ones, the example of a godly life and the testimony of a triumphant death. "And by it, he being dead yet speaketh."

Servant of God, well done, Thy glorious warfare's past;
The battle's fought, the victory's won, and thou art crowned at last.
G. A. Sellar

Another brief obituary from the newspaper belonging to the Bradshaws follows: "THEODORE WRIGHT – At the age of ninety-five, Mr. Theodore Wright, one of Campbelltown's most respected inhabitants, died on Tuesday last. Mr. Wright was one of the oldest settlers in that part of the country and was highly esteemed by all. He was always upright and exemplary in his behaviour, and his death is deeply regretted by those who know him."

4.16 Thomas Robins Wright (6, Elizabeth 5, Mary 4, Thomas 3, Clement 2, Stephen 1) born December 25, 1823; married Delilah Ballou, November 1857; and died August 29, 1908 in Oswego Falls, N.Y.

Thomas, like the rest of his brothers, received his education in the schools in Bedeque, wrote Doris Haslam, in *The Wrights of Bedeque:*

It was a four mile walk there, morning and evening. And like the others [brothers], he left school when he was sufficiently grown to help at home. One of the larger projects was helping his father and Uncle Nathaniel clear the site and build a saw mill located on his grandfather's [Nathaniel's] 250 acre Loyalist grant along the Dunk River. The 125 acre mill property was deeded to his cousin, George Wright, in 1854. When Thomas was twenty-five years old, he went to work with his Uncle Jesse Wright. Jesse [the husband of Sally Hooper] operated the grist mill in Bedeque. While he was living there, a visitor to the home painted such a glowing picture of opportunities in Fulton, N. Y. that Thomas set off July 12, 1850 for Fulton and arrived there on July 20 with the whole sum of three dollars in his pocket. He at once found employment in a saw mill, and before long he was operating a mill,

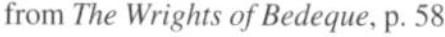

from *The Wrights of Bedeque*, p. 58

Thomas Robins Wright
(1823-1908)

from *The Wrights of Bedeque*, p. 58

Delilah (Ballou) Wright
(1834-1899), wife of
Thomas R. Wright

Parker and Wright, in partnership with Parker. Parker sold out his partnership to Schenech. The Wright & Schenech lumber business ran until 1884 when Thomas retired. He then hired men to clear off the lumbered areas for farmland. He was also a partner in Gilbert, Wright & Company, a custom grinding and feed mill bought in 1865. In public life, he filled many responsible positions. For many years he was president of the town of Granby and one of the supervisors.[80]

Thomas appears to be the first from his area in P.E.I. to go to Fulton and Oswego, N. Y.; many others followed. Delilah was born about 1834 in Warren County, N.Y. and died on April 26, 1899 at age 65 in Oswego Falls, N.Y. Both Thomas and Delilah are buried in Mt. Adnah Cemetery in Oswego Falls. The obituary from the local newspaper follows:

Wright - Thomas R. Wright died at his home on West First Street, August 29th, [1908] aged 84 years. He is survived by two sons, Jay, J. and Jesse Wright both of Syracuse. Funeral services were held Monday afternoon at his late residence; interment in Mt. Adnah.

In the demise of Mr. Wright, Fulton loses one of her oldest residents. He has resided in Fulton for the past 53 years. For years he was interested in the lumber business and has always taken an active interest in local affairs. He was popular with all classes, a man of sterling worth, and though he reached an advanced age, yet his demise was regretted by all who had the pleasure of his association or acquaintance.

4.17 Anne Wright (6, Elizabeth 5, Mary 4, Thomas 3,Clement 2, Stephen 1) born 1826; died that year. Within a year after Anne was born, her mother, Elizabeth died as well; cause of death unknown.

John, the father, was one of the first settlers of Searletown which was quickly settled when a new road to Bedeque was opened, "commencing near the 17th mile of the old Tryon Road and running ten miles to the West Branch of the Bedeque River." He was also one of the most public-spirited of Nathaniel's sons. Early in his adult life John was a Justice of the Peace which gave him the title "Squire." John Wright, served in the militia as a Lieutenant in the 2nd Battalion, was appointed a High Sheriff for Prince County, and a member of the Legislative Council, which gave him the title "Honorable." He was also a coroner, conducting inquests for many years. When he was over 80 years old, he was listed, albeit honorary, as Lt. Colonel in the 2nd Prince Co. Regiment.

As we have already seen earlier in this chapter, about four years after Elizabeth's death, John Wright married Mary Stewart. Mary was born c.1805 at Shipyard, Princetown, P.E.I. and died at Searletown on Dec. 20, 1877. John and Mary had one son and one daughter who were not Hooper descendants, but because the children's ages ranged from 4 to 18 years in 1831, Mary must have helped to raise several of them. A few of them no doubt grew up with John and Mary's daughter and son - Elizabeth Ann (called Eliza), born in 1833, and Dugald Stewart, born June 19, 1835.

Eliza married Nathaniel Huestis [See elsewhere in this book]. Dugald inherited the homestead, "Birch Grove," in Searletown, and farmed it and the Lewis Wright farm.[81] He also inherited his father's family's tradition for public service as he was appointed Justice of the Peace in 1871 and succeeded his father as High Sheriff of Prince County. Dugald married Beria Steward Black. His son, Fred, succeeded him many years later [See information elsewhere in this book].

4.2. Ann Robins (5, Mary 4, Thomas 3, Clement 2, Stephen 1)**,** born in 1789; [My information gives the same birth year for the two girls. Were they twins or born 10 - 11 months apart?] married John Craig, the son of William Craig and Kennedy Copeland, in 1810. John was born in 1788 and died in 1852. John had a general store and farmed in Lower Bedeque. Ann died young (1827); she lived only 17 years after her marriage), and John married (ii) Elizabeth Lee Owen of Malpeque. They had two sons and five daughters who would also be Hooper relatives as John Craig was a Hooper descendant. The last child of Elizabeth's was 36 years younger than the first child of Ann's; in other words, John Craig begat children for thirty-six years!]

The names of the seven children of John Craig and Ann Robins (surname Craig, sixth generation) are:

4.21 Mary Craig (6, Ann 5, Mary 4, Thomas 3, Clement 2, Stephen 1) born in 1811; "almost certainly married William Cale Schurman."[82]
4.22 Margaret Craig (6, Ann 5, Mary 4, Thomas 3, Clement 2, Stephen 1) born 1811. No further information.
4.23 William Craig (6, Ann 5, Mary 4, Thomas 3, Clement 2, Stephen 1) born 1813; married Jane Hooper, Major's 9th child, (5, Major 4, Thomas 3, Clement 2, Stephen 1) born 1815; [Ann's son married Ann's niece, a first cousin!]; died 1890. The reader will please note that William, the husband of Jane Hooper of the 5th generation is himself, through his birth to Ann Robins Craig, in the 6th generation.

For this family we will count the next generation as number 6 as though the line goes through Jane, and we will find the family of nine children listed arbitrarily under Jane Hooper, the daughter of Major of the 4th generation.
4.24 John Craig (6, Ann 5, Mary 4, Thomas 3, Clement 2, Stephen 1) born 1815. No further information known.
4.25 Alexander Craig (6, Ann 5, Mary 4, Thomas 3, Clement 2, Stephen 1) born 1817; died 1900. Nothing further known.
4.26 Sophia Ann Craig (6, Ann 5, Mary 4, Thomas 3, Clement 2, Stephen 1) born August 30, 1819 in Lower Bedeqeue; married her cousin, John Robins Wright (born c.1813) on March 31, 1842; died on July 3, 1898 in Searletown, P.E.I. John R. died on February 23, 1890 in Searletown.
4.27 James Craig (6, Ann 5, Mary 4, Thomas 3, Clement 2, Stephen 1) born 1822. No further information known.

4.3 Richard Robins (5, Mary 4, Thomas 3, Clement 2, Stephen 1) probably named for his grandfather Robins who came to P.E.I. with Thomas Hooper, was born in 1791 in Lower Bedeque, and married Harriett L. Ruston, who was born in Nova Scotia. They resided in Bedeque, P.E.I. They had five sons and three daughters, all of whom lived in various places around Bedeque. I have information on only one son:

4.31 Sandy Robins (6, Richard 5, Mary 4, Thomas 3, Clement 2, Stephen 1) married Elizabeth Crossman. The wedding was the only marriage performed by Alfred Schurman, Justice of the Peace.

4.4 Maria Robins (5, Mary 4, Thomas 3, Clement 2, Stephen 1) was born c.1793; married on March 11, 1821, to Thomas Moyse who was born in 1785 in Devon, England. Thomas was one of four seaman sons of Henry Moyse, a carpenter in Dover, England, who died on November 1, 1834 and was buried in St. Mary's churchyard in Dover. Thomas was a sea captain, and died in 1864. Maria was his second wife, the first wife dying on the way to visit the Schurman

home at the death of William, the Loyalist in 1819. Maria and Thomas lived and farmed in Central Bedeque. They had three girls and three boys. I know the name of only one son (surname Moyse, sixth generation):

4.41 Frederick Holland Moyse (6, Maria 5, Mary 4, Thomas 3, Clement 2, Stephen 1) born on October 29, 1829, on a farm in Wilmot Valley, P.E.I.; when he was about 12 years old, his family moved to Central Bedeque. He married Mary Crawford Wright on January 13, 1859. Mary was born on May 12, 1831 in Middleton, P.E.I. and died on January 19, 1919 in Central Bedeque. A brief obituary follows from the newspaper given by Mr. and Mrs. Malcolm Bradshaw: "The funeral of the late Mrs. Mary Moyse, who passed away at Central Bedeque on Sunday morning, will take place from the residence of her son, Mr. Thomas Moyse, Central Bedeque, this Tuesday afternoon at 2 o'clock to the Methodist Church, Centreville, thence to the Methodist Cemetery." Fred died on September 26, 1887 in Central Bedeque.

The fall after Fred and Mary were married, on November 15, 1859, Captain Thomas deeded the Central Bedeque farm to Fred and it was on this farm that he and Mary lived until he was accidentally killed in a threshing accident. He was operating one of the old-fashioned horse-powered mills when the belt slipped off and the mill started running wild with the horses. He applied the brake too heavily; the large fly-wheel broke and a piece hit him, causing his death almost instantly. His son Tom stopped the mill by jamming a stick under the revolving floor on which the horses were racing. The obituary, compliments of Mr. and Mrs. Malcolm Bradshaw, includes some of the above as well as additional details:

Death of Mr. F. H. Moyse
September 26, 1887

Quite a gloom was recently cast over Bedeque and vicinity by the sudden death of Mr. Frederick H. Moyse. While the deceased was engaged in threshing, on Monday fortnight last, the belt slipped off the machine, and before anyone could

reach the brake, the speed of the horses had increased to a run. Mr. Moyse immediately ran and threw his whole weight on the brake, and this together with the high speed, caused the fly wheel to burst, killing him instantly.

Mr. Moyse was one of Bedeque's most enterprising and successful farmers, and by his removal the community loses an esteemed brother, a generous neighbor, and a true, warm-hearted friend. His temperance principles were well-known, as for years he had been an advocate of total abstinence and had ofter been called upon to preside at temperance meetings and to speak from the temperance platform. He was one of the earliest promoters of temperance in Bedeque and took an active part in the organizing of Champion Division which is still existing in Centreveille.

For years he had been an active member of the Methodist Church, taking an important part in the various services and holding many offices of trust and responsibility. At the time of his death he was a member of the building committee of the new church now in course of construction in Centreville. He will long be missed by the church as a good and faithful brother and a wise and clever counselor. He leaves a wife and four [actually he had five] children to mourn the loss of a kind and loving husband and a careful and affectionate father. In their bereavement, the family has the respect and sympathy of all in the community. His funeral was on a Tuesday following his death, and his popularity and the esteem in which he was held could easily be seen by the large number who attended to pay their last respects to the deceased.

Fred and Mary had five children (seventh generation, surname Moyse).

4.5 John M. Robins (5, Mary 4, Thomas 3, Clement 2, Stephen 1) was born in 1795. No more information found.

4.6 Thomas Robins (5, Mary 4, Thomas 3, Clement 2, Stephen 1) born 1796; married in 1827, Isabella (called Belle) Beairsto, who was born in 1809 in Malpeque, P.E.I., and died in 1869. Thomas, who died in 1882, was a farmer and they lived in Central Bedeque. He and Isabella raised a family of three sons and seven daughters of whom I can account for only four (surname Robins, sixth generation):

4.61 One son died in infancy (6, Thomas 5, Mary 4, Thomas 3, Clement 2, Stephen 1)

4.62 Thomas Robins, Jr. (6, Thomas 5, Mary 4, Thomas 3, Clement 2, Stephen 1) (1836-Aug. 10, 1915), married Fanny Boyle [died Feb. 21, 1915, aged 83; both buried in Lower Bedeque Cemetery], and raised two sons, one of whom died of tuberculosis, a huge killer in those days. [Please see generation seven]
4.63 Nancy Robins (6, Thomas 5, Mary 4, Thomas 3, Clement 2, Stephen 1)**,** died 1855.
4.64 Mary Robins (6, Thomas 5, Mary 4, Thomas 3, Clement 2, Stephen 1) married, raised a large family, and died at age 42 of tuberculosis.

Tragedy struck this Robins family in 1855 when **Thomas Junior**, his sisters **Mary and Nancy**, and a friend, Miss Johnson of Margate, were returning from a visit with friends in Summerside. A storm blew up while they were crossing the ice to the Bedeque shore, a shortcut used in winter. Blinding snow caused Thomas to lose his way and they plunged through the ice. [With blinding snow one loses his sense of direction. The group actually was going in the direction from which they had come!] Thomas managed to rescue Mary and Nancy, but Miss Johnson could not be found. They started for a light on the shore, and Nancy, soon exhausted and nearly frozen to death, fell on the ice and would not go on. Mary, too, was nearly exhausted when they finally reached a house in Summerside. A search party found Nancy and Miss Johnson's frozen bodies the next day.[83]

Another source described the tragedy of the deaths under the heading of "Drownings in Summerside Harbour:" [In the year 1855] "... occurred the tragedy of the Robins family who, returning to Bedeque from a visit in Summerside over the unbushed ice, and bewildered by falling snow, drove into an opening at the mouth of the harbour. Two perished, but the remaining two, though badly frozen, managed to make their way back to the town."[84]

Mary lived to marry and raise a large family, but died of tuberculosis at the age of forty-two. Thomas, Junior, [who was born in 1836] lived to be seventy-nine and died in 1915. He never forgot his friend, Miss Johnson, and often talked of her. He later married Fanny Boyle and raised two boys. The sons, too, died of tuberculosis.

A much more detailed account of this same accident.appeared in 1890:

A Terrible Night on the Ice

(The Province Prize Story for Prince Edward Island in *Montreal Witness)*

A little more than thirty years ago when the now flourishing town of Summerside had grown only to the size of a small village, a very sad and tragic event happened on the ice in this harbor which for the time cast a deep gloom over the neighborhood.

The winter had just fairly set in and the first ice had completely closed up the navigation. It was about the time of the Christmas festivities, so much enjoyed by the young people in those days in the social and innocent pastime of sleigh-driving and visiting friends. At this time our railway was not thought of nor yet our telegraph and telephone system, now a seeming necessity of our every day life; hence the utility of so much sleigh driving in those days. In the narrative we are about to relate, we shall aim at giving nothing but the simple fact in every detail as there are many persons still living who recollect this unfortunate occurrence and therefore it is more necessary to be particular in this respect, only the names of the parties being withheld.

A party of four young persons [Thomas Robins, Mary Robins, Nancy Robins, and a friend, Miss Johnson, of Margate], all unmarried, consisting of two ladies, their brother, and lady friend, left their home in Bedeque to visit some friends residing in Summerside, intending to return home the same evening. Being early in the season, the ice had not yet been "bushed" or marked out for travelers, but this they did not mind as the day was fine, the ice fairly good, and the traveling light and enjoyable. Arriving early at their friend's house they spent a pleasant evening in social chat and rustic merriment, and it was not till some time after nine o'clock that they thought of returning home.

The night was not quite so fine as the day had been for a north-easterly wind had sprung up and was increasing with some snow falling, but no danger was apprehended as less than an hour's drive would put them over the dangers of the harbor's ice. But such good fortune was not in store for them. After getting fairly on the ice, they found that their former track was completely obliterated, and very soon every object was lost to their view, not even a solitary star could be seen to guide those lonely travelers over that icy waste.

For some time they drove on and on in the hope of seeing some object, but in vain. At length one of the ladies, growing restless and fearful that they were going astray, observed that either the wind had changed or they were going in the wrong direction. The young man then left the sleigh and tried to find where they were, but could discover nothing, and now fully realized that they had lost their way. He walked on cautiously leading the horse. The night, in the meantime, grew bitterly cold and stormy while their uncomfortable condition from cold and exposure made the situation each moment more perilous and the time painfully weary.

In this bewildered condition they slowly wandered about in hope of finding a landing and some shelter for the night, but in what direction they went, or over what dangers they may have passed can only be conjectured.

At last, without the least warning, they were all thrown headlong into the freezing water; horse, sleigh, driver and the three women were all plunged into the deep water without any hope of help. The young man, being in the prime of life, by sheer strength soon succeeded in getting out on the firm ice, and just then observed the glimmer of a distant light, but, to his dismay, he found that there was a sheet of open water between him and where he saw the light.

There appeared no other way of escape than to swim across the opening to the inner side, and this he succeeded in doing though with much difficulty owing to snow and thin ice obstructing his way. He had now reached the spot where his two sisters were struggling in the water, and one of them for a time clung to him with that tenacity so peculiar to drowning people, but the brother told her to make an effort to hold to ice until he could get out and then he would save them both. This she did and with great effort he succeeded in getting both his sisters out of the cold, deep water, but, unfortunately, the lady friend who was with them could not be reached for she seemed to have got entangled in the sleigh or harness and soon perished.

The brother and sisters then made towards the light, struggling on in their half-perishing condition in the face of a blinding snow-storm. This light was about a mile or more distant, and in their benumbed condition, they made but slow progress which became still slower as the elder of the two sisters momentarily grew fainter, and after bearing up bravely for nearly half a mile, she sank down never to rise again in this life urging her brother and sister to go on and save themselves, if possible. Nothing could be done but for the two remaining ones to push on towards the light, and this they did bravely although by this time there were two or three inches of snow on the ice, and the clothes they had on were frozen solid, but every moment brought them nearer relief, and after what seemed to them many long hours, they finally saw the shore and found they had at last got to land. Here again was another difficulty; no house was near enough for its inmates to hear their cries for help, so there was nothing left to be done but for the brother to leave his sister and seek help or else die there with her. With her advice, however, he climbed the

bank and found to his great surprise that he was again in Summerside though how it happened he could not understand. After a short time he got to a house, the alarm was soon given and the perishing woman was found in the snow and was promptly cared for.

At the time there were ship yards close by and all the men there employed turned out in search of the two persons who had perished. It was not yet daylight when the search began, and it was impossible to learn from the bewildered young man the direction in which they had met their misfortune. The party of searchers burnt tar barrels to aid them in their search, and parties traveled in different directions, but all to no purpose. Soon after daylight, however, some articles of clothing were found, a glove in one place and a victorine further in another, and so by following up this clue, the body of the sister [Nancy] who had perished on the ice was found. She had sunk down on her knees and had fallen forward on her face in her dying moments. A temporary bier was made with sticks and her remains carried to the hotel where her brother and sister were already being cared. for. After this one had been found, a party of men, following on in the direction indicated by the bits of clothing, soon found the remaining body and also the horse and sleigh, all of which were floating on the surface of the water, the woman and horse being cold in death.

It seemed that sometime after leaving Summerside on their way home, the driver became confused and, turning his horse toward the harbor's mouth, had made a right angle to the course he should have followed, and drove directly out towards the open sea, into an opening in the ice quite across the harbor.

At their home the parents had been very uneasy and the father, in the morning took a horse and drove with haste to Summerside, arriving shortly after the recovery of his dead child and her companion. The surviving daughter [Mary] being young, strong, and healthy, soon rallied and regained her former strength and in due time married and reared a family, some of whom are still living near by, the mother having passed away some years ago. The brother is still living, seeming little the worse of his terrible night's adventure on the ice.
Benjamin Howard, Summerside, P.E.I. [1890][85]

John Robins died very shortly after his sixth child was born, leaving his wife a widow at a young age. Mary Hooper Robins was the first recorded widow in Bedeque [1796]. In 1798 an official from Charlottetown took the first census in Bedeque since its settlement by the Loyalists. He found twenty-four families (not exactly a large population living in what are now the communities of North Bedeque, Central Bedeque, Centreville Bedeque, and Lower Bedeque).

As a local magistrate, William Schurman, the Loyalist, would be called upon to attest to affidavits and so on and hold small court. It was the most honoured position a country dweller could have. It made his advice sought, his interpretation respected, his opinions valued. Some cases with which he was involved were of a serious nature such as murder as well as many that were of a minor nature. Thomas Hooper, the Loyalist, also had been given the designation Esquire as had Major, the eldest son of Thomas with whom William had been associated in 1784 when Major was about twenty years old. William and Major appeared to have been partners for a time around 1810, perhaps owning a ship between them.

5.0 Thomas Hooper, Jr. (4, Thomas 3, Clement 2, Stephen 1), called Tommy, came from New Jersey to P.E.I. with his father in 1785 when he was about 13 years old. He married Elizabeth, called Betsy, Cole (1788 - June 10, 1866), daughter of Benjamin and Isabella Robins Cole, and granddaughter of Loyalist Richard Robins. Thomas Jr. and Betsy had seven children (surname Hooper, fifth generation):

5.1 Mary Hooper (5, Thomas Jr. 4, Thomas 3, Clement 2, Stephen 1) was born about 1807, and died in 1846); in January 1836 she married James Murray who was born c.1805 in North Bedeque, the son of David Murray and Elizabeth Penman. James died in North Bedeque in 1850. [As an aside, Benjamin Cole probably came to the Island of St. John with his mother and his stepfather, George Penman, who had been paymaster of the British forces under Lord Rollo when Rollo occupied the Island in 1758. George Penman and his family were living in the Port Hill area of P.E.I. prior to 1783. It is very possible that Elizabeth Penman was the stepsister of Benjamin Cole].[86] The reader may remember that Mary's cousin, Hugh Montgomery, (Ann's son) married James's younger sister, Elizabeth. James was a farmer in Bedeque. After Mary's death James married a lady called Zalah, who was born c.1826 and died after 1881. They had at least one

child who died in infancy. James died in 1850. Both he and Mary were interred in the Presbyterian Cemetery in North Bedeque. James and Mary had at least five children whose names I do not know (sixth generation)[87]

5.2 Ann Hooper (5, Thomas Jr. 4, Thomas 3, Clement 2, Stephen 1) was born on January 1, 1811 and died on March 2, 1846; on October 1, 1828 she married John "Cummyfoe" Baker Schurman (August 29, 1805-December 18, 1891), son of Isaac Schurman (born November 1774 in New Rochelle, N.Y.) and Mary Baker (born May 3, 1779 in Westchester County, N. Y.) of Central Bedeque, P.E.I. Ann's husband was a farmer/school teacher, an active temperance worker, an amateur poet, and a Commissioner of Deeds. He was a poor man most of his life, which was spent primarily in Bedeque, Freetown, and Summerside. He probably got his nickname from his frequent use of the expression "comme il faut" (as it should be; proper, correct) in response to his pupils' recitation! Ann and Cummyfoe had four daughters and two sons (surname Schurman, sixth generation):

5.21 Thomas Hooper Schurman (6, Ann 5, Thomas Jr. 4, Thomas 3, Clement 2, Stephen 1) was born June 12, 1832; married Mary Ann Baxter, daughter of George and Mary (Hewson) Baxter, on September 1, 1852 in St. Eleanors, P.E.I. She was born on July 26, 1831 in River Philip, Nova Scotia, and died in February 1906 in Summerside East. Thomas died on March 1, 1906 in Summerside East.

Thomas taught school as a young man, but soon settled to the life of a farmer. He was referred to as a teacher in probably only one record, the entry for his first child's baptism in 1863. Ross Graves in, *William Schurman, Loyalist ...*, provided an interesting and well-researched description of Thomas's life:

> ... He lived in Summerside East on what is called the Gillespie place where Lester Baglole lived in 1971. It was a portion of the farm of George Darby who was married to Olivia Hewson, an aunt to Thomas' wife. George Darby had no children living at the time he drew up the will (February, 1863- he died the follow-

ing year) and he left his homestead property to his wife, at whose death it was to be divided between his nephew George Darby Baxter and his niece Mary, the wife of Thomas Schurman. Thomas and Mary, who had been living with George and Olivia for some time and had named their first two children for the older couple, received the eastern portion of the property on which the Darby house was situated. It contained a hundred acres, divided in two equal lots by the line separating Lots 17 and 19. George Baxter's smaller portion of fifty acres lay on the west. Before going to live on the Darby farm Thomas and Mary may have lived for a time in Summerside. He had bought in 1855 a lot on Second Street from Joseph Green, the tavernkeeper. He sold it nearly twenty years later, long after we know he was settled in Summerside East.

Harvie's Island almanacs from 1868 through 1870 list Thomas as one of the four Commissioners of Small Debts for the Summerside district. Like his father, he was interested in temperance work. In 1871 he was "Temple Deputy" for the Wilmot division of the International Order of Good Templars. He wrote a series of articles, "History of the United Empire Loyalists who Settled in and around Bedeque," which appeared in one of the Summerside papers.... He was one of the executors of the will of his neighbour and brother-in-law, George Darby Baxter, in 1892.

Mary died [February 1906] a week before her husband [March 1, 1906] and two weeks before her son Howard (March 7, 1906). Her will, drawn up before Howard's death and probated May 14, 1906, left the farm to Howard, money to George, Olivia and Annie.[88] [One wonders if a communicable disease took their lives]

5.22 Mary Jane Schurman (6, Ann 5, Thomas Jr. 4,Thomas 3, Clement 2, Stephen 1), was born on April 26, 1834. She did not marry and died on January 25, 1917 in Central Bedeque. For years she lived at the home of her mother's nephew, Nelson Hooper (Alexander's son), in Lower Bedeque. When the property was sold she was supposed to go with it, but the new owner's wife refused to keep her and she was put out. Eventually Mrs. Leonard Schurman, whose mother was a Hooper, gave her a home. [Isabel or Isabelle Hooper Schurman's mother was Mary *Alice* Hooper, daughter of Alexander Hooper. Alice and Nelson were brother and sister.]

5.23 Elizabeth B. Schurman [a twin] (6, Ann 5, Thomas Jr. 4, Thomas 3, Clement 2, Stephen 1) was born on November 27, 1837; she died on January 30, 1848. The initial "B." appears on the gravestone, but she is called Elizabeth Ann in the Bedeque Presbyterian Church baptismal register. She and her two brothers and two sisters were baptized in 1843, her sister Isabella the following year.

5.24 Lemuel Schurman, [a twin] (6, Ann 5, Thomas Jr. 4, Thomas 3, Clement 2, Stephen 1) was born on November 27, 1837. He grew up in the household of his grandfather, Isaac Schurman, in Central Bedeque. The grandfather's will, dated 1849, left Lemuel two cows and a horse when he became twenty-one, if he remained with the family. He left the Island for Michigan, married Mary A. Luckey, lived in Negaunee, then in Ishpeming and was accidentally shot in the Michigan woods on January 3, 1893. His death notice, carried in the Island papers, stated that he left a family, but nothing was known of them. Carnegie Public Library in Ishpeming provided the account of the accident as carried in the town's weekly paper, *The Iron Ore*, for Saturday, January 7, 1893: "A man named Lemuel Schurman working at Walton's camp, Dexter, accidentally shot himself with a revolver Monday last. Death was instantaneous. A jury was selected and a coroner's inquest held. He has a brother in St. Paul. The funeral took place Friday, the remains being taken to Negaunee for interment.

5.25 Margaret Schurman (6, Ann 5, Thomas Jr. 4, Thomas 3, Clement 2, Stephen 1) was born on September 20, 1840 and died in 1893. She married Benjamin Wentworth. She was dismissed from the Bedeque Baptist Church to the Summerside Baptist Church in 1868, the same year her father's membership was similarly transferred. She and Benjamin appear to have settled in Oakdale, MA. [I believe that there is no such place in Massachusetts] She and Ida, the daughter of John and his second wife, moved to the United States, each daughter to a separate location with her husband. Ida moved to St. Paul, MN.

5.26 Isabella Hooper Schurman (6, Ann 5, Thomas Jr. 4, Thomas 3, Clement 2, Stephen 1) was born on November 30, 1842, baptized in 1844, and died on January 23, 1848. She is buried in the

North Bedeque Presbyterian Cemetery with her mother and her sister Elizabeth who died a week later. On the gravestone is a verse written by the father:

> The mother and two daughters dear
> Now side by side are laying here;
> Both old and young as you pass by,
> Do not forget that you must die.[89]

Within a year of the time that Ann and Cummyfoe were married in 1828 "financial difficulties prompted leaving the Island temporarily." A letter he wrote to his father from River Philip, Nova Scotia, in October 1829, indicates his intentions at that time were to settle elsewhere than on the Island:

> Dear Father
>
> I embrace this opertunity of writing to you to let you know we got safe over and have been well ever since and hope you are all the same, we was three days on the passage and one and a half we fasted. I feel quite satisfied to stop here but I want to hear from Ann I should like to hear If there was much disturbance after I left I do not think of going to Marimichy but if I have any thing to go there I would be glad If you would send it and sell it to the best advantage and send me the money....

Ross Graves, in *William Schurman, Loyalist ...*, wrote:

> John's uncle, an earlier John, had settled in River Philip some five years before, and no doubt John was staying with him. How long he remained, whether Ann joined him there, whether he went on to Miramichi [New Brunswick], and how he settled his affairs, we do not know. We do know he was in River Philip long enough to join the Baptist Church in that community, and that by 1834 he had returned to the Island.
>
> He and Ann settled on a hundred acre lot at the east end of Wilmot Valley and on the south side of the Blueshank Road. He obtained title to the lot in 1836 from his uncle Squire William, but had been living on it for some time. The 1841 census shows twenty of his hundred acres to be cleared land. He owned at that time four

cows, twenty sheep, four hogs, and a horse. His occupation is given in the census return as farmer as it is, for the last time, in the deed two years later by which he sold his property to Robert MacCaull for over twice what he had paid for it.

It was at this point that John left farming for teaching. His movements for the next eighteen years are difficult to trace, for he no doubt rented near the schools in which he taught."[90] [Ann died on March 2, 1846]

John married (ii) Sarah Ann Hyde, on October 8, 1856. They had two sons, the second of whom died the day that he was born, and a daughter, all of whom would not be Hooper relatives. About 1885 John and Sarah left the Island to live with their son Charles (1857 – 1934) in St. Paul, Minnesota. Charles had been in newspaper work all of his life, learning the business at the *Summerside Journal.* When the *Pioneer* was first established in Alberton he was a member of its staff. About 1879 or 1880 he went to St. Paul, MN; in October 1880 he bought the *West St. Paul Times* and continued as editor and publisher for forty-four years. In 1900 he was a member of the Minnesota legislature.

Ann died forty-five years before her husband, whose death occurred in West St. Paul, Minnesota in 1891.

5.3 Isabella Hooper (5, Thomas Jr. 4, Thomas 3, Clement 2, Stephen 1)) was born in 1813. She married William Wells, and they resided in Point de Brute, New Brunswick. Isabella was William's second wife, but I have no information on the name of the first wife, or whether they had any children. Isabella and William had one daughter who died when she was quite young.

5.4 Alexander Hooper (5, Thomas Jr. 4, Thomas 3, Clement 2, Stephen 1) was born in 1816; he married his cousin, Isabella Cole (1823-1906), daughter of James Cole and Margaret Clark, on December 18, 1845. Alexander died on July 1, 1894. [The reader may recall that James Cole was the son of Benjamin and Isabella (Robins) Cole] They lived in Lower Bedeque, P.E.I., and had four daughters and two sons. [I have the names of only two sons and one daughter in this document, surname Hooper, sixth generation]:

5.41 Mary *Alice* Hooper (6, Alexander 5, Thomas Jr. 4 , Thomas 3, Clement 2, Stephen 1) was born on September 13, 1850 in Lower Bedeque. She married William *Thomas* Wright, called Tom (Benjamin Wright,[4] William,[3] Nathaniel,[2] William (Loyalist),[1] on June 25, 1875. Thomas was born on February 9, 1850 in South Bedeque and died on March 19, 1924 in Lower Bedeque. Alice died there on April 10, 1921.

Tom and Alice were second cousins through the Coles. Alice was another descendant of Thomas Hooper who married a descendant of the Loyalist, William Wright. They lived on the Benjamin Wright homestead [which Tom inherited] in South Bedeque where their four children (seventh generation) were born. Tom and Alice provided Ben and Margaret, his second wife, with four grandchildren to entertain with stories of the pioneer days. There, their only son, Horace, brought his bride. The school district is now called Chelton, rather than South Bedeque. When Alice's brother's farm in Lower Bedeque came up for sale, Horace bought the farm from his Uncle Nelson Hooper, and the Chelton homestead [where Elmer and Margaret Pearson used to live] was sold to their neighbor, David Pearson.

After visiting their daughter Emma in Virden, Manitoba, Tom and Alice, in 1912, returned to the Island to assist Horace on the Lower Bedeque farm. There they spent the rest of their lives. Tom's obituary follows:

An exceptionally wide circle of our readers will join us in deep regret at the death of Mr. Thomas W. Wright of Bedeque. Mr. Wright who was 74 years of age, was taken ill whilst on a visit to his daughter, Mrs. Leonard Schurman of Central Bedeque, where he passed away on Wednesday night [1924]. The deceased gentleman was the son of the late Mr. Benjamin Wright and grandson of the late Mr. William Wright, a United Empire Loyalist and pioneer of the district. Throughout his life, he upheld the best traditions of the family and the old homestead, being one of the most prosperous and up-to-date farmers of that fine agricultural district; a good husband, a kind and indulgent father, a good neighbor and friend and held in the hightest esteem and respect of all classes in the district. There are left to mourn three daughters and one son, namely: Mrs. Minton Schurman of Butler, Manitoba; Mrs. Leonard Schurman of Central Bedeque; Mrs. Thomas Bolwin of Cabrie, Sask.; and Mr. Horace M. Wright of Bedeque; also two sisters Mrs. F. H. Leard of

Summerside and Mrs. Eliza Strang of New York to whom our sincere sympathy is extended. The funeral takes place today (Saturday) at 3 p.m. to the Methodist Church and cemetery at Bedeque, the remains being laid to rest beside those of his wife (nee Miss Mary Hooper, daughter of the late Mr. Alex Hooper) who predeceased him by three years.

5.42 Nelson Hooper (6, Alexander 5, Thomas 4, 3, Clement 2, Stephen 1) was born in 1856; he married (i) Carrie Stavert, daughter of Thomas Stavert of Wilmot; he married (ii) Eleanor Stavert, daughter of James Stavert of North Bedeque, who survived him.; he died on November 10, 1910 at the age of 54. Nelson lived in Lower Bedeque according to the 1881 Atlas. His obituary follows:

Announcement of the death on Thursday last of Nelson Hooper, one of the best known residents of Central Bedeque, came as a surprise and a shock to his many friends. He had been in excellent health until a week ago when he was suffering with a stomach hemorrhage which, notwithstanding the best medical treatment, continued at intervals until he passed away. He was a successful farmer, a public-spirited citizen and a man whom all esteemed most highly. He was fifty-four years of age and was twice married. His first wife was Miss Carrie Stavert, daughter of Thomas Stavert, Wilmot, who left one son; the second wife, who survives him, was Miss Eleanor Stavert, daughter of the late James Stavert, North Bedeque. One brother Robert of Vancouver, B. C., and one sister, Mrs. Thomas Wright [Mary Alice], Chelton, now visiting at Verden, Manitoba, survive. The bereaved family and relatives have the heartfelt sympathy of a large circle of friends. The funeral takes place Saturday at 2 o'clock.

5.43 Robert P. Hooper (6, Alexander 5, Thomas Jr. 4, Thomas 3, Clement 2, Stephen 1) resided in Vancouver, B.C. In the Ledger of Stephen Wright [preserved and given to the author in 2003 by Mr. and Mrs. Bradshaw] Robert Hooper's name appears as owing money for purchases from 1881-1884. No more information is known except at some time he must have moved to Vancouver, B.C.

5.5 Margaret Graham Hooper (5, Thomas Jr. 4, Thomas 3, Clement 2, Stephen 1) was born in 1819 in Lower Bedeque, P.E.I.; she married her cousin [according to Doris Haslam, p 60 of *The Wrights of Bedeque*], Benjamion Cole Wright (b. Feb. 20, 1820), as his sec-

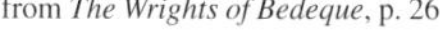

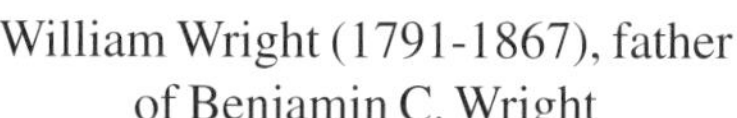

from *The Wrights of Bedeque*, p. 26

William Wright (1791-1867), father of Benjamin C. Wright

from *The Wrights of Bedeque*, p. 26

Isabella (Cole) Wright (1800-1867), wife of William Wright

ond wife, on February 1, 1864. Benjamin, son of William Wright and Isabella Cole, lived in South Shore Bedeque (Chelton), P.E.I. [It is interesting to note that Lavinia Davies Wright, who will be mentioned later, was also the child of William and Isabella (Cole) Wright.. Margaret was 45 years old (c.1864) when she married Benjamin. He had been married to Hannah White before he married Margaret.

An interesting aside on Margaret's middle name is that it may have come from the physician named James Graham, a forty-two year old bachelor who came from Edinburgh, Scotland to Bedeque in 1814. It is of interest to note, as well, that Ben had a brother whose middle name was Graham. Again, in 1823, the grandson of the first Nathaniel Wright, James Graham Wright, was born.[91] Dr. Graham began a thirty-five year practice which ended only in his death. He lived at Major Hooper's and had a practice even larger than the

Methodist missionary circuit.[92] Ben and Margaret had no children, but she helped to raise Ben's family (surname Wright) of five children whom he had had with Hannah.[93] One son (William *Thomas* Wright) married a Hooper:

Nancy E. Neal Coll.

Gravestone of Benjamin C. Wright (1820-1900) and his second wife, Margaret Graham Hooper (c.1819-1895)

- **George Wright**, born February 1, 1849; died young.
- **William *Thomas* Wright**, called Tom, born February 9, 1850 [family Bible: Feb. 8, 1851], married **Mary *Alice* Hooper.**
- **Annie Elizabeth Wright**, baptized on July 31, 1853 [family Bible says born April 4, 1855], did not marry; died December 8, 1873 in South Bedeque, buried in Lower Bedeque Cemetery.
- **Eliza Barratt Wright**, baptized July 20, 1857 [family Bible reads December 3, 1858] married Elijah Lewis Strang, lived in Searletown, then in New York.
- **Harriet Ella Beatrice Wright** (called Hattie) born May 23, 1860, married Frederick Holland Leard (whose obituary is included later) and lived all her married years in Summerside. Hattie and Holland lived in the large, comfortable house at the corner of Harvard and Granville Streets in Summerside where she kept boarders. Her obituary, thanks to Mr. and Mrs. Bradshaw, follows:

The death of Mrs. Holland Leard took place suddenly on Monday evening in the Prince County Hospital [June 10, 1929]. The deceased was a daughter of the late Benjamin and Hannah Wright, and was born in Bedeque, but has lived most of her life in Summerside. She was a lady of lovable and Christian character and is sur-

vived by an only sister, Eliza, Mrs. Strong [Strang] of New York, who has been informed by telegraph. There are also left to mourn two daughters, Anna, Mrs. William Schurman, of North Bedeque, and Georgie, Mrs. Ernest Large [probably named for her Uncle George who died young] of Summerside, to whom the *[Island] Farmer* tenders its sincere sympathy. The funeral had not been arranged at the time of our going to press at noon today (Tuesday).

An interesting piece of family history is presented, as related by Doris Haslam in *The Wrights of Bedeque*:[94]

Ben's South Shore [Chelton] farm lay between his father's farm and that of Hannah's older sister, Lydia, and husband John Pearson. Ben was the fisherman of the family. He was never happier than when he was out in his boat hauling in cod, mackerel, herring and lobsters. His sister, Priscilla, was heard to remark, "No need to turn around; you can always tell when Ben is in church." He and Hannah were members in good standing of the South Shore Wesleyan Class and subscribed to the "Wesleyan," and when Ben's father died, Ben succeeded him as Class leader. However, after his marriage to the Presbyterian wife [Margaret}, he seems to have relinquished the Class leadership to his brother-in-law, Busby Atkinson, who was reputed to be so powerful in prayer that "he made the devil fly howling from the house."[94]

[An interesting comment on Busby's name is that he was named for the Methodist minister Sampson Busby][95]

The obituary of Busby's widow, the former Christine Wright, who died on February 4, 1909 at the age of 81, is included from a local newspaper:

The death occurred on February 4th at Lowell, Mass., of Mrs. Christina Atkinson, aged 81 years, widow of the late Busby Atkinson who predeceased her about four years. A brother, James Wright, of Tryon, and two sisters, Mrs. Priscilla Callbeck and Mrs. John Howatt, of Bedeque, survive her. She also leaves to mourn her loss a son, Sergeant Thos. Atkinson of Lowell, Mass., and three daughters, Mrs. Wm. Ramsay, Bedeque; Mrs. Susan Lowther, Chelton; and Mrs. Chas. Hill, of Lowell, Mass. Though residing in Lowell for a number of years, she loved to visit her native place where her cheerfulness and kindliness made life more pleasant for all with whom she came in contact. She died as she lived, trusting in Jesus Christ for salvation with a firm hope of a glorious immortality.

The farm home was given the name "Thorndale Cottage," according to Doris Haslam." It was here that the oldest daughter [Annie Eliza beth] died in 1873. Her gravestone in the Lower Bedeque Cemetery is inscribed with this verse:

Dear sister, thou hast left us.
Here thy loss we deeply feel,
But 'tis God that has bereft us.
He can all our sorrows heal."

Tom inherited the homestead [of his father, Ben], married [Alice Hooper], and provided Ben [and his second wife, Margaret] with four grandchildren to entertain with stories of the pioneer days.

I found what to me is a most interesting article, written by Louis W. Pearson, who is mentioned later in this document in relation to a cow with a distended udder. When we first came to Chelton as property owners in 1987 the author of the following article had a cow grazing in his field which was just down the road from our cousin Thelma and Calvin's home where we stayed. The title of the article is "Women, Mice and Bears,"[96] and it is a story with which to entertain grandchildren:

Sir,
In reading Mr. W. I. Green's letter in your paper a few days ago on Women, Mice, and Bears, my memory freshened up on a Bear story which I often heard told when a young boy. When Lydia Wright, daughter of Stephen Wright, the Loyalist, left her ancestral home on the north side of Bedeque Bay about one hundred and thirty-five years ago as the bride of Capt. John Pearson, she was rowed across the Bay in a dory to Pope's Shore on the south side. They walked four miles through the forest to the shores of present-day Chelton. Bears were then almost as numerous as the passenger cars we in our day see turned upside down on highways under our new Temperance Act.

Lydia Pearson's "honeymoon" would be made up of such chores as taking care of the new log cabin, recently built as the new bridal home; helping her husband plant potato sets in around the stumps, garnering the harvest with the reaping hook, pushing a bigger bale under the pry to give John a new advantage under the stumps, and going a few yards from the log house to the shore for the lobsters for dinner, etc.

Lobsters in those days were as numerous on John Pearson's beach as bathers are today. They could be forked into baskets by the cartload without even getting

one's feet wet. No doubt those aristocrats of the rocks and the sea were often a three-times- a- day delicacy on the table of this newly married pioneer couple; and "breathes there a man with soul so dead" who wouldn't have dined with John and Lydia!

The years moved on in those days, just as now, and notwithstanding Lydia's busy life, she found time to make an occasional pilgrimage to the old home on the north side of Bedeque Bay. The only means of moving about in those days was on foot, so this was the "taxi" Lydia would take! She would walk this four-mile path through the forest to Pope'e Shore, then, standing on the edge of the bank, she would shout; and her beautiful, resonant voice, which it is said could be heard for a great distance on a calm day, would be picked up on the other side of the Bay, and her brothers would row over and take her across.

One fine sunny summer morning Lydia decided to take this trip. Making ready, she coddled her seven-months-old babe in her arms and started on her way. When about half way along this forest path a great bear stepped out of the undergrowth and crossed the path a short distance in front of her. Noticing Lydia, the bear turned, stepped back out of the path, faced her and stood as pat as Wolfe's men stood that memorable morning on the Plains of Abraham.

Had this bear been a mouse, according to Mr. Green, Lydia would have screamed, perhaps dropped her child, and run to who knows where. But as it was only a bear, then back on the path she stepped a little beyond, and proceeded on her way. The bear, perhaps dumbfounded at the courage of a woman, offered no attack; he sniffed his nose a few times, then disappeared into the forest.

On reaching Pope's Shore Lydia related her experience to her brother who, on hearing her voice, had rowed across to meet her. That evening on return she was accompanied by her two brothers with their guns, in the hope of meeting Bruin. But Bruin, on learning that it was no use for a bear to try to scare a woman, had gone his way, perhaps on a diplomatic errand to make a bargain with some mouse. Lydia survived this experience and lived years enough to see five stalwart sons and a daughter grow up to call her blessed; when at length, one warm summer evening, as the sun was nearing the west, like her father Stephen Wright who dropped dead on his barn floor, Lydia Pearson dropped dead in the yard. Thus came to a close the life of a brave and lovable woman, Chelton's first pioneer housewife.

Many years after Lydia's passing, the seven months old babe which lay perhaps sound asleep in its mother's arms when Lydia met the bear, and which she no doubt held tightly to her breast, became this writer's grandfather, and as I recall the tall stories I used to hear of bears and a bear's fondness for baby meat, I reflect on what a narrow escape I had of having no grandfather when Lydia Pearson met that bear on the forest path now one hundred and twenty-two years ago!

I am, sir, etc.

LOUIS W. PEARSON

Chelton, P. E. I.

Another story comes down to posterity about Lydia Wright (1793-1862), the granddaughter of William Wright, the Loyalist. She married (i) John Bell, and (ii) John Helix Pearson, who was born about 1790 in Arbroath, Scotland. [Part of the interest in the Pearsons stems from the fact that Alden and I have friends and acquaintances among the later generations of the Pearson family. Also, as explained later, Margaret Pearson was influential in the Hooper girls and their Allen cousins going to Massachusetts in the early years of the 20th Century]. Doris Haslam wrote, in *The Wrights of Bedeque*:

> Lydia, the oldest daughter of Stephen and Fanny (Lord) Wright, had eloped with John Bell when she was eighteen. Little is known of Bell except that he went away on a sailing vessel. When, after many years, he did not return, Lydia married John Pearson, a young Scottish mariner who, after surviving shipwreck off West Point, P.E.I., walked to Bedeque, stopping at her home enroute. According to a story handed down by the family, Bell did return once, saw how things were with his wife, and left South Shore (Chelton) for good, never to be heard of afterward. One day when John and Lydia were absent, a stranger called and asked the little Pearson boys for a drink of water. After drinking the water and talking to them, he pulled out his watch and gave it to one of the boys, then went on his way. When the parents returned, they were amazed. Why would a stranger be touring South Shore in those days and why would he give his watch in return for a mere drink of water? From the description the little boys gave their mother, and the presentation of the watch, it was surmised that the stranger was none other than John Bell. What would have happened had the two Johns met one cannot say![97]

During the summer of 1988 when we were first summer residents in Chelton, Ed Pearson, our neighbor across the paved street and down about three houses, was a great help to us in bringing his equipment to put large rocks in front of the twelve-foot drop from our back yard to the Northumberland Strait. We were concerned about the tides coming up the bank and taking valuable land away with it. Ed was such a good and helpful neighbor, but, alas, the tides were too strong for the rocks and many of them were washed away by the summer of 1989! It seems strange that Alden's ancestors and Ed's ancestors knew each other so many generations ago when they were all farmers tilling the soil for the first time!

In the fall of 2003 Ed and Kay Pearson visited and gave us a copy of "The History of Chelton, Lots #26 & #27" (revised in 1972). In the 18th century a boy named John Pearson lived in Scotland. He ran away from home when he was 13 years old to go to sea. He later became a Master Mariner. He was shipwrecked three different times near West Point, P. E. I. The last time he walked to North Bedeque and stayed at the home of a family named Wright. He married one of the Wright daughters and was persuaded to take up land. He cleared a spot, built a log house, and became the first settler of Lot #27. This was about the year 1800. At the time of settlement the land was owned by landlords and the settlers had to pay rent. Later the Government bought all the land and gave the settlers so many years to pay for their farms.

The community of Chelton, where Alden and I have our summer home, has an interesting history. "The farm owned by Chauncey and Louis Pearson [the man mentioned previously who had written about his ancestor meeting a bear] was the old Capt. John Pearson place," according to research published on the history of Chelton, in the Lots 26 and 27 area. A few excerpts from the local history, *The History of Chelton, Lots #26 & #27*, indicate the scope of information researched for the history:

> He [Capt. John Pearson] had a ship yard just south of where the picnic grounds now stand where he built a vessel called the "Sea Horse." When it was finished they hauled it by oxen out on to the ice and when the ice melted it naturally rested on the water ready for sailing. Mr. Pearson sailed this vessel himself.
>
> The next settler was William Wright. He settled in Lot # 26 on the farm now owned by Daniel McCardle. Through time he owned all the land over to the school. One of his daughters married a Callbeck and lived on the MacKenna place. One married an Atkinson and lived on the Sherry farm. To his sons, James and Benjamin, he gave the farms now owned by Daniel McCardle (the empty house on top of the hill) and the Chelton camp grounds.
>
> Barclays were the first settlers on the farm owned by Edward Gardiner and, in succession, Waldo Gardiner and Garth Toombs. Stewards settled on the land now owned by Roy Campbell.
>
> The first frame house to go up in Chelton is the one in which Louis Pearson lived and which was about 130 years old when it burned in 1961.

Michael Price was the name of the first settler on the farm now owned by Edward Pearson. Hugh Campbell settled on the Heber Schurman farm. A Mr. Gillespie had the Clark farm now owned by Helge Peterson. The place known as the Holland farm was first settled by Thomas Carruthers and stretched from Peterson's to Searletown Road and included Fred Clark's place and all the cottages along the shore.

At the time of settlement, Lots 26 & 27 formed a district known as the "South Shore" and the settlers had to walk to Bedeque for their mail. They kept after the Government for a Post Office of their own and about 1892 this was granted. As there was another South Shore, they had to change the district's name. At a school meeting the Hon. Mr. A. E. C. Holland suggested they call it "Cheltonham" after a place in England. This suggestion was adopted, but the "ham" disappeared at the school meeting and has not been heard of since.

Nathaniel Pearson was the first Postmaster, the office being in his home and which was later Louis Pearson's home. He received $10 a year for his work. The post office was discontinued when Rural Route delivery was commenced about 1912.

The first school house in Chelton was built on Capt. John Pearson's land near Louis Pearson's gate. Before it was built, the settlers' children went to the school at the cross roads (the road leading from Bedeque to Fernwood known as Sand Hill). The first teacher in Chelton was Artemis Leard from Bedeque. Each settler kept the teacher for three weeks as the salary paid was so small they [the teachers] could not pay board. The present schoolhouse was built by John Gardiner and William Wright in 1874 and was also used as a Methodist Meeting House. [It was torn down in 1994]

In 1950 the Bedeque Power Company was formed for the district of Lower Bedeque, Fernwood, and Chelton. It was built by volunteer labor, the only money spent being for equipment and the lineman to supervise putting up the wire, with power being brought from Summerside. In 1955 it was sold to the Maritime Electric Company.

The telephones were installed in 1925 and are being transferred to dial phones in July, 1972.

5.6 John R. Hooper (5, Thomas Jr. 4, Thomas 3, Clement 2, Stephen 1) married Ann C. Cousins, daughter of John F. Cousins and Ellen Montgomery, on February 23, 1848. They resided in Central Bedeque, P.E.I. John, with his wife and children [I do not know how many there were or what their names were], left Bedeque about 1857 and are thought to have lived in Iowa. He died after 1869.

5.7 Eliza Hooper (5, Thomas Jr. 4, Thomas 3, Clement 2, Stephen 1) was born about 1827; married John Walker in 1868, as his second wife. He was born March 28, 1827 and died on February 6, 1883 in Cape Traverse, P.E.I. John's first wife was Anne Bell, daughter of John Bell and Elizabeth Little. According to the genealogy of the Walker family, which Harold Cairns had researched, John and Anne had four sons and three daughters. Only two sons were named: Gavin, born in 1861 and Hugh, born June 24, 1856. John was another Walker to marry a Hooper, as he was the brother of Jane Walker, John Keir Hooper's wife. One would assume that Eliza, the daughter of Thomas Hooper and Elizabeth Cole, would have had responsibility to at least partially raise some of the children that John had with his first wife. John and Eliza lived in Augustine Cove, P.E.I. and had one daughter (sixth generation, surname Walker):

5.71 Eliza Ann Walker (6, Eliza 5, Thomas Jr. 4, Thomas 3, Clement 2, Stephen 1) died on February 10, 1896. John Walker, Eliza, and Eliza Ann are buried in the Church of Scotland Cemetery in Cape Traverse, P.E.I. No more information was given on date of birth or personal history.

Thomas and Elizabeth Robins, lived in Lower Bedeque, P.E.I. where they had both settled after coming to Canada to seek a new life. Mary Hooper married John Robins, Elizabeth's brother; Mary's brother, Tommy, married the niece of John Robins!

6.0 Rachel Hooper (4, Thomas 3, Clement 2, Stephen 1) was Thomas's youngest daughter and next-to-youngest child who did not marry. We know very little about her: we do not know her birth date, her death date, or anything about her activities or friendships. She is assumed to have lived in the homestead with her father and after his death lived with her brother, Elisha. This writer believes that she

did not exist as there appears to be *NO* factual material about her in print! This writer believes that she was confused with Rachel of the generation before her, Thomas's [the father's] sister, who did not leave New Jersey.

7.0 Elisha Hooper (4, Thomas 3, Clement 2, Stephen 1) was the baby who had recently been born (June 22, 1782) in New Jersey when the Patriots caused his mother's death (1782). He was brought up by his four sisters and came with three of those sisters to P.E.I. when he was about 4 ½ years old. He was baptized in Charlottetown on October 8, 1812 by the Rev. DesBrisay.[98] He was a farmer in Lower Bedeque and was appointed a lieutenant in the Prince County militia on January 23, 1813.[99] On April 19, 1858 he was appointed High Sheriff of Prince County. He was a Methodist and is buried in the Lower Bedeque Cemetery. On June 30, 1809 Elisha took Margaret Crosby as his bride. Margaret was born in 1781 and died on March 31, 1843. She came from Meadowbank, P.E.I., and was the daughter of William Crosby. Elisha died on March 18, 1860.

Thomas Hooper's sons, Major and Thomas Junior, lived near their father in Lower Bedeque. Major was almost opposite him and Thomas's land was a short distance up the road. After Thomas Senior's death, Elisha, the youngest son, inherited the home place and provided for his sister, Rachel,[100] [if, indeed, she ever existed].

The seven children of Elisha Hooper and Margaret Crosby, all born in Lower Bedeque, are as follows (surname Hooper, fifth generation):

7.1 Mathilda Ann Hooper (5, Elisha 4, Thomas 3, Clement 2, Stephen 1) was born in 1810 at Lower Bedeque, P.E.I.; she married Horatio Nelson Hope on January 15, 1835. Horatio was born in Liverpool, England in 1798, the son of Peter Hope and Ann Chrisholm; Horatio died in St. Eleanors, P.E.I. on January 23, 1867; she died in St. Eleanors on October 15, 1854 at the age of 44, after the birth of her thirteenth baby. Her body was brought back to Lower Bedeque for burial beside her grandfather, Thomas. Horatio was a farmer and a storekeeper. He is said to have been a godson of Admiral Nelson.

Mathilda Ann Hooper Hope died after her thirteenth child was born. Horatio then married a Mrs. Sarah (Emery) Holman, (1824-June 15, 1914). She and Horatio had a daughter, Susan Goodwin, born on February 22, 1858. Susan was a half-sister to the 13 children, but was not a Hooper descendant. Their thirteen children (sixth generation, surname Hope) were as follows:

7.11 Cuthbert Collingwood Hope (6, Mathilda Ann 5, Elisha 4, Thomas 3, Clement 2, Stephen 1), was born in 1836, and died February 19, 1850, at age 13 or 14.
7.12 Ann Hope, (6, Mathilda Ann 5, Elisha 4, Thomas 3, Clement 2, Stephen 1) was born in 1837. No further information.
7.13 Archibald Hope (6, Mathilda Ann 5, Elisha 4, Thomas 3, Clement 2, Stephen 1) was born c.1839 in St. Elcanors, P.E.I., and died in Mexico in 1877. No further information.
7.14 William Hope (6, Mathilda Ann 5, Elisha 4, Thomas 3, Clement 2, Stephen 1) No further information available.
7.15 Margaret Crosby Hope, (6, Mathilda Ann 5, Elisha 4, Thomas 3, Clement 2, Stephen 1) was born in 1843 (a twin) in St. Eleanor's. No further information available.
7.16 Constance Massy Hope (6, Mathilda Ann 5, Elisha 4, Thomas 3, Clement 2, Stephen 1), was born in 1843 (a twin) in St. Eleanor's, and died in 1920 at Angus, Ontario.
7.17 Delores DeGoray Hope (6, Mathilda Ann 5, Elisha 4, Thomas 3, Clement 2, Stephen 1), was born on October 17, 1845, and died on November 7,1865, at age 20. She was not married.
7.18 Lara Hope (6, Mathilda Ann 5, Elisha 4, Thomas 3, Clement 2, Stephen 1), was born in 1846, and died in November 1865, at age 19. [One wonders if Delores and Lara had diphtheria or measles]
7.19 Jennett Hope (6, Mathilda Ann 5, Elisha 4, Thomas 3, Clement 2, Stephen 1), was born on April 13, 1847. No further information.
7.20 Matilda Ann Hope (6, Mathilda Ann 5, Elisha 4, Thomas 3, Clement 2, Stephen1),was born on August 9, 1848. No further information.

7.21 Caroline Hope (6, Mathilda Ann 5, Elisha 4, Thomas 3, Clement 2, Stephen 1) No further information.
7.22 John Priestly Hope (6, Mathilda Ann 5, Elisha 4, Thomas 3, Clement 2, Stephen 1), was born on August 21, 1852, and died in 1929 in Mexico. No further information.
7.23 Isabella Rhymers Hope[101] (6, Mathilda Ann 5, Elisha 4, Thomas 3, Clement 2, Stephen 1), was born on May 13, 1854; she married Hugh James Massy, on October 10, 1881, and died on May 2, 1925. [Ross Graves writes that Isabella's great-great-grandfather was William Schurman, Loyalist. I find that her great-grandfather was Thomas Hooper, Loyalist.] Hugh was born on June 23, 1854 and died on July 23, 1934. Hugh James [he used both names] worked for two years in Nebraska, then attended St. Dunstan's College, Charlottetown. He became clerk of the county court for one of the Prince County circuits, and held this position for ten years. He was also an agent for the Confederation Life Insurance Co. for seven years.

Hugh James was a Justice of the Peace and a Commissioner for Taking Affidavits to be used in the Supreme Court. He was appointed town clerk for Summerside, P.E.I., holding that position for many years. He lived on the corner of Spring and Pleasant Streets. He and Isabella had two daughters (surname Massy, seventh generation).

7.2 Margaret Hooper (5, Elisha 4, Thomas 3, Clement 2, Stephen 1) was born on February 1, 1811, and died on August 11, 1889, at French Fort, P.E.I. She married Charles Robert Braddock on July 13, 1837. He was born on March 11, 1813 at "Nans Villa," Charlottetown Royalty, P.E.I., the son of Samuel Clark Braddock and Eleanor Saunderson, of French Fort [Scotchfort].[102] After settling at Scotchfort, Charles farmed the homestead, "Nan's Villa." He eventually bought saw and grist mills and employed a miller to operate the mills. He had several "occupations": a farmer, a miller, a mill owner, and a

Justice of the Peace. Margaret and Charles resided at "Nan's Villa," Mt. Stewart, and Scotchfort, P.E.I. They are buried at Mt. Stewart People's Cemetery. They had seven children (surname Braddock, sixth generation):

7.21 Elisha Charles Braddock (6, Margaret 5, Elisha 4, Thomas 3, Clement 2, Stephen 1) was born in 1839 in Southport, P.E.I., the oldest of seven children of Charles and Margaret. I have a copy of an interesting letter, compliments of Muriel Hooper Blanchard, from C. E. Braddock, who was fighting in the United States Civil War. I do not know to which aunt he was writing. [My birth record gives the name as Elisha Charles rather than Charles E. Braddock]:

Camp Bean in M.D. [Maryland] Oct. 4, 61 [1861]
Dear Aunt: [probably Aunt Sarah]
I thought I would write you a few lines today to let you know that I am well and hope these few lines may find you the same. I suppose you would like to know what kind of a country this is, well to begin with it is very hilly, very much like the Island. They raise plenty of fruit, but this was rather a poor season for apples, but a good one for peaches, all kinds of fruit grow here the soil is very poor and very stony, they raise but very little small grain, corn is the principal crop. There is not many grain in this state to support the inhabitants through the coming winter, sufferings here this winter among the poor class of people will be very great, there is more poor here at presant than I ever saw in my life. This is a great state for cotton and iron factories, this rebellion has caused them all to be stoped it has thrown thousands out of employment. There is a large iron factory close to our encampment which is now standing still which employed three hundred men [illegible] of all kinds is stoped in our Camp ground of an evening, there will sometimes be over a hundred poor men, women some peddling pies and milk, some bread and begging washing, they come to get our clothes, wash them, bring them back in fact they depend on the soldiers for a living. This winter the volenteers or soldiers are draped very different from others that I ever saw in frock coats, our caps, pants are fine black broadcloth, we have [illegible] suits our first was slate uniforms, grey pants [illegible] jackets. We got a new suit of black two weeks ago from goverment, we got three suites a year, fifteen dollars a month and at the close of the war we get 100 dolars and 160 acres of land the hundred dollars is bounty money. We get besides this each man receives in money five cents a mile for every mile he travels with the regiment from the place he inlisted and back again, we have traveled now about 2000 miles we started from Wisconsin and travelled through Mich., Indiana,

New York State, Pennsynamvia [sic] and we are now in M.D. our next move will be into Virginia there is some talk of going very soon, the weather here now is hot now as it would be in the middle of summer on the Island. I have been in fourteen different States I have seen a great many beautiful city and places, the city of Baltimore is the largest I ever saw, we were there seven days, it is the second largest in the United States, there is not a wodden building in the city, the houses are built of brick and stone, it is a splended city. It would take me a week to relate all that I have seen let alone write it. I have not seen John Hooper [I don't know who he is] for nearly two years he was then in Iowa but two persons from the Island one of them probly you know his name is Edward Ramsay from Bedeque the other is Wm Morrison they are here in this regiment in Camp to [illegible] that I have left there six years ago if we live through this war we are coming back together, this regiment's composed principly of men from Maine and Canada upper and lower parts, I am called to go on duty so I must finish give my love to all and except of mine.
C. E. Braddock

A genealogy friend of ours, who summers in Chelton, near us, is involved with the Civil War re-enactments in Virginia and surrounding states. He looked up some information about Charles Elisha Braddock and found the following: "He signed up in Wisconsin as a substitute for a rich man in 18—. He was in the 4th regiment, Co. C. On Feburuary 4, 1862 near Baltimore, he deserted." One wonders if he could stay in the United States, if he returned to Prince Edward Island, or what happened to him. His defection was four months to the day following this letter.

Apparently many young men went from Prince Edward Island to fight in the Civil War for a number of reasons. Some wanted adventure, others living in the United States were drafted, and still others offered themselves up or were crimped (kidnapped and enlisted) as substitute soldiers. Wealthy northerners who didn't want to go to war could buy the service of another man to fight for them. The G. A. R. (Grand Army of the Republic) *Journal* of Port Byron, N. Y. published "The First Decoration Day," by Rev. E. B. Olmstead. It is reprinted below, thanks to Mr. and Mrs. Bradshaw:

Immediately after the close of the war the soldiers stationed in the vicinity of the first Bull Run battlefield erected a rude monument to the memory of their comrades buried there, and on the 11th day of June, 1865, a large concourse of officers, soldiers, and citizens went from Washington, Alexandria, Arlington, and other points to dedicate it. While some preliminaries were being arranged, preparatory to the exercises, Mrs. Colonel Kimball, Mrs. Captain Norris and other ladies gathered wild flowers from the fields and hedges and while they were making wreaths and boquets, Captain E. B. Olmstead (now chaplain of Lockwood Post 175, at Port Byron, N.Y.) wrote the following little poem which the ladies insisted upon his reading during the dedication services:

Hang them there tenderly, though they may fade,
Others are blossoming down in the glade -
Smiling so lovingly out from the dell,
Close by the graves of the brave boys who fell.
National emblems - so simple and true,
Brightly arrayed in the "red, white, and blue."
Rainbow tints glow in these flowers fair,
Gushing with fragrance that perfumes the air.

Droop they caressingly over the brayes,
Weeping bright dew drops on unlettered graves;
Weeping for heroes confined 'neath the sod,
Whose souls are transferred to the gardens of God.

Cover then this monument with these wild-flowers
Gathered from nature's own heaven-decked bower;
Emblems of love for the honored at rest -
Emblems of hope for the realms of the blest.
Ever with coming of spring and its beauty,
Be it a loving and patriot duty
To deck every mound where a soldier reposes
With garlands of fairest and sweetest of roses.

Among the speakers of the occasion were Generals Logan and Howard who referred to the floral decorations and to the sentiment of the poem and expressed the hope that the monument might be annually visited and arrayed with floral tributes.

But the scene of June 11, 1865, was not again enacted on the Bull Run battle ground. Traitor hands tore down the monument and the dead were removed to Arlington where, the next year, mainly under the direction of General Howard, the graves of soldiers were decorated with flags and flowers. Thus began Decoration Day, the Memorial Day of the present.

The poem, "Home Again," was written in beautiful penmanship and included by the Bradshaws. This young man was indeed glad to be at home again!

Home again! Home again from a foreign shore;
And oh! it fills my heart with joy to meet my friends once more.
'Twas here I dropped the parting tear, to cross the ocean's foam;
But now I'm once again with those who kindly greet me home.
Happy hearts! Happy hearts with mine have laughed in glee;
And oh! the friends I loved in youth seemed dearer far to me;
Then if my guide should be the fate which bid me longer roam,
But death alone can break the tie which binds my heart to home.
Music soft! music sweet lingers round the place;
And oh! I feel the children's charm which time can ne'er efface;
Then give me back my homestead roof - I'll ask no palace dome -
For I can live a happy life with those I love at home.

1866

The background of a poem published in Charlottetown, on Feb. 27, 1869, is interesting. George Dowey, a sailor who had served with the Union Navy during the U.S. Civil War, later became a steward on the barque, *Clara Novello*. He had travelled around the continents of North America and Europe as a sea-faring man, and while in Charlottetown killed another sailor over a girl. His subsequent execution for the crime was the last public hanging in Prince Edward Island, and possibly Canada. His execution was also one of the most gruesome ever recorded. After two attempts failed (the first time the trap door fell the rope broke, and the second time the rope broke loose from a cleat), the sheriff, with the help of several constables, managed to hoist Dowie manually off the ground and secure him to the gallows where he hung forty minutes before being untied and pronounced dead.

LINES FROM GEORGE DOWEY TO HIS WIFE AND MOTHER

Weep, my poor old mother, weep. Let tears fall fast and free.
They will help ease your troubled heart of woe and agony.
Weep for the loss of your poor son who on a foreign shore

Now lies in iron fetters strong and ne're will see you more.
Poor mother, you I've ever loved through life's short changing scenes,
Whether on Africa's burning clime or midst the Arctic's winds.
Through storms and hurricanes on sea, through evils on the shore,
I shall my love e'er show to you until my dying hour.
How can I you, my dear, address, my only joy in life,
Who must a widow shortly be almost before a wife
The fountain of my heart is dry, no more my tears will flow,
And God alone doth only know how bitter is my woe.
It is not death that troubles me or causes me such pain
For I have faced it oftentimes upon the stormy main;
But it's the shame and sure disgrace which I to you have borne,
Which makes me now to rue the day I ever had been born.
Oh, then, my young and tender wife, it makes me blush with shame
To think when I am dead and gone you still must bear my name.
But, oh, remember, dearest Kate, to you I'll never lie
Although my hand has done the deed for which I am to die.
I never for an instant thought to use the fatal knife,
Nor would I for ten thousand worlds take a fellow-creature's life.
But there's *one* thing I'm guilty of, which pains me to confess,
That, in an evil hour, to you I've proved most faithless.
But, oh, my kind and loving wife, I suffer for it sore,
Nor will I cease to think of it until my dying hour.
Farewell, my mother, sad farewell, likewise my loving wife.
I leave you poor and desolate within this world of strife.
But He who doth the ravens feed and hears them when they cry
Will be to you a constant friend so I can calmly die.
And now, my dearest mother, let this your spirit cheer
Your son has been well-treated although a stranger here.
And from each Christian heart there doth a tearful prayer ascend
That Christ will take me to His home where Sabbaths have no end.

From the private archives of Malcolm and Edith Bradshaw comes a poem, entitled, "The Veteran Speaks," about another war, the Spanish-American War of 1898, in which several Islanders also participated:

Has Jimmie fetched the papers? An', Molly, what do they say?
Anything new an' startlin'? Air we goin' ter war terday?
Has they foun' the Cause o' the trouble? Air they makin' the matter plain?
How did the whole thing happen, an' what blowed up the *Maine*?

Lord in the heavens above us! but things air a-goin' wrong;
An' the song that singin' the babes ter sleep may be drowned in the battle song!
Thar's a wild an' a restless feelin' on the sea an' the rumblin' shore,
And the boys'll kiss yu good-bye some day an' never come home no more!
How long sence the war? It never has seemed so long ter me
Sence I follored Stonewall Jackson an' charged in the fight with Lee.
How long sence I jined my regiment an' marched 'cross the hills away
With the ol' band playin' "Dixie" an' the boys shoutin' back, "Hooray"!
Long enough for the frosts ter come an' sprinkle my hair with white;
Long enough for the friends we loved ter whisper a last "Good Night"
An' pass ter the peace unbroken an' yet, nor long, I say
Fer the band's still playin' "Dixie" an' the boys shoutin' back "Hoorah"!
No matter! The sky looks darker than I've seen it many a year,
But I'm glad that the boys still face it with never a finch o' fear!
I ain't so spry with my rifle now; my j'ints air stiff with pain;
But I wants ter know, I tell you, who blowed up the warship *Maine*?
I don't keer what he has suffered. I shet my eyes ter the past;
I'm fer my country, right or wrong, for my country first an' last!
Let 'em git down ter business; let 'em tell it, an' tell it plain:
Whose was the hand that done it? Who blowed up the warship *Maine*?
Peace? I'm fer peace, I tell you! I ain't a huntin' no fight,
But ef wrong's been done ter the country, we must battle our way ter right!
"Who are the ones that done it?" is passin' from lip ter lip;
It's a solid an' simple question, who blowed up the ship, the ship?
Read what the paper's printed. What does it say terday?
Air they any nigher ter mourn? Air they clearin' the mists away?
Let 'em git down ter business! an' ef it must be a storm
Han' me my gun, I tell you, an' trot out my uniform!
An' ef it comes ter the worst, we're ready, ready ter play our parts;
"We're one with the great, green country that blossoms around our hearts.
Here's one of a million vet'rans that's wantin' an answer plain.
Whose wuz the hand that done it? Who blowed up that warship *Maine*?"

7.22 Sarah Hooper Braddock (6, Margaret 5, Elisha 4, Thomas 3, Clement 2, Stephen 1) was born on November 12, 1840 in Southport (Notice how the names repeat!); she married Francis Dougherty on December 29, 1859. Francis died young.

7.23 Lemuel Braddock (6, Margaret 5, Elisha 4, Thomas 3, Clement 2, Stephen 1) was born in 1844; he was lost at sea in 1865.

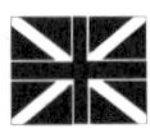

7.24 Horatio W. Hope Braddock (6, Margaret 5, Elisha 4, Thomas 3, Clement 2, Stephen 1), named for his grandfather, was born in 1845; he was a farmer and lived in Scotchfort, P.E.I.; Horatio died unmarried on April 16, 1885.

7.25 George Whelock Braddock (6, Margaret 5, Elisha 4, Thomas 3, Clement 2, Stephen 1) was born at Benstead, Lot 34 in November 1847; he died on March 14, 1849 at 1 year, 4 months old.

7.26 George William Braddock (6, Margaret 5, Elisha 4, Thomas 3, Clement 2, Stephen 1) was born in 1849; he died August 2 [one account reads Aug. 12], 1874 at Charlottetown. He did not marry.

7.27 Matilda Jane Braddock (6, Margaret 5, Elisha 4, Thomas 3, Clement 2, Stephen 1) was born in 1857 in St. Cuthberts; she married William Webster, and died in 1890 at Five Houses on the East River, P.E.I., an area now known as Fort Augustus. They had one son about whom I have no information (seventh generation).

7.28 Eleanor Braddock (6, Margaret 5, Elisha 4, Thomas 3, Clement 2, Stephen 1) was born on August 26, 1815 and died on October 25 of the same year.

7.3 Sarah Jewell Hooper (5, Elisha 4, Thomas 3, Clement 2, Stephen 1) was born on October 31, 1813, and died on February 8, 1900 at Mt. Stewart, P.E.I., named for her father's sister who stayed in New Jersey. On June 29, 1847, she married William Ewen Clark, M.L.A. He was born on September 9, c.1813, and died in 1881; he was the son of William Clark and Margaret MacEwen. They lived at Bedeque and Mt. Stewart. He was a merchant and a hotel keeper. Sarah's grandfather-in-law, William Clark (1765-1831), came by way of Boston to P.E.I. and settled in Darnley. He married Helen Simpson (1766-1852), a native of Dunderes, Morayshire, Scotland, and had a son, William Clark (1789 - 1845) ,who married Margaret McEwen, youngest daughter of Duncan and Janet (McLaren) McEwen, who

came from Perthshire on the ship *Falmouth* which landed at Stanhope Beach in June 1770. Their son, William Ewen Clark (1814 - 1881), and Sarah Jewell Hooper, his wife, were the parents of the following five children (surname Clark, sixth generation):

7.31 Margaret Elizabeth Clark (6, Sarah 5, Elisha 4, Thomas 3, Clement 2, Stephen 1), called Maggie, was born in 1849 at Darnley, P.E.I., and died on Feb. 6, 1917 in Summerside. Maggie married Elisha Hooper Wright. Doris Haslam, in *The Wrights of Bedeque*, wrote:

> Elisha was named for his granduncle, Elisha Hooper, the grandfather of his wife, Maggie. When Elisha was sixteen, he started his business career as a clerk in the Bedeque store of his cousin, Major Wright. Seven years later, he went into partnership with his brother, Norman, to conduct a general merchantile business under the name of Wright Bros. in Summerside, the little town formerly known as Green's Shore on Bedeque Bay, which owed its growth to the shipbuilding trade. In the 1880s Norman left Summerside to establish a branch business, Wright Bros. Commission and General Shipping Merchants. Elisha was owner of the *Jubilee*, a schooner of 76 tons, built in Georgetown in 1887. When his cousin, A. M. Wright's General Produce and Shipping business failed, Elisha and Isaac N. Schurman were appointed assignees and trustees of the estate, an appointment which entailed considerable work for the trustees. In *McAlpine's P.E.I. Directory* for 1909, he is listed as manager of Hall Mfg. Co. as well as of Wright Bros. on Water Street, with a home on Euston Street.
>
> Elisha moved to Victoria in 1911 to take charge of the business there. He and Maggie lived on Russell St., Victoria, in the large house he had bought from Capt. Archibald Lord.[103]

Maggie and Elisha had seven children (seventh generation, surname Wright). [See Doris Haslam's The *Wrights of Bedeque*, p. 106, for a continuation of this genealogy]

7.32 Sarah Eleanor Clark (6, Sarah 5, Elisha 4, Thomas 3, Clement 2, Stephen 1) was born in 1851; she married Francis C. Gamble. No further information available.

7.33 William Elisha Clark (6, Sarah 5, Elisha 4, Thomas 3, Clement 2, Stehen 1) was born in 1853 and died Dec. 24, 1865 at age 12.

7.34 Eva Clark (6, Sarah 5, Elisha 4, Thomas 3, Clement 2, Stephen 1) was born in 1858 at Bedeque; she died in 1944. She did not marry.
7.35 a daughter, died young.

7.4 William Hooper (5, Elisha 4, Thomas 3, Clement 2, Stephen 1) was born in 1815; he died on August 12, 1874. From what I gathered from Muriel Hooper Blanchard, he was a poor farmer, and was mentally handicapped; he was called "Black William," and lived with his brother Lemuel on the home farm until he leased a farm on the Dunk River where he lived until his death. He had burned the barn down. One day he went in his boat on the Dunk River, pulled the plug in the boat, and drowned. It would appear that he was another of the several Hoopers who was addicted to alcohol as the story is passed down in the family. In the 1700s and the 1800s "tipping the bottle too much" was apparently common. [Chapter Six in this genealogy addresses that issue].

7.5 Lemuel Crosby Hooper (5, Elisha 4, Thomas 3, Clement 2, Stephen 1) was born in 1818, and died September 13, 1885 at Bedeque, P.E.I. On July 22, 1852 he married Louisa Strong (1823-1895) of Greenville, Nova Scotia, the daughter of the Rev. John Bass Strong and Elizabeth Gamble (perhaps Gambee). Lemuel was a farmer who inherited the house of his father, Elisha, and his loyalist grandfather, Thomas Hooper, in Lower Bedeque. Lemuel and Louisa had four children (sixth generation, surname Hooper) as follows:

7.51 John *Herbert* Hooper (6, Lemuel 5**,** Elisha 4, Thomas 3, Clement 2, Stephen 1) was born on July 25, 1853; in 1913 he was living in Detroit, Michigan.
7.52 Henry Havelock Hooper (6, Lemuel 5, Elisha 4, Thomas 3, Clement 2, Stephen 1), was born on January 31, 1857; in 1913 he was living in California.

7.53 Charles Fredrick *Allison* Hooper (6, Lemuel 5, Elisha 4, Thomas 3, Clement 2, Stephen 1)**,** was born on May 25, 1858 in Lower Bedeque; he married Bessie Maria Moyse, on April 27, 1887, and died on October 18, 1945 in Freetown, P.E.I. Bessie, whose mother was a Wright, was born on December 3, 1862 in Central Bedeque, the daughter of Frederick Holland Moyse and Mary Crawford Wright, and died on May 24, 1943 in Freetown. According to Doris Haslam's research, "Allison and Bessie first lived on his home farm, the Elisha Hooper homestead in Lower Bedeque, owned in the 1970s by Conrod Plomp."

Elisha, in turn, had lived on "the home farm" of his father, Thomas. When Allison and Bessie sold the farm they moved to Central Bedeque where, according to Doris Haslam, in *The Wrights of Bedeque*, "Allison operated a blacksmith shop in a building which stood in the corner of Jesse Schurman's orchard, opposite his brother Ed Hooper's woodworking and carriage shop." She writes:

> The building was later moved by Ed's son, Leslie Hooper, and converted into a garage and many years laterward, the Fundamental Baptist Church was erected on the site. Allison's next move was to Searletown where he and his son Ellis operated the steam sawmill they bought from Wallace Bradshaw who had originally purchased it from Alpheus Wright and his son.[104] After Ellis enlisted in World War I Allison's other son, Fred, joined his father. They operated the mill for twenty-five years until it was sold to James K. Smith in 1939. It was in this mill in March, 1912, that a tragic accident occurred: Allison's brother, Ed, mentioned previously, was struck on the head by a flying board and died the next day. [A bit more information will be available in a few more paragraphs]
>
> Bessie and Allison went to Freetown to live with their daughter Lou and her husband Frank Deacon. In her later years Bessie became blind because of macular degeneration, but always being an industrious woman, she was not content to sit idle, so she knitted by the hour for the Red Cross, making innumerable pairs of socks for people she could never see. On his mother's side, Allison was a grandson of the Rev. John B. Strong, Wesleyan Missionary at Bedeque, 1818-1819, and pastor of the circuit from 1847 to 1850.[104]

I have a copy of an article from the *Pioneer*, compliments of Muriel Hooper Blanchard. It provides a wonderful sketch of Allison Hooper and his homestead:

Octogenarian Recalls Early Days in Province

On Saturday we had a very pleasant call from Mr. Allison Hooper of Searletown. Mr. Hooper is one of the oldest readers of these Papers. He informs us his father subscribed for the *Pioneer* in 1874. He read it as a young man at his father's fireside and has been a constant reader of both the *Pioneer* and the *Island Farmer* down through the intervening years to the present time.

Mr. Hooper is a descendant of Thomas Hooper, an Empire Loyalist who came to Prince Edward Island from New Jersey at the close of the Revolutionary War and settled on the land now partly occupied by the farm of Mr. William Stavert in Lower Bedeque. Five generations of Hoopers [Thomas,[3] Elisha,[4] Lemuel,[5] Allison,[6] Allison's children[7]] lived on that farm prior to its purchase by Mr. Stavert. Mr. Hooper states that when his great-grandfather took up the land granted to him, there were about ten acres cleared on it back from the river, upon which were the charred remains of some burnt building partly grown over by shrubbery, and the remains of an old orchard. The land had evidently been occupied and cleared by some early French settlers who had either burned the buildings when vacating the place, or they had been driven off and their buildings burned. [The latter is what the history books say] Back of and surrounding this clearing was the primeval forest. For many years after the occupancy of the land by Mr. Hooper, crude agricultural tools, axes, etc., and French coins were occasionally turned up near the sites of the burned buildings. Although now past his 80th year Mr. Hooper retains his faculties to a wonderful degree. Being blessed with an unusually retentive and reminiscent memory as well as being an entertaining conversationalist made Mr. Hooper's visit a very pleasant one which we hope he will repeat in the near future.

7.54 Edward Arthur Hooper (6, Lemuel 5, Elisha 4, Thomas 3, Clement 2, Stephen 1) was born on June 22, 1867 [another possible date of birth is June 3, 1866] in Lower Bedeqeue; he married Bessie Bagnall, who was born on June 1, 1864 in Central Bedeque; she died March 27, 1912 in Middleton. Ed was the son of Lemuel Crosby and Louisa (Strong) Hooper, making him a grandson of Rev. John B. Strong, Wesleyan missionary at Bedeque.

On his father's side, he was a great-grandson of Thomas Hooper, Loyalist, from New Jersey, who settled in Bedeque in 1784. Thomas's youngest son, Elisha (1782-1860), married Margaret Crosby (1784-1843) and was father of Lemuel who married Louisa Strong. Lemuel's sister, Matilda, Mrs. Horatio Nelson Hope, was mother of Isabella Hope who married Hugh Massy. [Rufus Bagnall, who has been quoted in this document, was the brother next in birth after

Bessie] Edward, a woodworker and a carpenter, went to the sawmill which his brother, Allison, had recently bought in Middleton. [In 1912 Wallace Bradshaw and his son Jesse sold their saw mill to Allison and Ellis Hooper. It was on the land that now belongs to Malcolm Bradshaw. Was Edward not sufficiently familiar with working the new-to-him equipment with no one else nearby?] As he was sawing he was struck on the head by a flying board. The diary of Jesse A. Wright of North Bedeque records, "Mar. 27, Wed. - Ed Hooper got hurt in mill this afternoon. Mar. 28, Thurs. - Ed Hooper died at 10 last night."[105] A description of the accident and a funeral notice follow:

Edward Hooper Killed in Sawmill at Middleton

A terribly sad accident occurred at Middleton, Wednesday afternoon by which Edward Hooper, a widely known and highly respected resident of that locality, lost his life.

The deceased was working in the steam sawmill owned by his brother Allison. At the time of the accident he was operating a circular saw and was alone, his brother being in the engine room. A Mr. Kehoe who happened to be passing at the time noticed that something unusual had occurred in the mill and went in to investigate. He found Mr. Hooper lying unconscious by a pile of lumber, a deep gash in his head which subsequent examination showed had been caused by a slab thrown off by the circular saw. The brother was hastily summoned, a doctor called in and everything possible done for the injured man, but he never regained consciousness and passed away about ten o'clock.

The deceased was about 45 years of age and was the son of the late Lemuel Hooper. He leaves to mourn his wife and two children, Leslie and Helen, both at home, three brothers Allison, above mentioned, Herbert in Detroit, Mich., and Henry in California. [Is Henry the father of the ball player who was with the Red Sox at one time?] The funeral takes place this Friday afternoon at 2:30.

The stricken family have the heartfelt sympathy of the whole community in their sudden and sad bereavement.

and ...

The funeral of the late Edward Hooper, whose death was reported in yesterday's *Guardian* as Edward Harper, took place yesterday afternoon at 2 o'clock from the late residence of the deceased and was very largely attended. Interment was made in the Methodist cemetery at Bedeque and the services at the house and

grave were conducted by Rev. Hammond Johnson assisted by Rev. A. O. Morse. The following were pallbearers: T. J. Enman, John Steward, Peter Barwise, Duncan Nicholson, Artemas Carvell, and John Murray.

7.6 Catherine Pope Hooper (5, Elisha 4, Thomas 3, Clement 2, Stephen 1) was born on July 23, 1819; she died on August 15, 1896. Catherine married Mark Butcher, son of William and Mary Butcher of St. James, Suffolk, England (1819-June 2, 1883), as his second wife, on July 3, 1849. Mark was a cabinet maker and a furniture maker and was in charge of the firm Butcher and Sons in Charlottetown. [On the first Friday that Alden and I were in P.E.I. in 2000, I saw an advertisement in the *Journal Pioneer* for an auction featuring furniture made by Mark Butcher's firm. We went in order to see these beautiful formal mahogany pieces which I thought would be really rare. We saw Joan Lefurgey there, and she told us that many pieces are auctioned from time to time. They certainly were beautifully made] Mark's first wife was Margaret Theodasia Chappell, daughter of Theopolius Chappell and Dorothy Bovyer, born 1811. Margaret died in April 1848, perhaps of typhoid fever. Mark and Margaret had nine children. The family had many tragic deaths: two children died of typhoid and two children died of diphtheria. Because Catherine Hooper Butcher must have raised or helped to raise most of the children, I will include them in the genealogy although they are not Hooper relatives (surname Butcher, sixth generation):

- **Margaret Theodasia Butcher**, born October 14, 1836; died October 23, 1870 of typhoid.
- **James Mark Butcher,** born 1838; baptized January 3, 1839; married Eliza Jane Gardiner (6, Mary 5, Major 4, Thomas 3, Clement 2, Stephen 1) on October 14, 1864. Eliza and James moved to Denver, Colorado. No more information available.
- **Patience Eliza Butcher,** born December 4, 1839; baptized August 23,1840; died July 13,1860 of diphtheria.
- **Maria Patience Butcher,** born about 1840; married James P. Searle, October 29, 1860.

- **William Jewell Butcher,** born 1842; died July 15, 1860 at age 18 ½ years. He apparently died of diphtheria, as well as Patience.
- **J.W. Butcher** (female), born 1843, married Angus Stewart August 3, 1863.
- **Mark Butcher,** born c.September 1845; died August 11, 1846 at age 11 months.
- **Theophilias Chappell Butcher,** born November 7, 1847; baptized May 2, 1848; died November 22, 1870 of typhoid, at age 22. He was probably a member of the firm, Butcher and Sons.
- **Hannah Butcher,** born c.1849; married Edison Daniel Dawson, on August 20, 1879.

Mark and Catherine lived in Charlottetown, P.E.I. and had six children, making Mark the father of fifteen children! (sixth generation, surname Butcher). These children are Hooper descendants. I know nothing further about these children:

7.61 Jane Butcher (6, Catherine 5, Elisha 4, Thomas 3, Clement 2, Stephen 1), was born April 3, 1850
7.62 Matilda Marie Butcher, (6, Catherine 5, Elisha 4, Thomas 3, Clement 2, Stephen 1) was born in 1852; she died on September 30, 1854.
7.63 Eunice Butcher (6, Catherine 5, Elisha 4, Thomas 3, Clement 2, Stephen 1) was born on August 4, 1855 (a twin)
7.64 Heatherington Butcher (6, Catherine 5, Elisha 4, Thomas 3, Clement 2, Stephen 1) was born on August 4, 1855 (a twin)
7.65 Sarah Butcher (6, Catherine 5, Elisha 4, Thomas 3, Clement 2, Stephen 1) was born in 1858.
7.66 Richard Johnson Butcher (6, Catherine 5, Elisha 4, Thomas 3, Clement 2, Stephen 1) was born on March 30, 1860.

A sister of Mark's, Betsy Maria Butcher, came to P.E.I. from St. James, Suffolk, England where she was born, and married George M. Wright, who died on February 1, 1848. Betsy outlived him by forty-four years. George died rather young after he and Betsy had had six children in nine years. George was named for the Wesleyan missionary who performed his baptism, the first Wright birth to be recorded in the baptismal records which were begun that year on the newly organized circuit.

The circumstances surrounding his death are interesting and will be included here, not because George is our relative, but because they most likely depict life of the times. George had come into full possession of one hundred and twenty-five acres in Lot 26 in 1854. This land was a part of the 250 acre inland grant given to his grandfather, Nathaniel Wright, to be equally divided among his six "dear sons." He had saw, grist, and carding mills which he operated until his early death from pneumonia. He had been on business in Charlottetown and on the way home stopped at the Warrens in North River because of a bad storm. Doris M. Haslam recalled the details of his death in *The Wrights of Bedeque*: "The Warrens were millers, too. It was a very cold, stormy time of year. His socks were frozen to the floor the night he slept there. On his return home he developed a bad cold and three days later, he was dead. The *Islander,* on March 22, 1867, recorded his obituary: 'At his residence, Freetown on the 13th of inflammation of the lungs, George M. Wright, Esq., aged 45 years.'"[106]

Doris M. Haslam continues:

> George had a very fine dog, an Irish setter. He followed the funeral procession to the burying ground, refused to leave, burrowed into the mounded earth and stayed there until the family came the next morning and took the faithful animal back home. His devotion was displayed on an earlier occasion. George had his arm badly scraped and could not get it to heal. The dog was nearby one day when the dressing was removed. He started to lick the wound. Every day when the dressings were changed the dog repeated his effective medication and the wound soon began to heal"[107]

A Summerside newspaper also recorded his death as follows: "At his residence, Freetown, on Wednesday the 13th inst. of inflammation of the lungs and congestion of the brain, Geo. M. Wright, Esq. aged 45 years. Besides the loss his friends sustain in his death, the poor will lose in him a generous and kind-hearted benefactor."

Betsy had grown up in Charlottetown and one week after her husband died, she bought a house and lot from William Butcher in Charlottetown (her father?) where her relatives were still living. By 1867 her brother Mark had already gained considerable recognition as a cabinet and furniture maker. The move to town gave her two sons the opportunity to apprentice with their uncle and to live at home with their mother and sisters. Her son, George Dudley Wright, became an apprentice at the cabinet-making trade serving with his uncle Mark four and a half years, and one as a journeyman, as well. Dudley also was mayor of the city of Charlottetown and served the city in other capacities for many years.[108]

Betsy's brief notice of death appeared in the newspaper in 1892: "Wright - at Charlottetown, Sept 26, Betsy M. Butcher, wife of the late George M. Wright, of Bedeque aged 66 years."

On my last visit to the Coles Building in Charlottetown in September 2000 to find more genealogical information, I saw a display of Queens Square, Charlottetown, in the lobby of the building. One picture had the words, "In 1867 after much bitter debate, Charlottetown replaced its now decrepit Round Market. The new building was designed by Mark Butcher." Apparently Mark was an architect as well as a splendid furniture maker. Next year I shall bring my camera hoping that the display is still there. [It wasn't!]

7.7 Jane Payne Hooper (5, Elisha 4, Thomas 3, Clement 2, Stephen 1) was born on October 15, 1822, and died on February 10, 1912. She did not marry. Jane made her home with her brother, Lemuel, who inherited his father's and his grandfather's house in Lower Bedeque, and with her niece [most probably Mrs. Maggie Clark Wright, the daughter of Sarah Jewel Hooper Clark, who was herself the daughter of Elisha Hooper 4], at Victoria, P.E.I., where she died.

She is buried in the Methodist Cemetery in Lower Bedeque, very near her father's and her grandfather's house. Jane had the tall monument placed in the cemetery. All four sides of the stone are inscribed: one side for Loyalist Thomas Hooper, her grandfather; one side for Matilda Ann Hooper, Elisha's first child who died after her 13th child was born; another side for William Hooper, Elisha's son, who drowned in the Dunk River, and the fourth side for her, Jane Payne Hooper, Elisha's last child.

Notes

1 Ada MacLeod, *Roads to Sumerside, the Story of Early Summerside and the Surrounding Area,* edited by Marjorie McCallum Gay, 1980, p. 13
2 George A. Leard, *Historic Bedeque. The Loyalists at Work and Worship in Prince Edward Island* (Bedeque, P.E.I.: Bedeque United Church, 1948), pp 20-21
3 Ibid., p. 30
4 Doris Haslam, *The Wrights of Bedeque, Prince Edward Island, A Loyalist Family (Summerside, P.E.I.: Doris Muncey Haslam, 1978)*, p. 44
5 Ibid., p. 31
6 Ibid., pp. 32-33
7 Ibid., pp. 89-90
8 Ibid., p. 91
9 Ibid., pp. 90-91
10 Ibid., p. 36
11 Ibid., pp. 36-37
12 Ibid., p. 92
13 Orlo Jones and Doris Haslam, eds., *An Island Refuge. Loyalists and Disbanded Troops on the Island of Saint John* (n.p.: Abegweit Branch of the United Empire Loyalist Association of Canada, 1983), p. 320
14 Doris Haslam, op. cit., pp. 93-95
15 Doris Haslam, op. cit., p. 98
16 Ibid.
17 Doris Haslam, op. cit., pp. 97-98
18 Orlo Jones and Doris Haslam, eds. , op. cit., p. 113
19 Ross Graves, *William Schurman, Loyalist of Bedeque, Prince Edward Island, and his descendants* (Summerside, P.E.I.: Harold B. Schurman, 1973), pp. 126-127

20 Doris Haslam, op. cit., p. 101
21 Orlo Jones and Doris Haslam, eds., op. cit., p. 330
22 Ibid., p. 101
23 George A. Leard, op. cit., p. 56
24 Ibid., p. 57
25 Vital Records, Public Archives and Records Office (PARO), Coles Building, Charlottetown, P.E.I.
26 Doris Haslam, op. cit., p. 88
27 Vital Records, Marriages, PARO, op. cit., p. 590
28 Public Archives and Records Office (PARO), Prince Edward Island, R. G. 19, Marriage Licenses; Box 1, Nov., 1886
29 Marriage Register #13, PARO, 1870-1887
30 Ross Graves, op. cit., p. 128
31 *Atlas of the Province of P.E.I., Canada,* (Winnipeg, Manitoba: Hignell Print ing Ltd., 1990), p. 42
32 Ibid.., p. 44
33 Ibid., p. 45
34 Ibid., p. 44
35 Vital Records, PARO, op. cit.
36 Ibid.
37 *Atlas of the Province of PEI, Canada,* op. cit., p. 45
38 File Drawer 105, PARO, op. cit.
39 Doris Haslam, op. cit., p. 38
40 Ibid., pp. 82-83
41 Rev. Janes Robertson, *History of the Mission of the Succession Church to Nova Scotia and P.E.I. 1847,* and Doris Haslam, op. cit., p. 38
42 Doris Haslam, op. cit., p. 37
43 Doris Haslam, op. cit., p. 107.
44 Ibid., pp. 107-108
45 Doris Haslam, op. cit., pp. 108-109.
46 Orlo Jones and Doris Haslam, eds., op. cit., pp. 299-300, 346
47 Doris Haslam, op. cit., pp. 110-111
48 Ibid., pp. 109-110
49 A. B. Warburton and D.A. MacKinnon, eds., *Past and Present of Prince Edward Is land* (Charlottetown: B.F. Bowen and Co., c.1905)
50 Orlo Jones and Doris Haslam, eds., pp. 30-31
51 Because Major's tenth child had six children, the designation is (1. Major; 10 Artemas, 10th child; 1 Artemas' first child in next generation).
52 Orlo Jones and Doris Haslam, eds., op. cit., pp. 329-330
53 Source uncertain; either Ross Graves, op. cit., or Doris Haslam, op. cit.

54 Taken from the genealogical abstract of Mrs. J. A. Newell, 100 Oak St, Gisborne, New Zealand, and Hooper Family files (found at Public Archives and Records Office, Charlottetown, P.E.I., Sept. 30, 1999)
55 Orlo Jones and Doris Haslam, eds., op. cit., p. 139
56 Doris Haslam, op. cit., p. 35
57 Orlo Jones and Doris Haslam, eds., op. cit., p 139
58 Ibid., p. 197
59 Doris Haslam, op. cit., p. 120
60 Ibid., p. 99
61 Ibid., p. 100
62 Ibid., p. 100
63 Ibid., p. 195
64 Ibid., p. 100
65 Ibid., p. 101
66 Ibid., p. 102
67 Ibid., p. 104
68 Ibid., p. 103
69 Ibid., p. 105
70 Ross Graves, op. cit., p. 73
71 Ibid., p. 228
72 Orlo Jones and Doris Haslam, eds., op. cit., pp. 238-239
73 Ibid., pp. 23-24
74 Ibid., p. 89
75 Doris Haslam, op. cit., p. 49
76 Ibid., p. 134
77 Malcolm and Edith Bradshaw, and at least one generation before them, had saved "local" newspaper clippings for years with articles of people whom they knew. In the summer of 2002 the author of this genealogy was the happy recipient of a copy of many, many of these clippings which have added substantially to the information, interest and integrity of this research. Not only were there Hooper "doings," in these papers, but much history and many events of the times were presented.
78 Doris Haslam, op. cit., pp. 50-51
79 Ibid., p. 25
80 Ibid., p. 58
81 Ibid., p. 59
82 Ross Graves, op. cit., pp. 221-222
83 Ibid., p. 104
84 Ada MacLeod, op. cit., pp. 42-43
85 The Province Prize Story for Prince Edward Island in *Montreal Witness*
86 Doris Haslam, op. cit., p. 831
87 Orlo Jones and Doris Haslam, eds., op. cit., p. 197

88 Ross Graves, op. cit., pp. 210-211
89 Information on the family of Ann Hooper and John Schurman is taken from Ross Graves, op. cit., pp. 46, 109-112
90 Ibid., pp. 109-110
91 Doris Haslam, op. cit., p. 62
92 George A. Leard, op. cit., p. 20
93 Ibid., p, 20, and Doris Haslam, op, cit., p. 61
94 Doris Haslam, op. cit., p. 60
95 Ibid., p. 65
96 *The Charlottetown Guardian,* issue unknown
97 Doris Haslam, op. cit., p. 41
98 St. Paul's Anglican Church records
99 Orlo Jones and Doris Haslam, eds., op. cit., p. 140
100 Ibid., p. 137
101 Ross Graves, op. cit., p. 227
102 Orlo Jones and Doris Haslam, eds., op. cit., p. 46
103 Doris Haslam, op. cit., p. 105.
104 Ibid., pp. 232-233
105 Ross Graves, op. cit., p. 227
106 Doris Haslam, op. cit., p. 76
107 Ibid., p. 77
108 Doris Haslam, op. cit., pp. 77-78

CHAPTER 8

Changing Life on Prince Edward Island in the Second Half of the Nineteenth Century and the Early Twentieth Century

The church held a prominent place in the lives of the people in the nineteenth century. Because the history of the Methodist Church in Bedeque seemed to have more information written about it, and more of the Hoopers attended there, that denomination will appear in this genealogy more often although some Hooper relatives were loyal to the Presbyterian Church, others to the Baptist Church, and still others to the Church of Scotland.

When the Methodists completed their new church in the village in 1848, many wondered what should be done with the old chapel down at the cemetery [in Lower Bedeque]. The new church was apparently a short distance behind the present corner store in Centerville, on the right side of the road going to Lower Bedeque. This is the same large property on which the third and current church now stands. Their question concerning a use for the old church was soon answered. The Sons of Temperance were gathering their forces and wanted a meeting place so the old church became the Temperance Hall, probably in 1850 or 1851.

The Aurora Division of the Sons of Temperance at Bedeque held a tea party on Wednesday, July 24, 1850, when a delegation from the Grand Division came with their brass band from Charlottetown to help to raise money for the hall. At two o'clock the picnic parade, which was marshalled near the post office (**Hooper's Inn**), and led

by John Arbuckle, sometime school visitor, but now in his official office of Grand Worthy Patriarch, marched smartly off to the grounds to the stirring music of the band and bag pipes, with the officers and members of the Grand Division followed by the Aurora Division marching two by two. This was followed in turn by carriages, carts, gigs, and wagons filled with happy people, big and little, for whom a tea-party was the biggest thing of the summer and a band something never heard before in Bedeque. Between five and six hundred people were fed that day, and as many addressed, with Rev. James Buckley, the Methodist minister and W. G. Strong, the Methodist local preacher, supplying the Bedeque oratory. George A. Leard, in *Historic Bedeque*, wrote:

> Temperance sentiment on the Island was fast coming to a head. The continent-wide abuse of liquor in the first half of the nineteenth century made it easy for those who sponsored real control to get a hearing. The Sons of Temperance organization on the Island was only four years old in 1852 when it petitioned the Government and had a bill introduced to provide for prohibition similar to that in effect in Maine, Massachusetts, and Rhode Island. The measure which passed the Assembly with a good majority lost out in the Council by one vote. Next year the drinking element marshalled their forces to stave off any effective action for nearly thirty years till the Scott Act became law.[1]

Mr. and Mrs. Bradshaw shared with me a newspaper clipping which perhaps is a good starting point to write about the last half of the nineteenth century. The Rev. Mr. Huestis, who was born in Nova Scotia, at the age of 23 years came to Charlottetown and offered himself for the ministry to the Rev. Mr. Strong who was the pastor of the Charlottetown Methodist Church. One year later Mr. Huestis entered the ministry. According to this undated news clipping, Rev. Mr. Huestis "came to Prince Edward Island and located at Bedeque":

> There were only three Methodist preachers stationed in this province at that time, one at Bedeque, one at Pownal, and the one in Charlottetown. Mr. Huestis's circuit included Margate, DeSable, Cape Traverse for the first year. In the second year he had an assistant which made four Methodist ministers on the Island. He was pastor at Bedeque from 1852-1854.

J. H. Meacham and Company, *Illustrated Historical Atlas of the Province of Prince Edward Island*, pp. 67-68

The western half of Lots 25 and 26 in 1880

The Bedeque Church was comparatively new then. It was the second church in the province and stood on the ground where the present church is located. The congregation numbered about two hundred. He had six local preachers, one of whom was the late Hon. William Strong, Summerside.

Mr. Huestis's influence was very strong in "adding to the church those who were being saved." When he was 78 years old Mr. Huestis returned to P.E.I for a visit and brought with him a poem which was published in the newspaper:

P. E. I SLAND

Beauteous Island, whose features still whisper of Scotland's proud vale in the long, long ago,
Lowly (illegible) Alpines desiring, Kissed by the Atlantic, fertilized by the snow.
Surcharged with the essence of pure vegetation and relics of oysters to nourish its life,
Thy riches and glory shine forth on the surface, supplying the needs of humanity rife.
Thy symmetrical trees with luxuriant foliage are fields of delight with unspeakable green,
Arrest the keen eye and surprise of the tourist who weary not tarrying to drink in the scene.
The voice of thy waving fields everywhere gladdens. Britain hears and outstretched are her arms,
Rejoicing to welcome thy cheeses and thy butter, though rarely allowed to gaze on thy charms.
Thy sons and thy daughters in spirit and features the Heather and Shamrock and Rose represent;
The pure AngloSaxon is power presiding, secure strength and progress, religion, content.
Not hating democracy, blending with loyalty in the Dominion existing today,
Grasping the hand of a kindred Republic while standing beneath Queen Victoria's sway.

Mail Delivery

For the early settlers, the mail service to Prince Edward Island was extremely slow and unreliable, especially in winter....Before 1827 the Island's single link with the mainland during winter was a twice-monthly courier service over the ice between Wood Islands and Pictou.

Later small ice boats were introduced to make the crossing from Cape Traverse to Cape Tormentine. This became a daily service, weather permitting, but "in 1856 there was weekly service. The mail was dispatched every Thursday at 9 a.m. and arrived every Friday at 6 p.m." in Springfield.[2]

In the fall of 1881, the failure of the Prince Edward Island Bank brought trouble to many households. Another calamity happened that year also: the first appearance of the potato bug, a specimen of which was on exhibition in the window of the P. C. Drugstore.

On the last week in April in 1882, the ice in the harbour was three feet thick and solid as in midwinter.

A Hooper descendant sat on the Summerside Town Council for 1883, along with six others: R. C. MacLeod; P. T. Fanning; D. Montgomery; H. A. Compton; John A. Sharpe; A. C. McDonald; and **Elisha Wright.**[3]

The crews carrying the mail across the Strait had to be hardy, powerful, courageous men....One can envision some of the hardships through the following entries:

> The winters of 1885 and 1886 were noted for the terrible time the ice boats had in crossing the strait; they got lost and were out all night in a storm and were all badly frostbitten. 1885 was the worst time. Adrift on the Ice [February 12, 1885]. About 9:30 a.m. on Wednesday last three boats with 22 men (including 7 passengers) left Cape Traverse for the opposite shore. The wind was blowing briskly from the east, the ice running west, the mercury below zero and a snowstorm prevailing which increased in violence as they advanced. Soon they lost their way, became exhausted, and were carried about the strait by wind and current. Towards evening, Cape Traverse light was seen, but the men were too much exhausted to make further effort. During the night a violent storm of sleet and hail came on, but before morning the wind turned N.W. the mercury falling to –15 degrees.

The following statement given by Mr. Fraser, druggist, was condensed from the *Examiner*:

> We left Cape Traverse board ice at 10:15 a.m. on Wednesday. The crews were composed as follows: Boat No. 1 - Newton Muttart, Hector Campbell, Mont Campbell, Eph Bell, Jas. A. Howatt. Boat No. 2 - Muncy Irving, Alex Muttart, Bluch Robinson, Wm. Howatt, Wm. Campbell. Boat No. 3 - Hanford Allen, Geo.

Allan, John Allan, (illegible) Trenholm; Daniel McGlashey. The passengers were Dr. McIntyre, M. P.; Souris; Jas. A. Morrison, Halifax; Aaron Wilson, S'side; Philip Farrell, Sturgeon, PEI; Mr. Glyddon, clerk in store of J. H. Myrick, Tignish; and Mr. Millet belonging to the States.

A snowstorm was setting in from the east, and weather looked threatening. The ice was running west at from three to four miles an hour. The boats were all good and well-built, but their equipment was totally inadequate. They were without axes and without any provisions. A small keg of water was all that was taken for 22 men and only two matches could be found. Not a lantern was attached to the boats. In fact there was no preparation whatever for the passage. There was a small pocket compass in possession of Muncey Irving which might or might not be accurate. On leaving the board ice Jas. A. Morrison fell through and got wet. His clothes froze stiff and he suffered from the start.

During the first hour the ice was rough and we experienced great difficulty pulling the boat over it; but after that we got into smooth ice. Our course was given by Capt Irving, and we kept this course for four hours. Whether intentionally or not, I feel confident the course was changed, and we continued our tiresome journey without getting a sight of land. Finally, at 5:30 p.m. we halted on a pan of ice, surrounded on three sides by water. Capt. Irving told us he did not know where we were. Consultation was held, deciding to retrace our steps a short distance from the open water. It was now blowing a half hurricane.

The pelting sleet and hail was hard to face, and we had to move back slowly to a place considered safe. Here we upset two boats, placed their gunwhales together, and placed the third with baggage to windward. Then taking some tin off the bottom of the boats they constructed a fireplace and prepared fuel of oars. These were soon consumed, and it was found necessary to break up one of the boats, but there was no axe. The work of breaking up the boat, considering it was strongly kneed and tinned, was a difficult job. It was now about 8. The hail and sleet were blinding and the cold intense. In company with Jas. Morrison, I spent the night outside - from 8 on Wednesday evening till 5 on Thursday morning. At times I would get down on a trunk, but the biting frost would keep me on the move. At five in the morning, I went inside the cabin to warm myself, and I earnestly pray to God I shall never witness such a scene as was then presented.

Strong men lay around the fire famished, shivering and exhausted while from the smoky cabin came prayers for relief, and blasphemies intermingled. Occasionally a man, overcome by suffocation, would dash out through the smoke and fall exhausted on the ice. Revived by the piercing cold air, he would again return to the smoky cabin. At midnight the wind shifted to the northwest, blew a hurricane, and the weather became colder than ever. During night only one of the crew (James Howatt) had his feet frozen, and he was given preference at the fire until they were thawed out. About 8 a.m. we changed the camp because the fire had melted the ice so thin it was dangerous. After this, one of the passengers had a pound of sweet

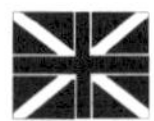

crackers on which the whole number broke their fast - being served with one cracker each. After this we heard a tremendous crash outside. The ice had parted about 15 feet from the cabin. In a short time there was a space of a mile between the pans. The waves then dashed where we had our cabin and broke it so rapidly that we had barely time to get up the boats and baggage and move away. In the center of the pan we pitched our tent again.

At noon on Thursday the cold was beyond endurance, the fuel nearly consumed. We reckoned on the balance of the boat, three trunks, a quantity of mail matter, etc. to last till Friday morning. By this time most of the men had given up all hopes of reaching land, and for my part, I think if we had to spend Thursday night in the Gulf there would be few remaining Friday morning. At this time few if any had hope of ever seeing land. One of the men became quite delirious and thus added to the horror of the scene. We were all then inside the camp, looking out at intervals. The passengers wished to move, thinking it best to die on the move than like rats in a hole. About 4 p.m. we were all lying about inside the boat half asleep when Muncy Irving sung out, "Land ho! not three miles away."

Everyone at once scrambled out and we saw the land. The news appeared to be taken quietly. The men were dazed from want of food and from being so long confined in the smoky camp. All went to work and we packed up everything in the two remaining boats and started for the shore which turned out to be six or seven miles away. Some were only able to follow the boat, holding on. But all kept along until we struck the board ice. It was a struggle for life. The two crews would often have to combine to move one boat. We had to row through some 300 yards of lolly. We had only four oars between the two boats, and our way was mostly made by rocking the boats in the lolly and one boat making way for the other. When we got to the board ice, we left the boats, the crew refusing to pull another inch.

Every man started for the shore without bags or baggage. There was no order of our going; the strongest went to the front and the weaker followed. It was about 8 p.m. when I reached the house. It was a regular hospital, everyone being more or less frozen. It was then seen that three of our number were missing and a party was sent out to search for them. They found Newton Muttart at a neighbor's house and Glyddon was found in a barn, hands and feet badly frozen. The other man, Sandy Muttart, was found in the marsh perfectly speechless, with his face badly frozen. The people at the house (Angus McPhail's) vied with one another in helping us. They spared no trouble and many of the passengers owe their lives to their prompt and kind attention. A motley-looking spectacle was 20 men sitting with their feet in dishes of cold water, trying to draw out the frost. Their walk from the board ice to shore (about two miles) was a severe task for many of the crew. It was the last struggle for life and many of the men had just power to move one limb in front of the other and barely conscious. Until morning the men could not tell to what degree they were frozen. Some of them had kept their limbs in water five or six hours.

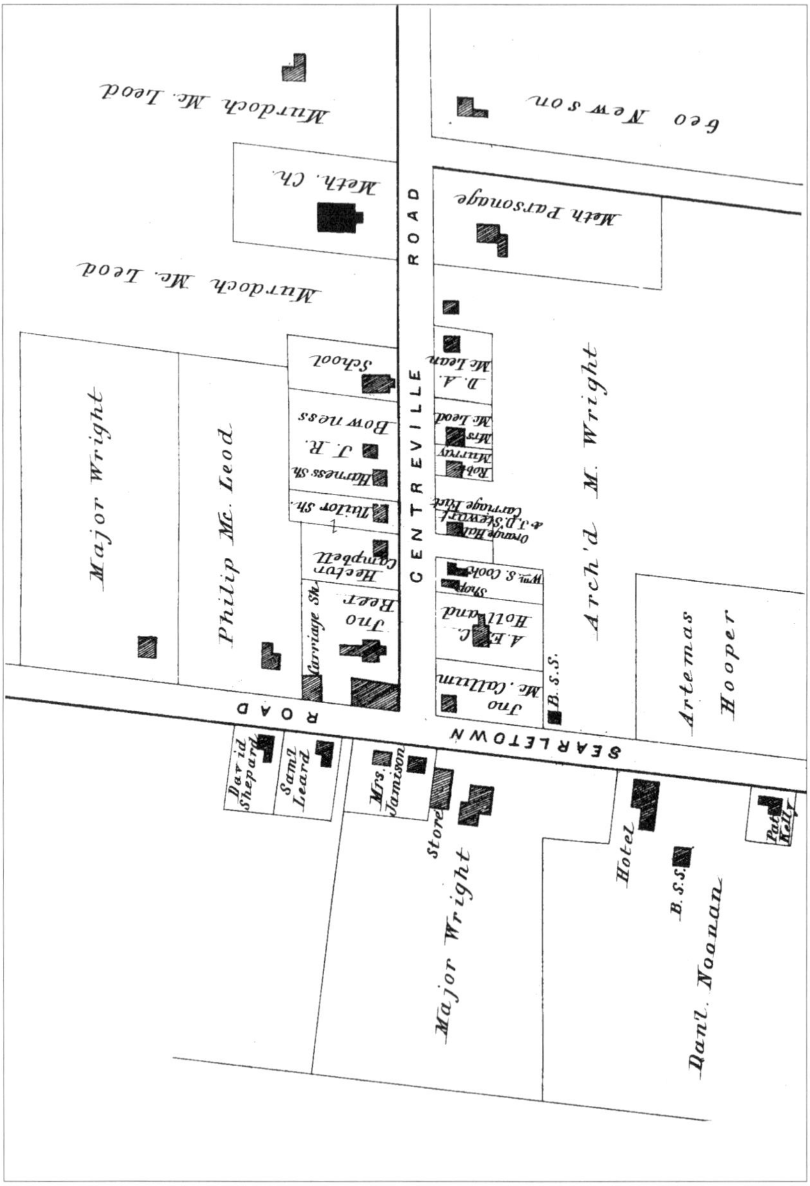

J. H. Meacham and Company, *Illustrated Historical Atlas of the Province of Prince Edward Island*, p. 31

Centreville Bedeque, Lot 26, P.E.I. in 1880

It was then found that all the crew and passengers, with the exception of Dr. McIntyre, the three Campbell brothers, Muncey Irving, Hanford Allan and Buncher Robertson were more or less frozen. Those who were most severely frozen were Glyddon, Millet, James Muttart, and James Morrison. My own injuries are but trifling compared with others. I am of opinion there was unnecessary delay in starting. Had they got away at 8 there would have been no difficulty in making the crossing, and the day was such when the start was made that it was almost madness to make it. That boats should start so inefficiently equipped is in my opinion nothing short of criminal. The conduct of the men will probably be investigated. Mr. Fraser declined to give any expression of opinion . The traveling public have now an opportunity of learning under what protection they cross the straits.

Dr. McKay arrived home last night and reports all the frost-bitten patients out of danger and doing well. Some of them will lose one or more fingers and toes, but they are not so far gone as was at one time reported. M. A. Wilson also returned last night, apparently not much the worse for his adventure.

Friday, February 11, 1887. Wind North-East with snow. No crossing this morning. 12:15 p.m. Captain Muttart left with three boats and mails. Captain Howatt (is) at Cape Tormentine. No crossing from there to-day. 4:15 p.m. Captain Muttart had to return. Crossing bad and snowing hard.

Another entry from December 3, 1890, compliments of Malcolm and Edith Bradshaw, reads:

The weather on the Island for the past two or three days has been the most severe for the time of year that has been known. On Monday a snow storm set in, accompanied by a gale which was as fierce as is experienced any time during winter. About four or five inches fell, but it is all in drifts. The wind was from the north, but coming on night, it veered to the westward. During the afternoon the tide rose till it reached all of 12 inches higher than the high tide of a week or two ago, but owing to the wind being off the shore but little damage was done. Muirhead's wharf was totally submerged, only a few feet of the shore end being uncovered. Half of the outer end of Holman's wharf was also under water and his old coal yard was all afloat. Queen's wharf had more than half of the outer end submerged. The water reached the top of the timber on the Railway abutment between these two wharves.

At the west end of the town the road, when the tide was at its height between five and six in the evening, had all of a foot of water over it for some distance while the grocery store and dwelling of Mr. John Martin was nearly all surrounded. The water reached the door sill and it is said another inch would have let the water pour in on the floor. Mr. James Grady's boats which had been hauled up to his house got afloat in his yard and were in danger of floating out to sea. At the railway wharf the

water was over the rails at the inner end of the coal shed, and at the outer end nothing but the mooring posts could be seen. Where the passengers land from the steamer some eight or ten inches were over the platform and the water was over the curbing, while the rails had some two feet of water over them at this point. The water was over the entire floor of the freight shed, and in Mr. Gordon's office was some three or four inches. There was considerable freight in this warehouse which we suppose will be more or less damaged. Between the freight and coal sheds, some heavy timber floated on to the wharf and some of the planks were torn up by the force of the water. Much of the floor in the outer freight shed was also lifted up and displaced.

The *St. Lawrence* and *M. A. Starr* lay at the wharf all day, but on the following morning the *St. Lawrence* left for Point du Chêne, getting through the ice which had made during the night fairly well and reached the Point. The latest account we have heard was that she had taken in some 14 cars of freight and got clear of that harbor at 11 p.m., and it is supposed she has steamed for Charlottetown. The *M. A. Starr* tried to get out on Tuesday night, but failed, and all Wednesday forenoon she was about a hundred yards off from the railway wharf. On Saturday evening the *Katie Steward* was towed out to the lighthouse and on Monday forenoon, the *F. C. Batt* went out with Captains Edward and Read to her, and has been unable owing to the ice to get back. Men walked ashore from her on Wednesday morning.

The tide on Monday was the highest ever known here and for the time of year, the weather has been the coldest. Through the night of Monday the thermometer registered 5 degrees below zero and on Tuesday night it was down to 8 ½ below. Some damage has been done at Stanley Bridge and the Steam Navigation Co's wharf at Charlottetown had some damage done to the covering, and other wharves there were submerged. About twenty yards of the embankment on the east end of the railway bridge at Morell was washed out, the *Examiner* says. The bridge at Midgell was almost similarly damaged to the extend of about 60 yards on one side and 20 on the other. The breastwork at St. Peter's was also damaged.

The *Princess of Wales*, the *Patriot* says, left Charlottetown at 6 o'clock on Monday morning for Pictou with several passengers and a quantity of freight. At that hour the weather looked somewhat threatening and rain was falling. Capt. Cameron, however, did not anticipate such a terrific storm as set in later. The steamer got as far as Caribou about ten miles from Pictou when the storm struck her. The wind was fair for her going in that direction , but the blinding snow storm prevented her from making Pictou harbor. Captain Cameron, seeing that the port could not be reached, put the boat about and headed for Charlottetown and kept her head on to the storm, battling with the wind, seas, and weather such as the *Princess* has seldom, if ever, experienced. This was kept up until the afternoon and when off Wood Islands, it was decided to anchor. The anchor was accordingly let go, but the chain snapped and away went the anchor and part of the chain to the

bottom of the Strait. Nothing could then be done but to steer to Charlottetown. The seas were tremendous, but in the face of this, Captain Cameron and Pilot Archibald Finlayson directed the steamer's course from the wheelhouse where they were being continually drenched with spray, and although soaking wet and unable to see even the lights of the block-house until abreast of it, still they stood to their post like true seamen and eventually safely docked the *Princess* at her wharf at 3 o'clock Tuesday morning. The *Princess* was thus seventeen hours fighting her way a distance of about forty miles.

On Wednesday morning she was unable to leave. Nothing but ice can be seen at Shediac, and the harbor in Summerside is to all appearance frozen up for the winter. A number of vessels are here partly loaded with potatoes and oats. At noon on Wednesday there was no word of the whereabouts of the *St. Lawrence*.

January 17, 1891 Wind North-East. Not blowing hard. Captain Muttart left Traverse six-fifteen with bags of mail. Captain Howatt left Tormentine six-fifty with sixty bags of mail. Captain Howatt returned to Tormentine for Monday's mail leaving at 11:30. Captain Muttart returned to Traverse with remainder of mail 21 bags left.

With the advent of the ice-breaking ferries, the era of the Ice Boats came to an end, but admiration for these brave, hardy men lives on.

In George A. Leard's *Historic Bedeque*, we read: "Centreville School in 1869 had been made a grammar school where the teachers, in distinction from those who taught the three R's, had to hold certificates of ability to teach Latin, Greek, and French. Grammar school teachers were paid £95 (British currency) or $380 a year. This was a good salary for those days. The assistant unmarried minister on the Bedeque circuit at this period got $86 for board money (evidently board was $1.65 a week) and $120 salary plus horse hire, while the superintendency minister received $600 plus transportation charges and children's allowances. Not all items were as cheap as board: the fare on Richard Bagnall's stage coach from Charlottetown to Summerside was nine shillings or $1.80."[4]
George A. Leard continued:

...about the same time (1869) that Bedeque acquired Grammar school status, the school trustees purchased the Temperance Hall, formerly the old chapel of Lower Bedeque, and, having double plastered it, etc., made it into a comfortable, two-roomed school. The old school, purchased by Murdock McLeod for a tailor shop after fire destroyed his first store, was moved some time in the eighteen-hundred

and eighties, to Central Bedeque. Placed on the west side of the Summerside road, a little north of the corner store, it continued as a tailor shop under the ownership of Colin Wright, with Charles Bearisto, well-known Freetown tailor, as manager, till 1890 when William Callbeck commenced a tailoring business on the corner, renting this property and continuing with Charles Bearisto as tailor. Four years later when a new Callbeck tailor shop was built on the opposite corner, the old school-tailor shop was sold to **Edward Hooper** who moved it back to face on the road to the Old Mill Bridge, where it stands today (1948), the busy workshop of his son **Leslie.** With the erection of a new school somewhere around the turn of the century, the one-time church-temperance-hall-school was sold to Solomon Bell, who, further altering it, moved it to his corner lot (now [1948] the home property of Walter Bowness) from where it was finally moved to the rear of the Bowness store to eventually be razed in the fire of 1938.[5]

...In visiting Bedeque you would almost think you were in the fashionable circles of London or Paris...so testified A.E.C. Holland Esq., before the Land Commissioner's Court in 1860. "Young men," he said, "are brought up well, driving about in fine carriages." Holland testifying as a landlord before the Commissioners, painted a rosy picture of plenty and prosperity under benevolent landlords. The most rancorous matter in early Island politics was that known as the Land Question. According to many politicians of that day, the system of landlords and rentals was responsible for all the evils of pioneer life, though the hardworking thrifty farmer made a success and the shiftless lazy one the reverse, whether free or lease holders."[6]

By the late 1860s "the ranks of the older ministers were thinning out," wrote George A. Leard, in *Historic Bedeque*:

On the 16th of May, 1870, the cold silence of death laid its rigor on Bedeque's pioneer missionary, the beloved John B. Strong, stilling that voice so charming to young childhood - so melodious in the hymns of Wesley and Watts - so eloquent and persuasive in the pulpit message, stilling it all but in memory where it lived well on towards the middle of the next century. During his last years in the church he had become "Father Strong" to more than his children. The conference custom of addressing the delegates as "Fathers and Brethren" seemed appropriate in 1862 for the ministerial representatives from P.E.I. district were, according to the minutes, four brethren "and Father Strong."

Father Strong had been a leader in social reform. At the last District meeting he attended in Charlottetown, he told the brethren he had been a teetotaler since 1828, something which few ministers or laymen of that generation could truthfully say.

In less than two years, "...a second grave received all that was mortal of his wife, Elizabeth," wrote Leard.

Mrs Strong died in Bedeque at the home of her daughter, Mrs. Lemuel Hooper, according to Leard, "in the same house and the same room where with her husband she had lodged fifty-three years previously. This was on the present [1948] William Stavert farm owned in 1819 by Elisha, youngest son of the pioneer Loyalist, Thomas Hooper...."

Leard continued:

...[Around 1870] Tryon, looking forward to a division of the overgrown Bedeque circuit, planned a parsonage to equal or surpass any on the Island, which, erected in 1872, still stands serene and poised, looking out over Tryon River. The division of the Bedeque-Tryon circuit would, of course, leave the Searletown parsonage off center as a minister's residence for the proposed Bedeque circuit. Accordingly some of the Bedeque members, led by "Brother David Rogers" of Freetown, moved that a new house for the minister be erected at Centreville. By October of 1872, the Island *Argus* of Charlottetown had the printed word that "The Wesleyans of Bedeque are about erecting a parsonage in vicinity of Centreville. What "are about erecting" meant is not wholly clear, but whether framed that fall or not, the Centreville parsonage was not completed till the next year. A two acre corner property on the road leading to Wright's mills was purchased from Jesse Wright Sr. for $194.60. The trustees of the new property- Stephen Wright, William G. Strong, John Beer, George Crosby, George Clark, Edmund Crosby, David Rogers, Busby Atkinson, Stephen Black, Jesse Wright, and Hiram Trueman included only one, Stephen Wright, Esq., who had been trustee of both the first and second "mission houses" as the early parsonages were called....[7]

The relocation of John Beer, Esq., in 1875, " ..."left a big store vacant on Centreville Corner (where William T. Bowness later built) and a gap in the offices of the church equaled only by Hon. W. G. Strong's departure from Central Bedeque the next year," wrote Leard:

...John Beer, well-known as merchant, farmer, magistrate, and local preacher, gave probably his best services to Centreville in the work of the Sunday School to which he was intensely devoted and in which he served as Superintendent and teacher during most of his eighteen years in Bedeque. As a farmer, who necessarily had to hire men to do most of the work, he was deeply concerned with preserving and improving soil fertility. A story is told of John Beer sitting as a magistrate in Tryon

on a case involving the piling of mussel mud on the side of the road to the inconvenience of the public. In his judgment he found for the defendant and said he'd like to see mussel mud, destined for the fields, piled not only on one side of the road, but on both, all the way from Tryon to Bedeque. John Beer's schooner frequently tied up at Hurd's Wharf to load much of the Bedeque produce shipped at this time. It was a period when store accounts, running for ten months, were settled once a year with potatoes and oats. Many accounts were never settled. This fact, together with a growing awareness that since the Railway went through by-passing Bedeque, the community would never be a big commercial center, probably accounted for Mr. Beer's moving. The quarterly meeting appointed Nelson Inman to take up the collection at Bedeque, in place of Mr. Beer, and Colin Wright to prepare for the Sacraments [Colin Wright and Isaac Wright were brothers].

William G. Strong who removed to Summerside in 1878 to continue a general merchandising business in a larger field of action, was still the Bedeque represntative in the Legislative Council and still continued as a local preacher for the Bedeque charge. Archibald M. Wright took his place as circuit steward, and brother Albert Craig's name was added to the list of prayer leaders at this time. At Strong's Corner Colin Wright who married a daughter of Wm. G. Strong took over the business which some years later became Wright and Craig. At Centreville John Beer's departure left Major Wright as sole merchant in the settlement, doing business at the same stand where he and Charles Gardiner had commenced many years previously [in the building which was recently the home of Brian and Brenda Beaton until it was demolished on October 1, 2002]. Major Wright commenced the good Bedeque custom of combining store and post office, having been postmaster as early as 1863.[8]

There are times when an obituary can reveal a great deal about the times in which the person lived. The information included within the following obituary was of interest to the writer:

GEO MUTTART OF P.E.I. Mr. George Muttart – long a consistent and useful member of the Methodist Church – departed this life at Augustine Cove, P.E.I., on Sunday, the 17th of May in the 57th year of his age [year not given]. His father was originally a Roman Catholic, and was converted and brought into the enjoyment of true religion by an interesting circumstance. A neighbor of his, who had recently experienced salvation, had occasion to go to the woods with his team, and being warm in the love of God, fell down to pour out his soul in prayer and thanksgiving, unconscious of the proximity of any human being. Providence, however, had guided Mr. Muttart near to the spot [where the man was praying and] hearing indistinctly a voice with which he seemed to be familiar, drew near to listen, fancying that his friend, of whose conversion he was ignorant, was swearing at his horses, but to his

great surprise, he heard the earnest supplications of a soul engaged with God. Deep was the impression made on his mind, resulting soon after in his own enlightment and conversion.

In 1880 Rev. George Harrison became pastor of Bedeque for the three year term. "The thirty-year-old Centreville church was in need of repairs which Mr. Harrison endeavoured to have done during his pastorate; but a slow-growing sentiment in the congregation argued that the church was too hard to heat, too boxy in style, too large for the smaller families," wrote George A Leard:

The smaller families were a fact. Nathaniel Wright, the father of Methodism, had eighty-five grandchildren while his eleven children (ten of whom had issue) averaged only twenty-two grandchildren each. A smaller, more modern church would be the cure for everything, thought some in a congregation which at this period was perhaps more or less in the spiritual doldrums. Thus, at Mr. Harrison's last trustee meeting, when the subscription list for repairing the chapel was presented, the question of repairs was laid over for further consideration. The fact that the sister congregation at Tryon had opened a beautiful new church (their third) that fall may have had some influence in the minds of the Bedeque trustees. A. M. Wright, John Craig, and Martin Black were perhaps the most ardent in the new church movement while Ewen Clark led a conservative minority who wished to retain the old church. George Clark of Wilmot and David Rogers of Freetown who resigned from the trustee board at this time were also probably opposed or wished to leave the decision solely with the Bedeque people....

Bedeque Methodist finances at this period missed Wm. G. Strong who before his removal to Summerside had handled them with a deft, sure touch. Supplementary aid in raising money was tried the last year of Mr. Harrison's stay when on December 28, 1882 a supper, or as the *Patriot* called it, a "Methodist tea" was served to the general public. Sixty-four dollars was realized the first evening with not quite half that amount in the second edition on New Year's night...."[9]

Sentiment in favour of a new church at Centrewille, first argued for in 1883, finally crystallized during the pastorate of Rev. E. C. Turner who came to Bedeque in 1886. Plans for the new church were secured that fall, and having the approval of the building committee were submitted to the congregation in February of 1887 for a final vote of approval: receiving which the trustees went ahead with commendable dispatch to erect the third and latest Methodist Church in Bedeque. The old church was dismantled, its pews moved into the Orange Hall where church services were held, and the building itself moved from its foundations to give room for the new one.

To those who like the things of life that have been hallowed with time, even to those who think new things are always best, there is something inexpressibly sad about an old home, or an old church, which has outgrown its usefulness and been condemned to meager uses. The church which was eventually sold to A. M. Wright for $100.00 to be used for a warehouse, was hauled from Centreville the next year, March 9,1888, over the ice to Coles' Wharf by thirty-two span of horses. But first the tower which was of no value except for firewood, was jacked up on one side and toppled neatly in the road, falling so straight the S on the weather vane was buried six inches in the roadbed. The church-warehouse was placed on the west side of the wharf near a building owned by R. T. Holman. Years later when Coles' Wharf was nearing the end of its commercial life, the warehouse was torn down and the frame taken across to Summerside to be incorporated into still another warehouse.

It is not as a warehouse that the old church is remembered by the few who sixty years after it was hauled away, can lean back in memory against the upholstery of the Jesse Wright square pew and hear again John Beer drilling them in scripture texts - or sitting perhaps in a gallery class of the Sunday School, may remember better (a child's mind being so constituted) more of what the teacher wore than of what he or she taught. In a description of the church's interior, given earlier in this history, no mention was made of the pews or where people sat. As in all churches of its day, the pews, with the exception of two or three reserved for visitors, were private property, sold at the time of the building of the church. To keep them private they were equipped with doors and latches and to make them more comfortable were often upholstered at the option of the owner. No chapel steward's pew-book to show the original owners or the changes of forty years, has been found so that what is known of the seating arrangement of the second church has come from memories which can focus sharply on the location of the family pew in which they sat, but naturally blur on a fuller picture of the general seating arrangement."[10]

This second chapel was used through the year 1887. It must have been located in close proximity to the present Bedeque United Church. The description of this second church is so beautifully narrated by George A. Leard, in his *Historic Bedeque*, that it was included only partially in Chapter Six, with Leard's added details below:

Writing proudly of the second chapel in 1849, Father Strong said it had sixty-six pews in all, seating five hundred. On the main floor of the church there were three rows of seats and two aisles. The middle row of pews had a division board in the center of each, making in effect two middle rows of seats. At the top of the church on the west side, Jesse Wright-at-the-mill had the first of four square pews which,

equal in size to two ordinary pews, had seats on three sides. The next was owned jointly by George Gardiner and William Wright of South Shore, with the third one in possession of Joseph Pope, later Wm. G. Strong. The fourth and last double pew on the west was occupied by Thomas Wright of Centreville and later his sons Solomon, Theodore, and Colin. There were possibly six single pews completing this row, which, continuing to the back of the church, were occupied respectively by David Edwards, Philips Callbeck, John Robinson, and Joseph Rogers with the last two pews reserved possibly for strangers. The west middle row of seats had one square pew at the top occupied by Joseph Black of Searletown and later his son Stephen. At the very back of this row in 1887 John A. Howat occupied the last seat or perhaps the second last, the back ones so often being reserved for strangers. The seats in front of him at one time were occupied respectively by Benjamin Wright, Horatio Wright, Lorenzo Wright, and J. R. Wright , with several intervening pews, owners of which have not been ascertained. At a later period W. A. Leard and Josph Morris occupied seats on this row, probably ones formerly owned by Lorenzo Wright and Horatio Wright.

In the Eastern middle row, Nelson Inman sat in the back seat, one time the pew of George M. Wright of Freetown. Successive pew-holders ahead of him included **Thomas Robins**, David Rogers, Jesse Schurman, **Lemuel Hooper**, George Clark and George Newsom with John Beer occupying the top box pew. The minister's pew was the top corner one on the East side with the Stephen Wright (Middleton) pew, later occupied by Martin Black, directly behind it. Stephen Wright, Esq. of Bedeque and Squire John Wright of Searletown occupied the two other box pews on this side with smaller pews behind occupied by Job Wright, Busby Atkinson, Fred Moyse, James Wright, Ewen Clark, and James Watt.

Large double doors on the east side of the tower provided the main entrance to the church. In the porch a stairs, commencing on the west side, wound up to the commodious gallery which, extending on two sides and one end of the church, was roomy enough in itself for quite a congregation, having five rows of seats at the back and three rows on the sides. The occupants of the gallery pews have only partially been ascertained. In the memory of those living, the gallery seats were but thinly occupied. Indeed the gallery was closed altogether a year or more before the last service was held in the church. [It would appear that the attendance had diminished considerably!]

The pews in the gallery, unlike those in the main body of the church, had no doors. The top front pew on the west side was occupied by J. R. Bowness and family, one of whom (William T.) remembers looking dizzily down at the people below. Directly across from the Bowness pew on the other side of the gallery was the Robert Inman seat with the William Cook pew immediately behind. Wm. Cook later sat downstairs on the west side in a pew near the Joseph Rogers' seat and took up the collection. George Crosby of Freetown, who also moved down later, and Charles Leard of Fernwood had front pews on the East side of the gallery. Other

gallery folks included George Doull of Wilmot, Mr. Wilkins of Lower Bedeque and Benjamin Pollard of Central Bedeque. The latter was a noted clock-maker and mechanic who lived to be very old and very feeble. He is remembered in Bedeque for a famous answer to a question asked by a neighbor whether he minded being left dinnerless and alone while his wife went out by the day to help earn the living. "Oh, no," he replied, "I'm fine as long as I have plenty of apple sass and the Wesleyan!"

The most prominent figure in the gallery was Nathaniel Huestis, who before there was a choir sat in a front pew on the east side of the gallery. When a hymn was announced he would rise, strike the pitch on a tuning fork and lead off in one of the glorious tunes of Methodism. Later, with the formation of a choir, his place was in the front pew of the south gallery with the choir on his left. The memory of their beautifully blended voices, leading the congregation in the singing of "My God, the Spring of All My Joys" to the tune of Lyngham, was something never to be forgotten. The church clock, attached to the gallery below where the choir sat, like most church clocks, never went. An organ came to the old church in the early eighteen hundred and seventies with Jesse Alexander Wright, nephew of Nancy and Nathaniel Wright, of North Bedeque (one of the most versatile men of his generation) as first organist, followed later on by Alice [Hooper] Wright who in turn was succeeded by Mrs. Colin Wright. Mrs. Wright was organist in 1886 when, the gallery being closed, the choir and organ moved downstairs to the Wm. Strong and adjoining pews.

Mrs. Wright was succeeded at the organ towards the close of the century by Minnie Leard who for a time shared the pleasant duties with Priscilla Schurman (later Mrs. J. Clarke MacQuarrie). Next in line of faithful melody-makers was Lulu Hooper who, during the four years previous to her marriage to Frank Deacon, presided at the Bedeque organ. She in turn was succeeded by Ethel Bell [Mrs. Wright Morris] who played for a year or two. The most outstanding record of Bedeque organists was that made by Louise Schurman (later Mrs. John Stuart) who for over thirty-five years made joyful music unto the Lord being succeeded in 1947 by Mrs. Wilfred Craig [the mother of Frances Howatt and Joan Wright]. A notable singing record is that of Thomas Moyse who, having joined the Methodist choir in 1883, celebrated his sixty-fifth anniversary in 1948. He followed in a singing tradition: his father, Frederick Holland Moyse of Central Bedeque, was precentor in the Presbyterian Church at North Bedeque before a revival and a Wright wife combined to make him a Methodist.

At the last service held in the old church in the spring of 1887, Rev. E. C. Turner, viewing his congregation from the high pulpit for the last time, preached from the text, "Now that which decayeth and waxeth old is ready to vanish away," [Hebrews 8:13] in a sermon which, while doubtless challenging his congregation to build a fine new house of worship, seems from the Scripture text to have been

also an apology for the removal of the old. The third and present church was built in the last eight months of 1887 with considerable despatch and without corner-stone laying ceremonies. [A newspaper article of the time read "The Methodist Church is progressing. Plasterer Philip Smith has commenced his work."]

The contractor, John MacCallum, a good Presbyterian from Lower Bedeque, had novel ideas on how to make thirty-eight hundred Methodist dollars build, finish, and pew a church, 50 x 31, with a vestry 30 x 24, and still yield a reasonable profit. One brilliantly conceived shortcut and money-saver was the erection inside the tower of the spire which was then hoisted into its place seventy-eight feet from the ground. This achievement, as remembered by Wm. T. Bowness, was accomplished with as much rope and tackle as would rig a ship! Of the carpenters who worked on the church only one, Ernest Gay then of Hampton, Va, had lived to see its 60th anniversary.

The pews in the new church, made by George Webber of Summerside, differed in every respect from those in the old. They were long and friendly and free with red plush cushions showing to advantage against the ash and walnut woods of which they were made. The chancel furniture of pulpit, table and chairs, costing seventy dollars, was from the shop of H. A. Compton. A new Bible (this one without Free Church marginal notes!) was on the pulpit for the first time, the gift of Hon. William G. Strong. It took precedence over James Connell's 1849 gift which went to the vestry for Sunday School and prayer meeting use. Another gift at this time was a set of collection plates from Wellington Burns of Summerside.

Calling the people to the dedicatory services of the new church on January 8, 1888, was a six-hundred pound bell, costing three hundred dollars, the gift of Hon. Benjamin Rogers, a native son, whose affection for the church and community of his youth thus found practical expression.

As the musical notes of the new bell died on the clear morning air, the choir occupying the corner to the west of the pulpit, with Mrs. Colin Wright presiding at the new organ, sang the anthem, "How Beautiful in Zion" as a processional, while the pastor, Rev. E. C. Turner accompanied by Rev. Job Shenton of Charlottetown and Rev. C. W Hamilton of Margate, marched impressively up the aisle. The sermon preached by the visiting Charlottetown pastor, as a prelude to the solemn service of dedication for Methodist Churches, was based on a text from Second Chronicles, twenty-ninth chapter and seventeenth verse, which by a strange coincidence, showed a similar day and month for the dedication of Solomon's Temple: "Now they began on the first day of the first month to sanctify, and on the eigth day of the month came they to the porch of the Lord."

The large morning congregation of "five hundred people" [perhaps the 1888 reporter exaggerated a little] who crowded the church and vestry to overflowing,, were in their places again for the afternoon service. Many of them were from other Prince County congregations which had been at one time part of the all-inclusive Bedeque circuit. Sharing in the services of the new church meant sharing of Sun-

day dinner in many hospitable homes in Bedeque. The theme of the afternoon service was Prayer, with Rev. C. W. Hamilton preaching from 1 Kings, Chapter 8, Verse 22. Appropriate anthems and hymns included "Prayer Is the Soul's Sincere Desire." At the evening service, the pastor of First Methodist Church, Charlottetown, spoke on the Kingdom from a text found in the second chapter of Daniel, forty-fourth and forty-fifth verses.

Only a few of those who attended the dedicatory services in 1888 could remember similar services in 1818 when the first church had been opened. One of these, Mrs. Nathaniel Wright of North Bedeque, known familiarly to the community as Aunt Nancy, and specifically as Big Nancy Wright, to distinguish her from her sister-in-law Little Nancy, generously contributed $300.00 to the new church. She and her brothers James Wright of Bedeque in his 85th year and Jesse Wright-at-the-mill in his 80th year would doubtless compare the comfort and beauty of the new church with the plank-bench homeliness of their father's barn where the first Methodist services had been held. Job Wright of Middleton and Frances Wright, wife to William Schurman, were the only ones of the Stephen Wright family to see the third house of worship. Nathaniel Huestis, in his 95th year with five more to go, probably brought the only adult memories of the beginnings of Methodism to the opening of the third church[11].

Thanks to the kindness of Mr. and Mrs. Bradshaw, the obituary of Nathaniel Huestis is included:

Early in the new year died the oldest man we were ever called upon to bury. Nathaniel Huestis [born 1794] died on Jan. 9th, 1894, in his 101st year. It scarcely seemed possible to be attending the funeral of one whose life spanned the distance between John Wesley and the present day. Two years after Wesley's death Bro. Huestis was born. A very faithful account of Mr. Huestis has already appeared in the *WESLEYAN*, but it is now for us to say that in his sickness he was perfectly at rest in Jesus. In his early days he was noted for his singing, and sometimes even during his sickness when he was left alone, he would sing some of the old hymns. He died very peacefully. His son placed him in as comfortable a position as possible, crossing his hands across his breast and laid down for two hours to sleep and when he returned he was in the same position, never having apparently moved and the face contained a smile and the soul had gone to Eternal Rest after being 60 to 70 years a member of the Methodist Church. [At the time of his death he lived in Albany, P.E.I.]

"Bedeque Methodists were never very much interested in their history," wrote George A. Leard:

Believing that life is a one way street, they were rightly concerned with what lay ahead on the High Way rather than thinking of a past they could not retravel. They might not agree with Winston Churchill that "the longer you can look back the further you can look forward," but even the least historically-inclined would admit, from a brief study of Bedeque Church annals, that history has important lessons for the open mind. One of these lessons, self-evident, though often overlooked, is the relative unimportance of church buildings which all church histories, including this one, seem to delight in telling about.[12]

The important thing [during the years 1886-1889]... was not the building of a new church. It was rather the "adding to the church of such as should be saved." The church is never a building apart from believers and (the pastor) was instrumental, by the Spirit's guidance and the powerful working of a revival throughout the whole circuit, in bringing nearly a hundred members into the body of Christ. Nearly a half were from Centreville Church, and while a few were teen-aged, most were of the age class which sixty years later would be called "young adult."

...The new members were soon given responsible offices in the church....In 1892 new cemetery trustees including Thomas Moyse, **Allison Hooper**, Albert Bell, **A.M. Wright**, **Colin Wright**, W. A. Leard, **A.T. Wright**, and Robert Price were appointed. In the same year the resignation of Morice Wright as chapel steward brought to that office William Callbeck who was to fill the position in the faithful manner required of stewards for fifty years....

The licensing of Thomas Moyse as a local preacher on trial by the Quarterly Meeting of December 15, 1892, marked the official beginning of a lay-preaching career unequalled for persuasive power and far-reaching results in the annals of Bedeque Church. The joy of bringing others to Christ has been the key note of a devoted life which has had expression in many other ways, but which counted personal evangelization the most satisfying of life's achievements. Mr. Moyse's moving testimony, before Presbytery in October, 1948, to the delight in sharing the Master's work, sometimes thought of as the minister's work only, will long be remembered by those who heard it. Mr. Harrison's three-year pastorate, ending in 1892, was unique in the fact that though funerals were conducted on other parts of the circuit, none were made to Lower Bedeque Cemetery. This ministerial term also saw the final payment made on the debt of the new church. Three of the trustees, **A. M. Wright**, **Major Wright**, and **Colin Wright** assumed responsibility for payment of the last $362. **Major Wright** and **Colin Wright** were the merchants and postmasters at this time at Centreville and Central Bedeque respectively.

The Bedeque Methodists were but little ahead of their older contemporary, the Bedeque Presbyterian congregation, who in 1891 erected what was also their third house of God. Built by Thomas Beattie and dedicated the next year, it was as fine an example of rural church architecture as any Presbytery of the Maritime Synod could boast. But as a fine house doesn't necessarily mean a fine home, so the real glory of the Presbyterian congregation was not in a building but in the body of believers who came every Lord's Day from the east and from the west, from the north and from the south, for many of them a six to ten mile drive, with a faithfulness pleasing to preachers and astounding to strangers.

The Lower Bedequers who came to church in the winter-time over the ice could not help but feel how convenient it would be to come over the water in the summer. Shortly after the building of the third church, a movement got under way which, in 1893, resulted in a petition signed by four hundred people asking the government to build a bridge and aboiteau from Howatt's Shore to Murray's Island, claiming that from eight hundred to a thousand acres of marsh land could be reclaimed. The dream never materialized though the agitation kept up for a number of years.

The new church was dedicated during the ministry of Rev. W. Tufts, the third pastor at North Bedeque. Rev. R. S. Patterson had completed his long unbroken ministry of fifty-six years in 1882 when death called for the seemingly tireless servant who, as preacher, farmer, schoolmaster, lawyer, and even sometimes physician, gave to his flock the fatherly care and example which only the word pastor in all its richest meaning could encompass. A generous man, tithing in his early years, and double-tithing (one-fifth) in later life, Mr. Patterson still managed to leave, as a monument to his industry, a sizeable estate at his death....

At Central Bedeque the Baptists, not feeling the need of discarding the ancient landmark, still clung to their old meeting-house. However in 1894 . . . the church was made to look like new by the addition of tower and vestry and a thorough renovation in furnishings and interior decoration. The congregation meanwhile used the Methodist Church for Sunday afternoon services. The mid-week prayer service has no early mention in Methodist records, being possibly first introduced into the community by the Baptist brethren who, in 1854 in their Bedeque record book, asked that Wednesday evening prayer meetings should be held "from house to house at seven o'clock in the summer and early candle light in winter...."

[At Bedeque Methodist] A total membership in 1894 of two hundred and fifty-two communicants with ten on trial, included one hundred at Bedeque, seventy-six at Searletown, twenty-four at South Shore [Chelton], six at Middleton and forty-six at Cape Traverse. South Shore and Searletown membership had been greatly augmented in 1892 with a large number of young people including Horace Wright, Nathaniel Pearson, **Major Lowther**, **Grace Lowther**, Emma Wright, Herman Myers, Fred Wright, Debbie Lowther, Leigh Lowther, James Arnett and many others who gave their lives to the Master at this time in special services held by Rev.

W. Harrison and whose contributions since then in personal dedication to the work of Bedeque and other churches have been truly magnificent. New members meant replacements as the old ones dropped out. Quarterly Board in 1895 was composed of seven stewards (financial managers), five society representatives (representing the church membership) and delegates from the trustee boards. Three Wrights (**Major**, Dugald and **A.T.**) three Muttarts (Capt. Lewis, Herbert, and William), two Leards (Artie and Lewis), and David T. Lowther, Robert Price, **John Craig**, and Christopher Smith made up the Board."[13]

The record of the death, on May 26, 1885, of the Honorable J. C. Pope, in a local newspaper was saved by the Bradshaws and is repeated here:

Yesterday morning the Summerside community received a shock by the news that Hon J. C. Pope was no more. For the last four years, Mr. Pope has labored under a disease which has completely laid him aside from either mental or physical effort. The lapse of time increased his malady, but so slow and gradual was his disease that the news of his death gave a shock to the community. Less than a half dozen years ago, Mr. Pope was among the foremost men in the Province and was, indeed, a prominent man in the Dominion. Since the death of Hon. George Coles, no man has fallen who figures more prominently in the public affairs of this Province. Deceased was a man of great push and energy. Some 25 years ago he conducted a large business in this place, principally in shipbuilding, and owned real estate in every part of the county. Mr. Pope was a Conservative in politics and we believe, honest and straight forward in dealing with his opponents. Though not a fluent or eloquent speaker, he expressed his view in a blunt, honest way that rarely failed to carry conviction.

Mr. Pope was born at Bedeque, June 11th, 1826. Having secured the best education practicable at that time, he made preparations to enter a business life at Centreville, but was diverted from his purpose by the following adventure: In 1849, he, in company with some 30 other young men, purchased a brig (the *Fanny*), loaded her with a suitable cargo, and sailed round Cape Horn to California. Arrived at their destination, they sold the vessel and cargo and proceeded to the gold mines on Sacramento River. Here disease and death overtook many of them. Mr. Pope escaped, and greatly reduced by fatigue, returned home in 1853, richer only in experience. [**Charles Nathaniel Wright**, son of **Martha Hooper Wright**, was another of the forty "adventurers" who sailed on that ship to California in 1849. See Chapter Seven. Unfortunately he died before the end of 1850 from yellow fever]

He (Mr. Pope) settled at Summerside (then called Green's Shore) and built the store now occupied by Mr.Strong on corner of Water and Central Streets. Besides a general mercantile business, he carried on extensive shipbuilding trade. This business he afterwards transferred to Cascumpec.

In 1857 he entered the local legislature and held his seat almost continuously till 1876 when he was defeated on the School question. He was leader of the Govt. from 1865 to 1868 and from 1870 to 1872. In 1873 he formed the administration which built the P.E.I. Railway. He entered the Dominion Parliament in 1876, received a seat in the Cabinet and was appointed Minister of Marine and Fisheries in 1878. He retained the office till compelled by failing health to retire sometime in 1881. In 1880 he was summoned from Ottawa to the deathbed of his brother, the late Hon. Judge Pope, to whom he was warmly attached. His nervous system is said to have received a shock by this painful event, from which it never fully recovered. In common with the community at large, we tender our sympathies to the sorrowing family.

Another "old-timer," born about 1826, was Philip Callbeck, no doubt related to the Callbecks still living in Central Bedeque. Thanks to the Bradshaws his obituary from a newspaper has been preserved:

DIED at Centreville, Bedeque, PHILIP CALLBECK, aged 49 years. Our deceased brother was a native of Tryon, and it might be said of him that he feared God from his youth. But it was not until the 28th years of his age that he fully responded to the call and invitation of the Gospel by opening the door of his heart and admitting that Saviour who for so long a time had gently knocked for admission.

This important event in his history took place during a revivial of religion with which the Church was favored under the pastorate of Br. G.O. Huestis, and which gracious visitation of the Spirit, was blessed, not only to our late brother, but to many others, some of whom have already joined the Church triumphant, and some are on the way, having a good hope through grace of a blissful immortality. His conversion to God was not problematical; he was thoroughly convinced of sin; his sorrow was godly, his repentance deep and evangelical, and his faith rested upon the blood and righteousness of Christ for pardon and acceptance. The language of his heart was "In my hand no price I bring, simply to Thy cross I cling; This all my hope and all my plea, for me the Saviour died."

Two poems (authors' names not given) were in the papers belonging to Mr. and Mrs. Bradshaw and will be shared here:

An Opportune Arrival

I told her when she went away that I was quite resigned to losing her
And she might stay six months, if so inclined.
She hasn't been away a week and everything's awry.
To friends I hardly care to speak and time drags slowly by.
The smallest trifles put me out. I mope from day to day.
My business is gone about in a half-hearted way.
At night when I go home to tea, the house seems lone and bare,
And it is quite a grief to me to find she isn't there.
I wrote last night and told her how I missed her, that my life
Was joyless and that I know now how much I loved my wife.
Ah, me! a wife has power to charm__ Who's that there at the door?
She puts round my neck a plump white arm! Thank heaven she's back once more!"

John White's Thanksgiving

"THANKSGIVING for what?" and he muttered a curse.
"For the plainest of food and an empty purse:
For a life of hard work and the shabbiest clothes
But it's idle to talk of a poor man's woes!
Let the rich give thanks. It is they who can;
There is nothing in life for a laboring man."
So said John White to his good wife Jane,
And o'er her face stole a look of pain.
"Nothing, dear John?" and he thought again;
Then glanced more kindly down on Jane.
"I was wrong", he said; "I'd forgotten you.
And I've my health and the baby, too."
And the baby crowed- 'twas a bouncing boy-
And o'er Janes face came a look of joy;
And he said to himself as he worked that day:
"I was wrong, very wrong; I'll not grumble again.
I should surely be thankful for baby and Jane."

The obituary from an old newspaper in the possession of Mr. and Mrs. Bradshaw, of the granddaughter of Daniel Green, a United Empire Loyalist, will be printed here:

Mrs. Gulielma M. Reid

There is something very beautiful in the picture of a long life filled with good deeds and crowned with a lovely character passing out at last full of years and honour and bearing the benediction of a whole community. Such a life was that of

Mrs. Gulielma M. Reid who died in Summerside on Wednesday last at the advanced age of 88 years, all of which had been spent in the town. She was born in the first building erected in Summerside – a log house put up by her grandfather, Daniel Green, a United Empire Loyalist who received from the British government a grant of the land afterwards called "Green's Shore." In her childhood, her father, Joseph Green, built "Summerside House," the earliest hotel, and here this gracious lady learned that art of dispensing hospitality which characterized her to the last hour of her life in this self-same home. She was a woman of keen intelligence and forceful personality – proficient in all housewifely arts and specially successful in the culture of flowers. But most of all was she loved for her kindness to the poor. In the days when nurses and doctors were not easily available, she was one of those "born nurses" who carried help and healing into afflicted homes, and until the hour of her last illness, she habitually went about, bringing food and clothing to the needy of all creeds. As she lay in her coffin there was a veritable procession of those who came telling, as they did of Dorcas in old time, of "the coats and garments" she had made for them. In her illness Mrs. Reid was tenderly nursed by her daughters, Mrs. H. H. Beer who, with her grandson, Mr. Bradford Beer and a brother Mr. W. Penn Green (now in his 90th year) are the survivors [Another daughter is not listed]. Her funeral service was beautifully conducted by her pastor, Rev. Mr. Rice and as the funeral procession wended its way to the old burial ground in Bedeque, there were many who felt that the passing of such a life should yield not sadness, but much of inspiration.

In another chapter this writer mentioned that many homes in the Centreville, Chelton, Searletown, and Lower Bedeque areas had names. Some of those names will be repeated here, courtesy of George A. Leard's earlier research in his book, *Historic Bedeque*:

Jesse Wright [husband of Sally Hooper Wright] at the mill, the last of the Nathaniel Wright family, died in 1894, leaving to those who took up his work in church and community notable examples of achievement. His home, *Castalia Grove*, bore one of the fanciest names of all Bedeque estates, with a classical allusion that only a few ever recognized. Castalia Street, for Centreville folk who wish to be precise, may still be used as it was in 1863 and earlier for the road which runs from the parsonage corner to the mill. All Bedeque farms had groves on them which for some owners in the middle of the last century seemed to suggest the name of their properties.

Besides Jesse Wright's *Castalia Grove*, there was at Lower Bedeque Hon. J.R. Gardiner's *Gordon Grove* - now [1948] the Barrett farm [John Gardiner's second wife was **Mary Hooper**]. *Holland Grove*, Bedeque, was named by its owner, A. E. C. Holland, Esq., for the famous estate of the same name in Charlottetown where

his uncle, Colonel John Frederick Holland, had lived. Squire John Wright [whose wife was **Elizabeth Robins**] at Searletown called his home *Birch Grove*, while his cousin John Wright of South West Bedeque, lived on *Mill Grove Farm.* The naming of Bedeque residences apart from inns probably did not start till the eighteen hundred and thirties. The earliest record of such appears in a newspaper marriage announcement in 1839 when Stephen Wright [husband of **Martha Hooper** Wright] was listed as of *Elm Vale*. This house, probably built in the same decade, still stands near the mills and is presently occupied by Wilfred Connolly [1948]. By 2003 the house and the mills had been demolished, perhaps many years before.

Other farm-home names included *Maplethorpe*, the residence of Major Wright, afterwards owned by Louis Holland and now [1948] by Albert Weeks [It was sold about 2001 to a couple from Montana,U.S.A. who operate a bed and breakfast there; *Avondale Cottage,* where Joseph Schurman resided; *Willow House* at Searletown where Joseph Black lived; *Fairview*, home of Jabez Wright, and *Riverside Farm*, North Bedeque, where Jesse A. Wright farmed the ancestral holdings of his greatgrandfather, William Wright, the Loyalist.

Centreville House and *Bedeque House* were famous in their day. *Centreville House*, one of the oldest residences in the village is now [2002] owned by Claire and Anthony Lockhart. "It was built, possibly as a farm home, by Thomas Hooper (son of Major Hooper) who later made it into an Inn, which, by virtue of the table spread by Mrs. Hooper, had quite a reputation among travelers toward the middle of the last [nineteenth] century. A map of 1863 shows A. A. MacKenzie, the school master, as proprietor of *Centreville House*, with the 1880 atlas having A. E. C. Holland as owner. Its history since then has been a motley of neglect and care woven on a warp of changing ownership. To most Bedequers it will be remembered best as the doctor's place, the residence and office of Dr. Sharp and his immediate successor, Dr. Moyse. [In 1948 it was occupied by our summer neighbor, Bud Craig's parents, Vernon and Augusta Craig]

Bedeque House, older and more famous than *Centreville House* was built at Wilmot in the early years of the nineteenth century, when the name Bedeque was an address for all residents of Townships 17, 19, 25, 26, and 27. Built for Alexander Campbell, Esq., merchant, shipbuilder, and Provincial Treasurer, it was for many years the largest and most imposing residence west of Charlottetown. Its second owner, Evan Thomas, Esq., converted it into an Inn with spacious accommodation for the travelling public. Hon. Alexander Laird, brother of Hon. David Laird of newspaper and political fame, was the third occupant of this fine property and doubtless feeling that a *Bedeque House* at Wilmot was geographically astray, he changed the name to *Laird House*. Its destruction by fire many years later removed an historic landmark from the property presently owned by Alban Lecky [1948].[14]

In George A.Leard's *Historic Bedeque*, we read:

Death came to many in this period, including Richard Cole, early merchant of Lower Bedeque, the sale of whose estate gives an idea of the typical farms of this period. The Cole farm, eventually to be owned by one with three distinct lines of Cole blood in his pedigree, the Hon. Horace Wright, was advertised for sale as having seventy-five acres in high state of cultivation, forty-five acres being manured with 'muscle-mud'[mussel-mud]. Between fifteen and twenty thousand cedar rails marked the line and crop fences of the farm, which was laid off in small fields. The house (35x26) on the property was completely finished to the garrett and the barn (50x40) housed a threshing machine costing 75 pounds. The orchard of apple and cherry trees adjoined a garden of fruit trees and currant bushes surrounded by a cedar picket fence. The property, situated next [to] the public road leading to Hurd's Wharf, was thought by the executors to be the best situation for either business or farming of any in the harbour of Bedeque."[15]

George A. Leard continued, in his *Historic Bedeque* (p. 85):

At North Carleton, or Seven Mile Bay, the first Methodist services were held sometime in the early eighteen hundred and seventies in Mrs. David Lowther's big kitchen, where the friends and neighbors sat on piano seats on Sunday afternoon to hear the Gospel preached, generally by a local preacher. Mrs. Lewis Trueman of Centreville can call up vivid childhood memories of Richard Hudson, Tryon's best loved local preacher, speaking in this kitchen which was her mother's. Deborah, the wife of David Lowther, was the first member of the Methodist Society in North Carleton.

The first class at North Carleton, formed in 1875, had Stephen R. Black as leader with a membership including Mrs. S. R. Black, Isaac Wright and wife, David T. Lowther and wife, Mrs. David Lowther, Mrs. James Penwarren, Wallace Thomas, Mr. and **Mrs. Charles Crossman** [these last two people must have been Alden's great-grandmother **Jane Walker Hooper Crossman**, whose husband **John Keir Hooper** had died suddenly in 1851, and her second husband, Charles Crossman], and Sarah M. Penwarren. The next year Quarterly meeting appointed Stephen Black "to take up collections in Carleton and to make necessary preparation for worship." With the opening around this time of a school situated on the David Lowther farm, preaching was transferred to the school house where once a month the folks gathered to sit on long desks with their feet in the seats and listen perhaps more attentively than those who in more favored places lounged in padded pews. In the North Carleton hall built in 1891 preaching was once a month with prayer meetings led by an exhorter on the other Sundays and a mid-week service every Wednesday evening. Special revival services conducted by Thomas Moyse

of Central Bedeque, newly licensed local preacher, in this hall in 1896 led many to a life-long dedication to Christ. The hall was used for both church services and Sabbath School, the latter under the devoted superintendency of the late Herman Myers, till 1922 when services were consolidated at Searletown.

The formation of a class at Carleton in 1875 came at a time in the history of the Bedeque Methodist circuit when the class system was slowly on the way out. Rev. Joseph Seller, shortly after his arrival in 1875, appointed several new leaders and tried in various ways to keep the classes going better, but two years later the report to Quarterly Board on the classes was 'not very satisfactory'. Classes were originally planned to give Methodists, always aware that there was no such a thing as a solitary Christian, the privilege and opportunity of meeting in small groups (seldom more than twenty) under the guidance of a devout leader for prayer, instruction, exhortation and, if necessary, rebuke. At their best they provided a careful oversight of the moral behaviour of every church member, a forum for discussion of mutual difficulties and a center where inspired lay leadership in prayer and earnest reasoning could often give clearer guildance than the pulpit. At its worst, the class meeting degenerated into an assembly of smug church members who used the time in telling God how to run the world instead of inquiring more closely into what His will was for them.

"In 1866 there were twenty-six classes on the Bedeque-Tryon circuit," wrote Leard.[16] Listed are the leaders and the meeting places, one of which might be interesting to our Hooper family: "Brother Horatio Wright, leader, at Mr. C. Crossman's Thursday evening." Several Hooper brothers-in-law are also mentioned as "Brothers" (meaning brothers in Christ) who were leaders in the Class Meetings. The reader will note that C. Crossman is the step-father of Adella, Major, and Sarah Hooper. Charles and **Jane Crossman** were probably living in North Carleton for another three or so years until **Major** could run the farm when they moved to Albany, a few miles away.

George A. Leard's comments on the Bedeque Circuit are very informative:

...The division of the circuit in 1873 left only twelve classes on the Bedeque circuit which two years later under Mr. Seller's reorganization had the following changes: Number One class at Central Bedeque with the pastor as leader and Ewen Clark as assistant met at Mrs. Callbeck's. At Centreville chapel the class, led for many years by Jesse Wright at the mill, was put under **Archibald M.** Wright's

leadership, and John Beer's class was conducted by George Crosby. Busby Atkinson of South Shore who succeeded to the leadership of the late Wm. Wright's class, met his small band in Chelton school on Sunday afternoon. Four classes at Searletown were under the leadership of Lewis Wright, Solomon Wright, Thomas Sobey and S. H. Trueman. The only woman to lead a class was **Jane Hooper** (spinster daughter of Elisha Hooper), who was appointed in 1876. Other class leaders of the period included **John Craig** at Middleton, David Rogers, with Edmund Crosby as Assistant, at Freetown, Charles Maxfield with James Wall as assistant at Newton, and George Clark at Wilmot.[17]

A rather strange article appeared in a local Island newspaper, c.1875-1878, about a rather shamefully silly disagreement between the Anglican priest and the Methodist minister:

BURIAL GROUNDS - ONCE MORE - This ghost has risen on another Island - the Island of Prince Edward. Rev. Joseph Sellers of Bedeque has presumed to enter a grave-yard, whether one of Episcopal legal, or doubtful, right, we are not aware - to bury "a parishioner." This act has led to a conflict - not in court, as the Bermuda case, but on paper. Rev. T. B. McLean [Anglican], lays about him, right and left, in gallant [?] style. Seriously this is rather sorry business. If ministers of Christ cannot address each other respectfully, cannot dispense with gross personalities, what will the world think of them? We have not seen previous letters, but this last one of Mr. McLean's is really pitiful.

George A. Leard's *Historic Bedeque* revealed a number of interesting observations and changes which took place during the ministry of Rev. W.W. Percival:

At Mr. Seller's last board meeting in June of 1878, Brothers F. Moyse and N. Inman were added to the list of prayer leaders. Mr. Seller was followed in parsonage and pulpit by Rev. W. W. Percival who like his predecessor was Island born. The changing pattern of Bedeque population for the period 1865-1877 was clearly shown in the trustee board. The 1865 members included Stephen Wright, Stephen Black, George Crosby, Jesse Wright [**the husband of Sally Hooper**], Wm. G. Strong, Wm. Wright Sr., **Lemuel Hooper**, J. R. Gardiner [**the husband of Mary Hooper**], Gabriel Strang, George Doull and John Howatt. By 1878 only the first five remained, and one of these, Wm. G. Strong, was living in Summerside. The others had been replaced by Wm. Wright Jr., **Martin Black, John Craig, Major Wright**, David Rogers, and George Clark. In December of 1877 the trustees took

the matter of heating the church under consideration and ruled that the pew holders (people who owned a pew) in the vicinity of Centreville should be requested to bring half a load of wood to the chapel yard and inform the chapel steward (Jesse Wright) through the sexton of its delivery.[18]

The death in 1877 of Dr. Frank Lawson after but a short practice of two years was a blow to all who liked a resident physician. Dr. Lawson, who settled in Centreville in 1875 when his newspaper card stated "advice to the poor gratis," was a native of Covehead and a surgeon of some experience having served in the American Civil War for which he drew a pension and which was possibly responsible for his death at the early age of thirty-nine. Another doctor at Bedeque at this period was J. H. Jamieson who lived in the house now owned by Mrs. Willoughby (1948) and occupied by Mrs. Percy Affleck. His dispensary, a small building between the house and Major Wright's store, was known as Jamiesons's apothecary shop. An earlier Bedeque physician was Francis Dyer Beer of Charlottetown, brother of John Beer, the merchant. Dr. Beer, who came to Bedeque in 1860, was married two years later to Louise Palmer, eldest daughter of Stephen Wright, Esq. of Elmvale [and his second wife Millicent]. On leaving in 1864 he was presented with an address signed by A. E. C. Holland, Alex Anderson, John Clay, Malcolm McFarlane, Francis Henderson and George Gardiner, in which the community regretted his departure after such a short stay. He replied, "the profession to which I belong is fraught with anxiety of mind and fatigue of body, but I always found in Bedeque warm-hearted friends to cheer and encourage me."[19]

The reader may recall that Dr. James Graham of Edinburgh, Scotland had come to Bedeque in 1814 and practiced medicine there for 35 years or until 1849 when he died at age 77. A young Dr. Potts of Charlottetown settled in Crapaud and Tryon. From there he extended his practice to Bedeque in 1849 when "the first doctor of the settlement had completed his last call and was awaiting his final visitor - death."[20]

George A. Leard wrote of Dr. James Conroy, proprietor of Conroy's Mills, known as Laird's Mills at Leard's time of writing *Historic Bedeque* in 1948:

[He] was a frequent visitor to Bedeque from 1830 till the time of his death in 1856. Asked one time by a witty Bedeque farmer to set a hen's leg, he gravely did so, making a return visit to see how the patient was doing. As a sample of his own humor, Dr. Conroy charged five pounds [£5] - and collected it! Dr. Tremaine of Tryon was another well-known medical adviser in Bedeque of a little later period.

The arrival in the late eighteen-hundred and seventies of John Sutherland, M.D. (1846-1908) brought to Bedeque the nineteenth-century doctor whose name would be best remembered among the 1948 residents. He lived in a house (first occupied by Dr. Beer) which had been built probably around 1860 by John Beer Esq. for his son Charles who died young. Many years later this house was to be a community-owned project to have its face lifted and modernized and be occupied by Dr. Wm. W. Tidmarsh.[21]

Occasionally one reads about a death of a child which is always sad. A boy by the name of Frank Ellis Kennedy, born in Summerside on November 25, 1870 was killed by a horse in New Annan, near Summerside on June 3, 1882. The child was only 11 years old.

Changing the subject to a much happier event, thanks to Mr. and Mrs. Bradshaw a wedding which was printed in the local newspaper is available for us to read:

The nuptials of Miss Bertha Walker, a daughter of Mr. Henry Walker of this town, and Mr. David McMurdo of the firm of Warren, Hicks & McMurdo Bros. took place last Tuesday evening at the residence of the bride's father amid the hearty congratulations of the numerous friends who witnessed the ceremony. Rev. Mr. Dickie was the officiating clergyman while the bride was attended by her cousin Miss Laura Cannon of St. Eleanors, the groom being assisted by Mr. William Craswell. Mrs. McMurdo was the recipient of a large, varied and costly lot of presents among which was a purse of $25 from the Presbyterian congregation as a recognition of her services as organist for some time past. The gathering was a happy one and it only broke up when the "wee sma oors" were reached. Mr. and Mrs. McMurdo began housekeeping in the residence recently vacated by Dr. Price. We wish them a happy and prosperous life." [Dr. Price was the husband of Catherine Gardiner who was the daughter of Mary Hooper Gardiner and the granddaughter of Major Hooper of generation 4)

Thanks to Malcolm and Edith Bradshaw a record was kept via the local newspaper of the farewell party given to Mr. and Mrs. Isaac Schurman:

A gathering of at least sixty of the inhabitants of North Bedeque met at Mr. James McMurdo's residence last Thursday evening to do honor to Isaac W. Schurman, Esq., Mrs. Schurman and family who are about removing to Carthage, Missouri. An address (which we hope to publish in a later issue) was presented to Mr. and

Mrs. Schurman, and accompanying this was a handsome silver-beaded ebony walking stick as a gift to Mr. Schurman while to Mrs. Schurman, a remembrance was given in the shape of a beautiful gold brooch. Mr. Schurman has been one of the Island's most progressive and intelligent farmers, and Mrs. Schurman one of the most pleasant and best of neighbors, and it is seldom regret is so deeply felt at the removal of a family from the community. We heartily join in the many expressions of good wishes.

John Beer had been an important person in the Bedeque Methodist Church. Only one more statement is given in reference to him in this genealogy, thanks to Mr. and Mrs. Bradshaw. "At the First Methodist Church, Charlottetown, on the 20th inst. by Rev. W. W. Brewer, assisted by Rev. T. J. Deinstadt of Moncton, Peter S. Macnutt of St. John to Miss Annie S. Beer, daughter of the late John Beer, of Charlottetown. [1892]."

An excerpt from the *Telegraph*, a newspaper in Saint John, New Brunswick [post-1892] mentions several people who have been included in this book, again thanks to Mr. and Mrs. Bradshaw:

The death of Mrs. Rebecca McCallum Deinstadt, wife of Rev. T. J. Deinstadt, [pastor at Bedeque Methodist Church from 1867-1870] occurred yesterday morning after an illness of several years. Mrs. Deinstadt was a daughter of the late John Beer of Charlottetown. She is survived by her husband, five daughters: Mrs. W. J. Wellington, New Rochelle, N. Y.; Mrs. L. B. C. McMann, Toronto; Mrs. R. Bell, Halifax; Miss Lillian and Miss Hazel Deinstadt, at home; one brother, G. Frank Beer of Toronto; and two sisters, Mrs. A. T. Wright [the former Harriet Beer] of Bedeque, P.E.I.; and Mrs. P. S. McNutt of Tacoma, Washington.

During his terms as pastor in several of the Methodist churches in the city and the provinces, Rev. Mr. Deinstadt, who is now in retirement, developed a broad acquaintanceship and the sympathy of a wide circle of friends will go out to him and the rest of the family in their bereavement.

There will be a service at the home 242 Duke Street this morning. Interment will be in Charlottetown.

Obviously, at least two of John Beer's children found their marriage partners in Bedeque! Considering the rather small population of Prince Edward Island, and the fact that it was separated by water from the rest of the world, it is no wonder that there was so much intermarriage among the "natives."

Mr. and Mrs. Bradshaw copied an unusual obituary from the newspaper, dated November 18, 1896:

The remains of the late Dr. Wall were taken from Charlottetown on Sunday afternoon by special train to Emerald, a large number of friends being on board. When the party reached Emerald [an Irish town] a large gathering of people were waiting both on foot and in carriages. The pall bearers were Dr. McNeill of Kensington, Dr. Robertson of Crapaud, Samuel Kennedy of Breadalbane, and John Hughes, Albert Craig, and Geo. R. McMahon of Emerald. The body was conveyed to the church near[by] when Rev. Mgr. Gillis of Indian River and Rev. J. J. McDonald of Kinkora conducted the funeral service after which the interment took place at Kinkora burying ground. On the Saturday evening previous the Emerald branch of the Benevolent Irish Society held a special meeting and passed the following resolution: "Whereas it has pleased Divine Providence to call, we trust, to a brighter and happier world our brother, Dr. Wall, be it resolved that this Society give expression to the loss it has sustained through his death. And be it further resolved that this resolution be inscribed in the minutes of the Society and a copy sent to the press for publication."

Another obituary from the files of the Bradshaws, dated 1899, was of an "old-time" gentleman who had been born in Ireland.:

The death of Mr. John Hayes, one of P.E. Island's veteran settlers, occurred on the 17th ult at the residence of his son, Mr. J. F. Hayes of Searletown. Until the last few years the deceased was an active, industrious man, endowed with a rugged constitution and had at his death attained the ripe old age of four score years and ten. He was born in the county of Antrim, Ireland, and emigratee to the Island in 1832 as mate of the bark *British Tar* which was wrecked off Sea Cow Head. Before coming here he traveled through many of the European countries, and in the course of his travels visited the home of Robbie Burns and conversed with Burns' sisters. He distinctly remembered having heard the firing of the cannon in a naval engagement about the time when Napoleon was routed on the field of Waterloo. When he came to this Island only one house stood where now is located the town of Summerside, while between here and Charlottetown, an ox path was the thoroughfare. In this province the [deceased] remained until his death with the exception of a few trips made to Newfoundland as mate in the ships of Messrs Pope and Lord. The deceased was a humorous and entertaining conversationalist and could relate many stirring incidents of the hardships undergone by the early settlers, and the general character of pioneer life in this province. He settled in Albany on a then greenwoods farm and had to clear in the forest a space whereon to build a house.

After years of toil he had the pleasure of seeing the forest converted into an arable farm, and there he remained during the greater part of his life. The deceased, who was a member of the Methodist Church, was well-known as a kind, inoffensive man. He leaves four sons and four daughters besides a number of grandchildren and greatgrand children to mourn his death.

Many Irish people came to P. E. I. from the "auld country." A short Irish joke and a letter follow, thanks to the Bradshaws: "According to the philosophers everything has two uses, a lower and a higher. Some very common people find this out for themselves, so far, at least, as the practical application of it is concerned. The daughter of the rector of the parish in East London over the border taught the choir boys a new tune at a Monday evening rehearsal, to be sung on the following Sunday. Sunday morning came."Well, Johnny," said Miss X, "I hope you haven't forgotten the tune for I depend much on you." "Naw, mum, not a bit. I've been a-skeering the crows with it all the week."

A "rale" Irish "letther" reads as follows:

Dear Nifus – O haven't sint ye's a letther since the last time I wrote to ye's because we've moved from the former place of livin' an' I dident know whither the letther would reach ye's or not. I now wid pleasure take up me pen to inform ye's of the death of ye's oun livin' uncle Kelpatrick who died suddenly afther a lingerin' illness of six months. The poor man was in violent conwulsions, lyin' perfectly quiet and spaachless, all the time talkin' incoherently an' callin' for wather. I had no opportunity to inform ye's of his death except I wrote to ye's thelast posht which wint off two days before he died, an' thin ye's would havbe posthage to pay. I am at a loss to tell what his death was occasioned at, but fear it waz his lasht illness. He niver was well ten days together durin' the hull time of his onfoinment. I am at a loss to tell what occasioned it, but I fear it was by atin' too much paze and gravey. Be that as it will, as soon as he breathed his lasht the docthers gave up all hopes ov his recovery.

The property now revolves to the next of kin, who all died some time age, so I expect it will be divided atween us. You know his property was very considerable, for he had a fine estate, which went for his debts, and the remainder he losht that on a horse race; but it would have won the race if the horse he run against had

not bin to fasht for him. I niver saw a man, ad' the docthers all say so, that tuk medicine better nor he did. He would as lave take bitther as swate if it only had a taste and appearance ov whisky punch, an' it would only put him in the humor for fightin'; but, poor soul, he'll niver ate nor drhink any more – an' yez haven't a living relashun but fwat was killed in the lasht war.

But I can't dwell on the mournful subjic an' sail me letther in black sail in wax an' put on it yer uncle's coat of arruus, so I beg ye's not to break the sail when ye's opin the letther till three or four days afthur ye's resaive it, by which ye's will have time to be prehpared for the sorrowful tidins. Yer ould seteheart sends her love to he's unbeknownst to me. When Geray McGee arrives in Aromiky, ax him for this letther, and if he don't know it from the rest tell him it's the wun that spakes of yer uncles death and is sail'd in black. I remain yer ould granmother.

ALLEGED SIGNS OF LUCK

- Dream of eggs, sign of money. Dream of snakes, sign of enemies.
- If you sing before breakfast you'll cry before supper.
- Dreaming of muddy or rushing water brings trouble.
- Finding a horseshoe or a four-leaf clover brings good luck.
- If you sneeze on Saturday, you do it for evil.
- She who takes the last stitch at a quilting will be the first to marry.
- If you can't make up a handsome bed, your husband will have a homely nose.
- If you spill the salt someone will be "mad" with you unless you put some of it in the fire.
- Stub your right toe, you are going where you are wanted; your left toe, where you are not wanted.
- If your right ear burns, someone is praising you; if your left ear, your friends are raking you over the coals.
- Returning to the house for a moment after having once started out will bring bad luck unless you sit down.
- If the rooster crows on the fence, the weather will be fair; if on the doorstep, he will bring company.
- If you see the new moon through the glass, you will have sorrow as long as it lasts. If you see it fair in the face, you'll have a fall; over the left shoulder, bad luck; over the right, good luck.

A Queer Race

I saw the queerest race today out at the county fair.
The riders all were tiny tots, the racers all were rare.
I saw a little wonsome maid with flying yellow hair
Hold fast and ride around a ring upon a big brown bear.
Another one laughed aloud in glee and raced around the track
And she was seated fearlessly upon a lion's back.
And one rode on a tiger fierce, another on a deer,
While others rode on prancing steeds without a sign of fear.
And round and round the track they rode, all at a rapid pace,
And no one beat, though all tried hard to win the funny race.
At last the racers came to rest. The music ceased to sound,
And all the little tots went home and left the merry-go-round!

Another interesting article, called "Black Your Heels," was published in the newspaper and will be included, compliments of Mr. and Mrs. Bradshaw:

It is interesting to go into some room filled with boys and girls and notice the heels of their boots and shoes. Many of them will be found to be brown and rusty. It is only a careful boy who blacks the heels of his boots. Most boys put their foot onto a chair or box, put a good shine on the parts of their boots that they can see easily, and go off with a good deal of satisfaction. Carelessness, that is what rusty heels means to make your heels. Look well to your heels. It would be all very well, seemingly, to neglect the heels if boys and girls could always face people. I know a good many persons who think if they can face the world well, appear honest, and kind and good, they are doing all that is required. Back out of sight, as they suppose, in the home perhaps, maybe in school or in business are the little dishonest, rude, or careless acts that "nobody sees." Is there nobody to see? What do you suppose the Lord thinks of these unshined moral "heels?" How short-sighted such people are! Do they suppose they can go along and never turn around? Do they suppose no one is ever to come *after*? Just because they are smart enough, or careless enough, or willfully blind enough to see only part, do they suppose no one else will see the whole?

During the early twentieth century, the books of Lucy Maud Montgomery, a native of Prince Edward Island, became popular. She won world fame with her first book, *Anne of Green Gables,* published in 1908. A local newspaper later printed her impending marriage, a copy of which was made by the Bradshaws:

The marriage of Miss Lucy Maude [sic] Montgomery, the talented Island authoress, to Rev. Ewen McDonald, pastor of the Presbyterian Church at Leasdale [sic], Ont., will take place at Park Corner today [July 5, 1911]. Rev. Mr. McDonald is a native of Valleyfield in this province and a nephew of Capt. Alex Cameron of the *S. S. Empress*. The marriage will take place at 12 o'clock noon at the home of Miss Montgomery's uncle, John Cameron. Rev. John Sterling, pastor of the Presbyterian Church, will officiate. At 4 o'clock the happy couple will leave for Summerside and will leave by the *Empress* on the following morning en route to England. They will travel for three months on their wedding tour after which they will return to Canada and make their home in Leasdale [sic].

A rather sweet poem entitled "The First Love and the Last" was included in the material from the Bradshaws:

Heigh-ho! 'Twas years ago yet by my chair tonight there stands a maid surprising fair -
The self-same maid, with waving nut brown hair who rent my boyish breast, my heart laid bare,
And stamped a never dying impress there - Sweet maid, she's there.
Heigh-ho! Oh, life! With all your toil and care, with all your hopes, your trials hard to bear,
Days of bright triumphs, nights of grim despair, your somber shades, your noon-time's brazen glare -
I do not forget all now, for she is there - Sweet maid, she's there
Heigh-ho! No, no; 'tis but a vision there - The maid has gone, but now a woman rare
Stands in her place. There's silver in her hair, and on her loving face are lines of care,
Yet sweeter far tonight than maiden fair is this dear one who smiles beside my chair - My wife, my wife!

Looking ahead to the beginning of the twentieth century we find many of the same people involved in the work of the Bedeque Methodist Church. George A. Leard wrote:

The exhorters and leaders in this first year of the new century included John Craig, Nelson Inman, D. S. Wright, A. S. Wright, Wm Callbeck, Lewis Trueman, D. T. Lowther, Lewis Leard, Henry Lowther, Robert Price, Thomas Hudson, Nathaniel Pearson, Herman Myers, Herbert Muttart, Major Lowther, and Wm. S. Muttart. None of them pretended eloquence in preaching, but all could conduct a

meeting, lead a discussion, drive home a religious truth and pray extemporaneously with considerable zeal. Enough were ready to serve so that no one individual was overworked...The local preachers, David Rogers and Thomas Moyse, were expected to give a more finished address to a more formal meeting than that which the exhorters led....

The new century brought its changes; and if the word streamlined had been in use in 1901, it might have described what happened to the Church setup when the three trustee boards for church, parsonage, and cemetery were amalgamated into one. The mid-week prayer meeting was still widely attended, possibly never more so than at the turn of the century. Family worship, conducted in a great many Bedeque homes, was also perhaps at the peak at this time. The old style of asking a blessing at the beginning of each meal and returning thanks at its close was giving ground in many homes to a short grace which required of the pudding no proof ere combining the thanks with the blessing.

The most enjoyable evenings in the social life of this period were those when gathered round the organ, the young and the old blending their voices in the Stephen Foster classics, or songs that told the simple, homey things of life like "The Old Oaken Bucket," "The One Hoss Shay," or "Bringing in the Sheaves." Sunday songs were found sometimes among the great hymns of the Church, but more often in the more sprightly publications of Moody and Sankey. For Sunday night church service, a fast mare and smart buggy were not absolutely necessary, but in many young hearts much to be desired and envied. One would have been a rash prophet indeed to suggest that in twenty-five years time on a summer Sunday morning the church yard would be be filled with gasoline buggies, yet the new century wasn't two years out- September 12, 1902- before Jesse A. Wright wrote in his diary: "Walter Doull brought an automobile here this p.m. I had a ride in it."

The next summer under the general guidance of a new minister, Rev. Neil MacLaughlan, Jesse A. Wright planned and directed the moving out of the end of the Church to provide an extra fifteen feet for choir and other purposes. It was nicely done under contract by Major Schurman at a cost of nearly $600 making a very pleasing chancel which was honoured with a re-opening on the first Sunday in Novemnber, 1903. Jesse Wright's devotion to the Centreville Church led to a gift of gas lamps in the same year (1906) that he became choir director. More important than church lights was the spiritual light shining on the circuit. The official board gave its formal thanks in June of 1905 to Brother Thomas Moyse for his work in connection with special services during the preceding winter.[22]

The name of David Rogers, Esq. has been prominent in the ongoing work of the Bedeque Methodist Church. The marriage of his youngest daughter, Annie, to John Stafford Walker, a fourth genera-

tion Walker (John [3], James [2], David [1]) took place on June 15, 1904. The newspaper account follows:

The marriage of Mr. J. Stafford Walker, son of John Walker, Esq., Freetown, to Miss Annie S., youngest daughter of David Rogers, Esq. [and his wife Louise Wright], Kentleth Lodge, Dunk River, was solemnized on Wednesday evening, the 15th June [1904] by Rev. H. S. Young, assisted by Rev. R. S. Whidden. The groom was supported by his brother, Mr. Patterson Walker, while Miss Hattie Carruthers of Bedeque acted as bridesmaid, with Miss Mamie Cairne as flower girl. The ceremony was performed in the presence of numerous relatives of bride and groom. The wedding march was pleasingly rendered by Miss Anna Rogers, Bedeque. The bride was becomingly attired in crème silk with bridal veil and flowers of val-de-lis. The presents to the bride were very beautiful and valuable. The church choir, of which she was organist, presented her with gold coin. The sumptuous wedding meal was most tastefully arranged by Miss Mattie Rogers with table decorations of apple blossoms. Aftrer the ceremony the happy couple repaired to their future residence, the beautiful Walker homestead in Freetown, followed by the best wishes of many friends for their future happiness.

Interestingly, only two weeks after the wedding described above, another wedding announcement was recorded in the newspaper provided by the Bradshaws, as follows:

Mr. Henry L. Rogers of Freetown was united in marriage to Miss F. Louise Wright, daughter of Isaac Wright, Esq., "Castalia Grove," Bedeque, on Wednesday evening, the 29th of June [1904], by Rev. F. A. Wightman of Alberton in presence of a large number of family and relatives. The attendants of the bride and groom were Miss Louie of Bedeque and Mr. Geo. Morris of Granville. Miss Lizzie Craig of Middleton rendered the wedding march and appropriate music. The bride was dressed in ivory white mousseline de soie with lace and carried blush roses. The bridal presents were exceedingly beautiful, several being received from friends abroad. After a sumptuous supper was served, the happy couple drove to their future residence, Kentleth Lodge, Freetown.

The notes from the Walker genealogy inform us that John and Annie had three children: Janet Louise, born September 3, 1906; Florence Elizabeth, born July 3, 1912; and John David, born September 16,

1913, who would be related to Jane Walker Hooper. The notes of Harold Cairns, who put together the Walker genealogy, read:

Staff was a successful farmer who took over the farm in Freetown from his father, John. He remained there until 1917 when he sold the farm. He moved to Freetown village and started in the store business with Robert C. Auld. He resided in the house that was built by Albert Craig which he purchased from Charles Taylor. He remained in the store business until 1921 when he sold his interest in the store to Mr. Auld and his house to Davis Baker. John S. Walker was the superintendent of the Sunday School in Freetown in 1919 which was then called the Freetown Union Sunday School. The Walkers were affiliated with the Methodist Church. After that he moved to Sidney, N. Y. where he operated a shoe store.

From the *Wesleyan*, in 1904, was taken the obituary of a former pastor of the Bedeque Methodist Church, thanks to Mr. and Mrs. Bradshaw:

FAREWELL TO THE VETERAN One of the grand old men of our common Methodism has stepped from the Alps to the everlasting hills, in the passing of the Rev. George O. Huestis, who left us with a smile on his face and a song in his heart a week ago yesterday. For so many years he has gone in and out amongst us, thrilling our hearts with his voice and pen that though bearing the weight of eighty-five years, he was so buoyant of spirit that his departure seemed an intrusion and we could not forgive death for the insult. Entering the ministry in 1846, he labored in New Brunswick, Prince Edward Island, and Nova Scotia till 1889 when he became a supernumerary, and for the last eight years has lived at Lunenburg, N. S. where he died. Several times was he honored as Chairman of District and was held in much esteem by his brethren in the ministry, and beloved by the people on the circuits where he labored. He was an ardent advocate of temperance and held for several years the highest positions in the gift of the Order of Sons of Temperance. He was the author of "Memorials of Wesleyan Missionaries and Ministers" and "Beginning of Methodism" and was a frequent contributor for many years to the columns of the *WESLEYAN*. Part of the past summer was spent in Prince Edward Island lecturing on temperance and attending the Camp Meeting at Berwick [which in 2002 was still continuing] when he seemed as vigorous as ever, but death came suddenly, for as he sat in his chair in his usual good health, "God's finger touched him, and he slept." Out into life with a new impulse the kind grey head and the young heart have gone, and we feel his passing because we loved him, but we shall

not weep beside a marble monument for we look beyond the clouds, and his best monument is in human hearts. Farewell to the chief! Hereafter in a brighter world where clouds are lost in visions and grief is changed to songs, we shall meet, and till then, we shall honor the veteran by doing noble things in a divine way.

A Golden Wedding Anniversary was held for Mr. and Mrs. Caleb Taylor in 1907 [with Mrs. Bradshaw giving the newspaper article saved from the files of her father-in-law or grandfather-in-law]:

The Golden Wedding of Mr. and Mrs. Caleb Taylor, Freetown, was celebrated on Tuesday evening, March 26th. About sixty of the older residents of Freetown and Bedeque attended. After partaking of the good things provided, a programme was carried out consisting of speeches, music, recitations, etc. The following address was read and fittingly replied to by Mr. and Mrs. Taylor:

Willow Wood Cottage
March 26, 1907
Dear Mr. and Mrs. Taylor,
Fifty years have rolled away since the magic words were spoken that made you two one. We, the undersigned on behalf of your many friends, desire to congratulate you on this, the jubilee of that auspicious event. During these many years you have retained unbroken the confidence and esteem of the entire community. Where sickness or bereavement or trouble of any kind came to any of our homes, you vied with each other both in ministering to the need or in extending kindly sympathy. You ever seemed to possess a happy aptitude to meet any and every condition - "rejoicing with those who do rejoice and weeping with those who weep." The claims of the Master were recognized by you. The advancement of His cause lay very near your hearts as evidenced by the liberal and hearty contributions given by you through all these years.

Mrs. Taylor is widely known for her labors of love in the Master's service. As Sunday School teacher, she has done much to develop Christian character in the young. You have lived to see many and great changes wrought by the hand of time. You have seen the almost unbroken forest transformed into broad acres of waving grain of various kinds, and the landscape dotted with comfortable homesteads. You have seen our kindly soil, which had been expending its energy in the production of timber, made through the help of a kind Providence, and the labor of the husbandman, produce liberally the choicest of food for man and beast. Your farm has been an object lesson to the whole community. Your fields give evidence of intelligent cultivation; neatness and thoroughness is in evidence everywhere. On all public questions you have taken a deep interest and every movement calculated to benefit the province and the people have had your hearty and loyal support.

Please accept as a slight token of our esteem and as a souvenir of this happy occasion, this small gift and coupled with it the earnest wish that the twilight of your journey may be long and pleasant - happy in the consciousness of the ever present One who "keepeth Israel and who slumbers not, nor sleeps."
Yours very truly,
Stewart Burns
Colin J. Schurman
Alexander Cairns
John Walker
J. Davis Schurman

Mrs. Taylor was dressed in her wedding dress of fifty years ago. An interesting feature was a charivari [a noisy demonstration accompanied by beating on drums and blowing on horns] conducted by the younger people of the community.

From the writing of George A. Leard, in his *Historic Bedeque,* we get a glimpse of the many changes that were coming about after the turn of the century:

The minister's salary was on the way up, gradually increasing from $750 in 1905 to $1,000 in 1911. Church union, though still a long was off, was the desire of the Bedeque Methodists as revealed in a plebiscite taken in 1912 which recorded a favourable vote of 238 to 4. Time's unrelenting hand was changing the faces around the congregation's council table. Major Wright, most successful of Centreville's merchants, died in 1907 and A. T. Wright in 1912. In the latter year, Calvin Leard and T. J. Inman were appointed relieving stewards, and John Stuart and Melvin Johnson ushers.

Information about another death was given by the Bradshaws and while it has nothing to do with a Hooper relative, it is related to the church that Alden's grandparents attended:

There passed away on Sept. 23rd [1912] in the 61st year of her age, Sarah Jane Compton of Albany. She was widely known as a person of a kind, loving and gentle disposition, always seeking the welfare of others before that of herself, and was highly esteemed by all who knew her on account of her beautiful character and Christian virtues. She was a consistent member of the Church of Scotland and a zealous admirer of the Word of God. She leaves to mourn a grief-stricken husband, one son Henry of Albany, and one daughter, Mrs. Bruce Wright, of Mission City,

B.C., also one brother William of Peters Road, and four sisters, Mrs. Malcolm Taylor of Portland, Oregon, Mrs. Henry Compton of Iris, Mrs. Geo. Hume of Brooklyn, and Mrs. Henry Bramhall of Carleton. The funeral service was conducted by her pastor, Rev. Jas. MacDougall, who spoke words of comfort and appreciation from Eph. 2:19, and interment took place in Cape Traverse cemetery.

An interesting article entitled, "Uses for Turpentine," was a part of the material given the author by Mr. and Mrs. Bradshaw:

Turpentine, either in resinous form or spirits of turpentine, has many household virtues will-known to the women on the frontier or isolated farm houses, but not so familiar to city housewives. Few barefoot boys are ignorant that a cut toe heals quickly if some resinous turpentine is used as a salve. But in cities spirits of turpentine can be more easily secured and is more convenient for application. In most cases it will produce the same effect.

Let the child suffering from the croup, or any throat or lung difficulty, inhale the vapor, and then rub the little sufferer's chest until the skin is red, ending by wrapping about it a flannel moistened with the fiery spirits. Relief will be almost instantaneous. Afterward sweet oil will save the skin.

Use spirits of turpentine for burns, the pain will disappear and healthy granulation will at once set in. It can be applied effectively on a linen rag.

Spirits of turpentine will take away the soreness of a blister very quickly. The skin will soon go down, and healing will begin as soon as the remedy is applied.

But outside of the family medicine chest, spirits of turpentine is a good thing to have at hand. It is the best dressing for patent leather; it will clean artists' clothes and workmen's garments from paint; it will drive away moths if a few drops are put into the closets and chests; it will persuade mice to find other quarters far away, if a little is poured into a mouse-hole. A tablespoonful added to the water in which linens are boiled will make the goods wonderfully white; a few drops will prevent starch from sticking; mixed with beeswax it will make the best floor polish, and mixed with sweet oil is unrivaled for fine furniture. The latter mixture should be two parts of sweet oil to one of turpentine.

The next three articles were from a newspaper submitted by Edith and Malcolm Bradshaw:

The Power of Children

One man was making unkind remarks about his mother-in-law, and the other man was taking it all in. After a while he put in his oar.

"You haven't any children, have you?" he inquired.

"No," was the reply; "what's that got to do with it?"
"More than you'll ever know until you have some."
"I fail to see it."
"Yes, and so did I at first, and I talked just as you do. Then when the youngsters came and began to grow up and to learn who their grandma was, and to look to her as their best friend; the one to shield them when they needed the parental spanking; the one to give them pennies when their parents thought they should not have them; the one who came and watched by them when they were sick; the one who was always good to them; the one grandma of all the world to the innocent, mischievous, all pervading kids, blamed if I didn't forget utterly that she was my mother-in-law, and got to calling her "grandma" just as the little ones did, and thinking about her just as they did, and finally, when the gray-haired old angel went to her rest, I grieved with the children and as sincerely as any of them."

A Brave Man's Weakness

He was all that's brave and manly; he had emulated Stanley, and had traversed wilds where white man ne'er had set his foot before. He just gloried in a battle, for he loved to hear the rattle of the bullets and the sounding of the cannon's deadly roar.

He would fight a hundred people; he would climb the highest steeple, though he knew by what rash act he was courting certain death; he would face a raging tiger; he would swim the turbid Niger, and he'd walk up to a cannon's mouth and never bate his breath.

There was nothing that could scare him; he had ventured in the harem of the wildest, fiercest pasha that e'er lived on Turkey's coast;
in a graveyard he had wandered late at night and there he pondered if it would be his fortune just to see a real ghost fight.

He was brave beyond all question; there ne'er had been suggestion that the stories of his boldness were not made up of the truth; but, alas his courage failed him, his courage really failed him for he didn't have the nerve to let a dentist pull his tooth.

Hard Things to Say

Probably you will be going to many a bright party at this happy season of the year. Now, perhaps you cannot sing, or play or recite, but you would like to do something to add to the general enjoyment. If so, just learn these funny sentences which follow so as to be able to repeat any one of them six times in succession rapidly. By asking your young friends to do the same, should there be a pause in the games, much fun can be obtained. Here are the sentences:
"Six thick thistle sticks."
"Flesh of freshly fried flying fish."

"Two toads, totally tired, tried to trot to Tedbury."
"The sea ceaseth, but it sufficeth us."
"Give Grimes Jim's great gilt gig whip."
"Strict, strong Stephen Stringer snared slickly six sickly, silky snakes."
"She stood at the door of Mrs. Smith's fish-sauce shop welcoming him in."
"Swan swam over the sea; swim, swan, swim; swan swam back again; well swam swan."
"A haddock, a haddock, a black spotted haddock, a black spot on the black back of a black spotted haddock."
"Susan shineth shoes and socks, socks and shoes shines Susan. She ceaseth shining shoes and socks, for socks and shoes shock Susan."

Mr. and Mrs. Bradshaw had also saved a March 1902 newspaper article of interest:

Earliest Opening of S'Side Harbor.
All Previous Records In Navigation Beaten Over and Over This Season.

Summerside Harbor is now open to summer navigation, what little ice that was left having gone seaward with the late northeast wind. The Strait being almost clear, the Northumberland will probably go on the Point du Chene route in a day or two. Never before this season did the ice leave our harbor in March, and never before did the people of Summerside, and the province in general, experience such quick dispatch in the mail and passenger service at this season of the year.

From the time that the *Stanley* was placed on the Summerside-Cape Tormentine route records in navigation during the winter season began. The year 1902 will remain a memorable one from the fact that it is the first year in which this part of the province has enjoyed direct communication with the outside world in the months of January, February, and March.

Last spring the *Stanley* broke open Summerside harbor on April 5th and left for Pictou [Nova Scotia] on April 8th with a cargo of produce. On the 9th of the month the harbor was clear to navigation. On April 12 the *Frank C. Batt* made her first trip of the season to Bedeque. On ___ day of the month the steamer *Elliot* arrived from Charlottetown and loaded produce for Sydney.and on the same day the schooner *Lois* arrived from Pictou with coal which was the earliest date known for a vessel to enter our port. The following day (the 18th) the schooner *–lephone* [probably the 73.3 foot, 70 ton schooner *Telephone* out of Port Medway, N.S., built in 1877] arrived coal-laden from Pictou, followed next day by the schooner *Malabar* also with coal from Pictou. Because of the amount of ice in Point du Chene harbor, it was not until April 21st that the *Northumberland* came from Charlottetown. The steamer attempted the following day to make Point du Chene, but failed and an-

other unsuccessful trial was made on April 24th, the winds being unfavorable holding the ice in that port all this time. On the 29th of the month the steamer was successful and on the following day, April 30th, the mails were transferred to the Point du Chêne route.

The following are the dates of the opening of Summerside harbor for the past twenty-one years. These dates are of the first arrival of the summer steamer:

1881............. April 25
1882............. May 11
1883............. April 23
1884 .... May 26
1885 ....April 27
1886............. April 26
1887............. May 7
1888............. April 12
1889......... April 17
1890......... April 19
1891......... April 26
1892.......... April 13
1893............. April 18
1894............. April 23
1895............. April 22
1896............. April 21
1897............. April 29
1898............. April 17
1899............. April 26
1900............. April 8
1901............. (*Stanley*) April 5
1902...............March (7th?)

An earlier Mr. Bradshaw had cut out of a local newspaper the following article, dated April 6, 1912:

Two Persons Probably Drowned in Dunk River. Horse and Sleigh Found in Channel, --- Fred McKenzie and Mrs. McCallum Missing and Supposed to be Drowned

Grim evidence of a double drowning accident was discovered on Tuesday evening when a horse and sleigh were found about three hundred yards below Dunk River Bridge, the horse drowned and the sleigh empty. Enquiries were at once set on foot and the horse and sleigh were identified as belonging to Fred McKenzie of Rose

Valley who, in company with a Mrs. McCallem of the same place, had that day been in Summerside.

William Callbeck of Central Bedeque communicated with the McKenzie family and arrangements were made on Wednesday to begin a thorough search at once in the locality in which the horse and sleigh were found. Accordingly, on Thursday, some thirty of the good people of Bedeque, who willingly tendered their services, were on the ground and with boats on the ice and by every means available, the search was begun. The search was continued all day and well into the night, but without success. It was resumed again in the morning, but up to the time of going to press no traces of the bodies had been found.

On inquiry we learn that Mr. McKenzie and Mrs. McCallum were in Summerside on Friday returning from a visit to friends in the western part of the Island. McKenzie had his horse stabled at Charles McDonald's and about 3:30 drove to St. Eleanors with the intention of selling his horse to Hubert Mills. His horse was a handsome stallion and valued by Mr. McKenzie at $500. He returned from St. Eleanors about 8:15 and drove again to Mr. McDonald's stable where he wished to feed his horse before proceeding homeward. Mrs. McCallum was then, and during McKenzie's visit to St. Eleanors, at the Empress Hotel. As it was then about Mr. McDonald's closing time, the latter advised McKenzie to feed at Mr. Matthew's livery stable. This he did, in the meantime calling at the Empress Hotel and asking Mrs. McCallum to be ready to leave for home on his return in a few minutes. Mr. Matthews informs us that McKenzie left his stable shortly after 9 o'clock and that he was perfectly sober. He, Mr. Matthews, advised him not to attempt the Dunk River ice as it was not safe. McKenzie called at the Empress Hotel at 9:30 when Mrs. McCallum joined him and they started, presumably for home. Neither of them has been seen since and there is no doubt that both found a watery grave near the spot where their horse and sleigh were found in the Dunk River.

Mr. McKenzie was a widower, aged about 45. He was a respectable farmer, honest and upright and highly esteemed in the community in which he lived. Mrs. McCallum was formerly Miss McDonald also of Rose Valley. Her husband is in Boston and she was visiting relatives and friends in Rose Valley. She had proposed leaving last Monday to rejoin her husband in Boston and it was intended that Angus McKenzie, a brother of the missing man, and Mrs. Kenneth McKenzie, wife of another brother, would accompany her.

The sad affair has elicited heartfelt sympathy for the bereaved relatives.

Several other deaths, sometimes odd, and unusually sad, [most with no dates given] were recorded in newspaper articles given to me by the Bradshaws. The first of these numerous death announce-

ments from the local press was taken from a Summerside newspaper, The *Island Farmer*, March 13, 1929, p.1.

1. Tragic Death

A tragic death occurred near Montague last week and was only discovered two or three days after the event. It appears an old spinster, age ninety, named Margaret Gillis, lived all alone in a shack in the manner of a recluse refusing to allow anyone to enter her house, and never ventured out except in the early part of the morning. Kind neighbors supplied her with sustenance, but she would only allow them to leave the food and water on the doorstep. She allowed no light to enter her habitation except what [came] through the door when opened for exit and entrance when receiving her food supplies. The windows inside were all covered with sacks and the interior had the darkness of a cave. As she had not been seen out in the morning for two or three days some neighbors called and, failing to receive any response, forced an entry and found the poor old woman, huddled up on a mat on the floor, the only bed she had, dead. The features were practically unrecognizable as rats had been doing their deadly work. The occurrence was reported to the Coroner who took necessary action. The house was found to be in a dreadfully unsanitary condition and there was not a scrap of food or a drop of water in it. It is almost unbelievable that in a Christian, civilized community like this such a state of affairs could exist.

2. A Suicide

A young farmer named McClean living at North River Bridge, committed suicide by cutting his throat last Thursday afternoon, says the *Examiner.* It appears that McLean, who has been melancholy for about a month past, went out to the cow stable to feed the cattle after doing which he committed the rash act which ended his career upon earth. His sister with whom he resided, not seeing him moving about the place when she went outside to give him some assistance with the cattle, called out his name. Not receiving any response she went inside the stable and there found him with his throat cut from ear to ear. Life was not quite extinct when this alarming discovery was made, and word was sent to town for Dr. S. R. Jenkins. The doctor got to the scene of the sad affair as soon as he could, but too late to be of service. McLean was dead. A jury was empanneled and an inquest was held by Dr. Conroy, Coroner. A verdict of "Death while laboring under a fit of temporary insanity" was returned.

3. Sad Death at Tryon

SAD DEATH AT TRYON - The sad death of Mr. Nathan Wood, age about fifty years, occurred Thursday night at Tryon. The late Mr. Wood who had been in ill health for the past two months left his home at noon Thursday telling his wife that he would take a walk in the adjoining woods. Tea time came around and as he did not return a search party went out after him, but was prevented from searching the

woods on account of the approaching darkness. Yesterday morning about 7 o'clock, the body of the unfortunate man was discovered by Messrs. F. Keard, C. Holland and others, hanging from a tree in the woods some three quarters of a mile from his home. Mental depression caused by ill health was no doubt responsible for the tragedy, though at the time Mr. Woods left home on Thursday, he appeared in cheerful spirits. Coroner Dr. N. R. Bovyer of Crapaud was called in and after viewing the remains, decided that an inquest was unnecessary. The deceased was respected in the community in which he lived and was a kind husband and father. He leaves to mourn a wife and two children to whom the deep sympathy of the province will be extended.

4. Dr. A.A. Black's Death

The saddest affair that has happened at Summerside for many a long day took place on Sunday evening. Dr. A. A. Black, who had not been home all day, telephoned to his wife at about half past six o'clock from his office and informed her that he had just taken poison. She in turn immediately telephoned to a doctor who, upon arriving at Dr. Black's office was informed by him that he had taken ten grains of strychnine which had already reached his feet and that therefore nothing the doctor could do could save his life. And the end came shortly afterwards. The late Dr. Black came to Summerside about six years ago and was reckoned one of the best veterinary surgeons in the province. He was perhaps the leading authority upon fox ailments and was the first to start a "fox hospital." There aristocrats of the reynard species were taken as in-patients. He also did a very extensive practice amongst the ranches. He was meat and food inspector for the town of Summerside and all his duties were discharged in an energetic and faithful manner. The late Mr. Black was only 55 years of age and was twice married. He leaves a widow to whom the entire sympathy of the community goes out, but no family. The funeral is taking place today (Tuesday) to his former home at Searletown. A very wide circle of friends will miss the deceased who was good-natured and obliging to all and honorable in all his dealings.

Sometime before the death of Dr. Black, Mrs. Christopher Smith, his mother-in-law, died. The obituary was published in a Summerside newspaper on April 14, 1916 and given to the writer by Mr. and Mrs. Bradhshaw:

One of the oldest and most esteemed members of the Summerside Methodist Church, Mrs. Christopher Smith, passed peacefully away on March 20th at the home of her son-in-law, Dr. A. A. Black, Summerside. Mrs. Smith was born at Crapaud on Feb. 21st, 1835, but the greater part of her life was spent at Searletown on the Bedeque Circuit, to which place she came in 1855 at the time of her marriage. It was in the old Searletown Church, under the ministry of the late John Prince, that both she

and her husband were soundly converted to God, and throughout her long life, her faith and confidence in God's love and mercy remained unshaken. Mrs. Smith was a woman of more than ordinary agility and manifested the greatest interest in everything that was good and ennobling. She knew by memory many of the choice passages of scripture and the choicest hymns. Her mind, too, was well-stored with much of the best in English literature. She was greatly interested in current events and followed the progress of the great war with unabated interest to the very last. During the past few years, owing to ill health, her activities had been somewhat restricted, but the welfare of Zion was ever uppermost in her thought. On the 18th the writer was talking with her, and heard her testify to her trust and confidence in her Savior. She seemed to be in her usual health. It was therefore with surprise that the announcement of her death was heard on the following day - not dead, but "Asleep in Jesus."

There are left to mourn, Mrs. A. A. Black with whom she made her home, Mrs. Gabriel Allen, Summerside, and Mrs. J. Bell, Cape Traverse, daughters, and one son, Dr. Percy F. Smith of Camorsa, Alberta. Interment took place at Searletown on Wednesday, March the 22nd.

Two period obituaries (no dates given) will be offered for their value in generosity and thoughtfulness to others:

1.

There passed away on Thursday morning [c.1914] at her home in Summerside in the 57th year of her age Helen Bell, wife of Mr. John H.Bell, K. C. The cause of death was congestion of the brain consequent upon the hardening of the arteries. Her death by herself was anticipated. She prepared for it and met it courageously - even cheerfully. She had supreme confidence that God rules in the hereafter and that in His hands all is well. She was a generous patroness of the Prince County Hospital. Just before she was stricken, she had completely furnished two rooms - one in the main building and one in the maternity ward. She was also in the habit of bringing in the poorer patients to be treated at her own expense. [She was a philanthropist, at least on a small scale] She died in the midst of her labors and administration to the welfare of others. It is understood that the bulk of her estate goes to the maintenance of trained nurses in country homes. The funeral will be held today (Saturday) at 2 p.m. Service in the Presbyterian Church at that hour. Please omit flowers. It was her wish.

2.

SUBSTANTIAL LEGACIES TO ISLAND RELATIVES – Word has been received by Mr. William McMurdo of Summerside that Mr. Robert Neill, who was a native of Kelvin, P.E.I. and died in California about two months ago, has left an estate val-

ued at upwards of $260,000 [dollars] and by his will several Island relatives are substantially remembered. After making ample provision for his sister who resided with and kept house for him and his brother, Mr. John Neill who also resides in California, the residue of the estate is left to be equally divided between his nephews and nieces, two of the latter of whom are daughters of Mr. John Neill and reside in California. The others are Mr. Norman McMurdo, Mr. James Clark and Miss Jessie Clark of Bedeque, Mrs. Hattie MacLean of Lot 16 and Mr. Lawson McMurdo, now residing in Ontario, each of whom will receive when the will is probated at least $25,000. The late Mr. Robert Neill, who was 77 years of age at the time of his death, left the Island as a young man and settled in California about fifty years ago where he bought a ranch and continually added to his estate until he became one of the best-known ranchers on the Pacific Coast. Apart from his cattle and hog raising activities, he made careful investments which brought him in a substantial income. By his will the whole estate is to be converted into cash and so divided amongst the beneficiaries.

Before the days of antibiotics, sulfa drugs, and immunizations, many people died from communicable or infectious diseases as illustrated by the following ten newspaper articles:

1.

The death occurred at his home at Fernwood yesterday afternoon of Herbert Leard, son of Chas. and Mrs. Leard, Fernwood. Deceased who was 46 years of age suffered from an attack of measles about two weeks ago which developed into pneumonia causing his death. He leaves to mourn besides an aged father and mother, a wife and two children. The funeral takes place at 2 p.m. tomorrow (Sunday) from his late residence to Bedeque Baptist Cemetery." [no date given]

2.

On Wednesday morning, the 28th instant (1866) after an illness of four days of Scarlet Fever, Ann Elizabeth, eldest daughter of the late Mr. William Craig of Middleton, Bedeque, in the Nineteenth year of her age. She was an affectionate and dutiful daughter and sister and an amiable companion and thereby endeared herself to all who made her acquaintance, and though surrounded by such attachments as make it very hard to give up all and be willing to go, yet she murmured not, her patience and resignation to the Divine Will failed not. She was triumphantly happy as she neared the wave of Jordan, and after most beautifully and touchingly inviting those who stood around her to love her Saviour who had done so much for her and to whom she was going, her spirit took its flight to make one more in that great company that has washed their robes in the blood of the Lamb and are ever before His throne. "Remember thy Creator in the days of thy youth."

3.

Many of our readers will learn with deep sorrow of the death of Benjamin B. Profit of Augustine Cove, which took place on Saturday last in the P.E. Island Hospital, Charlottetown. The deceased entered the hospital some time ago suffering from blood poisoning in the hand and although all was done for him that medical skill could do, he passed away. [Obviously blood poisoning is not a communicable disease, but before the days of effective medication like antibiotics, blood poisoning could not be treated] On Saturday afternoon the body was removed from the hospital and taken by train to Cape Traverse and thence forwarded to Augustine Cove. The remains were accompanied by Mrs. Profit who went to the city on Wednesday on learning that her husband was becoming worse. Mr. Profit was an energetic and hard -working man and was highly popular. The deceased was about fifty years of age and was born in New London. About fourteen years ago he removed to Alberton and four years ago located in Augustine Cove. Besides his widow he leaves to mourn a family of seven, some of whom are at home and some abroad. The children who reside abroad have been telegraphed for.

Pneumonia *may* not be a communicable disease, but, even in a person of reasonably young age, especially before antibiotics or other drugs were available, was often deadly:

4.

Joseph W. Wright The death occurred at Chelton Bedeque on March 24, [no year given] of Mr. Joseph Wright in the prime of life after a few days illness of pneumonia. For some years he had been engaged in piano tuning and in the occupation he was well-known and liked throughout the province. Many will remember him for he had a genial smile and a cheerful word of greeting for all, and left one feeling better for having met him. He leaves to mourn the loss of a kind husband and father a widow, formerly Miss Nina Lowther, of North Carleton, two daughters, Maude, now attending Prince of Wales College and Amy at home, and one son, Atkinson, at home. Also two brothers in theWest and one sister, Miss Maude Wright, Bedeque. On account of the serious illness of his little son, the funeral services were held in the Methodist Church, Bedeque. They were very largely attended and were conducted by Rev. Mr. Rice, Summerside.

In the second half of the century, residents, especially children, were still dying of communicable diseases. Infant mortality was high. The family of Jesse Wright of Middleton was a prime example of early childhood death: a daughter, Annie Clark, died at age six years

of diphtheria; a daughter, Mary Janetta, died at age four years from the same disease; a daughter, Jessie Agnes, died at age six weeks; and three-month-old John Wesley died. Annie Clark Wright and Mary Janetta Wright's deaths from diphtheria were graphically recorded by Ross Graves, writing in *William Schurman, Loyalist....*

5.

Diphtheria came to the settlement in the winter of 1881-1882, and two of his [Jesse Wright's] daughters took it. When their fever grew worse, a heavy snowstorm came along, making it difficult to get the services of a doctor. One was procured, but he could do nothing, and six-year old Annie died the evening of February 22nd. Jesse, realizing she was dying, carried her to the kitchen door to see her brothers and sisters who were not allowed to come near her. Since diphtheria had come to the home, the two girls had been kept as far as possible from the others, so contagious was the disease, so weak the defenses against it. Another blizzard set in, a protracted one, and they delayed taking the body to the cemetery at Lower Bedeque until the storm subsided. After a couple of days there was a lull. Jesse and his nephew John Hyde took the small coffin by horse and sleigh over the drifts to the burying ground several miles away, but the wind on that exposed rise above Bedeque Bay drove the snow as they tried to shovel it, and although they worked and worked they could not dig the grave. John Howatt, who lived nearby - he was later to marry Jesse's widow, to her family's disapproval came over to help. It was still an impossible task, and Mr. Howatt urged Jesse to leave the coffin in his barn until the next day, expecting the wind would have spent itself by then. Jesse had little choice, and may himself have stayed overnight at Howatt's. At any rate, when he reached home, the same day or the next, after an exhausting trip over the drifts, his wife met him at the door wth the news that four-year-old Mary had died during his absence. Jesse returned to the cemetery the next day and buried the two girls in one grave."[23]

Again, a newspaper report on the death of a Miss Amy Ross, of North Bedeque, dated Dec. 6, 1898:

6.

WE RECORD WITH SINCERE REGRET THE DEATH OF Miss Amy Ross, daughter of the late Mr. Murdock Ross of North Bedeque, which sad event took place early on Tuesday morning as the result of an attack of typhoid fever contracted about three months ago, soon after she returned from attending the last term of the Prince of Wales College. Miss Ross was a very promising student and had she lived would have done honor to a clever family. She was of a quiet and

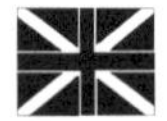

lovable disposition and won the confidence, good will, and respect of all who knew her. She leaves a widowed mother, four sisters, and three brothers, Theodore and George are attending Dalhousie College, Halifax. One sister, Miss Lottie, is at home; the others are Miss Sophie Ross, now a teacher in Honolulu, Hawaii; Miss Jennie Ross, B. A., teacher at Wolfville, N. S., and Miss Annie Ross, a Montreal Hospital nurse. The funeral takes place this (Thursday) morning at 11 o'clock. To the bereaved mother and family the *FARMER* tenders its sincere sympathy.

7.

On the 24th Sept. [no date] at Pugwash, of Typhoid Fever, Mary L. Stuart, aged 8 years and 3 months, younger daughter of Horatio and Margaret Wright.

8.

At Searletown on Saturday, November 13th [no year] of Spinal Meningitis, Annie Amelia,eldest daughter of D. S. Wright, aged 11 years and 8 months.

9.

DIED HUNTER - At the P.E.I. Hospital, Nov. 3rd, 1907, Maggie Hunter, music teacher, aged 47 years, a native of Nova Scotia. (Owing to quarantine at the Hospital, the funeral will take place from G. D. Wright's undertaking rooms today, Monday at 2:30 p.m.)

Here is an unusual newspaper article [undated], from the *Examiner*:

10.

A lie is a bad thing to run at large. It damages, ravages, devours more poison than a serpent; it often ruins not health, but reputation and usefulness. Every lie should be stopped, but whose business is it to chase a lie? Who let it loose? The man who let it loose is bound to catch it again; but a man of truth is under no obligation to chase and catch other people's lies. Suppose some man, or a dozen of men. sent forth a falsehood about me. Am I obliged to spend my days and years in chasing it and contradicting it? By no means; let those that make it attend to their own work or meet the responsibility in the reckoning day.

From the newspaper clippings of the Bradshaws we learn of a happier event: "On March 6, 1908 Mrs. Mary Wright, widow of the late Lewis Wright, Bedeque, celebrated her 92nd birthday recently at the home of her sister, Mrs. D. S. Wright of Summerside. Notwithstanding her great age, Mrs. Wright is still bright, cheerful, and companionable and takes a keen interest in the current events of the day."

Six years later Mrs. Wright's death notice appeared in the local press:

IN MEMORIAM MRS. MARY WRIGHT The death occurred in Searletown on Wednesday, the 4th inst. [1913] of Mrs. Mary Wright, widow of Mr. Lewis Wright, Searletown, and daughter of the late Mr. Joseph Black, Searletown [Mary Black Wright was the sister-in-law of Eliza Hooper Wright]. The deceased lady had attained a remarkable age, death coming on the day preceding her 98th birthday. To the last she retained all her faculties, mental and bodily with the exception of her hearing which for some years was slightly defective. She was a bright, charming, and intelligent conversationalist. For many years a function yearly looked forward to with pleasure by her many friends was the celebration of her birthday and on each occasion her pleasant reminiscences of by-gone days and her interest in current events made the birthday call a veritable pleasure both to herself and her friends. Her husband died several years ago. Since his death she resided with her sister and brother-in-law, the late Mrs. and Mr. Dugald Wright, until a little over a year ago, since which time she lived at the home of her nephew, Mr. Charles N. Black, Searletown, where she entered upon her eternal rest.

One brother, Captain Rufus R. Black, Taunton, Mass., survives her, the last of a large family. The late Mrs. Wright had a host of friends throughout the province and although her life was pleasantly and happily prolonged far beyond the common span, they will miss the kindly smile and the whole-hearted welcome that always greeted them on their visits to one whom all had learned to call "Aunt Mary." The funeral takes placd at 2 p.m. Saturday from the home of her nephew, Mr. Charles N. Black to Searletown Cemetery.

In Chapter Nine, the writer has mentioned the death of Berice Wright, the wife of Dugald Wright, son of John Wright by his second wife [John's first wife had been Elizabeth Robins of Hooper generation five]. His obituary appeared in a 1913 edition of the newspaper given by Mr. and Mrs. Bradshaw:

The funeral of the late ex-Sheriff Wright took place on Thursday afternoon. The remains were removed from his late residence and conveyed to the Methodist Church followed by a large number of citizens and friends from outside the town. Amongst them were Mr. Justice Haszard and the officials of the Supreme Court which was adjourned till 2:30 p.m. out of respect to the late sheriff. At the church an impressive service was held, the services being opened with singing by the choir the hymn,"Lead, Kindly Light" which was excellently rendered, followed with prayer by Rev. Mr. Fraser. After the reading of the Scriptures by Rev. Mr. Morse, the Rev. Mr. Strothard, pastor of the [Searletown] Church gave a pathetic address on the life

of the departed brother. After singing by the choir and benediction, those present were given an opportunity to view the remains, following which the casket containing all that was mortal of the respected Dugald S. Wright was removed to the hearse, when the funeral cortege proceeded to Searletown [Cemetery] where the remains were placed beside those of his wife who predeceased him some three years ago. On reaching Searletown, the remains were taken into the church where a short service was held, the Rev. Hammond Johnston, officiating, assisted by Rev. J. Strothard who accompanied the body to its last resting place. The choir rendered the hymn, "Asleep in Jesus." The church was filled with mourners. The pall bearers were John A. McKay, Thomas Frizzle, J. A.Brace, C. Edward Strong, Thos. L. Hinton, and John Dobson.

Another obituary from the Bradshaws contained very interesting information for the writer, as it clarified what had been a mystery: of how and why two young brothers from a small village on Prince Edward Island managed to attend the College of Veterinary Medicine at Cornell University. One's first thought was that there were *very* few schools for veterinary medicine in the northeast of the United States or Canada. The next thought is that there were many large animals such as cows, horses, and pigs that needed medical attention on Prince Edward Island. Soon the reader will find out how these two dove-tailed and led the two Robins gentlemen to pursue the course in veterinary medicine:

THE LATE MRS. ROBT. SCHURMAN OF FREETOWN When on Saturday, Nov. 29, 1913 Lydia Gouldrup Schurman, widow of the late Robert Schurman, passed away from the home of her son-in-law, Mr. Wm. Gordon Schurman at Lower Freetown, a really remarkable life reached its earthly termination. Mrs. Schurman was born more than eighty-seven years ago and had lived all her life on P. E. Island. Her long life was therefore largely coincident with the development of the Province of P. E. Island. It was the writer's privilege to know this good woman only during recent years when many years of suffering had wrecked the once strong body and at times cast a cloud over a mind of unusual strength. But from the interest which she evinced during these last years in the life about her, it is not difficult to imagine the thrill with which she entered into the interests of life in her youth. Two generations ago, she gave her heart and hand in marriage to the strong young man who had won her affections. They made their home at Freetown and in

that community the remainder of her long life was spent. She was the faithful helpmate of her husband. She looked well to the ways of the household. To this union were born six sons and two daughters, all of whom still live - a family who have and who are largely influencing the world of today.

If successful motherhood be the highest test of woman's service, surely the service rendered by this good woman has been unusual as the record of her children shows. The eldest son, J. Davis, was a successful farmer in P.E.Island, and locating later in Western Canada, he has made good there. The success of the second son, Major, is too well-known in Summerside and vicinity to call for any comment. The third son, Jacob Gould, has achieved international fame as scholar, author, teacher, administrator, public speaker, and diplomat. For twenty years he has been president of Cornell University, and for one year, he honorably filled the position of United States Minister to Greece. [He is the reason, I am sure, that two "Hooper" (Robins) sons went to Cornell to the Veterinarian College] His powerful personality had greatly influenced student life for a generation. The fourth son, Caleb, has made good in the business life of Chicago. The fifth son, Maynard F. is a highly respected citizen of Summerside and has also made good along his chosen industry. The youngest son, George W., a man of fine personality, is a lawyer of recognized high standing in the City of New York. Of the two daughters, the eldest became the wife of the Rev. D. G. McDonald many years ago, and the gracious touch of her life and the power of her personality has been felt in various communities where her husband has labored as a minister of the Gospel. The other daughter, the wife of Wm. Gordon Schurman of Lower Freetown, is a woman of great charm and strength of character, and during many years rendered to her invalid mother such service as only a fully sympathetic daughter can render to an afflicted mother.

And the success of the motherhood of this good woman is the more clearly realized when it is known that her husband died thirty-eight years since, when most of the family were at the age where parental guidance is most greatly needed. Nor were the interests of this good woman confined to her immediate family. Her helpful influence went out to all the community in which she lived. Her sympathies touched all life. Her Christian faith was simple, her religious convictions were strong, her spiritual life was deep and abiding. They were her support during many years of suffering. Hers was the type of religion that makes noble women.

The funeral services of Mrs. Schurman were held at the home of her son-in-law, Mr. Wm. Gordon Schurman, Lower Freetown, on Monday afternoon, Dec. 1. They were conducted by her pastor, the Rev. R. Osgood Morse. Suitable music, including a solo by Mrs. M. F. Schurman, was rendered. A suitable address was delivered by Pastor Morse in which he spoke especially of the sorrow, the sympathy, and the sacred joy of the occasion. The burial was in the Baptist cemetery at Central Bedeque where the three sons attending the funeral, J. Gould, Maynard F. and George W., with the son-in-law Wm. Gordon Schurman acted as pallbearers.

My interest was piqued by reading in his mother's obituary of J. Gould Schurman's professional involvment with Cornell University, as well as with many other well-known institutions and organizations. For this reason his biography, from the *National Cyclopedia of American Biography,* will be presented. To think that a young man from a tiny town in the smallest province of Canada could achieve such a leadership role on the world scene is absolutely amazing!

SCHURMAN, JACOB GOULD, educator and diplomat, was born in Freetown, Prince Edward Island, Canada, May 22, 1854, son of Robert and Lydia (Gouldrup) Schurman. His first paternal ancestor in America was Harmen Schurman, who came from the Netherlands to New Amsterdam before 1649, later moving to New Rochelle, N.Y. From Harmen, the descent was through Frederick and Christina Jans, Frederick and Elizabeth Thorne, Jacob and Anneteje Jeffers, Jacob and Jane Perescitee, Jacob and Magdalen Parent, William and Elizabeth Hyett, and Caleb and Mary Lefurgey, the grandparents of Jacob G.. Schurman. His great-great-grandfather Jacob and great-grandfather, William were loyalists in the Revolutionary War. As a result all their property was confiscated and at the end of the Revolution they were among those transported with their families by the British to St. John, New Brunswick, Canada, in 1783. A year later they settled on Prince Edward Island. Jacob G.. Schurman worked on his father's farm until he reached the age of twelve years, after which he was employed as clerk in a general store in Summerside, Prince Edward Island, for two years. In 1868 he entered the Summerside High School where a year later he won a two-year government scholarship at Prince of Wales College, Charlottetown. He next studied for two years at Acadia College in Nova Scotia where in 1873 he won the Canadian Gilchrist scholarship for three years' study in any British university. He chose the University of London where he was graduated A. B. in 1877 and M. A. in 1878, winning the highest honors in philosophy and political science. In 1877-78 he also studied in Paris and at the University of Edinburgh, taking a Sc. D. degree at the latter in 1878. Immediately thereafter he was awarded the Hibbert traveling fellowship open to graduates of all universities in Great Britain and Ireland, and spent two years at the universities of Heidelberg, Berlin, and Gottingen, and in Italy. While in Germany he majored in German philosophy and became acquainted with the foremost exponents of that discipline. After his return to Canada in 1880, he held the chair of English literature, political economy, and psychology at Acadia College for two years after which he served for four years as professor of English literature and metaphysics at Dalhousie College, Halifax, Nova Scotia. In 1886 he came to the United States as Sage professor of philosophy and head of that department at Cornell University. He became dean of the newly established Sage School of Philosophy in 1890 and

in 1892 was elected the third president of Cornell, serving in that capacity until 1920 when he resigned. During his administration Cornell developed into one of the leading educational institutions in this country, the student enrollment increasing from 1600 to 7350 and the faculty from 146 to 847, while various new schools or departments were added. Among Schurman's outstanding achievements at Cornell was the creation and implementation of a new relationship between the college and the State of New York whereby were established state colleges known as contract colleges, controlled by the trustees of Cornell and subject to their authority and administered by the president and the administrative staff of Cornell, although supported financially by the state. Starting with the College of Agriculture, the project was expanded so that it came to include the New York State College of Home Economics, New York State College of Veterinary Medicine, New York State College of Labor and Industrial Relations, and the New York State School of Nutrition. In all instances the state constructed commodious buildings to house these schools and colleges and furnished the finest and most modern libraries and equipment. Furthermore their salary scale attracted to the faculties the finest teachers and acknowledged leaders in their respective fields of knowledge. From time to time Schurman was given leaves of absence from Cornell to serve in various government posts. In 1899 he was appointed by William McKinley, then President of the United States, as president of the first U. S. Commission to the Philippine Islands. Schurman spent most of that year in the Philippines helping to organize administrative facilities and advising Washington with respect to future American policies to be pursued in the recently acquired archipelago. He was largely responsible for the four-volume report of the commission published in 1900. During 1912-1913, by appointment of William Howard Taft, he was U.S. minister to Greece and Montenegro. In the First World War he served on the New York State Food Commission and later carried out an overseas mission for the YMCA. In 1920 he was a member of the Frank A. Vanderlip commission to Japan, a non-governmental body invited to that country to observe its beauties, culture, and industry and thus to be in a position to speak with authority on Japan in the United States. In 1921 Warren G. Harding appointed Schurman minister to China. He was the first American envoy who made it a part of his duty to visit every consular office of the United States in that vast republic, and for this, and for his skill in handling problems that were inherent in the constantly changing aspects of internal Chinese politics, he won the high regard of official Washingon. Calvin Coolidge in 1925 transferred Schurman from Peking to Berlin as ambassador from the United States to Germany. He remained there until he retired from the Foreign Service in 1930 While in Berlin he became immensely popular with the German government and people and did much to restore friendly relations between the two recent enemies. In part this was due to his familiarity with German culture and philosophy and way of life. During this period he raised $500,000 with which to build a new academic building at the University of Heidelberg, and when it was completed and dedicated in

1931, the structure was named Schurman Hall in his honor. On that occasion he was decorated with the great golden state medal by the premier of Baden. He had previously been elected a member of the Prussian Academy of Sciences, being the only foreigner to receive that honor, and the German Academy of Munich. From 1891 to 1905 he was editor of *The Philosophical Review*. Schurman was the author of "Kantian Ethics and the Ethics of Evolution" (1881), "Agnosticism and Religion" (1886), "The Ethical Import of Darwinism" (1888), "A Generation of Cornell" (1898), "Philippine Affairs - A Retrospect and Outlook" (1902). "The Balkan Wars, 1912 and 1913" (1914), and "Why America's at War" (1917). He was also a contributor to many philosophical and other journals at home and abroad, and delivered the Stafford Little lectures at Princeton University in 1914 and lectures on international affairs at the California Institute of Technology in 1931-32. He was awarded honorary LL.D. degrees by Columbia University (1892), Yale University (1901), the University of Edinburgh (1902), Williams College (1908), Dartmouth College and Harvard University (1909), Brown University (1914), the University of Pennsylvania (1917), and the University of Missouri (1921), and honorary PhD degrees by Heidelberg and Marburg Universities in 1927. He was a member of numerous learned societies and belonged also to the University and Century clubs of New York city, the Cosmos Club, Washington, D. C. and the Town and Gown Club, Ithaca, N. Y. He became a naturalized citizen of the United States and for many years was a distinguished figure in the affairs of the Republican Party. He was a delegate-at-large to the Republican National Convention in 1912, serving on the resolutions committee, was an ardent Taft supporter in the successful contest with Theodore Roosevelt (for the Republican nomination for President). He was also vice-president of the Newark State Constitutional Convention in 1915. For many years he was in frequent correspondence with Republican Presidents of the United States and statesmen, prominent educators, men of letters and philosophers throughout the world. He was in demand as a public speaker not only at commencements, but on other occasions of importance, and his views on foreign affairs as well as on topics of domestic concern, commanded wide attention. His religious affiliation was with the Baptist Church. He was married in New York City, Oct. 1, 1884, to Barbara Forrest, daughter of George Munro, a publisher of that city, and had eight children: Catherine Munro, who married Raymond Ware; Robert; George Munro; Helen who married John Magruder; Jacob Gould; Barbara Rose who married Vladimir Petro-Palovsky; Dorothy Anna Maria, who married James S. Sisk; and one who died in infancy. Schurman died in New York City on Aug. 12, 1942.[24] [Another source said that he died in Bedford Hills, N.Y.]

Courtesy of the family of the late Harold B. Schurman

Jacob Gould Schurman
(1854-1942)

He was one of Prince Edward Island's most distinguished sons. Born in Freetown, he achieved international recognition during a brilliant career with the United States Foreign Service before his retirement in 1930.

Jacob Gould Schurman c.1868

Courtesy of the family of the late Harold B. Schurman

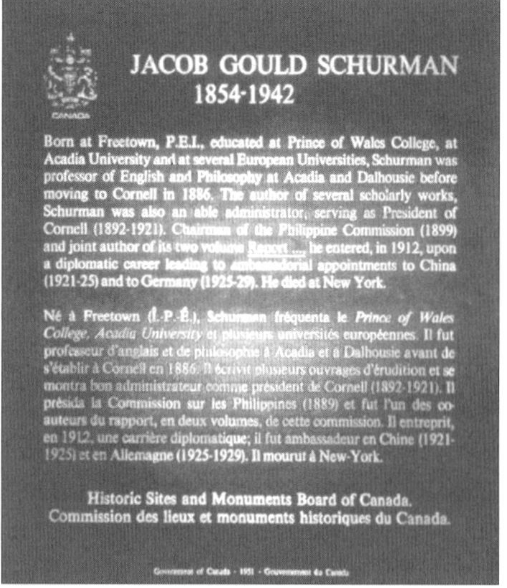

JACOB GOULD SCHURMAN
1854-1942

Born at Freetown, P.E.I., educated at Prince of Wales College, at Acadia University and at several European Universities, Schurman was professor of English and Philosophy at Acadia and Dalhousie before moving to Cornell in 1886. The author of several scholarly works, Schurman was also an able administrator, serving as President of Cornell (1892-1921). Chairman of the Philippine Commission (1899) and joint author of its two volume Report ..., he entered, in 1912, upon a diplomatic career leading to ambassadorial appointments to China (1921-25) and to Germany (1925-29). He died at New York.

Né à Freetown (Î.-P.-É.), Schurman fréquenta le *Prince of Wales College*, *Acadia University* et plusieurs universités européennes. Il fut professeur d'anglais et de philosophie à Acadia et à Dalhousie avant de s'établir à Cornell en 1886. Il écrivit plusieurs ouvrages d'érudition et se montra bon administrateur comme président de Cornell (1892-1921). Il présida la Commission sur les Philippines (1889) et fut l'un des co-auteurs du rapport, en deux volumes, de cette commission. Il entreprit, en 1912, une carrière diplomatique; il fut ambassadeur en Chine (1921-1925) et en Allemagne (1925-1929). Il mourut à New-York.

Historic Sites and Monuments Board of Canada.
Commission des lieux et monuments historiques du Canada.

Government of Canada · 1951 · Gouvernement du Canada

Plaque honoring Jacob Gould Schurman at Freetown, P.E.I., installed by the Historic Sites and Monuments Board of Canada

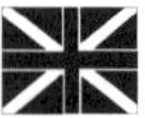

Prince Edward Island's Jacob Gould Schurman was so busy, so involved, so important in so many countries, and so intelligent, that he seems too good to be true!

In 1914 news came of the death of a Central Bedeque native. Also successful in his own right, but on a lesser scale than Jacob Gould Schurman, he, too, was an expatriate Islander living in the United States. The article was copied by Mrs. Bradshaw for this genealogy:

DEATH OF MR. ISAAC SCHURMAN One of the saddest duties that falls to the lot of one is to record the passing of his friends. The news has been conveyed to friends in Summerside of the death of Mr. Isaac W. Schurman, formerly of North Bedeque, but latterly of Texas, U.S.A. He had been ailing for some time, and it was no surprise to those around him when his spirit was removed. Mr. Schurman was born at North Bedeque seventy-seven years ago, was the son of the late Mr. William Schurman. He married Isabel Millar, daughter of the late Mr. Alex Millar and settled on the old home farm. In 1891 he moved with his family to Carthage, Missouri, and later to Winona, Texas, where he died on the 30th of Aug., 1914. His wife predeceased him by one year and five months. Mr. Schurman was a wholehearted man, and the removal of himself and his family from Bedeque was very keenly regretted, for he was a leader in every movement for the betterment of the community. His example as a farmer and stock-raiser was looked upon as being of the highest class. A kindly, courteous, hospitable, honorable gentleman who could always welcome a friend with a smile. Death came to him as a happy release and it was only a question of time to him to say goodbye at the threshold we all have to cross. He is survived by two sons: Stephen of Winona, Texas, and Norman at Webb City, Missouri, U.S.A. Mrs. K. McKae of Texas and Mrs. Ronald Campbell, Summerside, are his sisters. His youngest son, Elias, enlisted with the U.S. Army and went to the Phillippine Islands at the beginning of the Spanish War where he lost his life. His daughter who taught school in Summerside for some years, a highly educated and accomplished young lady was drowned in a railway wreck at Eden, Colorado, Aug. 7th, 1904. There is not a man who knew Mr. Schurman who will not feel extra sorrow on hearing of his removal from this earthly stage.

Just before Mr. and Mrs. Schurman left for the U.S.A. in 1891, their friends had given them a party. A local newpaper printed the following description of the occasion:

Some pleasant hours were spent (on the evening of the 10th inst.) at the well-ordered residence of Mr. James McMurdo of North Bedeque, on the eve of their [the Schurmans] departure for the United States. Over sixty ladies and gentlemen were present, and about 8 p.m. proceedings were commenced. Mr. Edward Clark was appointed chairman and briefly explained the object of so many coming together. James Carruthers, Esq., was called on to give voice to the meeting, and that gentleman responded in good and fitting terms. He referred to Mr. Schurman's high standing in the district; his uprightness and public spirit; his always taking front place in whatever was calculated to reform society or increase its comforts. He referred to the community's loss in his departure; and wished all kinds of prosperity to Mr. S. and his partner. Later in the evening, Hon. A. Laird spoke in much the same tenor. Mr. Wm. G. Taylor then read an address at the right moment, placing in Mr. Schurman's hand a silver-headed walking cane with the following inscription: "Presented to I.W. Schurman by his neighbors -1891." Mrs. McMurdo (the hostess) presented to Mrs. Schurman a handsome gold brooch, a parting gift from ladies in the community. During the evening, Mr. Schurman related how his ancestors (three or four generations back) had left the German Fatherland by the classic Rhine, and settled on the Hudson in New York State. Then forsaking their pleasant homes and orchards on account of loyalty to the British throne, had come to this untilled country to suffer years of poor living. After years of careful industry, comfort again rewarded their efforts; and now their descendants are returning to dwell under the aegis of the gridiron flag. The proceedings were abundantly interspersed with music, vocal and instrumental.

The next item on the program being announced, all sat down to an excellent spread, prepared by the generous hostess. This over, after reasonable time, the national anthem was fervently sung and the company departed.

Here are the address and reply: "Dear Sir, We learn with regret that you have decided to exchange the old home of your early life for another in a far-off land. The ties which years of friendly intercourse have formed and strengthened are not to be severed without a pang, and our feelings prompt us to show, in this manner, our appreciation of you as a neighbor, a citizen and friend. We ask you to accept this cane as a tangible memento of our esteem. We have admired your honest and honorable ways in business transactions, and your manly, straightforward course in public affairs. Kindness and large-hearted generosity were marked features of your character, and your hospitality extended almost beyond bounds. You heartily co-operated in schemes of moral advancement, while the needy found your hand and purse always open. The noble, true and honest you esteemed and supported; the base and fraudulent you heartily despised. Some persons are said to leave their country for its advantage, but in parting with you, we lose one of those who help to make English-speaking nations esteemed and honored in all lands.

Dear Sir, Our best wishes go to you and your esteemed family, and our earnest desire is that God will prosper you and yours in the distant home to which you are about starting. A person of your manly disposition and upright, sterling character will make friends elsewhere, but none more real and true than....Should you at any time return to the land of your childhoon, be assured of a kind hand and hearty welcome.

We regret also to see your estimable partner going out from among us. Her deeds of charity and goodness of heart will long be remembered in the community."

Dear Friends, We will miss you. Be assured your memory will not soon be allowed to perish.

With best wishes for the welfare of yourself and family, we remain very sincerely, William Taylor, Walter Hogg, Edward Taylor, George Clark, Even Clark, Edward Clark, Joseph Rogers, Angus McDonald, Thomas Stavert, John Mackinnon, Alex Laird, M.L.C., Jas. McMurdo, John A. Burrows, Thomas J. Humphrey, Daniel Cobb, Thomas S. Waugh, Peter B. Stavert, Herbert Hogg, James Carruthers."

Mr. Schurman responded to the generosity of his friends:

"Valued Friends: I feel to a disadvantage in replying to this unexpected and unmerited demonstration of your esteem and regard for Mrs. Schurman, myself, and family on the eve of our departure from you and the home of our childhood, coming as it does from those among whom I was born and spent my youth with its frivolities up to the years at least of mature manhood with its accompanying cares and responsibilities.

The feeling which prompted the expression of so high an estimate of our character we duly appreciate, but beg leave to disclaim all pretensions to so honorable a sphere in real-life, further than the moral effect resulting from the imperative conformance to (as far as the shortcomings of our fallen nature will permit) the divinely commanded precept which says "and as you would that men should do to you, do ye also to them likewise."

That we may be favored in the land of our adoption with kind and true friends, I do not doubt, but that will never erase from our memories our past associations with true, trusted and time-honored friends whose welfare and interests as far as practicable have been identified and interwoven with our own, and whom we may never again meet in this probationary sphere of duty as we are all on the threshold of eternity where "time shall be no longer."

Be assured, Dear Friends, that Mrs. Schurman and I gratefully appreciate this token of your respect and lasting friendship, and the "tangible memento" which is a most fitting emblem of your best wishes with us in our future home. The "Staff" is a very anciently chosen representation of Divine support.

But above all, we value your petition in our behalf to the moral Governonr of the universe whose "offspring we all are for He hath made of one blood all nations of men for to dwell on the face of the earth."

My Dear Neighbors, our uncontrollable thoughts will often return to the home of our youth, to roam in the agreeable memories of former associations with you as things of our valued past, perhaps not again to return. In conclusion, permit me to tender you our heartfelt obligation for this visible expression of your good will in a distant land.

Wishing you all farewell, I will ever remain in memory's reality, your neighbor and friend, ISAAC W. SCHURMAN"

The Bradshaws had saved a newspaper article concerning a birthday party of Mrs. Jesse Schurman:

They Celebrated the Occasion

In Central Bedeque, near the little village known as "Callback Corner," over the slope of the hill, nestling among the historic trees, lied [sic] the comfortable home of Mr. Jesse P. Schurman. This home has long been noted for its hospitality. Its doors seem ever open to friend and stranger alike. Truly the milk of human kindness doth flow within its gates.

On Thursday last a few friends met at this home to celebrate the occasion of Mrs. Schurman's birthday. Just before dinner was served she was presented with a substantial nickel-plated water kettle with the accompanying verse:

We meet again at your festive board on this your natal day;
And raise our voice with one accord. Good luck to you, we pray.
We bless the morn that you were born, You've cheered our rugged day.
In saddest hours you threw us flowers. Let's all shout, "Hip Hurrah!"
And now we wish to greet sincere your kind and worthy spouse
Who faithful proved nigh forty years. To him we make our bows.
We hope and trust with all our heart as the seasons come and go
You'll both be --- --- --- a part of creation ---- below.
To brighten up the rugged way, to cheer the faint and sinner,
But I fear that we have caused delay to your anniversary dinner.
This little gift we bring to you, "Tis filled with boiling water.
When e'er you have a grievance true, just use - it – as – you'd – oughter!"

The sentiment contained in the last few lines seemed to fill the heart of the host with fear for a moment, then a spirit of hilarity took possession. The sumptuous repast was partaken amid jovial remarks, cheers, and shouts of merriment. We feel

sure that even the great and mighty Kaiser Bill, whose birthday occurred on the same date, did not experience as much pleasure as did that humble little party on the hillside at Bedeque.

Another interesting newspaper article from the Bradshaws is entitled, **HOW TO BE HAPPY IF MARRIED – Mrs. Maeterlinck's Ten Commandments For Wives** [I wonder how this would work in today's changed society!]:

Paris, July 22 [no year] - Mrs. Maeterlinck, the actress and wife of the poet, says she has achieved married happiness under the most trying auspices, being guided by the following maxims:

The Ten Commandments

1– Matrimony is a combination of two imperfect personalities. The smart wife considers herself the most imperfect part of the combination.

2 – The part of the wife is: To look out, to anticipate, to give in, to amuse, to conciliate - in a manner she will contribute to the mental peace and the material welfare of her husband.

3- Don't allow a hired person to be your husband's caterer and possibly the destroyer of his health. Select his food and cook it.

4- See to his clothes, his laundry, his socks, and handkerchief.

5- Turn yourself into a marital barometer and anticipate electric storms. Play the lightning rod so no one gets hurt.

6- Be joyful when your husband is joyful, counteract his spells of distemper by being agreeable and pleasant.

7- When your husband comes home, don't bother him with affairs of the household or the neighbors or your own. When the meal was a success and he is rested, he will stand for anything.

8- Let your tongue be the assenter. Dissent only with your eyes.

9- If your husband has rheumatism, don't talk about dancing.

10- If you want to make your husband believe that you are superior to other women, excel as a cook.

More interesting advice was found in a newspaper clipping from Mr. and Mrs. Bradshaw. This time it pertains to keeping the son(s) at home happy and contented. It, too, was directed primarily at the mother in the household. It would appear that the mother of the family was expected to be the one that kept everyone happy! The article follows:

Make home a pleasant place for your boys. Don't be so afraid of your best parlor that they may not use it. Let them have plenty of warmth and light, and entertaining books to read, and musical instruments, and any parlor games they like.

Girls will stay at home if home be the dullest place under the moon, but boys will not. If their young companions are diminished, if they are checked when they laugh or sing, or make a noise, if they may not have the innocent freedom that they need under their parents' roof, then they will have freedom of some sort elsewhere. And there are always enough ready to beckon them to places where the bloom is brushed from youth's round cheek.

A young man *will* squeeze a little "fun" out of his life, and if you want him to be a credit to you and to himself, make it possible for him to enjoy himself in his home. Let the home be a place to live and breathe in, not merely a roof under which he may eat and sleep.

The Rev. F. A. Wightman, D. D., who had been the pastor at Bedeque Methodist Church from 1899-1903, married a parishioner. Her obituaries are included not only for the description of a beautiful person, but because of the unique way in which they are written. She died in 1916. These newspaper articles had been saved by Malcolm Bradshaw's father, Ellis, or his grandfather, Wallace:

Mrs. (Rev.) F. A. Wightman - Mrs. Wightman, wife of Rev. F. A. Wightman of the Methodist Church in Bathhurst, N. B., passed away at the parsonage on Friday morning. About fifteen months ago Mrs. Wightman developed symptoms of cancer, and a year ago she went to the Royal Victoria Hospital where an operation was performed. It was hoped a speedy recovery would follow, and for a time this seemed likely, but evidently the disease had gone too far and in October it gave evidence of return. The disease gradually made progress despite all that medical skill and attentive nursing could do. Mrs. Wightman, formerly Miss Lavinia Alice Crosby, was born near Bedeque, P.E.I., where she spent her early life. She was first married to Rev. Sanford B. Sweetzee, and after some years of widowhood she was united in marriage to Mr. Wightman.

After an impressive service held in the church on Friday evening, conducted by Rev. Dr. Harrison of Newcastle, assisted by local clergymen, the body was taken to P.E.I. for interment. The body, accompanied by the husband of the deceased, arrived in Summerside Saturday night and was forwarded to Bedeque where the funeral took place yesterday afternoon from the Methodist Church to the cemetery adjoining.

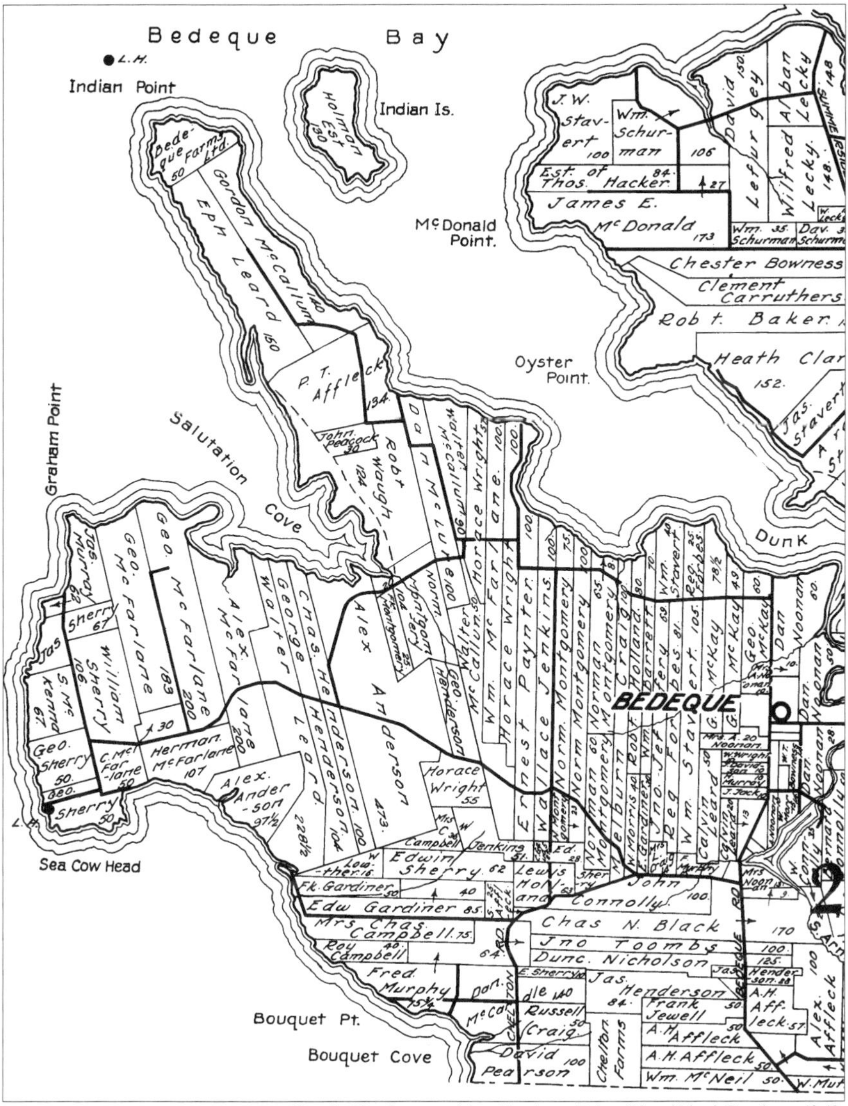

Cummins Map Company, *Atlas of Province of Prince Edward Island, Canada*, pp. 42-43

The western half of Lots 25 and 26, P.E.I., about 1928

The following obituary of Mrs. Wightman was written by Rev. William Harrison, D. D., pastor of the Methodist Church at Bedeque from 1889-1892:

On the early morning of May 5th, the beloved wife of Rev. F. A. Wightman of Bathurst, N. B. passed peacefully and with great hope to the home where the inhabitants never say "I am sick." After a year marked by much suffering, borne with a full and cheerful resignation, the patient sufferer passed to the painless and tearless life above. Mrs. Wightman, formerly Miss Lavinia Alice Crosby of Bedeque, P.E.I., entered upon the Christian life when a mere girl and to the close of an active and beautiful life maintained the character of a disciple of the Lord she served and loved so well. By her devotion, cheerfulness, sympathy and unceasing kindness she was specially fitted for the position which she occupied in the church for several years. Her religious life was a very happy experience and by the bright and attractive manner in which her inner life found expression she was a constant invitation to others to share with her the deep joy which was hers as the days and years passed away. It is no wonder that such a sunny and hopeful life won an appreciation far and wide irrespective of Church distinction of every kind. It is one of the mysteries of the present world that a character and career so useful in the home, in the community and Church should thus be stricken in its prine, but we are assured that some day the light will fall on all such painful problems and it is ours with patience and unshaken confidence and hope to wait for the coming blessed dawn of that morning which will not fail to lift the night of mystery and "justify the ways of God to man." An appropriate service, which was largely attended was held on Friday evening in the Bathurst Church which was conducted by Rev. Dr. Harrison of Newcastle, assisted by the pastors of the town. It is needless to say that the deepest sympathy has been expressed by the community and congregation for Mr. Wightman and his family in the sore bereavement which has come to them. The interment took place on Sabbath, the 7th inst. at her old home at Bedeque, P.E.I. Fitting and touching references were made to the character and work of our departed sister in the morning service of that day by the pastor, Rev. George Ayers.

Another obituary was provided for the daughter of Stephen Wright and his second wife, Millicent Palmer, who had married Francis Dyer Beer, M. D., a graduate of Harvard Medical School:

The death occurred in Charlottetown on Sunday [February 9, 1919] at the age of 78 years, of Mrs. Beer, wife of the late Dr. F. D. Beer, of Charlottetown. The deceased was the eldest daughter of the late Mr. Stephen Wright of Bedeque, and with her late husband had resided in Charlottetown from her young womanhood until her

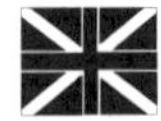

death. There are left to mourn two daughters, Mrs. Alexander Anderson of Albany, N. Y. and Mrs. John Longworth of Brandon, Manitoba, and two sons, Mr. F. Robert Beer of Seattle, and Col. George S. Beer, Bloemfontein, S. A. Two sisters and four brothers survive her, namely Mrs. F. W. Strong formerly of Summerside, now of Minto, N. B.; Mr. Edward Wright, New Annan; Mrs. Charles S. Wright, Victoria, P.E.I., and Mr. Maurice Wright, Vancouver, B. C. Funeral Tuesday by train to Sherwood, leaving G. D. Wright's parlors at 1:50 p.m.

A former P. E. Islander, Harry R. Wright, had moved west and died in 1921. The Bradshaws had also preserved his obituary:

ISLAND DOCTOR DIES IN CALGARY

Calgary, July 30, 1921. The funeral of the late Dr. Harry R. Wright, which took place from his home to the Central Methodist Church last Wednesday afternoon, was under the supervision and direction of Perfection Lodge, A. F. and A. M. and was attended by a large number of his friends and relatives. The late Dr. H. P. Wright is a native of Prince Edward Island and has resided in Calgary for the last fifteen years. He was a brother of Dr. Frank Wright of Vancouver, formerly of Calgary. He is survived by his widow and one son, Gordon, and a sister, Maud Wright, also of P. E. Island. The deceased was well-known on the Island and the news of his death will be received with many regrets by his large circle of friends and relatives who are still living on the Island. The funeral service was attended by many former residents of the Island among whom were Mr. and Mrs. D. A. MacLeod, Mr. and Mrs. J.T. McDonald, Dr. H. W. Wright, Dr. Coffin, the Misses Sadie and Gertrude MacDonald, sisters of Mrs. D. A. MacLeod, Mrs. B. F. Dingman, and many others.

While he was a resident in the West, the late Dr. Wright had built up an exceptionally large practice and he leaves behind him as large a circle of friends as anyone could wish. He was extremely popular among his co-workers and with his office staff and was a prominent member of many of the best clubs.

It was somewhat of a surprise to see so many people from Prince Edward Island attendant at the funeral. I really did not think there were so many men and women from the Island in Calgary.

One very noticeable feature was that all of the men from the Island who were attendant were well up in the business world and well-known to the public. Prince Edward Island has good reason to be proud of the many men who were born there and have gone out into the world and been successful in the name of Prince Edward Island. As an Islander I take this opportunity of offering to the bereaved doctor's family the sincere regrets and best wishes of all who knew him.

From a page of *Christian Union* is a short article called "Be Courteous," again compliments of Mr. and Mrs. Bradshaw:

There are a thousand little courtesies and salutations and compliments of life, but it would be well if there were still more of them. Bluntness does not mean honesty, and a recognition of whatever is good in men does not mean insincerity. It would be promotive of happiness if every time men descended in the morning they would look for that which is comely and praiseworthy, and single it out and tell it to their wives. Oh, if men would only court after they are married as they do before, what joy there would be! What praise there would be distributed among the community! But the faults of men are generally first thought of, and are condemned. There are a multitude of little, imperfect irregular things in human conduct; and a man says, "I am not one of those who goes around and flatters folks; I'll tell them what I think of them; if they have faults, I hit them strong." But it is not necessary to be hard and repellant and unsympathetic in order to be honest. There is good as well as evil in men, and it is surely as worthy of recognition.

On January 25, 1922 a local newspaper ran an obituary for Patrick Munsey. Thanks to the Bradshaws for the information about this apparently needless death:

Mr. Patrick Munsey was instantly killed at Borden on Wednesday morning, an empty freight car passing over his body. Just exactly how the accident happened is not known as it was not witnessed by anyone. Mr. Munsey was at work with the shunting crew at the time. He was badly mangled about the head and limbs. The deceased was a son of the late Mr. T. C. Munsey and is survived by his mother, two brothers Singleton and Frank W., both in Vancouver, and two sisters, Mrs. (Dr.) Tanton and Miss Sue Munsey, both of Summerside.

Even as late as 1926 when a person from the Island died off the Island, an incredible amount of time, it seems, was taken to transfer the body to the Island to be buried. Mr. Bradshaw had saved an article about the death of John Bell in Los Angeles, California:

Last Saturday morning the body of the late Hon. John H. Bell, accompanied by his niece, Mrs. Valentine Buckner, with whom he was staying when he met with his fatal accident, left Los Angeles, Calif., for home via Chicago. The remains should arrive at Summerside next Thursday night, in anticipation of which tentative fu-

neral arrangements have been made as follows: A short service will be held next Saturday afternoon at the residence of his niece, Mrs. H. M. Downing, Central Street, and thence to Trinity United Church [Summerside]. Interment in the People's Cemetery, where the remains will be laid to rest beside those of his wife who died at Summerside some twelve years ago. If the body does not arrive at Summerside until Friday night by any chance [which would make the transit of the body take almost one week!], the funeral will be held next Sunday afternoon.

Somewhere around this time many men were smoking cigarettes, of course of the unfiltered variety. Many were rolling their own. An article from the Bradshaw papers entitled, "The Little Black Devil," addresses the issue of smoking tobacco:

He hates both God and man. He is an unclean spirit. Last year he robbed men of over four hundred millions of dollars in this country alone. In our meeting last Thursday evening, one man out of whom he had been cast said that had ruined his teeth, injured his lungs, and robbed him of over five hundred dollars, besides the interest, through his diabolic agency. He dims the eyes, injures the throat, unstrings the nerves, benumbs the brain, pollutes the breath, poisons the blood, sows the seeds of dyspepsia, heart disease, consumption, and cancers in the system, and then laughs at his victim who tries to escape from his clutches. Selfishness, stinginess, peevishness, slavishness, filthiness, all delight to call him "Father." Drunkenness is his own pet nephew. Strong drink is his twin brother and they are often seen together. Inconsistent as it may seem, he sometimes goes to church and has often persuaded professed Christians to pay more for his support than for all benevolent purposes combined. His friends usually feel "too poor" to take a religious paper. Unlike wicked men and other "devils," he is to be annihilated at the end of the world. He can never enter heaven for 'tis written that "no unclean thing can enter there." His name is TOBACCO. Christ can cast him out. Will you let him?

Church Union in 1925 saw the union of the Presbyterian, Methodist and Congregationalists into a new, stronger, and hopefully more vibrant and useful church to the members. George A. Leard, writing in *Historic Bedeque*, described how this momentous event within the Methodist Church was accepted by the Bedeque Methodist congregations:

Church union came quietly at both Centreville and North Bedeque with no divisive action in either Methodist or Presbyterian Congregations. It brought its problems of local church government, and those of loyalties and change of membership due to geographical nearness which time and understanding eventually worked out. However, for a year or two very little change was evident. Rev. D. K. Ross at North Bedeque and Rev. P. A. Fitzpatrick at Centreville, pastors during the transitional period, shared with their people a feeling that nothing was lost save their church's denominational name which, like a bride's, is gladly surrendered to the larger loyalty of two families becoming one.

Was **Bedeque United** still a **Methodist Church**? Or was it Presbyterian? It was both. When represented in World Councils, North American Alliances, or Ecumenical Conferences, Bedeque, like all other United Churches, would count as either a Methodist or Presbyterian body, depending on who was calling the roll; or it might even count twice, in which case the counted could feel nothing else but flattered. In the last year of its solely Methodist life, before entering into the wider horizons of Union, Bedeque Methodist Circuit which had been born in a revival experienced another under the special service conducted by Mr. Foster, the Farmer Evangelist, from Maine: a fitting finale to its separate career.

...For the Church at Bedeque, known in the Year Book till 1937 as **Bedeque Center United Church,** the greatest event in its **United** history was the adherence of the staunch former Presbyterians from Lower Bedeque, Fernwood, and other near centers, who gradually switched their membership from North Bedeque United to Bedeque, helping make the latter church one of the strongest rural churches in the Maritimes. This has been recognized by the Presbytery of Prince Edward Island and the Maritime Conference which have appointed more lay representatives to General Council from Bedeque than from any other charge on the Island.

Bedeque's most frequent conference representative, Thomas Moyse, was the only Island Methodist layman to attend the birth of the United Church of Canada in Toronto, on the historic Sunday of June 10th, 1925. He had just previously sat in the last session of the Methodist General Conference to which he had been a delegate, in which capacity he was also sole Island representative in 1923. Mr. Moyse went again in 1928 to General Council which met in Winnipeg. Two years later at the next Council which met in London, Ontario, the Island Commissioner was Horace Wright, who brought further honour to Bedeque Church by being the first layman in Canada to be elected chairman of Presbytery, a post very capably filled by Mr. Wright for the P.E.I. Presbytery in 1933-34....

In many other activities of the church, including the Layman's Association and the Woman's Missionary Society, the men and women of Bedeque have been prominent in their devotion and leadership, showing by their deeds and words the motivating thought of their religious life. The history of their Church, written

every day in their personal and community activites, has a past for guidance, a future of hope, and a present full of immeasurable opportunity for doing God's will in Bedeque and elsewhere, as it is done in Heaven.[25]

Most obituaries are sad, and this one, again given to us by Mr. and Mrs. Bradshaw, regarding one of their own family whose death was in 1928, is no exception:

Mrs. Ellis Bradshaw of Middleton, P. E. I., departed this life on March 6th . She leaves a family of ten children, one being a baby only a few days old; also a husband and a large circle of friends to sorrow because of her sudden passing. The funeral was held on March 9th. Services were conducted by the pastor, Rev. A. J. Reynolds at the house, the United Church at Bedeque, and at the grave. The large attendance at the house and church showed the high esteem in which she was held. Favorite hymns were sung and a sermon appropriate to the occasion was preached at the church. Mrs. Bradshaw was a member of the Bedeque United Church for many years. She was greatly devoted to the interests of her family and home. Much sympathy is felt for the husband and bereaved children. [The family requested no flowers]

A March 16, 1929 clipping from the newspaper was preserved by the Bradshaws and is printed below. It is interesting for its portrayal of the the old saying that "A dog is man's best friend":

A heavy thunderstorm, accompanied by much rain, passed over the Island last Saturday night and was particularly severe in the eastern section. At Whim Cross Road, some five miles from Montague, at about 10 p.m., in the height of the electrical storm, the farm residence and barn owned by Mr. Freeman Miller were struck by lightening apparently about the same time. Mr. Miller and his wife were asleep in bed and possibly might have lost their lives except for their dog. The animal, hearing the crash, at once ran to their bedroom and grabbed Mr. Miller by his arm. He and his wife were able to leave the house in safety, but by this time, both buildings were in flames and both were totally destroyed. Mrs. Miller then went to a neighbour's house, and the dog, missing her and thinking she was still in the burning building, rushed in apparently with the intention of saving her, but the animal was so badly burned that he had to be mercifully dispatched to end his sufferings. Mr. Miller was unable to save any of the contents of the house, but succeeded in getting his livestock out of the barn in time. A quantity of hay, grain, and straw, and some implements, went up in smoke. The loss of over one thousand dollars was partly covered by insurance.

Notes

1 George A. Leard, *Historic Bedeque. The Loyalists at Work and Worship in Prince Edward Island* (Bedeque, P.E.I.: Bedeque United Church, 1948), p. 57
2 Springfield Historical Committee, The History of Springfield, [P.E.I.] 1828-1985. Revised and updated. (n.p.: Springfield Historical Committee, n.d.)
3 Marjorie McCallum Gay, ed. (Ada MacLeod notes), *Roads to Sumerside, the Story of Early Summerside and the Surrounding Area* (Summerside, P.E.I.: n.p., 1980), p. 70
4 Leard, op. cit., p. 79
5 Ibid., pp. 87, 89
6 Ibid., p. 66
7 Ibid., pp. 78-79
8 Ibid., p. 82
9 Ibid., p. 89
10 Ibid., pp. 89-92
11 Ibid., pp. 92-95
12 Ibid., p. 95
13 Ibid., pp. 97-99
14 Ibid., pp. 99-100
15 Ibid., pp. 53-54
16 Ibid. p. 85
17 Ibid., p. 86
18 Ibid., pp. 86-87
19 Ibid., pp. 86-87
20 Ibid.
21 Ibid.
22 Ibid., pp. 101-103
23 Ross Graves, *William Schurman, Loyalist of Bedeque, Prince Edward Island, and his descendants* (Summerside, P.E.I.: Harold B. Schurman, 1973), p. 41, 194-196
24 The *National Cyclopedia of American Biography*, pp. 491-492
25 George A. Leard, op. cit., pp. 104-106

CHAPTER 9

Generations Seven and Eight: Great-Great-Grandchildren and Great-Great-Great-Grandchildren of Thomas Hooper and His Wife

By the time that the children from the seventh and eighth generations were born, the numbers had increased tremendously and the Hooper-related population had spread out over thousands of miles in at least Canada and the United States; therefore, the number of people identified in this genealogy for the seventh and eighth generations is much smaller in percent than in some other generations because contact has been lost with many ancestors.

Many descendants of generations five and six who had moved to a distant location did not keep in touch well with their relatives who remained on P.E.I. We will start with the descendants in the seventh and eighth generation of Major, the oldest child of Thomas Hooper, and work down through Elisha. I will include only the names of those ancestors about whom I have information in the seventh and eighth generations.

Anyone having more information for inclusion into this genealogy is welcome to contact me by mail at 10 Peterborough Drive, Northport, New York 11768, by e-mail at NancyENeal@aol.com during the winter months, or by mail in Prince Edward Island during the summer months at R.R. 2, Albany, P.E.I. Canada COB 1AO. No more numerals precede the names. The reader will find genealogical descent following the names. As the surname Hooper appeared less

often, those of us "from away" would not have a clue initially who was related to whom!

The second and only child of Major Hooper and Ann Patterson to marry was **Martha** (5, Major 4, Thomas 3, Clement 2, Stephen 1) who married Stephen Wright (c.1801-1883), as his first wife. Martha (c.1797-1838) and Stephen had four children (sixth generation, surname Wright).

Major Wright (6, Martha 5, Major 4, Thomas 3, Clement 2, Stephen 1) married Adah Shreve and they had four children (seventh generation, surname Wright):

Mina Millicent Wright, called Millicent, (7, Major Wright 6, Martha 5, Major 4, Thomas 3, Clement 2, Stephen 1) born August 27, 1871 in Centreville Bedeque; did not marry; died in July 1956 in Vancouver, B.C.
Mary Beatrice Wright, called May, (7, Major Wright 6, Martha 5, Major 4, Thomas 3, Clement 2, Stephen 1) born September 2, 1873 [another source: 1872]; died April 18, 1906, less than two months after her mother passed away.
Stephen Charles Wright, called Tennie, (7, Major Wright 6, Martha 5, Major 4, Thomas 3, Clement 2, Stephen 1) born February 4, 1875; died August 16, 1877 in Centreville, aged about 2 ½ years.
Richmond Harold Wright, called Rich, (7, Major Wright 6, Martha 5, Major 4, Thomas 3, Clement 2, Stephen 1) born April 13, 1881; married Jane Crossan [Crossman?] June 25, 1913; d. Feb. 16, 1936, Vancouver, B.C. They had one child [eighth generation, surname Wright]:

Alan Douglas Wright (8, Richmond Harold 7, Major Wright 6, Martha 5, Major 4, Thomas 3, Clement 2, Stephen 1) born January 14, 1930 in Vancouver, British Columbia.

Ann *Eliza* Wright (6, Martha 5, Major 4, Thomas 3, Clement 2, Stephen 1) and Martin Black, had eight children, all born in Centreville Bedeque (surname Black, seventh generation) are:

Martha Louise Black, probably named for her grandmother, Martha Hooper Wright, (7, Eliza 6, Martha 5, Major 4, Thomas 3, Clement 2, Stephen 1), called Mattie, born February 28, 1857; did not marry. When her aunt Alice Wright, (Mrs. Joseph Pascoe) died in the Methodist parsonage, Mattie took charge of the parsonage and the Rev. Pascoe's young family. Mattie died on July 17, 1939 in Reading, MA at the home of her sister Elma.

Sarah *Elma* Black (7, Eliza 6, Martha 5, Major 4, Thomas 3, Clement 2, Stephen 1) born September 2, 1859 in Centerville Bedeque; married David Schurman, son of Peter and Janet (MacKay) Schurman as his third wife, on October 25, 1892 in Centreville Bedeque. David was born March 30, 1847 probably in Wilmot Valley, P.E.I. and died on August 2, 1935 in Reading, MA. David married (i) Mary Elizabeth McEwen on February 2, 1868 in the Anglican Church in St. Eleanor's, P.E.I.; they had four daughters two of whom died in infancy, another at the age of 20, and the second daughter at the age of 77 in Los Angeles, California. He married (ii) Amy Dobson on March 6, 1888 in Fredericton, N. B. and had twin girls, one of whom died young, the other became a nurse in 1911 at the Prince Edward Island Hospital in Charlottetown, and did not marry.[1] Because Elma married David Schurman in 1892, she probably raised Winnie who appeared to do very well as a nurse overseas in World War I, working in England, France, and Belgium. After the war she went to the United States and nursed in Cleveland, New York, and Boston. After she retired in 1960 she moved to Summerside.[2]

Elma lived in Reading, MA at least toward the end of her life, and died there on January 13, 1946. They had one son (surname Schurman), the only one of his children to be a Hooper relative.

Vernon Lionel Schurman (8, Elma Black 7, Eliza 6, Martha 5, Major 4, Thomas 3, Clement 2, Stephen 1) called Vern, born December 22,

1896 in Centreville Bedeque; married Ethel Elizabeth Higgins, daughter of Sandy J. and Bertha Alice (Leard) Higgins on April 7, 1928.[3]

Ann Wright Black, called Annie, (7, Eliza 6, Martha 5, Major 4, Thomas 3, Clement 2, Stephen 1) born June 18, 1861; did not marry; died March 15, 1884 in Centreville Bedeque.
Charles Nathaniel Black, called Charlie, (7, Eliza 6, Martha 5, Major 4, Thomas 3, Clement 2, Stephen 1) born May 17, 1863; died April 8, 1928 in Centreville Bedeque. [The reader may recall that Martha Hooper Wright had a son named Charles Nathaniel who died in California in 1850 on his search for gold] He married on November 18, 1903, Annie L. LePage who was born July 30, 1867 in Charlottetown and died August 16, 1933 in Centreville Bedeque. Charlie farmed the home farm until his death. It was then sold to Frank Jewell who passed it on to his son. The owner in the mid-1970s was Garth Toombs [from whom Alden and I bought our property in Chelton in 1987).
Laura Eliza Black (7, Eliza 6, Martha 5, Major 4, Thomas 3, Clement 2, Stephen 1) born August 23, 1865, did not marry; died March 4, 1915 in Centreville Bedeque.
Henry Ernest Black (7, Eliza 6, Martha 5, Major 4, Thomas 3, Clement 2, Stephen 1) born December 3, 1867/8; baptized May 1868. He studied at Baltimore College of Dental Surgery, Baltimore, MD and practiced his profession in Summerside until his early death on January 29, 1901 in Centreville Bedeque.
Millicent Wright Black, called Millie, (7, Eliza 6, Martha 5, Major 4, Thomas 3, Clement 2, Stephen 1) born October 24, 1869; did not marry; died November 27, 1896 in Centreville Bedeque.
Cecil Asher Black (7, Eliza 6, Martha 5, Major 4, Thomas 3, Clement 2, Stephen 1) born October 25, 1871; died December 14, 1874. One wonders how many of the deaths of these young people were due to tuberculosis or diphtheria.

In Chapter Seven, the sister-in-law of Eliza Black, Beria Black, was mentioned and, although she is not a Hooper descendant, her obituary will be recorded here, thanks to Mr. and Mrs. Bradshaw.

[Duglad Wright's father, John, had married (i) Elizabeth Robins (5, Mary 4, Thomas 3, Clement 2, Stephen 1) who died after her seventh child was born. It would appear that Mary, John's second wife, would have brought up Elizabeth's younger children as the oldest was only about 13 when his mother died. As Mary and John had one son and one daughter, the family must have lived together for at least a few years]:

MRS. DUGALD S. WRIGHT On Sabbath morning, February 27th, inst. [1910 at age 73] Berice, wife of Dugald S. Wright, Esq., of Summerside, passed from the shadows of earth into the brightness of everlasting day. Mrs. Wright, who was a daughter of the late Joseph Black, formerly of Amherst, N. S. , but who moved to Searletown, P.E.I., was born at Searletown Sept. 1837 and fifteen years later was born anew during the ministry of the late Rev. G. O. Huestis [minister at Bedeque from 1852-1854] and joined the Methodist Church of which she was ever after a faithful and valued member. She was of an unassuming yet intensely lovable disposition, ever devoted to her home, her church, and the broader interests of the kingdom of God. Her place in the sanctuary was rarely empty when she was able to be there and she loved and served her Saviour with a heart sincere. Just as she was passing away, her pastor, bending over her, asked: "Is the Lord Jesus with you, Mrs. Wright?" and with a smile of ineffable sweetness she replied: "Yes, He is always with me," and with this blessed confidence, she passed to be forever with the Lord, just as the Sabbath morning was breaking.

The funeral services which were conducted by the pastor, assisted by Rev. F. S. Bamford and Rev. Geo. Steel, were held at the home, Summerside, and then to Searletown where the remains were laid to rest. Besides her husband, she leaves to mourn two sons and a daughter and a large circle of relatives and friends.

A son of Dugald and Beria Wright, Leslie Asher Black Wright, was born on August 12, 1869 in Searletown; he married Henrietta Harper Russ, called Etta, on May 10, 1897. Etta was born on February 6, 1875. Leslie died on February 13, 1912. His obituary from a local newspaper, thanks to the Bradshaws, reads:

The many friends throughout this Province will hear with regret that Leslie A. Wright, the well-known and popular commercial traveler, passed away at his home in Summerside yesterday morning at 3 o'clock after an illness of about one month. Mr. Wright, who was only 42 years of age when called away, early in life went to Charlottetown and entered the employ of Stanley Bros. where he remained for

several years. Returning to Summerside he established the firm of McGougan and Wright. Selling out his interest to his partner, Mr. Wright removed to Montague where he established the firm of Wright and Crockett, retiring from business to become the Provincial representative of Brock & Patterson, St. John, which position he held up to his death. Being a young man of attractive personality and excellent business ability, Mr. Wright made many friends wherever he went. He was the oldest son of Dugald S. Wright, High Sheriff of Prince Country, and his wife is a daughter of Mrs. J. C. Russ now residing in Charlottetown. Besides his sorrowing wife and three children, a father, brother, and sister are left to mourn, and they will have widespread sympathy in the hour of trial. The funeral will be held tomorrow, Thursday, afternoon to Peoples Cemetery. Mr. Wright was a leading member of the I.O.O.F., and the brethren will take charge of the funeral.

The obituary, thanks again to the Bradshaws, of an older sister of Leslie A. Wright - Annie Olivia Delilah Wright - appears below:

At Searletown, Nov. 13th, 1875, of Spinal Meningitis, Annie Amelia [Annie Olivia], eldest daughter of D. S. Wright, Esq., and granddaughter of the late Hon. John Wright, aged eleven years and eight months. About a year and a half before her death she experienced the converting grace of God under the ministry of the Rev. J. S. Phinney. [who was the minister at the Bedeque Methodist Church from 1872-1875]. When she became afflicted she conversed with her mother concerning the subject of death with a calmness beyond her years saying, "I love Jesus and I know that He loves me and I am willing to die if it is the Lord's will." On another occasion when her physician told her that he could not save her, she replied, "I trust in Jesus to save me." On the day of her funeral the scholars of the Methodist Sabbath School with sadness stood beside the remains of their departed companion and sang the well-known lines beginning, "Sister, thou are mild and lovely," and then formed the procession to the grave. Thus in less than three short weeks those who had cheered the same home on earth were united in the Paradise above." (written by J. Seller, Bedeque, P.E.I., Jany. 13th, 1876) [Joseph Seller was the pastor at Bedeque Methodist Church from 1875-1878, following Mr. Phinney]

Mary Hooper (5, Major 4, Thomas 3, Clement 2, Stephen 1) married John Rhodes Gardiner (1798-1874) , as his second wife. Mary (1802-1890) was the first daughter of Major Hooper and his second wife, Catherine. Their daughter (sixth generation, surname Gardiner) was:

Adelaide Gardiner (6, Mary 5, Major 4, Thomas 3, Clement 2, Stephen 1) married Charles B. MacNeill, on November 24, 1859. Adelaide and Charles lived in Summerside and had one child (surname MacNeill, seventh generation):

Eva MacNeill (7, Adelaide 6, Mary 5, Major 4, Thomas 3, Clement 2, Stephen 1) about whom I have only the information that she was an only child, lived in Summerside, cared for her Aunt Mary Gardiner at the end of her Aunt Mary's life, and in 1920 was not married. A newspaper clipping from the Summerside newspaper dated Wednesday, December 9, 1914, read as follows: "Mrs. Alex McNeill and Miss Eva McNeill were passengers by the *Empress* from Summerside on Monday morning on their way to Montreal."

Sarah Sophia Hooper (6, Thomas 5, Major 4, Thomas 3, Clement 2, Stephen 1) married Archibald MacIntosh and they had the following children (surname MacIntosh, seventh generation):

Laura Legin MacIntosh (7, Sarah Sophia 6, Thomas 5, Major 4, Thomas 3, Clement 2, Stephen 1) born November 23, 1862 in Port Hill, P.E.I.; no further information available.

Alexander James MacIntosh (7, Sarah Sophia 6, Thomas 5, Major 4, Thomas 3, Clement 2, Stephen 1) born April 14, 1864 in Port Hill, P.E.I.; no further information available

Alice May Maud MacIntosh (7, Sarah Sophia 6, Thomas 5, Major 4, Thomas 3, Clement 2, Stephen 1) born December 29, 1865 in Port Hill, P.E.I.; no further information available

Major Hooper MacIntosh (7, Sarah Sophia 6, Thomas 5, Major 4, Thomas 3, Clement 2, Stephen 1) born August 12, 1868 in Port Hill, P.E.I.; married August 19, 1903 Cassie Mabel Simpson (born October 9, 1882, daughter of Jeremiah Simpson and Maysie Walker Clark; died 1969 in Halifax, N.S.); Major died January 5, 1945 in Waverly, N.S. They had five sons and one daughter (surname MacIntosh, eighth generation):

Archibald Jeremiah MacIntosh (8, Major Hooper 7, Sarah Sophia 6, Thomas 5, Major 4, Thomas 3, Clement 2, Stephen 1), born June 23, 1905; no further information

Charles Gordon MacIntosh (8, Major Hooper 7, Sarah Sophia 6, Thomas 5, Major 4, Thomas 3, Clement 2, Stephen 1), born September 6, 1907 in Bedeque, P.E.I.; no further information

Douglas Major MacIntosh (8, Major Hooper 7, Sarah Sophia 6, Thomas 5, Major 4, Thomas 3, Clement 2, Stephen 1), born July 13, 1909 in North Bedeque; married Beatrice Drysdale August 1, 1934. The Rev. Douglas Major MacIntosh was ordained as a minister in the Congregational Church. He lived in North Quincy, MA, U.S.A. Douglas and Beatrice had four children in the ninth generation [See Chapter 11].

Allan Simpson MacIntosh (8, Major Hooper 7, Sarah Sophia 6, Thomas 5, Major 4, Thomas 3, Clement 2, Stephen 1) born August 4, 1912; married January 12, 1945 to Aileen Winters. Allan lives/lived in Halifax, Nova Scotia, where he was a physician at the Victoria General Hospital. Allan and Aileen had five children (ninth generation). [See Chapter 11]

David Lloyd MacIntosh (8, Major Hooper 7, Sarah Sophia 6, Thomas 5, Major 4, Thomas 3, Clement 2, Stephen 1) born June 6, 1914; married Elaine Dickie. Dr. David Lloyd MacIntosh is an orthopedic surgeon who lives/lived in Toronto, Ontario. He and Elaine had three children (ninth generation). [See Chapter 11]

Marjorie MacIntosh (8, Major Hooper 7, Sarah Sophia 6, Thomas 5, Major 4, Thomas 3, Clement 2, Stephen 1) born January 31, 1920. No further information.

Major Gardiner Hooper (6, Thomas 5, Major 4, Thomas 3, Clement 2, Stephen 1), the fourth child of Thomas Hooper, and Pocahontas Millan, were married on February 21, 1870 in Lancaster, Iowa, U.S.A. They had four sons (surname Hooper, seventh generation):

Harry Franklin Hooper (7, Major Gardiner 6, Thomas 5, Major 4, Thomas 3, Clement 2, Stephen 1) born November 3, 1871; no further information available

Thomas Millan Hooper (7, Major Gardiner 6, Thomas 5, Major 4, Thomas 3, Clement 2, Stephen 1) born March 3, 1876 in Orleans, Nebraska, U.S.A. No further information

Stanton Blaine Hooper (7, Major Gardiner 6, Thomas 5, Major 4, Thomas 3, Clement 2, Stephen 1) born 1877 in Orleans, Nebraska, U.S.A. No further information

Louis Kent Hooper (7, Major Gardiner 6, Thomas 5, Major 4, Thomas 3, Clement 2, Stephen 1) born July 27, 1881. No further information

Ann Matilda Hooper (6, Thomas 5, Major 4, Thomas 3, Clement 2, Stephen 1) was the sixth child of Thomas Hooper. She married Andrew Campbell and they resided in Spokane, WA They had nine children (surname Campbell, seventh generation):

Daisy Campbell (7, Ann Matilda 6, Thomas 5, Major 4, Thomas 3, Clement 2, Stephen 1) first born; date and other data unknown

Maud Campbell (7, Ann Matilda 6, Thomas 5, Major 4, Thomas 3, Clement 2, Stephen 1) second born; date and other data unknown

Andrew C. Campbell (7, Ann Matilda 6, Thomas 5, Major 4, Thomas 3, Clement 2, Stephen 1) third born; date and other data unknown

William P. Campbell (7, Ann Matilda 6, Thomas 5, Major 4, Thomas 3, Clement 2, Stephen 1) fourth born; date and other data unknown

Nicholas Campbell (7, Ann Matilda 6, Thomas 5, Major 4, Thomas 3, Clement 2, Stephen 1) fifth born; date and other data unknown

Chauncy Campbell (7, Ann Matilda 6, Thomas 5, Major 4, Thomas 3, Clement 2, Stephen 1) sixth born; date and other data unknown

Charles Campbell (7, Ann Matilda 6, Thomas 5, Major 4, Thomas 3, Clement 2, Stephen 1) seventh born; date and other data unknown.

Haszard Campbell (7, Ann Matilda 6, Thomas 5, Major 4, Thomas 3, Clement 2, Stephen 1) eighth born; date and other data unknown
Oliver W. Campbell (7, Ann Matilda 6, Thomas 5, Major 4, Thomas 3, Clement 2, Stephen 1); died in 1892 in Schuyler, Nebraska. No other information known.

Charles Haszard Hooper (6, Thomas 5, Major 4, Thomas 3, Clement 2, Stephen 1) was the seventh child of Thomas and Maria Waitsill Gardiner Hooper. He and Christina Birch had eight children as follows (surname Hooper, seventh generation):

Sarah Jane Hooper (7, Charles 6, Thomas 5, Major 4, Thomas 3, Clement 2, Stephen1); born February 27, 1866 at Birch Hill, P.E.I.; died on May 6, 1875 at age 9 years.
Augusta Katherine Hooper (7, Charles 6, Thomas 5, Major 4, Thomas 3, Clement 2, Stephen 1); born March 20, 1868 at Birch Hill, P.E.I.
Thomas Percival Hooper (7, Charles 6, Thomas 5, Major 4, Thomas 3, Clement 2, Stephen 1); born on February 27, 1870 at Birch Hill, P.E.I.
Colin Leslie Hooper (7, Charles 6, Thomas 5, Major 4, Thomas 3, Clement 2, Stephen 1); born November 5, 1872 at Birch Hill, P.E.I.
Ernest Haszard Hooper (7, Charles 6, Thomas 5, Major 4, Thomas 3, Clement 2, Stephen 1); born March 21, 1875 at Birch Hill, P.E.I.
Ethel May Hooper (7, Charles 6, Thomas 5, Major 4, Thomas 3, Clement 2, Stephen 1); born April 27, 1879 at Birch Hill, P.E.I.
Charles Gardiner Hooper (7, Charles 6, Thomas 5, Major 4, Thomas 3, Clement 2, Stephen 1); born December 9, 1883 at Birch Hill, P.E.I.
Edmund Crosby Maxfield Hooper (7, Charles 6, Thomas 5, Major 4, Thomas 3, Clement 2, Stephen 1); born September 15, 1885 in Lot 5, P.E.I. My notes from Muriel Hooper Blanchard say, "killed March 11, 1918." One might assume that he was in World War I, but I am not certain.

Colin MacLennon Hooper (6, Thomas 5, Major 4, Thomas 3, Clement 2, Stephen 1) the eighth child of Thomas and Maria, had the following four children (surname Hooper, seventh generation):

Hollie (or Hallie) Winnifred Hooper (7, Colin 6, Thomas 5, Major 4, Thomas 3, Clement 2, Stephen 1), born November 14, 1869 in Nebraska, U.S.A.
Ethel Ann Hooper (7, Colin 6, Thomas 5, Major 4, Thomas 3, Clement 2, Stephen 1) born June 10, 1876 in Summerside, P.E.I.
Frank Bernard Hooper (7, Colin 6, Thomas 5, Major 4, Thomas 3, Clement 2, Stephen 1) born June 18, 1878 in Nebraska, U.S.A.
Fancheon Marie Hooper (7, Colin 6, Thomas 5, Major 4, Thomas 3, Clement 2, Stephen 1) born March 8, 1887 in Nebraska, U.S.A. I have no more information on the above family.

Ann Hooper, called Nancy, (6, Ann 5, Major 4, Thomas 3, Clement 2, Stephen 1) and James Clark had five children (surname Clark, seventh generation):

Wilfred D. Clark (7, Ann 6, Ann 5, Major 4, Thomas 3, Clement 2, Stephen 1) born 1869. No more information available
Gertrude Clark (7, Ann 6, Ann 5, Major 4, Thomas 3, Clement 2, Stephen 1) born 1871. No more information available
Frederick W. Clark (7, Ann 6, Ann 5, Major 4, Thomas 3, Clement 2, Stephen 1) born June 6, 1873; died September 6, 1902
James E. Clark (7, Ann 6, Ann 5, Major 4, Thomas 3, Clement 2, Stephen 1) born 1876 No more information available
Harriet L. Clark (7, Ann 6, Ann 5, Major 4, Thomas 3, Clement 2, Stephen 1) born October 31, 1882; died January 30, 1903. No more information available

Adella Jane Hooper (6, John 5, Major 4, Thomas 3, Clement 2, Stephen 1), first child of John Keir and Jane Walker Hooper, (1852-February 1, 1936), age 83. Adella married Christopher Lowther and had the following children (surname Lowther, seventh generation):

Major Hooper Lowther (7, Adella 6, John 5, Major 4, Thomas 3, Clement 2, Stephen 1), born 1874; married on January 6, 1907 to Adeline "Addie" Sinclair; died in Searletown in 1963. Mrs. Lowther was born in 1881 and died in 1950 after she had had a stroke. I have a copy of the newspaper report of Major and Addie's wedding, given to me by their daughter, Gladys Henderson. The news item read as follows:

The residence of Mrs. Sinclair, wife of the late Hon. Peter Sinclair, Summerfield, was the scene of a very happy event on Wednesday evening, the 6th, when there was solemnized by Rev. John Murray Clifton, the marriage of her eldest daughter, Janet Adeline, to Major Hooper Lowther of Searletown. The bride who was handsomely attired in an ivory lace robe over satin du chene, and who wore a bridal veil caught with orange blossoms, was attended by her sister, Miss Winnifred, who wore white with blue trimmings. The groom, the son of Christopher Lowther, Searletown, was supported by the bride's cousin, Dr. J. A. McMurdo, Summerside. Miss Ethel Walker of Kensington, another cousin of the bride, played the wedding march, "Lohengrin's bridal chorus." [Ethel Mae Walker was the daughter of William and Catherine (MacMurdo) Walker and was born on June 8, 1885 in Kensington; she married Frederick Hughes Clark of Wilmot Valley on November 11, 1909 in Kensington.] On the conclusion of the ceremony, the large number of guests assembled, being the immediate friends and relatives of the contracting parties, spent a very enjoyable evening. A musical selection rendered by Miss Lena Murray of Clifton, was much applauded, and added greatly to the evening's enjoyment. A large number of wedding presents were [sic] received, which in themselves, bear testimony to the popularity of the bride and groom.

Gladys told the author that her father went to the wedding with a horse and sleigh, but because of the January thaw when he was at the wedding, he and his new bride went home with a horse and wagon!

In response to my question, Gladys told me a bit about her father (Ada Hooper and Major Lowther were first cousins). On his farm he had horses, cows, pigs, and 300 hens at one time. The eggs were graded in Bedeque and the hens were sold in Moncton. At one time there were four generations living in the house on the Albany Road in Searletown: Major and Addie, his mother Adella who had an ex-

tension on the back of the house, Gladys and Neil, and two of their children. Gladys said that her father never spoke an unkind word! He enjoyed reading, especially poetry. He could be as "stubborn as a mule," however.

Alden's Aunt, Jennie Hooper, was very fond of her first cousin, Major. Each summer when she visited the Island from Massachusetts, where she lived, she and Major would read poetry and the Bible together. She often talked about Major. Of course, they had both grown up on the Island. Major had 100 acres of land that bordered the parents of our next-door cottage neighbor, Bud Craig [It is sometimes a small world!].

When Aunt Jennie visited in the summer, Gladys would drive her to Travellers Rest (a village) to visit a MacNeil woman who married a Matheson. This lady was apparently a former neighbor in North Carleton.

Major and Addie had two children (eighth generation, surname Lowther):

Gladys Winnifred Lowther (8, Major 7, Adella 6, John 5, Major 4, Thomas 3, Clement 2, Stephen 1); born January 24, 1914 in Searletown, P.E.I.; married (i) in Bedeque, P.E.I., in 1933, Neil Thomas Bradshaw, the son of Thomas Wright Bradshaw and Mary Pearl MacFadyen. Neil was born on July 20, 1907.

Neil is perhaps the person most responsible for our going to P.E.I. He and Gladys, Joan, and Garth had come to the North Shore of the Boston area in 1953, when Alden was in college, for a visit. Of course, Ada had them for a meal/meals and they got acquainted. Ada had not returned to "the Island" since she had left as a girl. Aunt Jennie used to go to "the Island" every year, and would stay at Gladys's and her father's (Major who was Ada and Jennie's first cousin). When Alden and I were ready to go to "the Island" in 1970, it was Neil with whom we corresponded. Gladys was most hospitable as was Neil when we arrived, and during our visit they would often entertain us in their home for dinner. We stayed on the campground that Joan

Bradshaw Lefurgey and her husband, Ross Lefurgey, and Bill Callbeck owned. After we left, Alden corresponded with Neil, and we returned the following year. Through the years Alden and Neil kept up a correspondence.

Neil had been a farmer. He farmed with his father-in-law on the original Gabriel Strang farm, one of the first to be settled in Searletown, P.E.I. In his later years he drove a school bus. I can remember that he went one summer (probably 1971) to pick up a new bus and drive it back to P.E.I. perhaps from Windsor, Ontario, for the school district.

Neil and Gladys sold the farm and built a new home about 1972 in Searletown on the way from Seven Mile Bay to Bedeque. It was built on property that they already owned on the southwest end of the farm on the North Carleton Road, and was a continuation of what they owned across the street from their Albany farm. The farmland was sold to his brother, Malcolm. Neil developed a heart condition, but it was cancer of the prostate which ended his life on July 16, 1975.

The house that Gladys's children grew up in had been her parents' home, and before that her grandparents.' I believe that the property is the same as that of John Wright and his wife Elizabeth Robins of the fifth generation of Hoopers. Gladys told me in the summer of 2001 that the extension that was put on the back of the house for Adella, Gladys's grandmother, was moved after she no longer needed it, and is now a house in its own right in Carleton. As one is going toward Borden, it would be on the right just past Allison and Bernice Harper's house on the other side of the street before turning the corner. At the same time Gladys told me that Adella raised turkeys for Christmas dinners when she lived in Searletown. One year, just before Christmas, some "people" in a sleigh came at night into the yard in the snow, took all the turkeys and went on their way. That year they made the profit from the turkey meat, not Mrs. Lowther!

Life on Prince Edward Island was changing in various ways for many people in the eighth generation, such as Gladys. By the late 1920s and early 1930s several families had telephones, and listening in on party lines became a diversion for some! Outhouses were still prevalent, but heated water was becoming popular as water was pumped into the house from the outside well to a barrel that was attached to the kitchen stove. Bleach was not needed as fabric would be put in the sun or on the snow in winter. In either case, the sun was a wonderful bleaching agent as it is today.[4] I look forward to putting my wash on the line in Chelton in the summer to get white things whiter! For that reason I do not want an electric dryer when I stay on the Island.

In the 1930s many families still had cows, horses, and sheep. The wool would be sent away to be processed after the children had combed it many times to get the debris out of it. The white yarn was used for knitting and the gray yarn was made into blankets. Lambing time was in April.

Gladys married (ii) Arnold Henderson, of Bedeque, on October 15, 1985. He died rather suddenly at Prince County Hospital in Summerside from a heart condition on November 16, 1993. I have a copy of his obituary:

Henderson

The death occurred at Prince County Hospital on Wednesday, November 17, 1993, of Arnold Henderson of Searletown in his 83rd year. Born at Bedeque, he was the son of the late James and Mabel (Wright) Henderson. He was employed at Callbecks Ltd. for 25 years, retiring in 1986. He was a member and elder of Bedeque United Church. Survived by his wife Gladys (Bradshaw) Henderson as well as five step-children: Joan Lefurgey, Wilmot; Janet Tredenick, Summerside; Garth Bradshaw, Mount Uniacke, N. S.; Carol Bell, Lower Sackville, N. S.; Norma Palmer, Summerside, as well as 15 step grandchildren. Predeceased by his first wife Ruth Carruthers. Resting at the Moase Funeral Home until noon Friday, then to the Bedeque United Church for funeral service at 2 p.m. Interment in the North Bedeque Cemetery. Visiting hours Thursday 2-4 and 7-9 p.m. Memorial donations to the Prince County Hospital equipment fund or Bedeque United Church would be appreciated.

An interesting aside is that Arnold's mother was the granddaughter of Stephen Wright and his second wife. Arnold is the great-great-great-grandson of Nathaniel Wright, Loyalist. Gladys is the great-great-great-granddaughter of Thomas Hooper. The two Loyalists came from New York and New Jersey, respectively, about the same time, in 1783 or 1784, became friends, and the intermarriages continued two hundred years later!

I would be remiss not to mention that within a few months of Arnold Henderson's death, Gladys sold her home in Searletown and moved to a lovely rented apartment which she furnished beautifully in Summerside where three of her daughters live in homes of their own. Summerside is about 15 miles from Searletown and Chelton. We miss the nearness of Gladys very much. We are on the phone often and stop in to see her frequently when we are in Summerside, but it is not the same as being able to walk up the back unpaved road for about two miles and be at her home in Searletown. We often stopped in the evening to visit [via an automobile]!

Gladys and Neil had five children (ninth generation, surname Bradshaw). See Chapter Eleven.

Carman Sinclair Lowther, (8, Major Hooper 7, Adella 6, John 5, Major 4, Thomas 3, Clement 2, Stephen 1) was the second child of Major Hooper Lowther and Adeline Sinclair. Born in Albany, P.E.I. on October 15, 1918, he worked in a Summerside Bank as a young man. He married Ruth Hilda Oliphant on August 29, 1945. In Belleville, Ontario, he ran an electrical business which his son William took over and still operates (1999).

"Carm" was a pilot instructor during World War II. He enjoyed sailing and travelling in his motor home; he also loved to read. When Carm, Ruth, and Suzanne were visiting Gladys, perhaps in 1989, they came for a short visit to see us and we were delighted to meet them. Carm and Gladys were close to each other as brother and sister.

Carman died on September 26, 1991 of lymphoma while Gladys and Arnold were on a trip to the west coast. Gladys was saddened that she was not available for the funeral of her dear brother. Carm and Ruth had two children (ninth generation, surname Lowther).

The second child of **Adella Hooper** and Christopher Lowther was **Grace Maud Lowther** (7, Adella 6, John 5, Major 4, Thomas 3, Clement 2, Stephen 1) born 1877; married on June 22, 1904 Archibald MacKenzie who died in 1964 in Searletown, P.E.I. Archie's father John, a tailor, was born in Scotland and married Bessie, the daughter of Squire George and Ann (MacIntosh) MacKay. Archie's grandfather, John MacKenzie and his wife Catherine MacLeod, were natives of Raasay, an island off the coast of the Isle of Skye, and came to P.E.I. around 1839, settling in Hartsville. Grace and Archie lived in a beautiful house in Kensington, next to the United Church on School Street. Grace died in 1957 in her 81st year. Their daughter Dorothy, who lived with them, built a house on a piece of the property after her parents died and sold the house that she and her sisters had grown up in. In July 1999, Dot gave me a copy of the newspaper report of the wedding of her parents. Because Dot has visual difficulties, I typed a copy of the wedding in very large print. How wonderful it is to have interesting records of such important family events! The news item reads:

On the evening of the 22nd June [1904], a pleasant company assembled at "The Willows," Searletown, the home of Mr. and Mrs. Christopher Lowther, to celebrate the nuptials of their only daughter, Grace Maud and J. Archibald MacKenzie of Springfield, Lot 67. The ceremony was performed by Rev. D. McLeod, cousin of the groom. The bride looked charming in a gown of white peau-de-soie and carried a shower bouquet of val-de-lis. She was attended by Miss Katie MacKenzie, Kensington, sister of the groom, who was attired in a dainty costume of white organdie. The groom was supported by Mr. Major Lowther, brother of the bride. The wedding march was beautifully rendered by Miss Aitken, Montague. Mrs. MacKenzie, who is a general favorite, was the recipient of many beautiful and valuable presents, among which was an elaborate silver celery dish from Aurora Division. Immediately after the ceremony, the wedding supper was served and at

an early hour the happy couple left for their future home in Springfield, followed by the best wishes of their many friends.

Grace Lowther (7, Adella 6, John 5, Major 4, Thomas 3, Clement 2, Stephen 1) and Archie MacKenzie had three daughters as follows (surname MacKenzie, eighth generation):

Florence MacKenzie (8, Grace 7, Adella 6, John 5, Major 4, Thomas 3, Clement 2, Stephen 1), born July 20, 1905; married Trevor Way, a dentist in Charlottetown, P.E.I. He died in 1987; she died in 1985. Florence, a registered nurse, and Trevor had one son (ninth generation, surname Way).

Dorothy Adella MacKenzie (8, Grace 7, Adella 6, John 5, Major 4, Thomas 3, Clement 2, Stephen 1) was born in Springfield, P.E.I. (Lot 67) on August 31, 1907. She and her two sisters grew up on a farm there until 1914 when they moved to Kensington where her father also farmed and eventually became quite successful in the fox farming industry.

Harold Cairns's research for his *Descendants of David Walker*, gives an interesting biography of Dorothy, known as "Dot":

After graduation from high school, Dot took a business course from Union Commercial in Charlottetown and went on to work at the Bank of Nova Scotia in Kensington for 17 years and the Bank of Nova Scotia in Ottawa for one year. Dot came home during the war years and worked at the original Prince County Hospital as the admitting clerk for seven years. When the new hospital was built (ca.1952), she took a job with the Town of Summerside, and it was from there that she retired in 1972.

Aside from her career, Dot was busy with volunteer work and involvement in her church, Kensington United. She has been a CGIT (Christian Girls in Training) leader, an explorer leader, and a choir member for over 50 years. Music has played a very important role in her life, she said. She enjoyed playing basketball, volleyball, and skating as well as travelling especially by train. She has visited many parts of the U.S. as well as the west coast of Canada.[5]

Dot did not marry. She had her house built about 1969 on School Street, Kensington on the lot next to her parents' house which had been sold. She lived there alone until May 2000 when she went into the Andrews Lodge as a resident. Dorothy had macular degeneration and could see very little. She was the first Islander to visit us in the summer of 1971 when she came to Long Island to see her cousin on her father's side in Bellerose, Nassau County. Dorothy died at Prince County Hospital, Summerside, P.E.I., October 24, 2005, aged 98 years. She was the last surviving member of the late J. Archibald and Grace M. (Lowther) MacKenzie. Interment was in People's Cemetery, Kensington.

Marjorie MacKenzie (8, Grace 7, Adella 6, John 5, Major 4, Thomas 3, Clement 2, Stephen 1), born 1911; married Ralph MacMillan who died July 31, 1989 in Summerside, P.E.I. She died in the summer of 1988 in Summerside. Marjorie and Ralph had three children (surname MacMillan, ninth generation).

Jane Walker Hooper (7, Major 6, John 5, Major 4, Thomas 3, Clement 2, Stephen 1) was named for her Hooper grandmother, John's wife; she was called "Jennie" by everyone but Dot MacKenzie, her cousin, who calls her Janie yet; she was born February 2, 1887 on the family farm in North Carleton, P.E.I. Jennie was baptized on July 13, 1890. She went to work in Haverhill, MA, with her cousin, Lila Allen, who lived next door. Later I will relate a story which is interesting to me regarding her travel and work in Massachusetts which became her home.

As I think of Jennie, it reminds me of why so many Islanders went to the "Boston States." While perusing the book, *If You're Stronghearted*, by Dr. Edward MacDonald, I found an interesting paragraph. In addition to going to the Prairie Provinces, many Islanders went South: "The pull of New England remained strong as well. Compared to the rest of the Maritimes, a disproportionate

number of Islanders settled in 'the Boston States' as the region was generally known. It was nearby; its economy was booming; it was culturally familiar; and it had cheap sea and rail links, as well as a long history of traffic with the Island."[6]

After her father's death in 1914, Jennie returned to North Carleton to run the farm for a few years with the help (?) of her two mentally handicapped brothers. After they were institutionalized and she sold the farm, Jennie returned to work in Haverhill, MA. She never married, and after her retirement as a seamstress, she made her home with her cousin, Lila Allen MacLeod, and Lila's daughter, Verna Clay, in Bradford, MA, a suburb of Haverhill, about an hour's drive from Saugus where Jennie's sister Ada lived. Aunt Jennie had been in and out of Hale Hospital in Haverhill several times. She died on January 25, 1968 at 4:30 a.m. of congestive heart failure. There is a reason for the detail as the reader will see later.

To digress again in telling about Aunt Jennie's summer trips to "the Island," I think it is interesting for the reader to know that the trip from Haverhill to P.E.I., a distance of about 12 hours by car today, was not always so easy. Aunt Jennie never had a car or a driver's license, but she went to her "roots" every summer for years and years. Many times she went with her cousin, Lila, Lila's husband Fulton, and their girls, Verna and Helen, in Fulton's car. During World War II when gasoline was rationed, she would take the train which went from Boston to P.E.I. with stops and changes from time to time. Recently Alden was given a train timetable by a neighbor who collects euphemia. This Boston and Maine timetable was one that Jennie would have used to go to Canada in 1945 or 1946. The train finally went on the ferry across the Northumberland Strait. Jenny would get off at Borden where the ferry docked, and Gladys or Major, Gladys's father and Jennie's cousin, would pick her up and take her to their home.

Ferry boats have been operating across Northumberland Strait since the late 1800s. I have a newspaper clipping from June 30, 1947, post-war, regarding the newest ferry at that time:

**New Car Ferry, *Abegweit*,
Formally Named Saturday
by Mrs. Jones, wife of the Island Premier**

Sorel, Que., June 28 - Heaviest ship ever built in a Canadian shipyard, the car ferry *Abegweit* was formally named today in ceremonies which preceded her entry into service as the main link between Prince Edward Island and the Mainland.

The Abegweit, world's largest ice-breaking car ferry, was named by Mrs. J. Walter Jones, wife of the Premier of Prince Edward Island. On the platform with Mrs. Jones were representatives of the Dominion Government, including Transport Minister Chevrier, the Department of Transport, Canadian National Railways and Marine Industires Limited, in whose Sorel yards the Abegweit was built.

Shortly after the naming ceremony, the streamlined diesel-electric ship continued her trials, after which she will be drydocked for final inspection and then will go into service between Borden, P.E.I., and Cape Tormentine, N.B. Operating across Northumberland Strait, she will carry 19 railway cars, 60 automobiles, and 950 passengers. She is expected to be in regular operation by mid-July.

The *Abegweit* was built by Marine Industries Limited to replace the *S. S. Charlottetown* which was sunk after striking a reef while en route to Saint John, N.B. for a refit. The new ship, like the *Charlottetown* and the *Prince Edward Island* which has been carrying on the service in recent years, will be operated by Canadian National Railways.

Completion of the *Abegweit* established a wide range of precedents in Canadian shipubuilding. As well as being the heaviest ship in Canadian ship-building history, she is the world's largest and most powerful ice-breaking car ferry, the first heavy diesel-electric ship built in Canada, and one of North America's largest all-welded vessels. In addition, she was launched last fall from the world's largest marine railway at the yards of Marine Industries here.

The *Abegweit* has a gross tonnage of 7,500 tons, which is in excess of the gross tonnage of 10,000 deadweight-ton freighters launched at Marine Industries and other Canadian shipyards during the War. She is 372 feet long with a breadth of 63 feet and a loaded depth of 19 feet. Her service speed is 17 knots.

Eight double diesel engines operate electric motors producing 12,500 horsepower to turn the *Abegweit's* four propellers - two of which are at the stern and two in the bow. The bow propellers help the ship to manoeuvre and in addition aid in ice-breaking by sucking water out from under the ice through which the ship's heavily-reinforced bow crushes.

The *Abegweit* carries a name long famous in Prince Edward Island - the name given to the Island by the Micmac Indians. Its literal translation is "The Home Cradled on the Waves."

Upwards of 2000 persons attended the ceremony.

The *M.V. Abegweit*, called the "Abby," was the largest of the three ferries traversing the Northumberland Strait, until 1997, when the "fixed link" [Confederation Bridge] was completed. She was a comfortable and rather luxurious vessel. The bridge that replaced it is one of the longest in the world.

Melvina Hooper, called Millicent, (7, Major 6, John 5, Major 4, Thomas 3, Clement 2, Stephen 1) was born November 19, 1889 at home in North Carleton.. She was baptized on July 13, 1890, by the Rev. John Goodwill. She was unmarried and died on December 12, 1910 [five years almost to the day after her mother's death] at age 21, probably of tuberculosis. Mr. MacQuarrie (one of the "old-timers," mentioned in the next chapter, and a neighbor and a long-time family friend) told us that she was also pregnant with Billy Doule's baby. Her pregnancy probably exacerbated the TB. Dr. Ballem signed the death certificate. Her tombstone in the Church of Scotland Cemetery in Cape Traverse lists her year of death as 1911; that date should read 1910.

I have a school picture, compliments of Jean Schurman, whose father, Heber, was in the class, taken perhaps about 1905. All five Hooper children are in the picture; it is the only picture of the family that I know of in existence. We treasure this picture! Thank you, Jean Schurman!

Norman Major Hooper (7, Major 6, John 5, Major 4, Thomas 3, Clement 2, Stephen 1) born March 29, 1894, the third child and first boy. He was baptized on December 10, 1896. Unmarried, he died March 29, 1929 [on his birthday] at age 35. Gladys told me in 2000 that as there were no family members remaining, his body was brought from Charlottetown by train to Albany and was picked up (probably by Major Lowther) and taken to the Lowther home in Searletown where he was laid out. Dr. Goodwill signed his death certificate. A horse and wagon took his body to the cemetery in Cape Traverse. Like Ada and his father, Norman had red hair. Norman was mentally handicapped to a greater degree than his brother, Robbie.

***Ada Ann Hooper** (7, Major 6, John 5, Major 4, Thomas 3, Clement 2, Stephen 1) born March 5, 1896; baptized November 9, 1897, by the Rev. J. Goodwill, baptismal name Annie Eva; married Charles Stone O'Neil of Boston, MA on August 20, 1921; died on January 25, 1968 at 9 p.m. at her home at 4 Park Street, Saugus, MA of an embolus to the lung. She had been in bed all day with what she thought was "the flu." She and her sister Jennie died the same day; Jennie's death was expected, Ada's was not. About 7 p.m. Ada had a very severe pain in a shoulder. She asked her husband to get her a hot water bottle, "as hot as you can get it." He brought it to her and started down the stairs, but before he got to the bottom of the stairs an embolus had gone to her lung and she was dead!

The last time that Ada had visited Jennie in the hospital, Jennie had been trying to say something that Ada couldn't understand - something about what was in a box at home. In retrospect, she was probably telling her sister to destroy the evidence that they had had mentally handicapped brothers on P.E.I. (both of whom were now dead).

Alden and Nancy Neal Coll.

Charles and Ada (Hooper) Neal (O'Neil),
leaving their home in Saugus, MA, Easter 1956

In any event, Verna found the "evidence" and Lila's girls and Ada's children were shocked to say the least by the knowledge! Lila had died over 2 ½ years earlier. No one had ever told Lila or Ada's children that there were two Hooper boys in the family. We all thought that Alden's mother had two sisters only, one of whom had died young. In fact, in answer to my pointed questions about her siblings, she stated that there were three girls, no boys in the family. Her embarrassment by the retardation of her brothers must have been *so* great that it overshadowed everything else - like being truthful. How awful for her and Jenny! They perhaps thought that retardation was something which was inherited as I recall how *very* upset she was when Lois was pregnant with her third child, Lynbeth, fearful that something would go wrong!

The visiting hours for Jennie from the Rogers Funeral Home in Haverhill were Friday evening, January 26 with the burial service at the funeral home on Saturday, January 27. I had never seen Aunt Jennie look lovelier than she did in her casket; she really looked beautiful and peaceful! Burial was in the Linwood Cemetery in Haverhill on Saturday afternoon. We had two funeral cars for the family; one (ours) was in an accident leaving the cemetery!

On Saturday evening, January 27, visiting hours were held for Ada at the Bisbee Funeral Home in Cliftondale, Saugus. All of the children and their spouses were there. The evening was bitterly cold yet long, long lines of people waited outside on the sidewalk to gain access inside to see Ada and visit with the family. It was a lovely tribute to her. On Sunday afternoon at 3 o'clock, the funeral service was held at the Cliftondale Church of the Nazarene with Dr. J. Glenn Gould, the minister who had married Charlie and Ada in 1921, officiating. The church was filled with family and friends. Because the gravediggers did not work on Sundays, Ada could not be buried until Monday morning in Peabody. The five children of Ada and Charles (surname O'Neil, eighth generation) are as follows:

Lillian Frances O'Neil (named for her Aunt Lillian [her father's sister], but called Frances, or Fran (8, Ada 7, Major 6, John 5, Major 4, Thomas 3, Clement 2, Stephen 1), born January 17, 1923 in the back part of the house her parents rented on Lincoln Avenue, Cliftondale, opposite the end of Park Street; married April 11, 1947 to Alwyn E. Stickney, born on March 30, 1926, son of William Stickney and Wilhelmina Froberg. Fran and Al live (2000) at One Elmwood Avenue, Saugus, MA where they have lived for about 50 years. After her children were partially grown, Fran worked in insurance agencies as a front office representative to the public. She retired in June 1990. [An update: the house in which they had lived for 55 years was sold on September 30, 2002, and they moved to a senior housing complex about two blocks from where they lived for so many years. Al died on October 10, 2002 of cancer of the colon and liver. He had symptoms only since late July 2002. Al was well-liked and his funeral was well attended. Fran and Al (surname Stickney, ninth generation) had three sons. (Please see Chapter Eleven)

Paul Austin O'Neil (8, Ada 7, Major 6, John 5, Major 4, Thomas 3, Clement 2, Stephen 1) born on September 3, 1926, in the same house in which Frances had been born, with Dr. Furbush again delivering the baby. Paul married Lois Anderson, daughter of Mr. and Mrs. Alfred Anderson, of New Canaan, CT, at the Church of the Nazarene in Norwalk, CT, on July 14, 1951. Paul received a bachelor of theology degree from Eastern Nazarene College and served as a minister in the Church of the Nazarene in Pittsfield, ME, Springfield, MA, Kansas City, MO, and Ashland, KY. In later years he was a sales representative for the Nazarene Publishing House and continues in that occupation in 2004 on a part time basis. Lois was an elementary school teacher and later a guidance counsellor in a high school. They have lived in Kentucky for over 30 years (2004). Paul and Lois have three daughters (ninth generation, surname O'Neil/Neal).

Millicent Neal (8, Ada 7, Major 6, John 5, Major 4, Thomas 3, Clement 2, Stephen 1) [notice the change in the surname] I gather that Lillian O'Neil Varney, Charlie O'Neil's older sister, was influential in his changing his surname. At the time, the Irish Catholics domi-

nated Boston politics. The name O'Neil was common among the firemen, the policemen, and the politicians. Apparently Lillian had a very strong personality and was decidedly persuasive. She, it would appear, did not want her brother's name to be associated with the Irish! Who knows why she cared as her name was no longer O'Neil, and *her* married name sounded waspy enough! Over the years I have come to believe that there is something unsavory about which to be embarrassed by association with the name Matthew Joseph O'Neil, Lillian's and Charlie's father. It appears that he may have left when Charlie was about six years old, not to be heard from again!

Millicent was the first of the O'Neil/Neal children to be born in a hospital, the Lynn Hospital, Lynn, MA and the first to come home to their new house at 4 Park Street, Cliftondale, a section of Saugus. At this time, and for a while previously, Charlie Neal worked as a machinist in the Round House of the Boston and Maine Rail Road. He did well financially, and they had saved for a new home which Alfred Haley, a neighbor at 15 Palmer Avenue, built for them. It is interesting to note that Mr. Haley's two daughters, Thelma and Geraldine, still live in their father's house (2005) whose property abuts the former Charlie and Ada Neal house. When we go to Saugus, we visit the Haley sisters as well as Fran and Al. For some reason, the Neals had only two bedrooms in their house which in 1927 would already seem inadequate.

Millicent, their third child, was born on May 16, 1928; married Herbert Mark White, son of William White and Vida Thistle (both born in 1900 in Newfoundland), on July 3, 1952; died on March 19, 1975 of cardiomyopathy (a viral infection of unknown origin of the heart muscle). She was sick for perhaps three years, was in bed much of the time, and was told by a cardiologist at Massachusetts General Hospital in Boston that her only option for living was a heart transplant. Of course, in 1974, that wasn't a very viable option; it was pretty much comparable to a death sentence. Despite her fatigue and her knowledge of the prognosis, she was an optimistic person with a great sense of humor, laughing a lot! She ruled the family from her bed! Millicent had a wonderful talent for creating a beautiful home;

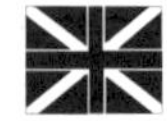

she said that color and contrast were very important. She and Herb bought their large, gorgeous home in Danvers in 1971, and she did a fantastic job decorating it tastefully. According to Alden she was always a hard-working student; she went to the North Shore Community College and earned an Associate degree. Alden was fond of his sister Millicent; he says she paved the way for him in school by being the good, conscientious student that she was, willing to take responsibility. Millicent and Herb have two children (ninth generation, surname White).

Alden Hooper Neal (8, Ada, 7, Major 6, John 5, Major 4, Thomas 3, Clement 2, Stephen 1) born January 30, 1933 in the Lynn Hospital, Lynn, MA; married Nancy Elizabeth Ellis, daughter of Harold Mervyn Ellis and Edith Florence Maxim of East Wareham, MA, on June 25, 1955. Alden earned a Bachelor of Arts degree from Eastern Nazarene College, a Master of Education degree from Bridgewater State College, and a Professional diploma (42 defined college credits beyond

Alden and Nancy Neal Coll.

New Year's Day at Alden and Nancy Neal's home in East Wareham, MA, 1956

Left to Right: Lois Neal, Ada Neal, Walter Olson, Lorraine Olson, and Paul Neal.

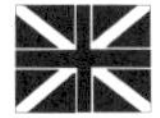

the master's degree) in reading from Hofstra University. In addition he took many graduate courses at C. W. Post, Long Island University. During his teaching career he taught children in grades 5 through 9 primarily. Nancy got her basic nursing education at the New England Deaconess Hospital in Boston, and earned the Bachelor of Nursing degree at Boston University and the Master of Nursing degree at Emory University in Atlanta, Georgia.

Alden's mother told the author that he had whooping cough when he was six months old, and she did not think that he would survive. Ruth Thornell (later to marry Fred Bagnell Essery whose families on both sides were from PEI), a neighbor and a friend from church, helped her with the housework and the child care. Many, many years later, Ada still talked about appreciating Ruth's help and didn't know how she could have coped had she not had Ruth's assistance. The Charles Neal family had 4 children 7 years of age and younger at this time. Alden and Nancy have two children (ninth generation, surname Neal).
Lorraine Ruth Neal (8, Ada 7, Major 6, John 5, Major 4, Thomas 3, Clement 2, Stephen 1) born January 6, 1934 in Lynn Hospital, Lynn, MA; married (i) Walter Olson, born May 1932 to Edwin and Carolyn Sumner Olson, on May 2, 1953. Walter was in the U. S. Army during the Korean War and left for active duty a few days after they were married. After he returned, he became a teacher and Lorraine worked in a bank and later played the organ in a lounge of a restaurant. Lorraine and Walter had two children (ninth generation, surname Olson).

Lorraine and Walter were divorced, and he later remarried and had two additional children who would not be Hooper relatives. Walter died on July 2, 1980 at Boston University Hospital after surgery. Lorraine married (ii) Roy Christie, son of LeRoy and Pauline Christie, of Boston, on December 29, 1979.

Robert Glover Hooper (7, Major 6, John 5, Major 4, Thomas 3, Clement 2, Stephen 1) born February 13, 1899 in North Carleton; baptized on November 4, 1900 by the Rev. Donald Campbell; unmarried; died on June 10, 1961 at age 60 in Charlottetown, P.E.I.. Dr. Penhold signed his death certificate. Robbie's body was taken to a

funeral home in Tryon. More people came for the visiting hours than were expected. He was mentally handicapped (but, according to Gladys, less severely than Norman) and had been in a Charlottetown institution, Riverside Hospital, as there was no one at home to care for him. Robbie would take the bus from Riverside, which was near the Charlottetown waterfront, to the Charlottetown Exhibition, for instance.

His name was of interest to me, and I did a bit of research on it. Here is what I found: Glover, according to Mr. MacQuarrie (one of the "old-timers" mentioned in the next chapter), was a family name between Summerside and Kensington. More importantly is the fact that Robert Glover was a person in the Walker family, a relative of Jane Walker Hooper, the grandmother of Robert Glover Hooper. Margaret Hetherington Walker (a third generation Walker in P.E.I.) married John Glover; Robert was born to them as their child in 1877 in Kensington, P.E.I. Both John Walker and Jean Weir, the parents of Jane, were born in Scotland and emigrated to Prince Edward Island in 1820. Jane Walker's brother, David, was the grandfather of Robert Glover, making Jane the great aunt.[7]

All of the Hooper children but Jennie and Ada are buried in the churchyard of the beautiful little Church of Scotland in Cape Traverse. You could see this church across Northumberland Strait on a clear day on the ferry going between Cape Tormentine, N. B., and Borden, P.E.I. [The last ferry run was on May 31, 1997] One can still see the white Church of Scotland from the Confederation Bridge as well.

Before leaving this family, I would like to present a possible explanation about the mental retardation of the two boys, Norman and Robert. Those who knew Norman and Robbie say that they did not have Downes Syndrome. [At least one of them, Robbie, had red hair as did Ada and their father] Mr. MacQuarrie had told us that Major Hooper was "not good with children." In the family were, first, two girls, then a boy, a girl, and a boy. It could be that the boys were rather rambunctious, annoying the father who wanted to put a stop to noisy, overactive behavior. Alden and I have a good friend from England who is in chemical research. He has done post-doc-

toral studies and is probably the most brilliant person we know. He suggested on a visit to P.E.I. that Major may have given or had his wife give the boys "the powders," not unheard-of in England at that time, to quiet them. The "powders" contained lead and would settle a small child with adequate dosage. We know today that ingestion of lead can lead to mental retardation. It's a theory which we will not be able to test, but it sounds reasonable as only the two boys were affected. According to those who knew the boys, Norman's retardation was more severe than Robbie's. Robbie could take the bus in Charlottetown and get around the city which was rather small when he entered the facility. [Ada was the only one of the Hooper's five children to marry and/or have children. None of her children, grandchildren, great-grandchildren or great-great-grandchildren are mentally handicapped.

How kind and generous Major Lowther was to have Norman's funeral held at his home. He also had Robbie's body brought from Charlottetown to the Tryon funeral home where several people came to visit. His kindness was directed because there was no direct-line family on the Island, but also because that is the kind of man that he was.

Sarah Hooper (6, John 5, Major 4, Thomas 3, Clement 2, Stephen 1) was the third and last child of John Keir Hooper and his wife Jane Walker Hooper. We know nothing of her childhood except that she and her two siblings lived on the farm in North Carleton and her father died before she was born. After she married James Edwin Allen [called Ed], her brother, Major, gave her two acres of his property (which adjoined his) on which to build a house. Ed was a wheelwright and apparently a very talented man in building things. He and Sarah had five children (surname Allen, seventh generation):

Walden *Keir Allen* (7, Sarah 6, John 5, Major 4, Thomas 3, Clement 2, Stephen 1), born May 22, 1887 in North Carleton; married Margaret *Alice* MacQuarrie, born July 24, 1888 in North Carleton, on November 29, 1916 in Searletown, P.E.I. Alice was the sister of

Mr. Fred MacQuarrie, one of the "old-timers" quoted in the next chapter. She was also the sister of Mary who was taking care of the Hoopers when Mrs. Hooper had measles, contracted measles herself, and died.

Keir and Alice lived in Halifax, Nova Scotia, where Keir was working on a drag line dredge. The author believes that his brother, Reuben, had a job in the same company. They returned to the Island and lived on a farm in Middleton which is near the former home of Alma and Keith Affleck. It was sold many years ago and was near the beginning of the back road going to Charlottetown.

Viola had some remembrances of her dad which I would like to include: when Keir was nine years old, his dad left the family, never to return or support. Keir worked very hard on a farm near where he lived for a time; he was paid very poorly and wasn't given much to eat. As an adult Keir worked on the ferry in the engine room, but when the political leaders changed, he lost his job. He worked on the ice boats that went from Cape Traverse to New Brunswick, he ran a steam shovel, and worked in a gold mine. Early in their marriage, Keir and Alice lived in Halifax where he worked on a drag line dredge,

Alden and Nancy Neal Coll.

W. Keir Allen (1887-1961) and his wife, M. Alice MacQuarrie (1888-1968), were married at Searletown, P.E.I. on November 29, 1916. They resided in Halifax early in their marriage and later moved to Middleton, P.E.I. to farm. Keir was a great-great grandson of Thomas Hooper, the Loyalist.

then returned to P.E.I. and settled on a farm in Middleton. Keir died on October 18, 1961 from a massive heart attack. Alice died on December 1, 1968 of cancer of the colon. Keir and Alice had three children all born in Middleton, P.E.I. (surname Allen, eighth generation):

Alma Elsie Allen (8, Keir 7, Sarah 6, John 5, Major 4, Thomas 3, Clement 2, Stephen 1); born December 28, 1920 in Middleton, P.E.I.; married Keith Affleck, born on November 13, 1917, in Centreville Bedeque, on December 23, 1944. Alma and Keith had two children (surname Affleck, ninth generation):

Everett Walden Allen (8, Keir 7, Sarah 6, John 5, Major 4, Thomas 3, Clement 2, Stephen 1) born June 20, 1922; married Marion Leone Stetson of Freetown, on August 5, 1950. She was born on August 22, 1926 in Freetown, daughter of Willard Stetson and Eva Drummond. Everett died February 8, 1964 as a result of an automobile accident. I will quote from the newspaper report of the collision:

Deaths of Four People Due to Collision, Coroner's Jury States

A verdict of death by collision was brought in last night by a coroner's jury in the deaths of Keith Willard Stetson and Mrs. Eva Stetson of Freetown and Everett Waldon Allen and Sheldon Waldon Allen, Middleton, which occured as the result of an accident on the evening of February 8, 1964. The jury found that the collision was between a 1958 Meteor driven by Everett Allen and Irving Oil tanker trailer driven by Leland Murray.

Following a deliberation of approximately an hour the jury recommended "that a tanker trailer of this type have a low guard to prevent cars from getting underneath and preventing accidents of this type in the future." A total of nine witnesses testified at the inquest, including Carlene Stetson, 11, South Freetown, one of the occupants in the Allen car the night of the fatal crash. Also testifying were Dr. Roy Taylor, Summerside; Dr. Daniel Stewart, Bedeque; Harry Taylor, Kensington; Joseph Arnold Murray, Carleton; Leland Murray, East Royalty, the driver of the tanker trailer; Cnst. Allen Burchill, R.C.M.P., Borden; Raymond Henry Arsenault, Carleton, and a Mr. Coffin, a garage mechanic from Carleton. In his testimony Mr. Murray, the driver of the truck, said that on the night of the collision that the road conditions were poor due to a heavy snow storm which also made for poor visibility. As he came into the turn where the accident occurred at the intersection of

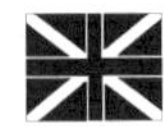

highway 1A and Highway 10, Mr. Murray, a veteran of 22 years of driving tractor trailers, said that the large vehicle "just didn't answer the wheel." He said that he had applied the brakes at the start of the turn and at the time of the collision the tractor was on the right side of the road. Mr. Murray was unable to say exactly where the trailer was at time of collision, but said that it possibly was on the white center line or perhaps a bit over the line. He said he couldn't tell, however, as there was about three inches of snow on the road and he was unable to tell where the centre line was. The driver testified that before the accident he was driving between 35 and 40 miles per hour and he didn't imagine he was driving any faster than 30 at the time of the collision. He said that as he was rounding the turn he saw a car coming through the cutting and "thought he was going to Bedeque." He added that it appeared as if the brakes had been applied on the car and "I pulled as far to the side of the road as I could." He heard the impact rather than felt it, Mr. Murray said.

Joseph Arnold Murray of Carleton, who along with his hired hand, Raymond Henry Arsenault, and Mr. Murray's son had been travelling some 50 yards behind the Irving truck for approximately ¾ of a mile prior to the accident, verified that the truck was travelling between 30 and 40 miles per hour prior to coming to the turn. Mr. Murray said that as the truck went into the turn the truck partially jacknifed, but the trailer stayed fairly steady. Having seen the lights of the oncoming car, Mr. Murray said, "I told my son there is going to be an accident." The witness testified that judging from where he was, the tractor was slightly over the white line. Mr. Arsenault also testified that the truck had slowed before the accident.

Carlene Stetson, one of the eight occupants in the car at the time of the crash, said she was in the back seat at the time of the accident and didn't recall how fast the car had been travelling at the time of the accident. Other survivors in the accident were Sheila Allen, daughter of Everett Allen, Mrs. Everett Allen, Mrs. Keir Allen, mother of Everett.

Dr.Daniel Stewart of Bedeque, who was called to the scene, testified that when he arrived at the scene Everett Allen was dead. Willard Stetson, he said, was still breathing, but died approximately 10 minutes after his arrival. The other occupants were taken by ambulance to Prince County Hospital where two were transferred to Halifax the following day, Mrs. Everett Allen and Mrs. Eva Stetson. Mrs. Stetson died there Feb. 11.

Coroner for last night's inquest was Dr. Charles Dewar, O'Leary. Also in attendance was Crown Prosecutor George R. McMahon. Members of the jury were Norman Leslie Reeves, foreman, North Bedeque; John Joseph Gallant, Albany; Patrick Leslie Smith, Kinkora; Sidney Charles Green, Central Bedeque; Horace Chesley Crossman, Central Bedeque; Lorne Everett Reeves, North Bedeque, and John Everett MacLellan, Kinkora.

Viola told the author that her brother and his family group were going home from having dinner at her home that evening. I recall Alden's mother being terribly distraught when she received the word of Everett's death. Ada and Keir were cousins who grew up next door to each other in North Carleton, P.E.I. Marion and Everett had two children (surname Allen, ninth generation).

Viola Celia Allen (8, Keir 7, Sarah 6, John 5, Major 4, Thomas 3, Clement 2, Stephen 1), born June 2, 1927; married Harry Edward Taylor, son of Major and Jessie Maude Taylor, born April 11, 1919, in Hamilton, P.E.I. They were married on June 30, 1948. Viola and Harry live in Kensington. In his early years Harry was a farmer in Hamilton. Then he went to work for Canadian National, working as a cook on the ferry that crossed Northumberland Strait. He retired several years ago. Viola worked for a time for the Tourist Bureau in Kensington and knows the sights to see on P.E.I.! Several years ago Viola and Harry sold their home and moved into an apartment where their grounds are maintained. Either one of them could easily live alone in their comfortable, 2-bedroom apartment. They have done their clearing out of outdated and unused articles and are ready for a good retirement. Alden and I have lots of fun playing cards and other games with Viola and Harry. Their kitchen or our dining room becomes converted into a place of laughter many times during the summer! We enjoy their company. They have two children (ninth generation, surname Taylor).

Reuben Sprague Allen (7, Sarah 6, John 5, Major 4, Thomas 3, Clement 2, Stephen 1), the second child of Sarah and Ed Allen, was born on June 6, 1890 in North Carleton; married Elizabeth Gertrude Francis, called Liza (September 23, 1891-June 1963); died November 5, 1962 at age 72. I have a copy of his obituary from a Halifax newspaper:

Former Carleton Man Dies in N. S.

Reuben S. Allen, well-known Halifax businessman, died at his home in Allen Heights, Head of St. Margaret's Bay, Monday at the age of 73 [he was actually 72].

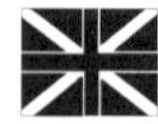

Alden and Nancy Neal Coll.

Reuben Sprague Allen and his sister, Vera Allen Hart (See p. 389)

Mr. Allen, who was founder of R. S. Allen Limited, excavating and demolition contractors, and president of the firm until his retirement last year, was born in Carleton, Prince Edward Island, and went to Halifax in 1905 [when he was only 15 years old!] to engage in construction work where he had since been a resident.

In 1955 Mr. Allen celebrated 50 years in the construction industry. Since his retirement, Mr. Allen had been developing his interest in Allen Heights, a subdivision he constructed in 1957-58.

Mr. Allen's son, Lloyd Allen, took over direction of the firm last year and is now president.

Son of the late James E. and Sarah Hooper Allen, Mr. Allen is survived by his wife, the former Elizabeth Francis, one son Lloyd, three [should be four] daughters, Thelma (Mrs. Calvin Clark), Dorothy (Mrs. D. F. Dorey), and Margaret, all of St. Margaret's Bay, and Jean (Mrs. Hubert Henderson) of Minneapolis, Minn; also one sister, Mrs. Fulton MacLeod [Lila] of Bradford, Mass., and 15 grandchildren.

The funeral will take place on Thursday in Halifax.

Rube had diabetes and, as his granddaughter Janet Murphy recalls, he would eat ice cream with the grandchildren, but they had to keep it a secret! She said that he was the best grandfather that a child could have! Rube died of a massive heart attack for which he was unable to get help. His devoted wife Liza died just a few months after Rube.

His daughter Thelma loved to tell humorous stories about "Dad" who was apparently a very generous man as well as, at times, a blunt person! Thelma could keep us laughing for a long time relating anecdotes about him! She has often told us of his presence and assistance in the great Halifax explosion which occurred in 1917. Alden remembers, when he was perhaps a teenager, Rube, Ada's first cousin, coming to Boston wearing a cowboy hat. He was a very distinguished person. Rube and Liza had five children (eighth generation, surname Allen), as follows:

Thelma Ethel Allen (8, Reuben 7, Sarah 6, John 5, Major 4, Thomas 3, Clement 2, Stephen 1) born May 31, 1913 in Halifax, N.S.; married Calvin Milo Clark, the son of Fred Clark and Lillian Doule, of Chelton, in November 1942 when Calvin was in the Canadian Forces during World War Two. Thelma died suddenly on June 14, 1999 in St. Margaret's Bay, Nova Scotia, where she and Calvin were visiting their daughter Barbara. Chelton, P.E.I. was not the same in the summer of 1999 without Thelma's presence. She had many physical problems with her eyes and her heart, and she had had two strokes from which she recovered well, but she was always an optimist. To hear her laughing and joking one would not know that there was

Remembrances of Calvin Clark:

1. A friendly, outgoing, generous man
2. A famlily man especially devoted to Thelma, his children, and Gail
3. Mr. "fix-it"
4. Not a clock watcher, but a man generous with his time
5. A great vegetable gardener, knowing how to get the most from the soil and the space
6. The man who immediately knew the person to contact for waterfront property on P.E.I. for the Neals
7. The overseer for building the Neal's cottage
8. The inventor of the wonderful cupboards between the studs on the walls - a great use of waste space. We have four or five such cupboards!
9. The builder of his own home in Chelton; then the person who added a dining room, then an enclosed sunroom toward Janet and Jim's, followed by an entryway to the kitchen with closets and storage space, and finally an oversized garage.
10. The teller of stories with Thelma about her mother and father as well as his work experiences at CBC and Sears
11. A parent proud of Janet's accomplishments in wallpapering, baking bread and birthday cakes, making donuts, etc.
12. A parent proud of the capable way Janet spotlessly cleaned their home in Chelton and the tasteful way that she arranged and re-arranged the furniture.

With Love,
Nancy and Alden Neal

anything wrong with her. Her memory was fantastic; she could relate at will funny episodes from the past which would put us in peals of laughter. Thelma was also a wonderful cook and to be invited to her home for dinner was a treat! She seemed to work at her cooking almost effortlessly! She is sorely missed! She shared great recipes that I will cherish and bought me several Maritime cookbooks. She, as well as her father, was a very generous person.

Calvin (August 3, 1920 - September 23, 2000) was the overseer of the building of our cottage. In July 1988, when we decided that we wanted to buy waterfront property to build a cottage, we were visiting Thelma and Calvin. It was he who telephoned Garth Toombs, who owned two waterfront lots across the cove from where Thelma and Calvin lived, to inquire about buying a lot. Garth came over in about 15 minutes, showed us the two lots which were side by side, and with a handshake and a $500.00 check drawn on a U.S. bank as a down payment on the property, we would be the owners of a waterfront lot. Sally chastised us for not buying both of them, but when we telephoned after we had arrived in New York, we found that the other lot had been sold to Margaret Ann and Bud Craig who became our very good neighbors. Interestingly, the reader may connect Bud's name (Charles) with a distant cousin of Alden. That's right, these neighbors are cousins [Hooper relatives]!

Calvin chose a builder for us, and we came to Chelton in April 1988 to meet him, staying at Thelma and Calvin's home. I had drawn up the plans over the winter, showed them to Donnie MacFarlane who started building the cottage in May 1988 with the help of Bannie Coughlin. They worked all summer on our cottage with Calvin as the overseer. While we owe a big debt of gratitude to Neil Bradshaw for keeping in touch with us early in our visits to P.E.I. and to Gladys for being so hospitable to our family, we would be remiss not to include the contributions of Calvin and Thelma in our decision to build and summer on the Island. Each year almost as soon as we left for "the mainland" Calvin came over to check the cottage and make certain that we had not left on any electric appliance, etc. In the last

Alden and Nancy Neal Coll.

The author and her husband enjoying their summer cottage at Chelton with friends and neighbors. L to R: Bob Johnson, Elaine Johnson _____, Alden Neal, Shirley Johnson (holding grandson, Cameron), Nancy Neal, and Charles "Bud" Craig.

Alden and Nancy Neal Coll.

Irish mossers are a common site along the Island shoreline, as the above post-card scene depicts, many of whom come all the way from Miminegash in West Prince to harvest the waters off Chelton beach.

years of their being in their Chelton home, they would be standing on their porch steps to wave goodbye about 5:55 a.m. as we left to get the ferry to the mainland and go home. They were dear friends as well as relatives.

In early June 1999 Calvin and Thelma sold their lovely, cozy home which he had built in the 1980s. Their daughter, Janet, had lived on waterfront property that adjoined theirs. By late May she and Jim had lost some land as the result of winter storms and decided to move. They bought land about a mile from their location and prepared to move their house to the new location. Calvin and Thelma would be unable to remain without the help of Janet who had done their housework and laundry for some years and so they put their house on the market. It sold very quickly and they moved temporarily to Gail's, their granddaughter in Summerside. Thelma and Calvin took a little vacation to visit their daughter, Barb, in Halifax. While there Thelma died suddenly in the night from a heart ailment of long-standing. Calvin was devastated, especially as he and Thelma were very close friends, both being very kind and helpful people.

In December he moved into an apartment in Summerside. When we arrived on the Island in mid-June we visited him and met his new "lady friend." He looked in wonderful health, tan and slender. What he had not told anyone was that he had been having bleeding for perhaps four years. Only Janet and Thelma knew about the bleeding, and as he was not willing to go to the doctor, there was not much that they could do about it. About two weeks after we initially saw him, he went to the doctor, was immediately hospitalized, transferred to Charlot-tetown Hospital where there were specialists, transferred to Halifax for a couple of days, then back to Charlottetown. He had a few surgical procedures to make him more comfortable, but his life expectancy was about three or four months. He had a few radiation treatments and lived just about three months from the time that he went to the doctor with his complaints.

His funeral service, as well as Thelma's, was held from the Bedeque United Church, the Rev. Barbara Wagner officiating, with burial in the Searletown Cemetery. In the short time of his known illness, he had lost nearly one-half of his body weight, was extremely weak and tired, and became incapable of thinking logically. The end was very sad for us all. Calvin and Thelma had many friends and acquaintances, and their funerals, as well as the visiting hours, were well attended. I have a copy of his obituary as it appeared in the *Journal Pioneer* [Summerside] on September 23, 2000, the day of his death:

CLARK—The death occurred at the Prince County Hospital, Summerside, Saturday, Sept. 23, 2000, of Calvin Clark of Summerside, formerly of Chelton, aged 80 years. A veteran of the Second World War, he was born in Summerside, the son of the late Fred and Lillian (Doull) Clark. [Calvin's mother had died less than a year before him at age 99!] Survived by daughters Barbara (Frank) Judge of Timberlea, N.S., and Janet (James) Murphy of Chelton and son David (Nancy) Clark of Freetown. Survived as well by nine grandchildren, seven great-grandchildren and brother Howard Clark of Chelton. Predecesed by his wife Thelma (Allen) Clark in 1999. Resting at the Moase Funeral Home, Summerside, until Monday, then to the Bedeque United Church for funeral service at 2 p.m. Interment in Searletown Cemetery. Visiting hours Sunday 2-4 and 7-9 p.m. Memorial donations to the Canadian Cancer Society or a charity of your choice would be appreciated.

Calvin and Thelma had three children (ninth generation, surname Clark). See Chapter 11.

Lloyd Allen (8, Reuben 7, Sarah 6, John 5, Major 4, Thomas 3, Clement 2, Stephen 1) born November 1914; married Louise Barkhouse of Bridgewater, Nova Scotia. Lloyd Allen took over the business of his father. He and Louise live in St. Margaret's Bay, Nova Scotia. Although they have had many (what would appear to be nearly insurmountable) health problems over the past 20 or so years, they are always bright, cheerful, and optimistic. He has had many surgeries, and she has had hip replacements because of arthritis and open heart surgery. They are two very remarkable and truly fantastic people who

are upbeat and so pleasant to hear from and be with. Thelma was very fond of her dear brother. Lloyd died on March 7, 2002, after a valiant battle for survival. Lloyd and Lousie have three daughters (ninth generation, surname Allen). See Chapter 11.

Margaret Arlene Allen, called Marg (8, Reuben 7, Sarah 6, John 5, Major 4, Thomas 3, Clement 2, Stephen 1), born April 1, 1921; married Aubrey Wagner; divorced about 15 years later. They had no children. Margaret was a nurse in Halifax for years, much of that time doing private duty. She and her sister, Jean, had "trained" at the same hospital in Halifax, Marg having just graduated when Jean entered. Marg lived with her parents and on their deaths, she continued to live in the very large house which Rube had had built on St. Margaret's Bay. She sold it about 1996 and bought a two bedroom condo in the Halifax area, and then started to spend some time in Clearwater, FL with her sister, Jean, in the winter. Marg had a heart attack in the winter of 1996/1997 in Florida and recovered well.

Dorothy Frances Allen, called Dot, (8, Reuben 7, Sarah 6, John 5, Major 4, Thomas 3, Clement 2, Stephen 1), born January 28, 1923; married Edmund Thomas (called Ted) Dorey; they live in St. Margaret's Bay. Dot had been a hairdresser. Once when she was visiting Thelma, with her sister Marg, Thelma brought them to our cottage for a visit, and we enjoyed meeting her. Dot and Ted have seven children (ninth generation, surname Dorey). See Chapter 11.

Emmajean Vivian Allen, called Jean (8, Reuben 7, Sarah 6, John 5, Major 4, Thomas 3, Clement 2, Stephen 1), born October 20, 1925; married Alexander Herbert Henderson; Jean lives in Clearwater, FL for most of the year. Her husband died many years ago. They had two children (ninth generation, surname Henderson). See Chapter 11.

How I wish I had written what Thelma had given me of her family information. I miss her very much, but at times like this when I am trying to put together her section of the family history I especially miss her as she always had dates and events at her fingertips without consulting any book. Her mind was as clear as a bell. She could and would have given me the dates and episodes of all the family. The

June that she died I was finally ready to make serious notes of her family, but I was too late, unfortunately, for writing it down although I did question her many, many times about her family genealogy. I should have written more information on paper rather than trying to carry some in my head. She told us several humorous stories about her father, and never tired of relating them! Rube, Ada's first cousin, must have been a bright, hard-working, very kind and generous man. He used to send $50.00 a month to his mother who died when he was 31, so he probably was not more than 25, perhaps less, at the time. His sister, Lila, was caring for their mother at that time.

Bertram W. Allen (7, Sarah 6, John 5, Major 4, Thomas 3, Clement 2, Stephen 1), the third son of Sarah and Ed Allen, was born in North Carleton, P.E.I. about 1893; married Eula Ogilvie; died prior to October 1961. I have a Halifax newspaper account of his life and obituary:

B. W. Allen

The death occurred Monday morning of Bertram W. Allen, 52 Columbus Street, after a short illness. He was 71.

Mr. Allen was born in P. E. I. and lived in Halifax for 50 years. He was employed as yard superintendent by R. S. Allen Ltd. at the time of his death, and previously was an employee of Halifax Shipyards Ltd.

He is survived by his wife, Eula M.; three daughters, Aletha, at home, Irene (Mrs. Robert Martinson) Halifax, and Marjorie, (Mrs. George Benoit) Woodlawn; five sons, Wallace, Wellington Station; Sinclair, Douglas, and Weldon, all of Halifax; and Oral, of Toronto; one sister, Lila, (Mrs. Fulton MacLeod), Bradford, Mass.; two brothers, Keir, Kinkora, P.E.I., and Reuben S., St. Margaret's Bay.

Remains are resting at Cruikshank's Funeral Home. The funeral will be held at 2 p.m. Wednesday from the funeral home, with Canon F. A. Heffler officiating [This would be an Anglican service]. Interment will be in Fairview Cemetery.

I do not have the year of Bert's death, but it was before October 1961 as Keir was still living when Bert died. He was 71 at his death and he could not have been born before 1891 so some numbers must be inaccurate. I believe this is the correct birth order of Bert's children (eighth generation, surname Allen):

Aletha Allen (8, Bert 7, Sarah 6, John 5, Major 4, Thomas 3, Clement 2, Stephen 1)

Wallace Allen (8, Bert 7, Sarah 6, John 5, Major 4, Thomas 3, Clement 2, Stephen 1) married Alice Bradley; he is now deceased. Wallace and Alice had eight children (surname Allen, ninth generation). His obituary appeared in a Halifax newspaper:

Two Car Collision Kills Wellington Man

A two car accident on the Bedford Highway early Saturday morning claimed the life of Wallace Wendal Allen [son of Bert Allen], 60, of Wellington, Halifax County. R.C.M.P. report Mr. Allen was the driver of a car which was in collision with a car occupied by Evelyn MacRae of Dartmouth at 12:30 a.m. near the Hammonds Plains Road Intersection.

Born in Halifax, Mr. Allen, a millwright at the Halifax shipyard for over 30 years, was the son of the late Bertram and Eula (Ogilvie) Allen. He was a member of Athole Lodge No. 15, Masonic Lodge A.F. and A.M.

Surviving besides his wife, the former Alice Bradley, are two daughters [ninth generation, surname Allen]: Judy (Mrs. Clemeth Decker), Dartmouth, and Heather (Mrs. David King), Bedford; four sons: Kenneth, Oakville, Ontario; David, Toronto; Brian, Wellington; Ralph, Nine Mile River, Hants County; three sisters: Aletha, Halifax; Mrs. Irene Martinson, Halifax; and Marjorie (Mrs. Gerard Benoit, Dartmouth); four brothers: Sinclair [who visited Thelma unannounced about the summer of 1991; she brought him to our cottage with his second wife; we had a delightful visit] and Douglas, Halifax; Weldon, Hilden (?), Colchester County; and Kenneth, Toronto; and eight grandchildren. The body is at the R. D. Lindsay Funeral Home, Bedford, where the funeral will be held Tuesday at 2 p.m., the Rev. Norman MacDougall officiating, assisted by Lic. Gordon Fraser. Interment will be in Hillcrest Memorial Gardens, Sackville. In lieu of flowers donations can be made to the charity of your choice. [This item is not dated]

Lila Blanche Allen (7, Sarah 6, John 5, Major 4, Thomas 3, Clement 2, Stephen 1) born July 6, 1892 in North Carleton, P.E.I.; married Fulton MacLeod (born in Long River, P.E.I. and died of a heart attack on June 21, 1961 in Haverhill, MA) on July 15, 1923. Lila was the child of Sarah who cared for her during her disability with arthritis, perhaps in the last seven or so years of her life. The reader may remember that Lila and Jennie had left the Island for Haverhill, MA prior to this period and the death of Major Hooper, Jennie's father.

After Major's death in 1914, Jennie came home to run the farm; Lila returned to care for her mother [the two homes were side by side]. Ada and Vera had gone to Haverhill to work in the City Farm, as Ada had written a card to Robbie from Haverhill early in 1913.

Within Alden and my memories, Lila and Fulton and their girls lived in Haverhill. Lila's cousin, Ada, lived in Saugus, about an hour's journey by car. I remember going to Lila's unannounced one Saturday afternoon with Alden, his mother, and perhaps Fran, and we were all invited to stay for a delicious baked bean supper, so typical of New England and probably of P.E.I. as well. Lila certainly had the P.E.I. hospitality! Lila, like Ada, was a very short lady - perhaps 4 feet, 9 inches. In her later years she was thin. She had a heart condition. In the last several years of their lives, Lila and Fulton had lived in Bradford, a suburb of Haverhill, with their daughter, Verna, whose husband had been killed in the Korean War. Lila died on May 30, 1965 as Verna and her friend, Laurie Perkins, whom she would marry the following year, were driving to her home after visiting us on Long Island, N.Y. I have the newspaper clipping of Lila's obituary:

Mrs. Lila B. McLeod

[Her surname was misspelled]

Mrs. Lila B. McLeod, 54 Williams St., Bradford, widow of Fulton G. McLeod, died Saturday night at her home.

She was born in North Carleton, Prince Edward Island, Canada, daughter of Edward [he was James Edwin] and Sarah (Hooper) Allen. She lived in Haverhill for 40 years and attended the Church of the Nazarene.

She leaves two daughters, Mrs. Verna C. Clay, Bradford, and Mrs. Helen E. Caswell, Haverhill; three grandchildren, several nieces and nephews, and cousins.

The funeral service was held this afternoon [no date on article] at 1:30 at the Tilton, Rogers and Gale Funeral Home, 334 Main St. The Rev. Harry E. Trask, pastor of the Church of the Nazarene, officiated.

A delegation attended from the Haverhill Office of the New England Telephone Company.

Bearers were Milton Hart, Kenneth Thurston, the Rev. Herbert White, A. E. Stickney, Maurice Clevesy, and Bradford Burnard.

Burial was in the Linwood Cemetery where Mr. Trask held a committal service.

Lila's daughter, Helen, said that her mother had had heart problems for years and that her heart finally gave out [She probably had congestive heart failure]. Lila and Fulton had two daughters (eighth generation, surname MacLeod):

Verna MacLeod (8, Lila 7, Sarah 6, John 5, Major 4, Thomas 3, Clement 2, Stephen 1) born August 31, 1927 in Haverhill, MA; married (i) Carleton B. Clay* on January 29, 1949. Carl was in the service during the Korean War and was killed in Korea on August 12, 1950. His remains were brought home, after what seemed like years of waiting, and buried in the Linwood Cemetery in Haverhill in March 1951. Verna worked for the telephone company. They had one child (surname Clay, ninth generation). See Chapter 11.

Verna married (ii) Wellman Laurie Perkins of Sherbrooke, Quebec, Canada, born 1934, on April 16, 1966 in Haverhill, MA. They had one child (surname Perkins, ninth generation).

Verna discovered that she had cancer of the cervix when she was pregnant with her second child. She was hospitalized for treatment after her child was born, and she seemed to do well; she was declared cancer-free. Occasionally when she was working on Sunday or on a holiday, she would call us on her break. It was always a pleasure to hear from Verna and catch up on the news! Verna died of cancer of the stomach in February 1977.

***ARMY REPORTS SERGEANT CLAY PRESUMED DEAD**

Had Been Missing in Action in Korea Since August 1950

A Haverhill GI decorated for bravery in World War II and missing in acton in Korea since August 12, 1950, was listed as "now presumed dead" by the Army today.

Sgt. Carleton B. Clay who was 26 when he was reported missing in Korea, was one of the first Haverhill men to go into action in that conflict. His wife, Mrs. Verna MacLeod Clay, 8 Fourth Avenue, said today she had been notified by the Army that her husband is now presumed dead. They have a daughter, Carlene, 4, who was born in 1949 after her father left for service in the Pacific and whom he has never seen.

Mrs. Clay said today the notice from the Army was something she had "expected, but dreaded." More than a year ago her hopes that her husband might have been taken a prisoner of war were raised when she thought she recognized him in a group picture of American GIs held by the Korean Reds. Mrs. Clay sent the picture to the American Prisoners of War Association, but she never received conftrmation that the picture was that of her husband and has never had a report that he might have been a prisoner of war. The last news Mrs. Clay received from her husband was a letter on August 6, 1950, six days before the Army listed him as missing in action in the Naktong River section of Korea. He was fighting with the 24th Infantry. She had received several letters from him prior to that date in which he described conditions in Korea and told of the conflict. In the August 6 letter, he gave her news that he had been promoted from corporal to sergeant, a promotion he said he had earned "the hard way."

Sgt. Clay, the son of Mrs. Doris Clay, 7 South Warren St., and Linwood S. Clay, who is in California, received a bronze star medal for heroism under fire while serving in Germany in World War II. He entered the Army in May, 1943 and was discharged in January, 1946. He served overseas for 24 months.

Sergeant and Mrs. Clay were married in January, 1949 and he re-enlisted in the service in May, 1949. He was sent to Japan two months later and in July, 1950, went from Japan to Korea.

Sergeant Clay was born in North Berwick, ME, and attended schools in North Andover. His parents moved to Haverhill when he was 16.

He has two sisters, Mrs. Laura Wallace and Miss Doris Clay, both of Haverhill, and three brothers, Linwood S. Clay, Jr., and John D. Clay, Haverhill, and William Clay, Hyattsville, Ind.

Helen MacLeod, (8, Lila 7, Sarah 6, John 5, Major 4, Thomas 3, Clement 2, Stephen 1) born on November 5, 1930; married Edward Caswell (born April 13, 1926) on April 14, 1956 in Haverhill. MA. Ed and Helen have two children (surname Caswell, ninth generation). See Chapter 11.

Vera Grace Allen (7, Sarah 6, John 5, Major 4, Thomas 3, Clement 2, Stephen 1) born December 2, 1900 in North Carleton, P.E.I. She married Elwood Hart when she was 15 (c.1915). When their fourth child, Milton, was four years old, Elwood left her and the family, never to return or support. Social programs from the federal government were not available at the time, so with four dependent children she worked in a laundry and other places in the Haverhill area to

suppprt her children. Vera opened a convalescent home and took, perhaps, four patients. I believe the story is that she tripped on a rug, fell, developed a blood clot, and died suddenly in March 1951. Alden's mother, her first cousin, described her as being very pretty It was Ada and Vera who came together from the Island to Haverhill to work in the City Farm sometime between 1912 and 1913. The two pairs of sisters and cousins were probably all like sisters, having lived side-by-side in North Carleton, P.E.I. In Massachusetts three of them lived in Haverhill and one in Saugus, about an hour's drive away.

Please allow me to digress to tell what I think is an interesting story of how the two sets of sisters, who were cousins to each other and who lived side by side in North Carleton, came to Haverhill, MA to work. Alden's brother, Paul, thinks that his mother, Ada, came when she was about 14; I think she probably came when she was 17, about 1914, when Jennie and Lila returned to the Island after Major Hooper died. It appears that neither of us is correct as just yesterday (April 1, 2000) Alden was looking through a collection of things that he had saved from his mother. He found a postcard which we had never noticed previously, of the Armory in Haverhill, MA addressed in his mother's handwriting to Master Robert Hooper, North Carleton, P.E.I. The postmark from Haverhill was May 6, 1913. At that time Vera would have been 12 as her birthday was in December of 1900 and Ada would have been 17. We are not certain if that date is close to the time that she arrived in the U.S.A. Their father was still living in 1913. The tone of the letter makes me think that she was not long separated from her brother, Robbie, who would have been 13 or 14 at the time. Here is what she wrote: "My Dear little Brother, I often think of you, dear, and wish I could put my arms around you, you sweet little dear. Be a good little boy and I will see you soon. Goodby, Dear. Ada Ann."

In Chelton, living very near where our cottage is, was the Pearson family. Alden had remembered that the sisters and cousins had worked for the Savages from P.E.I. One Saturday evening in late August of

1999, a large group of people, neighbors and former neighbors, were invited nearby for a pot-luck dinner with the traditional making of Indian bread in the campfire, and singing. Ed and Kay Pearson, former neighbors, were there. Just a few days prior to the pot-luck dinner, Cousin Viola Taylor had loaned me the two volumes of the genealogy, written by Doris Haslam, of the Wright family, Loyalists from New York. I squealed with glee to Alden when I found the link to Haverhill for Jennie and Ada and their cousins Lila and Vera.

When I saw Ed at the pot-luck, I made an appointment for Alden and me to go to their house early the next week to pursue this Savage lead. Fortunately we got there just days before Ed and Kay left for Vancouver for two months.

Captain John Pearson, born c.1790, was the first of his family to come to P.E.I., in 1820. He married Lydia Wright. They had many children, among them a son Edward. The Pearsons lived in South Shore Bedeque, now called Chelton. Edward and his wife, Elizabeth, had a daughter, Margaret (born January 25, 1860; died February 27, 1938), who went up to the States to work and met and married Louis Savage. Louis was superintendent of the House of Correction in Ipswich, MA before being appointed superintendent of the City Farm in Haverhill, MA. He held the latter position for 40 years![8]

Chelton is about 2 miles "as the crow flies" from North Carleton where the Hoopers and the Allens lived. Apparently there was little work for girls and women (except marriage) in those days. Farm life was hard, and the girls got no money for helping on the farm. They wanted to do something better for themselves. Here was a "neighbor" who was established in MA, whose husband was in a position of hiring personnel for the City Farm (called in those days "the poor farm" as it was mostly older, unhealthy, indigent people who lived there). Mr. Savage was looking for honest, healthy young people to work in various capacities in the institution. Alden remembers that there were a lot of elderly people, some poor, others chronically ill.

In the early days, the institution had a farm with cows, pigs, etc. Arrangements were made with someone whom they knew or knew of and they went by two's until the 4 of them were there. Marriage

took Ada, Lila, and Vera away, but Jennie stayed at the City Farm all of her working years. Room and board was included in the "wages" which probably were small. Jennie was a seamstress; Ada was a cook; Vera worked in the laundry; Lila's job we do not know. Alden's father, Charles O'Neil, came from a small town in southern New Hampshire to work in the big city of Haverhill where there were lots of jobs in the late teens and early 1920s. One of the places where he worked was at the infirmary doing I don't know what! He then worked as a machinist in several shops in the Havehill area. I am sure that he worked at other jobs as well, as he was ambitious.

He was an affable man who enjoyed going to dances and parties. Alden's dad left New Hampshire when he was about 15 or 16 as he didn't get along with his stepfather, Clarence Harris. Charlie referred to him as "Harris." He disliked him, but was polite to him. Charlie, his older sister Lillian, and his younger brother, Austin, all left New Hampshire. Charlie had a stepbrother, Ernest, who was eleven years younger than Charlie. Charlie had gone as far as grade 9 in school. Alden thinks that he left school because the family was poor and he didn't get along with his stepfather. Charlie later attended Franklin Union in Boston for two years. He often said that he had an 11th grade education. He especially loved algebra and geometry. Charlie encouraged his oldest daughter, Lillian Frances, to take the college course in high school which she did for one year, then changed to the business course.

Lillian and her two sisters took piano lessons on Saturdays from Mrs. Sweezey from Franklin Park, North Revere, for fifty cents a lesson. Daisy and Dawson Stewart owned a piano, but because they moved around a lot and lived in second and third floor tenements, it would be cumbersome to move the piano. The Neals kept the piano for the Stewarts, and it was still in the house in the late 1960s. For some reason Alden's father detested alcohol. Alden doesn't know the reason: it could be that Alden's grandfather, Matthew O'Neil, or his stepfather, was a boozer. Another possibility was that the temperance society was active at that time.

A group of people from the farm would take the street car to the Haverhill Nazarene Church. The old church could accomodate 400 people. Glen Gould, who was pastor of the Haverhill church then, received a call to Cliftondale. Because Annie Eva and Charlie were fond of him and his wife Mildred, they decided to move to Saugus when Charlie was working for the Boston and Maine Railroad. Then he started taking classes at Franklin Union.

Alden's parents were very close to Mildred Gould's parents, the Crosbys. Alden remembers them driving to his house in a 1939 spotless car from East Lynn for a visit about every three weeks. They were lovely, refined, dignified people. Alden thinks that one reason that Glen Gould moved to Saugus was to attend Boston University for his doctorate degree. He was a scholarly man with an excellent vocabulary. When he came to Cliftondale, he left a larger congregation in Haverhill.

To digress again, Aunt Jennie worked at the Haverhill Infirmary, as it became known, five and one-half days a week. She had a small private room and got her meals there. If we had to reach her by phone, we would call Haverhill 475, which was done only in emergencies. Usually on Saturdays Aunt Jennie would take the bus to downtown Haverhill's Water Street. She would do some shopping at Mitchell's, the big department store. Then she would walk up the hill to visit her cousins, Lila and Vera, in their homes. A cup of tea and some sweets awaited her where she was warmly received.

According to her nephew, Alden: "Once a month Jennie would take the Boston and Maine Railroad to Malden. Her brother-in-law, Charlie, would pick her up and she would spend the rest of Saturday until Sunday afternoon with her sister Ada and family. Immediately when she arrived at the house she would start working for Ada. The stove was never so clean as when Aunt Jennie visited! She thought of all of us often and constantly prayed for us."

Louis, Elmer, and Margaret Pearson of Chelton, P.E.I., all worked for a time at the City Farm where the uncle by marriage of the men (Louis Savage) was the administrator. As an addendum to the introduction of Margaret and Louis, their grandchild, Louis D. Savage

(named for his grandfather), became a physician and was living in 1976 in South Lynnfield, MA. Margaret and Louis also had a daughter, Helen Dodge Savage, born on June 23, 1898 in Haverhill, MA; married Harold E. Larkin on 9/11/1920, and died in December 1977. Harold and Helen had a son, Greg Larkin, for whom Lorraine [Neal] and Walter Olson named their son. Walter and Greg Larkin had been friends in Massachusetts from college days and probably before that time. It is certainly strange where genealogy takes us!

Going down memory lane again we think of several Pearsons who lived in our area, some in view of our cottage. Louis Pearson was a cousin of Elmer. Louis never married, but had a farm that was opposite the present Chelton Provincial Park. I remember in the 1970s, when we came to Chelton, seeing his cow with a hugely swollen udder day after day after day. Neighbors seemed to indicate that he was a strange man. Was I surprised when I read some of the things that he wrote in a book of genealogy. His writings were not those of a person "three bricks short of a load," but of an intelligent person who writes well. Later I found out that he went to college. Perhaps he had a dementia of old age or perhaps he didn't give a hoot about farming! In Chapter Seven of this document is an article written by Louis titled, "Women, Bears, and Mice."[9]

John and Lydia were the first settlers at South Shore Bedeque [as Chelton was called in the early days]. Their first home, a log cabin, was built near the site of the Chauncey Pearson house. Doris Haslam in *The Wrights of Bedeque* (pp. 41-42), writes:

> His next home, a frame house, was built on that part of the farm later owned by Louis Pearson. John's land was covered with maple and other hardwoods. He would be up before dawn, chopping and piling logs ready to burn. Long before he died he had his land all cleared and in cultivation. In the 1841 census John was listed as farmer and seaman. He was one of the crew which sailed with his brother-in-law, John Wright, on the *Lovely,* the schooner which John and William Wright had built to carry produce to the Miramichi, and (according to one descendant) even to the West Indies. John Pearson built vessels on the beach below Louis' farm. They were launched by hauling them with oxen out on the ice in the winter. In the spring they launched themselves.

The farm between Louis's and our former neighbor, Edward's, was Chauncey Pearson's, whom we did not know. Chauncey was Elmer's brother.

When Alden and I first went to P.E.I. in 1970 we stayed at the campground next to where the provincial park is now. Just about where the gate to the park entrance is was situated the house of Elmer and Margaret Pearson. They had been friends of Jennie's and knew Alden's mother. Lo and behold, Elmer and Margaret paid us a visit early one morning with melt-in-your-mouth home-made rolls dripping with butter, and a jar of home-made strawberry jam. This neighborliness started an acquaintance, and we stopped at their farmhouse which was very close to where we were camping. In my mind I can still see the large kitchen with many windows and a big black stove. It was a sunny and very pleasant home for a sunny and very pleasant couple. Elmer Pearson was the great-grandson of Lydia Wright Pearson who met the bear when she was walking through the woods with her baby. Edward told us that the house of Margaret and Elmer was demolished about 1976/1977 to make room for the small housing development planned, as lots were being subdivided and sold.

Some of the interest in the Pearsons stems from the fact that Alden and I have friends and acquaintances among the later generations of the Pearson family. Also, as explained later, Margaret Pearson was influential in the Hooper girls and their Allen cousins going to Massachusetts in the early years of the 20th century. An interesting story related in Chapter Seven will be repeated here. Lydia, the oldest daughter of Stephen and Fanny (Lord) Wright, had eloped with John Bell when she was eighteen. Little is known of Bell except that he went away on a sailing vessel. When, after many years, he did not return, Lydia married John Pearson, a young Scottish mariner who, after surviving shipwreck off West Point, P.E.I., walked to Bedeque, stopping at her home enroute. According to a story handed down by the family, Bell did return once, saw how things were with his wife, and left South Shore (Chelton) for good, never to be heard of afterward. Doris Haslam related in her book, *The Wrights of Bedeque*:

One day when John and Lydia were absent, a stranger called and asked the little Pearson boys for a drink of water. After drinking the water and talking to them, he pulled out his watch and gave it to one of the boys, then went on his way. When the parents returned, they were amazed. Why would a stranger be touring South Shore in those days and why would he give his watch in return for a mere drink of water? From the description the little boys gave their mother, and the presentation of the watch, it was surmised that the stranger was none other than John Bell. What would have happened had the two Johns met one cannot say![10]

During the summer of 1988, when we were first summer residents in Chelton, Ed Pearson, our neighbor across the street and down about three houses, was a great help to us. He brought his equipment and put large rocks in front of the twelve-foot drop from our back yard to the Northumberland Strait. We were concerned about the tides coming up the bank and taking valuable land away with it. Ed was such a good and helpful neighbor, but, alas, the tides were too strong for the rocks, and many of them were washed away by the summer of 1989! It seems strange that Alden's ancestors and Ed's ancestors knew each other so many generations ago when they were all farmers tilling the soil for the first time!

Another unusual and interesting interaction between the Neals and the Pearsons occurred in March 2001, when we were passengers on the *Princess Line* cruising through the Caribbean. The day before we were to land we were at the purser's office to pay whatever bills we had charged during the voyage. Alden was talking with the pleasant personnel lady and asked her if she knew if anyone from Prince Edward Island was on the cruise. She thought that there was a mate on board from P.E.I. and said that she would call him; his name was Arnold. Sure enough, it was Arnold Pearson, Ed and Kay's son who lived almost across the paved street from us when we were all in Chelton! He came to see us and we had a bit of a conversation. At the time of writing this section of the Hooper history (2001) he is to be married in the fall, and they will be living in his parents' former home where he grew up and which he has been remodeling!

The children of Vera and Elwood (surname Hart, eighth generation) are as follows:

Stanton Allen Hart (8, Vera 7, Sarah 6, John 5, Major 4, Thomas 3, Clement 2, Stephen 1) born about 1920; died 1938. I have the newspaper announcement of his death, which is much more of a listing of those who sent what kind of flowers than an obituary:

Allen S. Hart

The following were the floral tributes at the funeral of Allen S. Hart: Carnations and snapdragons, mother; lillies and snapdragons, brother; snapdragons, principal and teachers at the School Street school [this offering by the school personnel would make me think that Stanton might still be in school; he may have been born after 1920]; carnations, Bessie Fall and Clifford Wheeler; spray, Jennie Hooper and Ellen Truesdale; carnations and snapdragons, Church of the Nazarene; spray, John Alvin; carnations, Mrs. Charles Collins; carnations, Mrs. Emma Welch, Miss Besse Ackerman, Mrs. Lizzie Dorman, Miss Frances Dorman; carnations, Uncle Rube Allen and Uncle Bert Allen; carnations, the Maranda family [a member of this family was driving the car in which Stanton died]; spray, Mr. and Mrs. Fulton MacLeod and family; carnations, Mr. and Mrs. Charles Eastman, Mr. and Mrs. Oscar Eastman, Rose Eastman, Mr. and Mrs. George Demarais; spray, Cousin Nick; snapdragons and tulips, Mr. and Mrs. Chester Spurr; basket, Mr. and Mrs. Frank Blake and family, Mr. and Mrs. Jewett Benoit, Mr. and Mrs. Walter Pike and family, Mr. and Mrs. Horace Morehouse, Mr. and Mrs. Grover Cook and family, Mrs. Elizabeth Spinney, John Cronin, Miss Mary Burke, Mr. and Mrs. Edward Kennebrew, Mr. and Mrs. Freeman Shedd, Mr. and Mrs. Daniel Foley and family, Clovis Martel; Mr. and Mrs. George Hitchcock, Louise, Teresa, and Angie Cresple.

One wonders the motivation for only listing the flowers and flower-givers. Was it a sense of being overwhelmed or angry? Stanton was killed, probably instantly, in an automobile accident with Francis Maranda, who became the husband of Velma, driving the car.

Velma Hart (8, Vera 7, Sarah 6, John 5. Major 4, Thomas 3, Clement 2, Stephen 1) born about 1922; married Francis Maranda who died about 1995, living for many years and still there (2001) in Plainville, CT. She writes to us occasionally. Her health (1999) is not very good; she, like her grandmother, Sarah Hooper Allen, has arthritis badly. Alden remembers that when Velma was in high school she came to live with his family in Saugus for a while. He isn't sure of the reason. Was it to keep her away from a particular boy, to keep her

going to school, to give her a different environment for a while? Anyway, he remembers her as a very pretty girl. When she started to play hookie from school, his mother didn't want to take responsibility for her any more, and she went back to her mother in Haverhill. Velma and Francis lived in Plainville, CT. Toward the end of 2000 Velma spoke of going with her daughter and possibly her granddaughter to live in North Carolina next year. The update in the spring of 2003 is that her daughter, Gloria, moved to North Carolina and wanted to take Velma with her, but Velma refused. She is (2003) in a health care facility because she has Alzheimer's disease. Velma and Francis had two children (surname Maranda, ninth generation).

Walden S. Hart, called "Wadsie" by some of the family (8, Vera 7, Sarah 6, John 5, Major 4, Thomas 3, Clement 2, Stephen 1), was born on August 24, 1923 in Liberty, Maine; married a lady called Gladys; died October 13, 1978 [He was only 55 years old]. His obituary from the newspaper follows:

Walden S. Hart, 55, of Kellogg Drive, Mt. Clemons, Mich., died October 13, in Mt. Clemons. He was born Aug. 24, 1923, in Liberty, Maine. He was a World War II veteran and was employed as a modelmaker by Fisher Body Co. He lived in Mt. Clemons 32 years. He leaves his wife, Gladys; two sons, William, Interlachen, Mich., and Richard, Mt. Clemons; a brother, Milton Hart, Newtonville, and a sister, Mrs. Francis Maranda, Plainville, Conn. The funeral was Oct. 16 in Mt. Clemons, Mich. Burial was in West Newbury, Mass.

Milton Hart (8, Vera 7, Sarah 6, John 5, Major 4, Thomas 3, Clement 2, Stephen 1) born May 17, 1925; married (i) Rosemary Cram. They had two sons (surname Hart, ninth generation). Milton and Rosemary divorced. Milton married (ii) a lady called Eleanor. They had a son and a daughter (surname Hart, ninth generation).

Milton keeps in touch with Helen Caswell, his cousin. He has written sporadically to Alden in the last three or four years. He lives in southern Maine and is a landscape painter. In her living room Helen has a beautiful painting which he did. She also has several prints that he had done. Milton died on November 10, 2000 in the Mid-Coast Hospital in Brunswick, Maine, of cancer, probably origi-

nating in the abdomen. When Milton went to the physician in late August 2000, with what he thought might be a hernia, he was told that he had a fast-growing tumor and it was too late to do anything. His cousin, Helen and her husband, Ed Caswell, spent part of Milton's last two days with him in the hospital. Helen read him a lovely letter which had just come from his sister Velma. Helen sent us a copy of his obituary:

Milton H. Hart, 75

EDGECOMB - Milton H. Hart, 75, of Boothbay Road died Nov. 10, 2000 at Midcoast Hospital in Brunswick. Born in Liberty, he was a son of Elwood [Edwin] and Vera Allen Hart. He moved to Haverhill, MA, where he attended schools. He served in the Marine Corps in the Solomon Islands of the South Pacific during World War II; he was discharged as a corporal.

Mr. Hart was a machine designer for the NRC Co. in Newton, MA. In 1986 he moved to Maine where he painted. He had several gallery showings.

Surviving are three sons, Douglas and Steven, both of Massachusetts, and Peter of Virginia; a daughter, Peggy Hart Pace, of Illinois; a sister Velma Maranda of Plainville, CT; and grandchildren. A son, David, died previously.

Services will be held at 11 a.m. Wednesday [the 15th] at Bremen Union Church Route 32, Bremen, with the Rev. Charles Shotzberger officiating. Burial will be at 11 a.m. Thursday [the 16th] in Linwood Cemetery, Haverhill, MA. Arrangements are by Strong Funeral Home, Damariscotta [Maine].

The author's husband, Alden, found a similar obituary on the internet:

Milton H. Hart, 75, of Edgecomb died Friday, November 10 at Midcoast Hospital in Brunswick. A son of Edward [Edwin] and Vera (Allen) Hart, he was born May 17, 1925 in Liberty. As a youth, he moved with his family to Haverhill, MA where he attended schools. He entered the U.S. Marine Corps, serving in the South Pacific Solomon Islands during World War II. He was discharged as a corporal. Mr. Hart was employed as a machine designer, working for the NRC Company in Newton, MA. In 1986 he moved to Maine where he rekindled his passion for painting and was active with the ASMA. He had several gallery showings throughout the years.

Survivors include his children, Douglas and Steven Hart, both of Massachusetts, Peter Hart of Virginia and Peggy Hart Pace of Illinois; a sister, Velma Maranda of Plainville, CT.; and many grandchildren, nieces and nephews. A son David and two brothers predeceased him.

Services were held Wednesday, November 15, [2000] at the Bremen Union Church in Bremen, with the Rev. Charles Shotzberger officiating. He will be laid to rest on Thursday, November 16 at the Linwood Cemetery, Haverhill, MA. Arrangements are by Strong Funeral Home in Damariscotta. If desired, donations may be made to either the American Cancer Society or the Salvation Army in his memory [from the *Wiscasset* newspaper, November 16, 2000].

Thelma, Vera's niece, told the author that Vera had a baby boy who died as an infant of convulsions. [He may have been deprived of oxygen for too long]

The reader may recall Major Hooper Clark (6, Harriet Hooper Clark 5, Major Hooper 4, Thomas 3, Clement 2, Stephen 1) who went to Chicago at the approximate age of 13. There is a space of several years, but sometime later he went to New Zealand. In 1980 there were still Hoopers living in New Zealand according to a letter to the P.E.I. Public Archives and Records Office from a person who wanted to know about her ancestors on P.E.I.! In 2002 this writer tried to make contact, but was unable to do so.

Interestingly, information about NewZealand was recorded nearly one hundred and fifty years ago:

Robert Clare, a son of James Douglas Haszard [who may have been related to Eunice Haszard Gardiner], was a principal organizer of an expedition to New Zealand in November, 1858. Reports of the favourable New Zealand climate could have been an inducement to emigrate; also with decreasing opportunities at home many Islanders were seeking greener pastures. Land was a major political issue, much of it being tenure which restricted the access to farming for young Islanders. Thus, many of the more amibitious ones moved to accept the offer made by the recently appointed New Zealand agent in Prince Edward Island of "Land Orders to all persons of Good Character and Sober Steady Habits who will Emigrate at their own Cost from this Island to Auckland." Waste land was land bought from the Maori by the Crown for the purpose of settlement and each emigrant over 18 years was to select 40 acres of this land on paying 10 pounds Agents Fee. Children received 20 acres on application from a guardian.

A suitable ship was a first requirement and a brig of 174 tons was being built in Summerside by the shipyard of James C. Pope. She was the 67th ship registered in the Island in 1858 and was named *Prince Edward Island.*

The captain of the *Prince Edward Island* on its 14,000 mile voyage to New Zealand was Edward Nowlan; the ship's doctor was Dr. A. H. Boswell. They arrived in Auckland via the Cape of Good Hope, May 13, 1859 with ninety-eight passengers including children, thirteen of whom were Haszards." A son of Richard Bagnall was a member of the Legislative Assembly prior to emigrating with his family to New Zealand in 1862. They had eight sons and four daughters, two of whom were born in New Zealand where George died in 1889.

On February 12, 2004 this writer received an e-mail from Judith Newell, the greatgranddaughter of Major Hooper Clark. Judy lives in New Zealand and in the early 1980s brought her grandfather to P.E.I. She had received a letter from this writer about her genealogy. The mail had taken a long time to get to New Zealand. She sent this information: Major Clark had gone to Chicago from P.E.I. where he stayed for a while and married. He went to New Zealand and had some children among whom was William Clark who had five wives. Apparently one of these wives had a son, Clarence Charles Clark who, according to his daughter Judith Clark Newell who is mentioned in Chapter 11, was a compassionate man. Unfortunately our communication broke down and the addresses have been lost so further communication is not possible.

The first child of Sally Hooper and Jesse Wright, **Martha Ann Wright** (6, Sally 5, Major 4, Thomas 3, Clement 2, Stephen 1), born November 29, 1838, married Charles Wesley Strong. Martha Ann and Charles had five children (surname Strong, seventh generation):

Alan Wilmot Strong (7, Martha Ann 6, Sally 5, Major 4, Thomas 3, Clement 2, Stephen 1) born April, 1862 in Central Bedeque; died there January 8, 1864.

John Wesley Strong (7, Martha Ann 6, Sally 5, Major 4, Thomas 3, Clement 2, Stephen 1) born November 1863 in Central Bedeque; died March 21, 1865 in Summerside. [Please notice the names, Charles Wesley and John Wesley - a good Methodist family!]

Alan *Wilmot* Strong (7, Martha 6, Sally 5, Major 4, Thomas 3, Clement 2, Stephen 1) was born in 1866 in Summerside, P.E.I. The reader

will note that he was named the same as the first baby who died. In July 1894 he married Frances Bryson, daughter of Thomas MacFarlane and Louisa (Farrill) Bryson, born in March 1855 in Montreal, P.Q. and died there on April 22, 1938. Wilmot died on August 15, 1924 in Montreal. He graduated from McGill University in civil engineering. He was a gold medalist and a member of the British Engineering Society. He was head actuary with Sun Life Assurance Company Ltd. He and Frances lived in Montreal. Members of Frances's family were well-known druggists. They had one child (surname Strong, eighth generation):

Alan Bryson Strong (8, Alan *Wilmot* 7, Martha 6, Sally 5, Major 4, Thomas 3, Clement 2, Stephen 1) born September 6, 1897 in Montreal; married Teresa Gertrude Murphy, daughter of William and Hannah (Kelly) Murphy, on August 13, 1924. Teresa was born on September 16, 1901 in Montreal. Alan served with the Royal Flying Corps 1915-1918 and later attended McGill University. He was an accountant working in Montreal where he and Teresa lived. They had two children (surname Strong, ninth generation), both born in Montreal.

Jessie Wright Strong (7, Martha Ann 6, Sally 5, Major 4, Thomas 3, Clement 2, Stephen 1) born July 6, 1867 in Summerside; did not marry. She was a graduate of Mount Allison Ladies College, taught music in Summerside and was organist of the Methodist Church. For over forty years she was always in her place at the organ until a few weeks before her death.
Martha Jane Strong (7, Martha Ann 6, Sally 5, Major 4, Thomas 3, Clement 2, Stephen 1) born September 4, 1869 [church record August 5] in Summerside and died there May 20, 1870.

Archibald M. Wright (6, Sally 5, Major 4, Thomas 3, Clement 2, Stephen 1) and Kate Wright had five children (surname Wright, seventh generation):

Charles Gowan Wright (7, Archibald M. 6, Sally 5, Major 4, Thomas 3, Clement 2, Stephen 1) born May 20, 1868; married Janie Seaman, daughter of James and Mary (England) Seaman, on August 22, 1894. Janie was born on January 11, 1867 in Bideford, P.E.I. and died on August 16, 1944 in Summerside. Charles was an accountant in Malden, MA; Janie was a milliner. Again the Bradshaws provided the newspaper announcement of Charles's death:

> A telegraph received by Dr. Alex McNeill on Sunday last announces the death of Charles G. Wright, formerly of Summerside and latterly of Malden, Mass. No particulars were given. Deceased was a son of A.M. and Mrs. Wright, formerly of Bedeque and was for a number of years a prominent citizen in Summerside, being for a time book keeper in his father's shipping office and afterwards a member of the firm of Wright, Schurman & Co. For about three years past he was in delicate health. He leaves to mourn his father and mother, his wife (formerly Miss Janie Seaman, Summerside) and one brother Percy of St. Albans, Vermont.

After his death on May 14, 1914 in Malden, Janie returned to Summerside and assisted her mother in running the Seaman House on Second Street where many young bank clerks found a congenial "home away from home." After her mother's death, Janie continued there until she retired about 1937.

Frederick Hammond Wright, called Fred (7, Archibald M. 6, Sally 5, Major 4, Thomas 3, Clement 2, Stephen 1), was born September 22, 1869 in Centreville Bedeque, P.E.I. He married December 24, 1889, Cecilia Gertrude Warren, daughter of Samuel and Elizabeth (Robins) Warren. **Cecilia Warren** (7, Elizabeth Warren 6, Elizabeth Robins 5, Mary Hooper Robins 4, Thomas Hooper 3, Clement 2, Stephen 1) was born on P.E.I. Fred and Cecilia were third cousins through the Hoopers. Elizabeth's grandmother was Mary Hooper, from New Jersey, whose father was Thomas Hooper, Loyalist. Mary Hooper Robins was also an aunt of Fred's grandmother, Sally Hooper Wright. In 1896 Archibald M. sold the gristmill to Fred who operated it until the family business failed. Then the family moved to Medford, MA; Fred died on May 30, 1945 in Medford, MA, a sub-

urb of Boston. Fred and Cecilia had three sons (surname Wright, eighth generation):

Vernon Lorne Wright (8, Frederick Hammond 7, Archibald M. 6, Sally 5, Major 4, Thomas 3, Clement 2, Stephen 1) OR (8, Cecilia 7, Elizabeth Warren 6, Elizabeth Robins 5, Mary 4, Thomas 3, Clement 2, Stephen 1) born 1890; married Lena Crowe. They lived in Foxborough, MA where he was a salesman. He died on June 26, 1955 in Danvers, MA.

Percy Kaye Wright (8, Frederick Hammond 7, Archibald M. 6, Sally 5, Major 4, Thomas 3, Clement 2, Stephen 1) born 1891 in Centreville Bedeque, P.E.I.; married Alice Bruce. They lived in Malden, MA where he was a carpenter. He was killed by a train in 1931, in Malden, MA. They had one child, born in Malden, MA (surname Wright, ninth generation). See Chapter 11.

Edgar Allan Wright (8, Frederick Hammond 7, Archibald M. 6, Sally 5, Major 4, Thomas 3, Clement 2, Stephen 1) born November 15, 1896 in Centreville Bedeque, P.E.I.; married Esther Plaisted on October 18,1917. Esther was the daughter of Frank West and Emily Esther (Foster) Plaisted. She was born on April 5, 1897 in Beverly, MA. Edgar was a dental surgeon. He received his D.M.D.[Doctor of Medical Dentistry] [Depending on what dental college a person goes to he receives either a D.M.D. or a DDS (Doctor of Dental Surgery) degree] from Tufts Dental College in 1921 and F.A.C.D. [Fellow of the American College of Dentistry] in 1941. He served with the U. S. Navy Reserve in World War II with the rank of Lieutenant Commander. Esther attended finishing school, majoring in music, both piano and vocal, and has been a concert pianist. She has been president of the Y.W.C.A. and Regent of the D.A.R. in Beverly. Edgar practiced dentistry in Salem, and they lived at "Tooth Acres" in Beverly. They had three children (surname Wright, ninth generation).

Martha Louise Wright (7, Archibald M. 6, Sally 5, Major 4, Thomas 3, Clement 2, Stephen 1) born May 2, 1871; died 1873 in Centreville Bedeque. No more information found.

Percy Lemuel Wright (7, Archibald M. 6, Sally 5, Major 4, Thomas 3, Clement 2, Stephen 1) born June 27, 1875; married Mary Gardiner, daughter of George, sixth generation [the son of Mary Hooper Gardiner 5], and Sarah (Reid) Gardiner. Percy was an executive of American Express Company with his headquarters and place of residence in Detroit, MI. Mary and Percy were second cousins; their grandmothers were both daughters of Major Hooper, Loyalist. Percy died in Detroit, MI.

Charlotte May Wright, called Lottie, (7, Archibald M. 6, Sally 5, Major 4, Thomas 3, Clement 2, Stephen 1) born July 4, 1877; died April 15, 1899 in Oak Grove, MA [probably a section of Malden, MA]. Her remains were brought home by her brother to be interred in the Lower Bedeque Cemetery. The Summerside newspaper, thanks again to Mr. and Mrs. Bradshaw, provided some information: "The body of the late Miss Lottie May Wright whose death in Malden, Mass. was recorded yesterday, arrived yesterday evening accompanied by Mr. Percy Wright, brother of the deceased. The remains were conveyed to the former home in Bedeque where the funeral will take place this afternoon at 2 o'clock."

Harriet Ethelinda Wrght (6, Sally 5, Major 4, Thomas 3, Clement 2, Stephen 1) was the fourth child and the third daughter of Sally Hooper and Jesse Wright, as the reader may remember. Harriet married Lemuel Vickerson and had three sons and a daughter (surname Vickerson, seventh generation):

Henry Vickerson (7, Harriet 6, Sally 5, Major 4, Thomas 3, Clement 2, Stephen 1) born November 27, 1867; did not marry; died March 17, 1925 in Centreville Bedeque.

Charles Wright Vickerson, a twin (7, Harriet 6, Sally 5, Major 4, Thomas 3, Clement 2, Stephen 1), born June 5, 1870; died December 23, 1870 in Summerside, P.E.I.

Herbert James Vickerson, a twin, called Herb, (7, Harriet 6, Sally 5, Major 4, Thomas 3, Clement 2, Stephen 1), born June 5, 1870 in Summerside, P.E.I. He married Ethel Jane Locker, daughter of George Richard and Sarah (Burwash) Locker on August 28, 1903. Ethel was born on January 17, 1878 in Montreal, P. Q. Herb attended McGill University and worked in different electrical companies in Montreal where he and Ethel lived. Herb died on December 6, 1938 in Montreal, P.Q. They had two children, both born in Montreal (surname Vickerson, eighth generation):

George Locker Vickerson (8, Herbert Vickerson 7, Harriet Wright 6, Sally 5, Major Hooper 4, Thomas 3, Clement 2, Stephen 1) born September 6, 1904 in Montreal, Province of Quebec; on June 27, 1934 he married Anne Emma Davis, daughter of James Herbert and Annie Jane (Mundy) Davis. She was born on September 16, 1908 in Montreal. George graduated from McGill University in engineering in 1925. His career was always in the family business, G. R. Locker & Co., Montreal, which dealt with tiles and fireplaces. When George took over, he went into the field of industrial incinerators. He retired in 1969. Anne was a McGill University graduate from the School of Physical Education and taught in Montreal before her marriage. They have one child (ninth generation, surname Vickerson).

George and Anne Vickerson donated a draft rug, woven by Harriet, George's grandmother, to the P.E.I. Museum and Heritage foundation.

Herbert Frederick Vickerson (8, Herbert Vickerson 7, Harriet 6, Sally 5, Major 4, Thomas 3, Clement 2, Stephen 1), called Herb, born July 13, 1910 in Montreal, P. Q.; married Elma Rockwell Gibson, daughter of Frederick William and Abagail (Cleveland) Gibson,[11] on June 19, 1937. Elma was born on December 4, 1912 in Halifax, Nova Scotia. Herb and his brother George were in business together for many years: George, as an engineer, and Herb, as an accountant, in the family firm. When George retired in 1969, they disposed of

the business and Herb went to work for an international firm of chartered accountants, Touche Ross & Co. Elma worked part-time as a volunteer in the local library. Herb and Elma had two children (surname Vickerson, ninth generation), both born in Montreal, P.Q.

Martha Strong Vickerson (7, Harriet 6, Sally 5, Major 4, Thomas 3, Clement 2, Stephen 1) born July 30, 1872. She married George Seymour, a native of England, on September 2, 1902. Martha and George lived for many years in western Canada, then for a short period in Centreville before retiring to California. Martha died on January 31, 1935 in San Gabriel, California, and George died on March 2, 1938 in Southern California."[12]

Now we come to the line of **Ann Robins** (5, Mary 4, Thomas 3, Clement 2, Stephen 1), the second child and the second daughter of Mary Hooper Robins and John Robins, her husband. Ann (1790-1827) had married John Craig (1789-1852). They probably had seven children, of whom six are identified (sixth generation, surname Craig):

Margaret Craig (6, Ann 5, Mary 4, Thomas 3, Clement 2, Stephen 1) born 1811. No further information.
William Craig (6, Ann Robins 5, Mary Hooper 4, Thomas 3,Clement 2, Stephen 1) born 1813; married Jane Hooper (5, Major 4, Thomas 3, Clement 2, Stephen 1) born 1815 and died 1890, the ninth child of Major Hooper, which would make Jane in the 5th generation the same as Ann. William and Jane had nine children (sixth generation of Hoopers on Jane's side and seventh generation of Hoopers on William's side); therefore, we shall arbitrarily count the generations on Jane's side (sixth generation, surname Craig):

Major Craig (6, Jane 5, Major 4, Thomas 3, Clement 2, Stephen 1) (1841-1905) and his first wife, Ann Wright (born December 20, 1840 in Middleton), daughter of Ethelinda and Job Wright, were married on February 26, 1868. Ann died on July 20, 1871. They had one child (seventh generation, surname Craig):

Etha Craig (7, Major 6, Jane 5, Major 4, Thomas 3, Clement 2, Stephen 1) born February 7, 1870; died November 13, 1870 at age 8 months, 6 days.

Major Craig (6, Jane 5, Major 4, Thomas 3, Clement 2, Stephen 1) married (ii) Elizabeth Campbell of Cape Breton, N.S. Elizabeth died on November 1, 1879. They had four children (seventh generation, surname Craig):

Elizabeth Craig, called Lizzie (7, Major 6, Jane 5, Major 4, Thomas 3, Clement 2, Stephen 1), born March 14, 1846 or 1848.
Emma Craig (7, Major 6, Jane 5, Major 4, Thomas 3, Clement 2, Stephen 1) born November 23, 1852; died November 4, 1855 in Middleton, P.E.I.
Norman Craig (7, Major 6, Jane 5, Major 4, Thomas 3, Clement 2, Stephen 1) born 1878; married Maud Craig (1882 - ?); died 1932. Maud married (ii) William Barclay. Norman and Maud had three children (eighth generation, surname Craig):

Kenneth Craig (8, Norman 7, Major 6, Jane 5, Major 4, Thomas 3, Clement 2, Stephen 1) born 1915; married Margaret Williamson, born 1920. They had a son (ninth generation, surname Craig). Please see Chapter Eleven.
Alice Craig (8, Norman 7, Major 6, Jane 5, Major 4, Thomas 3, Clement 2, Stephen 1) born 1918; married Nicholas Schroeder, born 1920. They had three children (surname Craig, ninth generation). Please see Chapter Eleven.
Margaret Craig (8, Norman 7, Major 6, Jane 5, Major 4, Thomas 3, Clement 2, Stephen 1) born 1922; married Peter McGrenera, born in 1919. They had three children (surname McGrenera, ninth generation). Please see Chapter Eleven.

Lina Craig (7, Major 6, Jane 5, Major 4, Thomas 3, Clement 2, Stephen 1) was born in 1878. [Were Norman and Lina twins or were they 10 or 11 months apart?] and married Stewart Tighe (1876-1953); I have no record of children.

John Craig (6, Jane 5, Major 4, Thomas 3, Clement 2, Stephen 1) and Jane Schurman Wright, born October 18, 1843, had four children all born in Middleton (seventh generation, surname Craig):

Albert Theodore Craig, called Bert, (7, John 6, Jane 5, Major 4, Thomas 3, Clement 2, Stephen 1) born February 26, 1870; married Jennie (called Jane) Taylor (August 16,1876/7-April 1959) on February 17, 1896. Jane was the daughter of Caleb and Elizabeth (McPhee) Taylor of Freetown, P.E.I. Bert is listed in *Frederick's* 1889 Island directory as a clerk in his uncle Albert Craig's store, Freetown. The uncle moved to Emerald where he started another business, and Bert took over the Freetown general store until he sold the business to D. H. Auld and moved to Vancouver where he carried on an extensive lumbering business with his brother-in-law, Bruce Taylor, in British Columbia. He died in 1955 in Vancouver, B.C. Bert and Jane had four children (surname Craig, eighth generation):

Edna May Craig (8, Albert 7, John 6, Jane 5, Major 4, Thomas 3, Clement 2, Stephen 1) born December 24, 1896 (another account reads December 26, 1897) in Freetown; married Walter Cambridge (1898-1935). They lived in Vancouver and in California.[13] They had one daughter (ninth generation, surname Cambridge).

John *Harold* Craig (8, Albert 7, John 6, Jane 5, Major 4, Thomas 3, Clement 2, Stephen 1) born May 11, 1899/1900 in Lower Freetown, P.E.I.; married (i) Olive Brooks and had one son; married (ii) Neta Alberta Trites, daughter of Warren and Hazel (Horsman) Trites. Neta was born on February 2, 1913. They had twin daughters. Harold lived in and around Vancouver, B. C. He was a logger. His children by both marriages are ninth generation (surname Craig).

Annie *Louisa* Craig (8, Albert 7, John 6, Jane 5, Major 4, Thomas 3, Clement 2, Stephen 1) born December 17, 1906; married Charles (Max) May, born 1905 and died October 1971 in Vancouver where they lived. He was a salesman. Louisa died on December 24, 1951 in Vancouver. They had one child (ninth generation, surname May).
Dorothy Craig (8, Albert 7, John 6, Jane 5, Major 4, Thomas 3, Clement 2, Stephen 1) born June 16/17, 1908 in Vancouver, B.C.; married Stanley Clarke. Dorothy died in October 1945 at the young age of 37. Stanley was in the insurance business. He remarried after Dorothy's death. Dorothy and Stanley had one child (ninth generation, surname Clarke).

Colin Chesley Craig (7, John 6, Jane 5, Major 4, Thomas 3, Clement 2, Stephen 1) born March 6, 1872 in Middleton, P.E.I.; married on February 20, 1901 Mary *Louise* Wright, daughter of Archibald Thomas [Ann Hooper Montgomery's grandson] and Harriet Susannah (Beer) Wright. Louise was born on May 23, 1878 in Centreville Bedeque and died on February 11, 1973 in Summerside, P.E.I. Colin died in Middleton on October 2, 1936. The Malcolm Bradshaws provided a newspaper items about Colin. A Vacation in June 1929: "Mr. and Mrs. Colin Craig of Middleton are leaving today (Wednesday) on a trip to Vancouver, B. C., and points of interest on the Pacific Coast as far down as Portland, Oregon. Mr. and Mrs. Craig expect to be away at least two months. We wish them a very pleasant holiday."

Colin inherited the homestead in Middleton and farmed there all his life. It is still in the fifth generation of family as it is the summer home of his granddaughter, Louise Corbett, and her husband Gregory. Colin was Recording Steward for the Bedeque United Church from 1931 to 1939. He and his wife, Louise, were second cousins. This family is another in which both father and mother could be counted in the Hooper genealogy. Mary *Louise* Wright (seventh generation of Hoopers) is the daughter of Archibald T. Wright of the 6th generation, the granddaughter of Mary of the 5th generation and her husband Jim Wright, and the great-granddaughter of Ann Montgomery of the 4th generation and her husband John Montgomery. We will

refrain from tracing the ancestry through Ann Montgomery, however, and give genealogical credit to Jane through the Craigs! Colin and Louise had six children (eighth generation, surname Craig), all born in Middleton except the first and the last:

John *Wilfred* Wright Craig (8, Colin 7, John 6, Jane 5, Major 4, Thomas 3, Clement 2, Stephen 1) born November 5, 1902 at his grandfather Wright's in Centrville Bedeque; married Isabel Montgomery Martin (1898-?), daughter of Samuel M. and Catherine E. (MacPhail) Martin on November 30, 1927 in Valleyfield, P.E.I. The following wedding announcement is compliments of Mr. and Mrs. Bradshaw: "Craig-Martin - At Valleyfield on Nov. 30th, John Wilfred Craig, Bedeque, and Isabel Montgomery Martin, daughter of Mr. and Mrs. Samuel M. Martin, Heatherdale, by Rev. J. A. Lellan, assisted by Rev. John Stirling, Montague [1927]."

Wilfred and Isabel farmed in Middleton and retired in 1966 to Central Bedeque. They had five children (surname Craig, ninth generation). Please see Chapter 11.

William *Walter* Beer Craig (8, Colin 7, John 6, Jane 5, Major 4, Thomas 3, Clement 2, Stephen 1) born February 18, 1905 in Middleton; married Jennie Louise MacCallum, the daughter of Albert and Lucy (Hogg) MacCallum, on June 23, 1931. Jennie was born on June 23, 1905 in Lower Bedeque. They lived in Middleton on the home farm. Walter retired from farming in 1965 and he and Jennie moved to Centreville to his grandfather Wright's house. Their son William lived on the farm in Middleton. Jennie taught music in the schools and was organist at the Bedeque Methodist Church [and continued when it became the Bedeque United Church] for about 40 years. He was the caretaker of the North Bedeque Cemetery. We remember when Mr. and Mrs. Craig lived two houses from the Bedeque United Church and he grew and sold vegetables and raspberries. They had three children (surname Craig, ninth generation).

Harriet *Jean* Craig (8, Colin 7, John 6, Jane 5, Major 4, Thomas 3, Clement 2, Stephen 1) born July 6, 1908 in Middleton; married John Archibald Craig on July 9, 1944. John was the son of John Lemuel and Sarah Adeline (Ramsay) Craig. He was born on March 9, 1895 in Brooklyn, N.Y. and died September 23, 1957 in New York City. Jean attended Mount Allison Ladies College, Sackville, N. B., 1927-1928, then trained at St. John's Hosptial School of Nursing, Brooklyn, N.Y. and received her R. N. in 1932. John attended Polytechnic Institute and Pratt Institute, Brooklyn, N.Y. He was a test engineer in the marine division of Sperry Gyroscope, Inc. at Mineola, Long Island. They lived in Wantagh, N.Y. They had two children, both born in Brooklyn, N.Y. (surname Craig, ninth generation).

Chesley Archibald Craig (8, Colin 7, John 6, Jane 5, Major 4, Thomas 3, Clement 2, Stephen 1) born September 16, 1916; married (i) Muriel Katherine Leard, daughter of Earle Douglas and Helen *Blanche* (Leard) Leard. She was born July 23, 1916 in Central Bedeque. They lived in Middleton and in Moncton, N.B. before the marriage was dissolved. Chesley re-married twice more. His third wife was Florence Louise Wilkinson; they were married on October 29, 1954, and lived in Vancouver, B.C. Chesley had no children. He was an electrician. He and Florence were both killed in a highway fatality in November 1960.[14]

Florence Elizabeth Craig (8, Colin 7, John 6, Jane 5, Major 4, Thomas 3, Clement 2, Stephen 1) born September 15, 1919 in Middleton, P.E.I.; married Richard O'Donovan Sheridan, the son of James and Anne (Beattie) Sheridan, on February 21, 1953 in Vancouver, B. C. He was born on February 2, 1920 in Paisley, Scotland. Richard was a statistician with the Federal Government in Vancouver, B. C. He served in the Canadian Army during World War II. Florence entered the Prince Edward Island Hospital School of Nursing, but ill health prevented her from finishing the course. Florence and Richard had one child (surname Sheridan, ninth generation).

Marguerite Louise Craig (8, Colin 7, John 6, Jane 5, Major 4, Thomas 3, Clement 2, Stephen 1) born April 10, 1922 in Middleton, P.E.I.; married Peter Harrison, born on November 29, 1924 in Blackheath, London, England, on March 5, 1945. Peter was the son of Arthur and Emily May (Corps) Harrison. They lived in South Burnaby, B. C. where Peter was a Quality Control Supervisor with the Council of Forest Industries. They had four children (surname Harrison, ninth generation).

Lizzie May Craig (7, John 6, Jane 5, Major 4, Thomas 3, Clement 2, Stephen 1) born August 5, 1874; did not marry; lived at home and died there August 10, 1917 at 4:30 a.m.; buried August 12 at 2:30 p.m. From the newspaper: "We learn with deep sorrow that Miss Lizzie Craig, only daughter of Mr. John Craig of Middleton, passed away almost suddenly at her home there on Thursday night. The deceased young lady, who was a universal favorite, had been in poor health for some time, but her death came quite unexpectedly and as a great shock to the bereaved parents and relatives to whom the profound sorrow of the community is extended. The funeral will take place on Sunday at 2:30 p.m."

Sarah Jane Craig (7, John 6, Jane 5, Major 4, Thomas 3, Clement 2, Stephen 1) born December 22, 1875; died January 2, 1879 in Middleton.

The reader may remember that **Albert Craig** (6, Jane 5, Major 4, Thomas 3, Clement 2, Stephen 1) married Emmeline Crosby (1852-1919). Albert (1844-1912) and Emmeline had three children (surname Craig, seventh generation):

Blanche Craig (7, Albert 6, Jane 5, Major 4, Thomas 3, Clement 2, Stephen 1) born 1878; did not marry; died in 1963.

Claude Craig (7, Albert 6, Jane 5, Major 4, Thomas 3, Clement 2, Stephen 1) born 1881; married Cora Bell (1886-1963); deceased. Claude and Cora had two children (surname Craig, eighth generation):

Shirley Craig (8, Claude 7, Albert 6, Jane 5, Major 4, Thomas 3, Clement 2, Stephen 1) born 1919; married Peter Simpson (1921-1965). They had four children (surname Simpson, ninth generation).
Albert Craig (8, Claude 7, Albert 6, Jane 5, Major 4, Thomas 3, Clement 2, Stephen 1) born 1924; married Louise Williams (1926-). They had three children (surname Craig, ninth generation).

Nellie Craig (7, Albert 6, Jane 5, Major 4, Thomas 3, Clement 2, Stephen) born 1886; married Arthur Fraser (1881-1919); died 1962. Nellie and Arthur had three children in the (eighth generation, surname Fraser):

Constance Fraser (8, Nellie 7, Albert 6, Jane 5, Major 4, Thomas 3, Clement 2, Stephen 1) born 1913; married (i) Brock King (born 1912); divorced; married (ii) Paul Ashby (1909-1992); died in 1994. No further information.
Elizabeth Fraser (8, Nellie 7, Albert 6, Jane 5, Major 4, Thomas 3, Clement 2, Stephen 1) born 1914; married James Potts (1911-). They had two children (surname Potts, ninth generation).
Craig Fraser (8, Nellie 7, Albert 6, Jane 5, Major 4, Thomas 3, Clement 2, Stephen 1) born 1915; married Iris Hunt (1920-). They had three children (surname Fraser, ninth generation). See Chapter 11.

The reader may remember that **Charles Craig** (6, Jane Hooper 5, Major 4, Thomas 3, Clement 2, Stephen 1) was the fifth child of William Craig and Jane Hooper Craig. Charles (1849-1915) married Anne Montgomery (1860-1944). [Was Ann a grandchild of Hugh, Archibald or Donald Montgomery? (Charles Craig 6, William and Jane Hooper Craig 5, Hugh, Archibald or Donald Montgomery 4)] Charles and Anne had three children, (surname Craig, seventh generation):

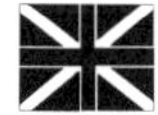

Earl Craig (7, Charles 6, Jane Hooper 5, Major 4, Thomas 3, Clement 2, Stephen 1) born in 1881; married Myrtle Crawford (1886-1963); died in 1944. Earl and Myrtle had four children (surname Craig, eighth generation):

Shirley Craig (8, Earl 7, Charles 6, Jane Hooper 5, Major 4, Thomas 3, Clement 2, Stephen 1) born 1919; married Leigh Begg, born in 1915. Shirley and Leigh divorced in 1966. They had two children (surname Begg, ninth generation).
Charles Craig (8, Earl 7, Charles 6, Jane 5, Major 4, Thomas 3, Clement 2, Stephen 1) born 1920; married (i) Elizabeth Hebb (1920-1962). Charles married (ii) Mary McEvenue (born 1925). I do not have information on any children of Charles and Mary. Charles and Elizabeth had five children (surname Craig, ninth generation).
Douglas Craig (8, Earl 7, Charles 6, Jane 5, Major 4, Thomas 3, Clement 2, Stephen1) born 1921; married Patsy Chenoweth, born 1924. Douglas and Patsy had four children (surname Craig, ninth generation).
Audrey Craig (8, Earl 7, Charles 6, Jane 5, Major 4, Thomas 3, Clement 2, Stephen 1) born 1931; married Richard Wright, born 1930. They had five children (surname Wright, ninth generation).

Vernon Craig (7, Charles 6, Jane 5, Major 4, Thomas 3, Clement 2, Stephen 1) born 1886; married Augusta Henderson, born 1888. They had four children (surname Craig, eighth generation):

Ralph Craig (8, Vernon 7, Charles 6, Jane 5, Major 4, Thomas 3, Clement 2, Stephen 1) born 1916; died 1916
Herbert Craig (8, Vernon 7, Charles 6, Jane 5, Major 4, Thomas 3, Clement 2, Stephen 1) born 1917; married Pauline Callbeck (1918-1976); died in 1969. They had four children (surname Craig, ninth generation).
Norma Craig (8, Vernon 7, Charles 6, Jane 5, Major 4, Thomas 3, Clement 2, Stephen 1) born 1919; married Ensor Bowness (1914-1962). They had one son (surname Bowness, ninth generation).

Charles Craig (8, Vernon 7, Charles 6, Jane 5, Major 4, Thomas 3, Clement 2, Stephen 1) born 1925 in Middleton, P.E.I.; married Margaret Ann Riley of Halifax, N.S. We were fortunate to live beside "Bud" Craig, as he is called, at the shore in Chelton. He and Margaret Ann had bought the other lot which was for sale beside ours. Had we bought the two lots we would never have had the pleasure of knowing the Craigs. In the summer of 2000 Bud told the author that his father was a progressive farmer. He had a horse and wagon, a tractor, and a car. He had a 100 plus acre farm in Middleton and owned shore lots from the Clark's to the MacQuarrie Road. He had cattle and milking cows.

Bud and Cousin Viola went to the same country school as they both lived in Middleton. He went into the Navy during World War II, then to Mount Allison in Sackville, New Brunswick to finish high school, then to Dalhousie University in Halifax which is where he met Margaret Ann who lived in Halifax.

In 1999 while on a tour in Spain with Margaret Ann, Bud became very sick and was hospitalized. Neither of them spoke Spanish and the hospital personal spoke very limited Enlgish. He had the diagnosis of cancer of the lung and after a stay in the hospital was flown home in a plane "for the sick and injured." Upon arriving at his home he knelt down and kissed the ground! His lung was removed and he had a couple of surgeries, but the disease had progressed too far even with the wonderful care that his wife gave him! He was able to come to the cottage in the summer of 2004. His death was about three weeks after we left the cottage in early October (November 2004). We shall miss him tremendously as he was a most wonderful and congenial neighbor! Bud and Margaret Ann have two children (surname Craig, ninth generation). See Chapter 11.

Sadie Craig (7, Charles 6, Jane 5, Major 4, Thomas 3, Clement 2, Stephen 1) born 1882; married James Norton (1884-1966); died in 1966. They had two sons (surname Norton, eighth generation):

Kenneth Norton (8 Sadie 7, Charles 6, Jane 5, Major 4, Thomas 3, Clement 2, Stephen 1) born in 1913; married Minnie McArthur, born in 1913. Kenneth and Minnie had two children (surname Norton, ninth generation).

Donald Norton (8, Sadie 7, Charles 6, Jane 5, Major 4, Thomas 3, Clement 2, Stephen 1) born in 1927; married Kathryn Mugridge, born in 1932. Donald and Kathryn had three children (surname Norton, ninth generation).

This concludes the children from Major through the eighth generation of whom this author has knowledge. Major was the first child in generation four of Thomas Hooper. What little knowledge of the family of Sarah (Thomas's child #2) I have has been included in chapter 7. I will continue with the children in the seventh and eighth generations of **Ann Hooper** (4, Thomas Hooper 3, Clement 2, Stephen 1), the third child of Thomas Hooper, Loyalist, and her husband, John Montgomery. Anne Hooper and John Montgomery's daughter, **Mary Montgomery** (5, Ann Hooper Montgomery 4, Thomas Hooper 3, Clement 2, Stephen 1), married James Wright. Mary and James Wright had ten children (surname Wright, sixth generation):

Jesse Nathaniel Wright, (6, Mary Montgomery Wright 5, Ann Hooper Montgomery 4, Thomas Hooper 3, Clement 2, Stephen 1) born Centreville Bedeque, Oct. 6, 1832; married Lavinia Davies Wright, on July 22, 1876; died May 12, 1892. They had one child (surname Wright, seventh generation):

Norman R. Wright (7, Jessie Nathaniel Wright 6, Mary Montgomery Wright 5, Ann Hooper Montgomery 4, Thomas Hooper 3, Clement 2, Stephen 1) born January 19, 1882 in Centreville Bedeque, P.E.I.; died May 4, 1885.

Ann Wright (6, Mary Montgomery Wright 5, Ann Hooper Montgomery 4, Thomas Hooper 3, Clement 2, Stephen 1) married Joseph C. Morris (1830-1896). Anne (1840-1921) and Joseph had five children (surname Morris, eighth generation):

Albert Morris (8, Ann Wright Morris 7, John Jesse 6, Mary Montgomery Wright 5, Ann Hooper Montgomery 4, Thomas Hooper 3, Clement 2, Stephen 1) born c.1867 in North Granville, P.E.I. and died in 1948 in Lower Bedeque, P.E.I. He did not marry and lived in Boston. He operated a tugboat for the Boston and Maine Railroad until he retired to live with his sister in Lower Bedeque.

James Wright Morris (c.1869-1948) (8, Ann Wright Morris 7, John Jesse 6, Mary Montgomery Wright 5, Ann Hooper Montgomery 4, Thomas Hooper 3, Clement 2, Stephen 1) married, on April 20, 1920, Lillian Jessie Ethel Bell (1880-1950). He was a farmer and carpenter. He resided in Banff, Alberta and Centreville Bedeque.

Elizabeth Jane Morris (8, Ann Wright Morris 7, John Jesse 6, Mary Montgomery Wright 5, Ann Hooper Montgomery 4, Thomas Hooper 3, Clement 2, Stephen 1), called Jennie, b. April 28, 1871; married Robert Barker Holland. They had two children (surname Holland, ninth generation).

Harriet Lea Morris (8, Ann Wright Morris 7, John Jesse 6, Mary Montgomery Wright 5, Ann Hooper Montgomery 4, Thomas Hooper 3, Clement 2, Stephen 1) born December 13, 1873 in Lower Bedeque. She did not marry and died November 30, 1961 in Greenvillle, New Hampshire. Harriet trained in the New England Hospital [in Boston]. She was matron of the hospital in Bellows Falls, New Hampshire and worked with the Victorian Order of Nurses in Sherbrook, P. Q. She changed to industrial nursing and was employed by a cotton mill in New Hampshire until she retired.

Cyrus Bradford Morris (8, Ann Wright Morris 7, John Jesse 6, Mary Montgomery Wright 5, Ann Hooper Montgomery 4, Thomas Hooper 3, Clement 2, Stephen 1) born December 16, 1876; married Florence Irving Mills, called Flossie. No more information available.

Harold Morris Holland (9, Jennie 8, Ann 7, John Jesse 6, Mary 5, Ann 4, Thomas 3, Clement 2, Stephen 1) born April 24, 1904 in Lower Bedeque, P.E.I. He married September 24, 1930 *Sibyl Lorna* Muriel Yeo, daughter of William Arthur and Eva Mae (Boates) Yeo. She was born December 30, 1907 in Tyne Valley, P.E.I. Harold and Lorna lived on the home farm in Lower Bedeque. He was a mechanic and served in the R.C. A. F. from November 1939, to September 1945. He sold the Lower Bedeque property around 1960 and moved to Chelton where he and Lorna retired. Harold and Lorna had four children (surname Holland, ninth generation).
James Wolfe *Chester* Holland (9, Jennie 8, Ann 7, John Jesse 6, Mary 5, Ann 4, Thomas 3, Clement 2, Stephen 1) was born on May 28, 1908, in Lower Bedeque, P.E.I. and died on February 5, 1967 in Derry, New Hampshire. He married, in July 1940, Madeline Peters, who was born February 26 (year unrecorded), in Everett, MA and died November 2, 1962 in Derry, N. H. When Chester left P.E.I. he went to Boston, MA and worked in Jordan Marsh department store. After serving with the American Air Force 1941-1946, he and Madeline moved to Derry, N. H. where he was general manager of a department store there. Chester and Madeline had three children (surname Holland, ninth generation).

Sarah Montgomery Wright (6, Mary Montgomery Wright 5, Ann Hooper Montgomery 4, Thomas Hooper 3, Clement 2, Stephen 1) born June 23, 1842; married Nov. 1, 1870, William Cyrus Morris (1841-1922), resided at North Granville, P.E.I. They had seven children (surname Morris, seventh generation):

John Bradford Morris (7, Sarah 6, Mary 5, Ann 4, Thomas 3, Clement 2, Stephen 1) born December 10, 1871; died in North Granville on September 8, 1872.
Mary Augusta Morris (7, Sarah 6, Mary 5, Ann 4, Thomas 3, Clement 2, Stephen 1) born April 9, 1873; died in North Granville [no date given].

Frederick Morley Morris (7, Sarah 6, Mary 5, Ann 4, Thomas 3, Clement 2, Stephen 1) born March 30, 1875; married (i) Edith Agnes Ann Elliott; married (ii) Ellen Peterson. They had one child (surname Morris, eighth generation):

Enid Virtine Morris (8, Frederick Morris 7, Sarah Wright Morris 6, Mary 5, Ann 4, Thomas 3, Clement 2, Stephen 1) born on September 14, 1911, in Regina, Sask. She married, on February 19, 1952, Ricardo Agostine Stradiotti, son of Gina Caesare and Carolikna Maria (Longi) Stradiotti. He was born on October 24, 1912, in Victoria, B.C. They lived in Vancouver, B. C. Ricardo was a partner in the firm of Stradiotti Bros. Ltd., tugboat operators. Enid and Ricardo had three children, all born in Vancouver, B. C. (surname Stradiotti, ninth generation).

Florence Ann Morris (7, Sarah 6, Mary 5, Ann 4, Thomas 3, Clement 2, Stephen 1) called Flossie; born December 1, 1877; married Rev. Benjamin Hedley Balderston. They had one child (surname Balderston, eighth generation):

Jean Morris Balderston (8, Florence Morris 7, Sarah Wright Morris 6, Mary Wright 5, Ann Montgomery 4, Thomas Hooper 3, Clement 2, Stephen 1) born on August 15, 1914 in Vancouver, B. C. She married, on November 9, 1940, Malcolm Nelson Brandon, son of James Roy and Esther Ann (Locke) Brandon. He was born on August 4, 1911 in Grand Forks, B. C. and died on March 30, 1977 in Nelson, B. C. Thy lived in Nelson, B. C. where Malcolm was a probation officer in the Attorney General's department. He served in the Royal Canadian Navy during World War II. Jean was a school teacher before her marriage.

George Huber Morris Sr. (7, Sarah 6, Mary 5, Ann 4, Thomas 3, Clement 2, Stephen 1) born April 19, 1880; married Florence Virtene Frost. They had three children (surname Morris, eighth generation):

George *Huber* Morris Jr. (8, George 7, Sarah Wright Morris 6, Mary Wright 5, Ann Montgomery 4, Thomas Hooper 3, Clement 2, Stephen 1) born on October 24, 1913 in Kensington, P.E.I. He married, on December 27, 1937, Reba Elizabeth Estabrook, daughter of Archibald James and Gertrude Sophia (Polly) Estabrooks. She was born on July 13, 1915 in Sackville, N. B.

Huber graduated from Mount Allison University with a Bachelor of Arts degree in 1936 and from Springfield College with a Masters of Education in 1937. He was employed with the Y.M.C.A. War Services 1943-1944. Afterwards he became vice-president in charge of personnel and industrial relations for the John Imglis Co., Ltd. Reba was an R. N. and has worked in Quebec City, Toronto, Charlottetown, and Bathurst, N. B. In 1976 they lived in Mississauga, Ontario.

Edith Virtine Morris (8, George Morris 7, Sarah Wright 6, Mary Wright 5, Ann Montgomery 4, Thomas Hooper 3, Clement 2, Stephen 1) was born on August 17, 1915 in Kensington, P.E.I. She married, September 16, 1939, Leslie Carey, son of Lesley C. Carey and Helen (Packard) Carey. He was born on July 13, 1915 in Sackville, New Brunswick. Edith graduated from Mount Allison with a Bachelor of Science degree in home economics and took a postgraduate course in dietetics at the Children's Hospital in Toronto, Ontario. She was engaged by the government of New Brunswick as a Youth Training Teacher and has worked in different communities in the province. Leslie is a professional engineer. They lived in Toronto in the 1970s.

Florence Elizabeth Morris (8, George Morris 7, Sarah Wright 6, Mary Wright 5, Ann Montgomery 4, Thomas Hooper 3, Clement 2, Stephen 1) born on November 27, 1913 in North Granville, P.E.I. She married Eldred Arthur Weeks, son of Leslie Stephen and Mabel Laura (Bradshaw) Weeks in 1936. Eldred was born on January 17, 1910 in Fredericton, P.E.I. They lived in Fredericton, P.E.I.. Eldred was a mechanic by trade, the owner and operator of Weeks & Sons Garage, Fredericton.

Ethel Maud Morris (7, Sarah 6, Mary 5, Ann 4, Thomas 3, Clement 2, Stephen 1) born December 4, 1881. She did not marry and died July, 1951 in North Granville P.E.I.
Cyrus Ray Morris (7, Sarah 6, Mary 5, Ann 4, Thomas 3, Clement 2, Stephen 1) born January 17, 1886; married Leah Alexandra MacKay. The reader may remember that a child of Mary Hooper Robins was Elizabeth Wright (called Lizzie) and a great-grandchild was Ellis Bradshaw. Please refer to Chapter 11.

Archibald Thomas Wright (6, Mary 5, Ann 4, Thomas 3, Clement 2, Stephen 1), called "A.T.,"(1844-1913) and his wife, Harriet Susannah Beer (1847-1936), had nine children, all born in Centreville Bedeque (surname Wright, seventh generation):

Alfred Beer Wright (7, A. T. 6, Mary 5, Ann 4, Thomas 3, Clement 2, Stephen 1) called Alfie, born February 19, 1872. He was drowned on November 28, 1885 on the new-formed ice in Wright's millpond.
James Walter Deinstadt Wright (7, A. T. 6, Mary 5, Ann 4, Thomas 3, Clement 2, Stephen 1) born February 19, 1873. He did not marry and died June 17, 1900 of tuberculosis in Centreville Bedeque, P.E.I. His obituary (courtesy of Mr. and Mrs. Bradshaw) was printed on June 17, 1900:

We record with sincere sorrow the death of Mr. J. Walter [Deinstadt] Wright, son of Mr. A.T. Wright of Bedeque, which sad event took place on Sunday at the early age of 27 years, after an illness of several years. In the fall of 1892 he left the Island for Carthage, Missouri, where he remained over a year. In the meantime his health had improved considerably, but not being altogether satisfied with the climate he went to Arkansas, bought a farm and engaged in general farming. During his stay in Arkansas, which was over two years, his health greatly improved. Being advised that there were better openings for young men out west, he left Arkansas and went to the Indian Territory. Here the climate did not agree with him, and he was seized with malarial fever, became very weak, and the doctors advised him to go to Arizona where he remained until last August when he decided to return to his native home. From the time of his arrival home, his health grew gradually worse until death ended his sufferings which he bore with Christian patience and resignation to the Divine will. He was a young man of more than average ability and but for ill

health would have made his mark. His manly Christian character endeared him to all who knew him. A mother and father, four brothers (three of them being a triplet) and one sister are left to mourn, to whom our sincere sympathy is tendered. The funeral took place on Tuesday afternoon and was largely attended."

Rebecca Jane Wright (7, A. T. 6, Mary 5, Ann 4, Thomas 3, Clement 2, Stephen 1) born October 6, 1874; died in Centreville Bedeque September 23, 1875.
John Beer Wright (7, A. T. 6, Mary 5, Ann 4, Thomas 3, Clement 2, Stephen 1) born December 31, 1875 [family Bible: Dec. 29, 1876]; died at Centreville, June 13, 1876 (family Bible: Jan. 12, 1877.
Mary Louise Wright (7, A. T. 6, Mary 5, Ann 4, Thomas 3, Clement 2, Stephen 1) born May 23, 1878; died Summerside, Feb. 11, 1973, married Colin Chesley Craig, born March 6, 1872, Middleton, P.E.I., died there, Oct. 2, 1936. [See *The Wrights of Bedeque*, p. 209]
Charles Dunlap Wright (7, A. T. 6, Mary 5, Ann 4, Thomas 3, Clement 2, Stephen 1), called Charlie, born November 2, 1879 in Centreville, P.E.I.; married (i) Areta Florence Myers, R.N., daughter of Mr. and Mrs. (nee MacCallum) Robert Myers. Areta was born in 1883 in Crapaud, P.E.I., and died on March 16, 1920 in Tryon in the Spanish influenza epidemic. Charlie married (ii) Janet *Edna* MacMurdo. Her obituary appeared in the newspaper and is copied here thanks to Malcolm and Edith Bradshaw:

Mrs. Charles D. Wright - On March 16, 1920, after a short illness, one of Tryon's elect ladies, Mrs. Charles D. Wright (nee Greta Florence Myers) at the early age of 37 years was summoned to her reward. Of a genial, kind and lovable disposition, her death has caused great sorrow. A bitterly bereaved church and community speak in hushed voices of the great loss.

In early youth she gave her heart to God and became a consistent member of the Methodist Church. The deceased was a graduate nurse and followed her professon in Florida previous to her marriage.

She was a woman of exceptional ability and sterling character. She was a worthy helpmate of her husband and she had the highest possible conception of the function and privilege of a Christian mother and felt that no sphere was comparable to it. In the remembrance of her character and the hallowed influence of her living she remains. The testimony of all who had the privilege of fellowship with her is that with true Christian patience and good hope she bore all the affliction.

It is a problem to know why such a useful and beautiful character should be removed from our midst when we think her usefulness, influence, and presence were most required. It must be that God has need of such spirits for higher and richer service. It is at least a comfort for us to believe and think this and in this belief we are submissive to His will.

Although scores of homes had illness at the time of the funeral, yet a goodly number assembled at the home on March 18 when the Rev. P. A. Fitzpatrick conducted the service. Interment was made at Crapaud. The deepest feelings of sympathy had been tendered by hosts of friends to the stricken ones.

A devoted husband and four dear little children are left to mourn an irreparable loss. Her father, Robert Myers of Victoria, her stepmother, two sisters, Mrs. A. D. Whitham, Calgary, Mrs. Russell Stordy, Crapaud, and one brother Oscar Myers of Halifax also surviving.

Charles Dunlop Wright was called "Charlie A. T.," to distinguish him from his father's cousin, Charles Stephen, who also lived in Centreville Bedeque. In 1900 Charlie's dad, A.T. Wright, bought his brother Jesse Wright's adjoining farm from John Galbraith who had bought it from Jesse's widow, Lavinia. Five years later, on December 18, 1905, Archibald T. conveyed the 100 acres to his son, Charlie. To this farm with its attractive shuttered home, he brought his bride, Areta, the golden-haired R.N. who had nursed him in the P.E.I. Hospital. Charlie sold his Bedeque farm and moved to one in Tryon near his grandfather James's birthplace, closer to Areta's relatives. Two years later the Spanish influenza epidemic took Areta's life, and Charlie was left a widower with four young children (surname Wright, eighth generation):

Harriet *Grace* Louise Wright (8, Charles Wright 7, Archibald Thomas 6, Mary Wright 5, Ann Hooper Montgomery 4, Thomas Hooper 3, Clement 2, Stephen 1) was born on June 11, 1909 in Centreville Bedeque; she married on March 19, 1936 Allan Stewart Mather who was born on November 12, 1899 in Banff, Alberta. Grace and Allan lived in Banff where their daughters (surname Mather) were both born. Allan was manager of the Bow River Boat House. Grace lived in an apartment in Calgary in the mid-1970s. Allan died in June, 1951 in Banff.

Charles Robert Wright (8, Charles Wright 7, Archibald Thomas 6, Mary Wright 5, Ann 4, Thomas 3, Clement 2, Stephen 1) born November 2, 1912 in Centreville; married on June 1, 1954, Mrs. Vivian Cecilia (Woods) Immel, daughter of Lloyd and Marion (Miller) Woods. Vivian was born on March 4, 1913 in Speers, Sask. Charles operated a large poultry farm in Surrey, B. C.

Norman Archibald Wright (8, Charles 7, Archibald Thomas 6, Mary 5, Ann 4, Thomas 3, Clement 2, Stephen 1) was born on February 18, 1914 in Centreville Bedeque, P.E.I. He married, on February 14, 1942, Mary Mattia, daughter of Guillio A. and Louisa (Malaspina) Mattia. She was born on March 9, 1914 in Vancouver, B. C. Norman was employed with the Canadian Pacific Railway in the baggage department. He and Mary lived in Medicine Hat, Alberta. They had two daughters (surname Wright, ninth generation).

Lilla Mabel Eleanor Wright (8, Charles 7, Archibald Thomas 6, Mary 5, Ann 4, Thomas 3, Clement 2, Stephen 1) born on May 17, 1918 in Tryon, P.E.I. Lilla was a graduate nurse (like her mother whom she would not have remembered), employed as a public health nurse in Victoria, B. C. No more information available.

Frank Norman Burwash Wright, first triplet, (7, Archibald Thomas 6, Mary Wright 5, Ann Hooper Montgomery 4, Thomas Hooper 3, Clement 2, Stephen 1) born April 14, 1884 in Centreville and died there in 1911. On June 2, 1908 he married Pearl Margaret Clark, daughter of Ewen and Rosara (MacGregor) Clark. A newspaper clipping, dated 1908, from Mr. and Mrs. Bradshaw, record the marriage of Frank and Pearl: "WRIGHT-CLARK - At Clark's Mills on June 2nd, by Rev. J. B. Gough, Pearl Clark, eldest daughter of Ewen and Mrs. Clark, to Frank N. Wright, son of A.E. Wright, Centreville." Frank farmed with his father, A.T., on the homestead until his sudden death that was the result of orchard spray poisoning. Pearl and the two girls went to live with her parents and lived there until she was married a second time to Frank Freeman Yeo of S.W. Lot 16. Pearl was born on April 10, 1885 in Wilmot Valley and died on December 15, 1950 in Arlington, MA.

By the turn of the century A. T.'s parents, infant son, and little daughter had all died. In June 1900, Walter died as well. Frank and Pearl had two children (surname Wright, eighth generation), born in Centreville:

Gladys Harriet Wright (8, Frank Wright 7, Archibald Thomas 6, Mary 5, Ann 4, Thomas 3, Clement 2, Stephen 1) born on April 5, 1909 in Centreville Bedeque; she married Edward *Bayfield* Ellis, son of L. Robert, Jr. and Flora Jane (Forbes) Ellis. Bayfield was born on May 24, 1895. He and Gladys were married on March 9, 1928. She died in Charlottetown on March 11, 1965. Gladys attended Prince of Wales College and taught school in Lot 16 and in Knutsford, P.E.I. before her marriage. She and Bayfield lived in O'Leary until 1952 when they moved to Charlottetown where he was on the staff of the Fruit and Vegetable Division, Canadian Department of Agriculture, and later became district inspector. Gladys was a portrait and landscape painter and a weaver of Elliscraft woven materials. When she was president of the P.E.I. Art Society, she became interested in securing a museum and gallery for P.E.I. and was the first to conceive the idea of a Centennial Memorial Building in Charlottetown, though her idea incorporated a modest structure with the main purpose to provide a museum and art gallery. She contacted the cultural groups in the city from which she had solid backing. At a public meeting in June 1958, she and Dr. Frank MacKinnon were named on the gallery committee. Dr. MacKinnon developed the idea of the present structure and was the prime mover in bringing about its erection. Gladys did not live to see the completion of the Fathers of Confederation Memorial Building. Gladys and Bayfield had five children (ninth generation, surname Ellis).

Frances Hope Marjorie Wright, called Frankie, (8, Frank 7, Archibald Thomas 6, Mary 5, Ann 4, Thomas 3, Clement 2, Stephen 1) born on May 25, 1911. [Doris M. Haslam wrote that Frankie's middle name was Hazel] She married Kenneth Alton Bruce, son of William and Lucy (Teasdale) Bruce. He was born on May 26, 1904

in Westborough, MA. Kenneth was a registered pharmacist and Frances was a registered nurse. They lived in Abington, MA. They had one daughter, Sharon (surname Bruce, ninth generation)

Elisha *Morris* St. Clair Wright, second triplet, (7, Archibald Thomas 6, Mary 5, Ann 4, Thomas 3, Clement 2, Stephen 1) born April 14, 1884 in Centreville. He married Eleanor Pearl Goodridge, daughter of James and Susan (Scott) Goodridge. Eleanor Pearl was born on April 30, 1893 in Edmonton, Alta and died in June 1971 in Calgary, Alta. Morris died on February 1, 1925 in Calgary. Morris and the third triplet brother, Jesse, left P.E.I. bound for Alberta. Morris settled in Calgary, a rapidly growing town then, and home to many other P.E. Islanders. He was a salesman for Toledo Scales Co. Morris and Eleanor had four children (surname Wright, eighth generation):

Marguerite Edna Wright (8, Morris 7, Archibald Thomas 6, Mary Wright 5, Ann Montgomery 4, Thomas 3, Clement 2, Stephen 1) was born on February 17, 1914 in Edmonton, Alberta and died in Calgary on June 16, 1968. She married (i) Ralph Washington Treasure, son of Theodore Treasure. Ralph was born on Feb. 22, 1911 in Chicago, Ill. They were later divorced. Marguerite married (ii) Patrick Campbell Hope. She and Ralph had one son (surname Treasure, ninth generation).

Eleanor Louise Wright (8, Morris 7, Archibald Thomas (6) Mary 5, Ann 4, Thomas 3, Clement 2, Stephen 1) born December 5, 1915 in Edmonton, Alberta; married Howard Bruce Hubble, Dec. 12, 1936, son of Bruce Edward and Minnie Adelaide (Street) Hubble. Bruce was born on June 1, 1912 in Kenlis, Sask. Bruce was employed with the Canadian National Hotels until his retirement. Then he became an apartment manager in Victoria, B. C. where he and Eleanor lived. They had three children (surname Hubble, ninth generation).

Leonard Thomas Wright (8, Morris 7, Archibald Thomas 6, Mary 5, Ann 4, Thomas 3, Clement 2, Stephen 1), called Len, born on May 31, 1918 at Calgary, Alberta. He married Jeanne Beatrice Desmarais, on Nov. 5, 1938. Jeanne Beatrice was born on June 15, 1918 in

Spalding, Sask., daughter of Edmund and Onada (Berube)Desmarais. Len was owner-manager of an insurance agency in Calgary where they resided. They had four children (surname Wright, ninth generation).

Claire Jean Wright (8, Morris 7, Archibald Thomas 6, Mary 5, Ann 4, Thomas 3, Clement 2, Stephen 1) born March 28, 1924 in Calgary; married Martin Simpson Hamilton, on Oct. 17, 1942. Martin was born on April 3, 1919 in Vancouver, B.C., son of Robert and Mary FitzPatrick (Dunn) Hamilton. Martin was an accountant. During World War II he served with the Canadian Army, 1939-1941, and with the Royal Canadian Air Force, 1941-1942. He and Claire lived in Calgary. They had five children (surname Hamilton, ninth generation).

James Morris Wright (8, Jesse Wright 7, Archibald T. Wright 6, Mary Wright 5, Ann Montgomery 4, Thomas Hooper 3, Clement Hooper 2, Stephen Hooper 1) was born on June 22, 1908 in Medicine Hat, Alberta. He married on August 29, 1939 Marie Elenor Wainwright, daughter of John Clark and Jennie Elizabeth (Jennett) Wainwright. Marie Elenor was born on August 28, 1908 in Edmonton, Alberta. The couple lived in vancouver, B.C. where Morris was in the clothing business for many years

Lemuel *Jesse* Davis Wright (7, Archibald Thomas 6, Mary 5, Ann 4, Thomas 3, Clement 2, Stephen 1) [third triplet] born April 14, 1884 in Centreville; married Gertrude Maggie Galloway, daughter of James Hadwin and Maggie Harriet Galloway. Gertrude Maggie was born on August 29, 1887 in Calgary and died there on March 2, 1971. By the end of the century A. T.'s parents, infant son, little daughter, and son Alfie had passed away.

The reader may recall that Jesse went with his brother Morris to Alberta. Jesse was a trainman with the C.P.R. (Canadian Pacific Railroad) and later a salesman in Calgary. He was badly gassed while serving in World War I, so severely that he was never well af-

terwards. However, with his wife's devoted care, he lived until 1953. Jesse and Gertrude had two sons (surname Wright, eighth generation).

James *Morris* Wright (8, Jesse 7, Archibald Thomas 6, Mary 5, Ann 4, Thomas 3, Clement 2, Stephen 1) born June 22, 1908 in Medicine Hat, Alta; married Marie Elenor Wainwright, daughter of John Clark and Jennie Elizabeth (Jennett) Wainwright. [See Doris Haslam's, *The Wrights of Bedeque*, Vol. 1, p. 204 for this line]
Clifford Charles Wright (8, Jesse 7, Archibald Thomas 6, Mary 5, Ann 4, Thomas 3, Clement 2, Stephen 1) born April 27, 1912 in Calgary, Alta [another account of birth is May 27, 1910]; married Grace Mary Cruickshank on October 26, 1941. Grace, the daughter of George Guthrie and Olive Cruickshank, was born on February 12, ?, in Hanna, Alberta [See Doris Haslam's *The Wrights of Bedeque*, Vol. 1, p. 332 for this line].

Ann Hooper (4, Thomas 3, Clement 2, Stephen 1) married John Montgomery and their son, Archibald Montgomery (5, Ann Montgomery 4, Thomas 3, Clement 2, Stephen 1), married Mary McKnight. Archibald and Mary had a son, Norman R. Montgomery (6, Archibald Montgomery 5, Ann Montgomery 4, Thomas 3, Clement 2, Stephen 1), who married Grace H. Brown. The lineage of their daughter follows (surname Montgomery, seventh generation):

Sylvina Annie Montgomery (7, Norman R. Montgomery 6, Archibald 5, Ann 4, Thomas 3, Clement 2, Stephen 1) was the great-granddaughter of Ann Hooper and John Montgomery. The daughter of Norman R. Montgomery and Grace Harriet (Brown) Montgomery, was born March 5, 1905 in Lower Bedeque, P.E.I. On October 3, 1934 she married Ernest Sedgewick Wright, called Ike, the son of Leslie Wright, born July 12, 1904 in Summerside. Ike was a radio technician. All his life, he was connected with the electric and radio business. He was one of the first radio hams to operate in the

Maritimes, and he maintained his own station up to the time of his death, on August 19, 1952. In company with Arthur Rogers, he was instrumental in bringing the Summerside radio station into being, and the call letters of the station - CJRW represent his name.[15]

Sylvina was a graduate of the Prince County Hospital School of Nursing in Summerside, and returned to nursing there following her husband's death. After she retired she lived in the family home on Central Street, Summerside. ["Through Ann Hooper, Sylvina is kissing kin to numberless Wrights."][16] Sylvina and Ike had one child (surname Wright), born in Summerside:

Marian Grace Wright (8, Sylvina 7, Norman 6, Archibald 5, Ann 4, Thomas 3, Clement 2, Stephen 1) born June 29, 1939; on September 2, 1961 she married Cyril James Jackman, the son of James Patrick and Madaline (Haggerty) Jackman. Cyril was born on May 1, 1940 in St. John's, Newfoundland. He was with the Armed Forces. He and Marian have been posted to R.C.A.F. stations in Sask, Gander, Nfld., and Summerside, P.E.I. They have five children (surname Jackman, ninth generation).

Margaret Montgomery (6, Daniel 5, Ann 4, Thomas 3, Clement 2, Stephen 1), granddaughter of Ann Hooper and John Montgomery, married Archibald Ellison and had five children (seventh generation, surname Ellison):

Flora Ellison (7, Margaret 6, Daniel 5, Ann 4, Thomas 3, Clement 2, Stephen 1) born 1856; married Alexander Cameron, born 1852 in Long River, P.E.I.; baptized in Alberton, P.E.I.; He was a hotel keeper and died in 1936(?). He and Flora lived in Elmsdale. She died in 1939. They are buried in the People's Cemetery in Kensington, P.E.I. Flora and Alexander had two children (surname Cameron, eighth generation):

Annie Cameron (8, Flora 7, Margaret 6, Daniel 5, Ann 4, Thomas 3, Clement 2, Stephen 1) married Carlyle Bell; born in Elmsdale, P.E.I. Annie has died, date unknown. No more information given.
Jack Cameron (8, Flora 7, Margaret 6, Daniel 5, Ann 4, Thomas 3, Clement 2, Stephen 1) married Hazel Weeks and worked as a post-master at C.F.B. Summerside (a Canadian Forces Base) Jack has died. No more information given.

Lois Ellison (7, Margaret 6, Daniel 5, Ann 4, Thomas 3, Clement 2, Stephen 1) born in 1860; married Alexander Green who was born in 1853 in Summerside, P.E.I. Alexander was a farmer who died in 1903. Lois died in 1943; they are interred in the Malpeque People's Cemetery, P.E.I. Lois and Alexander had two children (surname Green, eighth generation):

Mary E. Green (8, Lois 7, Margaret 6, Daniel 5, Ann 4, Thomas 3, Clement 2, Stephen 1) born May 8, 1892; married James Ramsay Lockerby who was born on April 21, 1892, the son of Frederick John Lockerby and Minne (Mary Jane?) Ramsay. James died on October 20, 1952; Mary died on October 15, 1977. They were both interred in the Malpeque People's Cemetery. No more information given.
Preston M. Green (8, Lois 7, Margaret 6, Daniel 5, Ann 4, Thomas 3, Clement 2, Stephen 1) born in 1895; married Olive Gillespie, daughter of William Gillespie and Elizabeth Preston; died in 1967. No more information given.

Sarah Ellison (7, Margaret 6, Daniel 5, Ann 4, Thomas 3, Clement 2, Stephen 1) born in 1863; married Malcolm MacGougan who was born in 1858, the son of Archibald MacGougan and Margaret Beairsto. Sarah and Malcolm lived in Kensington. Malcolm died in 1925 at the Kensington Nursing Home, P.E.I. Sarah died in 1948. Sarah and Malcolm had three children (surname MacGougan, eighth generation):

Annie Lois MacGougan (8, Sarah 7, Margaret 6, Daniel 5, Ann 4, Thomas 3, Clement 2, Stephen 1) born 1888; married Eliphalet Howatt who was born in 1882. He was a farmer, and they lived in French River, PEI. Annie died in 1978; Eliphalet died in 1970. No more information is available.

Keith MacGougan (8, Sarah 7, Margaret 6, Daniel 5, Ann 4, Thomas 3, Clement 2, Stephen 1) born in 1895. He married Rena Milligan who was born in Summerside. Keith died in 1969. No more information given.

Alfred MacGougan (8, Sarah 7, Margaret 6, Daniel 5, Ann 4, Thomas 3, Clement 2, Stephen 1) married (i) Beatrice McKenna; married (ii) Millicent MacNutt, born 1904, the daughter of Robert F. MacNutt and Lulu Rachel Cousins. They lived in Oyster Bed Bridge, P.E.I. Millicent died in 1982.

Lenora Ellison (7, Margaret 6, Daniel 5, Ann 4, Thomas 3, Clement 2, Stephen 1) No further information given.

Ann Montgomery Ellison (7, Margaret 6, Daniel 5, Ann 4, Thomas 3, Clement 2, Stephen 1) born in 1868; died June 2, 1880; buried in the Malpeque People's Cemetery, P.E.I.

We will continue with the descendants of **Mary Hooper Robins** (4, Thomas 3, Clement 2, Stephen 1), perhaps the fourth child of Thomas Hooper, Loyalist, and her husband, John Robins, (seventh and eighth generations):

Ingham Wright (7, Richard *Theodore* 6, Elizabeth 5, Mary 4, Thomas 3, Clement 2, Stephen 1) married (wife's name unknown); lived in Campbellton, P. E. I. apparently in his father's home and cared for his father until his father's death.

John Jesse Wright (7, Thomas Robins 6, Elizabeth 5, Mary 4, Thomas 3, Clement 2, Stephen 1) born in Oswego Falls, N.Y., no date given; married Anna Buell. The second name, Jesse, would be for John's granduncle, Jesse Wright, the husband of Sally Hooper. John and Anna lived in Oswego Falls, N. Y. and had two sons (surname Wright, eighth generation):

Howard Wright (8, John Jesse 7, Thomas Robins 6, Elizabeth 5, Mary 4, Thomas 3, Clement 2, Stephen 1) No further information given.

Thomas Wright (8, John Jesse 7, Thomas Robins 6, Elizabeth 5, Mary 4, Thomas 3, Clement 2, Stephen 1), an osteopathic physician who married on February 13, 1924, Carolyn Valentine, of Woodbridge, New Jersey. The Bradshaws gave a copy of a newspaper, The *Patriot,* of February 16, 1924, to this writer. Selective areas will be chosen. The progressive treatment of 1924 dims in light of 2003 techniques! Two articles follow:

FULTON YOUNG MAN STUDYING AT THE A. S. O. [American School of Osteopathy]

Thomas R. Wright, Fultonian of Twenty Years Ago, Writes Interestingly of His School - He Describes Operation – Fulton Boy Publishes Official College Paper, the A. S. O. Neuron – Has Conducted Restaurant and Soda Fountain to Earn Expense.

News of Fulton boys who are putting forth effort to make good in the various fields of endeaver into which they have stepped since leaving Fulton is always received with favor by The *Patriot.* In this connection it is pleasing to note that some of these boys feel like letting The *Patriot* know of themselves.

We received during the past week a chatty letter from Thomas R. Wright who twenty years ago removed with his parents, Mr. and Mrs. Jesse Wright, to Syracuse where the family home has since been although the family retains property in Fulton on the west side, opposite the knife works and on what is known as "Tom Wright's Hill." The writer of the letter is the grandson of Thomas Wright, well-known to the oldest residents of this city.

Four years ago young Thomas enteresd the American School of Osteopathy...[illegible] and graduated from that institution in June...

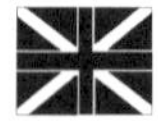

Young Wright has been under the necessity of earning a fair share of his expense money while at the school and to this end during the first two years, he conducted a restaurant and soda water fountain [business]. During the past two years he has published an official college paper, the "A.S.O. Neuron," a copy of which the young man enclosed in his interesting letter.

Of particular interest is a brief description given by Mr. Wright of an operation conducted at the college. This we give for its news value as to what field of work the former Fultonian is embarking upon.

Using no instruments except his fingers, Dr. J. D. Edwards of St. Louis operated to restore the hearing of a woman who had come all the way from Texas for treatment at his clinic at the American School of Osteopathy. Osteopathic physicians from many states are attending this clinic and also the senior students in that school among whom is Thomas R. Wright, formerly of Fulton.

Dr. Edwards originated the technique known as osteopathic finger surgery which includes work on eyes, ears, nose, and throat, and which has given both sight and hearing to many patients, some of the deaf having never heard before.

This Texas patient, 34 years old, has visited specialists from Colorado to Minnesota and back again, and the best of them had told her that nothing could be done. Some specialist, attempting to do something for a throat condition, had cut off her uvula, the little...[illegible] hanging down over the throat in the back of the mouth. The result was that the soft palate grew fast at the back shutting off all nose breathing. At the same time it interfered with the Eustachian tubes which pass from the ear to the throat and are essential to the sense of hearing.

Dr. Edwards stripped the soft palate loose from its abnormal attachment at the back, and almost immediately the woman could breathe through her nose which she had not been able to do for years. Tests made a little later showed improvement also in her hearing proper.

Other interesting cases were five deaf mutes back for examination after finger surgery treatment given them last year when Dr. Edwards held clinics. All showed remarkable improvement. Other cases of deafness were treated ranging in age from three years to nearly seventy, some of whom had never heard and whose hearing has been failing for a number of years.

Dr. Edwards opposes "tonsil slaughter," saying that unless a tonsil is rotten, it ought to be given a chance to make good. He believes in cleaning out adenoids and making conditions such that tonsils can function. In case they are infected he uses a pair of scissors of his own invention, with saw-like edges. He cuts two slits in the shape of a cross and then with a suction device "milks" out the infective material."

REVEALS MARRIAGE AT SURPRISE PARTY: THOS. WRIGHT, GROOM

The following clipping from the Elizabeth, N.J. paper of last week will be interesting reading for the numerous friends of Dr. Thomas R. Wright, former Fulton boy, who had made good in Elizabeth, and now had added new laurels by getting married. The clipping follows:

At a surprise party given at the home of her parents, Miss Carolyn Valentine, daughter of Mr. and Mrs. Frank R. Valentine of Woodbridge, announced her marriage to Dr. Thomas R. Wright of 421 Morris Avenue. The party was arranged by Mildred Valentine, a sister of the bride as a farewell gathering for her sister who was to have entered the Nurses' Training School of the Johns Hopkins Hospital at Baltimore this week.

The marriage, which was performed last Thursday afternoon in New York City, was kept secret until the announcement was made at the party Saturday evening. Rev. Chester J. Hoyt, pastor of St. James Methodist Church, was best man at the wedding, and Mrs. Jean Wallace Hazen of Maplewood was matron of honor. The ceremony was performed at the office of Rev. Dr. E. W. Chenowith, secretary of the Special Gift Department of the Board of Foreign Missions of the Methodist Church.

Dr. Wright who came to this city about a year ago is a graduate of the American School of Osteopathy in Kirk—, Missouri and has practiced at Morris Avenue where he and his bride will make their home. He is "Dad" of Veritas Chapter of the DeMolay boys. When the chapter was formed it was agreed among the members that Dr. Wright, a bachelor, was to be "Dad" of 155 boys. The boys were introduced last night to Mrs. Wright who was immediately accepted as the "Mom" of the chapter.

The only wedding trip taken by the couple was a [?] ride to New Brunswick [New Jersey] on the night of their wedding when a basketball team of Veritas Chapter had a game scheduled with the team of the New Brunswick Chapter. The bride was introduced as Miss Valentine and the unsuspecting boys knew nothing of their new mother until the regular practice was held last evening at the Armory.

Carolyn Valentine is a daughter of Mr. and Mrs. Frank Roseiter Valentine of Woodbridge, N. J. Mr. Valentine is a well-known fire brick manufacturer and is president of the National Refractors Manufacturing Association. Mrs. Wright is a graduate of the Colonial School, Washington, D. C., and attended Teachers' College, Columbia University from which she graduated in June, 1924.

Jay J. Robins (7, Thomas Robins 6, Elizabeth 5, Mary 4, Thomas 3, Clement 2, Stephen 1) married Belle Langdon. They lived in Syracuse. Jay died in March 1937. Further information is not available.[17]

Elizabeth Wright, called Lizzie, (7, Harriet Wright 6, Elizabeth [Robins] Wright 5, Mary [Hooper] Robins 4, Thomas Hooper 3, Clement Hooper 2, Stephen Hooper 1) born March 14, 1848 [another account 1846][18]; died October 28, 1934 at her daughter's in Albany. Harriet and Job Wright had two daughters, but because Emma, the younger daughter, died when Lizzie was 7 ½ years old, according to Doris Haslam, in *The Wrights of Bedeque*, "Lizzie came in for an extra share of attention. To give Lizzie the advantage of attending a young ladies' finishing school she was sent to stay with Harriet's brother and his wife in Oswego Falls, N. Y. While there Lizzie met and fell in love with Wallace Bradshaw [whom she married]. Before long, Lizzie and Wallace (whose father was Joseph Bradshaw and mother was Margaret Ballou) were living with her parents [Harriet and Job Wright] on the farm in Middleton which was made over to the young couple."[19]

In the November 3, 1898 edition of a local newspaper there was an item that stated: "Mrs. W. J. Bradshaw had the misfortune a short time ago to cut her arm very severely by falling against a window."

In 1912 W. J. Bradshaw and his son, Jesse, sold their saw mill to Allison and Ellis Hooper. This was on Malcolm Bradshaw's land. [More on this saw mill later.]

A hand-written note, dated Nov. 13, 1903, was given to me by Mr. and Mrs. Bradshaw. It read: "Poor Janie, wife of Ellis Bradshaw, died on Friday morning at 3:30 a.m. and was buried on Monday at 2 p.m. Nov. 16th, 1903. E.W.B." An obituary from a local newspaper reads, "The death occurred at Middleton on Nov. 13th, of Mrs. Jane H. Hyatt, beloved wife of Mr. Ellis Bradshaw. Deceased was a daughter of the late J. Jesse Wright of Middleton, and was a highly respected lady whom to know was to love and admire. She leaves a sorrowing husband and five children to mourn the loss of a devoted wife and mother." Mrs. Bradshaw was born on February 25, 1870.

Another notice, dated 1904, reads: "At Middleton, P.E.I., June 10th, of meningitis, Melbourne Bradshaw, aged 1 year and 10 months, son of Mr. Ellis Bradshaw."

A newspaper clipping from The *Patriot* in Fulton, N.Y. was saved and a copy given to this author by Malcolm and Edith Bradshaw about a trip that Mr. Wallace Bradshaw took back to Fulton:

BETTER THAN A LETTER

W. J. Bradshaw of Middleton, Prince Edward Island, and a former Fultonian, was in the city last week visiting his old-time friends and relatives. He says that since his last visit Fulton has made wonderful strides forward and he is pleased to see the substantial Federal building and the many new industrial buildings as well as an increase in the number of residences that have been erected.

Mr. Bradshaw has been a subscriber to The *Patriot* for over 25 years, and he says he could not keep house without it. He said: "Why, it's better than any letter that could be written, and we get it every Saturday in time to read on Sunday. Mrs. Bradshaw, who was a former student at Falley Seminary, is all taken up with the interesting letters printed from Prof. Underhill and others who attended that school. The *Patriot* keeps us in touch with the old home town, and we want to continue its weekly visits [dated September 1916]."

An obituary for Wallace (born in 1840), who died on January 29, 1918, follows, compliments of Mr. and Mrs. Malcolm Bradshaw:

Bradshaw - Died at his home in Middletown, Prince Edward Island, Jan. 29th, Wallace J. Bradshaw, aged 78 years. He is survived by his widow, one daughter and three sons, all of the same town; also a sister Mrs. I. M. White of Fulton.

Mr. Bradshaw was the son of Mr. and Mrs. Joseph Bradshaw of Fulton who resided in the house directly west of the Foster Brothers knife works on West First Street. The family consisted of the parents and five children, and Mrs. White is now the only survivor of the family.

About 50 years ago Mr. Bradshaw went to Canada where he married and settled down as a farmer. He had repeatedly made short visits to his old home town with which he kept in touch by receiving The *Patriot* every week for the half century of his Canadian residence. He was of a social nature and his visits were enjoyed by the writer as well as by the older people in Fulton who were his acquaintances in his boyhood days. He made a success of farming and was rated among the progressive agriculturalists of his adopted land. He was taken ill shortly after his last visit to Fulton in 1916 and had been in poor health since.

The *Wesleyan* printed: "Wallace Bradshaw of Middleton, P.E.I., one of the most prosperous and highly respected residents of the community, died on January 29th, aged 73 [should be 78]. He was a man of more than ordinary intelligence, well-read and public-spirited. He was a life-long member of the Methodist Church and gave generously towards the promotion of every worthy object. His death will be sincerely mourned not only by his immediate relatives, but by the whole community."

A third obituary was included, giving a bit more information:

> The death occurred on Tuesday last at his residence in Middleton of Mr. Wallace Bradshaw, a well-known and well-beloved resident of the community, at the age of 73 years [if born in 1840 he was 78 years]. He was a native of New York State, but came to the Island when a lad and settled at Middleton where he has always been a pillar of the Methodist Church and a man noted for his charitable and upright life. He is survived by a widow, formerly Miss Elizabeth Wright, three sons and one daughter namely Messrs Ellis and Thomas Bradshaw on the homestead; Jesse in the United States, and Mrs. Henry Cameron (Hattie) of Albany. The funeral which was largely attended, took place on Thursday afternoon." [Someone hand-wrote the date as January 29, 1918]

Wallace's widow, Lizzie, died at age 87, in 1934, at the home of her daughter, Hattie (Mrs. Henry Cameron), of Albany, P.E.I. Her obituary appeared in two newspapers, the dates of her death being given one week apart! It appears that the first listed here is from The *Patriot*, the newspaper from Fulton, N.Y.

> The death occurred of Mrs. Wallace Bradshaw of Middleton, at the home of her daughter, Mrs. Henry Cameron, at Albany on Sunday evening, Nov. 3rd, after an illness of three weeks. The deceased was before her marriage, Miss Elizabeth [perhaps named for her grandmother, Mary Hooper Robins's mother] Wright of Middleton, where she spent the most of her life in her native community. Mrs. Bradshaw was a kindly Christian lady, true and devoted to her family and kind and charitable to the many friends and all who came to her hospitable home."

The second obituary, taken from a Summerside, P.E.I. newspaper, reads: "**BRADSHAW** – At the residence of her daughter, Mrs. Cameron, Albany, on Sunday, Oct. 28, 1934, Mrs. Wallace Bradshaw. Funeral on Tuesday, at 2 p.m. Short service at the house, thence to Searletown Church. Interment Searletown Cemetery."

According to her grandson, Malcolm, she was about 87 years old when she died. When asked to describe her, he said: "She was average size, looked after herself pretty well, and had three boys and one girl" [eighth generation]. The children of Lizzie and Wallace (surname Bradshaw, eighth generation) are:

Ellis Bradshaw (8, Elizabeth 7, Harriet 6, Elizabeth 5, Mary 4, Thomas 3, Clement 2, Stephen 1), married Jane Hyatt, who died c.1887. After Jane's death, Ellis married a second time to Adeline Profitt (1883-1928). They had ten children (surname Bradshaw, ninth generation). Please see Chapter 11.
Thomas Bradshaw (8, Elizabeth 7, Harriet 6, Elizabeth 5, Mary 4, Thomas 3, Clement 2, Stephen 1) lived on the homestead.
Jesse Bradshaw (8, Elizabeth 7, Harriet 6, Elizabeth 5, Mary 4, Thomas 3, Clement 2, Stephen 1) owned a sawmill with his father in Middleton on the property where Malcolm Bradshaw lives (2003).
Harriet Bradshaw, called Hattie (8, Elizabeth 7, Harriet 6, Elizabeth 5, Mary 4, Thomas 3, Clement 2, Stephen 1), married Henry Cameron. They lived in Albany, P.E.I.

Emma Wright (7, Harriet 6, Elizabeth 5, Mary 4, Thomas 3, Clement 2, Stephen 1) born November 23, 1852; died November 4, 1855 in Middleton, P.E.I.

The eight children of **Sophia Ann Craig** (6, Ann Robins Craig 5, Mary Hooper Robins 4, Thomas 3, Clement 2, Stephen 1) and John Robins Wright, all born in Searletown, are as follows (surname Wright, seventh generation):

Ann Elizabeth Wright (7, Sophia Ann Craig Wright 6, Ann Robins Craig 5, Mary Hooper Robins 4, Thomas 3, Clement 2, Stephen 1) born March 10, 1843; baptized September 24, 1843; died at age 20 on December 5, 1863 in Searletown. She was named for her two grandmothers, a common custom in those days.

Mary *Louisa* Stewart Wright (7, Sophia Ann 6, Ann 5, Mary 4, Thomas 3, Clement 2, Stephen 1) born September 5, 1844; married David Rogers, as his second wife, on October 18, 1876. David's first wife was Mary Elizabeth Wright, Louisa's first cousin once removed. She died on March 16, 1903 in Freetown. Louisa's obituary follows:

Many of our readers will be pained to learn of the death of Mrs. Rogers, wife of Mr. David Rogers, Freetown, which occurred on Monday afternoon. Mrs. Rogers had been ill for some months and a few days ago was taken to the P.E.I. Hospital for treatment, but the physicians there held out no hope and she was brought back to her home where, in the midst of tender care and all that her family physician could do, she calmly awaited the end. Deceased was a devout Christian, beloved by a large circle of friends and acquaintances and her death will be sincerely mourned by the whole community. A sorrowing husband and one daughter, besides three step-daughters, Mrs. L.U. Fowler, North Bedeque; Mrs. Cairnes, Freetown, and Miss Mattie at home, and two step-sons, Picton in the Northwest, and Henry at home, survive her. She was a daughter of the late John R. [Robins] Wright, Searletown, and a sister of Messrs. Albert and Arthur Wright, Searletown, and James C. Wright, Summerside. To the bereaved relatives and friends, we tender our sincere sympathy.

A second obituary also appeared in the local press:

MRS. ROGERS, wife of David Rogers, Esq., Freetown, P.E.I., the highly esteemed local preacher of the Margate Circuit, entered into rest on March 16th, 1903, in her fifty-ninth year.

Mrs. Rogers never fully recovered from a severe sickness about two years ago, and about three months before her death began gradually to weaken. Her sickness did not seem serious at first, but during the last few weeks, her condition became alarming, and although all was done for her that could be done, she sank rapidly and finally passed away.

While her death is felt most of all by her family, yet she is greatly missed by the Methodist Church at Freetown of which she was a valued member, and by the ministers on the circuit whose home was always open to them. Mrs. Rogers was a type of Christian whose life adorned the doctrine of the Master: full of energy and faith; always ready to speak a kind word and to give a helping hand. She is missed by all who knew her. She was converted under the ministry of Rev. Richard Smith during his ministry in Bedeque [1864-1867].

The funeral services were conducted by the pastor assisted by Rev. Mr. Wightman of Bedeque, a former pastor.

In the death of Mrs. Rogers we feel that we have sustained a great loss, but her influence still lives to strengthen and to comfort those who are left behind. To the husband and children and the brothers we extend our heartfelt sympathy.

After her death David married a third time, to Louisa's cousin, Martha Maria Wright. All three of his wives were cousins to each other! Louisa and David had one daughter (eighth generation, surname Rogers):

Annie Sophia Rogers (8, Louisa 7, Sophia Ann 6, Ann 5, Mary 4, Thomas 3, Clement 2, Stephen 1), b. Jan. 24, 1879; married John Stafford Walker. They had three children (surname Walker, ninth generation). See Doris Haslam's book, *The Wrights of Bedeque*, Vol. 1, p. 253 for Annie's descendants.

Albert Solomon Wright (7, Sophia Ann 6, Ann 5, Mary 4, Thomas 3, Clement 2, Stephen 1) born February 8, 1847/8; married Elizabeth Catherine Atkinson, called Lizzie. Albert's farm was beside his father's farm.

Charles *Alonzo* Wright (7, Sophia Ann 6, Ann 5, Mary 4, Thomas 3, Clement 2, Stephen 1) born July 7, 1849; married Minnie Simmons. A personal news item from the Summerside newspaper (no date given) reads: "Personal - Alonzo Wright and wife, who had been visiting friends in Bedeque and vicinity, left Saturday morning for their home in New York State. Mr. Wright has not been on the Island for 9 years

previous to this summer; all together he has been a resident of the U. S. for 15 years. He is a native of Searletown and a brother of Mr. Jas. Wright in the Dominion Clothing Store, S'side." They had three children (surname Wright, eighth generation):

Jay Arthur Wright (8, Alonzo 7, Sophia Ann 6, Ann 5, Mary 4, Thomas 3, Clement 2, Stephen 1), b. Feb 21, 1880; d. July 28, 1883.
Arthur DeWitt Wright (8, Alonzo 7, Sophia Ann 6, Ann 5, Mary 4, Thomas 3, Clement 2, Stephen 1), b. Nov. 18, 1883; m. Elizabeth Cone. See Doris Haslam's *The Wrights of Bedeque*, Vol. 1, p. 146, for his descendants.
Beulah Sophia Wright (8, Alonzo 7, Sophia Ann 6, Ann 5, Mary 4, Thomas 3, Clement 2, Stephen 1), born October 11, 1890 in Oswego County, N.Y. She married Albert Renard who was born in Easton, PA. Beulah and Albert lived in Arlington or Lexington, MA. She met with a fatal accident about 1929 while running to catch a suburban train from a Boston station. She tripped and fell beneath the wheels of the morning train. There were no children. Albert remarried and had three children by the second wife, They would not be Hooper relatives.

Arthur Ramsay Wright, called Art, (7, Sophia Ann 6, Ann 5, Mary 4, Thomas 3, Clement 2, Stephen 1) born June 12, 1851; died October 13, 1856, in Searletown, P.E.I.
Thomas John Wright (7, Sophia Ann 6, Ann 5, Mary 4, Thomas 3, Clement 2, Stephen 1) born February 24, 1854; married Eugenia Evangeline Grant. He became a minister in the state of Washington. They had three children (surname Wright, eighth generation):

a son, died in infancy.
Louise *Pearl* Wright (8, Thomas Wright 7, Sophia Ann 6, Ann 5, Mary 4, Thomas 3, Clement 2, Stephen 1) born July 4, 1890 in Deer Isle, Maine. Pearl married James Alfred Tarte on November 6, 1912.

He was the son of John Frederick and Maryann Eleanor (Smith) Tarte. James Alfred was born on August 7, 1889 in Pleasant Valley, WA. Pearl had been a teacher in Shelton, Washington and in Whitehorn before her marriage. James was a farmer in Blaine, WA where he and Pearl lived until her early death following the birth of their second child. This little daughter, Doris, was brought up by her maternal grandparents, the Rev. and Mrs.Thomas Wright. After their death, she went to live with her father and his second wife. Pearl and James had two children (ninth generation, surname Tarte).

Thomas *Roe* Wright (8, Thomas Wright 7, Sophia Ann 6, Ann 5, Mary 4, Thomas 3, Clement 2, Stephen 1) was born on March 21, 1893 in Machias, Maine. Roe moved with his parents across the continent, finally settling in the state of WA. In Darrington he established the logging business, *Wright & Sons Inc.* On March 1, 1969 the business expanded with the purchase of Washington Trucking Inc. This larger business was operated by Roe and his three sons. His death occurred on November 19, 1972, and one month later, on December 16, 1972 his oldest son, Tom, died. Roe had served with the American Army in World War I. "He and the whole Wright family had and have a strong sense of duty to their home, family, and community."[20] He married, first, on June 18, 1919, Gretchen Henrietta VanderLinden, called Hattie, daughter of Govert O. and Jane VanderLinden. Gretchen was born on March 22, 1897 in Iowa. She died on February 13, 1939 in Ferndale, WA. Roe and Gretchen had five children (surname Wright, ninth generation).

James Craig Wright, called Jim, (7, Sophia Ann 6, Ann 5, Mary 4, Thomas 3, Clement 2, Stephen 1) born April 6, 1856. Jim did not marry. His father gave him a farm, but he preferred the small town life, and by 1889 was conducting a business on Water Street, Summerside, "Wright and Strong Tailors and Clothiers." Some time after 1904 his Tailor and Gents Furnishings business failed, and he left P.E.I., going to his brother's place, the Rev. Thomas John Wright, in the State of Washington. There he lived the remainder of his life and was buried in the Wright family plot in Enterprise, WA.

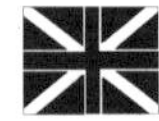

William Arthur Wright (7, Sophia Ann 6, Ann 5, Mary 4, Thomas 3, Clement 2, Stephen 1) born April 3, 1861; married Alice Alma Black.[21] They resided at Central Bedeque, Hampton, Bedeque, Charlottetown, Centreville-Bedeque, and Augustine Cove. He was a farmer, mail driver, and undertaker. They had one daughter, Louise Black, b. July 26, 1892 at Searletown (surname Wright, eighth generation):

Louise Black Wright (8, William Arthur Wright 7, Sophia Ann 6, Ann 5, Mary 4, Thomas 3, Clement 2, Stephen 1) She married Harold Keith Howatt, Dec. 20, 1921. He was born Oct. 29, 1891 at Augustine Cove, P.E.I. He was a veteran of the Great War, 1914-1919, and served with the 5th Canadian Siege Battery. He farmed on the family farm at Augustine Cove, P.E.I. Louise was killed in a highway accident, June 18, 1972, at North Bedeque, P.E.I.

The five children of **Frederick Holland Moyse** (6, Maria 5, Mary 4, Thomas 3, Clement 2, Stephen 1) and his wife Mary Crawford Wright (surname Moyse, seventh generation) were all born in Central Bedeque:

Edwin Farrow Moyse, called Ed, (7, Frederick 6, Maria 5, Mary 4, Thomas 3, Clement 2, Stephen 1), born July 25, 1860; married Annie Grant, on October 28, 1896; died October 1947 in Maine. Annie was born in 1884 in New Glasgow, N.S. and died in 1965 in Waterboro, Maine. Ed was a carpenter in the area of Waterboro where they made their home. Shortly before he died, he and Annie were forced to flee from a forest fire which was spreading rapidly towards their home. He rose from a sick bed, managed to get out of the house, but fell, exhausted, in the yard. Fortunately, a police cruiser came along at that moment and carried them to safely. The women and children were taken to a gravel pit and the pit was sprayed with water until the fire was brought under control.[22]

Bessie Maria Moyse (7, Frederick 6, Maria 5, Mary 4, Thomas 3, Clement 2, Stephen 1) born December 3, 1862; married Charles Frederick *Allison* Hooper, a descendant of Elisha.

Thomas Moyse, called Tom (7, Frederick 6, Maria 5, Mary 4, Thomas 3, Clement 2, Stephen 1) born October 25, 1864; married (i) Georgina Morrison Leard; married (ii) Alice Hart. No more information available.

Alpheus Stephen Moyse (7, Frederick 6, Maria 5, Mary 4, Thomas 3, Clement 2, Stephen 1) born March 22, 1867. One July day, as he was working near the house, a swarm of bees settled on his head. Frightened, he tried to beat them away, and they stung him horribly, resulting in his death when he was only 15 years of age.

Frederick *Ellis Moyse* (7, Frederick 6, Maria 5, Mary 4, Thomas 3, Clement 2, Stephen 1) born May 3, 1871; married Gladys Cady. They lived in Lynn, MA where Ellis practiced dentistry. He died on March 3, 1938.

Only two families of the children of **Thomas Hooper Schurman** (6, Ann 5, Thomas 4, 3, Clement 2, Stephen 1), son of John Baker Schurman and Ann Hooper, and Mary (Baxter) Schurman, appear in the seventh generation (surname Schurman, seventh generation):

George Darby Schurman (7, Thomas Hooper Schurman 6, Ann 5, Thomas 4, 3, Clement 2, Stephen 1) was born on November 17, 1852 in Summerside East, P.E.I. and died on June 1, 1913 in Lower New Annan, P.E.I. He married on May 22, 1876 (or May 27, 1877) in Wilmot, P.E.I., Mary Jane Silliker, daughter of James and Ann (Lefurgey) Silliker. She was born on January 28, 1850 in Wilmot, and died on May 19, 1944 in Lower New Annan. According to Ross Graves, in *William Schurman, Loyalist...*, "George was a farmer in Lower New Annan, which lies between Summerside and Kensington. He bought seventy acres there in 1881, adding to it by subsequent purchases in 1893 and 1899. His will, dated November 18, 1901, left the property to his wife. His vacant house stood north of where his son Harry lived in 1970.

Mary Jane's home was in Wilmot, between Read's Corner and the mouth of the Blueshank Road. Her mother, Ann Lefurgey (c. 1818-1882) wife of James Silliker (1820-1907) was a daughter of William Lefurgey (1788 – 1842) and his wife Catherine Munro (1791-1866). William was a brother to the two Lefurgey girls who married sons of William Schurman, the Loyalist."[23] George and Mary Jane had six children (surname Schurman, eighth generation):

Emma Vera Schurman (8, George Darby 7, Thomas 6, Ann 5, Thomas 4, 3, Clement 2, Stephen 1) born October 26, 1878 in Lower New Annan; married John *Henry* Moase on December 10, 1908 in Summerside, P.E.I. Henry, the son of John Lewis and Isabel (Burrows) Moase, was born on December 20, 1880 in Upper New Annan, and died on November 6, 1966 in Summerside. Henry was a farmer. He and Emma lived in Upper New Annan. They had two sons, both born in Upper New Annan (surname Moase, ninth generation).

Ray Schurman (8, George Darby 7, Thomas 6, Ann 5, Thomas 4, 3, Clement 2, Stephen 1) born December 31, 1879 in Lower New Annan; married (i) Ella Nora Montgomery, on April 8, 1903, in Travellers Rest, P.E.I. Ella Nora, born April 27, 1878, was the daughter of Benjamin and Emily Ann (Baker) Montgomery. Ray and Ella Nora had one daughter. They lived in Lower New Annan on the farm where Delbert Rayner lives in 2000. In 1906 they moved west and settled in Saskatchewan where Ray went into extensive farming. Ella Nora died in March 1917 in Dodsland, Saskatchewan. Ray married (ii) in Georgetown, P.E.I., Margaret MacConnell, daughter of Alexander MacConnell. They had one son (surname Schurman, ninth generation). Ray died December 18, 1938 in Dodsland, Saskatchewan.

Leonard Schurman (8, George Darby 7, Thomas 6, Ann 5, Thomas 4, 3, Clement 2, Stephen 1) born August 21, 1881 in Lower New Annan (another account reads July 22, 1881); married Mary Jane Horton, called Mamie, on March 25, 1907. Leonard and Mamie lived in Travellers Rest, then in Summerside. In 1909 they were living on First Street in Summerside; soon afterwards they left P.E.I. for Saskatchewan where they settled in Fairview, then moved to Dodsland.

Leonard was a carpenter. He and Mamie had four children, none of whose birth dates are given (surname Schurman, ninth generation). Leonard died on November 18, 1918 in Dodsland at the time of the great flu epidemic. Mamie married (ii) Elliott Cruickshanks and had one daughter, Helen, who would not be a Hooper relative. She married (iii) William Rowboat, and lived in Saskatoon.

Thomas Hooper Schurman (8, George Darby 7, Thomas 6, Ann 5, Thomas 4, 3, Clement 2, Stephen 1) born July 23, 1883 in Lower New Annan; married Leona Montgomery, sister to Ella Nora, on August 12, 1909 in North Bedeque. [Both girls are descendants, I feel certain, of Ann Hooper Montgomery, the great-grandmother of them and their brother Talmadge] Leona, the daughter of Benjamin and Emily Ann (Baker) Montgomery, was born on October 20, 1880 in Travellers Rest and died on June 27, 1963 in Charlottetown.

Harry James Schurman (8, George Darby 7, Thomas 6, Ann 5, Thomas 4, 3, Clement 2, Stephen 1) born January 16, 1886; died on November 12, 1971 in Lower New Annan. He married August 9, 1910 in Travellers Rest, Clara Jane Kelly, daughter of Malcolm Colin and Margaret Jane (Hogg) Kelly. She was born on September 21, 1889 in Travellers Rest, and died on January 23, 1957, in Summerside. They had no children. They lived on a portion of his father's property in Lower New Annan where Harry farmed and raised foxes and horses.

Flossie Blanche Schurman (8, George Darby 7, Thomas 6, Ann 5, Thomas 4, 3, Clement 2, Stephen 1) born November 10, 1888 in Lower New Annan, P.E.I.; married Benjamin DeWitt *Talmadge* Montgomery, brother to Ella Nora and Leona, and son of Benjamin and Emily (Baker) Montgomery, on December 24, 1911. He was born on June 25 [year unknown]. Flossie died on August 21, 1950 in Summerside, P.E.I.; Benjamin died on October 21, 1964, also in Summerside. They lived in Traveller's Rest. Talmadge was a farmer and at one time raised foxes. He was an elder in the North Bedeque United Church [which was Presbyterian until 1925]. They had three children (surname Montgomery, ninth generation).

Mary *Olivia* Schurman (7, Thomas Hooper Schurman 6, Ann 5, Thomas 4, 3, Clement 2, Stephen 1) born on September 5, 1855 and died on October 27, 1924 in Haverhill, MA. She married Richard K. Brace (1849-1925). They lived in Charlottetown where Richard had a store. In later years they separated. He remained in the city and Olivia boarded at Jesse Schurman's home in Central Bedeque, then went to live with her sister, Annie, in Massachusetts, and died there. Olivia and Richard had four children (surname Brace, eighth generation):

Nelson Brace (8, Olivia 7, Thomas 6, Ann 5, Thomas 4, 3, Clement 2, Stephen 1) was in the Boer War; settled in the United States.
Bertha Breadwood Brace (8, Olivia 7, Thomas 6, Ann 5, Thomas 4, 3, Clement 2, Stephen 1) born in 1880; did not marry; died in 1909.
Daisy Wesley Brace (8, Olivia 7, Thomas 6, Ann 5, Thomas 4, 3, Clement 2, Stephen 1) born in 1888; did not marry; died in 1909. Both of the girls were active in the Salvation Army. They settled in Bracebridge, Ontario, and were drowned in Sarnia while swimming. One got in difficulty and the other went to help her; both perished. They are buried in Bracebridge. Their gravestone there gives no dates, just their names and the verse from David's lament, "How lovely and pleasant in their lives, and in their death they were not divided." The dates are taken from the Brace Stone in the Sherwood, P.E.I. cemetery.
Roland Baxter Brace (8, Olivia 7, Thomas 6, Ann 5, Thomas 4, 3, Clement 2, Stephen 1) No further information.

John *Nelson* Schurman (7, Thomas 6, Ann 5, Thomas 4, 3, Clement 2, Stephen 1) born November 8, 1858; died unmarried on January 1, 1881 in Summerside East, according to the *Pioneer* for Wednesday, January 5, 1881. His death was the result of an accident; he was hoisting hay with a horse when one of the traces broke and hit him.

Annie Eliza Schurman (7, Thomas 6, Ann 5, Thomas 4, 3, Clement 2, Stephen 1) born August 26, 1862; married William Mutch, son of Benjamin and Elizabeth (Bishop) Mutch, in 1907, as his second wife. He was born in 1865. They had no children, and lived in Haverhill, MA where William had a chicken farm. He had married, first, in 1884, Minnie Callbeck, a sister to Lizzie Callbeck Johnson.[24]
Howard Lincoln Schurman (7, Thomas 6, Ann 5, Thomas 4, 3, Clement 2, Stephen 1) born June 14, 1865 [two months after U. S. President Lincoln's assassination]; lived at home and died unmarried on March 7, 1906, in Summerside East.

Mary Ann Baxter and her husband, Thomas Hooper Schurman, both died before their children, Mary a week before her husband and two weeks before her youngest son. Her will had been drawn up before Howard's death and probated May 14, 1906, leaving the farm to Howard and money to the other three children.

We continue with **Alexander Hooper's** (5, Thomas 4, 3, Clement 2, Stephen 1) descendants (surname Hooper seventh generation):

Emma Alicia Wright (7, Mary *Alice* Hooper Wright 6, Alexander 5, Thomas 4, 3, Clement 2, Stephen 1) born on April 1, 1876 in Chelton; on September 18, 1901, she married Milton Raymond Schurman, born December 11, 1875 in Central Bedeque and died March 30, 1930 in Winnipeg, Manitoba. Emma died on December 14, 1969 in Marysville, New Brunswick.

Emma and Milton settled in Virden, Manitoba where he kept store for many years. Later they farmed for four or five years in Butler, Manitoba. Then they went to Bird's Hill, a suburb of Winnipeg, where Milton resumed storekeeping. After his death, Emma returned to Central Bedeque and lived with her sister Belle (Mrs. Leonard Schurman) for ten years, after which she went to a home maintained by the Jehovah's Witness group in Marysville, N.B. Emma and Milton had two daughters, both born in Virden, Manitoba (surname Schurman, eighth generation):

Dorothy Evelyn Schurman (8, Emma 7, Mary Alice 6, Alexander 5, Thomas 4, 3, Clement 2, Stephen 1) born June 22, 1906; died in Virden, Manitoba, November 1907.
Dorothy Mary Ray Schurman (8, Emma 7, Mary Alice 6, Alexander 5, Thomas 4, 3, Clement 2, Stephen 1) born September 20, 1915; killed in a car accident in Winnipeg on August 22, 1926.

Horace Melville Wright (7, Mary *Alice* Hooper Wright 6, Alexander 5, Thomas 4, 3, Clement 2, Stephen 1) born January 7, 1879 in South Bedeque (now Chelton); married Minnie May Ross, daughter of Daniel and Elizabeth (Rogers) Ross. She was born in Stanley Bridge, P.E.I. on August 27, 1880 and died on January 24, 1953 in Lower Bedeque. He died on January 20, 1951 in Charlottetown, P.E.I. Horace graduated from Prince of Wales College with a First Class Teacher's Diploma. He taught school for three years before going to Western Canada for one year. He returned to the family farm in Chelton where he and Minnie lived until he acquired, on October 21, 1907, the 215 ¼ acre farm of his uncle, Nelson Hooper [his mother's brother] in Lower Bedeque.

Horace became interested in politics early in life. He first entered the political arena as a candidate for the Farmer's Progressive Party, but was defeated. In 1927 he was elected to the P.E.I. Legislature as a Liberal member of Fourth Prince, and in 1930 he became a Minister without Portfolio in the Lea government. Throughout his political career he was very active. At various times he was Chairman of the Workmen's Compensation Board, President of the War Labour Board, President of the Executive Council, as well as being Liberal representative for many years in the P.E.I. Legislature for the Fourth District of Prince. He was successful as a fox rancher and a farmer (for many years he was President of the Potato Growers' Association), he was a leader in the community, an ardent and vocal advocate of Temperance, and a leader in Sunday School and Tuxis Boys' work. In all these endeavours he was ably encouraged and assisted by Minnie. Horace and Minnie had four children (surname Wright, eighth generation):

William *Ross* Wright (8, Horace 7, Mary *Alice* Hooper Wright, Alexander 5, Thomas 4, 3, Clement 2, Stephen 1) born December 7, 1906 in Chelton, P.E.I.; married Dorothy Alice Brown, called Brownie, daughter of Frank and Martha Brown. Brownie was born on February 14, 1912 in Ottawa, Ontario. Ross and Brownie were married on November 26, 1937.

Ross attended Prince of Wales College in Charlottetown and taught for several years. Then he entered Dalhousie University to study medicine. He graduated M.D.C.M. in 1934, and after post-graduate study he settled in Fredericton, N.B. where he practiced ophthalmology. He was a Fellow of the Royal College of Surgeons, a past-president of the Canadian Otolaryngology Society, and a past-president of the N. B. Medical Society. Brownie was a registered nurse, having graduated from the Montreal General Hospital School of Nursing in 1935. They had three children, all born in Fredericton (surname Wright, ninth generation).

Winnifred Isabel Wright (8, Horace 7, Mary *Alice* Hooper 6, Alexander 5, Thomas 4, 3, Clement 2, Stephen 1) born April 10, 1909 in Lower Bedeque; she was office manager for Rogers Foam Corporation, joining the company in 1952. Before that time she had worked for five years with a Certified Public Accountant until called home because of her father's heart attack in December 1950. Shortly after her father's death she returned to her position in Boston where she lived at 1463 Beacon St., Brookline, MA.

Horace Melvin Wright (8, Horace 7, Mary *Alice* Hooper Wright 6, Alexander 5, Thomas 4, 3, Clement 2, Stephen 1) born June 27, 1913 in Lower Bedeque; married Helen Cecilia Archibald, daughter of the Rev. Leith Prescott and Jessie Margaret (Semple) Archibald, on June 3, 1936. Helen was born on January 5, 1916 in Economy, N.S. Horace was the farmer of the family and inherited his father's "Fairhaven Farms" in Lower Bedeque, a farm which had been his great-grandfather Hooper's [apparently Alexander's]. He was assisted by two of his four sons in a large dairy operation. Helen's father was pastor of the Bedeque United Church Circuit from 1927 until 1931. Her grandfather, the Rev. William Prescott Archibald, at one time was a Pres-

byterian minister on the Cavendish charge. [The reader may remember that the Methodist and the Presbyterian churches in Canada merged in 1925.] Horace and Helen had five children (surname Wright, ninth generation).

John *Sidney* Wright (8, Horace 7, Mary *Alice* Hooper Wright 6, Alexander 5, Thomas 4, 3, Clement 2, Stephen 1) born June 14, 1919 in Lower Bedeque; married Minnie Isabel Powers Hunt, daughter of Arthur and Margaret (Conrad) Hunt, on April 6, 1944. Minnie was born on September 21, 1921 in Lunenburg, N.S. She graduated from a diploma course in nursing at Acadia University in Wolfville, N.S. in 1940, and from the St. John School of Nursing in 1943. She took the exam to be a registered nurse and practiced her profession for many years. Sidney graduated from Dalhousie University in Halifax, N.S. with a Bachelor of Science degree in 1940, M.D.C.M. in 1943, R.C.A.M.C. 1943-1946, and conducted a general medical practice in North Sydney, N.S. from 1946 to 1948. He took specialist training in General Surgery 1948-1951, C.R.C.S. in 1950. He became a Fellow of the American College of Surgeons in 1959. He has been in private practice in Moncton, N.B. since 1951. Sidney and Minnie lived in Riverview, N.B. They had three children (surname Wright, ninth generation).

Isabelle Jane Wright, called Belle, (7, Mary *Alice* 6, Alexander 5, Thomas 4, 3, Clement 2, Stephen 1) born November 7, 1880, in Lower Bedeque and died on April 11, 1962 in Central Bedeque. In Chelton, on October 21, 1902, Belle married Leonard Abraham Schurman, son of Abraham, grandson of Caleb, great-grandson of William, the Loyalist. Leonard was born on December 14, 1877 in Central Bedeque and died on August 19, 1961 in Charlottetown. They lived on the home farm in Central Bedeque where Leonard had lived all of his life and dwelled in the house which his father had willed him. In the will Leonard had also received the 150 acre farm and the stock and the farming utensils. The house was owned in the mid-1970s by Warren Chapman. Belle and Leonard had four children (surname Schurman, eighth generation):[25]

Leith Wright Schurman (8, Isabelle 7, Mary Alice 6, Alexander 5, Thomas 4, 3, Clement 2, Stephen 1) born November 7, 1904 in Central Bedeque; did not marry. He lived on the homestead at Central Bedeque, the south portion of the lot first settled by his great-great-grandfather, William Schurman, the Loyalist. In 1965 he sold 124 acres of the 127 acres to Sidney Green, a Schurman descendant, who sold the house and an acre or so to Warren Chapman and retained the farmland. Leith reserved two acres on which he lived in a house trailer in the mid-1970s. Leith also retained an acre for his sister Lillian on which her house stood.

Hilda Alice Schurman (8, Isabelle Wright Schurman 7, Mary *Alice* Hooper Wright 6, Alexander 5, Thomas 4, 3, Clement 2, Stephen 1) born August 21, 1907 in Central Bedeque; married Leslie Ernest Hooper on June 22, 1927. Leslie was the son of Edward Arthur (of the sixth generation of Hoopers) and Bessie (Bagnall) Hooper. This is how his line runs: (Leslie 7, Edward 6, Lemuel 5, Elisha 4, Thomas 3, Clement 2, Stephen 1). He was born on June 15, 1899 in Central Bedeque, and died on January 3, 1974 in Summerside. Hilda and Leslie lived in Central Bedeque in a house that Leslie bought from the Royal Silver Black Fox Ranch Company and moved to a lot beside his shop. According to Frances Howatt, a long-time Bedequer, Leslie lived five houses toward route 1 (or 1A) counting the corner Callbeck home in Central Bedeque, on the same side of the road. Leslie operated a woodworking shop and garage for many years prior to working in Summerside as a garage mechanic.

The shop had an interesting history. Originally the Bedeque schoolhouse, it was situated at the bridge between Central Bedeque and Centreville. It was purchased by Murdock MacLeod and used for a tailor shop; it was moved to Central Bedeque by Colin Wright around 1880 and used again as a tailor shop. When it was on the Colin Wright property Miss Mame Schurman gave music lessons in it! In 1894 it was bought by Leslie's father, Edward, who moved it to his property and used it for a carriage shop before his son outfitted it for woodworking.

Leslie's great-grandfather, on the Hooper side, was Thomas Hooper, Loyalist, who settled in Bedeque in 1784. Thomas's youngest son, Elisha (1782-1860) married Margaret Crosby (1780-1843) and was the father of Lemuel (1816-1885) who married Louisa Strong (c.1823-1895), a daughter of the Rev. John Bass Strong, a Wesleyan missionary at Bedeque, 1818-1819, and pastor of the circuit, 1847-1850. Louisa's brother, Charles, married Martha Wright, and her nephew, Fred Strong, married another Martha Wright. Her niece and namesake, Sarah *Louisa* Strong, married Colin Wright, a cousin of Leslie's mother, Hilda. Louisa was the daughter of William Gambee and Sarah (Bousfield) Strong. At the Cape Traverse United Church annual turkey dinner in September 2000, I sat across the table from Elizabeth Reagh. Elizabeth, whom I met that evening, was a very interesting person. She is a barrister, a solicitor, and a mediator in Charlottetown. In the course of conversation, she told me that her great-great-grandfather was the Rev. John Strong of Bedeque!

I would like to share a rather interesting story about Colin Wright as it appears in *William Schurman, Loyalist...*, by Ross Graves (Vol. 1, p. 118):

> Colin Wright [1847-1933] was storekeeper and postmaster in Central Bedeque for many years. The first merchant in that community, his great-grandfather, William Schurman, the Loyalist, set up shop soon after his arrival in the 1780s and today - nearly 200 years later - Central Bedeque is the home of Callbeck's Ltd., the largest country store in the province, owned and managed by two of William's descendants. [In 1993, or thereabout, Callbeck's store moved to Summerside and became Callbeck's Home Hardware.] Colin's tenure lies midway between these points. He began his storekeeping career in the late 1860s as a clerk for William Strong, who then owned the store at Central Bedeque corner. When in 1876 Mr. Strong moved to Summerside to operate another store, Colin took over the Central Bedeque business. Soon after this he entered into partnership with Albert Craig, a brother to his brother-in-law, John Craig. The business carried on under the firm name of Wright and Craig until 1880, in which year the partnership was dissolved, Albert Craig moving on to Freetown to keep store there. Colin continued to operate the store until he sold out to William Callbeck, grandfather of the present owners. Mr. Callbeck also took over a tailor shop which Colin had started.... [The building used for tailoring was the workshop of Leslie Hooper]

The year Colin acquired sole control of the business at Central Bedeque he also acquired a wife, the daughter of the previous owner. One elderly Wright descendant can remember the name "S. L. Wright" on the packages of tea in Colin's store. This suggests that the business or a portion of it may have been in Louisa's name for a time. She was organist in the Methodist Church, Centreville Bedeque, for many years. Her grandfather, Rev. John B. Strong, was minister of the Bedeque circuit from 1818 to 1819 and again from 1847 to 1850.

Colin's house stood across the road from his store....The house was torn down in 1968. Louisa's unmarried sister, Mary Strong, lived with them. After Louisa's death [12/01/1908, both buried in Lower Bedeque Cemetery] Mary kept house for Colin, and after Colin's death lived on in the house, eventually moving to Summerside."[26]

Mr. and Mrs. Bradshaw shed a bit of light on Louisa's death as a result of an obituary published in a Summerside newspaper:

We regret to learn of the death of Mrs. Colin Wright of Central Bedeque which sad event occurred on Monday night after a prolonged illness. Deceased, who was 54 years of age, was a daughter of the late Hon. G. W. Strong, Summerside. One sister, Miss Mary Strong, and four brothers, Messrs. Frederick W., John B., C. E., and Henry P., survive. The funeral will take place on Thursday at 2 p.m.

Another obituary, however, for the same person, is a bit different:

The death took place suddenly at her home in Centreville early yesterday morning of Mrs. Colin Wright. Deceased had not been in the best of health for some years, but her death was not expected. Mrs. Wright, who was about fifty-four years of age, was a daughter of the late Hon. Wm. G. Strong, Summerside. Besides her husband, one sister, Miss Stirling, and four brothers, Fred W., John B., R. Edward, and Henry P., all of Summerside, survive her. Funeral tomorrow at two o'clock." [Newspapers don't always have all the details correct as the reader can see from the above minor contradictions]

Leslie E. Hooper and Hilda A. (Schurman) Hooper had one child (surname Hooper, ninth generation).

Verna Millicent Schurman (8, Isabelle 7, Mary *Alice* 6, Alexander 5, Thomas 4, 3, Clement 2, Stephen 1) born August 6, 1912 in Cen tral Bedeque; on September 22, 1951 she married Clarence *Earl* Hun-

ter, son of George Albert and Grace (Patrick) Hunter. Earl was born September 27, 1907 in Saskatoon, Sask. They lived in Scarborough, Ontario where Earl worked for the Massey-Ferguson Company. Verna was a dietician at Wycliffe College, Toronto, before her marriage. After marriage she had worked in the cafeteria of Consumers Gas Company. They had one child (surname Hunter, ninth generation).
Lillian Isabel Schurman (8, Isabelle 7, Mary *Alice* 6, Alexander 5, Thomas 4, 3, Clement 2, Stephen 1) born March 25, 1920 in Summerside; married Harold Sidney Clark, son of Edwin and Anita (Riley) Clark, on March 3, 1944, in Central Bedeque. Harold was born on December 8, 1923 in Summerside. Lillian died on December 12, 1971 in Charlottetown, P.E.I. Lillian and Harold lived on a portion of her father's farm (Leonard's) in Central Bedeque. He had reserved an acre for them. Harold worked in Charlottetown with Tidewater Seafoods, Inc., and at a canning plant in Victoria, P.E.I. They had four children (surname Clark, ninth generation), all born in Summerside.

Annie Helen Wright (7, Mary *Alice* Hooper Wright 6, Alexander 5, Thomas 4, 3, Clement 2, Stephen 1) born May 25, 1888 in South Bedeque; married Thomas Leslie Baldwin, called Tom, son of Levi and Sarah (Hare) Baldwin, on June 17, 1911. He was born in North Augusta, Ontario on January 23, 1888, and died on November 20, 1970 in Cabri, Saskatchewan She died in Cabri on February 7, 1964. Tom was a farmer in Cabri. Like so many young men from Ontario and the Maritime Provinces, he homesteaded in Western Canada. Annie met and married him while out west on a visit to her sister Emma. Annie and Tom had two children, both born in Cabri, Sask. (surname Baldwin, eighth generation):

Carmen Floyd Baldwin (8, Annie 7, Mary *Alice* 6, Alexander 5, Thomas 4, 3, Clement 2, Stephen 1) born August 23, 1912; married Jeanne Iva Duguid, daughter of George and Susan Bertha (Barter) Duguid, on June 8, 1940. Jeanne was born on July 22, 1919 in Cabri,

Sask. Carmen succeeded his father on the home farm where he and Jeanne lived. They had four children (surname Baldwin, ninth generation).

Reita *Inez* Baldwin (8, Annie 7, Mary *Alice* 6, Alexander 5, Thomas 4, 3, Clement 2, Stephen 1) born October 6, 1918; married, in 1947, Edward Leaf, called Ed, son of Fred and Mame Leaf. Ed was born on July 29, 1902 in Beresford, South Dakota. In the mid-1970s Ed and Reita lived in Swift Current, Sask. where he had retired.

Alex Frank C. Hooper (7, Robert 6, Alexander 5, Thomas 4, 3, Clement 2, Stephen 1) born in 1880 in Summerside; moved with his parents to Vancouver in 1899; died on April 30, 1916 in France in World War I. An obituary provided by Mr. and Mrs. Bradshaw reads:

> Very many old friends of the family at Summerside and the surrounding district will regret to learn that Mr. Alex Frank C. Hooper, only son of Mr. and Mrs. Robert P. Hooper, formerly of Summerside and now of Vancouver, B. C., was killed in action in France on April 30th. The deceased, who at the time of his death was 36 years of age, went to Vancouver with his parents from Summerside about 17 years ago, and enlisted there early in the war in the 29th Batttalion. His parents and one sister, Miss Ina M. Hooper, are left to mourn.

Ina M. Hooper (7, Robert 6, Alexander 5, Thomas 4, 3, Clement 2, Stephen 1) No further information found.

This concludes the children of whom I have knowledge through the eighth generation from Thomas Jr., the fifth child of Thomas, in generation four. The reader may recall that Rachel, presumably the sixth child of Thomas and Mrs. Hooper, did not marry, but lived initially with her father and after his death stayed on in the same house where Elisha and his family lived. The reader may also recall that this writer believes that Rachel, daughter of Thomas of generation three, did not in fact exist, but that she lived in the previous generation.

We will proceed to the descendants of **Elisha Hooper**, the last child of Thomas and his wife, Margaret Crosby (seventh generation).

Isabella Hope (6, Mathilda Ann 5, Elisha 4, Thomas 3, Clement 2, Stephen 1) is the only one of Mathilda Ann Hooper Hope's thirteen children about whom I have any further information (seventh generation, surname Massy):

Muriel Alexander Massy (7, Isabella Rhymers Hope 6, Mathilda Ann 5, Elisha 4, Thomas 3, Clement 2, Stephen 1) born September 15, 1884; did not marry; died April 17, 1909.
Dolores DeGoray *Hope* Massy (7, Isabella Rhymers Hope 6, Mathilda Ann 5, Elisha 4, Thomas 3, Clement 2, Stephen 1) born around 1900. The DeGoray in Hope's name was for her mother's sister who had died in 1865 at the age of 20. Hope was a nurse in Los Angeles, did not marry, and died in Los Angeles, California.

The reader may recall that **Margaret Elizabeth Clark** (6, Sarah Jewel Hooper 5, Elisha Hooper 4, Thomas 3, Clement 2, Stephen 1), called Maggie, was the granddaughter of Elisha Hooper. Her husband, Elisha Hooper Wright, was named for his granduncle. Maggie was Elisha's first wife; after her death on February 6, 1917, he married (ii) on July 1, 1922, Mrs. Claudine (Smith) Taylor. Maggie and Elisha Wright had seven children (surname Wright, seventh generation) as follows:

Ewen Bruce Wright (7, Margaret Elizabeth Clark 6, Sarah Jewel Hooper 5, Elisha Hooper 4, Thomas 3, Clement 2, Stephen 1) born October 12, 1874; died of diphtheria on November 14, 1879.
Mary Eleanor Wright (7, Margaret Elizabeth Clark 6, Sarah Jewel Hooper 5, Elisha Hooper 4, Thomas 3, Clement 2, Stephen 1) born January 26, 1877 in Summerside; married James, called Jim, Haywood Prichard on September 2, 1902; died April 20, 1958 in

Montreal, Quebec. Jim was born September 9, 1874 in Wales and died in June 1945 in Summerside. He worked for Hall Manufacturing Co. and CN Fox Breeders Association. Mary Eleanor and Jim had five children (eighth generation, surname Prichard):

Mary *Constance* Wright Prichard (8, Mary Prichard 7, Margaret Clark 6, Sarah Hooper 5, Elisha Hooper 4, Thomas 3, Clement 2, Stephen 1) born June 26, 1903 in Campbellton, N. B.; married Rutherford J. Conrod, called Jack, on September 21, 1927; died on April 19, 1945 in Summerside, P.E.I. Jack was born to William Humphrey and Leah E. (Rutherford) Conrod in Halifax, N.S., on February 23, 1902, and died there on July 9, 1966. When Jack and Connie were first married, they lived in the United States, but returned to Summerside. Jack married (ii) Dorothy Justyn Metzler, on August 29, 1946. He was an accountant-bookkeeper. He and Dorothy lived in Halifax. He was known as "Mr. Tennis." He developed Junior Tennis on his own and made tennis a real thing for youngsters in all of Nova Scotia. This was quite a challenge for a severe diabetic. Dorothy was a school teacher. Connie and Jack had two children (surname Conrod, ninth generation).

Arthur Pearson Wright Prichard (8, Mary Prichard 7, Margaret Clark 6, Sarah Hooper 5, Elisha Hooper 4, Thomas 3, Clement 2, Stephen 1) born 1904; died June 16, 1925 in Bangor, Maine, as the result of a motorcycle accident.

Sarah *Hope* Eleanor Prichard (8, Mary Prichard 7, Margaret Clark 6, Sarah Hooper 5, Elisha Hooper 4, Thomas 3, Clement 2, Stephen 1) born December 15, 1908 in Summerside; married Harold K. Watchorn on March 18, 1944. He was born September 13, 1906 in Merrickville. They had a son (surname Watchorn, ninth generation). Hope and Harold divorced in August 1945. In the 1970s she lived at 1414 Drummond St., Montreal, P.Q.

Norman Elisha Wright Prichard (8, Mary Prichard 7, Margaret Clark 6, Sarah Hooper 5, Elisha Hooper 4, Thomas 3, Clement 2, Stephen 1) born July 8, 1910 in Summerside, P.E.I.; married Glenda Louise Muttart, daughter of Willard Webb Muttart and Jennie Eliza-

beth Smallwood, on January 23, 1936. Glenda was born December 24, 1913 in Summerside. Norman served in the R.C.A.F. from 1940 to 1947, and was employed in the Department of Parcel Post Delivery. The children (surname Prichard, ninth generation) were all born in Summerside. Please see Chapter 11.

Reginald James Haywood Prichard (8, Mary 7, Margaret Clark 6, Sarah Hooper 5, Elisha Hooper 4, Thomas 3, Clement 2, Stephen 1), called Reg, was born on February 11, 1914 in Summerside, P.E.I. He married, on April 16, 1941, Mary Rita Matthews, daughter of Henry J. and Rose M. Matthews. Mary was born on October 9, 1918 in Montreal, P.Q. They lived in the 1970s at 4550 Oxford Avenue, N.D.G. Montreal. Reg was a real estate broker and successful in an enterprise owning properties in the old Montreal district of Dorchester Street, West. He served with the Royal Montreal Regiment in W. W. II 1939-1941. Reg and Mary had two children (surname Prichard, ninth generation), both born in Montreal, P.Q.

Sarah Clark Wright (7, Margaret Elizabeth Clark 6, Sarah Jewel Hooper 5, Elisha Hooper 4, Thomas 3, Clement 2, Stephen 1) born c.1879; died April 13, 1896, aged 17, in Summerside.

Eva *Constance* Wright (7, Margaret Elizabeth Clark 6, Sarah Jewel Hooper 5, Elisha Hooper 4, Thomas 3, Clement 2, Stephen 1) born 1881 in Summerside; married Harry Tinson Holman, son of Robert Tinson and Ellen MacEwen Holman, on September 30, 1903. Harry was born in 1875 in Summerside and died there in 1950. Constance died in Charlottetown on December 7, 1971. Harry and Constance lived on Beaver Street in Summerside. As a boy Harry went into the family business, a general store, in Summerside, called R. T. Holman Ltd. When she took her summer trip to the Island, for many years Aunt Jennie used to shop there to bring back an English bone china cup and saucer to me. [I assume that she brought bone china cups and saucers to each of her nieces as well] On the death of his father, Harry and his brother, J. LeRoy, carried on and expanded the business. He was Chairman of the Board of Trustees of Prince County

Hospital for twenty-five years. He was the founder of the Summerside Board of Trade, the Summerside Golf Club, and the Summerside Curling Club. Constance and Harry had six children, all born in Summerside (surname Holman, eighth generation):

Gerda Ellen Holman (8, Constance 7, Margaret Elizabeth Clark 6, Sarah Jewel Hooper 5, Elisha Hooper 4, Thomas 3, Clement 2, Stephen 1) born on September 22, 1904; married (i) Reginald Knight Morrison (called Reg), son of James Arthur and Georgia Squarebriggs Morrison. Reg was born on October 7, 1903 in Summerside and died there on May 11, 1977. Gerda and Reg had two children (surname Morrison, ninth generation); later they were divorced. Gerda married (ii) David Chandler Murray, son of Hugh and Susan (Chandler) Murray. David was born May 4, 1922. This marriage ended in separation. Gerda died in Sacramento, California on February 19, 1976.

Margaret Constance Holman (8, Constance 7, Margaret Elizabeth Clark 6, Sarah Jewel Hooper 5, Elisha Hooper 4, Thomas 3, Clement 2, Stephen 1) born in 1906, and died May 19, 1916 [g.s. says 1915]

Katherine Keltie Holman (8, Constance 7, Margaret Elizabeth Clark 6, Sarah Jewel Hooper 5, Elisha Hooper 4, Thomas 3, Clement 2, Stephen 1) born on August 19, 1907; married Ralph Comingo Hebb.

Hilda Wright Holman (8, Constance 7, Margaret Elizabeth Clark 6, Sarah Jewel Hooper 5, Elisha Hooper 4, Thomas 3, Clement 2, Stephen 1) born on February 6, 1909; married Judson Timmis Nichols.

Harry Tinson Holman, Jr. (8, Constance 7, Margaret Elizabeth Clark 6, Sarah Jewel Hooper 5, Elisha Hooper 4, Thomas 3, Clement 2, Stephen 1) born on October 12, 1912; married Velda Jane Reeves; the date of Harry's death is not known to me. Velda was still living in Summerside in 2004.

Alan Hathaway Holman (8, Constance 7, Margaret Elizabeth Clark 6, Sarah Jewel Hooper 5, Elisha Hooper 4, Thomas 3, Clement 2, Stephen 1) born on May 19, 1915; married (i) Jean Riddell Crichton; married (ii) Mrs. Helen Marion (Judson) Hogan. In the book *The*

Wrights of Bedeque, by Doris M. Haslam, I see no information on J. LeRoy, with whom Harry carried on the business of their father.

Annie Louisa Wright (7, Margaret Elizabeth Clark 6, Sarah Jewel Hooper 5, Elisha Hooper 4, Thomas 3, Clement 2, Stephen 1) was born on June 1, 1883 in Summerside, and died March 6, 1951 in Campbellton, N.B. On July 4, 1911 she married Reginald Kilgour Shives, son of Kilgour and Maria Somers (Mills) Shives. Reginald was born on April 20, 1885 in Saint John, N.B. and died on July 9, 1971 in Campbellton. Annie and Reginald lived in Campbellton where he was a coal and lumber dealer. They had two children, both born in Campbellton (surname Shives, eighth generation):

.

Robert Alexander Kilgour Shives (8, Annie Louisa Wright 7, Margaret Elizabeth Clark 6, Sarah Jewel Hooper 5, Elisha Hooper 4, Thomas 3, Clement 2, Stephen 1) was born on October 12, 1917; married Valerie Howard Scarborough.

Mary Louise Shives (8, Annie Louisa Wright 7, Margaret Elizabeth Clark 6; Sarah Jewel Hooper 5, Elisha Hooper 4, Thomas 3, Clement 2, Stephen 1) was born on January 6, 1922; married Roderick Chalmers Craig.

Lora Lee Wright (7, Margaret Elizabeth Clark 6, Sarah Jewel Hooper 5, Elisha Hooper 4, Thoma 3, Clement 2, Stephen 1) was born on July 29, 1885 in Summerside. She married Frank Arnold Lewis, the son of John Henry and Elizabeth Stanfield (Lowe) Lewis, on September 14, 1914. Frank was born on January 3, 1885 in Watertown, MA. He and his brother, John, were co-owners of Lewis Cleaners and Dyers, Inc. in Worcester, MA. During W.W. II he was stationed at Fort Devens in Ayer, MA. After he retired he took art courses in the Adult Education Department of the Plymouth, MA school system and had his paintings displayed (which he considered quite an accomplishment) to the public at 88 years of age. At that time Lora was a patient in a nursing home. They had two daughters (surname Lewis, eighth generation):

Constance Elizabeth Lewis (8, Lora Lee Wright 7, Margaret Elizabeth Clark 6, Sarah Jewel Hooper 5, Elisha Hooper 4, Thomas 3, Clement 2, Stephen 1) was born on October 3, 1915 in Worcester, MA; married Charles Joseph Lane on November 11, 1941. He was born on August 15, 1912 in Arlington, MA, the son of Daniel Michael Lane and Mary Burns Lane. They lived in Plymouth, MA where Charles was a real estate broker. They had five children (surname Lane, ninth generation).

Lora Eleanor Lewis (8, Lora Lee Wright 7, Margaret Elizabeth Clark 6, Sarah Jewel 5, Elisha Hooper 4, Thomas 3, Clement 2, Stephen 1) was born on January 25, 1918; married a Mr. Ponagoulis and lived in the 1970s at 6 Cushman Street, Plymouth, MA. No further information available.

Wilfred Clark Wright (7, Margaret Elizabeth Clark 6, Sarah Jewel 5, Elisha Hooper 4, Thomas 3, Clement 2, Stephen 1) was born on May 13, 1889 in Summerside and died on October 1, 1972 in Charlottetown, P.E.I. He married Mrs. Gladwys S. (Lord) MacDonald, daughterof Artemas and Margaret Pennefeather Stukely (Gray) Lord, on April 24, 1920. She was born on March 5, 1881 in Charlottetown and died there on August 21, 1974. Wilfred was a clerk in his father's business before enlisting in the Lord Strathcona Light Horse at the beginning of World War I. He was wounded and brought home in 1917. He sat with Justice Matheson on the exemption board for conscription enacted that year as respresentative for Prince County. His later years were spent in Souris where he was a railway clerk with the Canada Post Office Department. Gladwys and he retired to Charlottetown. They had one son (surname Wright, eighth generation) born in Charlottetown, P.E.I.:

Wilfred Artemas Wright, called Artie, (8, Wilfred 7, Margaret Elizabeth Clark 6, Sarah Jewel 5, Elisha Hooper 4, Thomas 3, Clement 2, Stephen 1) was born on May 22, 1921; married Mary *Caroline* Sinclair. No further information available.

The reader may recall **Charles Frederick *Allison* Hooper** (6, Lemuel Crosby 5, Elisha 4, Thomas 3, Clement 2, Stephen 1) who with his wife, Bessie Moyse Hooper, had three children (surname Hooper, seventh generation):

Lulu May Hooper (7, Charles Frederick *Allison* 6, Lemuel Crosby 5, Elisha 4, Thomas 3, Clement 2, Stephen 1) born May 15, 1888 in Lower Bedeque; married Frank Harrison Deacon, the son of Marcus and Marion (Edwards) Deacon, on October 19, 1910. Frank was born on July 2, 1886 in Freetown, P.E.I. and died there on November 15, 1950. Lou died in Charlottetown on February 11, 1977.

Frank was a farmer. He and Lou lived on the farm his father bought when he moved from North Wiltshire to Freetown. Lou was an organist in the Bedeque Methodist Church before her marriage, and in the Freetown church until she moved to Charlottetown in 1951. She continued her ministry of music in the Spring Park United Church which she helped to organize. "Her gardens in Freetown and Charlottetown were a sight to behold. She was a keen exhibitor at all the flower shows, winning many awards."[27] Lou and Frank had four children (surname Deacon,eighth generation), all born in Freetown:

Grace Eileen Deacon (8, Lulu 7, Charles Frederick *Allison* 6, Lemuel Crosby 5, Elisha 4, Thomas 3, Clement 2, Stephen 1) born May 16, 1912; married John Lowell Hickox (called Jack) on December 21, 1940. Jack was born to William *Franklin* and Catherine (MacLeod) Hickox. He was born May 22, 1910 in Springfield, P.E.I.

Frank *Morris* Deacon (8, Lulu 7, Charles Frederick *Allison* 6, Lemuel Crosby 5, Elisha 4, Thomas 3, Clement 2, Stephen 1) born February 2, 1915; married on October 4, 1945, Beatrice May Smith, (called Bea) daughter of Walter and Elizabeth V. MacMurdo (Robson) Smith. She was born August 4, 1916 in Halifax, Nova Scotia.

Morris attended Prince of Wales College and taught school for five years in P.E.I. During W. W. II, he served with R.C.N.V.R.P.O. (Wireless), 1940-1945. He graduated with a Bachelor of Science degree in agriculture from Macdonald College, McGill University in

1949, and was employed as a personnel administrator with headquarters in Halifax. He and Bea lived in Dartmouth, Nova Scotia.
Hilda Elizabeth Deacon (8, Lulu 7, Charles Frederick Allison 6, Lemuel Crosby 5, Elisha 4, Thomas 3, Clement 2, Stephen 1) born June 9, 1918 in Freetown; married George Howard Lewis , born May 28, 1916 in Freetown, on June 21, 1941 in Freetown. George attended Prince of Wales College in Charlottetown. He was a potato inspector for the provincial government. He was also a deacon in the Baptist Church in Charlottetown. Hilda's grandfather, Allison Hooper, was a brother to Edward Hooper, who married Bessie Bagnall, a cousin to George's grandfather. They had three children (surname Lewis, ninth generation).
Allison Marcus Deacon (8, Lulu 7, Charles Frederick Allison 6, Lemuel Crosby 5, Elisha 4, Thomas 3, Clement 2, Stephen 1) born April 28, 1924; married Muriel Frizzell.

Fredrick Lemuel Hooper, called Fred (7, Charles Frederick Allison 6, Lemuel Crosby 5, Elisha 4, Thomas 3, Clement 2, Stephen 1) born May 6, 1893 in Lower Bedeque; married Sarah Mary Lewis, called Sadie (daughter of Joseph Rogers Lewis and Eliza Taylor, born in Freetown on March 26, 1896), on January 1, 1918; died April 19, 1966 in Kensington, P.E.I. Sadie died on February 12, 1970 in Summerside. Fred was a miller and a merchant living in Kensington. At one time Fred had a saw mill next to and in the back of the farm owned by Major Lowther, and then by Neil Bradshaw on the Albany Road. Fred assisted his father in the operation of the steam sawmill. After the mill was burned to the ground, they rebuilt, making it a water-powered saw mill. In 1939, it was sold and Fred moved to Summerside to operate a saw mill there. There were two houses and the saw mill situated on the west branch of the Dunk River, but by 2000 one would never know that the area was used. Later, Fred worked at G. S. Blakeslie Machine Shop in Toronto. When he returned to the Island, he settled at Pownal where he conducted a general store, and Sadie was postmistress. Sadie had ancestors who were

Loyalists from New York. Fred and Sarah had two daughters (surname Hooper, eighth generation):

Marjorie Louise Hooper (8, Fredrick Lemuel 7, Charles Fredrick Allison 6, Lemuel Crosby 5, Elisha 4, Thomas 3, Clement 2, Stephen 1) born March 21, 1920 in Searletown, P.E.I.; married Delbert Ernest Rayner, the son of Ernest Charles Rayner and Harriet Lee Williams of Worcester, MA, U.S.A., on October 18, 1941. He was born on November 16, 1913 in Worcester, MA He was a farmer; in later years, he and Marjorie had a trailer park in New Annan off the highway between Summerside and Kensington. "Rayner's Camp Ground" was situated on the shore end of their farm at Webber's Cove, an inlet of Richmond Bay. In the mid-1970s Delbert worked as a potato inspector for the Department of Agriculture. He and Marjorie live in New Annan, P.E.I. (2000). Marjorie is an energetic, enthusiastic, interesting person. When I visited her in September 2000, to get further genealogical information on her branch of the family, Marjorie told me that her ophthalmologist in Charlottetown told her to take zinc for her macular degeneration, and the degeneration has not progressed. The reader may recall that Marjorie's grandmother, Bessie Hooper, became blind from macular degeneration. Marjorie and Delbert have six children (surname Rayner, ninth generation).

Muriel Elizabeth Hooper (8, Frederick 7, Charles 6, Lemuel 5, Elisha 4, Thomas 3, Clement 2, Stephen 1) born October 24, 1924 in Searletown; married Joseph Arthur Blanchard, on January 12, 1949. He was born on December 29, 1905 at St. Louis, P.E.I., the son of Oliver Blanchard and Marie Ann Poirier. They lived in Travellers Rest, P.E.I. Over the years Muriel has been very generous in sharing genealogical information with me. I had written to her in the winter of 1999, but had not visited her that summer. I planned to make one of my first visits to Muriel in 2000 especially to thank her for the booklet containing a lot of copies of Hooper historical papers that she had given me. About the end of June 2000 I had telephoned Gladys Henderson to inquire if she would like to visit Muriel with me. She told me that Muriel had been in a manor for a few months,

but had fallen out of bed a couple of weeks previously. She had seemed better and was considering returning to her apartment. I decided to wait for the visit. On July 9, I received a phone call from Gladys that Muriel had died suddenly the previous night. She had been tired and gone to bed early. Before 11 p.m. she was found dead in her bed. The *Journal Pioneer* published the following obituary:

BLANCHARD—The death occured at the Wedgewood Manor, Summerside, on Saturday, July 8, 2000, of Muriel E. Blanchard, formerly of Lefurgey Avenue, Summerside, aged 75 years. Daughter of the late Frederick and Sarah Mary (Lewis) Hooper. Wife of the late Arthur Blanchard of Summerside. Sister of Marjorie (Delbert) Rayner of Lower New Annan and sister-in-law of Genevieve (Gen) Noonan of Summerside. Also surviving are several nieces and nephews. Resting at the Davison Funeral Home, Kensington. A private commital service will be held at the Lower Bedeque Cemetery. No visitation or funeral service by personal request. If so desired, contributions may be made to the Heart and Stroke Foundation.

On July 21, 2000 another announcement was made in the *Journal Pioneer:* "MURIEL E. BLANCHARD A private family commital service for the late Muriel E. Blanchard of Summerside was held on Monday, July 10, from the Davison Funeral Home, Kensington, to the Lower Bedeque Cemetery, Lower Bedeque, where the service was conducted at 4 p.m. by Rev. Don MacPherson." She was buried in the cemetery of her great-great-great-grandfather, beside her husband, Arthur, who had died in 1986 The stone reads: "SPR Arthur Blanchard R.C.E. 1905-1986."

I am most grateful to Muriel for sharing so generously of her family information and stories. She provided much of the basic information for this study; I had to dig after using what she gave me, but without it, the impetus for this genealogy would not have been propelled. She has been acknowledged as an ardent genealogist and has had her findings published in several books. Muriel, I am truly sorry that I did not make a stronger attempt to visit you and share my thoughts and thanks with you one last time!

Ellis Moyse Hooper (7, Charles Fredrick Allison 6, Lemuel Crosby 5, Elisha 4, Thomas 3, Clement 2, Stephen 1) born October 20, 1896 in Bedeque, was the third child of Allison and Bessie Hooper; died March 20, 1917 in service to his country during World War One. Two articles in 1915 appear in the local newspaper and will be repeated here thanks to Mr. and Mrs. Bradshaw:

On Thursday evening next the boys of the 105th will be given a rousing farewell by the citizens of Summerside. The proceedings will take place at 7 p.m. on the school grounds and all friends of the boys in the country are heartily invited to join in the cheering. They will have ample time to return on the express trains the same evening. There will be a civic address and addresses by prominent speakers; also choruses by the school children and music by the Summerside Band. Should Thursday evening be wet, the event will take place on the following evening.

Private Ellis Hooper and Lloyd Bradshaw spent a very pleasant evening with a large number of their friends at Middleton Hall on Thursday, June 1st. Mr. Colin Craig presided and the evening passed all too quickly with singing, readings, amberola, violin, and banjo music. The boys were each presented with a military watch, fountain pen, New Testament, and purse. Mr. Calder responded for them with a very excellent patriotic talk. An abundance of ice cream and cake was enjoyed by all, and after singing "God save the King" and giving three cheers for the boys in khaki, the company dispersed.

A popular song about 1915 was a marching song written for the Siege Battery lads by R. Mahar, Darnley, to the tune of "Tramp, Tramp, Tramp, the Boys Are Marching":

We are leaving this fair Isle, and we're very sorry, too!
But wherever duty calls us we must go;
We are true Canadian lads and we scorn the traitor cads
Who would let their friends be ravished by the foe.
Chorus: Tramp! Tramp! Tramp! we all are marching.
Cheer up, loved ones, we will win. And beneath the Union Jack
We will drive the Kaiser back, then we'll hang him on the gates of old Berlin!
We are going far away, far from those we love so dear,
To relieve our comrades fighting at the front. In our struggle with the Huns,
We will stand behind our guns; Altogether we will help to bear the Brunt.
Chorus: Tramp! Tramp! Tramp, etc.

Now you chaps that are at home, You should join the colors, too,
But you seem to lack the courage and the grit. Do you think that it is right
To refuse to go to fight When you're big and strong and altogether fit?
Chorus: Tramp, Tramp. Tramp. etc.

A poem, "For King and Country," was written by Fred P. Duffy, Charlottetown:

A soldier boy was leaving for the battlefield in France
To fight for King and Country and glad he had the chance.
Donned in a suit of khaki the brave lad he sailed away
While friends at home were praying for his safe return some day.
Just about a year ago the brave laddie crossed the sea
To fight for King and Country and to bring us liberty.
Now on the field at Flanders where the shots and shells do rend'
He's wishing every moment that the war was at an end.
So maybe we can aid them in the nation's deadly strife.
So join our brave defenders and thus help to save their life,
For England needs our aid, boys; yes, she needs us one and all.
To save her from disaster we must answer to the call.

The following news item appeared in a local newspaper about Ellis M. Hooper's death in France:

BEDEQUE – The first one of the membership of the Bedeque Methodist Church to make the supreme sacrifice for his King and country was Ellis Hooper, youngest and dearly beloved son of Mr. and Mrs. Allison Hooper. He was seriously wounded while fighting "somewhere in France," March 29, and died the following day. He was a young man of exceptionally fine character and gave every promise of being a noble, useful man.

When the annual roll call was held in our church last May, Ellis, who was then in training with his regiment (105th) sent the following verse for his response: "Wherewithal shall a young man cleanse his ways? By taking heed there according to Thy Word." What a thoughtful testimony from one so young! Surely he would find peace and safety trusting in His Word.

The sympathy of the entire church goes out to his bereaved parents, his brother Fred, and his sister, Mrs. Frank Deacon, both residing in Freetown.

In a book given to me by Muriel Hooper Blanchard there is a page about Ellis Moyse Hooper (undated)":

In the casualty list issued at Ottawa last Tuesday night appeared the name of Private Ellis Hooper amongst the wounded. A telegram to his father, Mr. Allison Hooper, of Bedeque, added the ominous word "dangerously" and on Wednesday this was followed by another telegram conveying the sad news that Private Hooper was dead. He was one of the finest soldiers and best liked boys of the late 105th Battalion and had the honor, probably on that account, of being one of the first draft from the 105th to go into the trenches in Northern France. He helped materially, as so many Islanders are doing, in freeing that country from the murderous Hun and in re-establishing throughout the world the rights of freedom and justice, so dear to every British heart. The nobility of his sacrifice must assuage the sorrow of his bereaved relatives, to whom our deepest sympathy, coupled with gratitude to the dear hero for all that he had done, is extended. Private Ellis Hoooper is buried in the Searletown Cemetery. [This is highly unusual. There may be a gravestone there for him but, almost certainly, he lies in a military cemetery in France]

Several newspaper articles, from Mr. and Mrs. Bradshaw, related to World War I, will be quoted here:

My Mother

With heavy heart and trembling lips she reads the letter through.
Don't worry, dearest mother mine, I'm off to fight the foe.
I'll have to cross the ocean wide and stand in battle line,
But cheer up, ma'am, a man ne'er died, I've heard, before his time.
She checks the tears that seek to flow and gently heaves a sigh.
God, give me strength, my duty do, and bless my darling boy!
Till he'll return my grief I'll hide where others ne'er will see.
With smiles I'll cheer the other boys; a mother brave I'll be.
And now the day of peace has come. She waits with pride and joy
Among the throngs of mothers loyal to her soldier boy.
He did his duty nobly and happily blest is she
To be the mother of such a son and he her son to be.

(Mrs. M. J. N., Haliburton, P.E.I.)

KILLED IN ACTION - The many friends of Mr. and Mrs. Henry Lowther of North Carlton will be sorry to hear of their only son Charles who was killed the 25th September. He enlisted in the 105th and was sent to France in the first contingent.

He was a quiet, unassuming young man who, although he was much needed at home, saw the need of his country and has made the supreme sacrifice. He leaves to mourn his father and mother and two sisters.

Mrs. H. H. MacKenzie, nee Miss Marie MacLeod, is in Summerside, the guest of Mrs. H. H. Beer. Mrs. MacKenzie has just returned from England having been in France for almost four years. She enlisted when the war first started and intends spending part of the winter in Florida.

Mrs. F. McNeill, nee Miss Marion Sharp, returned from overseas last Friday night and is visiting her mother, Mrs. John Sharpe, at Summerside. Mrs. MacNeill, who was married in England about a year ago, left Summerside over four years ago for the front, being one of the first brave nursing sisters to volunteer for war service, and did much strenuous work amongst the wounded in the hospitals in France.

SOLDIERS HONORED – On Tuesday evening a reception was held in Middleton Hall in honor of Mr. Lloyd Bradshaw, returned soldier. Mr. James McCardle gracefully presided and called upon Mr. Colin Craig who on behalf of the community presented Mr. Bradshaw with a signet ring. In his address Mr. Craig feelingly referred to Mr. Bradshaw's comrade, Mr. Ellis Hooper, whose life was given as a part of the price of our dearly-bought liberty. A pleasing feature of the evening was an address by Prof. J. A. Clark concerning his work in connection with the Knaki University.

Solos by Mrs. Jenkins and Mr. Fraser accompanied by Mrs. Earle Leard were heartily enjoyed by all. A similar reception was tendered recently to Messrs. McKenna, Johnston, and McCardle, Middleton boys whose sacrifices will not be forgotten. Rev. J. J. MacDonald and Mr. Theodore Ross kindly assisted in the entertainment. Two boys, natives in this locality, have not yet reached their homes, but their home-coming is expected to be the signal for a demonstration that will prove that Middleton is not unmindful of the fact that "we are not our own, but we have been bought with a price."

Red, White and Blue

Britannia, the Gem of the ocean, the home of the Brave and the Free;
The Shrine of each Patriot's devotion, a World offers Homage to Thee!
Thy mandates make Heroes assemble when Liberty's forces stand in view;
Thy Banners make Tryanny tremble When borne by the Red, White, and Blue,etc.

When war waged its wide desolation and threatened our land to deform,
The ark then of Freedom's foundations, Britannia rode safe through the storm.
With her garland of victory o'er her when so proudly she bore her bold crew

With her flag proudly floating before her, the boast of the Red, White, and Blue, etc.

The wind cup, the wine cup bring hither and fill you it up to the brim.
May the wreath they have won never wither nor the Star of their glory grow dim!
May the service united ne'er sever and hold to their colors so true!
The Army and Navy forever! Three cheers for the Red, White, and Blue!

Thank God for Peace! November 11, 1918

With heart and soul and voice Thy people, Lord, rejoice!
The night of pain is past; Thy day has dawned at last.
We thank Thee for Thy gift of peace. Oh, build us now to Thine increase!
Far-scattered lie our dead. Their glory ne'er shall fade.
To keep Life's soul alive they died that we might live.
Like Kings they died and now in Peace they build again to Thine increase.
To every broken home with cheer and comfort come!
Console the hearts bereft with joy of mercies left!
So, through our sorrows shall Thy peace build all our hearts to Thine increase.

Leslie Ernest Hooper (7, Edward Arthur 6, Lemuel Crosby, Elisha 4, Thomas 3, Clement 2, Stephen 1) born June 15, 1899 in Central Bedeque; died January 23, 1974 in Summerside; married Hilda Alice Schurman, daughter of Leonard Abraham and Isabel Jane (Wright) Schurman, on June 22, 1927. Leslie was a machinist. He and Hilda lived in Central Bedeque in a house that Leslie bought from the Royal Silver Black Fox Ranch Company and moved to a lot beside his shop. Leslie operated a woodworking shop and garage for many years prior to working in Summerside as a garage mechanic. The shop had a long and interesting history, as told earlier in this chapter.[28] Hilda is also of the Hooper lineage (generation eight). Her line is through Thomas Hooper (generation four), and Alexander (generation five). [Unfortunately, generations six and seven are unknown to me]. Leslie and Hilda [tracing the line through Leslie] had one child (surname Hooper, eighth generation):

Helen Leona Hooper (8, Leslie 7, Edward Arthur 6, Lemuel Crosby 5, Elisha 4, Thomas 3, Clement 2, Stephen 1) born September 4, 1930 in Central Bedeque. Helen was a bookkeeper with M. F. Schurman Company before moving to Toronto where she was an accountant with Ultramar, an oil company.

Helen Louise Hooper (7, Edward Arthur 6, Lemuel Crosby 5, Elisha 4, Thomas 3, Clement 2, Stephen 1); born April 21, 1903; married Alfred Charles Pfeiffer, son of Conrad and Christina (Schick) Pfeiffer, on October 26, 1940 in Babylon, Long Island, New York. Alfred was born on May 9, 1892 in Stapleton, Staten Island, N. Y. and died on January 24, 1964 in Bay Shore, N.Y. Helen and Alfred lived in Bay Shore. Alfred was an insurance agent with Northwestern Life Insurance Co., 1938-1942; an inspector with Republic Aviation Corporation 1942-1957; then an employee of the town of Islip until his death. Helen was killed in an automobile accident in St. Stephen, N. B. on September 8, 1967, while travelling to visit relatives (probably her brother, Leslie, in Central Bedeque) on Prince Edward Island. Helen and Alfred had one child (surname Pfeiffer, eighth generation):

Marilyn Ann Pfeiffer (8, Helen 7, Edward 6, Lemuel 5, Elisha 4, Thomas 3, Clement 2, Stephen 1) born on August 31, 1942 in Bay Shore, N.Y. She graduated from the State University of New York, at New Paltz, 1964, taught at Sayville, Long Island, N.Y. and lived in Oakdale, N.Y. No further information. Marilyn is the last descendant of Elisha Hooper of whom I have knowledge.

Notes

1 Harold Cairns, *Descendants of David Walker (*Breadalbane, P.E.I., n.p., n.d.), pp. 13-14
2 Ross Graves, *William Schurman, Loyalist of Bedeque, Prince Edward Island, and his descendants* (Summerside, P.E.I.: Harold B. Schurman, 1973), p. 245
3 Doris Haslam, *The Wrights of Bedeque, Prince Edward Island, A Loyalist Family* (Summerside, P.E.I.: Doris Muncey Haslam, 1978), p. 194
4 Edward MacDonald, *If You're Strong-hearted: Prince Edward Island in the Twentieth Century(Charlottetown, P.E.I.: P.E.I. Museum and Heritage Foundation, 2000)*
5 Harold Cairns, op. cit.
6 Edward MacDonald, op. cit., p. 48
7 *The Charlottetown Guardian*, issue unrecorded
8 Doris Haslam, op. cit., p. 212
9 Ibid., see p. 212 for genealogical data on Lewis
10 Ibid., p. 41
11 Ibid., p. 340
12 Doris Haslam, op. cit., p. 111
13 Ibid., pp. 209 and 342
14 Ibid., p. 209
15 Ibid., p. 255
16 Ibid., p. 255
17 Ibid., p. 59
18 Ibid., p. 50
19 Ibid., pp. 49-50
20 Ibid., p. 255
21 Ibid., p. 56, and pp. 147-148
22 Ibid., p. 130
23 Ross Graves, p. 347
24 Ibid., pp. 211-212
25 Ibid., pp. 435-436
26 Ibid., p. 118
27 Doris Haslam, op. cit., p. 378
28 Ibid., pp. 355-356

CHAPTER 10

Talking with "Old-Timers"

Earlier in this genealogy I wrote of the wonderful opportunity that Alden and I had in 1970 and 1971, when we first went to P.E.I., to meet with people who had known Grammy's father and family. Alden's dear cousin, Gladys Bradshaw, took us around to meet several of these "old-timers" who had not yet passed on to their reward. The family of Mr. Fred MacQuarrie (who was himself about seventy-five years old at that time) had lived two doors down and across the street (toward Searletown) from the Hoopers as a boy. Here are some of his memories:

Fred MacQuarrie's Memories

Major Hooper was not very good with children. One Sunday morning when Major and Mary Hooper were at church, neighbor boys [they were the Allen boys, Major's nephews from next door] let their hens from the backyard into their living room and closed the doors and windows so that the hens could not get out. When Major and Mary came home, what a mess and a smell were in the living room!

Mrs. Allen (Sarah Hooper Allen, Thelma Clark's grandmother and Major's sister) was taller than Major Hooper who was small. He was inoffensive.

Jennie [Hooper] and Alice [MacQuarrie, Fred MacQuarrie's sister and Viola Taylor's mother] planned parties (dances). Only Methodist and Church of Scotland people [I'm not sure of the context here; it may mean that they were the ones invited].

Billy Doule [Aunt Norma's, Mrs. Clark's, and Mrs. MacQuarrie's brother] went with Millie [Hooper] who probably had tuberculosis. Billy didn't have a horse so he went with someone who did! Millie went to Tom Allen's, who was related to Crossman. That's where Billy met her. (Later there is a spoken report of a pregnancy with the two)

Ed Allen [Sarah's husband] was a wheelwright. He left home when Vera, [the youngest of 5 children] was 4 years old. He went to Oxford, Nova Scotia.

Mrs. MacDonald's people lived on MacDonald's Point [just across the cove from where we built our cottage]. Dr. Sinclair from Summerside married someone of Mrs. Hooper's family, a niece. Mrs. Hooper was not Roman Catholic after her marriage [Muriel Hooper Blanchard also thinks that she had been Roman Catholic and that is why she and Major were married by a justice of the peace]. Major was short. His wife was a little taller and round-shouldered.

The MacQuarries, the Hoopers, and the Allens were all neighbors. The Hoopers had about 100 acres of land with lots of hardwood, maple, etc. Hooper had another lot at a distance that he sold. There was an orchard of apple, cherry, and pear trees. When Major had picked all the cherries he could, we boys would climb the tree and get the ones further up. The Hooper boys were not much good on the farm. They were both slow. Major was O.K. He had dark hair, maybe a reddish cast. The boys and Ada had red hair. Mrs. Hooper was dark-haired, medium heavy, not fat or lean. A very nice woman. She did plain cooking. She was fairly strong and well. Major wasn't sick much. He grew blue potatoes with stable manure and seaweed. Now people use fertilizer and spray and poison to kill the tops in the fall. They don't rotate crops five ways now. Arsenate of lime killed potato bugs. Major and Mary were never seen to drink. [That is in direct opposition to Muriel's account of Major, handed down by family tradition. Perhaps Mr. MacQuarrie wanted to present as good a picture as he could to us!] Ed Allen drank a lot. He used to paint sleighs. The Allens had two acres.

The MacQuarrie girl [his sister] went to take care of the Hoopers [when the mother was sick] and caught measles and died of the after- effects [This is true as Viola was telling me in the summer of 1998, not knowing about her aunt caring for Mrs. Hooper, that she died of the measles as a very young woman].

The boys played baseball and house games such as love in the dark, pass a button, jinks up (one cent on the table, one on the floor under the table, and pass the cent.)

Ronald MacDonald lived at Gordon Point looking across to Borden. Austin MacDonald is Ronald MacDonald's grandson. [He lives in Bedeque] Gordon MacDonald was Austin's father, a sister (?) to Mary and Gordon. [So it was Ronald, Gordon, Austin]

Austin Doule was at Tom Allen's a lot. Ada might have got the name from there. [Paul's middle name is Austin] Glover was a family name found in use between Summerside and Kensington. Major had a barn with animals - cows, a horse. They churned butter. There was a lovely large dining room with lovely oil cloth on the table.

Jennie had turkeys, ducks, cows, and a horse, a barn, goose and gossling, a house with a shed in the back yard. The kitchen was big, on an "ell," a pantry, a large dining room. Upstairs were three or four bedrooms. Outdoors was a pump and an outhouse.

The Hoopers had old clocks, but the children destroyed them.

The Church of Scotland minister came to preach in a hall. The Hoopers went there.

The location of the hall was at the corner of the Searletown Road and "lovers' lane." According to Mr. MacQuarrie, Mary Ann had a brother Billy and another brother who were no good. Both Mr. MacQuarrie and Mr. McGrath told of a sister (no name given) who went from the Brook Road to Mary Ann's house to borrow a cup of buckwheat flour. The trip was perhaps a mile each way. About the time that she left Hooper's, a terrible snow storm came. Mrs. Hooper thought that she made it home; whoever was at the MacDonald's house thought that she was at Hooper's [of course, there was no telephone then]. The next morning she was found dead at the side of the brook road with the cup of buckwheat flour clutched to her chest. I searched the Summerside newspaper unsuccessfully for this account. With two area men telling the same story twenty years apart, it would seem that there must be truth to it.

Mr. MacQuarrie told us that he himself plowed 80 out of 100 acres of his property with two horses and a single plow. When we took her to the Amish area of Pennsylvania in 1964, Alden's mother told us that it reminded her of P.E.I. with the teams of horses plowing the fields.

Mr. and Mrs. MacQuarrie had four children, only one of whom lived to adulthood:

- *Arthur* Frederick Seaman, born August 23, 1920; died July 2, 1936 in Searletown, when he was hit by a car when riding a bicycle.
- Cecilia Doul, stillborn, on September 14, 1921.
- Charles *Lloyd*, born April 17, 1926; died February 15, 1927 in Searletown.

- *Harold* Waldo, born September 29, 1928; married Barbara Palmer; died of cancer of the lung in 1999.

I have Fred's obituary. The first part provides a wonderful bit of genealogical material for the family historian:

It was with sadness that family, friends and relatives learned of the passing at Prince County Hospital of Fred A. MacQuarrie on March 25, 1989, following a brief illness.

He was born on May 27, 1890 in North Carleton, P.E.I., the son of James and Celia (Schurman) MacQuarrie. He attended school in North Carleton.

He married, on January 28, 1920, Gwen Doull who predeceased him in May, 1987. They farmed in Searletown where their home was always open to friends, neighbours and relatives.

Following his wife's death, he made his home with his son, Harold, and daughter-in-law, Barbara. He was predeceased by two sons, Arthur and Lloyd; also by two sisters, Mary [who died from measles after caring for Mrs. Hooper] and Alice (Mrs. Keir Allen). Besides his son Harold and wife Barbara, he leaves four grandchildren and two great-grandchildren.

The funeral and committal service was held at the Moase Funeral Home at 1:30 p.m. on March 28th, conducted by Rev. James Abernathy. Hymns sung were "The Lord Is My Sheperd" and "I to the Hills."

Active pallbearers were Howard Clark, John Doull, Reg Hamill, Charles Schurman, David Doull, and Lloyd MacDonald.

Honorary pallbearers were Keith Affleck, Calvin Clark, Robert Carruthers, John Parker, Harry Taylor, Carl Wright, Fulton Hamill, and Lorne Platts.

Interment was in Free Church of Scotland Cemetery, Cape Traverse. [This is the same cemetery where Alden's Hooper grandparents, an aunt, and two uncles are buried]

Card of Thanks

The family of the late Fred MacQuarrie wish to thank friends, neighbors, and relatives for their help during our recent bereavement. Thanks to Drs. Lloyd and Harold Molyneaux, to nurses and staff of Fourth Floor, Prince County Hospital; to Moase Funeral Home; organist and choir members. Thanks also to those who sent cards, flowers, gave charitable donations, and brought food to the house. Your kindness will long be remembered. Harold, Barbara, and Family.

Mr. Clark's Memories

Mr. Clark, Calvin and Howard's father, age 82, said: "Major Hooper was barely five feet tall, weighed maybe 115 pounds. He was a farmer - perhaps [grew] an acre of potatoes. He had a barn with some animals."

Aunt Norma's Memories

Aunt Norma, aged 84, of Linden Street, Summerside, the mother of Shirley MacDonald, had known Major. She told us: "Major was sedate, quiet. If you were alone with him, he would talk, but in a group, he would be quiet. He wasn't the marrying kind a second time.... Dances were held at the Hooper's. They'd play games. People would take advantage of Major."

Aunt Gwen MacQuarrie's Memories

Mrs. MacQuarrie (Aunt Gwen, Aunt Norma's sister) remembers the procession from home to church when Major died. There was no embalming. He was taken in a wagon by a horse to the cemetery in Cape Traverse, a distance of perhaps seven miles. She recalls that he died in the summer. She said that he was sick for awhile, that it was not sudden, but doesn't know the cause of his death. [This description also appears at variance from the one that Muriel gave. Aunt Gwen's memory may well be poor after all those years. One wonders if his body was "planted" in the earth or if a casket [a wooden box] had been made for him. He died in 1914.

The reader may recall that the Church of Scotland worship took place just west of where the Hoopers lived in earlier times, but Major Hooper, his wife, and three children are buried in the Church of Scotland Cemetery in Cape Traverse. "This group of people were commonly called 'MacDonaldites' after the minister who established the Island churches of that denomination."[1]

Arnold McGrath's Memories

In 1991 we met Mr. Arnold McGrath, who lived across the street and back in the woods a bit from the St. Peter's-Seven Mile Bay (R.C.) Church. We were coming home from picking raspberries in Augustine Cove at the Howatt's Farm on a late hot August morning when Alden stopped the Toyota truck in front of the Seven Mile Bay Roman Catholic Church. He had had the hatch-back open to ventilate the berries as they are fragile. As we were planning to go home down the dirt road, he wanted to close the hatch so that the berries would not get the road dust on them. As it happened, a man was standing on the other side of the road, and Alden, being the friendly, outgoing person that he is, started a conversation with him. It was Mr. McGrath, born in 1910, who had lived in the area forever and seemed to enjoy relating much history of the area and the people to us! He was an Irishman who loved to talk. I do believe much of what he said because he was right on target about some things that we know, but I suspect that what he didn't know he made up or he told a tale about another person/family about whom he had heard and related it to the one being mentioned!

We wanted to know more about the Major Hoopers and the Mac/McDonalds. Anyway, he was very kind and generous to meet us another time when we taped what he said. Here is the transcript of what he told us in the basement of St. Peter's Church in Seven Mile Bay on the evening of August 20, 1991:

> I served mass for 75 years under 26 pastors. Mary Ann McDonald was the daughter of John McDonald. There were three girls and a boy in the family.
>
> Major's sister was Sarah, married Ed Allen. She was a fine woman. They got the lot from Major and built the house there. Ed Allen built the house from nothing. He was a fine builder, a first-class carpenter. He was always drunk; he drank a lot. Mr. Fraser owns the house now on two acres of land.
>
> Major had four children [whom he named. He left out Millicent, who he said died young.] The two boys were not crazy, but a lot of people around didn't want them around there. A man by the name of Cal MacQuarrie got papers from Dr. Bell and took the boys to Riverside. I told Dr. Bell at the time that they didn't belong there; they should never have went there.

He didn't like the idea either, but Cal MacQuarrie was bound to do it. I said, "Be sure you keep the right fella there!" I didn't say fellas; I said fella! Dr. Bell caught on right away what I meant! [I'm not sure of the year that the boys went to Riverside or even if they went together, but Mr. McGrath was probably too young to have the quoted opinion and to express it to Dr. Bell of Cape Traverse whom he called the best doctor on Prince Edward Island. Perhaps his father expressed this opinion]

The two girls were away to the states. I never heard tell of them in years. Gladys [Bradshaw] told me one time that Jennie was home and was asking for me. I never saw Jennie from the time she left [the Island for good. Their houses were perhaps one-half mile apart]. Ada came home, what was it, three or four years ago? It was more than twenty? Ada was a thick-set person. She had reddish hair just like Robert. Norman's was black like Jennie's. They called Ada "Reddy" [for the red fox] when she was going to school.

Next came what I think was one of those generic stories that could be attributed to anyone in order to get a laugh:

Jennie was pretty well grown. Old Father MacIntyre was the priest. He noticed that Ada [I wasn't sure if he was talking about Jennie or Ada] was sometimes late for school and told her to say a little prayer: "Hail Mary, full of grace, may I not be late for school again." She'd say it to herself. One morning she was late for school, but she said the little prayer to herself going up the steps when she fell at the top step. "God damn it, don't push me"! she said, and no one knew what she meant! [He was chuckling as he finished it!]

I went to school where Ada went. Ada and Heber [Schurman] were older. There was one classroom from grade one to grade nine or ten. That school went down for a chicken coup. Andy, Margaret, Lila and I carried the seats into the "new school" when it was built. I was one of the oldest kids then. The new school [which is now a house] was built on the same location. The old school went down to Harry Alder; he bought it for a chicken coup and hauled it off down across the fields, down to Parkerstown, just over there. He put it in the field there and I think it burned down - yes. Fred [MacQuarrie] went to that school, too; he lived in Searletown. Gwen [who became his wife] was a Doule, a sister of Mrs. Fred MacQuarrie . [She WAS Mrs. Fred MacQuarrie!]. She went to Carleton to school. Her father was a shoemaker in Carleton. There was no fooling in school. If you did, you got a strapping and stood in the corner. The teachers were Jennie Bell, Mary McCardle, and Gladys Murphy Mullins.

If a woman was seen smoking, she was a lunatic! She'd get a slap in the mouth in a minute.

[The Hoopers] used to go to Searletown to church; Presbyterian, they called it in them days. She was Roman Catholic, but she always went to church with him. Mary Ann was a fine woman. My mother knew her well. She was a thin woman with dark hair. She was always around the house; she never moved out [apparently didn't go visiting often]. Nothing ever worried her; she was happy-go-lucky.

Jennie was a hard worker, a fine woman. She pitched hay, forking hay on the wagon with the boys. She seen that the crops were looked after. She was in charge of the boys and the farm. Major was happy-go-lucky. If he didn't get the hay in, that was fine. He was a harmless man, a great neighbor. No one would say anything about it.[?] "O, it's all right, all right"! If a neighbor's cattle broke out, he would work all night to get them back in the field again. Major was a great man. He had red hair.

The young men played tricks on him on Hallowe'en. They went to steal apples. One night they put a rope across between two apple trees just high enough to catch him under the chin. The boys waited in the street. He was a strong man, thickset, about five feet, eight inches, 180 pounds. [Remember that Mr. McGrath was 4 years old when Major Hooper died. Whatever Arnold McGrath said about Major he either made up or remembered from what his mother or father, Jim McGrath, said. It is interesting that Gladys and her family call him Arnold McGraw] Major walked up, hit the rope, and went in a tumble, heels in the air. He could have broke his neck. He said, "You needn't run. I got whoever you are." They were standing out by the road.

Here is another tall tale which was undoubtedly originally told about someone else other than Major:

One hot summer day Major was painting outside. He was wearing a heavy coat. Pop went by and saw him. He asked him why he was wearing the heavy coat in the summertime. Major said, "The directions say for best results, use a heavy coat." Pop said, "It don't mean that a'tall, Major. It means use a heavy coat of paint."

Major had cherries, plums, apple trees all over. He had a horse, cattle, pigs, turkeys, and chickens. The turkeys roosted in the trees. One year the fox came out of the woods and got them all, killed them. I heard Mum talk about it. Lots of foxes around in them days.

Ada might drive with her father with the horse and wagon to Summerside. Going across the ice is shorter down back of Bowness's store. They don't use the ice any more. You'd see 100 teams on the ice. They'd haul [inaudible] out there, too.

Alden asked him about how his grandmother's grave would have been dug in the winter-time:

Men aren't born anymore; they're too lazy now. They got to use machines now-a-days. No neighborly love now! You pay $75.00 for a machine to dig the grave for you. Five or six men would gather up [and dig the grave]. You get that today in an odd place, but it's very rare.

Dr. Dougherty was the doctor in Cape Traverse in them days. He was the doctor when I was born and the doctor for the Hoopers, too. I was born on a Monday in a blinding snow storm, and the doctor didn't get there till I was born. My father knew Mrs. Dan McDonald, and she came up and stayed till I was born. When the doctor came, everything was over. It was a lost trip! [laugh]

I never heard tell that Major drank liquor. He never wasted money on liquor. [This statement is contradictory to what Muriel has been told by her Hooper relatives] Oh, maybe, he'd have a drink on election day. [That was apparently a popular thing to do as it appears in another section of this paper] Don Pearson, married to a MacQuarrie, lived next to the Hoopers.

Keir Allen and Rube built the CN Hotel in Charlottetown. One day I was driving around and saw Keir. I went back and Keir said, "Do you want a job, Arnold? There's all kinds of work if you want to work." Bert was a great man [Rube's and Keir's brother]; Lila and Vera [their sisters] were lovely girls. I think Lila went to work in the Poor Farm, too. The Allens were a great family.

Fred Hooper [he was Muriel's father] was a third cousin to Major; I heard him tell it. He had a mill. Once he got caught with a tractor cultivating a field that time and a hurricane came across and upset the tractor, and he was underneath it. He lived.

There were hospitals [in the old days], but people didn't bother going because the care was terrible. Now there are too many patients for the number of nurses. There's no remorse today for a person to die as far as the doctor is concerned. Dr. Bell, from Cape Traverse, would go near crazy when he lost a patient. "What did I do wrong?" he'd ask. He was the best doctor Prince Edward Island ever had. He forgot more than these doctors will ever know. He came home from the war, the first one, and died in 1954/56.

Major Lowther was a lovely man, just like Gladys - kind and sympathetic.

John McDonald was Mary Ann's father. They called him Cranberry McDonald because lots of cranberries grew down where he lived. They don't grow there any more. In 1924/1925 Cranberry Point that jutted out into the strait was washed out in a winter storm. It's all gone now. In the field there was a well. We used to get water out of the well there. Now it went one-half mile into the sea; The Point's all washed off of there. Cut the Wright's woods right off there. Trees all lying out there. There was a high tide and ice smashed everything out.

Her (Mary Ann's) mother died early; I never heard her name. They must be buried here. They were Catholics. The kids were alone with their father - three girls and a boy [I had heard two girls and two boys]. One girl died [the buckwheat flour girl], one married a Strong in Summerside or else Mary Ann's mother was a Strong, I don't remember, it was so long ago, and Mary Ann. The son's name was Norman [I don't think this is correct. At least it contradicts what Mr. MacQuarrie told us]. I think Mary Ann's mother and father married in Scotland and came to P.E.I. Cyprine [Cyprian] McDonald married John McDonald's sister. Cyprine had a big farm They had eight sons and one girl. The girl married William Muttart, Everett's grandfather. McDonald's Point was named for Cyprine. Seven sons died in eight years of TB [I have seen in the archives in Charlottetown that Jane, the mother, and according to Mr. McGrath, the sister of John, and several of her children died within a short time of tuberculosis].

My grandfather came to the Island from County Waterford, Ireland. There's a school up on the Island here by the name of Waterford. My grandfather built that school and he called the district Waterford. That was 1825.

Mr. McGrath took us down the Brook Road almost next to the church and showed us the location of Mary Ann's house. One road comes up from the shore, another road goes across through the woods there. There is no building there now, but the house used to be on the north-west corner near that intersection, according to Mr. McGrath. He said that the Cyprian McDonalds, who lived in the same general area only facing to Borden, were related to Mary Ann's family. Cyprian's wife, Jane, was the sister to Mary Ann's father, John. In other words, when Jane married, she did not change her name! He said that they were all Scottish Roman Catholics. He thinks that John and Mary Ann's mother married in Scotland and came from there directly to P.E.I. According to Mr. McGrath:

A large house was built for Crockett [near the junction of the Brook Road and the road leading in from "MacQuarrie Road"]. There was a dispute about where the Borden pier would go, so Crockett built a large house for guests [He thought the pier might go there at MacDonald's Point or Cranberry Point and he wanted to be positioned well for making money, the entrepreneur that he was!]. He built a big hotel; in the last five years they took the third story off all together. Crockett gave one daughter ________, a Profitt who died, and she married Alder Wright. Wilbur sold the place to Garth Toombs in Bedeque and moved out there, and he died, and Mrs. Wright got married again. Now the woman who owns it is Kathy West. She

bought the house and made a tourist home of it. [About 2003 the daughter of Lila Wilson bought the house and has a bed and breakfast there]

Hamp Allen, not related to Ed Allen, had two sons, Suddy and Winston, and two daughters, Lila and Winny, who lived down the Brook Road.

We went to swim down to the crik here. [In the winter] it would be 20-30 degrees below zero Fahrenheit in the old days when I was 16 or so. This metric business, that's crazy; that's for the birds. They don't know what they're talking about! They can't give you the weather today. Joe McDowell (McDonald?) and I walked the ten miles across the strait to Tormentine, then skated there and walked the 10 miles back when I was 16 and he was 18. It was a lovely Saturday morning in 1926. Away we went; the ice was as glib as could be! I was born in 1910, went to school in 1915. Everybody around here knows me.

The MacDonald girl came to Hooper's for buckwheat flour one day. As she was leaving a snowstorm came up, and she got lost on her way back [It was perhaps a one mile walk]. My father and Nee Lila (?) found her down behind the old school, about half way down the field. They saw her toes sticking in the snow bank. The storm had struck and a little can of flour [was] sitting on her breast. I always heard Pop talk about that! Ya! I thought her name was Jennie, Jane or Jennie. The brother was Norman McDonald who felt some guilt [for not going up to get the flour].

Henry Lowther was Gladys' uncle. Henry, Wallace, and Major were brothers.

I'm sure that this is from a poor memory. Major Lowther and Grace were brother and sister and the only children of Adella and Christopher Lowther.

Some 20 years previously, Mr. MacQuarrie had told us essentially the same story, without the finders of her body being identified! I searched several years of the Summerside newspapers to find an article about this tragedy as it would appear to be noteworthy, but I was able to find nothing. It had to be between the time of Mary Ann's marriage to Major Hooper in 1886 and the time that she died in 1905.

This is the end of Mr. McGrath's tale. I think it is remarkable for a man of about 80 to have such a good memory especially about people whom he did not know!

From what I can put together from "old-timers," Mr. Fred MacQuarrie and Mr. Fred Clark, Mary Ann's father, John "Cranberry" McDonald, two no-account brothers, one named Billy, and one sister (before she froze to death after getting the buckwheat flour from the Hoopers, her sister's family) lived in a poorly kept house near where the Brook Road intersects with the present dirt road coming in from "MacQuarrie's Road." Their account is in contradiction with Mr. McGrath's. The other men, Mr MacQuarrie and Mr. Clark, were probably 10-20 years older than Mr. McGrath and knew the Hoopers and perhaps the Mac/McDonalds. Mr. Clark was born c.1899 and died around 1984, Mr. MacQuarrie was born in 1890 and died about 1989, and Mr. McGrath was born in 1910 and died about 1997.

I am very happy with the information that I got from the "old timers"; in retrospect, however, I should have asked many more specific questions. After talking with them and listening to them, however, I feel as though there is now some meat on the bones of the skeletons!

Jean's, Joyce's and Charlie Schurman's parents are also old timers whose acquaintance we made. Mr. and Mrs. Schurman (Heber and Sadie) lived just up the lane and down the road from our cottage. We used to visit there and still visit Jean and her brother and sister-in-law who summer across the road. We can see Jean's home from our windows and yard. Next door to them on the same side of the street was the home of Ed and Kay Pearson where their son and his wife now live. It was Ed's relatives who we believe encouraged Ada and Jennie to go to Haverhill to work.

Mr. Clark, Howard and Calvin's father, was another "old-timer" whom we knew. He lived just down the lane and down the road in the other direction from Schurman's and Pearson's. Howard now (2004) lives alone with his dog on his father's acreage. Next to him are Shirley and Bob MacDonald, our friends and neighbors. We have been surrounded by friends, relatives, and kindly neighbors for which we are most grateful.

Notes

1 Doris Haslam, *The Wrights of Bedeque, Prince Edward Island, a Loyalist Family* (Summerside, P.E.I.: Doris Muncey Haslam, 1978)

CHAPTER 11

Generations Nine, Ten, Eleven, and Twelve

By the time that the children from the seventh and eighth generations were born, the numbers had increased tremendously and the Hooper- related population had spread out over thousands of miles across Canada and the United States, and elsewhere. The last three generations of Hooper descendants, about whom I have been able to find information from a variety of sources, are fewer in percentage than the first eight generations. The reasons are many, but a primary one seems to be that people have scattered over many thousands of miles and have not necessarily been faithful correspondents with their relatives who have stayed near the places of their birth. Also, today's generations are highly mobile and often move several times in a lifetime in order to pursue careers.

Doris Haslam and Ross Graves have provided much information in their research, which they have published, sections of which have been quoted in this book. The information in their books, however, ends in the early to mid-1970s. Gratitude also goes to Helen Caswell, Thelma Clark, and Gladys Bradshaw Henderson, all second cousins of Alden's, for their contributions on their lines of the family.

As in the previous chapters on the Hooper genealogy, this chapter will begin with the descendants of Major Hooper, fourth generation, and continue through those of his youngest sibling, Elisha. The Hooper descendants in generation nine will be followed by their chil-

dren - generation ten, their grandchildren - generation eleven, and their great-grandchildren - generation twelve, if they are known. The listing, however, will actually be from the earliest direct-line descendant about whom I have information - Stephen Hooper.

Family size is generally smaller in generations nine, ten, eleven, and twelve; in fact, most families have two children, thanks to the cost of living and good family planning techniques. As mentioned in Chapter Nine, as the surname Hooper disappeared, those of us "from away" would not have a clue initially who was related to whom!

Anyone having more information for inclusion in this genealogy is welcome to contact me by mail at: Nancy E. Neal, 10 Peterborough Drive, Northport, New York 11768 U.S.A.

The first, to my knowledge, in the ninth generation is a descendant of Major Hooper. In January 2004, I received an e-mail from a New Zealand lady who had been trying for some time to contact her relatives in Prince Edward Island. This is the way her genealogy looks: **Judith Clark Newell** (9, Charles Clarence Clark 8, William Clark 7, Major Hooper Clark 6, Harriet Hooper Clark 5, Major Hooper 4, Thomas Hooper 3, Clement Hooper 2, Stephen Hooper 1). The reader may recall a young man, the second child of Harriet Hooper and her husband Richard Clark, born on December 5, 1845, who left home at a rather early age and eventually went (via Chicago and a marriage or two) to New Zealand (Chapter 7). Judith described *her father* as a compassionate man. Judith has at least one daughter living in New Zealand, and at least one granddaughter, but our connection for more information seems to have been broken.

The next family from the fourth generation is the family of Mary Hooper and her husband, John Robins.

A great-great-great-grandchild of John and Mary (Hooper) Robins was Ida Helena Bradshaw, daughter of Ellis Hoffman Bradshaw and his second wife, Adeline Profitt. Ellis was a farmer and they resided in Middleton, P.E.I. Ellis had six children by his first wife, Jane Hyatt Wright, and eleven children by his second wife, Adeline Profitt.

Ida Helena Bradshaw, called Ida (9, Ellis Bradshaw 8, Elizabeth Wright 7, Harriet 6, Elizabeth Robins Wright 5, Mary Hooper Robins 4, Thomas Hooper 3, Clement Hooper 2, Stephen Hooper 1), daughter of Adeline (Addie) Profitt, and her husband, Ellis Hoffman Bradshaw, married Harry Walsh MacKay. Ida and Harry had eight children (surname MacKay, tenth generation):

Georgie Marion MacKay (10, Ida Bradshaw 9, Ellis Bradshaw 8, Elizabeth Wright 7, Harriet 6, Elizabeth Robins Wright 5, Mary Hooper Robins 4, Thomas Hooper 3, Clement Hooper 2, Stephen Hooper 1) was born on December 11, 1937 in Campbellton, P.E.I. She was married to Russell Reginald McInnis, born on January 9, 1933, son of Wilbur Russell and Muriel Ellen (Green) McInnis, in St. Lawrence, P.E.I. Russell was a carpenter. They had ten children (surname McInnis, eleventh generation):

Christine Ida McInnis (11, Georgie 10, Ida 9, Ellis 8, Elizabeth Wright 7, Harriet 6, Elizabeth Robins Wright 5, Mary Hooper Robins 4, Thomas Hooper 3, Clement Hooper 2, Stephen Hooper 1), born October 17, 1956 in Alberton, P.E.I. No further information.

Carolyn Joy McInnis (11, Georgie 10, Ida 9, Ellis 8, Elizabeth Wright 7, Harriet 6, Elizabeth Robins Wright 5, Mary Hooper Robins 4, Thomas Hooper 3, Clement Hooper 2, Stephen Hooper 1), was born in Montreal, P.Q., Sept. 27, 1957. No further information.

Connie Muriel McInnis (11, Georgie 10, Ida 9, Ellis 8, Elizabeth Wright 7, Harriet 6, Elizabeth 5, Mary Hooper Robins 4, Thomas Hooper 3, Clement Hooper 2, Stephen Hooper 1), born July 25, 1959, in O'Leary, P.E.I. No further information.

Reggie Harry McInnis (11, Georgie 10, Ida 9, Ellis 8, Elizabeth Wright 7, Harriet 6, Elizabeth 5, Mary Hooper Robins 4, Thomas Hooper 3, Clement Hooper 2, Stephen Hooper 1), born October 2, 1960, in O'Leary, P.E.I. No further information.

Wade Wilbur McInnis (11, Georgie 10, Ida 9, Ellis 8, Elizabeth Wright 7, Harriet 6, Elizabeth 5, Mary Hooper Robins 4, Thomas

Hooper 3, Clement Hooper 2, Stephen Hooper 1), born August 30, 1962, in O'Leary, P,E,I. No further information.

Rhonda Lynn McInnis (11, Georgie 10, Ida 9, Ellis 8, Elizabeth Wright 7, Harriet 6, Elizabeth 5, Mary Hooper Robins 4, Thomas Hooper 3, Clement Hooper 2, Stephen Hooper 1), born April 25, 1965, in O'Leary, P.E.I. No further information.

Irma Sylvia McInnis (11, Georgie 10, Ida 9, Ellis 8, Elizabeth Wright 7, Harriet 6, Elizabeth 5, Mary Hooper Robins 4, Thomas Hooper 3, Clement Hooper 2, Stephen Hooper 1), born September 11, 1966 in O'Leary, P.E.I. No further information.

Scott Russell McInnis (11, Georgie 10, Ida 9, Ellis 8, Elizabeth Wright 7, Harriet 6, Elizabeth 5, Mary Hooper Robins 4, Thomas Hooper 3, Clement Hooper 2, Stephen Hooper 1), born October 30, 1967, in O'Leary, P.E.I. No further information.

Norma Lee McInnis (11, Georgie 10, Ida 9, Ellis 8, Elizabeth Wright 7, Harriet 6, Elizabeth 5, Mary Hooper Robins 4, Thomas Hooper 3, Clement Hooper 2, Stephen Hooper 1), born April 4, 1969, in O'Leary, P.E.I. No further information.

Amy Georgia McInnis (11, Georgia 10, Ida 9, Ellis 8, Elizabeth Wright 7, Harriet 6, Elizabeth 5, Mary Hooper Robins 4, Thomas Hooper 3, Clement Hooper 2, Stephen Hooper 1), born September 2, 1973, in O'Leary, P.E.I. No further information.

Norma Eileen MacKay (10, Ida Bradshaw 9, Ellis 8, Elizabeth Wright 7, Harriet 6, Elizabeth Robins Wright 5, Mary Hooper Robins 4, Thomas Hooper 3, Clement Hooper 2, Stephen Hooper 1) born April 2, 1941 in Campbellton, P.E.I. She married October 30, 1959 Orville Condley, who was brought up by his grandparents, Mr. and Mrs. George Condley, of Long River, P.E.I. He died November 1974 in Summerside, P.E.I. Orville was a laborer in Summerside, where Norma and the five children lived in 1976 (surname Condley, eleventh generation). All were born in Summerside:

Catherine Condley (11, Norma MacKay 10, Ida Bradshaw 9, Ellis 8, Elizabeth Wright 7, Harriet 6, Elizabeth Robins Wright 5, Mary Hooper Robins 4, Thomas Hooper 3, Clement Hooper 2, Stephen Hooper 1) called Cathy, born in 1960.
June Condley (11, Norma MacKay 10, Ida Bradshaw 9, Ellis 8, Elizabeth Wright 7, Harriet 6, Elizabeth Robins Wright 5, Mary Hooper Robins 4, Thomas Hooper 3, Clement Hooper 2, Stephen Hooper 1), a twin, born in 1961.
Joyce Condley (11, Norma MacKay 10, Ida Bradshaw 9, Ellis 8, Elizabeth Wright 7, Harriet 6, Elizabeth Robins Wright 5, Mary Hooper Robins 4, Thomas Hooper 3, Clement Hooper 2, Stephen Hooper 1), a twin, born in 1961.
Kent Condley (11, Norma MacKay 10, Ida Bradshaw 9, Ellis 8, Elizabeth Wright 7, Harriet 6, Elizabeth Robins Wright 5, Mary Hooper Robins 4, Thomas Hooper 3, Clement Hooper 2, Stephen Hooper 1), born in 1963.
Kelly Lee Condley (11, Norma MacKay 10, Ida Bradshaw 9, Ellis 8, Elizabeth Wright 7, Harriet 6, Elizabeth Robins Wright 5, Mary Hooper Robins 4, Thomas Hooper 3, Clement Hooper 2, Stephen Hooper 1), born in 1965. No further information.

Marjorie Reta MacKay (10, Ida Bradshaw 9, Ellis Bradshaw 8, Elizabeth Wright 7, Harriet 6, Elizabeth Robins Wright 5, Mary Hooper Robins 4, Thomas Hooper 3, Clement Hoper 2, Stephen Hooper 1) was born on June 6, 1943 in Campbellton, P.E.I. She married on January 5, 1963 James Frederick Rix, son of John Burton and Barbara (Matthews) Rix. He was born on October 10, 1942 in Miminegash, P.E.I. and died on October 22, 1971 in the Victoria General Hospital, Halifax, Nova Scotia. Marjorie and James lived in Ebbsfleet, P.E.I. James was a machine operator. His death was caused by an accident at his work at the plant of Hayes Paving Company, Alma, P.E.I. In 1976 Marjorie lived with her four sons in their home in Ebbsfleet, P.E.I. The four sons of Marjorie and James (surmane Rix, eleventh generation), all born in O'Leary, are as follows:

Dennis James Rix (11, Marjorie Reta 10, Ida Bradshaw 9, Ellis Bradshaw 8, Elizabeth Wright 7, Harriet 6, Elizabeth Robins Wright 5, Mary Hooper Robins 4, Thomas Hooper 3, Clement Hooper 2, Stephen Hooper 1) born on October 11, 1963.
Timothy Ross Rix (11, Marjorie Reta 10, Ida Bradshaw 9, Ellis Bradshaw 8, Elizabeth Wright 7, Harriet 6, Elizabeth Robins Wright 5, Mary Hooper Robins 4, Thomas Hooper 3, Clement Hooper 2, Stephen Hooper 1) born on December 10, 1965.
Stacey John Rix (11, Marjorie Reta 10, Ida Bradshaw 9, Ellis Bradshaw 8, Elizabeth Wright 7, Harriet 6, Elizabeth Robins Wright 5, Mary Hooper Robins 4, Thomas Hooper 3, Clement Hooper 2, Stephen Hooper 1) born on March 25, 1969.
Edward Lloyd Rix (11, Marjorie Reta 10, Ida Bradshaw 9, Ellis Bradshaw 8, Elizabeth Wright 7, Harriet 6, Elizabeth Robins Wright 5, Mary Hooper Robins 4, Thomas Hooper 3, Clement Hooper 2, Stephen Hooper 1) born on October 2, 1970.

Sylvia Mae MacKay (10, Ida Bradshaw 9, Ellis Bradshaw 8, Elizabeth Wright 7, Harriet 6, Elizabeth Robins Wright 5, Mary Hooper Robins 4, Thomas Hooper 3, Clement Hooper 2, Stephen Hooper 1) was born on February 7, 1947 in Campbellton, P.E.I. She married Brian Dubickas, son of Zigmus and Jane (Shillinglow) Dubrickas, on August 16, 1969. Brian was born on January 6, 1947 in Newtongrange, Midlothian, Scotland. In 1972 they lived in New Glasgow, Nova Scotia where Brian was a machinist with Michelin Tire Company. They had two children (surname Dubickas, eleventh generation):

David Ross Dubickas (11, Sylvia 10, Ida Bradshaw 9, Ellis Bradshaw 8, Elizabeth Wright 7, Harriet 6, Elizabeth Robins Wright 5, Mary Hooper Robins 4, Thomas Hooper 3, Clement Hooper 2, Stephen Hooper 1), born June 5, 1970 in Toronto, Ontario.
Rhoda Jane Dubickas (11, Sylvia 10, Ida Bradshaw 9, Ellis Bradshaw 8, Elizabeth Wright 7, Harriet 6, Elizabeth Robins Wright 5, Mary Hooper Robins 4, Thomas Hooper 3, Clement Hooper 2,

Stephen Hooper 1) born July 15, 1973 in Fort Saskatchewan, Sask., Canada.

Nancy Lynn MacKay (10, Ida Bradshaw 9, Ellis Bradshaw 8, Elizabeth Wright 7, Harriet 6, Elizabeth Robins Wright 5, Mary Hooper Robins 4, Thomas Hooper 3, Clement Hooper 2, Stephen Hooper 1) born on Spetember 16, 1948 in Campbellton, P.E.I. On October 5, 1968 she married Robert Paul Beattie, son of Robert Leslie and Stella Mary (Chatterton) Beattie. He was born on August 23, 1946 in Doncaster, England. Paul was a supply technician in the Canadian Armed Forces (R. C. A. F.) as a corporal. In 1976 they were living in Lahr, Germany. Nancy was a licensed nurses' aid and worked part time at the Base Hospital. They had three children (surname Beattie, eleventh generation), two born in Summerside, P.E.I:

Paula Lynn Beattie (11, Nancy Beattie 10, Ida Bradshaw 9: Ellis Bradshaw 8, Elizabeth Wright 7, Harriet 6, Elizabeth Robins Wright 5, Mary Hooper Robins 4, Thomas Hooper 3, Clement Hooper 2, Stephen Hooper 1) born on November 8, 1969.
Robert Gregory Beattie (11, Nancy Beattie 10, Ida Bradshaw 10, Ellis Bradshaw 8, Elizabeth Wright 7, Harriet 6, Elizabeth Robins Wright 5, Mary Hooper Robins 4, Thomas Hooper 3, Clement Hooper 2, Stephen Hooper 1) born October 17, 1970.
Douglas Peter Beattie (11, Nancy Beattie 10, Ida Bradshaw 9, Ellis Bradshaw 8, Elizabeth Wright 7, Harriet 6, Elizabeth Robins Wright 5, Mary Hooper Robins 4, Thomas Hooper 3, Clement Hooper 2, Stephen Hooper 1) born in 1975.

Robert Francis Bell (10, Cottie Bradshaw 9, Ellis Bradshaw 8, Elizabeth Wright 7, Harriet 6, Elizabeth Robins Wright 5, Mary Hooper Robins 4, Thomas Hooper 3, Clement Hooper 2, Stephen Hooper 1) was born on April 27, 1937 in Searletown, P.E.I. He married Carrie Eileen Ross, daughter of Herbert and Eileen (Ahearn) Ross. She was born on July 16, 1941 in Bordon, P.E.I. In 1976 they lived in Cape Traverse, P.E.I. He was employed by the Canadian National

Raiload Ferry Service in Borden, P.E.I. They had ten children (eleventh generation, surname Bell):

Susan Lynn Bell (11, Robert 10, Cottie Bradshaw 9, Ellis Bradshaww 8, Elizabeth Wright 7, Harriet 6, Elizabeth Robins Wright 5, Mary Hooper Robins 4, Thomas Hooper 3, Clement Hooper 2, Stephen Hooper 1) born on September 26, 1958.

Wayne Robert Bell (11, Robert 10, Cottie Bradshaw 9, Ellis Bradshaw 8, Elizabeth Wright 7, Harriet 6, Elizabeth Robins Wright 5, Mary Hooper Robins 4, Thomas Hooper 3, Clement Hooper 2, Stephen Hooper 1) born on September 14, 1959; died on August 19, 1965.

Catherine Ann Bell (11, Robert 10, Cottie Bradshaw 9, Ellis Bradshaw 8, Elizabeth Wright 7, Harriet 6, Elizabeth Robins Wright 5, Mary Hooper Robins 4, Thomas Hooper 3, Clement Hooper 2, Stephen Hooper 1) born October 2, 1960.

James Donald Bell (11, Robert 10, Cottie Bradshaw 9, Ellis Bradshaw 8, Elizabeth Wright 7, Harriet 6, Elizabeth Robins Wright 5, Mary Hooper Robins 4, Thomas Hooper 3, Clement Hooper 2, Stephen Hooper 1) born September 16, 1962.

Sandra Darlene Bell (11, Robert 10, Cottie Bradshaw 9, Ellis Bradshaw 8, Elizabeth Wright 7, Harriet 6, Elizabeth Robins Wright 5, Mary Hooper Robins 4, Thomas Hooper 3, Clement Hooper 2, Stephen Hooper 1) born March 20, 1964.

Sharon Lee Bell (11, Robert 10, Cottie Bradshaw 9, Ellis Bradshaw 8, Elizabeth Wright 7, Harriet 6, Elizabeth Robins Wright 5, Mary Hooper Robins 4, Thomas Hooper 3, Clement Hooper 2, Stephen Hooper 1) born March 16, 1965.

Nancy Ellen Bell (11, Robert 10, Cottie Bradshaw 9, Ellis Bradshaw 8, Elizabeth Wright 7, Harriet 6, Elizabeth Robins Wright 5, Mary Hooper Robins 4, Thomas Hooper 3, Clement Hooper 2, Stephen Hooper 1) born September 20, 1966.

Barbara Arlene Bell (11, Robert 10, Cottie Bradshaw 9, Ellis Bradshaw 8, Elizabeth Wright 7, Harriet 6, Elizabeth Robins Wright

5, Mary Hooper Robins 4, Thomas Hooper 3, Clement Hooper 2, Stephen Hooper 1) born March 13, 1969.
Robert Allan Bell (11, Robert 10, Cottie Bradshaw 9, Ellis Bradshaw 8, Elizabeth Wright 7, Harriet 6, Elizabeth Robins Wright 5, Mary Hooper Robins 4, Thomas Hooper 3, Clement Hooper 2, Stephen Hooper 1) born October 22, 1970.
Tracy Dawn Bell (11, Robert 10, Cottie Bradshaw 9, Ellis Bradshaw 8, Elizabeth Wright Bradshaw 7, Harriet 6, Elizabeth Robins Wright 5, Mary Hooper Robins 4, Thomas Hooper 3, Clement Hooper 2, Stephen Hooper 1) born January 5, 1972.

Donald Archibald Bell (10, Cottie Bradshaw 9, Ellis Bradshaw 8, Elizabeth Wright Bradshaw 7, Harriet Wright Wright 6, Elizabeth Robins Wright 5, Mary Hooper Robins 4, Thomas Hooper 3, Clement Hooper 2, Stephen Hooper 1) was born on June 15, 1940 in Searletown, P.E.I. On December 28, 1965 he married Kathryn Alice Jeffery, daughter of Hudson Harold and Jean (Montgomery) Jeffery. She was born on March 23, 1942 in Lower Bedeque, P.E.I. In 1976 Donald and Kathryn lived in Cornwell where Donald was a subcontractor in carpet and furniture maintenance. Kathryn graduated from Prince of Wales College, Charlottetown, in 1960, and taught school in Lower Bedeque, P.E.I, Calgary, Alberta, Saint John, New Brunswick, Moncton, New Brunswick, and Mississauga, Ontario. They had two children (surname Bell, eleventh generation):

Christine Luanne Bell (11, Donald 10, Cottie Bradshaw 9, Ellis Bradshaw 8, Elizabeth Wright Bradshaw 7, Harriet Wright Wright 6, Elizabeth Robins Wright 5, Mary Hooper Robins 4, Thomas Hooper 3, Clement Hooper 2, Stephen Hooper 1) born on June 16, 1970.
Tanya Dawn Bell (11, Donald 10, Cottie Bradshaw 9, Ellis Bradshaw 8, Elizabeth (Lizzie)Wright Bradshaw 7, Harriet Wright Wright 6, Elizabeth Robins Wright 5, Mary Hooper Robins 4, Thomas Hooper 3, Clement Hooper 2, Stephen Hooper 1) born July 19, 1973. No further information.

Audrey Alice Bell (10, Cottie Bradshaw 9, Ellis Bradshaw 8, Elizabeth (Lizzie) Wright Bradshaw 7, Harriet Wright Wright 6, Elizabeth Robins Wright 5, Mary Hooper Robins 4, Thomas Hooper 3, Clement Hooper 2, Stephen Hooper 1) was born on November 8, 1941 in Searletown, P.E.I. She married James Allan MacIsaac, son of Emmett and Margaret (Kenney) MacIsaac. He was born on August 30, 1938 in Summerside, P.E.I. In 1976 they lived in Central Bedeque, P.E.I. Allan was a mechanic. They had three children (surname MacIsaac, eleventh generation):

Michael Allen MacIsaac (11, Audrey Bell 10, Cottie Bradshaw 9, Ellis Bradshaw 8, Elizabeth (Lizzie) Wright Bradshaw 7, Harriet Wright Wright 6, Elizabeth Robins Wright 5, Mary Hooper Robins 4, Thomas Hooper 3, Clement Hooper 2, Stephen Hooper 1) was born on April 5, 1964 in Toronto, Ontario. No further information.
Lori Michelle MacIsaac (11, Audrey Bell 10, Cottie Bradshaw 9, Ellis Bradshaw 8, Elizabeth (Lizzie) Wright Bradshaw 7, Harriet Wright Wright 6, Elizabeth Robins Wright 5, Mary Hooper Robins 4, Thomas Hooper 3, Clement Hooper 2, Stephen Hooper 1) was born on April 7, 1965 in Toronto, Ontario. No further information.
Kelley Anne MacIsaac (11, Audrey Bell 10, Cottie Bradshaw 9, Ellis Bradshaw 8, Elizabeth (Lizzie) Wright Bradshaw 7, Harriet Wright Wright 6, Elizabeth Robins Wright 5, Mary Hooper Robins 4, Thomas Hooper 3, Clement Hooper 2, Stephen Hooper 1) was born on September 12, 1968 in Charlottetown, P.E.I. No further information.

Darlene Joyce Bell (10, Cottie Bradshaw 9, Ellis Bradshaw 8, Elizabeth (Lizzie) Bradshaw 7, Harriet Wright Wright 6, Elizabeth Robins Wright 5, Mary Hooper Robins 4, Thomas Hooper 3, Clement Hooper 2, Stephen Hooper 1) was born on September 19, 1943 in Searletown, P.E.I. She married on November 19, 1966, Eldon Joseph Arsenault, son of Alyre Joseph and Emma (Enman) Arsenault. He was born on April 15, 1943 in Kinkora, P.E.I. In 1976 they lived in Barrie, Ontario, where Eldon was a foreman at Allan G. Cook Con-

struction, Ltd. They had three children, all born in Toronto, Ontario (surname Arsenault, eleventh generation):

David Joseph Arsenault (11, Darlene Bell 10, Cottie Bradshaw 9, Ellis Bradshaw 8, Elizabeth (Lizzie) Bradshaw 7, Harriet Wright Wright 6, Elizabeth Robins Wright 5, Mary Hooper Robins 4, Thomas Hooper 3, Clement Hooper 2, Stephen Hooper 1) was born on August 23, 1967.
Cindy Anne Arsenault (11, Darlene Bell 10, Cottie Bradshaw 9. Ellis Bradshaw 8, Elizabeth)Lizzie) Bradshaw 7, Harriet Wright Wright 6, Elizabeth Robins Wright 5, Mary Hooper Robins 4, Thomas Hooper 3, Clement Hooper 2, Stephen Hooper 1) was born on June 3, 1968.
Leanne Elizabeth Arsenault (11, Darlene Bell 10, Cottie Bradshaw 9, Ellis Bradshaw 8, Elizabeth (Lizzie) Bradshaw 7, Harriet Wright Wright 6, Elizabeth Robins Wright 5, Mary Hooper Robins 4, Thomas Hooper 3, Clement Hooper 2, Stephen Hooper 1) was born on August 21, 1970. No further information about this family.

Judith Ann MacKay (10, Reta Bradshaw 9, Ellis Bradshaw 8, Elizabeth (Lizzie) Bradshaw 7, Harriet Wright Wright 6, Elizabeth Robins Wright 5. Mary Hooper 4, Thomas Hooper 3, Clement Hooper 2, Stephen Hooper 1) was born on February 22, 1959 in O'Leary, P.E.I. She married on March 25, 1972, Roman Shyan Sereda, son of William and Helen (Hadzamon) Shyan. He was born on January 25, 1945 in Czechoslovakia. In 1976 Judith and Roman lived in Toronto, Ontario. He was employed at Statmos Industrial Sales. Roman's father was in the Ukraine Partisan Underground and was killed before Roman was born. His mother married Paul Sereda who adopted Roman and changed his name to Sereda. Judith and Roman had one child (surname Sereda, eleventh generation):

Christopher Roman Sereda (11, Judith MacKay 10, Reta Bradshaw 9, Ellis Bradshaw 8, Elizabeth (Lizzie) Wright Bradshaw 7, Harriet Wright Wright 6, Elizabeth Robins Wright 5, Mary Hooper Robins 4, Thomas Hooper 3, Clement Hooper 2, Stephen Hooper 1) No further information given.

Donna Ruth Bradshaw (10, Wallace Bradshaw 9, Thomas Bradshaw 8, Elizabeth (Lizzie) Wright Bradshaw 7, Harriet Wright Wright 6, Elizabeth Robins Wright 5, Mary Hooper Robins 4, Thomas Hooper 3, Clement Hooper 2, Stephen Hooper 1) was born on February 24, 1943 in Moncton, New Brunswick. On June 30, 1962 she married John Leonard McNally, son of John Leonard and Vera Margaret (Morrison) McNally. He was born on April 30, 1939 in Summerside, P.E.I. In 1976 John worked on the carferry between Borden, P.E.I. and Cape Tormentine, New Brunswick. He and Donna lived on Carol Avenue in Summerside and had three children (surname McNally, eleventh generation) all born in Summerside:

Karen Virginia McNally (11, Donna 10, Wallace Bradshaw 9, Thomas Bradshaw 8, Elizabeth (Lizzie) Wright Bradshaw 7, Harriet Wright Wright 6, Elizabeth Robins Wright 5, Mary Hooper Robins 4, Thomas Hooper 3, Clement Hooper 2, Stephen 1) was born on February 22, 1963.

John Scott McNally (11, Donna 10, Wallace Bradshaw 9, Thomas Bradshaw 8, Elizabeth (Lizzie) Wright Bradshaw 7, Harriet Wright Wright 6, Elizabeth Robins Wright 5, Mary Hooper Robins 4, Thomas Hooper 3, Clement Hooper 2, Stephen Hooper 1) was born on July 4, 1970.

Michael Wallace McNally (11, Donna 10, Wallace Bradshaw 9, Thomas Bradshaw 8, Elizabeth (Lizzie) Wright Bradshaw 7, Harriet Wright Wright 6, Elizabeth Robins 5, Mary Hooper Robins 4, Thomas Hooper 3, Clement Hooper 2, Stephen Hooper 1) was born on June 6, 1973.

The **Neil Bradshaw** (9, Thomas 8, Elizabeth (Lizzie) Wright Bradshaw 7, Harriet Wright Wright 6, Elizabeth Robins 5, Mary Hooper Robins 4, Thomas Hooper 3, Clement Hooper 2, Stephen Hooper 1) family is the second family that has the only children (to this writer's memory) who can be presented in this genealogy from both the mother's and the father's perspective! They will be accounted for here as well as with the **Major Lowther** family [Gladys's family], also Hooper descendants: (See page 525)

Joan Lowther Bradshaw (10, Neil 9, Thomas 8, Elizabeth (Lizzie) Wright Bradshaw 7, Harriet Wright Wright 6, Elizabeth Robins 5, Mary Hooper Robins 4, Thomas Hooper 3, Clement Hooper 2, Stephen Hooper 1) was born on June 29, 1934 in Summerside, P.E.I. She married William Ross Lefurgey, born September 5, 1933 in Summerside, son of Osbourne Bayfield and Katherine (Gordon) Lefurgey, on December 28, 1955. Joan and Ross live in a beautiful home that they had built for them c.1992. Joan is a registered nurse and works out of the office of the chaplain at the new hospital in Summerside (2004). Ross is a builder of summer furniture which he sells from his home. They have three sons (surname Lefurgey, eleventh generation), all born in Summerside, P.E.I.:

Nial Ross Lefurgey (11, Joan 10, Neil 9, Thomas 8, Elizabeth (Lizzie) Wright Bradshaw 7, Harriet Wright Wright 6, Elizabeth Robins Wright 5, Mary Hooper Robins 4, Thomas Hooper 3, Clement Hooper 2, Stephen Hooper 1) was born on June 28, 1956, married Arlene Marie Whalen, born April 1, 1959 on February 8, 1980. Arlene works at the Summerside Tax Centre, a government office. Nial and Arlene have two children (surname Lefurgey, twelfth generation):

Matthew Nial Lefurgey (12, Nial 11, Joan 10, Neil Bradshaw 9, Thomas 8, Elizabeth (Lizzie) Wright Bradshaw 7, Harriet Wright Wright 6, Elizabeth Robins Wright 5, Mary Hooper Robins 4, Thomas 3, Clement Hooper 2, Stephen Hooper 1) born May 22, 1982.

Mary Ellen Lefurgey (12, Nial 11, Joan 10, Neil Bradshaw 9, Thomas 8, Elizabeth (Lizzie) Wright Bradshaw 7, Harriet Wright Wright 6, Elizabeth Robins Wright 5, Mary Hooper Robins 4, Thomas 3, Clement Hooper 2, Stephen Hooper 1) born April 26, 1984

Alan *Shane* Lefurgey (11, Joan 10, Neil 9, Thomas 8, Elizabeth (Lizzie) Wright Bradshaw 7, Harriet Wright Wright 6, Elizabeth Robins Wright 5, Mary Hooper Robins 4, Thomas Hooper 3, Clement Hooper 2, Stephen Hooper 1) born March 31, 1961. Shane married Janet Estelle Parker and lives in Summerside where he operates a "not new" (used) sports shop. He also has assembled bicycles for a large store in Summerside. He and his family live in Summerside. Shane and Janet have two children (surname Lefurgey, twelfth generation):

Jonathan Shane Lefurgey (12, Shane 11, Joan 10, Neil Bradshaw 9, Thomas 8, Elizabeth (Lizie) Wright Bradshaw 7, Harriet Wright Wright 6, Elizabeth Robins Wright 5, Mary Hooper Robins 4, Thomas Hooper 3, Clement Hoper 2, Stephen Hooper 1) born on September 18, 1986.

Amanda Jane Lefurgey (12, Shane 11, Joan 10, Neil Bradshaw 9, Thomas 8, Elizabeth (Lizzie) Wright Bradshaw 7, Harriet Wright Wright 6, Elizabeth Robins Wright 5, Mary Hooper Robins 4, Thomas Hooper 3, Clement Hooper 2, Stephen Hooper 1) born on January 10, 1989.

Garth Lefurgey (11, Joan 10, Neil Bradshaw 9, Thomas 8, Elizabeth (Lizzie) Wright Bradshaw 7, Harriet Wright Wright 6, Elizabeth Robins Wright 5, Mary Hooper Robins 4, Thomas Hooper 3, Clement Hoper 2, Stephen Hooper 1) born on February 27, 1971; married Jennifer Johnson in June 2001. Garth has a sense of humor and a stage presence, and has been asked to be the master of ceremonies at wedding receptions. In 2002 he was employed by Callbeck's Hardware store. Garth and Jennifer have one son (surname Lefurgey, twelfth generation):

Brycen Ross Lefurgey (12, Garth 11, Joan 10, Neil Bradshaw 9, Thomas 8, Elizabeth (Lizzie) Wright Bradshaw 7, Harriet Wright Wright 6, Elizabeth Robins Wright 5, Mary Hooper Robins 4, Thomas Hooper 3, Clement Hooper 2, Stephen Hooper 1) born on March 13, 2003.

Mary *Janet* Bradshaw (10, Neil Bradshaw 9, Thomas 8, Elizabeth (Lizzie) Wright Bradshaw 7, Harriet Wright Wright 6, Elizabeth Robins Wright 5, Mary Hooper Robins 4, Thomas Hooper 3, Clement Hooper 2, Stephen Hooper 1) born on October 20, 1935 in Searletown, P.E.I. She married John Wesley Tredenick, son of Irving and Elizabeth Louise (Palmer) Tredenick. He was born on March 29, 1935 in Sumerside. John left home soon after the fifth child was born and did not return. For many years Janet was the secretary to the principal at Three Oaks Senior High School in Summerside, retiring in 2002. Janet and John divorced in 1971. They had five children (surname Tredenick, eleventh generation):

Brian John Tredenick (11, Mary *Janet* 10, Neil Bradshaw 9, Thomas 8, Elizabeth (Lizzie) Wright Bradshaw 7, Harriet Wright Wright 6, Elizabeth Robins Wright 5, Mary Hooper Robins 4, Thomas Hooper 3, Clement Hooper 2, Stephen Hooper 1) born September 6, 1955 in Charlottetown, P.E.I.; married Cynthia Kennedy, on August 8, 1986. Brian and Cynthia have three children (surname Tredenick, twelfth generation):

Brittany Ann Tredenick (12, Brian 11, Mary *Janet* 10, Neil Bradshaw 9, Thomas 8, Elizabeth (Lizzie) Wright Bradshaw 7, Harriet Wright Wright 6, Elizabeth Robins Wright 5, Mary Hooper Robins 4, Thomas Hooper 3, Clement Hooper 2, Stephen Hooper 1) born March 7, 1989.

Andrea Breann Tredenick (12, Brian 11, Mary *Janet* 10, Neil Bradshaw 9, Thomas 8, Elizabeth (Lizzie) Wright Bradshaw 7, Harriet Wright Wright 6, Elizabeth Robins Wright 5, Mary Hoper Robins 4, Thomas Hooper 3, Clement Hooper 2, Stephen Hooper 1) born September 8, 1990.

Jarret Kennedy Tredenick (12, Brian 11, Mary *Janet* 10, Neil Bradshaw 9, Thomas 8, Elizabeth (Lizzie) Wright Bradshaw 7, Harriet Wright Wright 6, Elizabeth Robins Wright 5, Mary Hooper Robins 4, Thomas Hooper 3, Clement Hooper 2, Stephen Hooper 1) born May 2, 1992.

Kent Bradshaw Tredenick (11, Mary *Janet* 10, Neil Bradshaw 9, Thomas 8, Elizabeth (Lizzie) Wright Bradshaw 7, Harriet Wright Wright 6, Elizabeth Robins Wright 5, Mary Hooper Robins 4, Thomas Hooper 3, Clement Hooper 2, Stephen Hooper 1) born November 29, 1957 in Montague, P.E.I.; married (i) Barbara Ramsay. Kent and Barbara had two children (surname Tredenick, twelfth generation):

Chelsea Mary Ellen Tredenick (12, Kent Bradshaw 11, Mary *Janet* 10, Neil Bradshaw 9, Thomas 8, Elizabeth (Lizzie) Wright Bradshaw 7, Harriet Wright Wright 6, Elizabeth Robins Wright 5, Mary Hooper Robins 4, Thomas Hooper 3, Clement Hooper 2, Stephen Hooper 1) born March 20, 1984.

Jamie Lynn Tredenick (12, Kent Bradshaw 11, Mary *Janet* 10, Neil Bradshaw 9, Thomas 8, Elizabeth (Lizzie) Wright Bradshaw 7, Harriet Wright Wright 6, Elizabeth Robins Wright 5, Mary Hooper Robins 4, Thomas Hooper 3, Clement Hooper 2, Stephen Hooper 1) born October 7, 1985

Kent and Barbara divorced, and Kent married (ii) Katherine Pendergast, who had a son, Jared Pendergast, born October 7, 1985, by an earlier marriage. Kent and Katherine have one child (surname Tredenick, twelfth generation):

Erin Kellie Elizabeth Tredenick (12, Kent Bradshaw 11, Mary *Janet* 10, Neil Bradshaw 9, Thomas 8, Elizabeth (Lizzie) Wright Bradshaw 7, Harriet Wright Wright 6, Elizabeth Robins Wright 5, Mary Hooper Robins 4, Thomas Hooper 3, Clement Hooper 2, Stephen Hooper 1) born September 26, 1996.

Susan Janet Tredenick (11, Mary *Janet* 10, Neil Bradshaw 9, Thomas 8, Elizabeth)Lizzie) Wright Bradshaw 7, Harriet Wright Wright 6, Elizabeth Robins Wright 5, Mary Hooper Robins 4, Thomas Hooper 3, Clement Hooper 2, Stephen Hooper 1) born July 8, 1960 in Amherst, Nova Scotia; married Gregory Campbell, on July 31, 1985. Susan and Gregory have two children (surname Campbell, twelfth generation):

Nichole Susan Campbell (12, Susan 11, Mary *Janet* 10, Neil Bradshaw 9, Thomas 8, Elizabeth (Lizzie) Wright Bradshaw 7, Harriet Wright Wright 6, Elizabeth Robins Wright 5, Mary Hooper Robins 4, Thomas Hooper 3, Clement Hoper 2, Stephen Hooper 1) born September 17, 1988.
Nolan Gregory Campbell (12, Susan 11, Mary *Janet* 10, Neil Bradshaw 9, Thomas 8, Elizabeth (Lizzie) Wright Bradshaw 7, Harriet Wright Wright 6, Elizabeth Robins Wright 5, Mary Hooper Robins 4, Thomas Hooper 3, Clement Hooper 2, Stephen Hooper 1) born December 1, 1990.

Shauna Tredenick (11, Mary *Janet* 10, Neil Bradshaw 9, Thomas 8, Elizabeth (Lizzie) Wright Bradshaw 7, Harriet Wright Wright 6, Elizabeth Robins Wright 5, Mary Hooper Robins 4, Thomas Hooper 3, Clement Hooper 2, Stephen Hooper 1) born June 5, 1963 in Summerside, P.E.I.; married Stephen Myles, on June 24, 1989. Shauna and Stephen have two children (surname Myles, twelfth generation):

Alexander Morgan Myles (12, Shauna 11, Mary *Janet* 10, Neil Bradshaw 9, Thomas 8, Elizabeth (Lizzie) Wright Bradshaw 7, Harriet Wright Wright 6, Elizabeth Robins Wright 5, Mary Hooper Robins 4, Thomas Hooper 3, Clement Hooper 2, Stephen Hooper 1) born January 24, 1993.
Mark Stephen Myles (12, Shauna 11, Mary *Janet* 10, Neil Bradshaw 9, Thomas 8, Elizabeth (Lizzie) Wright Bradshaw 7, Harriet Wright

Wright 6, Elizabeth Robins Wright 5, Mary Hooper Robins 4, Thomas Hooper 3, Clement Hooper 3, Clement Hooper 2, Stephen Hooper 1) born on March 25, 1994.

Scott Renwick Tredenick (11, Mary *Janet* 10, Neil Bradshaw 9, Thomas 8, Elizabeth (Lizzie) Wright Bradshaw 7, Harriet Wright Wright 6, Elizabeth Robins Wright 5, Mary Hooper Robins 4, Thomas Hooper 3, Clement Hooper 2, Stephen Hooper 1) born on July 2, 1964 in Sumerside, P.E.I. He married Michele Quinn, on September 4, 1993, at a beautiful service at the United Church in Summerside where the author of this genealogy was the organist. They live in Quebec (2000). Scott and Michele have one child (surname Tredenick, twelfth generation):

Shaelyn Michele Tredenick (12, Scott 11, Mary *Janet* 10, Neil Bradshaw 9, Thomas 8, Elizabeth (Lizzie) 7, Harriet Wright Wright 6, Elizabeth Robins Wright 5, Mary Hooper Robins 4, Thomas Hooper 3, Clement Hooper 2, Stephen Hooper 1) born August 5, 1998.

Carman *Garth* Bradshaw (10, Neil Bradshaw 9, Thomas 8, Elizabeth (Lizzie) 7, Harriet Wright Wright 6, Elizabeth Robins Wright 5, Mary Hooper Robins 4, Thomas Hooper 3, Clement Hooper 2, Stephen Hooper 1) born May 2, 1941 in Searletown, P.E.I.; married (i) Flora *Arlene* Fraser (born on April 11, 1944 in North Sydney, Nova Scotia) in 1968. They had no children. Arlene died in 1980 from cancer of the stomach. Garth married (ii) Jill Stultz, born 1948, in 1982. They live in Mt. Uniacke, Nova Scotia. Garth and Jill have one daughter (surname Bradshaw, eleventh generation):

Lindsay Rose Bradshaw (11, Garth 10, Neil Bradshaw 9, Thomas 8, Elizabeth (Lizzie) Wright Bradshaw 7, Harriet Wright Wright 6, Elizabeth Robins Wright 5, Mary Hooper Robins 4, Thomas Hooper 3, Clement Hooper 2, Stephen Hooper 1) born on September 5, 1983. Lindsay's passion (as well as her work) is participating in an equestrian sport [2002].

Carol Jean Bradshaw (10, Neil Bradshaw 9, Thomas 8, Elizabeth (Lizzie) Wright Bradshaw 7, Harriet Wright Wright 6, Elizabeth Robins Wright 5, Mary Hooper Robins 4, Thomas Hooper 3, Clement Hooper 2, Stephen Hooper 1) born in Summerside, P.E.I. on July 20, 1944; married Thane Arthur Bell, son of Gilbert Cedric and Lillian Elizabeth (Craig) Bell, on August 6, 1966. He was born on February 26, 1944. Carol graduated from the nursing program at the Prince County Hospital in Summerside and lives (2000) in Lower Sackville, Nova Scotia. She moved within the city of Halifax in 2002 and works for the Red Cross Blood Donor Center. Carol and Thane were divorced about 2000. Thane lives in Toronto. Carol and Shane had three children (surname Bell, eleventh generation):

Shannon Elizabeth Bell, called Beth, (11, Carol 10, Neil Bradshaw 9, Thomas 8, Elizabeth (Lizzie) Wright Bradshaw 7, Harriet Wright Wright 6, Elizabeth Robins Wright 5, Mary Hooper Robins 4, Thomas Hooper 3, Clement Hooper 2, Stephen Hooper 1) born on August 27, 1970.

Kyler Thane Bradshaw Bell (11, Carol 10, Neil Bradshaw 9, Thomas 8, Elizabeth (Lizzie) Wright Bradshaw 7, Harriet Wright Wright 6, Elizabeth Robins Wright 5, Mary Hooper Robins 4, Thomas Hooper 3, Clement Hooper 2, Stephen Hooper 1) born on December 25, 1972. Kyler is married and has one child.

Kara Ann Bell (11, Carol 10, Neil Bradshaw 9, Thomas Bradshaw 8, Elizabeth (Lizzie) Wright Bradshaw 7, Harriet Wright Wright 6, Elizabeth Robins Wright 5, Mary Hooper Robins 4, Thomas Hooper 3, Clement Hooper 2, Stephen Hooper 1) born on July 20, 1977.

Norma Ardene Bradshaw (10, Neil Bradshaw 9, Thomas Bradshaw 8, Elizabeth (Lizzie) Wright Bradshaw 7, Harriet Wright Wright 6, Elizabeth Robins Wright 5, Mary Hooper Robins 4, Thomas Hooper 3, Clement Hooper 2, Stephen Hooper 1) born in Summerside, P.E.I. on September 19, 1946; married Lloyd Harold Palmer, the son of Harold Lloyd and Verna Mae (MacFadyen) Palmer, on April 21, 1963 in the Bedeque United Church, P.E.I. For many years Lloyd was a

captain on the ferry boat that traveled between Borden, P.E.I. and Cape Tormentine, N.B. Then he went to Nova Scotia to do similar work. Norma and Lloyd have three children (surname Palmer, eleventh generation):

Christopher Lloyd Palmer (11, Norma 10, Neil 9, Thomas Bradshaw 8, Elizabeth (Lizzie) Wright Bradshaw 7, Harriet Wright Wright 6, Elizabeth Robins Wright 5, Mary Hooper Robins 4, Thomas Hooper 3, Clement Hooper 2, Stephen Hooper 1) born on October 4, 1968 in Summerside. He graduated from the University of P.E.I. in Charlottetown. He married a nurse and they have two children (surname Palmer, twelfth generation).
Kendra Ardene Palmer (11, Norma 10, Neil 9, Thomas Bradshaw 8) Elizabeth (Lizzie) Wright Bradshaw 7, Harriet Wright Wright 6, Elizabeth Robins Wright 5, Mary Hooper Robins 4, Thomas Hooper 3, Clement Hooper 2, Stephen Hooper 1) born August 25, 1971; married Stephen Gaudet, on September 5, 1998. [The writer of this genealogy played the organ at their wedding in the Summerside United Church] Kendra is a graduate of Dalhousie University and is an occupational therapist. She and Stephen have two children (surname Gaudet, twelfth generation):

Kate Kristina Gaudet (12, Kendra 11, Norma 10, Neil 9, Thomas Bradshaw 8, Elizabeth (Lizzie) Wright Bradshaw 7, Harriet Wright Wright 6, Elizabeth Robins Wright 5, Mary Hooper Robins 4, Thomas Hooper 3, Clement Hooper 2, Stephen Hooper 1) born on December 19, 1999.
A daughter (12, Kendra 11, Norma 10, Neil 9, Thomas Bradshaw 8, Elizabeth (Lizzie) Wright Bradshaw 7, Harriet Wright Wright 6, Elizabeth Robins Wright 5, Mary Hooper Robins 4, Thomas Hooper 3, Clement Hooper 2, Stephen Hooper 1) born on September 2, 2002.

Grant Neil Palmer (11, Norma 10, Neil 9, Thomas Bradshaw 8, Elizabeth (Lizzie) Wright Bradshaw 7, Harriet Wright Wright 6, Elizabeth Robins Wright 5, Mary Hooper Robins 4, Thomas Hooper 3,

Clement Hooper 2, Stephen Hooper 1) born on April 18, 1978. Grant studied hotel administration.

Doris Erlene Clark (10, Annie Bradshaw 9, Thomas Bradshaw 8, Elizabeth (Lizzie) Wright Bradshaw 7, Harriet Wright Wright 6, Elizabeth Robins Wright 5, Mary Hooper Robins 4, Thomas Hooper 3, Clement Hooper 2, Stephen Hooper 1) was born Aug. 13, 1932 in Summerside, P.E.I. She married Sept. 18, 1958, Eugene Joseph Mathew Mockler, son of Lawrence Mathew and Blanche Elizabeth Mockler. He was born Dec. 30, 1936 in Grand Falls, N.B. Doris and Eugene live at 86 Alexander Street, Fredericton, N .B. Eugene is a barrister and part time lecturer at the University of New Brunswick Law School. Children (eleventh generation, surname Mockler), all born in Fredericton, N.B.:

Gary Thomas Mockler (11, Doris Clark 10, Annie Bradshaw 9, Thomas Bradshaw 8, Elizabeth (Lizzie) Wright Bradshaw 7, Harriet Wright Wright 6, Elizabeth Robins Wright 5, Mary Hooper Robins 4, Thomas Hooper 3, Clement Hooper 2, Stephen Hooper 1), b. Aug. 1, 1961.

Alan Eugene Lawrence Mockler (11, Doris Clark 10, Annie Bradshaw 9, Thomas Bradshaw 8, Elizabeth (Lizzie) Wright Bradshaw 7, Harriet Wright Wright 6, Elizabeth Robins Wright 5, Mary Hooper Robins 4, Thomas Hooper 3, Clement Hooper 2, Stephen Hooper 1), a twin, b. Jan. 1, 1963.

Andrew Earl Mockler (11, Doris Clark 10, Annie Bradshaw 9, Thomas Bradshaw 8, Elizabeth (Lizzie) Wright Bradshaw 7, Harriet Wright Wright 6, Elizabeth Robins Wright 5, Mary Hooper Robins 4, Thomas Hooper 3, Clement Hooper 2, Stephen Hooper 1), a twin, b. Jan. 1, 1963.

Kimberley Jo-anne Mockler (11, Doris Clark 10, Annie Bradshaw 9, Thomas Bradshaw 8, Elizabeth (Lizzie) Wright Bradshaw 7, Harriet Wright Wright 6, Elizabeth Robins Wright 5, Mary Hooper Robins 4, Thomas Hooper 3, Clement Hooper 2, Stephen Hooper 1), b. Apr. 29, 1969.

Douglas Bradshaw Clark (10, Annie Bradshaw 9, Thomas Bradshaw 8, Elizabeth (Lizzie) Wright Bradshaw 7, Harriet Wright Wright 6, Elizabeth Robins Wright 5, Mary Hooper Robins 4, Thomas Hooper 3, Clement Hooper 2, Stephen Hooper 1) was born Aug. 21, 1935 in Augustine Cove, P.E.I. He married in 1960, Katharine Joan Estabrooks, daughter of Holland Theodore and Helena Beatrice (McCoomb) Estabrooks. She was born May 22,1936 in Woodstock, N.B. They live at 165 Ridgeway, St. Renforth, N.B. Douglas graduated with a B.A. degree from the University of New Brunswick in 1957. He is a contractor, owner and manager of a building and real estate business. Children (eleventh generation, surname Clark), all born in Saint John, N.B.:

Brian Douglas Clark (11, Douglas Clark 10, Annie Bradshaw 9, Thomas Bradshaw 8, Elizabeth (Lizzie) Wright Bradshaw 7, Harriet Wright Wright 6, Elizabeth Robins Wright 5, Mary Hooper Robins 4, Thomas Hooper 3, Clement Hooper 2, Stephen Hooper 1), b. Mar. 2, 1961.

Larry William Clark (11, Douglas Clark 10, Annie Bradshaw 9, Thomas Bradshaw 8, Elizabeth (Lizzie) Wright Bradshaw 7, Harriet Wright Wright 6, Elizabeth Robins Wright 5, Mary Hooper Robins 4, Thomas Hooper 3, Clement Hooper 2, Stephen Hooper 1), b. Feb. 18, 1963.

Jeffrey Allyson Clark (11, Douglas Clark 10, Annie Bradshaw 9, Thomas Bradshaw 8, Elizabeth (Lizzie) Wright Bradshaw 7, Harriet Wright Wright 6, Elizabeth Robins Wright 5, Mary Hooper Robins 4, Thomas Hooper 3, Clement Hooper 2, Stephen Hooper 1), b. June 18, 1964.

Heather Ann Clark (11, Douglas Clark 10, Annie Bradshaw 9, Thomas Bradshaw 8, Elizabeth (Lizzie) Wright Bradshaw 7, Harriet Wright Wright 6, Elizabeth Robins Wright 5, Mary Hooper Robins 4, Thomas Hooper 3, Clement Hooper 2, Stephen Hooper 1), b. Oct. 19, 1969.

Mabel Adele Clark (10, Muriel Bradshaw 9, Thomas Bradshaw 8, Elizabeth (Lizzie) Wright Bradshaw 7, Harriet Wright Wright 6, Elizabeth Robins Wright 5, Mary Hooper Robins 4, Thomas Hooper 3, Clement Hooper 2, Stephen Hooper 1) was born, Nov. 9, 1932 in Cape Traverse, P.E.I. She married Lloyd Cameron, son of Angus Cameron. The marriage ended in divorce. Lloyd is a bank manager. Adele lives at 4 Ashburn Crescent, Charlottetown, P.E.I. Children (eleventh generation, surname Cameron):

Randall Arthur Cameron (11, Adele Clark 10, Muriel Bradshaw 9, Thomas Bradshaw 8, Elizabeth (Lizzie) Wright Bradshaw 7, Harriet Wright Wright 6, Elizabeth Robins Wright 5, Mary Hooper Robins 4, Thomas Hooper 3, Clement Hooper 2, Stephen Hooper 1), b. Sept. 9, 1952 in Charlottetown. P .E.I.

Roma Kim Cameron (11, Adele Clark 10, Muriel Bradshaw 9, Thomas Bradshaw 8, Elizabeth (Lizzie) Wright Bradshaw 7, Harriet Wright Wright 6, Elizabeth Robins Wright 5, Mary Hooper Robins 4, Thomas Hooper 3, Clement Hooper 2, Stephen Hooper 1), b. Apr. 19, 1954 in St. Stephen, N.B.

Donald Arthur Clark (10, Muriel Bradshaw 9, Thomas Bradshaw 8, Elizabeth (Lizzie) Wright Bradshaw 7, Harriet Wright Wright 6, Elizabeth Robins Wright 5, Mary Hooper Robins 4, Thomas Hooper 3, Clement Hooper 2, Stephen Hooper 1) was born Oct. 22, 1933 in Cape Traverse, P.E.I. He married Juliet Badal Salim, daughter of Badal Salim and Katerina Hakim Salim. She was born May 21, 1946 in Baghdad, Iraq. Donald is an airplane pilot. He worked for Air Canada in Newfoundland and Saskatchewan, from 1952-55, and was a pilot for Canadian Pacific Airlines in B.C. and the Yukon 1955-59. He went to the U.S., was a pilot in California until 1963, freelanced as an airplane pilot in Lebanon and Jordan, flew out of Ireland with a charter company flying round-the-world flights (people, freight, pregnant horses from England to Japan, etc.), returned to the U.S., and in 1966 settled in Boston and joined Northeast Airlines, now Delta Airlines. Currently he is flying a Boeing 727 Jet across the U.S. out of

Boston. He lives at 52 Puritan Road, Swampscott, Mass. He met Juliet in Baghdad in 1964. Her family emigrated to England in 1965 and they were married in London in January 1966. The marriage ended in divorce. One child (eleventh generation, surname Clark):

Monique Lisa Clark (11, Donald Clark 10, Muriel Bradshaw 9, Thomas Bradshaw 8, Elizabeth (Lizzie) Wright Bradshaw 7, Harriet Wright Wright 6, Elizabeth Robins Wright 5, Mary Hooper Robins 4, Thomas Hooper 3, Clement Hooper 2, Stephen Hooper 1), b. Sept. 5, 1969 in Lynn. Mass.

Roger Russell Clark, called Buddy (10, Muriel Bradshaw 9, Thomas Bradshaw 8, Elizabeth (Lizzie) Wright Bradshaw 7, Harriet Wright Wright 6, Elizabeth Robins Wright 5, Mary Hooper Robins 4, Thomas Hooper 3, Clement Hooper 2, Stephen Hooper 1) was born May 7, 1935 in Charlottetown, P.E.I. He married, March 9, 1957, Winnifred Mary Cameron, daughter of Donald and Winnifred (Jennings) Cameron. She was born November 11, 1935 in Moncton, N.B. Buddy and Winnifred live at 6345 York Street, Halifax. N .S. He is a marketing officer for the Nova Scotia government. He received a B.Sc. (geology) degree from Mount Allison University, Sackville, N.B.; he was a pilot officer (R.C.A.F.) 1956, and an airline pilot with Nordair Limited, Montreal 1959-1965. Children (eleventh generation, surname Clark):

Wendy Dawn Clark (11, Buddy Clark 10, Muriel Bradshaw 9, Thomas Bradshaw 8, Elizabeth (Lizzie) Wright Bradshaw 7, Harriet Wright Wright 6, Elizabeth Robins Wright 5, Mary Hooper Robins 4, Thomas Hooper 3, Clement Hooper 2, Stephen Hooper 1), b. July 18, 1958 in Moncton. N.B.

Peter Allen Clark (11, Buddy Clark 10, Muriel Bradshaw 9, Thomas Bradshaw 8, Elizabeth (Lizzie) Wright Bradshaw 7, Harriet Wright Wright 6, Elizabeth Robins Wright 5, Mary Hooper Robins 4, Thomas Hooper 3, Clement Hooper 2, Stephen Hooper 1), b. June 25, 1959 in Montreal, P.Q.

Susan Mary Clark (11, Buddy Clark 10, Muriel Bradshaw 9, Thomas Bradshaw 8, Elizabeth (Lizzie) Wright Bradshaw 7, Harriet Wright Wright 6, Elizabeth Robins Wright 5, Mary Hooper Robins 4, Thomas Hooper 3, Clement Hooper 2, Stephen Hooper 1), b. June 20, 1961 in Montreal, P .Q.
Steven Arthur Clark (11, Buddy Clark 10, Muriel Bradshaw 9, Thomas Bradshaw 8, Elizabeth (Lizzie) Wright Bradshaw 7, Harriet Wright Wright 6, Elizabeth Robins Wright 5, Mary Hooper Robins 4, Thomas Hooper 3, Clement Hooper 2, Stephen Hooper 1), b. November 1, 1962 in Montreal. P.Q.
Christopher Andrew Clark (11, Buddy Clark 10, Muriel Bradshaw 9, Thomas Bradshaw 8, Elizabeth (Lizzie) Wright Bradshaw 7, Harriet Wright Wright 6, Elizabeth Robins Wright 5, Mary Hooper Robins 4, Thomas Hooper 3, Clement Hooper 2, Stephen Hooper 1), b. September 30, 1970 in Halifax. N.S.

Frances Enman Clark (10, Muriel Bradshaw 9, Thomas Bradshaw 8, Elizabeth (Lizzie) Wright Bradshaw 7, Harriet Wright Wright 6, Elizabeth Robins Wright 5, Mary Hooper Robins 4, Thomas Hooper 3, Clement Hooper 2, Stephen Hooper 1) was born May 26,1937 in Charlottetown, P.E.I. She married Douglas Wendall Cudmore, son of Wendall Roy and Maud Cudmore. He was born September 27, 1936 in Charlottetown. Douglas is a medical doctor. He graduated M.D.C.M. from Dalhousie University and is practicing (obstetrics, gynecology) in Halifax. He and Frances live at 1208 Blenheim Terrace. Children (eleventh generation, surname Cudmore):

Heather Jane Cudmore (11, Frances Clark 10, Muriel Bradshaw 9, Thomas Bradshaw 8, Elizabeth (Lizzie) Wright Bradshaw 7, Harriet Wright Wright 6, Elizabeth Robins Wright 5, Mary Hooper Robins 4, Thomas Hooper 3, Clement Hooper 2, Stephen Hooper 1), b. July 10, 1962.
Stephen Geoffrey Cudmore (11, Frances Clark 10, Muriel Bradshaw 9, Thomas Bradshaw 8, Elizabeth (Lizzie) Wright Bradshaw 7, Harriet

Wright Wright 6, Elizabeth Robins Wright 5, Mary Hooper Robins 4, Thomas Hooper 3, Clement Hooper 2, Stephen Hooper 1), b. February 18, 1964.

Linda Joanne Cudmore (11, Frances Clark 10, Muriel Bradshaw 9, Thomas Bradshaw 8, Elizabeth (Lizzie) Wright Bradshaw 7, Harriet Wright Wright 6, Elizabeth Robins Wright 5, Mary Hooper Robins 4, Thomas Hooper 3, Clement Hooper 2, Stephen Hooper 1), b. May 14, 1968.

Andrew Douglas Enman Cudmore (11, Frances Clark 10, Muriel Bradshaw 9, Thomas Bradshaw 8, Elizabeth (Lizzie) Wright Bradshaw 7, Harriet Wright Wright 6, Elizabeth Robins Wright 5, Mary Hooper Robins 4, Thomas Hooper 3, Clement Hooper 2, Stephen Hooper 1), b. October. 31, 1971.

Paul Hamilton Clark (10, Muriel Bradshaw 9, Thomas Bradshaw 8, Elizabeth (Lizzie) Wright Bradshaw 7, Harriet Wright Wright 6, Elizabeth Robins Wright 5, Mary Hooper Robins 4, Thomas Hooper 3, Clement Hooper 2, Stephen Hooper 1) was born July 8, 1943 in Charlottetown, P.E.I. He married January 31, 1970, Rosalie Anne Waters, daughter of Ralph Angus and E. Thelma (Anderson) Waters. She was born June 28, 1945 in Saint John, N.B. They live in Halifax, N .S. Paul is a medical doctor, a physician. He attended Dalhousie University and received a B.Sc. degree in 1965, an M.D. degree in 1970, and a L.M.C.C. He served in the Canadian Armed Forces with the rank of captain, 1970-1973. Rosalie is a registered nurse, a graduate of Saint John General Hospital in 1967. She received a P.H.N. degree (Public Health Nursing) from Dalhousie University in 1968. Children (eleventh generation, surname Clark):

Jeffrey Hamilton Clark (11, Paul Clark 10, Muriel Bradshaw 9, Thomas Bradshaw 8, Elizabeth (Lizzie) Wright Bradshaw 7, Harriet Wright Wright 6, Elizabeth Robins Wright 5, Mary Hooper Robins 4, Thomas Hooper 3, Clement Hooper 2, Stephen Hooper 1), b. August 6, 1970 in Halifax, N .S.;

Gregory Arthur Clark (11, Paul Clark 10, Muriel Bradshaw 9, Thomas Bradshaw 8, Elizabeth (Lizzie) Wright Bradshaw 7, Harriet Wright Wright 6, Elizabeth Robins Wright 5, Mary Hooper Robins 4, Thomas Hooper 3, Clement Hooper 2, Stephen Hooper 1), b. April 4, 1972 in Ottawa, Ontario

Linda Jane Clark (10, Muriel Bradshaw 9, Thomas Bradshaw 8, Elizabeth (Lizzie) Wright Bradshaw 7, Harriet Wright Wright 6, Elizabeth Robins Wright 5, Mary Hooper Robins 4, Thomas Hooper 3, Clement Hooper 2, Stephen Hooper 1) was born March 24, 1946 in Charlottetown, P.E.I. She married May 18, 1968, Alan Pierce Godfrey, son of Charles Henry and Catherine Irene (MacEachern) Godfrey. He was born September 27, 1945 in Charlottetown. They live in Marshfield, P.E.I. Alan is a wildlife biologist. He graduated B.Sc. in Agriculture from McGill, 1968, M.Sc. (Biology) from Acadia in 1971. He is working with the P.E.I. Department of Environment. Children (eleventh generation, surname Godfrey), both born in Charlottetown, P.E.I.:

Jennifer Louise Clark Godfrey (11, Linda Jane Clark 10, Muriel Bradshaw 9, Thomas Bradshaw 8, Elizabeth (Lizzie) Wright Bradshaw 7, Harriet Wright Wright 6, Elizabeth Robins Wright 5, Mary Hooper Robins 4, Thomas Hooper 3, Clement Hooper 2, Stephen Hooper 1), b. November 25, 1972.
Alexander Pierce Godfrey (11, Linda Jane Clark 10, Muriel Bradshaw 9, Thomas Bradshaw 8, Elizabeth (Lizzie) Wright Bradshaw 7, Harriet Wright Wright 6, Elizabeth Robins Wright 5, Mary Hooper Robins 4, Thomas Hooper 3, Clement Hooper 2, Stephen Hooper 1), b. August 17, 1974.

Dianne Gay Bradshaw (10, Ivan Bradshaw 9, Thomas Bradshaw 8, Elizabeth (Lizzie) Wright Bradshaw 7, Harriet Wright Wright 6, Elizabeth Robins Wright 5, Mary Hooper Robins 4, Thomas Hooper 3, Clement Hooper 2, Stephen Hooper 1) was born March 28, 1941 in Charlottetown, P.E.I. She married October 31, 1964, Reginald David

Webb, son of Reginald Warren and Dorothy Elva (MacPherson) Webb. He was born January 12, 1942 in Charlottetown, P.E.I. They live at 57 Prescott Street, Westphal, Dartmouth, Nova Scotia. Reginald is a superintendent of LeRoy Engineering Ltd. Children (eleventh generation, surname Webb):

Kristen Luane Webb (11, Dianne Gay Bradshaw 10, Ivan Bradshaw 9, Thomas Bradshaw 8, Elizabeth (Lizzie) Wright Bradshaw 7, Harriet Wright Wright 6, Elizabeth Robins Wright 5, Mary Hooper Robins 4, Thomas Hooper 3, Clement Hooper 2, Stephen Hooper 1), b. April 19, 1966 in North Sydney, N.S.
Marcia Lyn Webb (11, Dianne Gay Bradshaw 10, Ivan Bradshaw 9, Thomas Bradshaw 8, Elizabeth (Lizzie) Wright Bradshaw 7, Harriet Wright Wright 6, Elizabeth Robins Wright 5, Mary Hooper Robins 4, Thomas Hooper 3, Clement Hooper 2, Stephen Hooper 1), b. April 1, 1970 in Halifax, N.S.

Grant Charles Llewellyn (10, Wanda Bradshaw 9, Thomas Bradshaw 8, Elizabeth (Lizzie) Wright Bradshaw 7, Harriet Wright Wright 6, Elizabeth Robins Wright 5, Mary Hooper Robins 4, Thomas Hooper 3, Clement Hooper 2, Stephen Hooper 1) was born April 2, 1942 in Summerside, P.E.I. He married December 17, 1966, Donna Georgina Swan, daughter of George Arthur and Kathleen Cavell (MacLeod) Swan. She was born January 28, 1944 in New Glasgow, N.S. Grant and Donna live in Riverview, N.B. Grant is a medical doctor. He graduated from Dalhousie Medical School and practiced as a general practitioner for two years. He took a four year post graduate in diagnostic radiology with emphasis on nuclear study at Winnipeg General and St. Boniface Hospital, Winnipeg. He is, 1976, practicing in Moncton, N.B. Donna graduated from the Halifax Pathological Institute in 1963 as a registered technologist, and worked there till 1966. Children (eleventh generation, surname Llewellyn):

Sean Michael Llewellyn (11, Grant Llewellyn 10, Wanda Bradshaw 9, Thomas Bradshaw 8, Elizabeth (Lizzie) Wright Bradshaw 7, Harriet

Wright Wright 6, Elizabeth Robins Wright 5, Mary Hooper Robins 4, Thomas Hooper 3, Clement Hooper 2, Stephen Hooper 1), b. November 30,1968 in Halifax, N.S.

Gregory Mark Llewellyn (11, Grant Llewellyn 10, Wanda Bradshaw 9, Thomas Bradshaw 8, Elizabeth (Lizzie) Wright Bradshaw 7, Harriet Wright Wright 6, Elizabeth Robins Wright 5, Mary Hooper Robins 4, Thomas Hooper 3, Clement Hooper 2, Stephen Hooper 1), b. March 1, 1970 in Fredericton, N.B.

Stephanie Dawn Llewellyn (11, Grant Llewellyn 10, Wanda Bradshaw 9, Thomas Bradshaw 8, Elizabeth (Lizzie) Wright Bradshaw 7, Harriet Wright Wright 6, Elizabeth Robins Wright 5, Mary Hooper Robins 4, Thomas Hooper 3, Clement Hooper 2, Stephen Hooper 1), b. December 30,1970 in Fredericton, N.B.

Gary William Llewellyn (10, Wanda Bradshaw 9, Thomas Bradshaw 8, Elizabeth (Lizzie) Wright Bradshaw 7, Harriet Wright Wright 6, Elizabeth Robins Wright 5, Mary Hooper Robins 4, Thomas Hooper 3, Clement Hooper 2, Stephen Hooper 1) was born April 2, 1944 in Oshawa, Ontario. He married June 8, 1968, Carol Margaret Rose Smith, daughter of Charles Anthony and Melita Clare (Solymos) Smith. She was born September 9, 1945 in North Battleford, Sask. They live at 1119 Smythe St., Fredericton, N.B. Gary graduated in Business Administration from the University of New Brunswick. He is engaged in the national expansion of the Wandlyn Motor Inns. Carol graduated from the University of Saskatchewan in 1966. She taught school for three years in Calgary, Alta. and at Priestman Street School in Fredericton. Child (eleventh generation, surname Llewellyn):

Lita Karen Llewellyn (11, Gary Llewellyn 10, Wanda Bradshaw 9, Thomas Bradshaw 8, Elizabeth (Lizzie) Wright Bradshaw 7, Harriet Wright Wright 6, Elizabeth Robins Wright 5, Mary Hooper Robins 4, Thomas Hooper 3, Clement Hooper 2, Stephen Hooper 1), b. February 14, 1975 in Fredericton, N.B.

Wilbur Henry Cameron (10, Lorne Cameron 9, Harriet Bradshaw 8, Elizabeth (Lizzie) Wright Bradshaw 7, Harriet Wright Wright 6, Elizabeth Robins Wright 5, Mary Hooper Robins 4, Thomas Hooper 3, Clement Hooper 2, Stephen Hooper 1) was born January 15, 1933 in Albany, P.E.I. He married February 16, 1957, Kathleen Bernice Connick, daughter of Walter William and Mary (McMahon) Connick. She was born November 30, 1937 in Norboro, P.E.I. They live in Kinkora, P.E.I. Wilbur spent one year in Northern Alberta, and worked in Toronto three years erecting steel scaffolding, before returning to the Island to work as a deck hand on C.N. Ferry Service at Borden. Children (eleventh generation, surname Cameron):

Brian Wilbur Cameron (11, Wilbur Cameron 10, Lorne Cameron 9, Harriet Bradshaw 8, Elizabeth (Lizzie) Wright Bradshaw 7, Harriet Wright Wright 6, Elizabeth Robins Wright 5, Mary Hooper Robins 4, Thomas Hooper 3, Clement Hooper 2, Stephen Hooper 1), b. August 9,1957 in Toronto, Ontario.

David William Cameron (11, Wilbur Cameron 10, Lorne Cameron 9, Harriet Bradshaw 8, Elizabeth (Lizzie) Wright Bradshaw 7, Harriet Wright Wright 6, Elizabeth Robins Wright 5, Mary Hooper Robins 4, Thomas Hooper 3, Clement Hooper 2, Stephen Hooper 1), b. July 29, 1958 in Summerside, P.E.I.

Michael Peter Cameron (11, Wilbur Cameron 10, Lorne Cameron 9, Harriet Bradshaw 8, Elizabeth (Lizzie) Wright Bradshaw 7, Harriet Wright Wright 6, Elizabeth Robins Wright 5, Mary Hooper Robins 4, Thomas Hooper 3, Clement Hooper 2, Stephen Hooper 1), b. August 14, 1959 in Charlottetown, P.E.I.

Richard Joseph Cameron (11, Wilbur Cameron 10, Lorne Cameron 9, Harriet Bradshaw 8, Elizabeth (Lizzie) Wright Bradshaw 7, Harriet Wright Wright 6, Elizabeth Robins Wright 5, Mary Hooper Robins 4, Thomas Hooper 3, Clement Hooper 2, Stephen Hooper 1), b. March 8,1961 in Bonshaw, at Dr. MacLeod's.

Mary Lorna Cameron (11, Wilbur Cameron 10, Lorne Cameron 9, Harriet Bradshaw 8, Elizabeth (Lizzie) Wright Bradshaw 7, Harriet Wright Wright 6, Elizabeth Robins Wright 5, Mary Hooper Robins

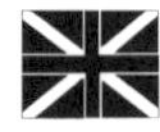

4, Thomas Hooper 3, Clement Hooper 2, Stephen Hooper 1), b. August 16, 1962 in Charlottetown, P.E.I.

Charles Lorne Cameron (11, Wilbur Cameron 10, Lorne Cameron 9, Harriet Bradshaw 8, Elizabeth (Lizzie) Wright Bradshaw 7, Harriet Wright Wright 6, Elizabeth Robins Wright 5, Mary Hooper Robins 4, Thomas Hooper 3, Clement Hooper 2, Stephen Hooper 1), b. November 2, 1963 in Charlottetown, P.E.I.

Harriet Jean Cameron (10, Lorne Cameron 9, Harriet Bradshaw 8, Elizabeth (Lizzie) Wright Bradshaw 7, Harriet Wright Wright 6, Elizabeth Robins Wright 5, Mary Hooper Robins 4, Thomas Hooper 3, Clement Hooper 2, Stephen Hooper 1) was born on August 14, 1935 in Albany, P.E.I. [See Chapter 9]

On November 21, 1953 Harriet married Garnet Marven MacDonald, son of Roy and Florence Alice (Bell) MacDonald. He was born on November 28, 1928 in Albany, P.E.I. In the mid-1970s they lived in Albany, P.E.I. Garnet was a ticket agent for the Canadian National Railroad at Borden, P.E.I. He had been a farmer until 1972. Harriet and Garnet had three children (surname MacDonald, eleventh generation):

Donna Jean MacDonald (11, Harriet Cameron 10, Lorne Cameron 9, Harriet Bradshaw 8, Elizabeth (Lizzie) Wright Bradshaw 7, Harriet Wright Wright 6, Elizabeth Robins Wright 5, Mary Hooper Robins 4, Thomas Hooper 3, Clement Hooper 2, Stephen Hooper 1) was born on August 22, 1954 in Winnipeg, Manitoba. She graduated from Dalhousie University, with a Bachelor of Nursing degree, in 1976, and then worked in Halifax, Nova Scotia. No further information.

Gary Marven MacDonald (11, Harriet Cameron 10, Lorne Cameron 9, Harriet Bradshaw 8, Elizabeth (Lizzie) Wright Bradshaw 7, Harriet Wright Wright 6, Elizabeth Robins Wright 5, Mary Hooper Robins 4, Thomas Hooper 3, Clement Hooper 2, Stephen Hooper 1) born January 11, 1957 in Summerside, P.E.I. He was attending the University of P.E.I. in the mid-1970s.

Janelle Shirley MacDonald (11, Harriet Cameron 10, Lorne Cameron 9, Harriet Bradshaw 8, Elizabeth (Lizzie) Wright Bradshaw 7, Harriet Wright Wright 6, Elizabeth Robins Wright 5, Mary Hooper Robins 4, Thomas Hooper 3, Clement Hooper 2, Stephen Hooper 1) born on August 22, 1966 in Summerside, P.E.I. No further information.

Shirley Lucy Cameron (10, Lorne Cameron 9, Harriet Bradshaw 8, Elizabeth (Lizzie)Wright Bradshaw 7, Harriet Wright Wright 6, Elizabeth Robins Wright 5, Mary Hooper Robins 4, Thomas Hooper 3, Clement Hooper 2, Stephen Hooper 1) was born on June 28, 1937 in Albany, P.E.I. She married Donald Ray Thomson, son of John David and Mildred Alice Olive (McInnis) Thomson. He was born on July 3, 1937 in Roseville, P.E.I. In the mid-1970s they lived in Markham, Ontario where Donald was an auto mechanic. They had three children (surname Thomson, eleventh generation):

John William Thomson (11, Shirley Cameron 10, Lorne Cameron 9, Harriet Bradshaw Cameron 8, Elizabeth (Lizzie) Wright Bradshaw 7, Harriet Wright Wright 6, Elizabeth Robins Wright 5, Mary Hooper Robins 4, Thomas Hooper 3, Clement Hooper 2, Stephen Hooper 1) was born on October 25, 1964 in Toronto, Ontario. No further information.

Carol Lynn Thomson (11, Shirley Cameron 10, Lorne Cameron 9, Harriet Bradshaw Cameron 8, Elizabeth (Lizzie) Wright Bradshaw 7, Harriet Wright Wright 6, Elizabeth Robins Wright 5, Mary Hooper Robins 4, Thomas Hooper 3, Clement Hooper 2, Stephen Hooper 1) born in Toronto on October 25, 1966; died there on July 5, 1967.

Bruce Donald Thomson (11, Shirley Cameron 10, Lorne Cameron 9, Harriet Bradshaw Cameron 8, Elizabeth (Lizzie) Wright Bradshaw 7, Harriet Wright Wright 6, Elizabeth Robins Wright 5, Mary Hooper Robins 4, Thomas Hooper 3, Clement Hooper 2, Stephen Hooper 1) born on August 8, 1969 in Scarborough, Ontario. No further information.

Winston Dawson Cameron (10, Lorne Cameron 9, Harriet Bradshaw Cameron 8, Elizabeth (Lizzie) Wright Bradshaw 7, Harriet Wright Wright 6, Elizabeth Robins Wright 5, Mary Hooper Robins 4, Thomas Hooper 3, Clement Hooper 2, Stephen Hooper 1) was born on May 20, 1943 in Albany, P.E.I. On March 19, 1966 he married Judith Ann Mota (called Judy), daughter of Albert N. and Emily (Bernard) Mota. In the mid-1970s they lived in Bay Ridge, Ontario where Winston was a police constable. They had three children (surname Cameron, eleventh generation):

Kirk Bradley Cameron (11, Winston Cameron 10, Lorne Cameron 9, Harriet Bradshaw Cameron 8, Elizabeth (Lizzie) Wright Bradshaw 7, Harriet Wright Wright 6, Elizabeth Robins Wright 5, Mary Hooper Robins 4, Thomas Hooper 3, Clement Hooper 2, Stephen Hooper 1) born on September 21, 1966 in Toronto, Ontario.
Sandra Lynn Cameron (11, Winston Cameron 10, Lorne Cameron 9, Harried Bradshaw Cameron 8, Elizabeth (Lizzie) Wright Bradshaw 7, Harriet Wright Wright 6, Elizabeth Robins Wright 5, Mary Hooper Robins 4, Thomas Hooper 3, Clement Hooper 2, Stephen Hooper 1) was born on August 26, 1971 in Scarborough, Ontario.
Judson Michael Cameron (11, Winston Cameron 10, Lorne Cameron 9, Harriet Bradshaw Cameron 8, Elizabeth "Lizzie" Wright Bradshaw 7, Harried Wright Wright 6, Elizabeth Robins Wright 5, Mary Hooper Robins 4, Thomas Hooper 3, Clement Hooper 2, Stephen Hooper 1) was born on February 2, 1974 in Scarborough, Ontario.

George Frederick Palmer (10, Maysie Cameron 9, Harriet Bradshaw Cameron 8, Elizabeth (Lizzie) Wright Bradshaw 7, Harriet Wright Wright 6, Elizabeth Robins Wright 5, Mary Hooper Robins 4, Thomas Hooper 3, Clement Hooper 2, Stephen Hooper 1) was born on February 7, 1943 in Summerside, P.E.I. He married, on August 6, 1966, Ruby Dale Morrison, daughter of John Albert and Ora Jean (Rose) Morrison. She was born on March 21, 1945 in Charlottetown,

P.E.I. In 1965 he joined the Canadian Armed Forces where he was an electrical technician. In the mid-1970s they lived in Aylesford, Nova Scotia. George and Ruby had a child (surname Palmer, eleventh generation):

Wendy Lynn-Ann Palmer (11, George Palmer 10, Maysie Cameron 9, Harriet Bradshaw Cameron 8, Elizabeth (Lizzie) Wright Bradshaw 7, Harriet Wright Wright 6, Elizabeth Robins Wright 5, Mary Hooper Robins 4, Thomas Hooper 3, Clement Hooper 2, Stephen Hooper 1) was born on February 27, 1970 in Berwick, Nova Scotia.

Wesley Cameron Palmer (10, Maysie Cameron 9, Harriet Bradshaw Cameron 8, Elizabeth (Lizzie) Wright Bradshaw 7, Harriet Wright Wright 6, Elizabeth Robins Wright 5, Mary Hooper Robins 4, Thomas Hooper 3, Clement Hooper 2, Stephen Hooper 1) was born on May 30, 1946 in Summerside, P.E.I. On July 18, 1964 he married Dawn Mabel Muttart, daughter of Harold Frederick and Norma Elizabeth (Small) Muttart. Dawn was born on November 11, 1946 in Summerside, P.E.I. They lived in Boutilier's Point, Halifax County. Wesley was a civilian electronic systems technician (communications) for the Department of National Defense. They had two children (surname Palmer, eleventh generation) born in Halifax, Nova Scotia:

Shirley Norma Palmer (11, Wesley Palmer 10, Maysie Cameron 9, Harriet Bradshaw Cameron 8, Elizabeth (Lizzie) Wright Bradshaw 7, Harriet Wright Wright 6, Elizabeth Robins Wright 5, Mary Hooper Robins 4, Thomas Hooper 3, Clement Hooper 2, Stephen Hooper 1) born on December 22, 1964.
John Wesley Palmer (11, Wesley Palmer 10, Maysie Cameron 9, Harriet Bradshaw Cameron 8, Elizabeth (Lizzie) Wright Bradshaw 7, Harriet Wright Wright 6, Elizabeth Robins Wright 5, Mary Hooper Robins 4, Thomas Hooper 3, Clement Hooper 2, Stephen Hooper 1) born on August 6, 1972. No further information given.

Lila Glee Cameron (10, Wallace Cameron 9, Harriet Bradshaw Cameron 8, Elizabeth (Lizzie) Wright Bradshaw 7, Harriet Wright Wright 6, Elizabeth Robins Wright 5, Mary Hooper Robins 4, Thomas Hooper 3, Clement Hooper 2, Stephen Hooper 1) was born on July 2, 1928 in Lansing, Michigan. She married Douglas Weldon McGeouch, son of Leonard Pierce and Beatrice (Latimer) McGeouch on August 1, 1945. Douglas was born on November 29, 1926 in Saint John, New Brunswick. They moved to Windsor, Ontario where Douglas was a welder and steam fitter. They had one child (surname McGeouch, eleventh generation):

David Walter McGeouch (11, Lila Glee Cameron 10, Wallace Cameron 9, Harriet Bradshaw Cameron 8, Elizabeth (Lizzie) Wright Bradshaw 7, Harriet Wright Wright 6, Elizabeth Robins Wright 5, Mary Hooper Robins 4, Thomas Hooper 3, Clement Hooper 2, Stephen Hooper 1) was born in Saint John, New Brunswick, on September 29, 1946. David married Roberta Claire Harwood, daughter of Robert Wesley and Clara Ilene (Harris) Harwood, on November 18, 1967. Roberta was born on December 19, 1947 in Windsor, Ontario.. David and Roberta lived in Windsor where David was employed as a police constable by the Windsor Police Department. They had one child (surname McGeouch, twelfth generation):

Heather Louise McGeouch (12, David McGeouch 11, Lila Glee Cameron 10, Wallace Cameron 9, Harriet Bradshaw Cameron 8, Elizabeth (Lizzie) Wright Bradshaw 7, Harriet Wright Wright 6, Elizabeth Robins Wright 5, Mary Hooper Robins 4, Thomas Hooper 3, Clement Hooper 2, Stephen Hooper 1) was born on September 21, 1970, in Windsor, Ontario. No further information given.

Miriam Jean Cameron (10, Wallace Cameron 9, Harriet Bradshaw Cameron 8, Elizabeth (Lizzie) Wright Bradshaw 7, Harriet Wright Wright 6, Elizabeth Robins Wright 5, Mary Hooper Robins 4, Thomas Hooper 3, Clement Hooper 2 Stephen Hooper 1) was born on June 4, 1932 in Middleton, P.E.I. She married, on November 26,

1948, Roy William Abbott, son of Robert Hartwell and Susan Pearl (Rodgers) Abbott. He was born on November 3, 1918 in Malpeque, P.E.I. They lived in Windsor, Ontario where Roy was a steamfitter. He served in the Canadian Army in World War II, from April 1941 - February 1946. They had three children (surname Abbott, eleventh generation) all born in Windsor, Ontario.

Robert Wallace Abbott (11, Miriam Cameron 10, Wallace Cameron 9, Harriet Bradshaw Cameron 8, Elizabeth Wright Bradshaw (Lizzie) 7, Harriet Wright Wright 6, Elizabeth Robins Wright 5, Mary Hooper Robins 4, Thomas Hooper 3, Clement Hooper 2, Stephen Hooper 1) born on March 31, 1951. No further information given.
Nancy Lynne Abbott (11, Miriam Cameron 10, Wallace Cameron 9, Harriet Bradshaw Cameron 8, Elizabeth Wright Bradshaw (Lizzie) 7, Harriet Wright Wright 6, Elizabeth Robins Wright 5, Mary Hooper Robins 4, Thomas Hooper 3, Clement Hooper 2, Stephen Hooper 1) born on January 29, 1954. No further information given.
Stephen Roy Abbott (11, Miriam Cameron 10, Wallace Cameron 9, Harriet Bradshaw Cameron 8, Elizabeth Wright Bradshaw (Lizzie) 7, Harriet Wright Wright 6, Elizabeth Robins Wright 5, Mary Hooper Robins 4, Thomas Hooper 3, Clement Hooper 2, Stephen Hooper 1) born on February 17, 1958. No further information given.

Phyllis Mae Cameron (10, Wallace Cameron 9, Harriet Bradshaw Cameron 8, Elizabeth "Lizzie" Wright Bradshaw 7, Harriet Wright Wright 6, Elizabeth Robins Wright 5, Mary Hooper Robins 4, Thomas Hooper 3, Clement Hooper 2, Stephen Hooper 1) born on April 13, 1935 in Albany, P.E.I. She married Watson John Dunlop, son of Watson Robert and Catherine Angelina (Wedge) Dunlop, on February 18, 1955. John was born on July 27, 1927, in Saint John, New Brunswick. Phyllis and John lived in Windsor, Ontario. He was a soldier with the Canadian Armed Forces from 1945 until 1972 when he retired. He served in the infantry during the Korean War and was with the Medical Corps and the Service Corps. Phyllis and John had three children (surname Dunlop, eleventh generation):

Watson *John* Dunlop (11, Phyllis 10, Wallace Cameron 9, Harriet Bradshaw Caameron 8, Elizabeth Wright Bradshaw (Lizzie) 7, Harriet Wright Wright 6, Elizabeth Robins Wright 5, Mary Hooper Robins 4, Thomas Hooper 3, Clement Hooper 2, Stephen Hooper 1) born on December 16, 1955 in Saint John, New Brunswick. No further information.

Brian Douglas Dunlop (11, Phyllis 10, Wallace Cameron 9, Harriet Bradshaw Cameron 8, Elizabeth Wright Bradshaw (Lizzie) 7, Harriet Wright Wright 6, Elizabeth Robins Wright 5, Mary Hooper Robins 4, Thomas Hooper 3, Clement Hooper 2, Stephen Hooper 1) born December 11, 1957 in Windsor, Ontario. No further information.

Katherine Phyllis Dunlop (11, Phyllis 10, Wallace Cameron 9, Harriet Bradshaw Cameron 8, Elizabeth Wright Bradshaw (Lizzie) 7, Harriet Wright Wright 6, Elizabeth Robins Wright 5, Mary Hooper Robins 4, Thomas Hooper 3, Clement Hooper 2, Stephen Hooper 1) born June 3, 1960 in Barrie, Ontario. No further information.

The next known and recorded family in the ninth generation is the family of the **Rev. Douglas Major MacIntosh** (8, Major Hooper MacIntosh 7, Sarah Sophia 6, Thomas 5, Major 4, Thomas 3, Clement 2, Stephen 1), who was a minister in the Congregational Church and had lived in North Quincy, MA, U.S.A. Douglas and his wife Beatrice had four children (surname MacIntosh, ninth generation):

Marian Lynn MacIntosh (9, Douglas MacIntosh 8, Major Hooper MacIntosh 7, Sarah Sophia 6, Thomas 5, Major 4, Thomas 3, Clement 2, Stephen 1), born October 24, 1937; no further information.

John D. MacIntosh (9, Douglas MacIntosh 8, Major Hooper MacIntosh 7, Sarah Sophia 6, Thomas 5, Major 4, Thomas 3, Clement 2, Stephen 1), born April 5, 1942; no further information.

Kathryn MacIntosh (9, Douglas MacIntosh 8, Major Hooper MacIntosh 7, Sarah Sophia 6, Thomas 5, Major 4, Thomas 3, Clement 2, Stephen 1), born April 4, 1947; no further information.

Alexander L. MacIntosh (9, Douglas MacIntosh 8, Major Hooper MacIntosh 7, Sarah Sophia 6, Thomas 5, Major 4, Thomas 3, Clement 2, Stephen 1), born January 28, 1951; no further information.

The five children of **Allan Simpson MacIntosh** (8, Major Hooper MacIntosh 7, Sarah Sophia 6, Thomas 5, Major 4, Thomas 3, Clement 2, Stephen 1) (ninth generation, surname MacIntosh) are:

Hugh D. MacIntosh (9, Allan Simpson 8, Major Hooper MacIntosh 7, Sarah Sophia 6, Thomas 5, Major 4, Thomas 3, Clement 2, Stephen 1) born July 1947; no further information.
Gillian R. MacIntosh (9, Allan Simpson 8, Major Hooper MacIntosh 7, Sarah Sophia 6, Thomas 5, Major 4, Thomas 3, Clement 2, Stephen 1), born December 1, 1949; no further information.
Malcolm N. MacIntosh (9, Allan Simpson 8, Major Hooper MacIntosh 7, Sarah Sophia 6, Thomas 5, Major 4, Thomas 3, Clement 2, Stephen 1) born March 5, 1951; no further information.
Colin W. MacIntosh (9, Allan Simpson 8, Major Hooper MacIntosh 7, Sarah Sophia 6, Thomas 5, Major 4, Thomas 3, Clement 2, Stephen 1) born January 13, 1953; no further information.
Clare McCulla MacIntosh (9, Allan Simpson 8, Major Hooper MacIntosh 7, Sarah Sophia 6, Thomas 5, Major 4, Thomas 3, Clement 2, Stephen 1) born August 22, 1956; no further information.

The three children of **David Lloyd MacIntosh, M.D.** (8, Major Hooper MacIntosh 7, Sarah Sophia 6, Thomas 5, Major 4, Thomas 3, Clement 2, Stephen 1) and his wife Elaine (surname MacIntosh, ninth generation) are:

F. Douglas MacIntosh (9, David MacIntosh 8, Major Hooper MacIntosh 7, Sarah Sophia 6, Thomas 5, Major 4, Thomas 3, Clement 2, Stephen 1) born November 5, 1947. No further information.
Ian B. MacIntosh (9, David MacIntosh 8, Major Hooper MacIntosh 7, Sarah Sophia 6, Thomas 5, Major 4, Thomas 3, Clement 2, Stephen 1) born December 16, 1949. No further information.

Ann S. MacIntosh (9, David 8, Major Hooper MacIntosh 7, Sarah Sophia 6, Thomas 5, Major 4, Thomas 3, Clement 2, Stephen 1) born May 15, 1953. No further information.

Chronologically, the next family about whom I have information is the family of **Gladys (Lowther) Bradshaw** (8, Major Lowther 7, Adella 6, John 5, Major 4, Thomas 3, Clement 2, Stephen 1) and Neil Bradshaw, who had five children. Information about this family was recorded previously in this chapter using Neil Bradshaw's lineage. It will be recorded here from Gladys's background (surname Bradshaw, ninth generation):

Joan Lowther Bradshaw (9, Gladys Lowther 8, Major Lowther 7, Adella 6, John 5, Major 4, Thomas 3, Clement 2, Stephen 1) born June 29, 1934 in Searletown, P.E.I.; married on December 28, 1955 to William Ross Lefurgey, son of Osbourne Bayfield and Katherine (Gordon) Lefurgey. Ross was born on September 5, 1933 in Summerside, P.E.I. Joan taught school for a year before entering the nursing program at Prince County Hospital in Summerside. Joan and Ross have three children (tenth generation, surname Lefurgey):

Nial Ross Lefurgey (10, Joan Bradshaw 9, Gladys Lowther 8, Major Lowther 7, Adella 6, John 5, Major 4, Thomas 3, Clement 2, Stephen 1) born June 28, 1956; married Arlene Marie Whalen, born April 1, 1959, on February 8, 1980. In 2000 Nial and his family lived in Charlottetown where he was a meat cutter for a supermarket and Arlene commuted to Summerside where she worked at the Summerside Tax Centre, a government office. The two children of Nial and Arlene (surname Lefurgey, eleventh generation) are:

Matthew Nial Lefurgey (11, Nial Lefurgey 10, Joan Bradshaw 9, Gladys Lowther 8, Major Lowther 7, Adella 6, John 5, Major 4, Thomas 3, Clement 2, Stephen 1) born May 22, 1982

Mary Ellen Lefurgey (11, Nial Lefurgey 10, Joan Bradshaw 9, Gladys Lowther 8, Major Lowther 7, Adella 6, John 5, Major 4, Thomas 3, Clement 2, Stephen 1) born April 26, 1984

Alan Shane Lefurgey, called Shane, (10, Joan Bradshaw 9, Gladys Lowther 8, Major Lowther 7, Adella 6, John 5, Major 4, Thomas 3, Clement 2, Stephen 1) born March 31, 1961; married Janet Estelle Parker, born September 6, 1962, on November 19, 1983. Shane has a store called "New to You" for sports equipment. He also assembled bicycles for a large store in Summerside. He and his family live in Summerside. Shane and Janet have two children (surname Lefurgey, eleventh generation):

Jonathan Shane Lefurgey (11, Shane Lefurgey 10, Joan Bradshaw 9, Gladys Lowther 8, Major Lowther 7, Adella 6, John 5, Major 4, Thomas 3, Clement 2, Stephen1) born September 18, 1986.
Amanda Jane Lefurgey (11, Shane 10, Joan 9, Gladys 8, Major 7, Adella 6, John 5, Major 4, Thomas 3, Clement 2, Stephen 1) born January 10, 1989.

Garth Lefurgey (10, Joan Bradshaw 9, Gladys Lowther 8, Major Lowther 7, Adella 6, John 5, Major 4, Thomas 3, Clement 2, Stephen 1) born February 27, 1971; married, June 2001, Jennifer Johnson. Garth has a sense of humor and a stage presence and has been asked to be the master of ceremonies at wedding receptions. He was employed by Callbeck's Home Hardware in Summerside [2002]. Garth and Jennifer have one son (surname Lefurgey, eleventh generation):

Brycen Ross Lefurgey (11, Garth Lefurgey 10, Joan Bradshaw 9, Gladys Lowther 8, Major Lowther 7, Adella 6, John 5, Major 4, Thomas 3, Clement 2, Stephen1), born on March 13, 2003.

Mary *Janet* Bradshaw (9, Gladys Lowther 8, Major Lowther 7, Adella 6, John 5, Major 4, Thomas 3, Clement 2, Stephen 1) born October 20, 1935 in Searletown, P.E.I.; married John Wesley Tredenick, son of Irving and Elizabeth Louise (Palmer) Tredenick, on January 13, 1955. He was born on March 29, 1935 in Summerside. Janet and John divorced in 1971. Until her retirement in 2001 Janet was secretary to the principal at Three Oaks Senior High School in Summerside. Janet and John had five children (surname Tredenick, tenth generation):

Brian John Tredenick (10, Janet Bradshaw 9, Gladys Lowther 8, Major Lowther 7, Adella 6, John 5, Major 4, Thomas 3, Clement 2, Stephen 1) born September 6, 1955 in Charlottetown, married Cynthia Kennedy, on August 8, 1986. Brian and Cynthia have three children (surname Tredenick, eleventh generation):

Brittany Ann Tredenick (11, Brian Tredenick 10, Janet Bradshaw 9, Gladys Lowther 8, Major Lowther 7, Adella 6, John 5, Major 4, Thomas 3, Clement 2, Stephen 1) born March 7, 1989.
Andrea Breanne Tredenick (11, Brian Tredenick 10, Janet Bradshaw 9, Gladys Lowther 8, Major Lowther 7, Adella 6, John 5, Major 4, Thomas 3, Clement 2, Stephen 1) born September 8, 1990.
Jarrett Kennedy Tredenick (11, Brian Tredenick 10, Janet Bradshaw 9, Gladys Lowther 8, Major Lowther 7, Adella 6, John 5, Major 4, Thomas 3, Clement 2, Stephen 1) born May 22, 1992.

Kent Bradshaw Tredenick (10, Janet Bradshaw 9, Gladys Lowther 8, Major Lowther 7, Adella 6, John 5, Major 4, Thomas 3, Clement 2, Stephen 1) born November 29, 1957 in Montague, P.E.I.; married (i) Barbara Ramsay. Kent and Barbara had two children (surname Tredenick, eleventh generation):

Chelsey Mary Ellen Tredenick (11, Kent Tredenick 10, Janet Bradshaw 9, Gladys Lowther 8, Major Lowther 7, Adella 6, John 5, Major 4, Thomas 3, Clement 2, Stephen 1) born March 20, 1984.

Jamie Lynne Tredenick (11, Kent Tredenick 10, Janet Bradshaw 9, Gladys Lowther 8, Major Lowther 7, Adella 6, John 5, Major 4, Thomas 3, Clement 2, Stephen 1) born October 7, 1985.

Kent married (ii) Katherine Pendergast, who had a son, Jared Pendergast, born October 7, 1985, by an earlier marriage. Kent and Katherine have one child (surname Tredenick, eleventh generation):

Erin Kellie Elizabeth Tredenick (11, Kent Tredenick 10, Janet Bradshaw 9, Gladys Lowther 8, Major Lowther 7, Adella 6, John 5, Major 4, Thomas 3, Clement 2, Stephen 1) born September 26, 1996.

Susan Janet Tredenick (10, Janet Bradshaw 9, Gladys Lowther 8, Major Lowther 7, Adella 6, John 5, Major 4, Thomas 3, Clement 2, Stephen 1) born July 8, 1960 in Amherst, Nova Scotia; married Gregory Campbell, on July 31, 1985. Susan and Gregory have two children (surname Campbell, eleventh generation):

Nicole Susan Campbell (11, Susan Tredenick 10, Janet Bradshaw 9, Gladys Lowther 8, Major Lowther 7, Adella 6, John 5, Major 4, Thomas 3, Clement 2, Stephen 1) born September 17, 1988.
Nolan Gregory Campbell (11, Susan Tredenick 10, Janet Bradshaw 9, Gladys Lowther 8, Major Lowther 7, Adella 6, John 5, Major 4, Thomas 3, Clement 2, Stephen 1) born December 1, 1990.

Shauna Tredenick (10, Janet Bradshaw 9, Gladys Lowther 8, Major Lowther 7, Adella 6, John 5, Major 4, Thomas 3, Clement 2, Stephen 1) born June 5, 1963 in Summerside, P.E.I.; married Stephen Myles, on June 24, 1989. Shauna and Stephen have two children (surname Myles, eleventh generation):

Alexander Morgan Myles (11, Shauna Tredenick 10, Janet Bradshaw 9, Gladys Lowther 8, Major Lowther 7, Adella 6, John 5, Major 4, Thomas 3, Clement 2, Stephen 1) born January 24, 1993.

Mark Stephen Myles (11, Shauna Tredenick 10, Janet Bradshaw 9, Gladys Lowther 8, Major Lowther 7, Adella 6, John 5, Major 4, Thomas 3, Clement 2, Stephen 1) born March 25, 1994.

Scott Renwick Tredenick (10, Janet Bradshaw 9, Gladys Lowther 8, Major Lowther 7, Adella 6, John 5, Major 4, Thomas 3, Clement 2, Stephen 1) born July 2, 1964 in Summerside, P.E.I.; married Michele Quinn, on September 4, 1993. They live in Quebec (2000). Scott and Michele have one child (surname Tredenick, eleventh generation):

Shaelynn Michele Tredenick (11, Scott Tredenick 10, Janet Bradshaw 9, Gladys Lowther 8, Major Lowther 7, Adella 6, John 5, Major 4, Thomas 3, Clement 2, Stephen 1) born August 5, 1998.

Carman Garth Bradshaw (9, Gladys Lowther 8, Major Lowther 7, Adella 6, John 5, Major 4, Thomas 3, Clement 2, Stephen 1) born on May 2, 1941 in Searletown, P.E.I.; married (i) Flora Arlene Fraser (born on April 11, 1944 in North Sydney, Nova Scotia) in 1968. They had no children. Arlene died in 1980 from cancer of the stomach. Garth married (ii) Jill Stultz, born 1948, in 1982. They live in Mt. Uniacke, Nova Scotia. Garth and Jill have one daughter (surname Bradshaw, tenth generation):

Lindsay Rose Bradshaw (10, Garth Bradshaw 9, Gladys Lowther 8, Major Lowther 7, Adella 6, John 5, Major 4, Thomas 3, Clement 2, Stephen 1) born September 5, 1983. In 2002 Lindsay's passion (and work) is participating in an equestrian sport.

Carol Jean Bradshaw (9, Gladys Lowther 8, Major Lowther 7, Adella 6, John 5, Major 4, Thomas 3, Clement 2, Stephen 1) born in Summerside, P.E.I. on July 20, 1944; married Thane Arthur Bell, son of Gilbert Cedric and Lillian Elizabeth (Craig) Bell, on August 6, 1966. He was born on February 26, 1944. Carol graduated from the nursing program at the Prince County Hospital in Summerside

and lives (2000) in Lower Sackville, Nova Scotia. Carol and Thane were divorced in 1998. Thane lives in Toronto, Ontario with a second wife. Carol and Thane had three children (surname Bell, tenth generation):

Shannon Elizabeth Bell, called Beth, (10, Carol Bradshaw 9, Gladys Lowther 8, Major Lowther 7, Adella 6, John 5, Major 4, Thomas 3, Clement 2, Stephen 1) born August 27, 1970.
Kyler Thane Bradshaw Bell (10, Carol Bradshaw 9, Gladys Lowther 8, Major Lowther 7, Adella 6, John 5, Major 4, Thomas 3, Clement 2, Stephen 1) born December 25, 1972.
Kara Ann Bell (10, Carol Bradshaw 9, Gladys Lowther 8, Major Lowther 7, Adella 6, John 5, Major 4, Thomas 3, Clement 2, Stephen 1) born July 20, 1977.

Norma Ardene Bradshaw (9, Gladys Lowther 8, Major Lowther 7, Adella 6, John 5, Major 4, Thomas 3, Clement 2, Stephen 1) born on September 19, 1946 in Summerside, P.E.I.; married Lloyd Harold Palmer, the son of Harold Lloyd and Verna Mae (MacFadyen) Palmer, on April 21, 1963 in the Bedeque United Church, P.E.I. Norma and Lloyd were divorced in 1982. They had three children (surname Palmer, tenth generation):

Christopher Lloyd Palmer (10, Norma Bradshaw 9, Gladys Lowther 8, Major Lowther 7, Adella 5, Major 4, Thomas 3, Clement 2, Stephen 1) born October 4, 1968.
Kendra Ardene Palmer (10, Norma Bradshaw 9, Gladys Lowther 8, Major Lowther 7, Adella 6, John 5, Major 4, Thomas 3, Clement 2, Stephen 1) born August 25, 1971; married Stephen Gaudet, on September 5, 1998. Kendra is an occupational therapist. Kendra and Stephen have two children (surname Gaudet, eleventh generation):

Kate Kristina Gaudet (11, Kendra Palmer 10, Norma Bradshaw 9, Gladys Lowther 8, Major Lowther 7, Adella 6, John 5, Major 4, Thomas 3, Clement 2, Stephen 1) born December 19, 1999

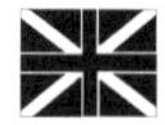

a son (11, Kendra Palmer 10, Norma Bradshaw 9, Gladys Lowther 8, Major Lowther 7, Adella 6, John 5, Major 4, Thomas 3, Clement 2, Stephen 1), born September 2002.

Grant Neil Palmer (10, Norma Bradshaw 9, Gladys Lowther 8, Major Lowther 7, Adella 6, John 5, Major 4, Thomas 3, Clement 2, Stephen 1), born April 18, 1978.

Carman Sinclair Lowther (8, Major Lowther 7, Adella 6, John 5, Major 4, Thomas 3, Clement 2, Stephen 1)) and his wife, Ruth, had two children (surname Lowther, ninth generation):

Suzanne Marguerite Lowther (9, Carman Lowther 8, Major Lowther 7, Adella 6, John 5, Major 4, Thomas 3, Clement 2, Stephen 1) was born June 20, 1948; married (i) Paul Campbell, on August 15, 1970, separated 1974, divorced 1977, no children; married (ii) Kevin McVeigh, on June 2, 1979; Kevin and Suzanne had one child (surname McVeigh, tenth generation):

Lisa Anne McVeigh (10, Suzanne Lowther 9, Carman Lowther 8, Major Lowther 7, Adella 6, John 5, Major 4, Thomas 3, Clement 2, Stephen 1), born October 3, 1983.

Suzanne married (iii) Robert G. Bowman, on June 28, 1997. They lived in Ottawa, Ontario. Robert died suddenly in January 2001, from cerebral hemorrhage. Suzanne and her mother visited us briefly in 2002 when they were visiting Gladys Henderson, Suzanne's aunt.

William Carmen Lowther (9, Carman Lowther 8, Major Hooper Lowther 7, Adella 6, John 5, Major 4, Thomas 3, Clement 2, Stephen 1), born March 10, 1951; married (i) Penni Clark, on April 20, 1974; divorced 1984, married (ii) Joanne Ouellette, on August 27, 1993. Joanne had two children born in the 1970s, but they would not be Hooper descendants.

The reader may recall that **Grace Lowther** and **Archibald MacKenzie** had three daughters (surname MacKenzie, eighth generation): **Florence MacKenzie** (8, Grace 7, Adella 6, John 5, Major 4, Thomas 3, Clement 2, Stephen 1), a registered nurse, married Trevor Way, had one son, David; **Marjorie MacKenzie,** the middle daughter (8, Grace 7, Adella 6, John 5, Major 4, Thomas 3, Clement 2, Stephen 1), married Ralph MacMillan, and had three children (surname MacMillan, ninth generation), and **Dorothy MacKenzie** (8, Grace 7, Adella 6, John 5, Major 4, Thomas 3, Clement 2, Stephen 1), the youngest daughter, did not marry,

David Way (9, Florence 8, Grace 7, Adella 6, John 5, Major 4, Thomas 3, Clement 2, Stephen 1) born March 28, 1941. On our first visit to P.E.I., Gladys had taken us to meet her cousin, Florence, and Alden's second cousin. Florence was very gracious and, in the P.E.I. manner of the times, invited us to dinner. Trevor, her husband, was a dentist in Charlottetown. Their son, David, died in 1998 at age 47.

Marjorie Helen MacMillan, called Helen, (9, Marjorie 8, Grace 7, Adella 6, John 5, Major 4, Thomas 3, Clement 2, Stephen 1), born March 19, 1938 in Charlottetown; married William Campbell Callbeck, born March 27, 1934, on September 23, 1961. Helen is a registered nurse. Helen and Bill had three children (surname Callbeck, tenth generation) and live in Central Bedeque, P.E.I.:

Mary *Lynn* Callbeck (10, Helen 9, Marjorie 8, Grace 7, Adella 6, John 5, Major 4, Thomas 3, Clement 2, Stephen 1) born August 19, 1962; married, in 1991, Gregory Read Pheeney, of Fredericton, New Brunswick, born 1963. Lynn and Greg have two sons (surname Pheeney, eleventh generation) and live in Bedford, Nova Scotia:

Harrison Callbeck Pheeney (11, Lynn 10, Helen 9, Marjorie 8, Grace 7, Adella 6, John 5, Major 4, Thomas 3, Clement 2, Stephen 1) born December 1994 in Halifax, Nova Scotia.

Alexander John Pheeney (11, Lynn 10, Helen 9, Marjorie 8, Grace 7, Aeella 6, John 5, Major 4, Thomas 3, Clement 2, Stephen 1) born in 1996.

Jennifer Ann Callbeck (10, Helen 9, Marjorie 8, Grace 7, Adella 6, John 5, Major 4, Thomas 3, Clement 2, Stephen 1) born April 22, 1964; married, in 1989, Robert Bloise Colpitts, of Fredericton, New Brunswick. Jennifer and Bloise live in Halifax and have twin boys (surname Colpitts, eleventh generation) born in Halifax, in December 1998:

William Daniel Colpitts (11, Jennifer 10, Helen 9, Marjorie 8, Grace 7, Adella 6, John 5, Major 4, Thomas 3, Clement 2, Stephen 1) born December 1998.
Campbell John Colpitts (11, Jennifer 10, Helen 9, Marjorie 8, Grace 7, Adella 6, John 5, Major 4, Thomas 3, Clement 2, Stephen 1) born December 1998.

John William Callbeck (10, Helen 9, Marjorie 8, Grace 7, Adella 6, John 5, Major 4, Thomas 3, Clement 2, Stephen 1) born June 28, 1966; married Tracy Ruth MacNevin, born 1967, in 1993; died on August 1, 1995 as a result of a motorcycle accident in Bedeque. He and Tracy had one daughter (surname Callbeck, eleventh generation):

Jonna Ruth Callbeck (11, John 10, Helen 9, Marjorie 8, Grace 7, Adella 6, John 5, Major 4, Thomas 3, Clement 2, Stephen 1) was born, on January 11, 1996, five months after her father was killed. She was named for her father and her father's Callbeck grandmother. Tracy and Jonna live in Bonshaw, P.E.I. Tracy works at Summerside Tax centre. John had been employed at Callbeck's Home Hardware Store in Summerside.

John *Roger* MacMillan (9, Marjorie 8, Grace 7, Adella 6, John 5, Major 4, Thomas 3, Clement 2, Stephen 1) born 1943; married Margaret Diana Poapst, born 1954, in 1976. They live in Halifax and have no children.

David *Ross* MacMillan, (9, Marjorie 8, Grace 7, Adella 6, John 5, Major 4, Thomas 3, Clement 2, Stephen 1) born 1948; married (i) Catherine Elizabeth Morgan, in 1964. Ross and Catherine were divorced in 1988. Ross married (ii) Barrie Sheila Cochlan, in 1991. They live in Calgary, Alberta. Ross and Catherine had two children (surname MacMillan, tenth generation):

Laura Shawn MacMillan (10, Ross 9, Marjorie 8, Grace 7, Adella 6, John 5, Major 4, Thomas 3, Clement 2, Stephen 1) born in 1979.

Ryan Ross MacMillan (10, Ross 9, Marjorie 8, Grace 7, Adella 6, John 5, Major 4, Thomas 3, Clement 2, Stephen 1) born in 1980.

Chronologically, the next known persons for whom I have information in generation nine are the grandchildren of **Ada Hooper** and Charles O'Neil/Neal:

Wayne Paul Stickney, (9, Frances 8, Ada 7, Major 6, John 5, Major 4, Thomas 3, Clement 2, Stephen 1) born January 16, 1948 in Malden, MA; married Linda Johnson in July 1970, at the Episcopal Church in Melrose, MA. Linda was the daughter of Dr. Dan Johnson, an anesthesiologist, and his wife, Naomi. Wayne graduated from Gordon College and Linda is a graduate of Wheaton College, both in MA. Linda is a teacher and Wayne has been an appraiser of property for banks. They reside in Naples, FL. Wayne and Linda have two children (surname Stickney, tenth generation):

Peter Stickney (10, Wayne 9, Frances 8, Ada 7, Major 6, John 5, Major 4, Thomas 3, Clement 2, Stephen 1) Peter graduated from the University of Florida in Gainsville in dentistry in May 2000. He is working as a dentist in 2002 in Naples, FL, the town where his parents live. In July 2003, Peter married another dentist, Robin.

Erin Stickney (10, Wayne 9, Frances 8, Ada 7, Major 6, John 5, Major 4, Thomas 3, Clement 2, Stephen 1) born April 20, 1976; graduated from the University of Florida at Gainsville with a bachelor's degree in August 1999. Erin is working in Naples, FL (2002) in a bank.

Gary Neal Stickney (9, Frances 8, Ada 7, Major 6, John 5, Major 4, Thomas 3, Clement 2, Stephen 1) born on February 7, 1951 in the Malden Hospital, Malden, MA; married (i) August 1973, Carol Hedquist, adopted daughter of Henry and Mildred Hedquist, at the Church of the Nazarene, in Melrose, MA. Gary and Carol divorced, and Gary married (ii), in 1992, Tristi Davis, a registered nurse. They live in Reading, MA. Gary has his own business installing garage doors and windows and he does siding, a skill he learned years ago from his uncle, Herb White. Gary and Carol had three children (surname Stickney, tenth generation):

Shawn Stickney (10, Gary 9, Frances 8, Ada 7, Major 6, John 5, Major 4, Thomas 3, Clement 2, Stephen 1) born November 18, 1973. Shawn and his wife, Tina, were married on June 11, 2000. Tina had been married and divorced and had one child, born in 1995, whom Shawn is adopting, but she will not be a Hooper descendant. In March 2000 Shawn was diagnosed with cystic fibrosis. He works (2002) for his father, Gary Stickney; Tina is a registered nurse. At the end of 2004 they are buying a house in Saugus, MA that had belonged to his grandmother's friend and had been vacant for years.

Scott Stickney (10, Gary 9, Frances 8, Ada 7, Major 6, John 5, Major 4, Thomas 3, Clement 2, Stephen 1) born June 16, 1979; he and his wife, Lauri (born c.1972), were married on September 1, 2002 at the Melrose Church of the Nazarene. They live in Everett with her mother (2002).

Sarah Stickney (10, Gary 9, Frances 8, Ada 7, Major 6, John 5, Major 4, Thomas 3, Clement 2, Stephen 1) born July 11, 1982. Sarah has a child (surname Stickney, eleventh generation):

Tyler Stickney (11, Sarah 10, Gary 9, Frances 8, Ada 7, Major 6, John 5, Major 4, Thomas 3, Clement 2, Stephen 1) born June 8, 1998.

Bradley Scott Stickney (9, Frances 8, Ada 7, Major 6, John 5, Major 4, Thomas 3, Clement 2, Stephen 1) born January 18, 1958 in the Melrose Hospital, Melrose, MA. He and his wife, Barbara, were married in Dorchester, MA, in August 1980. They live in Rockland, MA. Brad and Barbara have two daughters (surname Stickney, tenth generation):

Amanda Stickney (10, Bradley 9, Frances 8, Ada 7, Major 6, John 5, Major 4, Thomas 3, Clement 2, Stephen 1) born February 15, 1983. Amanda graduated from high school in 2001.
Laura Stickney (10, Bradley 9, Frances 8, Ada 7, Major 6, John 5, Major 4, Thomas 3, Clement 2, Stephen 1) born October 2, 1984. Laura graduated from high school in 2002.

The three daughters of **Paul** (8, Ada 7, Major 6, John 5, Major 4, Thomas 3, Clement 2, Stephen 1) and **Lois Anderson Neal** (surname Neal, ninth generation) are:

Lola Ann Neal (9, Paul 8, Ada 7, Major 6, John 5, Major 4, Thomas 3, Clement 2, Stephen 1) born August 5, 1958 in Springfield, MA; married Frank Brickey, on September 3, 1987 in Ashland, Kentucky. Lola received a Master of Business Administration from Morehouse State College in Kentucky. Frank works in a Kentucky prison as a supervisor in the shop where the prisoners make things. Lola and Frank have two children (surname Brickey, tenth generation), both of whom do very well in school:

Hunter Frank Brickey, Jr. (10, Lola 9, Paul 8, Ada 7, Major 6, John 5, Major 4, Thomas 3, Clement 2, Stephen 1) born June 13, 1991.
Lauren Brickey (10, Lola 9, Paul 8, Ada 7, Major 6, John 5, Major 4, Thomas 3, Clement 2, Stephen 1) born February 1993.

Lisa Jane Neal (9, Paul 8, Ada 7, Major 6, John 5, Major 4, Thomas 3, Clement 2, Stephen 1) born April 2, 1962 in Springfield, MA; married Keith Gillim, born October 27, 1964, son of James Keith and Judith (Mayer) Gillim on December 11, 1993 in Kentucky. Lisa has a Doctor of Education degree from Wayne State University in Detroit, Michigan; Keith's degree is in management from Rochester College. Lisa and Keith have four children (surname Gillim, tenth generation):

Lydia Jane Gillim (10, Lisa 9, Paul 8, Ada 7, Major 6, John 5, Major 4, Thomas 3, Clement 2, Stephen 1) born April 11, 1995.
Austin Frederick Gillim (10, Lisa 9, Paul 8, Ada 7, Major 6, John 5, Major 4, Thomas 3, Clement 2, Stephen 1) born August 3, 1997.
Anderson Keith Gillim (10, Lisa 9, Paul 8, Ada 7, Major 6, John 5, Major 4, Thomas 3, Clement 2, Stephen 1) born December 11, 1999.
Christian Leighton Gillim (10, Lisa 9, Paul 8, Ada 7, Major 6, John 5, Major 4, Thomas 3, Clement 2, Stephen 1) born January 2002.

Lynbeth Jean Neal (9, Paul 8, Ada 7, Major 6, John 5, Major 4, Thomas 3, Clement 2, Stephen 1) born October 27, 1967 in Springfield, MA. She graduated from Transylvania College in Lexington, KY and then from Ohio State University, in Columbus, with a Doctor of Optometry degree. While at the university, Lyn met John Lorey, who was also studying optometry. They were married and have two children (surname Lorey, tenth generation):

John Lorey, called Jack, (10, Lynbeth 9, Paul 8, Ada 7, Major 6, John 5, Major 4, Thomas 3, Clement 2, Stephen 1) born April 1997.
Julia Lexington Neal Lorey (10, Lynbeth 9, Paul 8, Ada 7, Major 6, John 5, Major 4, Thomas 3, Clement 2, Stephen 1) born August 1, 2000. The family has been stationed in Germany for about three years as John has an armed service commitment. In the summer of 2004 he was transferred to Hawaii where his family is with him.

Millicent Neal (8, Ada 7, Major 6, John 5, Major 4, Thomas 3, Clement 2, Stephen 1) married Herbert White and they had two children (surname White, ninth generation):

Kevin Mark White (9, Millicent 8, Ada 7, Major 6, John 5, Major 4, Thomas 3, Clement 2, Stephen 1) born April 3, 1957, in Melrose, MA; married (i) Valerie Rosen, on June 10, 1984. They were divorced about 1988. Kevin lives in Magnolia, MA and works in the insurance industry in Boston. Kevin and Valerie have a son (surname White, tenth generation):

Jesse White (10, Kevin 9, Millicent 8, Ada 7, Major 6, John 5, Major 4, Thomas 3, Clement 2, Stephen 1) born December 6, 1985. Jesse thinks that December is his lucky month; it is his birthday, it is Hanukkah, it is Christmas, and he celebrates all three!

Kevin White married (ii) Holly Ann Kissane in Simsbury, CT on October 20, 2001. Kevin's father and sister performed the ceremony, and we were able to attend the wedding in a large chapel in Simsbury, CT. They had a beautiful reception in Farmington, CT. Holly travels for Talbots. Kevin and Holly have one child (surname White, tenth generation):

Kathleen Grace White, called Katie, (10, Kevin 9, Millicent 8, Ada 7, Major 6, John 5, Major 4, Thomas 3, Clement 2, Stephen 1) born March 7, 2002. Katie has absolutely gorgeous outfits!

Janet White (9, Millicent 8, Ada 7, Major 6, John 5, Major 4, Thomas 3, Clement 2, Stephen 1) born October 22, 1960 in Melrose, MA; married Richard Munn, from Stevenage, England, on November 1, 1980. Janet graduated from Asbury College in Kentucky. She and Richard have been Salvation Army officers since 1987, when they finished their training in Saugerties, New York. They are now (2000) living in Portland, Maine, where they are in charge of the Salvation Army in Maine, New Hampshire, and Vermont. Janet re-

minds us of her mother as she keeps a BEAUTIFUL home and knows how to decorate it well! It is such a pleasure to visit them as they are intelligent, sincere, and lovely people. Janet and Richard have two children (surname Munn, tenth generation):

Nealson Munn (10, Janet 9, Millicent 8, Ada 7, Major 6, John 5, Major 4, Thomas 3, Clement 2, Stephen 1) born April 14, 1985 in Saugerties, New York. Neal, as he likes to be called, graduated from high school in June 2003, and started at Gordon College in Wenham, MA in September 2003. He is an excellent student.
Olivia Francis Munn (10, Janet 9, Millicent 8, Ada 7, Major 6, John 5, Major 4, Thomas 3, Clement 2, Stephen 1) born October 16, 1987 in Camden, New Jersey. When we were visiting the Munn family in 2002, Olivia was carrying to school a huge armful of books that she had been using to do her homework! She is also an excellent student in the ninth grade.

Alden Neal (8, Ada 7, Major 6, John 5, Major 4, Thomas 3, Clement 2, Stephen 1) and **Nancy (Ellis) Neal** have two children (surname Neal, ninth generation):

Sally Rebecca Neal (9, Alden 8, Ada 7, Major 6, John 5, Major 4, Thomas 3, Clement 2, Stephen 1) born March 8, 1958 at Southside Hospital, Bay Shore, New York; graduated from Davidson College with a Bachelor of Arts degree in psychology; from Wake Forest University with a Bachelor of Accountancy degree; and from Columbia University in New York City, with a Master of Business Administration. She works (2002) for Accenture in New York City and lives on the upper east side of Manhattan. Sally was made a partner in the firm in 2000, and since 2000 especially, she has traveled extensively for her company to Europe, South Africa and Australia, as well as within the United States and Canada. In 2004 Sally is employed as a Chief Financial Officer at a branch of the United Nations and travels for the U.N. to many different countries, having just returned from Bangkock, Thailand. She is very generous with her parents, her brother, and her nieces.

Alden and Nancy Neal Coll.

The Munn Family, L to R : Richard, Olivia, Janet, and Nealson, in 2003. Janet is the daughter of Herbert and Millicent (Neal) White.

Charles Ellis Neal (9, Alden 8, Ada 7, Major 6, John 5, Major 4, Thomas 3, Clement 2, Stephen 1) born April 20, 1961 at Southside Hospital in Bay Shore, New York; graduated from Wake Forest University with the Bachelor of Arts degree in communications. In his senior year of college he worked for a radio station in Winston Salem, North Carolina; he has a wonderful voice for the radio! After graduation he lived in Europe for several years, choosing the capital cities of London, Madrid, and Rome. On April 25, 1992, Charles married Nathalie Daubin, of Montreal du Gers, France, in a beautiful ceremony which six of us from the U.S.A. attended. Nathalie's father owned and operated a restaurant in the village, and her mother and her brother, who was a chef for the governor of the province, catered the dinner for fifty people before the wedding, as well as the reception for hundreds, which lasted from 9 p.m. until 5 a.m. From 6 p.m. until 8 p.m. there was also an outdoor reception. We had a wonder-

ful week in France. Sally and her friends stayed longer and explored the country in a bit more depth than we did.

Charles had met Alden and me in Bordeaux, several days before the wedding, and had taken us to the Pyrenees where we had a picnic with delicious goats' cheese, French bread, and wine, among other things. The day after the wedding many of the guests had a picnic in the country, a town or two away from the Daubin's, on a gorgeous day. We also went to another village where a flower show, which was magnificent, was featured. Nathalie's dad had rented a house for the six of us to live in for the week.

In France the only "legal" wedding is the one performed by the Justice of the Peace. This wedding was held in the Village Hall at 4:30 followed by the church wedding almost next door, performed by twin priests, one of whom was pastor of the parish during Nathalie's growing-up years. Nathalie's older brother was in the band for the French navy. He played trumpet for the processional march, and he and Charles's mother played an organ and trumpet duet during the signing of the register in the fourteenth century church.

Nathalie is a flight attendant for American Airlines. Charles has written four books, the last of which is in its second printing, on Armagnac; he is considered the authority on that spirit. Charles and Nathalie have two daughters (surname Neal, tenth generation) and live in San Francisco, CA (1996):

Juliette Daubin Neal (10, Charles 9, Alden 8, Ada 7, Major 6, John 5, Major 4, Thomas 3, Clement 2, Stephen 1) born October 2, 1995, at New York Hospital - Cornell Medical Center, division of New York Lying-In Hospital, at 8:50 p.m. At the time that Juliette was born, the hospital insurance allowed patients who had routine deliveries, to stay one day and one night in the hospital. (Actually Nathalie stayed until October 4th, in the morning because her baby's birth was in the evening of October 2nd.) I went home with Charles, Nathalie, and beautiful Juliette, and stayed about three days in their Queens apartment until Nathalie's parents arrived from France.

Alden and Nancy Neal Coll.

Sally and Charles Neal, at Christmas time. They are the daughter and son of Alden Neal and his wife, Nancy (Ellis) Neal, the author.

Rosalie Louise Neal (10, Charles 9, Alden 8, Ada 7, Major 6, John 5, Major 4, Thomas 3, Clement 2, Stephen 1) born September 8, 1997 at California Pacific Medical Center in San Francisco, California, at 12:50 a.m. I had flown from P.E.I. to San Francisco, a twenty-four hour jaunt by planes (three of them), and two automobile rides, a few days before the expected birth. Rosalie took her sweet time coming into this world, while Nathalie made plum jam and I took Juliette for long walks!

Both girls have been attending the French-American School, in San Francisco since 2001, and are excellent students. Half of the day is spent in studying in French and half in English. They have an advantage over many students because their mother has spoken French to them at home since they were born. They come twice a year to visit us in New York, during school vacation, from 1 ½ to 2 ½ weeks each time.

Lorraine Neal (8, Ada 7, Major 6, John 5, Major 4, Thomas 3, Clement 2, Stephen 1), and her first husband, Walter Olson, had two children (surname Olson, tenth generation):

Donna Ruth Olson (9, Lorraine 8, Ada 7, Major 6, John 5, Major 4, Thomas 3, Clement 2, Stephen 1) born July 9, 1957 in the Quincy Hospital, Quincy, MA; married William (Bill) Thorburn, son of Warren and Joan Thorburn of Lexington, MA. Donna and Bill had met at Gordon College from which they both graduated. Donna and Bill have two daughters (surname Thorburn, tenth generation):

Jennifer Thorburn (10, Donna 9, Lorraine 8, Ada 7, Major 6, John 5, Major 4, Thomas 3, Clement 2, Stephen 1) born November 27, 1982. Jennifer graduated from Gordon College in 2004.
Kimberly Thorburn (10, Donna 9, Lorraine 8, Ada 7, Major 6, John 5, Major 4, Thomas 3, Clement 2, Stephen 1) born September 29, 1984. Kim has finished two years at Gordon College (2004).

Greg Olson (9, Lorraine 8, Ada 7, Major 6, John 5, Major 4, Thomas 3, Clement 2, Stephen 1) born October 14, 1961; married Judy Cross on September 21, 1985 in Bangor, Maine. Greg and Judy met at Gordon College from which they both graduated. Judy was a teacher in elementary school. They lived in Andover, MA for several years and in 1999 moved to western Virginia. In 2003 they moved back to MA, living in Acton. Greg and Judy have triplets, born on August 23, 1992 at Beth Israel Hospital, in Boston, MA. The triplets are listed according to birth order (surname Olson, tenth generation):

Neal Olson (10, Greg 9, Lorraine 8, Ada 7, Major 6, John 5, Major 4, Thomas 3, Clement 2, Stephen 1) born August 23, 1992.
Lauren Olson (10, Greg 9, Lorraine 8, Ada 7, Major 6, John 5, Major 4, Thomas 3, Clement 2, Stephen 1) born August 23, 1992.
Brett Olson (10, Greg 9, Lorraine 8, Ada 7, Major 6, John 5, Major 4, Thomas 3, Clement 2, Stephen 1) born August 23, 1992. In the fall of 2000 Brett had surgery on his legs because he had trouble walking.

The family of **Sarah Hooper** (6, John 5, Major 4, Thomas 3, Clement 2, Stephen 1) and James *Edwin* Allen is is next, chronologically, in the Hooper genealogy.

Alma Elsie Allen (8, Keir 7, Sarah 6, John 5, Major 4, Thomas 3, Clement 2, Stephen 1), married Keith Affleck. Alma and Keith had two children (surname Affleck, ninth generation):

Harold Keith Affleck (9, Alma 8, Keir 7, Sarah 6, John 5, Major 4, Thomas 3, Clement 2, Stephen 1) born January 11, 1952; married Virginia Ann McGuigan, born April 28, 1952, on June 23, 1979. Harold worked on the car ferry crossing Northumberland Strait from Borden to Cape Tormentine. They lived in Charlottetown and had no children. In 2003 they moved to an area outside Summerside in order to be able to help his mother and father with the activities of daily living.
Darryl Alma Affleck (9, Alma 8, Keir 7, Sarah 6, John 5, Major 4, Thomas 3, Clement 2, Stephen 1) born January 31, 1956. Darryl had five children (surname Affleck, tenth generation):

Chrystal Dawn Affleck (10, Darryl 9, Alma 8, Keir 7, Sarah 6, John 5, Major 4, Thomas 3, Clement 2, Stephen 1) born October 16, 1978. Chrystal was murdered in Charlottetown in July 2002.The Charlottetown *Guardian* had an article in the paper a few days after

Chrystal's death: "Man Struggles to Cope after Partner's Murder. Months after slaying of Chrystal Beairsto, police get lab results "in dribs and drabs."

Al MacKenzie said he can't come to terms with the tragic loss of his partner, Chrystal Beairsto. It has been one month since the body of the twenty-three-year-old mother of two was found in a wooded area along the Confederation Trail in Charlottetown. MacKenzie said the period has been one of immense pain. "Words can't describe the amount of pain I'm in," he told The *Guardian* Tuesday. "I'm going to go to counseling to try to cope with it. It's really, really hard. I can't describe what I'm going through right now. I can't lay her to rest. I can't let go of her. It's so hard to let go." MacKenzie said he tried to return to work, but found the pain was too intense there. "It's the last place that I saw her," he said. He said he spent his 15 minute coffee break at Walmart with Beairsto on the afternoon of Saturday, July 27.

Chrystal's body was found by a passerby at about 5:30 p.m. the following day. MacKenzie said waiting for police to make an arrest has also been difficult. "It's been really tough," he said. Richard Collins, deputy chief of the Charlolttetown police, said Tuesday he will discuss how the case is developing later this week. "This investigation is progressing and we hope to do an update with the media later on in the week on Friday," he said. "At that point in time we will disclose some information as to how it pertains to the investigation and how it is going." Collins said investigators have been getting lab results "in dribs and drabs." Last week P.E.I. Crime Stoppers mounted a poster campaign to assist the Charlottetown Police Department with its investigation of the case." As of May 2004, no suspect has apparently been found.

a baby daughter (10, Darryl 9, Alma 8, Keir 7, Sarah 6, John 5, Major 4, Thomas 3, Clement 2, Stephen 1), died very young.

Larry John Affleck, a twin, (10, Darryl 9, Alma 8, Keir 7, Sarah 6, John 5, Major 4, Thomas 3, Clement 2, Stephen 1), born January 4, 1981.

Lisa Alma Affleck, a twin, (10, Darryl 9, Alma 8, Keir 7, Sarah 6, John 5, Major 4, Thomas 3, Clement 2, Stephen 1), born January 4, 1981.
Angela Lindsey Affleck (10, Darryl 9, Alma 8, Keir 7, Sarah 6, John 5, Major 4, Thomas 3, Clement 2, Stephen 1), born May 1987.

Marion Leone Stetson and **Everett Walden Allen** (8, Keir 7, Sarah 6, John 5, Major 4, Thomas 3, Clement 2, Stephen 1) had two children (surname Allen, ninth generation):

Sheila Marilyn Allen (9, Everett 8, Keir 7, Sarah 6, John 5, Major 4, Thomas 3, Clement 2, Stephen 1) born December 29, 1953; married Wendell Cameron, born December 29, 1953 (same date, Sheila in the Prince County Hospital in Summerside and Wendell in the Queen Elizabeth II Hospital in Charlottetown). They have two children (surname Cameron, tenth generation):

Walden Cameron (10, Sheila 9, Everett 8, Keir 7, Sarah 6, John 5, Major 4, Thomas 3, Clement 2, Stephen 1) born April 8, 1980. In 2003 he worked for the Call Center in Halifax, N. S.
Janalee Dawn Cameron (10, Sheila 9, Everett 8, Keir 7, Sarah 6, John 5, Major 4, Thomas 3, Clement 2, Stephen 1) born March 18, 1983. In 2003 she worked for the Call Center in Summerside.

Sheila and Wendell were divorced in 2001. She lives in their home in Freetown, P.E.I. and he lives in Summerside. Sheila's mother, Marion, is living with her (2001). Marion's vision is extremely poor, but she is a very "upbeat" person. In the fall of 2004 Sheila organized a series of three Wednesday evening "Musical Sessions" at her church, Freetown United. They were so successful that the series is going longer into the fall, if not into the winter! The Freetown United ladies are noted for their wonderful sweets and desserts and the abundant refreshments that they had prepared did them justice!

Sheldon Walden Allen (9, Everett 8, Keir 7, Sarah 6, John 5, Major 4, Thomas 3, Clement 2, Stephen 1) born February 22, 1957 in Summerside; died on February 9, 1964 in an automobile accident in which his father and other relatives also died. Please see Chapter 9.

Viola Celia Allen (8, Keir 7, Sarah 6, John 5, Major 4, Thomas 3, Clement 2, Stephen 1), born June 2, 1927; married Harry Edward Taylor, son of Major and Jessie Maude (Morrison) Taylor, born April 11, 1919, in Hamilton, P.E.I. They were married on June 30, 1948 Viola and Harry live in Kensington. They have two children (surname Taylor, ninth generation):

Alan Taylor [as Viola spells it; he spells it Allen, however, to relate to his ancestors as he is interested in genealogy] (9, Viola 8, Keir 7, Sarah 6, John 5, Major 4, Thomas 3, Clement 2, Stephen 1) born June 27, 1950. For many years Alan and his partner, Rick, lived in a suburb of Toronto. In 1996 when Rick retired from his employment at Eatons they moved to Chelton, P.E.I., bought property and a trailer, and built a house which was completed about 2001.

Ferne Alice Taylor (9, Viola 8, Keir 7, Sarah 6, John 5, Major 4, Thomas 3, Clement 2, Stephen 1) was born on May 22, 1954 in Summerside; married Douglas Layton Profitt, on April 7, 1987. Doug was born on March 10, 1953 in Summerside and was the son of Layton Ellis Profitt and Jean Adams. Ferne and Doug live in Kensington. He is the warehouse foreman for hardware and lumber at Schurman's in Kensington (2002) and Ferne is the secretary to Mental Health Services in Summerside. They have one daughter (surname Profitt, tenth generation):

Heather Profitt (10, Ferne 9, Viola 8, Keir 7, Sarah 6, John 5, Major 4, Thomas 3, Clement 2, Stephen 1) born August 28, 1986 in Summerside. Heather is a lovely girl and a good athlete. She was a candidate for Miss Kensington in 2003 and graduated from Kensington High School in 2004. She started college at St. Francis Xavier in Antigonish, Nova Scotia in the fall of 2004.

Reuben Sprague Allen (7, Sarah 6, John 5, Major 4, Thomas 3, Clement 2, Stephen 1), the second child of Sarah Hooper and James Edwin (called Ed) Allen, was born on June 6, 1890 in North Carleton; married Elizabeth Gertrude Francis, called Liza (September 23, 1891-June 1963); died November 5, 1962 at age 72. They had five children (surname Allen, eighth generation):

Thelma Ethel Allen (8, Reuben 7, Sarah 6, John 5, Major 4, Thomas 3, Clement 2, Stephen 1) born May 31, 1913 in Halifax, N.S.; married Calvin Milo Clark, the son of Fred Clark and Lillian Doule, of Chelton, in November 1942 when Calvin was in the Canadian Forces during World War Two. Thelma died suddenly on June 14, 1999 in St. Margaret's Bay, Nova Scotia, where she and Calvin were visiting their daughter Barbara. He died in 2000. Their children (surname Clark, ninth generation) are:

Barbara Ann Clark (9, Thelma 8, Reuben 7, Sarah 6, John 5, Major 4, Thomas 3, Clement 2, Stephen 1) born April 28, 1947 in Halifax, Nova Scotia; on November 27, 1965 she married Francis (called Frank) Nelson Judge who was born on July 7, 1944 in Halifax, Nova Scotia, the son of Harold and Evelyn Judge. Frank is a welder. He and Barbara live in Timberlea, Nova Scotia. They have three children (surname Judge, tenth generation):

Glenn Allen Judge (10, Barbara 9, Thelma 8, Reuben 7, Sarah 6, John 5, Major 4, Thomas 3, Clement 2, Stephen1) born on March 1, 1966 in Halifax, N.S.; Glenn and his wife are divorced. They have one child (surname Judge, eleventh generation):

Sean Judge (11, Glenn 10, Barbara 9, Thelma 8, Reuben 7, Sarah 6, John 5, Major 4, Thomas 3, Clement 2, Stephen 1) born in 1990.

Stephen Nelson Judge (10, Barbara 9, Thelma 8, Reuben 7, Sarah 6, John 5, Major 4, Thomas 3, Clement 2, Stephen 1) born November 28, 1970 in Halifax, N.S. Stephen is not married (2001).

Kelly Ann Judge (10, Barbara 9, Thelma 8, Reuben 7, Sarah 6, John 5, Major 4, Thomas 3, Clement 2, Stephen 1) born October 31, 1974 in Halifax, N.S. In 2000 Kelly is in the process of divorce; they had no children.

Janet Lee Clark (9, Thelma 8, Reuben 7, Sarah 6, John 5, Major 4, Thomas 3, Clement 2, Stephen 1) born August 27, 1949 in Halifax, N.S.; married on January 29, 1968, James Milo Murphy, son of James and Helen Murphy, of Borden, P.E.I. Jim was born in Borden on February 8, 1939. He was a welder for Curran and Briggs in St. Eleanor, P.E.I. for many years, until 2004, when he retired. Janet and Jim have three children (surname Murphy, tenth generation):

Gail Lillian Murphy (10, Janet 9, Thelma 8, Reuben7, Sarah 6, John 5, Major 4, Thomas 3, Clement 2, Stephen 1) born April 24, 1966 in Halifax, N.S.; married Edward Sherry, on October 14, 1986. They lived in Hamilton, P.E.I. where he was a farmer. Gail and Edward were divorced in November 1989. She works at the Summerside Tax Centre and resides in Bedeque. Gail and Edward's two children (surname Sherry, eleventh generation) are:

Evan Sherry (11, Gail 10, Janet 9, Thelma 8, Reuben 7, Sarah 6, John 5, Major 4, Thomas 3, Clement 2, Stephen 1) born April 20, 1987 in Summerside.
Sarah Sherry (11, Gail 10, Janet 9, Thelma 8, Reuben 7, Sarah 6, John 5, Major 4, Thomas 3, Clement 2, Stephen 1) born April 1, 1989 in Summerside, P.E.I.

Katherine Ann Murphy, called Kathie, (10, Janet 9, Thelma 8, Reuben 7, Sarah 6, John 5, Major 4, Thomas 3, Clement 2, Stephen 1) born November 25, 1968 in Summerside. Kathie became a hairdresser and lives in Summerside.
Gregory Thomas Murphy (10, Janet 9, Thelma 8, Reuben 7, Sarah 5, Major 4, Thomas 3, Clement 2, Stephen 1) born December 24, 1969 in Halifax, Nova Scotia. He married Shari Oulton MacKay, on

January 16, 1993. Shari was born on April 1, 1965. She had been married previously and had two children with Mr. MacKay, her first husband. They are: Tara Beth MacKay, born September 11, 1986; and Eric Webster Lawrence MacKay, born July 26, 1989. They would not be Hooper relatives. Greg is a truck driver for Linkletter Farms (2000). Greg and Shari have one daughter (surname Murphy, eleventh generation):

Breanne Murphy (11, Gregory 10, Janet 9, Thelma 8, Reuben 7, Sarah 6, John 5, Major 4, Thomas 3, Clement 2, Stephen 1) born May 19, 1994 in Summerside, P.E.I.

David Allen Clark (9, Thelma 8, Reuben 7, Sarah 6, John 5, Major 4, Thomas 3, Clement 2, Stephen 1) born March 23, 1953, in Halifax, Nova Scotia. On January 14, 197- he married (i) Peggy Richardson, in Glenmargaret, Nova Scotia. Peggy was born on Jan. 14, 1956. Peggy graduated as an R. N. They lived in Halifax and had a daughter (surname Clark, tenth generation):

Rebecca Clark (10, David 9, Thelma 8, Reuben 7, Sarah 6, John 5, Major 4, Thomas 3, Clement 2, Stephen 1), born January 17, 1972 in Halifax. In 1999 Rebecca lived in Bedeque. She has three children (eleventh generation):

a daughter (11, Rebecca 10, David 9, Thelma 8, Reuben 7, Sarah 6, John 5, Major 4, Thomas 3, Clement 2, Stephen 1), born in 1992.
Morgan, a girl, (11, Rebecca 10, David 9, Thelma 8, Reuben 7, Sarah 6, John 5, Major 4, Thomas 3, Clement 2, Stephen 1), born in 1995.
a son (11, Rebecca 10, David 9, Thelma 8, Reuben 7, Sarah 6, John 5, Major 4, Thomas 3, Clement 2, Stephen 1), born in 1998.

David and Peggy were divorced on January 5, 1982. On December 7, 1984 David married (ii) Nancy Kennedy. She was born on August 28, 1955. David and Nancy have two children (surname Clark, tenth generation) and live in Freetown, P.E.I. (1999):

Sean Clark (10, David 9, Thelma 8, Reuben 7, Sarah 6, John 5, Major 4, Thomas 3, Clement 2, Stephen 1) born July 7, 1985 in Halifax, Nova Scotia.
Ashley Clark (10, David 9, Thelma 8, Reuben 7, Sarah 6, John 5, Major 4, Thomas 3, Clement 2, Stephen 1) born January 28, 1987 in Halifax, Nova Scotia.

Lloyd Allen (8, Reuben 7, Sarah 6, John 5, Major 4, Thomas 3, Clement 2, Stephen 1) and his wife, Louise Barkhouse, had three daughters (surname Allen, ninth generation):

Sandra Ann Allen (9, Lloyd 8, Reuben 7, Sarah 6, John 5, Major 4, Thomas 3, Clement 2, Stephen 1) date of birth unknown.
Wendy Lou Allen (9, Lloyd 8, Reuben 7, Sarah 6, John 5, Major 4, Clement 2, Stephen 1) date of birth unknown.
Linda Elizabeth Allen (9, Lloyd 8, Reuben 7, Sarah 6, John 5, Major 4, Thomas 3, Clement 2, Stephen 1) date of birth unknown.

Dot Allen (8, Reuben 7, Sarah 6, John 5, Major 4, Thomas 3, Clement 2, Stephen 1) married Ted Dorey; they had seven children (surname Dorey, ninth generation):

Steven Dorey (9, Dot 8, Reuben 7, Sarah 6, John 5, Major 4, Thomas 3, Clement 2, Stephen 1)
Allen Dorey (9, Dot 8, Reuben 7, Sarah 6, John 5, Major 4, Thomas 3, Clement 2, Stephen 1)
Thomas Dorey (9, Dot 8, Reuben 7, Sarah 6, John 5, Major 4, Thomas 3, Clement 2, Stephen 1)
Margaret Dorey (9, Dot 8, Reuben 7, Sarah 6, John 5, Major 4, Thomas 3, Clement 2, Stephen 1)
Elizabeth Dorey (9, Dot 8, Reuben 7, Sarah 6, John 5, Major 4, Thomas 3, Clement 2, Stephen1)
Robin Dorey (9, Dot 8, Reuben 7, Sarah 6, John 5, Major 4, Thomas 3, Clement 2, Stephen 1)

Rebekah Dorey (9, Dot 8, Reuben 7, Sarah 6, John 5, Major 4, Thomas 3, Clement 2, Stephen 1)

In the early 1990s Dot came with her sister, Marg, to visit their sister, Thelma. We had the pleasure of their company at our cottage.

Jean Allen (8, Reuben 7, Sarah 6, John 5, Major 4, Thomas 3, Clement 2, Stephen 1) married Alexander Henderson and they had two children (surname Henderson, ninth generation):

Brawn Henderson was adopted by Jean and Alexander and so is not genetically a Hooper descendant.
John Allen Henderson (9, Jean 8, Reuben 7, Sarah 6, John 5, Major 4, Thomas 3, Clement 2, Stephen 1) date of birth unknown.

Verna MacLeod (8, Lila 7, Sarah 6, John 5, Major 4, Thomas 3, Clement 2, Stephen 1) married (i) Carl Clay, and they had one child (surname Clay, ninth generation):

Carlene Clay (9, Verna 8, Lila 7, Sarah 6, John 5, Major 4, Thomas 3, Clement 2, Stephen 1) born August 22, 1949 in Haverhill, MA; married July 1, 1967 Richard E. Segeberg. Carlene and Richard, called Dick, had seven children (surname Segeberg, tenth generation):

Eric Benjamin Segeberg, called Rick, (10, Carlene 9, Verna 8, Lila 7, Sarah 6, John 5, Major 4, Thomas 3, Clement 2, Stephen 1) born January 27, 1968 in Biloxi, Mississippi. Rick married Brenda Stevens on May 17, 1990. They have a girl and a boy (surname Segeberg, eleventh generation):

Jessica Segeberg (11, Eric 10, Carlene 9, Verna 8, Lila 7, Sarah 6, John 5, Major 4, Thomas 3, Clement 2, Stephen 1) born in 1991.
Taylor Segeberg (11, Eric 10, Carlene 9, Verna 8, Lila 7, Sarah 6, John 5, Major 4, Thomas 3, Clement 2, Stephen 1) born in 1994.

Shelly Lynn Segeberg (10, Carlene 9, Verna 8, Lila 7, Sarah 6, John 5, Major 4, Thomas 3, Clement 2, Stephen 1) born December 4, 1969 in Taipei, Taiwan. [Her father, Dick, was in the military.]
Wendy Rebecca Segeberg (10, Carlene 9, Verna 8, Lila 7, Sarah 6, John 5, Major 4, Thomas 3, Clement 2, Stephen 1) born August 8, 1972 in Oklahome City, Oklahoma; married Jared Newlun on February 14, 1995. They have four boys (surname Newlun, eleventh generation):

Jashon Newlun [male] (11, Wendy, 10, Carlene 9, Verna 8, Lila 7, Sarah 6, John 5, Major 4, Thomas 3, Clement 2, Stephen 1) born in second half of 1996.
Tanis Newlun [male] (11, Wendy 10, Carlene 9, Verna 8, Lila 7, Sarah 6, John 5, Major 4, Thomas 3, Clement 2, Stephen 1) born in second half of 1998.
Deacon Clay Newlun [fraternal boy twins] (11, Wendy 10, Carlene 9, Verna 8, Lila 7, Sarah 6, John 5, Major 4, Thomas 3, Clement 2, Stephen 1) born February 2002.
Zander Davis Newlun [fraternal boy twins] (11, Wendy 10, Carlene 9, Verna 8, Lila 7, Sarah 6, John 5, Major 4, Thomas 3, Clement 2, Stephen 1) born February 2002.

Tricia Lee Segeberg (10, Carlene 9, Verna 8, Lila 7, Sarah 6, John 5, Major 4, Thomas 3, Clement 2, Stephen 1) born June 10, 1974 in Fraserburg, Scotland. Tricia has a boy and a girl (surname Segeberg, eleventh generation):

Joshua Segeberg (11, Tricia 10, Carlene 9, Verna 8, Lila 7, Sarah 6, John 5, Major 4, Thomas 3, Clement 2, Stephen 1) born 1991.
Sage (11, Tricia 10, Carlene 9, Verna 8, Lila 7, Sarah 6, John 5, Major 4, Thomas 3, Clement 2, Stephen 1) born September 1997.

Becky Ann Segeberg (10, Carlene 9, Verna 8, Lila 7, Sarah 6, John 5, Major 4, Thomas 3, Clement 2, Stephen 1) born June 21, 1975; died June 21, 1975.

Heath Bradford Segeberg (10, Carlene 9, Verna 8, Lila 7, Sarah 6, John 5, Major 4, Thomas 3, Clement 2, Stephen 1) born July 18, 1977 in Portsmouth, New Hampshire. On April 15, 2000 Heath married Camille Orme, at Gig Harbor, Washington. They have one child (surname Segeberg, eleventh generation):

Nathan Heath Segeberg (11, Heath 10, Carlene 9, Verna 8, Lila 7, Sarah 6, John 5, Major 4, Thomas 3, Clement 2, Stephen 1) born November 13, 2000.

Ryan Brent Segeberg (10, Carlene 9, Verna 8, Lila 7, Sarah 6, John 5, Major 4, Thomas 3, Clement 2, Stephen 1) born January 29, 1981 in Biloxi, Missisippi.

Verna (MacLeod) Clay married (ii) Laurie Perkins and they had one child (surname Perkins, ninth generation):

Cheryl Perkins (9, Verna 8, Lila 7, Sarah 6, John 5, Major 4, Thomas 3, Clement 2, Stephen 1) born January 3, 1967. When Verna went to the doctor during her pregnancy, she learned that she had cancer of the cervix, and after the birth of Cheryl was treated successfully at the Massachusetts General Hospital. Verna worked for the telephone company. During one of her breaks from work, she would occasionally call us, and it was always a pleasure to hear from her. Again the boom dropped when she was diagnosed with cancer of the stomach in 1976. She died in February 1978, leaving her eleven-year-old daughter in the care of Laurie, Verna's husband.

Helen MacLeod (8, Lila 7, Sarah 6, John 5, Major 4, Thomas 3, Clement 2, Stephen 1) and Ed Caswell had two children (surname Caswell, ninth generation):

James Edward Caswell (9, Helen 8, Lila 7, Sarah 6, John 5, Major 4, Thomas 3, Clement 2, Stephen 1) (called Jim) born February 3,

1958; married Mary Harrison, in Shrewsbury, MA, on June 2, 1982. Jimmy and Mary had a son and a daughter (surname Caswell, tenth generation):

James Caswell (10, James 9, Helen 8, Lila 7, Sarah 6, John 5, Major 4, Thomas 3, Clement 2, Stephen 1) born November 14, 1987
Sarah Caswell (10, James 9, Helen 8, Lila 7, Sarah 6, John 5, Major 4, Thomas 3, Clement 2, Stephen 1) born 1989.

Janice Elizabeth Caswell (9, Helen 8, Lila 7, Sarah 6, John 5, Major 4, Thomas 3, Clement 2, Stephen 1) born January 18, 1960, married Roy Barlow, on July 22, 1989, in Shrewsbury, MA. Janice is a hiker and has been walking the Appalachian Trail. She and Roy have no children.

Velma Hart (8, Vera 7, Sarah 6, John 5, Major 4, Thomas 3, Clement 2, Stephen 1) married Francis Maranda and they had two children (surname Maranda, ninth generation):

Leonard Maranda (9, Velma 8, Vera 7, Sarah 6, John 5, Major 4, Thomas 3, Clement 2, Stephen 1) born c.1940.
Gloria Maranda (9, Velma 8, Vera 7, Sarah 6, John 5, Major 4, Thomas 3, Clement 2, Stephen 1) born after 1940. In early 2003 Gloria moved from Connecticut to North Carolina and wanted to take her mother with her, but her mother would not go. Velma lives now in a nursing home or an assisted living facility in Ct. (2003). She apparently has Alzheimer's Disease. We hear from her at Christmas.

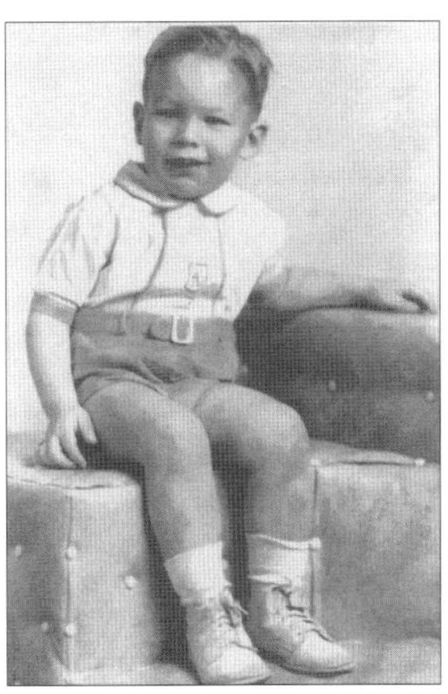

Alden and Nancy Neal Coll.

Leonard Maranda, c.1943-1944

Walden Hart (8, Vera 7, Sarah 6, John 5, Major 4, Thomas 3, Clement 2, Stephen 1) and his wife, Gladys, had two sons (surname Hart, ninth generation):

William (Bill) Hart (9, Walden 8, Vera 7, Sarah 6, John 5, Major 4, Thomas 3, Clement 2, Stephen 1) born in the late 1940's; married a French girl and had two daughters. Bill is living in France in 2000.
Richard (Rick) Hart (9, Walden 8, Vera 7, Sarah 6, John 5, Thomas 3, Clement 2, Stephen 1) date of birth unknown, but probably in the late 1940's.

Milton Hart (8, Vera 7, Sarah 6, John 5, Major 4, Thomas 3, Clement 2, Stephen 1) and his wife, Rosemary, had two sons (surname Hart, ninth generation):

Douglas Hart (9, Milton 8, Vera 7, Sarah 6, John 5, Major 4, Thomas 3, Clement 2, Stephen 1) lives in Massachusetts (2000). No further information available.
Steven Hart (9, Milton 8, Vera 7, Sarah 6, John 5, Major 4, Thomas 3, Clement 2, Stephen 1) lives in Massachusetts in 2000. No further information available.

Milton and Rosemary divorced. He married (ii) a lady called Eleanor, and they had two sons and a daughter (surname Hart, ninth generation):

Peter Hart (9, Milton 8, Vera 7, Sarah 6, John 5, Major 4, Thomas 3, Clement 2, Stephen 1) lives in Virginia (2000). In the late summer of 2004 Peter came to Prince Edward Island briefly to visit his cousin, Allen Taylor. As I recall he was interested in his father's genealogy and planned to return to the Island when he had more time. His second wife had recently had a baby, but no details are known.
Peggy Hart (9, Milton 8, Vera 7, Sarah 6, John 5, Major 4, Thomas 3, Clement 2, Stephen 1) married a Mr. Pace and lives in Illinois (2000). No further information available.

David Hart (9, Milton 8, Vera 7, Sarah 6, John 5, Major 4, Thomas 3, Clement 2, Stephen 1) Milton had adopted David. David was married and had a daughter. He died young, before his father. David would not be a Hooper relative.

The reader may recall that **Sally Hooper Wright** (5, Major 4, Thomas 3, Clement 2, Stephen 1), wife of Jesse, had a daughter, **Martha Ann** (6, Sally 5, Major 4, Thomas 3, Clement 2, Stephen 1), who married Charles Wesley Strong. Their child, **Alan *Wilmot* Strong** (7, Martha 6, Sally 5, Major 4, Thomas 3, Clement 2, Stephen 1), married a woman named Frances, from Montreal, where they lived. Wilmot and Frances had one child, **Alan** (8, Wilmot 7, Martha 6, Sally 5, Major 4, Thomas 3, Clement 2, Stephen 1), who married Teresa Murphy and lived in Montreal. Alan and Teresa had two children, both born in Montreal (surname Strong, ninth generation):

Diane Clare Strong (9, Alan 8, Wilmot 7, Martha 6, Sally 5, Major 4, Thomas 3, Clement 2, Stephen 1) born June 7, 1935; married, on July 11, 1959, Hugo Louis, son of Pieter and Anna (Bael) Louis, of Holland. He was born July 19, 1933 in Pati, Java. Diana received her B. A. in 1966 from Carleton University, with a major in sociology, and was a consultant with Manpower Planning. Hugo is an electrical engineer with the Corporation of Engineers of Quebec. In the pursuit of their respective careers, they have moved back and forth between Montreal and Ottawa.

Richard Norman Strong (9, Alan 8, Wilmot 7, Martha 6, Sally 5, Major 4, Thomas 3, Clement 2, Stephen 1) born June 11, 1941; married Joy McConnell, born in Aylmer, P.Q. He is a teacher in Humber College, Toronto, Ont.

Percy K. Wright (8, Frederick 7, Archibald M. 6, Sally 5, Major 4, Thomas 3, Clement 2, Stephen 1), born Centerville Bedeque, 1891; died Malden, MA, 1931, where he was a carpenter. He married Alice Bruce, and they had one child, born in Malden, MA (surname Wright, ninth generation):

Richard Wright (9, Percy 8, Frederick 7, Archibald M. 6, Sally 5, Major 4, Thomas 3, Clement 2, Stephen 1) (no date of birth given); served in the U. S. Navy in World War II; died in the service of his country.

Edgar Wright (8, Frederick 7, Archibald M. 6, Sally 5, Major 4, Thomas 3, Clement 2, Stephen 1), born Nov. 15, 1896, Centerville Bedeque; married Esther Plaisted, daughter of Frank West and Emily Esther (Foster) Plaisted; Esther was born on April 5, 1897, at Beverly, MA. They had three daughters (surname Wright, ninth generation):

Betty Plaisted Wright (9, Edgar 8, Frederick 7, Archibald M. 6, Sally 5, Major 4, Thomas 3, Clement 2, Stephen 1) born February 1919 in Beverly, MA; married James L. Dallas.

Emily Foster Wright (9, Edgar 8, Frederick 7, Archibald M. 6, Sally 5, Major 4, Thomas 3, Clement 2, Stephen 1) born June 1921 in Beverly, MA; married Gregory George Dobrenchuck.

Gloria Esther Wright (9, Edgar 8, Frederick 7, Archibald M. 6, Sally 5, Major 4, Thomas 3, Clement 2, Stephen 1) born March 30, 1933 in Salem, MA; married July 30, 1959, Marc Raphael Gutwirth, son of Charles and Regine Gutwirth. He was born September 7, 1919 in The Hague, Holland. He was instantly killed on June 14, 1966 in an automobile accident in Hamilton, N.Y. He was an associate professor of classics, and taught at Dartmouth College, the University of Pittsburgh, and Colgate University. Gloria received a B. A. degree from McGill University in 1955, and an M. A. from Radcliffe College in 1962. She taught Latin at the Windsor School in Boston, MA and lived in Beverly. She completed the writing of a book which she and Marc were working on at the time of his death.

George Vickerson (8, Herbert 7, Harriet 6, Sally 5, Major 4, Thomas 3, Clement 2, Stephen 1) and his wife, Anne, had one daughter (surname Vickerson, ninth generation):

Nancy Jane Vickerson (9, George 8, Herbert 7, Harriet 6, Sally 5, Major 4, Thomas 3, Clement 2, Stephen 1) born March 6, 1939; married (i) June 6, 1959; marriage later annulled; married (ii) John Howe Boynton.

Herbert Vickerson (8, 7, Harriet 6, Sally 5, Major 4, Thomas 3, Clement 2, Stephen 1) and his wife, Elma, had two children (surname Vickerson, ninth generation) both born in Montreal, P.Q.:

Frederick Herbert Locker Vickerson, called Fred (9, Herbert 8, 7, Harriet 6, Sally 5, Major 4, Thomas 3, Clement 2, Stephen 1) born April 23, 1942; married Gail Royer. No further information.
Gail Muriel Vickerson (9, Herbert 8, 7, Harriet 6, Sally 5, Major 4, Thomas 3, Clement 2, Stephen 1) born January 12, 1948; married Dr. Robert DuBois Schwartz. No further information.

The reader may recall that **Jane Hooper** (5, Major 4, Thomas 3, Clement 2, Stephen 1), the ninth child of Major, married William Craig.

Kenneth Craig (8, Norman 7, Major 6, Jane 5, Major 4, Thomas 3, Clement 2, Stephen 1) married Margaret Williamson and they had one son (surname Craig, ninth generation):

Donald Craig (9, Kenneth 8, Norman 7, Major 6, Jane 5, Major 4, Thomas 3, Clement 2, Stephen 1) born 1963. No further information.

Alice Craig (8, Norman 7, Major 6, Jane 5, Major 4, Thomas 3, Clement 2, Stephen 1) married Nicholas Schroeder, and they had three children (surname Shroeder, ninth generation):

Laura Shroeder (9, Alice 8, Norman 7, Major 6, Jane 5, Major 4, Thomas 3, Clement 2, Stephen 1) born 1949. No further information.

Brian Shroeder (9, Alice 8, Norman 7, Major 6, Jane 5, Major 4, Thomas 3, Clement 2, Stephen 1) born 1952. No further information.
Bruce Shroeder (9, Alice 8, Norman 7, Major 6, Jane 5, Major 4, Thomas 3, Clement 2, Stephen 1) born 1954. No further information.

Margaret Craig (8, Norman 7, Major 6, Jane 5, Major 4, Thomas 3, Clement 2, Stephen 1) married Peter McGrenera and they had three children (surname McGrenera, ninth generation):

Shannon McGrenera (9, Margaret 8, Norman 7, Major 6, Jane 5, Major 4, Thomas 3, Clement 2, Stephen 1) born in 1956. No further information.
Katherine McGrenera (9, Margaret 8, Norman 7, Major 6, Jane 5, Major 4, Thomas 3, Clement 2, Stephen 1) born in 1959. No further information.
Robert McGrenera (9, Margaret 8, Norman 7, Major 6, Jane 5, Major 4, Thomas 3, Clement 2, Stephen 1) born in 1961. No further information.

Wilfred Wright Craig (8, Colin 7, John 6, Jane 5, Major 4, Thomas 3, Clement 2, Stephen 1) and Isabel Martin had five children (surname Craig, ninth generation):

John Craig Sr.(9, Wilfred 8, Colin 7, John 6, Jane 5, Major 4, Thomas 3, Clement 2, Stephen 1), the eldest child, born 1928; married Mary Morgan (1930-1965). John and Mary had two children (surname Craig, tenth generation):

John Craig Jr.(10, John Sr. 9, Wilfred 8, Colin 7, John 6, Jane 5, Major 4, Thomas 3, Clement 2, Stephen 1) born 1953. No further information.
Mary Jane Craig (10, John Sr. 9, Wilfred 8, Colin 7, John 6, Jane 5, Major 4, Thomas 3, Clement 2, Stephen 1) born 1955. No further information.

Olive Craig, the second child of Wilfred and Isabel, (9, Wilfred 8, Colin 7, John 6, Jane 5, Major 4, Thomas 3, Clement 2, Stephen 1) born 1930; married Robert Wells (1929-). Olive and Robert had four children (surname Wells, tenth generation):

Donald Wells (10, Olive 9, Wilfred 8, Colin 7, John 6, Jane 5, Major 4, Thomas 3, Clement 2, Stephen 1) born 1952. No further information.
Louise Wells (10, Olive 9, Wilfred 8, Colin 7, John 6, Jane 5, Major 4, Thomas 3, Clement 2, Stephen 1) born 1954. No further information.
David Wells (10, Olive 9, Wilfred 8, Colin 7, John 6, Jane 5, Major 4, Thomas 3, Clement 2, Stephen 1) born 1958. No further information.
Dianne Wells (10, Olive 9, Wilfred 8, Colin 7, John 6, Jane 5, Major 4, Thomas 3, Clement 2, Stephen 1) born 1960. No further information.

Louise Craig, the third child of Wilfred and Isabel, (9, Wilfred 8, Colin 7, John 6, Jane 5, Major 4, Thomas 3, Clement 2, Stephen 1) was born in 1933; she married Gregory Corbett, who was born in 1931. The summer home of Louise and Gregory is the home (which has been modernized) of her father, Wilfred. They have two children (surname Corbett, tenth generation):

Craig Corbett (10, Louise 9, Wilfred 8, Colin 7, John 6, Jane 5, Major 4, Thomas 3, Clement 2, Stephen 1) born 1951.
Bryan Corbett (10, Louise 9, Wilfred 8, Colin 7, John 6, Jane 5, Major 4, Major 4, Thomas 3, Clement 2, Stephen 1) born 1956.

Catherine Craig, the fourth child of Wilfred and Isabel, (9, Wilfred 8, Colin 7, John 6, Jane 5, Major 4, Thomas 3, Clement 2, Stephen 1) born 1935; married John Bonnell, and had three children (surname Bonnell, tenth generation):

Elizabeth Bonnell (10, Catherine 9, Wilfred 8, Colin 7, John 6, Jane 5, Major 4, Thomas 3, Clement 2, Stephen 1) born 1958. No further information.
Mary Bonnell (10, Catherine 9, Wilfred 8, Colin 7, John 6, Jane 5, Major 4, Thomas 3, Clement 2, Stephen 1) born 1960. No further information.
John Bonnell (10, Catherine 9, Wilfred 8, Colin 7, John 6, Jane 5, Major 4, Thomas 3, Clement 2, Stephen 1) born 1963. No further information.

Arthur Craig, the fifth and last child of Wilfred and Isabel Craig, (9, Wilfred 8, Colin 7, John 6, Jane 5, Major 4, Thomas 3, Clement 2, Stephen 1) born 1937; married Shirley Green, who was born in 1939. Arthur died very suddenly in 1998. Shirley lives in Middleton and is secretary at a school in Middleton. Arthur and Shirley had three children (surname Craig, tenth generation):

Janet Craig (10, Arthur 9, Wilfred 8, Colin 7, John 6, Jane 5, Major 4, Thomas 3, Clement 2, Stephen 1) born 1960.
Allan Craig (10, Arthur 9, Wilfred 8, Colin 7, John 6, Jane 5, Major 4, Thomas 3, Clement 2, Stephen 1) born 1962.
JoAnn Craig (10) Arthur 9, Wilfred 8, Colin 7, John 6, Jane 5, Major 4, Thomas 3, Clement 2, Stephen 1) born 1963.

[In the summer of 2004 this writer had the pleasure of meeting two of Shirley's grandchildren, but I am uncertain which child belongs to which daughter] **Nicholas Jessome** (11) about age 16, is an unusually talented young man. He substituted as organist at the Bedeque United Church one or two Sundays and did very well in the summer of 2004. He is a senior in high school and seems very mature and motivated. His cousin, a girl age 14, played the violin during the offertory. She plays totally by ear as she does not read a note of music. They both came with their grandmother, Shirley, to a choir get-together/party in August. This writer does not know which person is a child of which mother.

Walter Craig (8, Colin 7, John 6, Jane 5, Major 4, Thomas 3, Clement 2, Stephen 1) and his wife, Jennie MacCallum, had three children (surname Craig, ninth generation):

Joan Annette Craig (9, Walter 8, Colin 7, John 6, Jane 5, Major 4, Thomas 3, Clement 2, Stephen 1) born May 9, 1934; married Eldon Campbell Wright, who was born on May 4, 1924, in Middleton. He died suddenly, in June 1998. Joan and Eldon had four children (surname Wright, tenth generation):

Marlene Wright (10, Joan 9, Walter 8, Colin 7, John 6, Jane 5, Major 4, Thomas 3, Clement 2, Stephen 1) born 1958.
Thomas Wright (10, Joan 9, Walter 8, Colin 7, John 6, Jane 5, Major 4, Thomas 3, Clement 2, Stephen 1) born 1960.
James Wright (10, Joan 9, Walter 8, Colin 7, John 6, Jane 5, Major 4, Thomas 3, Clement 2, Stephen 1) born 1961.
Robert Wright (10, Joan 9, Walter 8, Colin 7, John 6, Jane 5, Major 4, Thomas 3, Clement 2, Stephen 1) born 1964.

[When Alden and I became summer residents at first on the Island we picked raspberries in Mr. Craig's backyard. Going toward the village store from the United Church, he and his wife lived about four houses closer to the village store. He also had a vegetable garden and sold assorted vegetables]

Frances Marie Craig, the second child of Walter and Jennie, (9, Walter 8, Colin 7, John 6, Jane 5, Major 4, Thomas 3, Clement 2, Stephen 1) born 1935; died October 2005; married Cooke Howatt, in 1953, and had three children (surname Howatt, tenth generation):

David Howatt (10, Frances 9, Walter 8, Colin 7, John 6, Jane 5, Major 4, Thomas 3, Clement 2, Stephen 1) born 1961; married; has two children (surname Howatt, eleventh generation):

Jennie Howatt (11, David 10, Frances 9, Walter 8, Colin 7, John 6, Jane 5, Major 4, Thomas 3, Clement 2, Stephen 1).
a son (11, David 10, Frances 9, Walter 8, Colin 7, John 6, Jane 5, Major 4, Thomas 3, Clement 2, Stephen 1).

Kimberley Howatt (10, Frances 9, Walter 8, Colin 7, John 6, Jane 5, Major 4, Thomas 3, Clement 2, Stephen 1) born 1962; married Brian Affleck, son of Robert and Georgie Affeck. Kimberley is a laboratory technician and lives in Moncton, New Brunswick (2003) with her husband and two children (surname Affleck, eleventh generation).
Ruth Anne Howatt (10, Frances 9, Walter 8, Colin 7, John 6, Jane 5, Major 4, Thomas 3, Clement 2, Stephen 1) born 1963; married Kenneth Waugh; lives in Lower Bedeque (2003). Ruth Anne is a registered nurse and works at Prince County Hosptial. Kenny works for Stuart Affleck in the potato business. Ruth Ann and Kenny have three children (surname Waugh, eleventh generation):

Bethany Waugh (11, Ruth Anne 10, Frances 9, Walter 8, Colin 7, John 6, Jane 5, Major 4, Thomas 3, Clement 2, Stephen 1) born 1989. Bethany was working in the village store in Bedeque in the summer of 2004.
Logan Waugh (11, Ruth Anne 10, Frances 9, Walter 8, Colin 7, John 6, Jane 5, Major 4, Thomas 3, Clement 2, Stephen 1) born August 1990.
Hilary Waugh (11, Ruth Anne 10, Frances 9, Walter 8, Colin 7, John 6, Jane 5, Major 4, Thomas 3, Clement 2, Stephen 1) born December 1993.

William Craig, called Bill, (9, Walter 8, Colin 7, John 6, Jane 5, Major 4, Thomas 3, Clement 2, Stephen 1) born 1943; married (i) Vivian Bassett (born 1946); Bill is married again. He lives in Halifax, Nova Scotia.

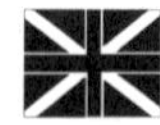

Jean Craig (8, Colin 7, John 6, Jane 5, Major 4, Thomas 3, Clement 2, Stephen 1)and her husband, John Archibald Craig, had two children (surname Craig, ninth generation), both born in Brooklyn, New York:

John Edgar Craig, called Jack, (9, Jean 8, Colin 7, John 6, Jane 5, Major 4, Thomas 3, Clement 2, Stephen 1) born March 12, 1947; married December 9, 1967 Linda Louise Ley, born August 31, 1948. They lived in California in the mid-1970s.
Florence Louise Craig (9, Jean 8, Colin 7, John 6, Jane 5, Major 4, Thomas 3, Clement 2, Stephen 1) born March 8, 1949.

Florence Craig (8, Colin 7, John 6, Jane 5, Major 4, Clement 2, Stephen 1) and her husband, Richard Sheridan, had one child (surname Sheridan, ninth generation):

Patrick Richard Sheridan (9, Florence 8, Colin 7, John 6, Jane 5, Major 4, Clement 2, Stephen 1) born December 19, 1955 in Vancouver, B. C. Patrick is a mechanic.

Marguerite Louise Craig (8, Colin 7, John 6, Jane 5, Major 4, Thomas 3, Clement 2, Stephen 1) and Peter Harrison had four children (surname Harrison, ninth generation):

Wayne Craig Harrison (9, Marguerite 8, Colin 7, John 6, Jane 5, Major 4, Thomas 3, Clement 2, Stephen 1) born September 16, 1948; married Cherry Dawn Sadgrove.
Janet May Harrison (9, Marguerite 8, Colin 7, John 6, Jane 5, Major 4, Thomas 3, Clement 2, Stephen 1) born February 19, 1950; married Peter John Fisher.
David Arthur Harrison (9, Marguerite 8, Colin 7, John 6, Jane 5, Major 4, Thomas 3, Clement 2, Stephen 1) born October 25, 1953. His grandfather's family Bible reads October 20th. No further information.

Beverly Ann Harrison (9, Marguerite 8, Colin 7, John 6, Jane 5, Major 4, Thomas 3, Clement 2, Stephen 1) born July 29, 1955; married, on June 20, 1975, Deryl Fell, son of Joseph and Lorraine Fell. He was born on June 6, 1954 in Burnaby, B. C. Deryl s a salesman. They live in Burnaby. A child was due in February 1977. No further details available.

Shirley Craig (8, Claude 7, Albert 6, Jane 5, Major 4, Thomas 3, Clement 2, Stephen 1) married Peter Simpson and had four children (surname Simpson, ninth generation):

Claudia Simpson (9, Shirley 8, Claude 7, Albert 6, Jane 5, Major 4, Thomas 3, Clement 2, Stephen 1) born 1943. No further information available.
Robert Simpson (9, Shirley 8, Claude 7, Albert 6, Jane 5, Major 4, Thomas 3, Clement 2, Stephen 1) born 1945. No further information available.
Diane Simpson (9, Shirley 8, Claude 7, Albert 6, Jane 5, Major 4, Thomas 3, Clement 2, Stephen 1) born 1951. No further information available.
Gregory Simpson (9, Shirley 8, Claude 7, Albert 6, Jane 5, Major 4, Thomas 3, Clement 2, Stephen 1) born 1953. No further information available.

Albert Craig (8, Claude 7, Albert 6, Jane 5, Major 4, Thomas 3, Clement 2, Stephen 1) and Louise Williams had three daughters (surname Craig, ninth generation):

Lynda Craig (9, Albert 8, Claude 7, Albert 6, Jane 5, Major 4, Thomas 3, Clement 2, Stephen 1) born 1950. No further information.
Bonnie Craig (9 Albert 8, Claude 7, Albert 6, Jane 5, Major 4, Thomas 3, Clement 2, Stephen 1) born 1951. No further information.
Deborah Craig (9, Albert 8, Claude 7, Albert 6, Jane 5, Major 4, Thomas 3, Clement 2, Stephen 1) born 1954. No further information.

Elizabeth Fraser (8, Nellie 7, Albert 6, Jane 5, Major 4, Thomas 3, Clement 2, Stephen 1) married James Potts and they had two children (surname Potts, ninth generation):

David Potts (9, Elizabeth 8, Nellie 7, Albert 6, Jane 5, Major 4, Thomas 3, Clement 2, Stephen 1) born in 1948.
Catherine Potts (9, Elizabeth 8, Nellie 7, Albert 6, Jane 5, Major Hooper Thomas 3, Clement 2, Stephen 1), born 1952. No further information about these generation nine children.

Craig Fraser (8, Nellie 7, Albert 6, Jane 5, Major 4, Thomas 3, Clement 2, Stephen 1) and his wife, Iris Hunt, had three children (surname Fraser, ninth generation):

John Fraser (9, Craig 8, Nellie 7, Albert 6, Jane 5, Major 4, Thomas 3, Clement 2, Stephen 1) born 1946.
Susan Fraser (9, Craig 8, Nellie 7, Albert 6, Jane 5, Major 4, Thomas 3, Clement 2, Stephen 1) born 1951.
Duncan Fraser (9, Craig 8, Nellie 7, Albert 6, Jane 5, Major 4, Thomas 3, Clement 2, Stephen 1) born 1955.

Shirley Craig (8, Earl 7, Charles 6, Jane 5, Major 4, Thomas 3, Clement 2, Stephen 1) married Leigh Begg; they had two children (surname Begg, ninth generation):

Lynn Begg (9, Shirley 8, Earl 7, Charles 6, Jane 5, Major 4, Thomas 3, Clement 2, Stephen 1) born 1940; married James Charles, born 1939. They had one child (surname Charles, tenth generation):

Brian Charles (10, Lynn 9, Shirley 8, Earl 7, Charles 6, Jane 5, Major 4, Thomas 3, Clement 2, Stephen 1) Birth date not known.

Vicki Begg (9, Shirley 8, Earl 7, Charles 6, Jane 5, Major 4, Thomas 3, Clement 2, Stephen 1) born 1948. No further information found.

Charles Craig (8, Earl 7, Charles 6, Jane 5, Major 4, Thomas 3, Clement 2, Stephen 1) married Elizabeth Hebb, and they had five children (surname Craig, ninth generation):

David Craig (9, Charles 8, Earl 7, Charles 6, Jane 5, Major 4, Thomas 3, Clement 2, Stephen 1) born 1944. No further information found.
Carolyn Craig (9, Charles 8, Earl 7, Charles 6, Jane 5, Major 4, Thomas 3, Clement 2, Stephen 1) born 1948. No further information found..
Gordon Craig (9, Charles 8, Earl 7, Charles 6, Jane 5, Major 4, Thomas 3, Clement 2, Stephen 1) born 1951. No further information found.
Jeffrey Craig (9, Charles 8, Earl 7, Charles 6, Jane 5, Major 4, Thomas 3, Clement 2, Stephen 1) born 1953. No further information found.
Katherine Craig (9, Charles 8, Earl 7, Charles 6, Jane 5, Major 4, Thomas 3, Clement 2, Stephen 1) born 1956. No further information available.

The only information available on the children of Douglas and Patsy Craig, and Audrey and Ritchie Craig, is the name and the birth year.

Douglas Craig (8, Earl 7, Charles 6, Jane 5, Major 4, Thomas 3, Clement 2, Stephen 1) and his wife, Patsy Chenoweth, had four children (surname Craig, ninth generation):

Andrea Craig (9, Douglas 8, Earl 7, Charles 6, Jane 5, Major 4, Thomas 3, Clement 2, Stephen 1), born 1948.
Kristine Craig (9, Douglas 8, Earl 7, Charles 6, Jane 5, Major 4, Thomas 3, Clement 2, Stephen 1), born 1950.
Dougal Craig (9, Douglas 8, Earl 7, Charles 6, Jane 5, Major 4, Thomas 3, Clement 2, Stephen 1), born 1952.
James Craig (9, Douglas 8, Earl 7, Charles 6, Jane 5, Major 4, Thomas 3, Clement 2, Stephen 1), born 1964.

Audrey Craig (8, Earl 7, Charles 6, Jane 5, Major 4, Thomas 3, Clement 2, Stephen 1) married Richard Wright, and they had five children (surname Wright, ninth generation):

Craig Wright (9, Audrey 8, Earl 7, Charles 6, Jane 5, Major 4, Thomas 3, Clement 2, Stephen 1), born 1952.
Sandrea Wright (9, Audrey 8, Earl 7, Charles 6, Jane 5, Major 4, Thomas 3, Clement 2, Stephen 1), born 1955.
Allison Wright (9, Audrey 8, Earl 7, Charles 6, Jane 5, Major 4, Thomas 3, Clement 2, Stephen 1), born 1957.
Charles Wright (9, Audrey 8, Earl 7, Charles 6, Jane 5, Major 4, Thomas 3, Clement 2, Stephen 1), born 1961.
Malcolm Wright (9, Audrey 8, Earl 7, Charles 6, Jane 5, Major 4, Thomas 3, Clement 2, Stephen 1), born 1963.

Herbert Craig (8, Vernon 7, Charles 6, Jane 5, Major 4, Thomas 3, Clement 2, Stephen 1), (1917-1969), and Pauline Callbeck (1918-1976) had four children (surname Craig, ninth generation):

Mary Norma Craig (9, Herbert 8, Vernon 7, Charles 6, Jane 5, Major 4, Thomas 3, Clement 2, Stephen 1), born 1945; married Arnold Reeves, born 1945. Mary and Arnold divorced. They had three children (surname Reeves, tenth generation):

Craig Reeves (10, Mary 9, Herbert 8, Vernon 7, Charles 6, Jane 5, Major 4, Thomas 3, Clement 2, Stephen 1), born 1964.
Judy Reeves (10, Mary 9, Herbert 8, Vernon 7, Charles 6, Jane 5, Major 4, Thomas 3, Clement 2, Stephen 1), born 1963.
Christopher Reeves (10, Mary 9, Herbert 8, Vernon 7, Charles 6, Jane 5, Major 4, Thomas 3, Clement 2, Stephen 1), born 1966.

Linda Craig (9, Herbert Craig 8, Vernon Craig 7, Charles Craig 6, Jane Hooper Craig 5, Major Hooper 4, Thomas Hooper 3, Clement Hooper 2, Stephen Hooper 1), born 1948.

Beryl Craig (9, Herbert Craig 8, Vernon Craig 7, Charles Craig 6, Jane Hooper Craig 5, Major Hooper 4, Thomas Hooper 3, Clement Hooper 2, Stephen Hooper 1), born 1949; married Howard Francis (1947-1980). Beryl and Howard had two children (surname Francis, tenth generation):

Parker Francis (10, Beryl Craig Francis 9, Herbert Craig 8, Vernon Craig 7, Charles Craig 6, Jane Hooper Craig 5, Major Hooper 4, Thomas 3, Clement 2, Stephen 1) Birth date unknown.
Mary Francis (10, Beryl Craig Francis 9, Herbert Craig 8, Vernon Craig 7, Charles Craig 6, Jane Hooper Craig 5, Major Hooper 4, Thomas 3, Clement 2, Stephen 1) Birth date unknown.

Varge Craig (9, Herbert 8, Vernon 7, Charles 6, Jane 5, Major 5, Major Hooper 4, Thomas 3, Clement 2, Stephen 1), born 1954; married Melanie Weist, born 1953. No further information.

Norma Craig (8, Vernon 7, Charles 6, Jane 5, Major 4, Thomas 3, Clement 2, Stephen 1), born 1919; married Ensor Bowness (1914-1962). Norma and Ensor Bowness had one son (surname Bowness, ninth generation):

John Bowness (9, Norma 8, Vernon 7, Charles 6, Jane 5, Major 4, Thomas 3, Clement 2, Stephen 1) John (1956-1996) had a motorcycle accident when he was a teenager that left him a quadraplegic. Norma is a nurse and cared for her son at home in Summerside until he died. She now resides at Wedgewood Manor, Summerside, P.E.I.

Charles "Bud" Craig (8, Vernon 7, Charles 6, Jane 5, Major 4, Thomas 3, Clement 2, Stephen 1) and Margaret Ann Riley (our Chelton neighbors) had two children (surname Craig, ninth generation):

Susan Craig (9, Charles 8, Vernon 7, Charles 6, Jane 5, Major 4, Thomas 3, Clement 2, Stephen 1) born 1953 in Halifax, Nova Scotia; married Edward Arsenault, who was born in 1954. They have three children (surname Arsenault, tenth generation) and live in Miscouche, P.E.I.:

Jason Arsenault (10, Susan 9, Charles 8, Vernon 7, Charles 6, Jane 5, Major 4, Thomas 3, Clement 2, Stephen 1) born 1975 in Summerside, P.E.I. Jason is a hairdresser in Summerside in his father's shop. Jason married his bride in the summer of 2002 in a beautiful outdoor wedding at the home of his grandparents, Bud and Margaret Ann Craug, who had recently had their deck extended toward their Northumberland Strait frontage.
Jared Arsenault (10, Susan 9, Charles 8, Vernon 7, Charles 6, Jane 5, Major 4, Thomas 3, Clement 2, Stephen 1) born in 1977 in Summerside, P.E.I. Jared is in Alberta working in the oil fields (2001-2004).
Michael Arsenault (10, Susan 9, Charles 8, Vernon 7, Charles 6, Jane 5, Major 4, Thomas 3, Clement 2, Stephen 1) born 1986 in Summerside, P.E.I. In the summer of 2004 Michael worked in the oil fields in Alberta, and in the fall he went to St. Francis Xavier College in Antigonish, Nova Scotia.

William Craig (9, Charles 8, Vernon 7, Charles 6, Jane Hooper 5, Major Hooper 4, Thomas 3, Clement 2, Stephen 1), born in 1955 in Corner Brook, Newfoundland. Bill married Ellen White, born in 1955. Bill and Ellen live in Calgary, Alberta and were divorced c.1998. They have two sons (surname Craig, tenth generation):

Tyler Craig (10, William 9, Charles 8, Vernon 7, Charles 6, Jane 5, Major 4, Thomas 3, Clement 2, Stephen 1), born in 1984.
Bradley Craig (10, William 9, Charles 8, Vernon 7, Charles 6, Jane 5, Major 4, Thomas 3, Clement 2, Stephen 1), born in 1986.

Kenneth Norton (8, Sadie 7, Charles 6, Jane 5, Major Hooper 4, Thomas 3, Clement 2, Stephen 1)) and Minnie McArthur had two children about whom I have no further information other than their births (surname Norton, ninth generation):

Carol Norton (9, Kenneth 8, Sadie 7, Charles 6, Jane 5, Major Hooper 4, Thomas 3, Clement 2, Stephen 1), born 1940.
James Norton (9, Kenneth 8, Sadie 7, Charles 6, Jane 5, Major 4, Thomas 3, Clement 2, Stephen 1), born 1948.

Donald Norton, (8, Sadie 7, Charles 6, Jane 5, Major Hooper 4, Thomas 3, Clement 2, Stephen 1) married Kathryn Mugridge and had three children (surname Norton, ninth generation). Information stops with the year of their births:

Craig Norton (9, Donald 8, Sadie 7, Charles 6, Jane 5, Major 4, Thomas 3, Clement 2, Stephen 1), born 1960.
Kenneth Norton (9, Donald 8, Sadie 7, Charles 6, Jane 5, Major 4, Thomas 3, Clement 2, Stephen 1), born 1963.
Elizabeth Norton Ann (9, Donald 8, Sadie 7, Charles 6, Jane 5, Major 4, Thomas 3, Clement 2, Stephen 1) born 1966.

This concludes the children from Major through the eleventh generation of whom I have knowledge. We will proceed to the known children in the ninth generation of **Ann Hooper** (4, Thomas Hooper 3, Clement Hooper 2, Stephen Hooper 1), the third child of Thomas Hooper, Loyalist, and her husband John Montgomery. Unfortunately, many gaps exist in these generations:

Grace Wright (8, Charles Wright 7, Archibald Thomas Wright 6, Mary Montgomery Wright 5, Ann Hooper Montgomery 4, Thomas Hooper 3, Clement Hooper 2, Stephen Hooper 1) and her husband, Allan Mather, had two daughters and lived in Banff, Alberta (surname Mather, ninth generation):

Susan Louise Mather (9, Grace Wright Mather 8, Charles Wright 7, Archibald Thomas Wright 6, Mary Montgomery Wright 5, Ann Hooper Montgomery 4, Thomas Hooper 3, Clement Hooper 2, Stephen Hooper 1) born January 13, 1937; married Allyn McMaster Humphreys. No further information.
Mary Lee Mather (9, Grace 8, Charles 7, Archibald Thomas 6, Mary 5, Ann 4, Thomas 3, Clement 2, Stephen 1) born March 22, 1939; married Michael Burgess. No further information.

Norman Archibald Wright (8, Charles 7, Archibald Thomas 6, Mary Wright 5, Ann 4, Thomas 3, Clement 2. Stephen 1) and his wife, Mary Mattia, had two daughters (surname Wright, ninth generation):

Eva Janet Wright (9, Norman 8, Charles 7, Archibald Thomas 6, Mary Wright 5, Ann 4, Thomas 3, Clement 2, Stephen 1) born on September 25, 1944; married (i) Barry C. Freeman, and married (ii) Harold E. Hubka.
Doreen Mae Wright (9, Norman 8, Charles Wright 7, Archibald Thomas 6, Mary 5, Ann 4, Thomas 3, Clement 2, Stephen 1) born December 3, 1946; married Murray J. Munsie. No further information.

Gladys Wright (8, Frank Wright 7, Archibald T. Wright 6, Mary 5, Ann 4, Thomas 3, Clement 2, Stephen 1) and Bayfield Ellis had five children, (surname Ellis, ninth generation):

Marion Luella Ellis (9, Gladys 8, Frank Wright 7, Archibald T. Wright 6, Mary 5, Ann 4, Thomas 3, Clement 2, Stephen 1), born October 29, 1929; married William Archibald MacMurdo.
Shirley Pearl Ellis (9, Gladys 8, Frank Wright 7, Archibald T. Wright 6, Mary 5, Ann 4, Thomas 3, Clement 2, Stephen 1), born April 20, 1931; died April 13, 1932 in O'Leary.
Marjorie Elaine Ellis (9, Gladys 8, Frank Wright 7, Archibald T. Wright 6, Mary 5, Ann 4, Thomas 3, Clement 2, Stephen 1), born August 15, 1932; married Thomas Dickson, Jr., son of Thomas and

Katharine (Shaw) Dickson, on August 7, 1965. They moved to Bridgeton, N.J. where Thomas was one of the founders of Airwork Corporation in Millville, N. J. in 1946. He was the vice-president and general manager of the company.

Margaret Jean Ellis, called Peggy, (9, Gladys 8, Frank Wright 7, Archibald T. Wright 6, Mary 5, Ann 4, Thomas 3, Clement 2, Stephen 1), born on August 10, 1935; married Robert Adrian Smith.

Ewan Douglas Ellis (9, Gladys 8, Frank Wright 7, Archibald T. Wright 6, Mary 5, Ann 4, Thomas 3, Clement 2, Stephen 1), born on March 26, 1938; married Clarice Joanne Compton.

Marian Wright (8, Sylvina 7, Norman 6, Archibald 5, Ann Hooper Montgomery 4, Thomas 3, Clement 2, Stephen 1) married Cyril Jackman. They had five children (surname Jackman, ninth generation):

Dianne Marie Jackman (9, Marian 8, Sylvina 7, Norman 6, Archibald 5, Ann Hooper Montgomery 4, Thomas 3, Clement 2, Stephen 1), born May 2, 1962 in Summerside.

Michael James Jackman (9, Marian 8, Sylvina 7, Norman 6, Archibald 5, Ann Montgomery 4, Thomas Hooper 3, Clement 2, Stephen 1), born July 16, 1963 in Summerside, P.E.I.

Robert John Jackman (9, Marian 8, Sylvina 7, Norman 6, Archibald Montgomery 5, Ann 4, Thomas Hooper 3, Clement 2, Stephen 1), born November 5, 1965 in Cudworth, Sask.

Paul Richard Jackman (9, Marian 8, Sylvina 7, Norman 6, Archibald Thomas Montgomery 5, Ann 4, Thomas Hooper 3, Clement 2, Stephen 1), born June 16, 1969 in Gander, Nfld.

David Ernest Jackman (9, Marian 8, Sylvina 7, Norman 6, Archibald 5, Ann 4, Thomas 3, Clement 2, Stephen 1), born October 8, 1970 in Summerside, P.E.I.

We will continue with the known descendants of **Mary Hooper Robins** (4, Thomas Hooper 3, Clement Hooper 2, Stephen Hooper 1), probably the fourth child of Thomas Hooper, Loyalist, and her husband John Robins:

Janet Louise Walker (9, Annie Rogers 8, Louisa Wright Rogers 7, Sophia Ann Craig Wright 6, Ann Robins Craig 5, Mary Hooper Robins 4, Thomas Hooper 3, Clement Hooper 2, Stephen Hooper 1) born September 3, 1906 in Freetown, P.E.I. She married Benjamin Ellis, son of Ewan H. and Margaret (Richards) Ellis, on June 3, 1930. Benjamin was born on December 17, 1907 in Dolgelly, Wales. Louise was named for her two grandmothers. She and Ben lived in Sydney, N. Y. where he was business manager at Sydney Central School for forty-one years. Ben and Louise had two children, both in Sydney, N. Y. (surname Ellis, tenth generation):

Florence Janet Ellis (10, Louise Ellis 9, Annie Rogers 8, Louisa Wright Rogers7, Sophia Ann Craig Wright 6, Ann Robins Craig 5, Mary Hooper Robins 4, Thomas Hooper 3, Clement Hooper 2, Stephen Hooper 1), born November 5, 1933; married Charles A. Flyzik.

Margaret Annie Ellis (10, Louise Ellis 9, Annie Rogers 8, Louisa Wright Rogers 7, Sophia Ann Craig Wright 6, Ann Robins Craig 5, Mary Hooper Robins 4, Thomas Hooper 3, Clement Hooper 2, Stephen Hooper 1), born May 12, 1936; married William Charles Aubrey.

Florence Elizabeth Walker (9, Annie Rogers 8, Louisa Wright Rogers 7, Sophia Ann Craig Wright 6, Ann Robins Craig 5, Mary Hooper Robins 4, Thomas Hooper 3, Clement Hooper 2, Stephen Hooper 1), born July 3, 1912 in Freetown, P.E.I. She married, on January 6, 1947, Rudolph William Guta Sr., son of John and Mary (Nusek) Guta. Rudolph was born on August 26, 1908 in Gloversville, N. Y. Florence graduated from St. Mary's School of Nursing in New

York City in 1934. She nursed in several hospitals until enlisting in the U. S. Army Nursing Corps in June 1943. She was Captain and Chief Nurse of an Army Hospital in Iceland for one and one-half years during World War II. She left the service in December 1945.

Rudolph graduated from Ohio State University in Columbus, Ohio in June 1933, and worked in Gloversville, N. Y. until recalled to active service in the U. S. Army in April 1942. He served as Captain, Company Commander in the Infantry in the European Theatre of Operations until his discharge from the army in May 1945. Then he was employed as a Field Director of the American Red Cross. In the mid-1970s he and Florence lived in West Barrington, R.I. They had one child (surname Guta, tenth generation):

Rudolph William Guta, Jr. (10, Florence Walker Guta 9, Annie Rogers 8, Louisa Wright Rogers 7, Sophia Ann Craig Wright 6, Ann Robins Craig 5, Mary Hooper Robins 4, Thomas Hooper 3, Clement Hooper 2, Stephen Hooper 1), born September 2, 1948; married on December 18, 1971, Susan Kay Hoch, daughter of Gerald and Geraldine Hoch. Susan was born on September 19, 1951 in Columbia, PA. Rudolph, Jr. attended the University of Rhode Island for one year prior to enlisting in the U. S. Air Force. He served from January 1968, until his discharge as Sgt. in August 1971. His last tour of duty was in Thailand where he spent one year. He then was employed in computer maintenance for the Honeywell Corp. Susan graduated from Wheaton College in Illinois in December 1971 and taught third grade in 1973 in the Greendale School in Greenfield, Wisconsin, where they lived.

John David Walker Sr. (9, Annie Rogers 8, Louisa Wright Rogers 7, Sophia Ann Craig Wright 6, Ann Robins Craig 5, Mary Hooper Robins 4, Thomas Hooper 3, Clement Hooper 2, Stephen Hooper 1), born September 16, 1913 in Freetown, P.E.I. He married, on August 1, 1939, Emily Jean Bond, daughter of Elmer J. and Ina May (Hill) Bond. Ina was born on August 1, 1914 in Syracuse, N. Y. John graduated in 1936 from Ohio State University in business adminis-

tration. He served from February 1943 to February 1946 in World War II with the 97th Infantry in the European Theatre, before being sent to Japan with the Army of Occupation. In the mid-1970s he was National Accounts Manager and Military Sales Manager for the Norwich Pharmaceutical Company, in Norwich, N. Y. He and Emily lived in Norwich. They had four children (surname Walker, tenth generation):

a twin daughter Walker, born September 16, 1940 in Watertown, N. Y.; died at birth.
a twin daughter Walker, born September 16, 1940 in Watertown, N. Y.; died at birth.
John David Walker, Jr. (10, John David Walker 9, Annie Rogers 8, Louisa Wright Rogers 7, Sophia Ann Craig Wright 6, Ann Robins Craig 5, Mary Hooper Robins 4, Thomas Hooper 3, Clement Hooper 2, Stephen Hooper1), born September 22, 1945 in Watertown, N.Y. He married, on April 29, 1972, Elaine Louise Orr, daughter of Miles Dan and H. Rita (Rooney) Orr. Elaine was born on August 14, 1951 in Washington, D. C. John David and Elaine lived in Silver Springs, Maryland in the mid-1970s where he was a microbiologist ecologist (PhD) with Martin Marietta Corp. He received his PhD from the University of Maryland. Elaine worked at the time in the Government Accounting Office in Washington, D. C. She has a Master of Science degree in politial science. No more information available.
Susan Jean Walker (10, John David Walker 9, Annie Rogers 8, Louisa Wright Rogers 7, Sophia Ann Craig Wright 6, Ann Robins Craig 5, Mary Hooper Robins 4, Thomas Hooper 3, Clement 2, Stephen 1) born September 16, 1950 in Boston, MA. No further information.

Arthur DeWitt Wright, Jr. (9, Arthur Wright 8, Alonzo Wright 7, Sophia Ann Craig Wright 6, Ann Robins Craig 5, Mary Hooper Robins 4, Thomas Hooper 3, Clement Hooper 2, Stephen Hooper 1),

born March 14, 1921 in Utica, N. Y. He married Ann Carol McDonough on January 26, 1952. Arthur was a journalist and lived in Weston, MA in the mid-1970s. Their summer home was on Cape Cod. They had two children (surname Wright, tenth generation):

Elizabeth Ann Wright (10, Arthur Wright, Jr. 9, Arthur Wright 8, Alonzo Wright 7, Sophia Ann Craig Wright 6, Ann Robins Craig 5, Mary Hooper Robins 4, Thomas Hooper 3, Clement Hooper 2, Stephen Hooper 1) born May 16, 1957.
Arthur DeWitt Wright III (10, Arthur Wright, Jr., 9, Arthur Wright 8, Alonzo Wright 7, Sophia Ann Craig Wright 6, Ann Robins Craig 5, Mary Hooper Robins 4, Thomas Hooper 3, Clement Hooper 2, Stephen Hooper 1), born April 7, 1959. No further information.

Pearl Wright (8, Thomas Wright 7, Sophia Ann Craig Wright 6, Ann Robins Craig 5, Mary Robins Hooper 4, Thomas Hooper 3, Clement Hooper 2, Stephen Hooper 1) married James Tarte in 1912. Pearl and James had two daughters (surname Tarte, ninth generation):

Myrna Jean Tarte (9, Pearl Wright Tarte 8, Thomas Wright 7, Sophia Ann Craig Wright 6, Ann Robins Craig 5, Mary Robins Hooper 4, Thomas Hooper 3, Clement Hooper 2, Stephen Hooper 1), died in infancy.
Doris Jean Tarte (9, Pearl Wright Tarte 8, Thomas Wright 7, Sophia Ann Craig Wright 6, Ann Robins Craig 5, Mary Hooper Robins 4, Thomas Hooper 3, Clement Hooper 2, Stephen Hooper 1) born on December 13, 1918 in Bellingham, Washington. Pearl died a few days after Doris was born. Doris was brought up by her maternal grandparents, Thomas and Eugenia Wright, and lived with them until she was sixteen, in 1934, the year her grandmother passed away. Her grandfather, the Rev. Thomas Wright, had died the previos year (1933). After her grandparents died, she lived with her father and his second wife. Doris was also a teacher, like her mother, graduating from Western Washington State University with a Bachelor of Arts

degree, in 1951; then she taught in Bellingham, WA as her mother had done. On June 8, 1941 Doris married Frank Nicholas Chorvat, called Fritz, the son of Joseph Martin and Anna (Trubiroha) Chorvat. He was born on April 11, 1913 in Chicago, Illinois. Fritz was also a teacher. He was principal of Shukson Middle School in Bellingham, WA until his retirement in 1975. He had received his Master of Arts degree from Western Washington State College in 1963. During World War II he had served in the U. S. Navy. Doris and Fritz had four children (surname Chorvat, tenth generation):

Michael Francis Chorvat, called Mike, (10, Doris Chorvat 9, Pearl Wright Tarte 8, Thomas Wright 7, Sophia Ann Craig Wright 6, Ann Robins Craig 5, Mary Hooper Robins 4, Thomas Hooper 3, Clement Hooper 2, Stephen Hooper 1), born January 30, 1943 in Bellingham, Washington; married Shirley Ann Robbins, daughter of Percy Preston and Beulah Mae Simmons Robbins, on May 11, 1968. Shirley Ann was born on December 29, 1942 in Concord, California. Michael graduated in June 1965 from the U. S. Air Force Academy at Colorado Springs, Colorado and spent one and one-half years as an Air Force Navigator in Vietnam. In 1972 he received his Master of Engineering degree from Oklahoma State University. He became part of a missile tracking team at Fort Lowry in Colorado. Shirley had been a dental assistant for several years and an airline stewardess for two years. Mike and Shirley have two children (surname Chorvat, eleventh generation):

Stacy Jean Chorvat (11, Michael 10, Doris Tarte Chorvat 9, Pearl Wright Tarte 8, Thomas Wright 7, Sophia Ann Craig Wright 6, Ann Robins Craig 5, Mary Hooper Robins 4, Thomas Hooper 3, Clement Hooper 2, Stephen Hooper1) No further information.

a child Chorvat (11, Michael 10, Doris Tarte Chorvat 9, Pearl Wright Tarte 8, Thomas Wright 7, Sophia Ann Craig Wright 6, Ann Robins Craig 5, Mary Hooper Robins 4, Thomas Hooper 3, Clement Hooper 2, Stephen Hooper1) The name and information about this second child was not available.

For clarification, **Sophia Ann Craig** (6, Ann Robins Craig 5, Mary Hooper Robins 4, Thomas Hooper 3, Clement Hooper 2, Stephen Hooper 1) was the fifth child of Ann Robins and her husband, John Craig, who was also a Hooper relative. Sophia Ann married her cousin, John Robins Wright. See Chapter 7.

Frank Nicholas Chorvat, Jr. (10, Doris Tarte Chorvat 9, Pearl Wright Tarte 8, Thomas Wright 7, Sophia Ann Craig Wright 6, Ann Robins Craig 5, Mary Hooper Robins 4, Thomas Hooper 3, Clement Hooper 2, Stephen Hooper 1), born May 3, 1944 in Chicago, Illinois; married Sandra Louise Stull, daughter of Mack Vernon and Hazel (Marx) Stull, on September 30, 1967. She was born on December 31, 1946 in St. Paul, Minnesota. After Frank served with the United States Army in Germany, he and Sandra settled in Bellingham, Washington where she did secretarial work at the police department and in the comptroller's office in Bellingham. Frank was a member of the Fire Department in Bellingham. They had three children, all born in Bellingham (surname Chorvat, eleventh generation):

Jason Paul Chorvat (11, Frank, Jr. 10, Doris Tarte Chorvat 9, Pearl Wright Tarte 8, Thomas Wright 7, Sophia Ann Craig Wright 6, Ann Robins Craig 5, Mary Hooper Robins 4, Thomas Hooper 3, Clement Hooper 2, Stephen Hooper 1), born July 1, 1969. No further information.

Joseph Christian Chorvat (11, Frank, Jr. 10, Doris Tarte Chorvat 9, Pearl Wright Tarte 8, Thomas Wright 7, Sophie Ann Craig Wright 6, Ann Robins Craig 5, Mary Hooper Robins 4, Thomas Hooper 3, Clement Hooper 2, Stephen Hooper 1), born August 8, 1971. No further information.

Timothy James Chorvat (11, Frank Jr. 10, Doris Tarte Chorvat 9, Pearl Wright Tarte 8, Thomas Wright 7, Sophia Ann Craig Wright 6, Ann Robins Craig 5, Mary Hooper Robins 4, Thomas Hooper 3, Clement Hooper 2, Stephen Hooper 1), born April 26, 1973. No further information.

Cynthia Jeanne Chorvat, called Cindy (10, Doris Tarte Chorvat 9, Pearl Wright Tarte 8, ThomasWright 7, Sophia Ann Craig Wright 6, Ann Robins Craig 5, Mary Hooper Robins 4, Thomas Hooper 3, Clement Hooper 2, Stephen Hooper 1), born April 5, 1954 in Bellingham, WA; on October 18, 1975 she married Richard Blain Batdorf, called Rick, son of Donald Cameron and Carol Virginia (Swanstrom) Batdorf. He was born on June 1, 1953. Cindy graduated from Washington State University in Pullman, WA as a math/science major. She worked at Seattle First National Bank in charge of New Accounts. Rick worked for the city at the sewage processing plant. They lived in Bellingham in the mid-1970s.
Christopher Thomas Chorvat (10, Doris Tarte Chorvat 9. Pearl Wright Tarte 8, Thomas Wright 7, Sophia Ann Craig Wright 6, Ann Robins Craig 5, Mary Hooper Robins 4, Thomas Hooper 3, Clement Hooper 2, Stephen Hooper 1), born January 3, 1956 in Bellingham, Washington. In the mid-1970s he was a college student. No further information.

Roe Wright (8, Thomas Wright 7, Sophia Ann Craig Wright 6, Ann Robins Craig 5, Mary Hooper Robins 4, Thomas Hooper 3, Clement Hooper 2, Stephen Hooper 1) and Gretchen Henrietta VanderLinden had five children (surname Wright, ninth generation):

Pearl Marie Wright (9, Roe Wright 8, Thomas Wright 7, Sophia Ann Craig Wright 6, Ann Robins Craig 5, Mary Hooper Robins 4, Thomas Hooper 3, Clement Hooper 2, Stephen Hooper 1), was born April 18, 1920 in Ferndale, Washington and died there on July 21, 1927.
Thomas Grover Wright, called Tom, (9, Roe Wright 8, Thomas Wright 7, Sophia Ann Craig Wright 6, Ann Robins Craig 5, Mary Hooper Robins 4, Thomas Hooper 3, Clement Hooper 2, Stephen Hooper 1), born January 10, 1922 in Ferndale, WA; married Athlene Gertrude D'Amico on November 3, 1945 in Concrete, WA. Tom died in Seattle, WA on December 16, 1972. Tom was a logger and worked with his father and brothers in the family business, Wright

and Sons, in the State of Washington. Tom and Athlene had two daughters (surname Wright, tenth generation):

Rose *Ellen* Wright (10, Thomas Grover Wright 9, Thomas *Roe* Wright 8, Thomas Wright 7, Sophie Ann Craig Wright 6, Ann Robins Craig 5, Mary Hooper Robins 4, Thomas Hooper 3, Clement Hooper 2, Stephen Hooper 1) born on September 24, 1946 in Burlington, Washington. She married, on November 24, 1965, John Douglas Grems, son of Colis Robert and Viola Mae (Dunker) Grems. He was born on September 9, 1943 in Seaside, Oregon, and was in the U. S. Navy from 1964 to 1968 during the Vietnam War. John and Ellen were owners of Permalume Plastic Corp. which they purchased in the 1970s from Mr. C. R. Grems. They lived in the mid-1970s in Vancouver, Washington. They had two children (surname Grems, eleventh generation), both born in Oak Harbour, Washington:

John Douglas Grems VI (11, Rose *Ellen* Wright 10, Thomas Grover Wright 9, Thomas *Roe* Wright 8, Thomas Wright 7, Sophia Ann Craig Wright 6, Ann Robins Craig 5, Mary Hooper Robins 4, Thomas Hooper 3, Clement Hooper 2, Stephen Hooper 1), born August 27, 1966. No further information.

Michelle Rene Grems (11, Rose *Ellen* 10, Thomas Grover Wright 9, Thomas *Roe* Wright 8, Thomas Wright 7, Sophia Ann Craig Wright 6, Ann Robins Craig 5, Mary Hooper Robins 4, Thomas Hooper 3, Clement Hooper 2, Stephen Hooper 1), born on November 11, 1967. No further information.

Mary Lou Wright (10, Thomas Grover Wright 9, Thomas *Roe* Wright 8, Thomas Wright 7, Sophia Ann Craig Wright 6, Ann Robins Craig 5, Mary Hooper Robins 4, Thomas Hooper 3, Clement Hooper 2, Stephen Hooper 1) was born on February 5, 1948, in Sedro Woolley, Washington. She married Elmer Wood, son of Horace and Martha Emaline (Wyatt) Wood, on October 4, 1970. Elmer was born on January 1, 1937 in Waynesville, North Carolina. Elmer and Mary

lived in Mt. Vernon, Washington (state) where he was a carpenter. They had two children (surname Wood, eleventh generation):

Laura Cecilia Wood (11, Mary Lou Wright Wood 10, Thomas Grover Wright 9, Roe Wright 8, Thomas Wright 7, Sophia Ann Craig Wright 6, Ann Robins Craig 5, Mary Hooper Robins 4, Thomas Hooper 3, Clement Hooper 2, Stephen Hooper 1), born on January 1, 1972, in Sedro Woolley, (state of) Washington. No further information.
Patricia Louise Wood (11, Mary Lou Wright Wood 10, Thomas Grover Wright 9, Roe Wright 8, Thomas Wright 7, Sophia Ann Craig Wright 6, Ann Robins Craig 5, Mary Hooper Robins 4, Thomas Hooper 3, Clement Hooper 2, Stephen Hooper 1), born on June 5, 1974 in Mt. Vernon, (state of) Washington. No further information.

Floyd Grant Wright (9, Roe Wright 8, Thomas Wright 7, Sophia Ann Craig Wright) 6, Ann Robins Craig 5, Mary Hooper Robins 4, Thomas Hooper 3, Clement Hooper 2, Stephen Hooper 1) born December 25, 1923; married Marjorie Julia Ann Rhoades, daughter of John and Rose (Jaynes) Rhoades. Marjorie was born on October 27, 1925 in Nooksack, WA. She is a registered nurse. Floyd managed the logging part of the family business, Wright and Sons, since his father's death. They lived in Everett, WA and had three daughters (surname Wright, tenth generation):

Delaine Joy Wright (10, Floyd Wright 9, Roe Wright 8, Thomas Wright 7, Sophia Ann Craig Wright 6, Ann Robins Craig 5, Mary Hooper Robins 4, Thomas Hooper 3, Clement 2, Stephen Hooper 1), born April 19, 1950; died August 18, 1950.
Cheryl Ann Wright (10, Floyd Wright 9, Roe Wright 8, Thomas Wright 7, Sophia Ann Craig Wright 6, Ann Robins Craig 5, Mary Hooper Robins 4, Thomas Hooper 3, Clement Hooper 2, Stephen Hooper 1), born October 24, 1951; married Theodore Allen Cloer, called Ted, son of Theodore and May (Gentry) Cloer, on July 9, 1970. Cheryl and Ted were divorced in May 1976. They had two children,

(surname Cloer, eleventh generation), both born in Everett, Washington. No further information:

Darell Thomas Cloer (11, Cheryl Ann Wright Cloer 10, Floyd Wright 9, Roe Wright 8, Thomas Wright 7, Sophia Ann Craig Wright 6, Ann Robins Craig 5, Mary Hooper Robins 4, Thomas Hooper 3, Clement Hooper 2, Stephen Hooper 1), born January 25, 1971. No further information.

Terrence Roy Cloer (11, Cheryl Ann Wright Cloer 10, Floyd Wright 9, Roe Wright 8, Thomas Wright 7, Sophia Ann Craig Wright 6, Ann Robins Craig 5, Mary Hooper Robins 4, Thomas Hooper 3, Clement Hooper 2, Stephen Hooper 1), born March 31, 1973. No further information.

Nancy Gretchen Wright (10, Floyd Wright 9, Roe Wright 8, Thomas Wright 7, Sophia Ann Craig Wright 6, Ann Robins Craig 5, Mary Hooper Robins 4, Thomas Hooper 3, Clement Hooper 2, Stephen Hooper 1), born January 15, 1956. No further information.

Arthur Wright (9, Roe Wright 8, Thomas Wright 7 Sophia Ann Craig Wright 6, Ann Robins Craig 5, Mary Hooper Robins 4, Thomas Hooper 3, Clement Hooper 2, Stephen Hooper 1), a twin, born on September 27, 1927 in Ferndale, Washington; married Esther Marguerite Hansen, on May 12, 1951. Esther was born on March 12, 1931 in Seattle, Washington, the daughter of Henry Lillemoen and Margarethe (Hendriksen) Hansen. Esther and Art lived in Darrington, Washington. Art was in partnership with his brother, Floyd, in the logging business, Wright & Sons, Inc., begun by their father and expanded to include Washington Trucking, Inc. Art managed the trucking of heavy machinery, building materials, bulk cement, bulk products, and state-wide affairs connected with the business. His community interests included education. He had been director of the school board for fourteen years. Art served in the U. S. Merchant Marines, in 1945, the U. S. Army 1949-1952, the Korean War, M. P.- 45th Division (Japan and Korean duty). Art and Esther

have four children (surname Wright, tenth generation) born in Everett, WA:

Grant Arthur Wright (10, Art Wright 9, Roe Wright 8, Thomas Wright 7, Sophia Ann Craig Wright 6, Ann Robins Craig 5, Mary Hooper Robins 4, Thomas Hooper 3, Clement Hooper 2, Stephen Hooper 1) called Art, born on July 3, 1953; he married Deborah Jean Stone, daughter of Marion and Barbara (Reynolds) Stone. Jean was born on November 1, 1952 in Sedro Wooley, WA. Art completed a two-year diesel school course in Diesel Mechanics at Seattle Community College. He worked with the family firm in the Washington Trucking Dept. which did all types of heavy trucking. Art and Deborah lived in Everett, WA. No further information.

Thomas Henry Wright (10, Art Wright 9, Roe Wright 8, Thomas Wright 7, Sophia Ann Craig Wright 6, Ann Robins Craig 5, Mary Hooper Robins 4, Thomas Hooper 3, Clement Hooper 2, Stephen Hooper 1), called Tom, was born on March 22, 1955. He took an automotive course at Everett Community College and worked the night shift at E. A. Nord Company, as well.

Heide Andrine Wright (10, Art Wright 9, Roe Wright 8, Thomas Wright 7, Sophia Ann Craig Wright 6, Ann Robins Craig 5, Mary Hooper Robins 4, Thomas Hooper 3, Clement Hooper 2, Stephen Hooper 1) was born on August 20, 1957. She was the valedictorian of her high school graduating class in 1975 and went to the University of Washington. No further information.

Kristian Erik Wright, called Kris (10, Art Wright 9, Roe Wright 8, Thomas Wright 7, Sophia Ann Craig Wright 6, Ann Robins Craig 5, Mary Hooper Robins 4, Thomas Hooper 3, Clement Hooper 2, Stephen Hooper 1), was born on December 15, 1959. No further information.

Jane *Arliss* Wright, a twin, (9, Roe Wright 8, Thomas Wright 7, Sophia Ann Craig Wright 6, Ann Robins Craig 5, Mary Hooper Robins 4, Thomas Hooper 3, Clement Hooper 2, Stephen Hooper 1) was born September 27, 1927 in Ferndale, WA.; married Bernard

Sturgulewski, Jr., son of Bernard and Mary Prawdzik Sturgulewski, both of Augustow, Poland. Bernard was born on March 11, 1919 in Chicago, Ill. and died on December 2, 1968 in Iliamna, Alaska. Arliss graduated from the University of Washington with a B.A. degree in economics and business as an accounting major, and was employed as an accountant and office manager. Bernard was a civil and construction engineer with the U. S. Army Corps of Engineers and was active in a supervisory role of major defense and communication projects in Alaska in the 1950s until his tragic death in an airplane crash. In the Anchorage area he had played a major role in reconstruction activities which were necessitated by the 1964 Alaskan Earthquake. Arliss and Bernard lived in Anchorage where she stayed after his death and was engaged in local civic government and state affairs. They had one child (surname Sturgulewski, tenth generation):

Bernard Roe Sturgulewski (10, Arliss Wright 9, Roe Wright 8, Thomas Wright 7, Sophia Ann Craig Wright 6, Ann Robins Craig 5, Mary Hooper Robins 4, Thomas Hooper 3, Clement Hooper 2, Stephen 1) born on March 15, 1957 in Anchorage, Alaska, and named for his father and two grandfathers. He was a good athlete and planned to major in civil engineering at the last update in the mid-1970s.

Emma Schurman (8, George 7, Thomas 6, Ann Hooper Schurman 5, Thomas Hooper 4, 3, Clement Hooper 2, Stephen Hooper 1) married John Henry Moase, in 1908, in Summerside, P.E.I. They had two sons, both born in Upper New Annan (surname Moase, ninth generation):

George Lewis Moase (9, Emma Schurman 8, George 7, Thomas 6, Ann Hooper Schurman 5, Thomas Hooper 4, 3, Clement Hooper 2, Stephen Hooper 1) born August 31, 1909; married Edith Louise MacQuarrie Johnson, on January 25, 1933, in Charlottetown, P.E.I. They lived on the home farm in Upper New Annan and had no children.

Sterling Ray Moase (9, Emma Schurman Moase 8, George Schurman 7, Thomas Hooper Schurman 6, Ann Hooper Schurman 5, Thomas Hooper 4, 3, Clement Hooper 2, Stephen Hooper 1) born on October 15, 1918; did not marry; lived on the home farm in Upper New Annan.

Ray Schurman (8, George Schurman 7, Thomas Schurman 6, Ann Hooper Schurman 5, Thomas Hooper 4, 3, Clement 2, Stephen 1) married (i) Ella Nora Montgomery, of Travellers Rest, P.E.I., had one daughter (surname Schurman, ninth generation):

Myra Montgomery Schurman (9, Ray Schurman 8, George Schurman 7, Thomas Schurman 6, Ann Hooper Schurman 5, Thomas Hooper 4, 3, Clement 2, Stephen 1), born March 25, 1904; married Joseph McCormick.

After Ella died in 1917, Ray married (ii) in Georgetown, P.E.I., Margaret MacConnell, daughter of Alexander MacConnell. They had one son (surname Schurman, ninth generation):

George Gould Schurman (9, Ray Schurman 8, George 7, Thomas 6, Ann Hooper Schurman 5, Thomas 4, 3, Clement 2, Stephen 1) born June 12, 1922; married Edith Smith. No further information.

Leonard Schurman (8, George 7, Thomas 6, Ann Hooper Schurman 5, Thomas Hooper 4, 3, Clement Hooper 2, Stephen Hooper 1) and his wife, Mamie, started their married life in Travellers Rest, then moved to Summerside, P.E.I., and soon afterwards left for Saskatchewan where he was a carpenter. They had four children (surname Schurman, ninth generation), none of whose birth dates are given:

Frederick Wyatt Schurman (9, Leonard Schurman 8, George 7, Thomas 6, Ann Hooper Schurman 5, Thomas Hooper 4, 3, Clement Hooper 2, Stephen Hooper 1) lived in Saskatoon, Saskatchewan.

Ray Schurman (9, Leonard Schurman 8, George 7, Thomas 6, Ann Hooper Schurman 5, Thomas Hooper 4, 3, Clement Hooper 2, Stephen Hooper 1) was a plumber and lived in Sarnia, Ontario.
Helen Schurman (9, Leonard Schurman 8, George 7, Thomas 6, Ann Hooper Schurman 5, Thomas Hooper 4, 3, Clement Hooper 2, Stephen Hooper 1) married John Bock.
Valerie Schurman (9, Leonard Schurman 8, George 7, Thomas 6, Ann Hooper Schurman 5, Thomas 4, 3, Clement 2, Stephen 1) No further information was given.

We go now to the descendants of **Alexander Hooper** (5, Thomas Hooper 4, 3, Clement 2, Stephen 1).

William Ross Wright, M D. (8, Horace 7, Mary Alice Hooper Wright 6, Alexander Hooper 5, Thomas Hooper 4, 3, Clement 2, Stephen 1) and his wife, "Brownie," a registered nurse, had three children (surname Wright, ninth generatiom), all born in Fredericton, New Brunswick:

Eileen Patricia Wright (9, William Ross 8, Horace 7, Mary Alice Hooper Wright 6, Alexander Hooper 5, Thomas Hooper 4, 3, Clement 2, Stephen 1) was born August 3, 1938; married, June 17, 1967 Herbert Frederick Wallace, son of Robert Wallace. Herbert was born in 1937 in Unity, Sask. Pat studied at the Montreal General Hospital and received her R. N. in 1960; she attended Dalhousie University and graduated in 1967 with a Bachelor of Nursing and a diploma in Nursing Administration and Public Health. She has a Master's degree in Nursing Services Administration from the University of Alberta, 1975, and became the Executive Director of Nursing at Royal Alexandra Hospital in Edmonton, Alberta. Herbert graduated from the University of Saskatchewan and from Dalhousie University with a PhD in chemical engineering, in 1968. He was a research chemical engineer with Sherritt Gordon, Fort Saskatchewan, Alberta. They lived in Edmonton.

Mary Frances Wright (9, William Ross 8, Horace 7, Mary Alice Hooper Wright 6, Alexander Hooper 5, Thomas Hooper 4, 3, Clement 2, Stephen 1) born on June 25, 1941; married Colin Steward Paterson. No more information given.
Diane Marie Wright (9, William Ross 8, Horace 7, Mary Alice Hooper Wright 6, Alexander Hooper 5, Thomas Hooper 4, 3, Clement 2, Stephen 1) born January 23, 1946; married Michael George Forse. No more information available.

Horace Melville Wright (8, 7, Mary Alice Hooper Wright 6, Alexander Hooper 5, Thomas 4, 3, Clement 2, Stephen 1) and Helen Archibald, who lived at Horace's father's "Fairhaven Farms" in Lower Bedeque had five children (surname Wright, ninth generation):

Ronald Horace Wright (9, Horace 8, 7, Mary Alice Hooper Wright 6, Alexander Hooper 5, Thomas 4, 3, Clement 2, Stephen 1) was born on June 6, 1939; married Susanne Elizabeth Salome.
Kenneth Alan Wright (9, Horace 8, 7, Mary Alice Hooper Wright 6, Alexander Hooper 5, Thomas 4, 3, Clement 2, Stephen 1) was born on November 13, 1942. On June 28, 1969 he married Linda Elaine Smith, the daughter of John Henry and Sarah Elizabeth (Donnelly) Smith. Linda was born in Gladstone, Manitoba, on September 23, 1943. She graduated from UPEI and taught in Montague and Charlottetown before her marriage. Alan also taught in Montague for two years before they went to Manitoba where he taught in Portage la Prairie.
Jeanie Isabel Wright (9, Horace 8, 7, Mary Alice Hooper Wright 6, Alexander Hooper 5, Thomas Hooper 4, 3, Clement 2, Stephen 1), born April 9, 1947; married Deric Alexander Affleck.
John Ross Wright (9, Horace Wright 8, 7, Mary Alice Hooper Wright 6, Alexander Hooper 5, Thomas Hooper 4, 3, Clement 2, Stephen 1) was born on October 24, 1949; married, on August 19, 1972, Charlene Ann Green, daughter of Sidney Charles and Phyllis Georgie (Reeves) Green. Charlene was born on September 24, 1953 in Summerside. John graduated with a Bachelor of Science degree from Mount Allison

University in 1971, and received the Bachelor of Education degree in 1973 from the University of New Brunswick, after which he farmed with his father. Charlene graduated with a Bachelor of Arts degree from the University of New Brunswick in 1974, and from UPEI with a Bachelor of Education in 1975. She taught in Lower Freetown.

Paul William Wright (9, Horace Wright 8, 7, Mary Alice Hooper Wright 6, Alexander Hooper 5, Thomas 4, 3, Clement 2, Stephen 1), born on September 25, 1956. He worked on the farm with his father and brother, John.

Dr. John Sidney Wright (8, Horace Wright 7, Mary Alice (Hooper) Wright 6, Alexander Hooper 5, Thomas Hooper 4, 3, Clement 2, Stephen 1) and his wife, Minnie (Hunt) Wright, had three children (surname Wright, ninth generation):

John Peter Wright (9, John Sidney 8, Horace Wright 7, Mary Alice (Hooper) Wright 6, Alexander Hooper 5, Thomas Hooper 4, 3, Clement 2, Stephen 1), born on May 15, 1945; married Jean Stratton MacDonald.

David Archibald Wright (9, John Sidney Wright 8, Horace Wright 7, Mary Alice Hooper Wright 6, Alexander Hooper 5, Thomas Hooper 4, 3, Clement 2, Stephen 1), born May 22, 1948 in North Sydney, Nova Scotia. In 1972 he married Margaret Young. No further information.

Sarah Margaret Wright, called Sally, (9, John Sidney Wright 8, Horace Wright 7, Mary Alice Hooper Wright 6, Alexander Hooper 5, Thomas Hooper 4, 3, Clement 2, Stephen 1), born June 10, 1954 in Moncton, New Brunswick. She attended Dalhousie University, majoring in arts and music. In 1976 she was in London, England, on a scholarship doing a year's post-graduated work at Guild Hall of Music and Drama.

Hilda Alice Schurman (8, Isabelle Wright Schurman 7, Mary Alice Hooper Wright 6, Alexander Hooper 5, Thomas Hooper 4, 3, Clement Hooper 2, Stephen Hooper 1) married Leslie Hooper. Hilda and Leslie are both Hooper descendants. Leslie's line runs (7, Edward 6, Lemuel 5, Elisha 4, Thomas 3, Clement 2, Stephen 1) They had one child (surname Hooper, ninth generation):

Helen Leona Hooper (9, Hilda 8, Isabelle 7, Mary Alice Hooper Wright 6, Alexander Hooper 5, Thomas Hooper 4, 3, Clement 2, Stephen 1) was born on September 4, 1930 in Central Bedeque. Helen was a book keeper with M. F. Schurman Company before going to Toronto where she was an accountant with Ultramar, an oil company.

Verna Schurman (8, Isabelle Wright Schurman 7, Mary Alice Hooper Wright 6, Alexander Hooper 5, Thomas Hooper 4, 3, Clement 2, Stephen 1) and Earl Hunter had one child (surname Hunter, ninth generation):

Gregory Earl Hunter (9, Verna Schurman 8, Isabelle Wright Schurman 7, Mary Alice Hooper Wright 6, Alexander Hooper 5, Thomas Hooper 4, 3, Clement 2, Stephen 1) was born on August 22, 1952 in Toronto, Ontario. He graduated from the University of Waterloo with a Bachelors degree in math (computer science and statistics) in 1976, and a Masters degree in math (statistics) in 1977. He has been employed with IBM Canada as a programmer/operator, maintenance programmer, development programmer, systems engineer, and marketing research analyst.

Lillian Isabel Schurman (8, Isabelle 7, Mary Alice Hooper Wright 6, Alexander Hooper 5, Thomas Hooper 4, 3, Clement 2, Stephen 1) married Harold Sidney Clark, and had four children (surname Clark, ninth generation), all born in Summerside:

Kenneth Harold Clark (9, Lillian 8, Isabelle 7, Mary Alice Hooper Wright 6, Alexander Hooper 5, Thomas Hooper 4, 3, Clement 2, Stephen 1) was born on October 25, 1945; married, on May 21, 1966, in Halifax, Judith Elaine Harris, daughter of Raymond and Lillian Harris. Judith was born on January 27, 1945 in Clyde River, Nova Scotia. They lived in Dartmouth, Nova Scotia. Kenneth was in the Canadian Forces (Navy). No further information.
Gordon Leonard Clark (9, Lillian 8, Isabelle 7, Mary Alice Hooper Wright 6, Alexander Hooper 5, Thomas Hooper 4, 3, Clement 2, Stephen 1), born on January 17, 1948. He worked on the Borden-Cape Tormentine carferry and at Campbell & Burns Cannery, Central Bedeque. No further information.
Richard Lowell Clark (9, Lillian 8, Isabelle 7, Mary Alice Hooper Wright 6, Alexander Hooper 5, Thomas Hooper 4, 3, Clement 2, Stephen 1) was born on September 11, 1952. Richard worked in construction in Charlottetown; he also attended Dalhousie University. No further information.
Cheryl Isabel Clark (9, Lillian 8, Isabelle 7, Mary Alice Hooper Wright 6, Alexander Hooper 5, Thomas Hooper 4, 3, Clement 2, Stephen 1) was born on January 2, 1954; married Brian Smith of New Brunswick. No further information.

Carmen Floyd Baldwin (8, Annie 7, Mary Alice 6, Alexander 5, Thomas 4, 3, Clement 2, Stephen 1)) and his wife, Jeanne Iva Duguid Baldwin, had four children (surname Baldwin, ninth generation):

Helen Faye Baldwin (9, Carmen 8, Annie 7, Mary Alice 6, Alexander 5, Thomas 4, 3, Clement 2, Stephen 1) was born on December 6, 1944; on May 20, 1967 she married Carmen Bernard Olsen, son of John and Marion (Haskins) Olsen. He was born on April 9, 1944 in Cabri, Saskatchewan. Helen was a legal secretary and a housewife. Carmen had been a welder and a coffee vendor. Later he became an assistant manager of Topline Feed Mille. They lived in Swift Current, Sask.

Vernon Floyd Baldwin (9, Carmen 8, Annie 7, Mary Alice 6, Alexander Hooper 5, Thomas 4, 3, Clement 2, Stephen 1) was born on November 27, 1947; married Donna Mae Murray. No further information.

Linda Jeanne Baldwin (9, Carmen 8, Annie 7, Mary Alice 6, Alexander 5, Thomas 4, 3, Clement 2, Stephen 1) was born on April 8, 1950; married Douglas Wayne Roth. No further information.

Carol Elaine Baldwin (9, Carmen 8, Annie 7, Mary Alice 6, Alexander 5, Thomas 4, 3, Clement 2, Stephen 1) was born on October 13, 1953; married Robert Hill. No further information.

This concludes the children of whom I have knowledge up through the eleventh generation from Thomas, Jr., the fifth child of Thomas, in generation four. Because the sixth child of Thomas Hooper 3, Rachel, (if she did indeed exist which I seriously doubt) did not marry, we will proceed to the descendants of **Elisha Hooper** (4, Thomas 3, Clement 2, Stephen 1**),** the last child of Thomas, and his wife, Margaret Crosby:

Mary Constance Wright (8, Mary Prichard 7, Margaret Clark 6, Sarah Hooper 5, Elisha 4, Thomas 3, Clement 2, Stephen 1) married Rutherford J. Conrod, called Jack. They had two daughters (surname Conrod, ninth generation):

Mary Constance Conrod, called Connie, (9, Constance Wright 8, Mary Prichard 7, Margaret Clark 6, Sarah Hooper 5, Elisha 4, Thomas 3, Clement 2, Stephen 1) born July 19, 1928; married Quentin Wayne Wenaus. No further information.

Barbara Rutherford Conrod (9, Constance Wright 8, Mary Prichard 7, Margaret Clark 6, Sarah Hooper 5. Elisha 4, Thomas Hooper 3, Clement Hooper 2, Stephen Hooper 1) born March 17, 1932; married Frederick Charles Hine, called Buzz. No further information.

Sarah Hope Prichard (8, Mary Prichard 7, Margaret Clark 6, Sarah Hooper 5, Elisha Hooper 4, Thomas 3, Clement 2, Stephen 1) married Harold K. Watchorn. They had one son (surname Watchorn, ninth generation):

C. Leslie F. Watchorn (9, Hope 8, Mary Prichard 7, Margaret Clark 6, Sarah Hooper 5, Elisha Hooper 4, Thomas 3, Clement 2, Stephen 1) born January 13, 1945 in Montreal, P.Q.; married Nancy Elizabeth Prichard, daughter of Sheldon and Ethel (McCaig) Prichard, on February 12, 1970. He graduated from McGill University in 1965 with honors in math. In the 1970s he was an actuary with the Sun Life Insurance Company in Montreal, P.Q.

Norman Elisha Wright Prichard (8, Mary 7, Margaret Clark 6, Sarah Hooper 5, Elisha Hooper 4, Thomas 3, Clement 2, Stephen 1) and his wife, Glenda Louise Muttart, had five children as follows (surname Prichard, ninth generation):

Arthur Norman Prichard (9, Norman 8, Mary 7, Margaret Clark 6, Sarah Hooper 5, Elisha Hooper 4, Thomas 3, Clement 2, Stephen 1), born July 1, 1938; married Karen Marlene Preston, daughter of Harold Lancelot and Lillian Doris (Willet) Preston, on September 20, 1969. Karen was born on September 11, 1946 in Toronto, Ontario. In the 1970s they lived at 75 Gulliver Crescent, Bramlea, Ontario where Arthur was manager of a parts department.

Mary *El*izabeth Prichard (9, Norman 8, Mary 7, Margaret Clark 6, Sarah Hooper 5, Elisha 4, Thomas 3, Clement 2, Stephen 1), called Betty, born December 16, 1940; married Donald Richard Aubin. No further information.

Judith Hope Prichard, called Judi, (9, Norman 8, Mary 7, Margaret Clark 6, Sarah Hooper 5, Elisha 4, Thomas 3, Clement 2, Stephen 1), born November 9, 1944/5; married James Wayne Newson. No further information given.

a son (9, Norman 8, Mary 7, Margaret Clark 6, Sarah Hooper 5, Elisha 4, Thomas 3, Clement 2, Stephen 1), stillborn.

Norman Kent Prichard (9, Norman 8, Mary 7, Margaret Clark 6, Sarah Hooper 5, Elisha 4, Thomas 3, Clement 2, Stephen 1), born April 3, 1951; worked with an oil exploration company in the Canadian north in the 1970s.

Reginald Prichard, called Reg (8, Mary 7, Margaret Elizabeth Clark 6, Sarah Jewel Hooper 5, Elisha Hooper 4, Thomas 3, Clement 2, Stephen 1) and Mary Prichard had two children (surname Prichard, ninth generation), both born in Montreal, P.Q.:

Sandra Hope Prichard (9, Reginald 8, Mary 7, Margaret Elizabeth Clark 6, Sarah Jewel Hooper 5, Elisha Hooper 4, Thomas 3, Clement 2, Stephen 1) born May 9, 1942; married Ronald Bertram Pickering. No further information.

James Haywood Prichard, called Jim (9, Reginald 8, Mary Wright 7, Margaret Elizabeth Clark 6, Sarah Jewel Hooper 5, Elisha Hooper 4, Thomas 3, Clement 2, Stephen 1) born December 25, 1945. Jim served with the U. S. Marines. In 1969 he married Linda Eunice McLaughlin, who was born in Montreal. No further information.

Constance Lewis (8, Lora Lee Wright 7, Margaret Elizabeth Clark 6, Sarah Jewel 5, Elisha Hooper 4, Thomas 3, Clement 2, Stephen 1) and Charles Lane had five children (surname Lane, ninth generation) and lived in Plymouth, MA:

Linda Gail Lane (9, Constance 8, Lora Lee Wright 7, Margaret Elizabeth Clark 6, Sarah Jewel 5, Elisha Hooper 4, Thomas 3, Clement 2, Stephen 1) born December 2, 1942 in Boston, MA.; married Joseph F. Schneider, on April 22, 1959. He was born in February 1934 in Plymouth, MA, the son of Joseph F. and Caroline C. Schneider. They have three children (surname Schneider, tenth generation) and live in Plymouth, MA (1970s):

Laurie Ellen Schneider (10, Linda 9, Constance 8, Lora Lee 7, Margaret Elizabeth Clark 6, Sarah Jewel 5, Elisha Hooper 4, Thomas 3, Clement 2, Stephen 1), born November 24, 1960 at Plymouth, MA. No further information.

Anthony Allan Schneider (10, Linda 9, Constance 8, Lora Lee Wright 7, Margaret Elizabeth Clark 6, Sarah Jewel 5, Elisha Hooper 4, Thomas 3, Clement 2, Stephen 1), born December 5, 1962 at Plymouth, MA. No further information.

Jodi-Beth Schneider (10, Linda 9, Constance 8, Lora Lee Wright 7, Margaret Elizabeth Clark 6, Sarah Jewel 5, Elisha Hooper 4, Thomas 3, Clement 2, Stephen 1), born September 11, 1964 at Plymouth, MA.

Loralee Wright Lane (9, Constance 8, Lora Lee Wright 7, Margaret Elizabeth Clark 6, Sarah Jewel 5, Elisha Hooper 4, Thomas 3, Clement 2, Stephen 1), born May 11, 1947 at Hyannis, Cape Cod, MA. She married John Petrie Draper, on January 17, 1970 at Canton, MA. He is the son of Walter S. and Mary Pennfield Draper. They lived in Foxboro, MA (1970) and have one son (surname Draper, tenth generation):

Andrew Pennfield Draper (10, Loralee 9, Constance 8, Lora Lee 7, Margaret Elizabeth Clark 6, Sarah Jewel 5, Elisha Hooper 4, Thomas 3, Clement 2, Stephen 1), born July 26, 1970 in Norwood, MA. No further information.

Jeffrey Michael Lane (9, Constance 8, Lora Lee Wright 7, Margaret Elizabeth Clark 6, Sarah Jewel 5, Elisha Hooper 4, Thomas 3, Clement 2, Stephen 1), born March 19, 1948 in Marblehead, MA. No further information.

Dale Lewis Lane (9, Constance 8, Lora Lee Wright 7, Margaret Elizabeth Clark 6, Sarah Jewel 5, Elisha Hooper 4, Thomas 3, Clement 2, Stephen 1), born August 27, 1949 at Salem, MA. On May 6, 1969, he married Kathleen Murphy, who was born in Boston, MA. Dale is

a supervisor for Old Colony Gas Company. He and Kathleen had a baby girl (surname Lane, tenth generation), born in Boston. Dale and Kathleen were divorced in 1971. No further information:

Sharon Marie Lane (10, Dale 9, Constance 8, Lora Lee 7, Margaret Elizabeth 6, Sarah Jewel 5, Elisha 4, Thomas 3, Clement 2, Stephen 1) Date of birth unknown.

Barry Mark Lane (9, Constance 8, Lora Lee Wright 7, Margaret Elizabeth Clark 6, Sarah Jewel 5, Elisha 4, Thomas 3, Clement 2, Stephen 1), born September 26, 1954. No further information on this family.

Lulu Hooper (7, Charles Fredrick *Allison* Hooper 6, Lemuel Hooper 5, Elisha Hooper 4, Thomas 3, Clement 2, Stephen 1) and Frank Deacon had four children. I have information on only one child (surname Deacon, eighth generation):

Allison Deacon (8, Lulu Hooper Deacon 7, Charles Fredrick *Allison* Hooper 6, Lemuel Hooper 5, Elisha Hooper 4, Thomas 3, Clement 2, Stephen 1). There is no information available to me on Allison, other than there was at least one daughter (surname Deacon, ninth generation):

Carol Edith Deacon (9, Allison Deacon 8, Lulu Hooper Deacon 7, Charles Fredrick *Allison* Hooper 6, Lemuel Hooper 5, Elisha Hooper 4, Thomas 3, Clement 2, Stephen 1), born on December 4, 1950 in Moncton, New Brunswick. On December 28, 1970, she married Gary David Craswell, born July 20, 1947, in Charlottetown, P.E.I. the son of Merrill Harrison and Janet Muriel (Swan) Craswell. In the mid-1970s Gary was technical director at the Confederation Centre in Charlottetown. Carol was a staffing officer with the Civil Service Commission of the provincial government. Both were enrolled in the public administration course at UPEI. They had one child (surname Craswell, tenth generation):

Krista Alyson Craswell (10, Carol 9, Allison Deacon 8, Lulu Hooper Deacon 7, Charles *Allison* Hooper 6, Lemuel Hooper 5, Elisha Hooper 4, Thomas Hooper 3, Clement Hooper 2, Stephen Hooper 1), born on February 12, 1977, in Charlottetown, P.E.I.

Hilda Elizabeth Deacon (8, Lulu Hooper Deacon 7, Charles Fredrick *Allison* Hooper 6, Lemuel Hooper 5, Elisha 4, Thomas 3, Clement 2, Stephen 1), married George Howard Lewis; they had three children (surname Lewis, ninth generation):

George Howard Lewis (9, Hilda Deacon Lewis 8, Lulu Hooper Deacon 7, Charles Fredrick *Allison* Hooper 6, Lemuel Hooper 5, Elisha 4, Thomas 3, Clement 2, Stephen 1), born on June 20, 1946; died the same day.

Lana Lou Lewis (9, Hilda Deacon Lewis 8, Lulu Hooper Deacon 7, Charles Fredrick *Allison* Hooper 6, Lemuel Hooper 5, Elisha 4, Thomas 3, Clement 2, Stephen 1) born May 15, 1948; married, on June 4, 1971, in Charlottetown, John Emerson Churchill, son of the Rev. E. C. Churchill. She attended Acadia University in Nova Scotia.

Jennie Isabel Lewis (9, Hilda Deacon Lewis, Lulu Hooper Deacon 7, Allison Hooper 6, Lemuel Crosby Hooper 5, Elisha 4, Thomas 3, Clement 2, Stephen 1), born February 14, 1950; attended the University of P.E.I.

Patricia Louise Deacon (9, Allison Deacon 8, Lu Hooper Deacon 7, Charles Allison Hooper 6, Lemuel 5, Elisha 4, Thomas 3, Clement Hooper 2, Stephen Hooper 1), born April 22, 1949, in Moncton, New Brunswick. In 1967 she married (i) Glydon Garry Dennis, son of Edgar and Joyce Dennis. He was born on October 18, 1949 in Charlottetown, P.E.I. The marriage of Patricia and Glydon ended in divorce. On March 21, 1973 Patricia married (ii) David George Walters, born on May 14, 1947, son of George Albert and Esther Lucas (MacDougall) Walters. David graduated from the Nova Scotia

Technical College, in 1975, as a mining engineer. David legally adopted Patricia's two children. In the mid-1970s they lived in Halifax, Nova Scotia. Their two children (surname Dennis, tenth generation) are:

Catherine Anne Dennis (10, Patricia 9, Allison Deacon 8, Lu Hooper Deacon 7, Charles Allison Hooper 6, Lemuel 5, Elisha 4, Thomas 3, Clement 2, Stephen 1), born October 31, 1967 in Charlottetown, P.E.I.
Mark Allison Dennis (10, Patricia 9, Allison Deacon 8, Lulu May Hooper Deacon 7, Charles Allison Hooper 6, Lemuel 5, Elisha 4, Thomas 3, Clement 2, Stephen 1), born October 11, 1968 in Charlottetown, P.E.I.

Marjorie Hooper (8, Fredrick Hooper 7, Charles Allison Hooper 6, Lemuel Hooper 5, Elisha 4, Thomas 3, Clement 2, Stephen 1). In the summer of 2000 Gladys Henderson took this writer to visit Marjorie, a cousin, at her home just east of Summerside. She and her husband, Delbert Rayner, have six children (surname Rayner, ninth generation):

Joyce Elaine Rayner (9, Marjorie 8, Fredrick Hooper 7, Charles Allison Hooper 6, Lemuel Hooper 5, Elisha 4, Thomas 3, Clement 2, Stephen 1), born April 17, 1945 in Summerside, P.E.I. On April 30, 1966 she married Roger Charles Newman, who was born on June 15, 1944, in London, England. His parents are Edmund John and Freda Mary (Braziel) Newman. Roger was a member of the Canadian Armed Forces (Navy). Joyce and Roger live (2000) in Cumberland, Ontario and have the following children (surname Newman, tenth generation):

Darcy Charles Newman (10, Joyce Newman 9, Marjorie Hooper Rayner 8, Frederick Hooper 7, Allison Hooper 6, Lemuel Hooper 5, Elisha Hooper 4, Thomas 3, Clement 2, Stephen 1), born September 2, 1969 in Edmonton, Alberta; married Tracy Sims, on September 24, 1993. They have two sons (surname Newman, eleventh generation):

Kyle Thomas Charles Newman (11, Darcy 10, Joyce Newman 9, Marjorie Rayner 8, Frederick Hooper 7, Allison 6, Lemuel 5, Elisha 4, Thomas 3, Clement 2, Stephen 1), born May 21, 1996.
Brett Darcy David Newman (11, Darcy 10, Joyce Newman 9, Marjorie Rayner 8, Frederick Hooper 7, Allison 6, Lemuel 5, Elisha 4, Thomas 3, Clement 2, Stephen 1), born November 22, 1998.

Todd Roger Newman (10, Joyce Newman 9, Marjorie Hooper Rayner 8, Frederick Hooper 7, Allison Hooper 6, Lemuel Hooper 5, Elisha Hooper 4, Thomas Hooper 3, Clement 2, Stephen 1) born November 26, 1971 in Ottawa, Ontario. No further information.

Frederick Ernest Rayner (9, Marjorie Hooper 8, Frederick Hooper 7, Allison Hooper 6, Lemuel Hooper 5, Elisha 4, Thomas 3, Clement 2, Stephen 1), born April 2, 1946 in Summerside, P.E.I.; married (i) Judy Mae Compton, daughter of George Watson and Sadie Mae (Mills) Compton, on January 18, 1969. Judy was born on June 26, 1947 in Summerside, P.E.I. Fred and Judy's marriage ended in divorce in Moose Jaw, Sask. No further information. Fred married (ii) Deane Denn, on February 15, 1975. Fred and Judy had one child (surname Rayner, tenth generation). Fred was in the R.C.M.P. in Ontario until 1997. He had spent ten years in Newfoundland, including St. Johns. He and Deane have two children (surname Rayner, tenth generation), and live in Fall River, N.S.

Tanya Christine Rayner, by Fred's first marriage, (10, Frederick Rayner 9, Marjorie Hooper Rayner 8, Frederick Hooper 7, Allison Hooper 6, Lemuel Hooper 5, Elisha Hooper 4, Thomas Hooper 3, Clement Hooper 2, Stephen Hooper 1), born on May 26, 197?. No further information.
Sherri Lee Rayner, by Fred's second marriage, (10, Frederick Rayner 9, Marjorie Rayner 8, Frederick Hooper 7, Allison Hooper 6, Lemuel Hooper 5, Elisha Hooper 4, Thomas 3, Clement 2, Stephen 1), born on December 17, 1975. No further information.
Frederick Scott Rayner, by Fred's second marriage, (10, Frederick Rayner 9, Marjorie 8, Frederick Hooper 7, Allison Hooper 6, Lemuel Hooper 5, Elisha Hooper 4, Thomas 3, Clement 2, Stephen 1), born on May 20, 1978.

Linda Lou Rayner (9, Marjorie 8, Frederick 7, Allison 6, Lemuel 5, Elisha 4, Thomas 3, Clement 2, Stephen 1), born November 12, 1947 in Summerside. Linda married Douglas MacArthur MacKay [a Wright descendant], on November 18, 1967, at the North Bedeque United Church. Doug was born on August 14, 1945. They have three sons (surname MacKay, tenth generation) and live in Brackley, P.E.I.:

Randall Douglas MacKay (10, Linda 9, Marjorie 8, Frederick 7, Allison 6, Lemuel 5, Elisha 4, Thomas 3, Clement 2, Stephen 1), born November 25, 1969; married Elizabeth Drennan, who was born on February 8, 1975 in New Germany, Nova Scotia, son of Tom and Valerie Drennan. Tom is a teacher. Randall is a graphic designer in Charlottetown, P.E.I. Randall and Elizabeth have a son (surname MacKay, eleventh generation):

Patrick Ian MacKay (11, Randall 10, Linda 9, Marjorie Hooper Rayner 8, Frederick 7, Allison 6, Lemuel 5, Elisha 4, Thomas 3, Clement 2, Stephen 1), born November 2, 1999.

Robert Kenneth MacKay (10, Linda 9, Marjorie 8, Frederick 7, Allison 6, Lemuel 5, Elisha 4, Thomas 3, Clement 2, Stephen 1) born on April 11, 1972. On January 5, 1995 Robert married Tammy MacLean in London, Ontario. Tammy had been married previously to Shannon Grinton, and had two children [who would not be Hooper relatives]: Cory Grinton, born September 12, 1989 and Amanda Grinton, born June 2, 1992. The children live in Cornwell, P.E.I. with their father, who works for H & R Block in Charlottetown. Robert and Tammy have three sons (surname MacKay, eleventh generation):

Robert Andrew MacKay, called Drew, (11, Robert 10, Linda 9, Marjorie 8, Frederick 7, Allison 6, Lemuel 5. Elisha 4, Thomas 3, Clement 2, Stephen 1), born on December 12, 1995.
Caleb Morgan MacKay (11, Robert 10, Linda 9, Marjorie 8, Frederick 7, Allison 6, Lemuel 5, Elisha 4, Thomas 3, Clement 2, Stephen 1), born on January 29, 1998.
Benjamin Douglas MacKay (11, Robert 10, Linda 9, Marjorie 8, Frederick 7, Allison 6, Lemuel 5, Elisha 4, Thomas 3, Clement 2, Stephen 1), born on October 29, 1999.

Duane Michael MacKay (10, Linda 9, Marjorie 8, Frederick 7, Allison 6, Lemuel 5, Elisha 4, Thomas 3, Clement 2, Stephen 1), born on June 5, 1975. On June 20, 1998 Duane married Lorrie Gaudet, born in Nova Scotia. They were separated in October 1998, and divorced in October 1999. There were no children. In 2000 he was living at home with his parents.

Alan Lewis Rayner (9, Marjorie Hooper Rayner 8, Frederick Hooper 7, Allison Hooper 6, Lemuel 5, Elisha 4, Thomas 3, Clement 2, Stephen 1), born June 29, 1949 in Summerside. On August 29, 1970, he married Brenda Elizabeth Waite, born December 22, 1951 in Summerside, daughter of Lorne Raymond and Lucy Evelyn (Ramsay) Waite. Alan and Brenda live in Fredericton, New Brunswick and have three children (surname Rayner, tenth generation):

Derek Michael Rayner (10, Alan 9, Marjorie 8, Frederick 7, Allison 6, Lemuel 5, Elisha 4, Thomas 3, Clement 2, Stephen 1), born on October 17, 1973.
Kevin Alan Rayner, a twin, (10, Alan 9, Marjorie 8, Frederick 7, Allison 6, Lemuel 5, Elisha 4, Thomas 3, Clement 2, Stephen 1), born on November 4, 1976.
Karen Brenda Rayner, a twin, (10, Alan 9, Marjorie 8, Frederick 7, Allison 6, Lemuel 5, Elisha 4, Thomas 3, Clement 2, Stephen 1), born on November 4, 1976. No further information.

Gordon Ellis Rayner (9, Marjorie Hooper Rayner 8, Frederick Hooper 7, Allison 6, Lemuel 5, Elisha 4, Thomas 3, Clement 2, Stephen 1), born July 21, 1952 in Summerside; married (i) Shirley Davis on August 25, 1979. They have twins (surname Rayner, tenth generation):

Carley Davis Rayner (10, Gordon Rayner 9, Marjorie Hooper Rayner 8, Frederick Hooper 7, Allison 6, Lemuel 5, Elisha 4, Thomas 3, Clement 2, Stephen 1) born on August 22, 1982. I met Carley when I was visiting her grandmother in 2000 and gathering information for this genealogy. She is interested in music and is a freshman at U.P.E.I. in Charlotteotwn. What a lovely girl she appears to be!
Shannon Leigh Rayner (10, Gordon 9, Marjorie 8, Frederick 7, Allison 6, Lemuel 5, Elisha 4, Thomas 3, Clement 2, Stephen 1), born on August 22, 1982; died on February 12, 1983. Gordon and Shirley divorced in December 1986.

Gordon married (ii) Brenda Waugh, on June 25, 1988. They have one child (surname Rayner, tenth generation) and live in Lower New Annan, P.E.I.:

Chelsee Lee Rayner (10, Gordon Rayner 9, Marjorie Hooper Rayner 8, Frederick Hooper 7, Allison Hooper 6, Lemuel 5, Elisha 4, Thomas 3, Clement 2, Stephen 1), born April 17, 1992.

Amy Louise Rayner (9, Marjorie 8, Frederick 7, Allison 6, Lemuel 5, Elisha 4, Thomas 3, Clement 2, Stephen 1), born in Summerside on June 22, 1957; married Shannon Murray, on October 4, 1991. They live in Warren Grove, P.E.I. There were no children (2000).

Muriel Hooper (8, Frederick Hooper 7, Allison Hooper 6, Lemuel 5, Elisha 4, Thomas 3, Clement 2, Stephen 1) and Joseph Arthur Blanchard married in 1949, and lived in Traveller's Rest, P.E.I. where their children were born (surname Blanchard, tenth generation):

Nelson Vaughan Blanchard (9, Muriel Hooper Blanchard 8, Frederick Hooper 7, Allison Hooper 6, Lemuel 5, Elisha 4, Thomas 3, Clement 2, Stephen 1), born May 29, 1949, apparently lived very briefly.

infant Blanchard (9, Muriel Hooper Blanchard 8, Frederick Hooper 7, Allison Hooper 6, Lemuel 5, Elisha 4, Thomas 3, Clement 2, Stephen 1), born October 22, 1950; did not survive.

Sarah Elizabeth Blanchard (9, Muriel Hooper Blanchard 8, Frederick Hooper 7, Allison Hooper 6, Lemuel 5, Elisha 4, Thomas 3, Clement 2, Stephen 1) born October 26, 1951; lives in Summerside and works at Cavendish Farms in Kensington, P.E.I. Sarah is the only surviving child of Arthur and Muriel (Hooper) Blanchard.

Infant, born November 29, 1959; did not survive.

About 1988 I went to Muriel's apartment in Kensington. She was outdoors as I approached her, identified myself, and started to talk with her. It was she who gave me the inspiration to write this genealogy. She also was a tremendous help by giving me much of the information that had been helpful to her, and that she had gathered over the years. I made several visits to see her and she was always helpful.

Muriel was in a manor for a short time before her death. She seemed to be feeling better, but was tired and went to bed early. When the attendant checked on her at 11 p.m. she was dead. The funeral was private, only for her family. The minister of the United Church

at North Bedeque officiated at the short service at the Lower Bedeque Cemetery where she was buried next to her husband who had died several years previously.

Without Muriel's assistance and encouragement this genealogy would not have been written as she supplied me with some materials and the motivation to continue. Accolades also go to my dear husband, Alden Hooper Neal, who has spent many, many lonely evenings with the television or with a book while I was engrossed in "the Hoopers."

THOSE WITH UNKNOWN CONNECTIONS TO STEPHEN HOOPER

Over the course of several years, while this genealogy was being assembled, I ran across many Hooper individuals and families about whom I know little. Quite possibly, somewhere back in the Hooper family's past, these people have a common ancestry, but at present their relationship to the Loyalist Hoopers of Bedeque is not known. But, an obsession with genealogical relationships does not allow me to simply ignore them. Consequently, I decided to include these individuals here in the hope that the information might benefit someone:

Fred *Jesse* Hooper, born April 4, 1873 in Trowbridge, England, the son of Henry and Johanna Hooper, married Catherine Frances Pearson, called Kate. He was her second husband; the first husband, George Clough, was born in 1859 in China, Maine, and died on December 7, 1902 in Kingston, N. H. [As an aside, Catherine was the granddaughter of Lydia Wright Pearson who appears in this document because of her adventure with a bear. Kate was also the sister of Margaret Pearson of Chelton, P.E.I., who married Louis Dodge Savage, the superintendent of the City Farm in Haverhill, MA where Jennie, Ada, Lila, and Vera (Alden's mother, aunt, and cousins) went to work. They would have known the Pearson family of Chelton, P.E.I. as they lived about 1 ½ miles "as the crow flies" from each other] George

was superintendent of the Amesbury Infirmary in Amesbury, MA for nineteen years; Kate was the matron. Jesse, the second husband. was also a superintendent of the Amesbury Town Infirmary as was George, the son of George and Catherine.[1]

***Fred* Witcher Hooper**, born July 5, 1906 in Amesbury, MA, was the son of the aforementioned Jesse and Kate.[2] He married Mary Ella Adams, the daughter of Carl Leslie and Hazel Gertrude (McLain) Adams. Mary Ella was born on March 30, 1907 in Searsmont, ME. Fred worked in the shipyard at Bath, ME from 1942 until 1944, and was with the Maine Forest Service until he retired. Mary was a telephone operator and lived in Belfast. Fred and Mary Ella had two sons (surname Hooper):

***Ernest* Adams Hooper** (of Fred, of Jesse, of Henry Hooper) born September 12, 1933 in Liberty, Maine. He married Ernestine Beverley Jewett, daughter of Forest and Linda Jewett. She was born on January 3, 1935 in Liberty. In the mid-1970s they lived in Washington, ME. Ernest was employed at Marriner's Inc. in Camden, and Ernestine worked at Penobscott Poultry Co., Belfast, ME. Ernest and Ernestine had four children (surname Hooper):

Lawrence Douglas Hooper (of Ernest, of Fred, of Jesse, of Henry Hooper) born October 17, 1953 in Belfast, ME
Beverley Ann Hooper (of Ernest, of Fred, of Jesse, of Henry Hooper) born February 4, 1955 in Hope, ME.
Kathleen May Hooper (of Ernest, of Fred, of Jesse, of Henry Hooper) born September 15, 1959 in Montville, ME.
Wayne Ernest Hooper (of Ernest, of Fred, of Jesse, of Henry Hooper) born March 3, 1961 in Belfast, ME.

***Douglas* Fred Hooper** (of Fred, of Jesse, of Henry Hooper) born April 13, 1937 in Liberty, ME; married Ada Marie Simmons, daughter of Charles and Margaret Simmons. She was born on July 7, 1938 in Belmont, ME. In the mid-1970s they lived in Belfast, ME where

Doug was part owner of *Doug and Ray's Sunoco Station*. He is supposed to have served in the U. S. Army for two years during World War II [How is this possible as he would have expressed his age in a single digit?] Doug and Ada have two children (surname Hooper):

Lori Ann Hooper (of Douglas, of Ernest, of Fred, of Jesse, of Henry Hooper) born June 14, 1963.
Kevin Douglas Hooper (of Douglas, of Ernest, of Fred, of Jesse, of Henry) born April 17, 1967.

I have a clipping from a newspaper, dated March 7, 1925, about a baseball player by the name of **Harry Hooper**. I don't know how he connects to Thomas Hooper, but I feel there is a connection:

Harry Hooper Playing Better Than Ever

Chicago, March 7 [1925]. Some ball players, like old wine, seem to improve with age. Take, for instance, Harry Hooper, veteran outfielder of the White Sox.

Hooper came into the majors back in 1909. For several seasons he was a member of the famous Boston Red Sox outfield, composed of Hooper, Speaker, and Lewis which has often been called one of the game's greatest. In 1921 he was traded to Chicago where he has since remained.

Despite his 16 seasons of active service, Hooper appears to be improving instead of going back. A glance at his batting record for the past 10 years will vouchsafe that remark.

In 1914 Hooper hit .258, a remarkable low figure for a regular outfielder. Five years later, or in 1919, he clouted .267, a jump of nine points. And, another five years -1925- found him hitting .328, a leap of 61 points.

Thus over a stretch of 10 years Hooper succeeded in elevating his average a total of 70 points. In other words, he reached a higher figure in the batting columns last season than he has ever done during his major league career.

(Hooper is a native of Morell, P.E.I. and a relative of Mrs. R. H. Jenkins of Charlottetown)

There are several other people whose connection to Thomas Hooper I do not know. These people arrived early on the Island of St. John, as Prince Edward Island was then known. I do believe that there is a connection between some of them and the Thomas Hooper family, however, and would be grateful if someone could give me a

clue how to include them in this genealogy. These are the names of the additional people whose relationships are not connected to this genealogy. The P.E.I. atlas, from which my data have been extracted, was apparently collated in 1928:[3]

- Lot 49, Pownal, Queen's County, **Mrs. Maria Hooper**, post of fice Pownal, rural route. Children: **William, Seymour, Garfield, Mary, Ethel, Gertrude** (p.72)
- Lot 31, 32, Queen's County, **George W. Hooper**, post office Milton; wife, Pearl, children: **Phillis, Maurice, Joyce, Noel, Dorothy, Garth, Rollin, Louise** (pp. 60-61)
- Lot 31, 32, Queen's County, **H. P. Hooper**, post office Milton, wife Minnie (pp. 60-61)

Finally, in conclusion, J. Clinton Morrison, of Crescent Isle Publishers, Summerside, discovered the following interesting notice of death in a 1922 magazine:[4]

Hooper - At Charlottetown, on Sept. 22, Brenton, son of Henry C. Hooper. A brother who was killed in the World War [1914-1918] was born on the same day of the month and the same hour as Brenton, February 4, and both died in the 29th year of their age. He [Brenton] leaves a widow (Winnifred Connolly), his parents, a sister and three brothers.

Notes

1 Doris Haslam, *The Wrights of Bedeque, Prince Edward Island, a Loyalist Family* (Summerside, P.E.I.: Doris Muncey Haslam, 1978), p. 347

2 Ibid., p. 213

3 *Atlas of Province of Prince Edward Island., Canada*, (Toronto: Cummins Map Co., c.1928). Re-published as: *Atlas of Province of Prince Edward Island Canada* (Charlottetown, P.E.I.: Prince Edward Island Museum & Heritage Foundation, 1990, printed by Hugnell Printing Limited, Winnipeg, Man.)

4 The *Maple Leaf*, October 1922, p. 214

Appendices

MINISTERS AT BEDEQUE METHODIST CHURCH (1818-1925)
AND BEDEQUE UNITED CHURCH (1925-2002)

J. B. Strong 1818-1850
David Rogers 1851-1906*
G. O. Huestis 1852-1854
John Prince 1858-1861
S. W. Sprague 1861-1864
Richard Smith 1864-1867
R. Wedall 1867-1870
T. J. Dienstadt 1867-1870
Paul Prestwood 1870-1872
John Phinney 1872-1875
Joseph Sellar 1875-1878
George Harrison 1889-1883
Joseph Pascoe 1883-1886
E. C. Turner 1886-1889
William Harrison, D.D., 1889-1892
W. J. Kirby 1892-1895
Thomas Moyse 1892-1955
George Palmer 1895-1899
F. A. Wightman, D.D. 1899-1903
Neil MacLauglan 1903-1906
George Steel, D.D. 1906-1910
Hammond Johnson 1910-1914
George Ayers 1914-1918
George Somers 1918-1922
P. A. Fitzpatrick 1922-1927
A. J. Reynolds 1927-1931
L. P. Archibald 1931-1935
Arthur Organ 1935-1937
Ralph Barker 1937-1942
J. M. Baxter 1942-1947
Burton Crowe 1947-1955
George K. Ward 1953-1955
Garth Cowper-Smith 1955-1959
H. B. O'Brien 1959-1960
R. M. Cameron 1960-1969
A. H. Mitton 1969-1978
A. G. N. Ware 1978-1984
Samuel P. Shields 1984-1985
Russell F. Burns (1985-1991)
Barbara Wagner 1991-2005

*Lay Minister

A LISTING OF GRAVESTONES OF HOOPER DESCENDANTS IN THE SEARLETOWN CEMETERY (WITH NO INTENDED ORDER), TRANSCRIBED BY THE AUTHOR IN THE SUMMER OF 2001

- John Craig 1842 – 1925. In Loving Memory of Jane S. Wright, Beloved Wife of John Craig, died September 11, 1880 AET [aged] 37 and their daughter Sarah Jane, died January 2, 1870 AET 3
  "Jesus Lover of my soul, let me to Thy bosom fly
  Where the nearer waters roll still support and comfort give."
- In memory of Colin Craig, died October 3, 19?? (illegible) His wife Mary Louise Wright, May 23, 1878-Feb. 11, 1973 Always Remembered
- Wallace J. Bradshaw, born November 11, 1844; died January 29, 1918 At Rest, But Not Forgotten. Elizabeth Wright, wife of Wallace Bradshaw March 11, 1847-? / 28/ 1934
- Neil Bradshaw born July 20, 1907; died July 16, 1975.
- Gabriel Strang died July 3, 1884, age 28.
- John R. Wright, died Feb. 23, 1890 AET 76
- John T. Ramsey, died September 21, 1839. In the middle of life we are in death.
- Hudson Louther 1900-1980 (?) The Lord is My Shepherd. Chauncey, their son 1885-1955
- David J. Pearson 1855-1938. His wife Jennie Leard 1862-1944
- George Wright 1866-1931. Mary A. Trueman 186?-1944. Their children (illegible)
- In Memory of Lewis Wright who deprted this life Mar. 13, 1877 in the 71st year of his life. Blessed Are The Dead Who Die In The Lord From Henceforth. Yea, Saith The Spirit That They May Rest From Their Labours And Their Works Do Follow Them. Also his wife Mary Black born March 5, 1816; died March 4, 1914.
- Lucy Irving G. daughter of J. Nelson and Eliza Wright, born August 14, 1876, died March 18, 1891.
- In Memory of Solomon Wright died (illegible) 1886, aged 77
- Dugald S. Wright born June 19, 1835; died November 20, 1912
- Emma Huestis, born February, 1856; died June, 1920

- In memory of Annie Amelia died November 13, 1875, aged 12 days, of Dugald S. and Beria S. Wright
- Annie I. Cameron 1901-1977, wife of Kenneth E. Stright. Kenneth E. Stright 1902-1992
- Nathaniel C. Pearson 1857-1938.
- Mary Ellen Howatt, wife of Nathaniel 1855-1924
- Earl P. Pearson 1897-1977. His wife Amy Belle Cairns 1903-1977. His brother Louis W. Pearson 1883-1977 The Lord is My Sheperd. [This is the gentleman whose ancestor met the bear while going through the woods] See Chapter 7
- Charles Heber Schurman, 1897-1977. His wife Sadie J. Arnett 1901-1998
- Hiram Truman died April 21, 1895 AET 67. Also his wife Typhena Black died January 12, 1911 AET 83. In the middle of life we are in death.
- Reginald Wright Bradshaw November 16, 1916-October 12, 1991. His wife Mary Grace Wright October 27, 1926-
- Elizabeth Trueman, June 20, 1857-February 2, 1942
  Lewis W. Trueman, January 3, 1869-June 29, 19--

LEDGER ENTRIES FOR SOME HOOPER DESCENDANTS, TAKEN FROM STEPHEN WRIGHT'S STORE LEDGER, AT BEDEQUE, 1879-1886

58

Lemuel Hooper

Date	Day	Particulars	Dr. $	Dr. ¢	Cr. $	Cr. ¢
		Carried from old ledger page 530				
1879 Nov	5	To amt a/c rend 16.42 Dec 24 Sawing 7¾ Shingles 80¢ 6.20	22	62		
1880 Jany	24	" Sawing 178 feet Pine .56 By pine logs .56		56		56
March	18	" Sawing 150 feet H Bds 32¢ .48 do 80 feet mill flooring .40		88		
		" do 237 feet H Wd .94 By log lost .94		94		94
"	24	To 1 M Shingles 1.60 By Oliver Goodwin 2.50	1	60	2	50
May	26th	By Henry Sawing Shingles 8.75 By 6 Loads Sawdust .96			9	81
		" Sleigh Runners Charged in Moulton .40				40
		To Balance			12	39
			26	60	26	60
1880 Octr	15th	To Balance pr a/c rend 12.39 1881 May 14th By Son Working 7.80	12	39	7	80
1881 May	14	" Sawing 8¾ M Shingles 75¢ 6.56 Balance 11.15	6	56	11	15
			18	95	18	95
" Nov	22	To Balance a/c rend 11.15	11	15		
1882 April	28	" Sawing 169 feet Sp Bds 32¢ .54 June 6th To Sawing 326 feet Pk 25¢ .81	1	35		
" June	26	" Sawing 235 feet H W Pk 25¢ .51 Sawing 189 feet M flooring .94	1	45		
" "	"	" Saw 187 feet Bds 32¢ .59 Sawing 289 feet Pine 32¢ .92 Saw 329 feet Pk 1.31	2	82		
" "	30	" Sawing 168 feet 2 inch Pk 25¢ .42 July 7th Sawing 101 ft Pine Bds .32		74		
" July	7th	" Sawing 128 feet Pine .38 July 8th To Sawing 339 feet Hardwood 40¢ 1.35 a/c rend Sept 22/82	1	73		
1883 March	28	To Sawing 127 feet Pk 25¢ .31 April 2 Saw 239 ft Pk 25¢ .59		90		
" April	3	" Sawing 149 ft Pk 25¢ (4th) .47 Saw 123 ft Pk .30		77		
" "	14	" Saw 221 feet Pk 25 .55		55		
1883 Oct	24th	To Bal a/c pr a/c rend	21	46		
1884 Feby	26	By Cash 15.00 April 21 To Saw 67 ft Oak 32¢ .21 Balance		21	21	67
			21	67		
" Oct	27	To Balce pr a/c rend 6.67 a/c Nov 19/85 1886 Apl 9 Saw 2¼ M Shingles 60¢ 1.35 a/c Oct 23/86	8	02		
1887 March	18	To Saw 244 ft Pine 30¢ .73 May 2 Saw 245 ft Pine 30¢ .73	1	46		
" July		" Saw 313 ft Scantling 22¢ .68 Aug 30 Saw 13½ M Shingles 60¢ 8.10 a/c Feb 14/88	8	78		
1890		" By cash 5.00 Scow 7 days 2.00 2 Double Loads Sawdust 1.00			8	00
1891 April		" By cash at settlement 10.26 with Edwd			10	26
			18	26	18	26
" Augt	25	To Carding 10½ lb wool 34¢ .36				

83

Robert Hooper

Year / Month	Day	Particulars		Dr.		Cr.
		Old Ledger 403				
1881 April	30th	To Sawing 475 ft Hardwood 1.52 32¢ Aug 13 To Sawing 216 ft Rafters .75		2	27	
" Aug	20	" Sawing 148 feet Bds .47 32¢ Sawing 300 feet plank .90 30¢		1	37	
" [illegible]	23	" Sawing 300 feet plank .90 30¢ Sawing 141 feet Sp Bds .63 32		1	53	
1881 Nov	25	To Amt pr a/c Rend		5	17	
1882 July	22	" Sawing 3 M Shingle 2.40 80¢ Nov 17th By Cash 7.57		2	40	7.57
1883 May	3	To Sawg 379 feet Bds 1.22 32¢ a/c Rend Sept 73/82 4th Sawg 1614 feet Bds 32¢ 5.16		6	37	
" "	5	" Sawg 789 feet Bds 2.53 32¢ Sawg 4844 feet Pickets 10¢ 4.84		7	36	
" "	7	" " 391 feet Hw 1.56 40¢ May 8 Sawg 370 feet Hw 35¢ 1.29		2	85	
" "	8	" " 171 " Pine .54 32¢ Sawg 348 feet P.Pk 25¢ .87 a/c Rend Oct 26/83		1	41	
				17	93	18.00
1884 May	7th	By Cash 16.00 By mistake 2.00				

Job Wright Junr (Middleton)

Year / Month	Day	Particulars		Dr.		Cr.
1886 July	13	To Carding 17 lbs Wool 32¢ .55				

34

Alexander Hooper

Month	Day	Particulars	Dr.	Cr.
		Old ledger ~~84~~ 478		
April	30th	To Sawing Sleigh ~~Runners~~ Benches .50 Sawing 116 ft H.W. .37	87	
"	"	" Sawing 303 ft Mill flooring 1.51 July 14 Carding 13¼ wool 3¢ .44	.95	
Nov	17	By Cash 2.82 ~~1883 April 4~~ a/c end day 73/52	2.82	2,82
April	4	To Saw'g 104 feet Bd. 32¢ .33 Saw'g 198 feet half inch .63	96	
	5	" Saw'g 353 feet Bd. 32¢ 1.12 6th Saw'g 230 feet Bd. 32¢ .73 Saw'g 66 ft half inch .21	2 06	
	12	" Saw'g 144 feet Bd. 32¢ .46 14th Saw'g 561 feet Bd. 32 1.79	2.25	
Nov	16th	By Cash 5.27 a/c Oct 25th 1883 .44	5.27	
		1884 April 23 Saw'g 126 ft H.W. 35¢	.44	5.27
April	23	To Ripping 12 H. Bars .10 July 2 Saw'g 226 ft Studs 1 Sills 32¢ .72 a/c Oct 27/84	.83	
Dec	6	By Cash 1.26	1 26	1,26
April	18	To Saw'g 745 ft fencing 30¢ 2.23 Saw'g 106 ft bds 30 .31	2.54	
"	19th	" Saw'g 1576 ft bds 30¢ 4.72 Saw'g 896 fencing 30 2.68	7.40	
"	"	" Saw'g 208 ft Rafters 30¢ .62 (21st) Saw'g 537 ft boards 30¢ 1.61	2.23	
"	21st	" Saw'g 671 ft fencing 30¢ 2.01 26 Saw'g 35 ft fencing .10	2.11	
May	1	" Saw'g 254 ft bds 30¢ .75 25th Saw'g 38 Cedar Posts 4¢ 1.52	2.27	
June	1	By Cash 10.00 1887 March 28 Saw'g 751 ft boards 30¢ 2.25	2.25	10.00
March	29	To Saw'g 343 ft boards 30¢ 1.03 30 Saw'g 1296 ft boards 30¢ 3.88	4.91	
April	4	" Saw'g 376 ft boards 30¢ 1.12 June 14 Saw'g 29½ M Shingles 17.70	18.82	
July	28	" Saw'g 936 ft 3x5 Scantling 24¢ 2.24 Saw'g 406 ft 3x4 Scantling 24 .97	3.21	
March	4	By amt settled .19 19		
			45.74	

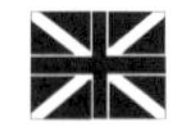

161

Major Hooper

Date	Day	Particulars		Amount
1881 Nov	29	To Balance from New Ledger page 521 (4 9c furnished) 2.27 1882 July 7 To Cardg 11½ lbs Wool .37		2,64
1883 July	11	To Carding 9 lbs Wool 3¼ .29 a/c Nov 21/83 1884 June 17 Cardg 21 lbs Wool 3¼ .68		.97
1884 July	24	" Carding 6½ lbs Wool 3¼ .20 Dec Interest .25		.45
1886 June	18	To Carding 27 lbs Wool 3¼ .87 (21) Cardg 21 lbs Wool 3¼ .68 a/c Dec 20/84		1.55
" Decemr	9	By Cash 5.61		

An Arthur J. Newsome photograph, Charlottetown, P.E.I./Jean Schurman Coll.

A photograph, very likely of a school group at North Carleton School c.1902. Four of the five Hooper siblings, children of Major C. Hooper and his wife, Mary Ann MacDonald, of Searletown are situated as follows: back row, far left - Jane Walker Hooper, called **Jennie**; middle row, second left - Annie Eva Hooper, called **Ada** (mother of Nancy E. Neal's husband, Alden Neal); middle row, third left, next to Ada - **Robert G.** Hooper; bottom of photo, far left, between middle and front rows - Melvina Hooper, called **Millicent;** the fifth sibling, **Norman M.**, is quite possibly one of the boys in the front row, seated.

Bibliography

Simpson, Harold H. *Cavendish: Its History, Its People*. Amherst/ Truro, N.S.: Harold H. Simpson and Associates Limited, second printing, 1974.

Graves, Ross. *William Schurman, Loyalist, of Bedeque, Prince Edward Island, and his descendants*. Summerside, P.E..I.: Harold B. Schurman, 1973.

Haslam, Doris Muncey. *The Wrights of Bedeque, Prince Edward Island, a Loyalist Family*. 2 Vols. Summerside, P.E.I.: Doris Muncey Haslam, 1978.

Hooper, H.H., and L.U. Fowler. "Bedeque and Its People." *Prince Edward Island Magazine*, June, August and September, 1900

Jones, Orlo and Haslam, Doris. *An Island Refuge. Loyalists and Disbanded Troops on the Island of Saint John*. n.p.: Abegweit Branch of the United Empire Loyalist Association of Canada, 1983.

Leard, George A. *Historic Bedeque. The Loyalists at Work and Worship in Prince Edward Island*. Bedeque, P.E.I.: Bedeque United Church, 1948.

MacFadyen, Jean. *For The Sake Of The Record*. Summerside, P.E.I.: East Prince Historical Group, n.d.

MacLeod, Ada (author) and Gay, Marjorie McCallum (ed.) *Roads to Summerside. The Story of Early Summerside and the Surrounding Area*. Summerside, P.E.I.: n.p., 1980.

Morrison, J. Clinton, Jr. *Robert W. Morrison, Sr., Emigrant from the Highlands, and His Descendants, 1831-1978. The Genealogy of a P.E.I. Family.* St. Eleanor's, P.E.I.: J. Clinton Morrison, Jr., 1978.

National Cyclopedia of American Biography, "Schurman, Jacob Gould."

Index

B

D

E

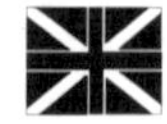

F

G

I

J

K

L

M

N

O

P

Q

R

S

T

Y